THE MERCHANT NAVY

HISTORY OF THE GREAT WAR

BASED ON OFFICIAL DOCUMENTS

BY DIRECTION OF THE HISTORICAL
SECTION OF THE COMMITTEE OF
IMPERIAL DEFENCE

THE
MERCHANT NAVY

Vol. I

BY
ARCHIBALD HURD

The Naval & Military Press Ltd

Published by
The Naval & Military Press Ltd
5 Riverside, Brambleside, Bellbrook
Industrial Estate, Uckfield, East Sussex,
TN22 1QQ England
Tel: +44 (0) 1825 749494
Fax: +44 (0) 1825 765701
www.naval-military-press.com

PREFACE

When the peace was broken on August 4th, 1914, nothing suggested that British merchant seamen would fare worse than their predecessors of the Napoleonic era, and the statement that they would be compelled to face perils in intensity and variety unparalleled in human experience would have been rejected as unbelievable in face of all the efforts made at The Hague to humanise warfare. Events falsified all anticipations.

After the comparative failure of the attack on commerce by surface craft—cruisers and auxiliary cruisers—the enemy became convinced that in the submarine he had found the means of cutting the communications of the British Empire, and of shutting off from the European battle-fields the essential supplies without which the troops could not continue to fight. The use of the submarine for commerce destruction involved the infraction of international law as well as the ignoring of the code of humanity, since these small craft, packed with machinery and equipped for war, were unable to accommodate the crews of ships sunk, whether by torpedo, gunfire, or bombs. The German flag had already been banished from the highways of the world. So, in desperation, it was decided, whatever the loss of human life might be, and without respect for considerations of law, however widely recognised, to embark on a policy which, rightly or wrongly, became generally known as piracy.

This decision changed the whole aspect of the War so far as merchant seamen were concerned. As the campaign made progress it became apparent that the British merchant seamen were being forced by circumstances, over which neither they nor the British naval authorities had any control, into the forefront of the struggle by sea. They had entered the Mercantile Marine with no thought that they would be exposed even to such trials and sufferings as their predecessors sustained during the previous Great War, for there had been much talk at various international Conferences of ameliorating the conditions of warfare; they found themselves involved in a conflict waged by a merciless enemy with large and newly-developed resources. The seamen were defenceless, for this emergency had not been foreseen either by the Admiralty, by the shipowners, or by the seamen themselves. As the campaign continued, the Germans found that their best hope of success lay in discharging their torpedoes without warning, leaving the crews, and in some cases passengers, at the mercy of the elements.

In these conditions it was thought appropriate that an official history should be prepared, placing on record for all time the manner in which British seamen, refusing to be cowed by the enemy's threats, confronted a ruthless foe, regarding their own lives as cheap if, in spite of the perils they willingly faced, the stream of ocean traffic, necessary alike for naval, military, and economic reasons, were maintained. This history was consequently undertaken, at the suggestion of the Board of Trade, under the authority of the Historical Section of the Committee of Imperial Defence towards the close of 1917, the proposal receiving the cordial support of the Admiralty and the Ministry of Shipping.

The ordeal to which the men of the British Mercantile Marine submitted with generous patriotism can be appreciated only if it is described in an appropriate setting, ignoring neither the plans of the naval authorities for the protection of merchant shipping, elaborated in the years before the outbreak of war, nor the measures afterwards adopted to enable merchant shipping to resist with better hope of success the enemy's policy. On the other hand, no attempt has been made to deal with the naval operations undertaken by the Admiralty for the protection of this country's sea communications, except in so far as they immediately concerned the Mercantile Marine, nor with the economic effects of the naval war on ocean-borne trade. The former subject has been treated in the companion work by Sir Julian Corbett, and Mr. C. Ernest Fayle has become responsible for the latter.

While British seamen, uncovenanted to the State, had never had to confront such an ordeal as that of **1915–18**,

PREFACE

it would be to misunderstand the history of the British Mercantile Marine, of which little has been written, to conclude that never before had sailors of the Merchant Service taken part in our wars, creating traditions handed down from generation to generation with increasing pride. On the contrary, the Merchant Navy was the defence of the nation's sea interests and its bulwark against invasion before the Royal Navy had any existence, and after the foundation of the Royal Navy it continued to bear no small share in the sea defences of the country. It has been thought not inappropriate to the story which these volumes tell to give in very brief summary, as a preliminary chapter, some account of the contribution of British merchant seamen in the past to this country's maritime history; this summary furnishes a fitting background to the unexampled record of high courage, uncomplaining suffering, and in thousands of instances martyrdom, which the late struggle has provided as an example and inspiration to future generations. The theme is a great one, and there is a tendency to forget that the Merchant Navy was the creator of the Royal Navy.

As soon as the task of preparing this History was undertaken, it became apparent that, if the record were strictly confined to the experiences of merchant seamen in passenger and cargo-carrying ships, it would convey an inadequate impression of the dauntless courage, fine resource, and dogged endurance of the men serving by sea, who were exposed to the full fury of the enemy's campaign, and of the wide range of the services they rendered. The Germans determined to hold up, or destroy, merchant shipping, and their failure is traceable alike to the spirit exhibited by the crews of merchant vessels and to the manner in which merchant seamen, fishermen, yachtsmen, and others responded to the Admiralty's invitation when it was decided to build up a new Navy to deal with the new problems created by the submarine and mine. And thus it happens that this History embraces an account of the operations of the Auxiliary Patrol, constituting one of the most remarkable aspects of the war by sea.

Acknowledgment is made of the assistance rendered by Lieutenant-Commander E. Keble Chatterton, R.N.V.R., in the preparation of this portion of the History. He was associated with that phase of the war by sea for three winters and three summers, and obtained first-hand knowledge of the sterling work done by the merchant seamen as belligerents in circumstances of much danger and difficulty. With his aid, an attempt has been made to convey an impression of the elaborate organisation which was gradually created by the Admiralty, ultimately comprising nearly 4,000 vessels, and of the high standard of seamanship of officers and men.

Little has hitherto been revealed of the activities of the Auxiliary Patrol. Now, with the advantage of official records, the veil can be lifted and particulars given of some of the most stirring incidents of the war by sea. It must be apparent that the story—a typical British story of a fight against heavy odds—has been little more than half told in the limited space available in this book.

The writing of this record of the ordeal of British merchant seamen would have been impossible had it not been for the cordial help received from officers of the Royal Navy who, while serving at the Admiralty or elsewhere, were brought into intimate association with the Merchant Service, from the officials of the Marine Department of the Board of Trade, of the Ministry of Shipping, and of the Admiralty, from the Registrar-General of Shipping and Seamen, and from many others, to whom acknowledgment is made.

Full use has also been made of the records of the various departments.

CONTENTS

INTRODUCTION

Mistaken conception of the Merchant Navy—Traditions and romance—Significance of sea power—Growth of the world's war fleets—Influence of the steam-engine—Responsibilities of merchant shipping on the outbreak of war . . . . pp. 1—7

CHAPTER I

THE MERCHANT NAVY OF THE PAST

I. THE FIGHTING MERCHANTMEN

The Cinque Ports and Home Defence—The Laws of Oleron—Merchantmen at the Battle of Sluys—War and piracy—Issue of letters of marque—Appointment of Admirals—The Merchant Adventurers—Sebastian Cabot—English seamen in the Narrow Seas—The Hanseatic League—The foundation of the Royal Navy—Elizabethan voyagers—Drake and the Spanish Main—The defeat of the Spanish Armada—The "Adventurers for the Discovery of the Trade of the East Indies "—The rivalry of the Dutch
pp. 8—44

II. THE MERCHANT FLEET IN THE REVOLUTIONARY AND NAPOLEONIC WARS

Enemy's war on sea-borne commerce—Heavy losses of merchant shipping—Successes of French corsairs—Unreadiness of the Channel Fleet—Spirited defence by British merchant seamen—The risks of commerce in war time—Unwieldy British convoys—Man-power of the Merchant Navy—The effect of impressment—The *guerre de course* after Trafalgar—The fight of the *Windsor Castle*—The escape of the *Shaw*—The *Antelope* and the *Atlante*—Consideration for prisoners—The value of Dunkirk, Calais, Boulogne, and Dieppe—Raids on shipping in the English Channel—British merchantmen captured, 1793-1812 . . . pp. 44—69

III. THE DEVELOPMENT OF THE MERCHANT NAVY, 1815-1914

The aftermath of the War—Prosperity and sea power—The influence of the Navigation Laws and the movement for repeal—The competency of masters and officers—Mr. Joseph Hume's agitation—Legislation to promote safety at sea—The Foreign Office inquiry of 1843—Mr. Samuel Plimsoll and "coffin-ships"—The work of reform—Growth of the Merchant Navy, 1818-74—The rivalry of the United States—Effect of the Civil War—Progress of ameliorative legislation—Responsibilities of the Board of Trade—Strength of the British Mercantile Marine on the outbreak of the War, 1914—Liners and tramps—Expansion of the world's sea-borne commerce—Distribution of the Merchant Fleet . . . pp. 70—97

CONTENTS

IV. THE MEN OF THE MERCHANT NAVY

Changed relations of the Royal Navy and the Mercantile Marine—Unpopularity of impressment—The Registry of seamen—Deterioration of the personnel—Reports from British Consuls—Discreditable conditions—Increase in the number of apprentices—A new scheme of registration and its failure—Repeal of the Manning clauses of the Navigation Laws—Establishment of a Voluntary Naval Reserve—A chequered history—New scheme of training of the Royal Naval Reserve introduced in 1906—The country's resources in seamen . . . . . pp. 97—116

CHAPTER II

ON THE EVE OF THE WAR

The position of the merchant seamen—Discussions at The Hague—Germany's deceptive declarations—Professions of respect for the code of humanity—Right of conversion on the high seas—The Admiralty's suspicions—A policy of defensive armament—Germany's varied resources for a war on commerce—British merchant ships detained in German ports before the outbreak of war—British protests—The enemy's Naval Prize Code—The status of merchant seamen—The German declaration of July 22nd, 1914—Merchant seamen as prisoners of war—The opening of hostilities—Loss of the s.s. *San Wilfrido* . . . pp. 117—136

CHAPTER III

CRUISER ATTACKS ON SHIPPING

The KÖNIGSBERG's attack on merchantmen—A British master's early experiences—The DRESDEN as a commerce destroyer—Chase of the Pacific Steam Navigation Company's s.s. *Ortega*—A fine exhibition of seamanship—Escape of the armed merchant cruiser KAISER WILHELM DER GROSSE from the North Sea—Experiences of the officers and men of the s.s. *Galicia*—Consideration for women and children—Operations of the KARLSRUHE off Parnambuco—An enforced cruise—A British captain's diary—A lucky escape—Misfortunes of a defensively armed merchantman—The fate of the sailing-ship *Wilfred M.*—Capture of the armed merchant cruiser KRONPRINZ WILHELM—Operations of the PRINZ EITEL FRIEDRICH—The sinking of the American s.s. *William P. Frye*—Capture of the s.s. *Elsinore* by the LEIPZIG—Marooned on an island . . pp. 137—185

CHAPTER IV

THE EXPLOITS OF THE "EMDEN"

Captain von Müller's resource and courtesy exaggerated—Record of the EMDEN's captures—Raid in the Bay of Bengal—A passenger's experiences—A rich harvest—A British master's diary—The attack on the

CONTENTS

oil-tanks at Madras—Captain von Müller's change of scene—Treatment of British seamen—Escape of the s.s. *Glenturret*—Destruction of the EMDEN—The gunboat GEIER's only capture—Rescue of the s.s. *Southport*—A notable exploit—Total captures by enemy cruisers—No lives sacrificed
pp. 186—209

CHAPTER V

THE PROTECTION OF MERCHANT SHIPPING

I. STRATEGIC POLICY

The responsibilities of the Navy—The Royal Commission on the Supply of Food and Raw Material in Time of War—Changes in naval conditions owing to the introduction of steam—Command of the sea essential—Concentration of force the key to security—Losses of merchantmen anticipated—Shipowners and the risks of war—An enemy's difficulties—Linking up the Admiralty and the Merchant Service—No fear of starvation . . . . pp. 210—216

II. PRE-WAR ARRANGEMENTS

Action of the Committee of Imperial Defence—The basic principle of British defensive policy—Oversea ports and their protection—The danger of panics—Limitation of local defence—An enemy's probable policy—Harbours of refuge—The compilation of the War Book—Admiral of the Fleet Sir Arthur Wilson's declaration—Influence of a policy of concentration of naval force . . . . pp. 216—223

III. THE CREATION OF THE TRADE DIVISION OF THE WAR STAFF

A Royal Commission's recommendation ignored—A reversal of policy—Captain Henry Campbell's Memorandum on an intelligence service for the main trade routes—The creation of a Trade Division—Its growth and organisation—Relations between the Admiralty and the Merchant Navy
pp. 224—228

IV. THE WAR INSURANCE SCHEME

Mr. Austen Chamberlain's Committee of 1907—A fresh inquiry undertaken in 1913—Formation of Mutual Insurance Associations, or Clubs, changes the situation—Government action and the avoidance of publicity—Co-operation between the State and the Clubs suggested—Estimate of probable losses—Basis of the value of shipping to be accepted—Proposals for the insurance of cargoes—" An administratively practicable scheme "—Prompt action on the outbreak of war . . . . pp. 228—239

V. ADMIRALTY DIRECTIONS TO SHIPPING

Communications opened with ships and shipowners—Co-operation of other State departments—Counsels of weakness rejected—Merchant shipping urged to continue its operations—A policy of dispersion of shipping adopted—Why the convoy system was impracticable—Early instructions to merchant shipping—The " sea is free to all "—Re-establishing confidence amongst shipowners—An official review of the first two months of the War—The opening of the New Year—Activities of the Operations Division of the War Staff—Daily voyage notices to the Mercantile Marine . . . . pp. 239—252

CHAPTER VI

THE ORGANISATION OF THE AUXILIARY PATROL

Scarcity of small craft for purposes of patrol—Influence of the submarine and mine—Organisation of the New Navy—Lord Beresford's foresight—Trawlers organised for war purposes—An Admiralty Committee appointed—The purchase of trawlers in 1910—Manning policy—Progress of recruiting—The mobilisation scheme—The trawler section on the outbreak of war—A notable achievement . . . pp. 253—267

CHAPTER VII

THE APPEARANCE OF THE SUBMARINE

Development of a new policy for attacking sea-borne commerce—The sinking of the s.s. *Glitra*, the first merchant ship to be destroyed by a submarine—The achievement of U21 in the English Channel—Germany's decision to ignore international law and the code of humanity—Interview with Grand Admiral von Tirpitz in December 1914—Germany's declaration of the War Zone on February 4th, 1915—The reply of the British Government—The attack on the s.s. *Laertes*—The British seamen's ordeal—Enemy threats treated with contempt—The rising toll of lives lost—Merchant ships attacked by aeroplanes—Vessels torpedoed without warning—The escape of the s.s. *Vosges*—The s.s. *Falaba* torpedoed and sunk—A court of inquiry—The tragedy of the s.s. *Fulgent* . pp. 268—317

CHAPTER VIII

THE AUXILIARY PATROL AT WORK

Mine-laying by the Germans—Operations of British mine-sweepers—Maintaining a swept channel—The needs of the Grand Fleet—Trawlers in a new rôle—Steam-yachts requisitioned—The Motor-Boat Reserve—Clearing three German minefields—The menace of the submarine—An anti-submarine trawler flotilla—Protecting merchant shipping—A new naval command at Dover—Hunting for submarines—Expansion of the mine-sweeping service—Escape of the Norddeutscher Lloyd liner *Berlin*—A minefield laid off Tory Island—Foundering of H.M.S. AUDACIOUS—Impressment of Liverpool tugs as patrols—Exploration of a new minefield—The Gorleston raid—Activity in the English Channel—U18 sunk by a trawler—Incursions into Scapa Flow—The raid on Scarborough
pp. 318—366

CONTENTS xiii

CHAPTER IX

THE GROWTH OF THE SUBMARINE MENACE

The enemy's dependence on the mine and submarine—An attack upon the Grand Fleet—Additional armed trawlers fitted out—The development of the " indicator net "—An extended scheme of patrol introduced—The nucleus of the drifter fleet—Submarine attack off the Mersey—Reorganisation of the patrol area—The war zone declaration and its influence on the patrol—Netting the Straits of Dover—Destruction of a submarine by the steam trawler *Alex Hastie*—Encounters with submarines—The value of the modified sweep—The fighting spirit of the British crews—The enemy's reply to the indicator net—Loss of fishing-vessels and crews—Protective measures devised by the Admiralty—Further changes in the Auxiliary Patrol—The discovery of an enemy minefield . pp. 367—409

CHAPTER X

THE SINKING OF THE " LUSITANIA "

The " Blue Ribbon of the Atlantic "—Enemy warning of an attack on the *Lusitania* ignored by passengers—An unarmed ship, with 1,959 people on board—Lord Mersey's judgment supported by an American judge—The cross-Atlantic voyage—Warnings from the Admiralty as to the presence of submarines off the Irish coast—Captain Turner's decision—The enemy's attack without warning—A passenger's experience—Scene on board the doomed ship—Heroic conduct of an able seaman—The first officer's exertions to save life—Captain Turner's explanation—The official inquiry and judgment—Reception of the news in Germany pp. 410—428

CHAPTER XI

THE ADVENT OF THE OCEAN-GOING SUBMARINE

The concentration of enemy craft off the Irish coast to attack the *Lusitania*—The disposition of patrol vessels—The S.O.S. signal and the response—Rescue of the survivors—Fine service of unarmed fishing-vessels—Increasing constriction on the enemy's movement owing to the activity of the patrol—A well-devised scheme—The introduction of the hydrophone—The fighting spirit of the new Navy—Entrapping the submarine—The harvest of the sea—Trawler sea-fights—A submarine's cowardly action—Destruction of the U-boat—Rescue of a merchant ship and a valuable cargo . . . . pp. 429—449

INDEX . . . . pp. 451—473

LIST OF ILLUSTRATIONS

	FACING PAGE
After a Mine Explosion	134
The Sinking of a Merchant Ship	146
The White Star Liner "Olympic" (from the Air)	202
Survivors from a Torpedoed Ship	270
A Drifter Fleet at Sea	320
Flagship of a Drifter Fleet	330
A Drifter on Patrol	358
Net Mines being thrown Overboard	374
Throwing a Lance-bomb	392
The Cunard Liner "Lusitania" off Brow Head	416
Grave of Victims of the "Lusitania" at Queenstown	426
Laying Nets from Drifters to catch Submarines	438

THE
MERCHANT NAVY

INTRODUCTION

A HISTORY of the part which merchant seamen took in the war by sea, from its dramatic opening on August 4th, 1914, to its close over four and a half years later, would be incomplete were no attempt made to fill in the background against which the stirring events of those years must stand out in due perspective. Without such an historic setting it would be difficult to appreciate the character and extent of the services which British seamen, non-combatants and unpledged to the State, rendered with fine patriotism, never-failing resource, and a hardihood unparalleled even in British annals.

During the long period of peace after the conclusion of the Napoleonic War, the British Merchant Navy was regarded as a trading organisation—that and nothing more. The authority which the State had exercised in the past had been in general of two kinds—protective and economic. Throughout the latter half of the nineteenth and the first decade of the twentieth century, it tended to interest itself increasingly in shipping, and especially to regulate it more closely in the interest of the persons (passengers and crews) carried in the ships, with a view to safeguarding life. The restricted powers formerly vested in the Admiralty were transferred to the Board of Trade and exercised by that department, overburdened with many and varied responsibilities, with sagacity and restraint, the aim being to discourage as little as possible the individualistic enterprise of the shipping industry.

It was forgotten by the British people that the British Merchant Navy had a war history dating back to a period anterior to the founding of the Royal Navy. No one recalled the part which merchant seamen had borne in former wars, or remembered that in earlier periods of British history the merchant sailor had stood between this country and the invader when little or no progress had been made in the organisation of a fighting Navy as a State institution. The Merchant Navy was thought to be an organisation without traditions and with little remaining romance, owing to the advent of steam, which had replaced sail power. That was a narrow and mistaken view, as events were to show. Just as in the great period of the nation's expanding self-consciousness the Merchant Navy was the finest embodiment of the national spirit, so when the war clouds burst in the summer of 1914, the real character of the British merchant seamen was revealed as the flash of artillery lit up the battle-fields on the Continent of Europe. These sailors were recognised as no ordinary men engaged merely in facilitating the barter and exchange of a commercial community, but as belonging to a great brotherhood, instinct with patriotism and proud of the traditions dating back, in unbroken and glorious sequence, to the early years of British history.

When the present struggle began, two great national forces, the Navy and the Army—the latter supported by Territorials—were recognised, and supported out of public funds. Within a few months of the opening of hostilities, the King, in a message of appreciation of the services of the merchant seamen, referred to " his Merchant Navy," subsequently appointing Captain H. J. Haddock, C.B., one of the most distinguished senior officers of the Mercantile Marine, as an aide-de-camp, and the Prime Minister, in a self-revealing phrase, described the Merchant Navy as " the jugular vein of the nation." Its officers and men in a short time set up a record of daring, resource, and fine seamanship, so conspicuous, even when studied against the background of past centuries, that it was necessary to amend the statutes and introduce new regulations in order to enable suitable recognition to be given to them. The merchant sailor, unassuming and modest, took his stand, with the full recognition of an aroused and grateful public opinion, beside the men of the ancient fighting services.

During the years of fierce naval competition which preceded the War, when the talk was of Dreadnoughts, sea power was thought to be a matter of men-of-war—battleships, cruisers, destroyers, and submarines—organised in fleets, squadrons, or flotillas, and manned by highly trained officers and men. So long as the country possessed a supreme Navy, any other deficiency was of minor importance. The relationship between the Royal Navy and the Mercantile Marine had undergone a radical change since the close of the last Great War, to be reflected in the public attitude towards the Merchant Fleet. The former had become independent of the latter as a source of manpower, owing to the introduction of a system of continuous naval service in the middle of the nineteenth century. It was concluded that, since the necessity of compulsory service had disappeared, the value of the Merchant Fleet as an auxiliary force in time of war had been reduced, though its place as a food-carrier from distant markets was realised by open-eyed statesmen. Mahan, fresh from the study of naval history, had made, it is true, a significant declaration. "Sea power," he remarked, "primarily depends upon commerce which follows the most advantageous road; military control follows upon trade for its furtherance and protection. Except as a system of highways joining country to country, the sea is an unfruitful possession. The sea, or water, is the great medium of circulation established by Nature, just as money has been evolved by man for the exchange of commerce. Change the flow of either in direction or amount, and you modify the political and industrial relations of mankind."[1] This writer was groping after a truth, but even he was blind to the essential character of the functions of a merchant navy, or, rather, did not associate cause with effect. He and other writers, in common with Governments throughout the world, failed to trace the wide influence exerted, on the one hand, by conscription for military purposes, and, on the other, by the introduction of steam as the motive power for men-of-war.

When Napoleon decided to make a levy on the population of France in order to raise a vast army which was to dominate Europe, he laid the foundations of a system which rendered a long war in future years impossible except with the aid of sea carriage. Before that development, armies and navies made relatively small demands upon

[1] *Naval Strategy* (Mahan).

the man-power of the nations engaged, and those nations were in large measure self-supporting. Europe had had its Hundred Years' War. Maritime commerce was still in its infancy during the Revolutionary and Napoleonic Wars. The Continent of Europe was engaged in hostilities almost without interruption for a period of nearly a quarter of a century without being brought to a condition of famine, so great were its resources. Between 1815 and 1914, however, the standard of living in Western Europe had been raised; industrialism had grown at the expense of agriculture; and increasing reliance had been placed upon the ship of commerce, acting as the link between the highly developed nations of the West and the States overseas, which still continue to produce a surplus of food-stuffs and raw materials.

In war-time conscription, as the late struggle was to reveal, withdraws from essential industries all the able-bodied men of a State; it blights agriculture and depresses trade; it converts producers into consumers. Moltke, after the Franco-Prussian War, admitted that long-drawn-out contests would in future be checked by the economic exhaustion which wars on the scale of national man-power would involve, since, from the moment such a struggle opened, a State, in developing fighting energy on a broad national basis, would begin subtracting from its economic strength. But in this respect, as German writers were among the first to recognise, a maritime Power necessarily enjoys advantages over a land Power, so long as it is able to use the pathways of the sea to replenish its supplies of food and raw material from neutral markets. Conscription casts fresh burdens on sea power, and, in particular, on that form of sea power represented by the ship of commerce.

But that is not the only change which occurred during the nineteenth century. The great development of military power on shore was accompanied by a vast growth of military strength by sea. Owing to the advent of steam, the typical man-of-war of the Nelsonian era disappeared, and was replaced by the coal or oil consuming vessel. Mahan [1] remarked, long before the Great War opened, that, "The days when fleets lay becalmed are gone, it is true; but gone are the days when, with four or

[1] *Naval Strategy* (Mahan).

five months of food and water below, they were ready to follow the enemy to the other side of the world without stopping. Nelson, in 1803–5, had always on board three months' provisions and water, and aimed to have five months'—that is, to be independent of communications for nearly five months. If it is sought to lessen the strategic difficulty by carrying more coal, there is introduced the technical drawback of greater draught, with consequent lower speed and more sluggish handling, a still more important consideration. The experience of Admiral Rodjestvensky in this matter is recent and instructive. His difficulties of supply, and chiefly of coal, are known : the most striking consequence is the inconsiderate manner in which, without necessity, he stuffed his vessels with coal for the last run of barely a thousand miles. That he did this can be attributed reasonably only to the impression produced upon his mind by his coaling difficulties, for the evident consequence of this injudicious action was to put his ships in bad condition for a battle which he knew was almost inevitable." Those words indicate that the American historian was approaching a realisation of the changes which had occurred in the character of naval power, rendering it dependent on auxiliaries for food, ammunition, and stores ; but, on the other hand, he under-estimated the extent to which the ship of commerce loaded with coal and operating with the ship of war engaged in attacking commerce, as in the case of the EMDEN and other enemy cruisers, could provide a measure of compensation for the restrictions on naval warfare traceable to the development of the swift-running steam-engine with its enormous consumption of fuel.

All those considerations were inadequately recognised before the War opened in 1914, which was at last to involve in its horrors, directly or indirectly, practically all the nations of the Continent of Europe, was later on to draw in Japan and China, and at last to bring the United States and other American Republics into the arena. Even Mahan did not go farther than to suggest that " a broad basis of mercantile maritime interests will doubtless conduce to naval efficiency by supplying a reserve of material and personnel." Events were to show that his anticipation of reliance being placed upon the Mercantile Marine for men to anything like the same extent as during the wars of the eighteenth and nineteenth centuries was based upon an under-appreciation of the varied responsibilities devolving upon a merchant navy as soon as the maritime State whose flag it carries becomes engaged in warfare. The books of British writers upon war policy may be studied in vain for a just appreciation of the essential part which the British Mercantile Marine necessarily assumed as soon as this country become involved in varied war activities overseas.

Soon after the declaration of war, the British Mercantile Navy was confronted with responsibilities which in character and extent were without parallel in maritime history.

1. Owing to circumstances which need not be examined in this connection, the Royal Navy was without defended bases of supply on the east coast *vis-à-vis* to Germany. Consequently, as soon as the Grand Fleet was mobilised, heavy demands were made upon the Mercantile Marine for ships to carry fuel (coal and oil), ammunition, stores, food, and everything required for the prosecution of the war in home waters. At the same time, other ships were requisitioned for the support of naval power in the outer seas.

2. The resources of the Royal Navy—large as they were—proved inadequate to maintain the patrol which it became necessary to organise in order to make the blockade of the enemy effective. Some of the swiftest liners were, therefore, taken up and commissioned under the White Ensign, and from the varied resources of the Merchant Navy the Auxiliary Patrol was organised.

3. As the military commitments of the country increased, a large volume of mercantile tonnage was required for transport purposes. Transport facilities had to be provided for the Gallipoli Expedition, the army at Salonika, the forces based on Egypt, the operations in Mesopotamia and Palestine, and the campaign in East Africa. Shipping was also requisitioned for the troops engaged in routing the Germans out of their Pacific possessions, and other ships were employed in maintaining the military lines of communication between the mother-country and India, New Zealand, Australia, South Africa, Canada, and Newfoundland. Hospital carriers had to be fitted out.

4. Storeships had to be found for the growing armies

engaged in all the widely separated theatres of war to carry the vast assortment of material ranging from heavy guns and horses to bomb-throwers and medical comforts.

5. As the British Army grew in size, a vast expansion occurred in the munition movement in the British Isles, in India, and in Canada, as well as in the United States, and a large number of ships were soon engaged exclusively in conveying ores and other raw materials over the seas.

6. At the same time, the sea-dependent people of the British Isles, numbering over forty million persons, had to be fed, and, owing to the isolation of Russia with its surplus grain production, the cutting off of beet sugar from Germany, and the dangers which threatened navigation between the British Isles and Scandinavia, new sources of supply had to be opened up, involving longer voyages, and therefore the employment of a larger amount of tonnage.

It was a fortunate circumstance that this country possessed about half the merchant shipping of the world; otherwise it would have been seriously hampered in the prosecution of the War. It is also a fortunate circumstance that its merchant ships possessed officers and crews who were not to be frightened by the enemy threats or acts.

The British Navy has never wanted historians; its history has been written from every standpoint; but the historian to give full credit to the British Merchant Navy, with its fine achievements in peace and in war, has not yet arisen. In approaching the study of the part taken by the Merchant Navy in the Great War, it has been thought pardonable to supply a background, consisting of a short survey of the place which British merchant seamen have filled in the evolution of the British people, a brief record of the heroic services they have rendered in successive wars, and particularly in the Revolutionary and Napoleonic Wars, and some details of the gradual development of the Mercantile Marine during the nineteenth century. A contrast may thus be provided between the conditions existing in former wars and those with which the British seaman, unarmed and undefended, was confronted when, in performance of his peaceful duty, he was suddenly called upon to meet the menace of the raider, the mine, and, above all, the submarine.

CHAPTER I

THE MERCHANT NAVY OF THE PAST

I. THE FIGHTING MERCHANTMEN

OF all the lessons taught to the inhabitants of these islands by the Great War, none can have been more completely mastered than this—that they owe their very existence to the two branches of the great Sea service—the Mercantile Marine bringing them the bulk of their supplies, and the Royal Navy, the " sure shield " of that vital traffic as well as of the homeland itself. Viewed in the light of this immense debt of gratitude, the two branches are seen to be essentially one, the fighting arm but an extension of the Mercantile Marine ; and the modern separation of functions takes its proper place as a natural evolution from the days when our sea battles were fought by vessels temporarily converted from merchantmen to men-of-war. That condition did not mark in any degree the centuries which immediately followed the Roman occupation. Sunk in internecine strife, and the prey to successive piratical invasions, England had then no effective share in the sea-borne commerce of which the Mediterranean was the secular home; and in constructing and maintaining the Fleet which has given him such a high place in our naval history, King Alfred was dealing with a simple though formidable problem of invasion, and, taking an accurate strategical view of the situation, he placed his first line of defence off his coasts. His policy was vigorously carried on by Athelstan, and though from time to time merchant shipping was drawn upon by the Saxon kings for their war fleets, it may be said generally that the basis of the navies of these troublous centuries was essentially a military one. The change came with the return to greater national security, and the consequent growth of maritime enterprise, and the incorporation of

SEAMEN OF THE CINQUE PORTS

the famous Cinque Ports by the Conqueror—a step directly due to the fear of a Danish invasion—may conveniently be taken as inaugurating the unity of the two branches of the sea service.

Upon the seamen of the Cinque Ports—Dover, Sandwich, Romney, Winchelsea and Rye (the list was extended later)—were conferred certain unique commercial and maritime privileges on condition of their raising a powerful force of fifty-seven ships properly manned and equipped for use in any sudden emergency. The period of service (fifteen days) could be extended at the King's pleasure, but in such event the cost was to be borne by the Royal Treasury. The fleet thus created was actively maintained by William Rufus, and it contributed its full share to the great expedition undertaken by Richard I to recover the Holy Land from the Saracens. In this enterprise over 200 merchant vessels were enrolled for the task of transporting the Crusaders; and, disastrous as it proved in some respects, the expedition had notable consequences for the country's maritime progress. In the critical days which followed the death of King John, the Cinque Ports Fleet covered itself with immortal glory by the prominent part it took in the defeat of the French Armada dispatched from Calais under Eustace the Monk. Responding to the patriotic appeal of Hubert de Burgh, the stout sailors and fishermen of Dover manned all the vessels, large and small, lying in the harbour, and, having taken the knights and men-at-arms on board, sailed out to meet the enemy. The battle, as recorded by Matthew Paris, took place off Sandwich. The English sailors proved their better seamanship by getting the weather gauge, and when the cross-bowmen and archers had discharged their arrows under these favourable conditions and quick-lime had been thrown at close quarters, the Frenchmen were rammed and boarded. Such a picture presents the mariners of the southern ports in the most favourable colours. Their brilliant share in the exploit won them a generous extension of their already existing rights, but it has to be admitted that the position of the seamen of the Cinque Ports as a privileged class was productive of many evils which must be set off against their great services to the nation. The privilege now conferred upon them—in itself a foreshadowing of the custom of issuing Letters of Marque

—of annoying " the subjects of France and all they met of whatever nation," simply meant the right to plunder any and every foreign merchant ship. The example found so many imitators that before long the Channel was swarming with pirates, the strong preying on the weak, "until the evil had grown to such an enormous extent that the most stringent measures were found necessary to sweep the seas of the marauders."[1] Moreover, the Cinque Ports were not free from the jealousy characteristic of a privileged class, and feuds with other ports, and notably with Yarmouth, broke out again and again, often marked by savage energy.

We get a picturesque hint of the beginnings of maritime enterprise under the Saxon kings in Athelstan's grant of the rank and privileges of Thane to any merchant or mariner who should successfully accomplish three voyages on the high seas; but for long after the Conquest the limits of British overseas trade appear to have been the entrance to the Baltic in the north and the ports of the Bay of Biscay to the south, nor did our wool trade with Flanders reach its high prosperity till a later date. Richard's last crusade, therefore, has a special significance as the first extended voyage of English ships, and it furnished results far removed from its idealistic purposes. For the first time since the Roman occupation the English now entered into trade relations with the Levant (though English ships did not penetrate there till much later); and not only was a new stimulus applied to the growth of English shipping, but the attempt was made to codify by regular enactment the rules of the sea.

The famous *Laws of Oleron*, generally attributed to Richard himself,[2] but almost certainly derived from a French source, are of great interest for the light they throw on life on board the sea-going merchant ship of the period. The articles covered all matters relating to mercantile shipping—questions of total loss, damage, demurrage, harbour regulation, fishing, and the like—and in particular defined for the first time the duties and qualifications of the Master of the ship. The Master was put in charge of, and held answerable for, everything on board, and he was required to understand thoroughly the

[1] *The British Merchant Service* (Cornewall Jones).
[2] For a full discussion of this question, see *The Black Book of the Admiralty*, in the edition of Sir Travers Twiss.

art of navigating his vessel, for the specific reason that he might thereby control the pilot, who was the Second Officer on board a merchantman. Nor could any sailor leave the ship without his consent. Navigation in the days before the compass was largely a matter of practical experience, and of this fact the second article of the Code affords a striking illustration; for it was there laid down that if a vessel was delayed in port by unfavourable weather, or by the failure of the wind, the Master had to call the ship's company together, and take their opinion on the situation, and in the event of a division of opinion he was to abide by the voice of the majority. This rule, in fact, applied to every emergency by which the Master might be confronted. It is interesting to note that such a regulation in a modified form remained in active force for centuries; indeed, one of the charges brought by his detractors against Sir Francis Drake in the period of his great voyages was that, by his attitude towards his officers, he had on occasion treated this obligation with contempt. But Drake, a giant among sea captains and self-reliant to his finger-tips, was a law unto himself in such matters. Here, surely, in this thirteenth-century code we perceive the beginnings of that spirit of freedom under discipline which has become traditional in the Mercantile Marine, a spirit which found such rich expression in Elizabethan times, and helped to make the British the first seamen of the world.

The same principle, born as it were of the breath of the sea, is traceable in the article defining with amusing particularity the relations of the Master with the crew. It was the Master's duty to keep peace among his men. If one called another a liar at table, he was to be fined fourpence, but if the Master himself so offended he was mulcted in twice the amount. For impudently contradicting the Master, a seaman was fined eightpence. A single blow from the Master was to be accepted by a sailor without retaliation, but a second blow gave him the right to defend himself. On the other hand, if a sailor struck the first blow, he was either to pay a heavy fine or lose his hand. Finally, if a sailor received abuse from the Master, he was advised to hide himself in the forecastle; but if the Master followed him into that retreat—the Englishman's house at sea in the proverbial sense of his castle—then the victim was entitled to stand on his defence.

This significant recognition of the rights of the common sailor went hand-in-hand with strict discipline, and order and good conduct were maintained with mediæval severity. Damage to the ship due to a sailor's absence without leave was punishable with a year's imprisonment; a fatal accident due to the same cause involved a flogging—a flogging of the period—and actual desertion meant branding in the face with a red-hot iron. Other offences, including such human weaknesses as swearing and gambling, often incurred brutal penalties in the Middle Ages, and the punishment of keel-hauling, which seems to have been first practised by the English in the twelfth century, survived into modern times, as we know from the pages of Captain Marryatt.

By the Oleron Code, a defaulting pilot—the navigating officer of the time—was allotted treatment in full proportion to the responsibility of his task. If through his ignorance his vessel miscarried in entering a port, and if he were unable to render full satisfaction for the damage or loss, then he paid for the mishap with his head; and if the Master or the merchants on board chose to exact the penalty there and then, they were not to be called on to answer it in law. Furthermore, any pilot who, in connivance with the "lords of the coast," ran his ship on shore, was to be hanged on a high gibbet at the place of destruction, as a caution to other vessels that might pass thereby. Against any "lord of the coast" involved in such a crime drastic measures were laid down. His goods were to be confiscated by way of restitution, while he himself was to be fastened to a stake in the midst of his mansion and the whole building committed to the flames. In the Middle Ages wreckers infested the shores, and the sense of this ever-present menace to shipping is fully expressed in the severe treatment reserved for those who plundered a ship or murdered castaway mariners. They were to be "plunged into the sea till they were half dead, and then drawn out from the sea and stoned to death." A notable example of the common practice of the impressment of sailors occurred in the following reign at a time when King John was preparing an expedition to Ireland. For the transport of the soldiers, the seamen of Wales were ordered to repair to Ilfracombe on pain of hanging and forfeiture of goods. This power of the Crown was continuously exercised up to the beginning of the nineteenth century. Though never a statutory right, and occasionally challenged as an illegality, it is implied in numerous statutes, and was judicially regarded as a part of the Common Law of the Realm.

Like the fight off Sandwich of 1217, the Battle of Sluys, early in the reign of Edward III, was a triumph for the merchantmen of England. The French King's fleet, largely composed of Norman ships, reinforced by a Genoese squadron, were massed in the harbour at the entrance to the canal leading to the great mart of Bruges—so vast in numbers, says Froissart, that " their masts seemed to be like a great wood." King Edward attacked with a fleet drawn from the various ports of the kingdom, and carrying a large force of archers and men-at-arms. A fierce struggle, lasting all day and renewed the following morning, ended in a complete victory, with capture or destruction of nearly all the French vessels, though the Genoese mercenaries escaped in the night. The Harleian MSS. have preserved for us the list of the Armada with which, six years later, the King blockaded Calais. Exclusive of those of "forrayne Countreyes in this Ayde," the roll shows a total of 707 vessels, and of that number only twenty-five were King's ships. The detailed list is of great interest, also, as an indication of the relative prominence of the different maritime towns. The famous Cinque Ports, their harbours already beginning to silt up, were far out-distanced by the West Country. Sandwich, Winchelsea, Dover, Rye, and Hythe, together muster an average of fifteen ships each, but Fowey—a place of little importance to-day, but then a centre of the tin industry—sent 47; Dartmouth—whence Chaucer's shipman haled—32; Plymouth, 26; Bristol, 22; and Looe, 20. On the other hand, the modern Welsh ports of Cardiff and Swansea were represented by only one ship each, and Liverpool did not even appear in the tally.

The Battle of Sluys marked the beginning of that exhausting attempt at Continental conquest known as the Hundred Years' War, itself followed by the devastating civil strife of the Wars of the Roses. The long struggle with France interrupted trade and checked maritime enterprise, though it helped powerfully to evoke a new spirit of national consciousness at a time when municipal institutions were beginning to decay and our mercantile policy was undergoing a drastic change. Apart from the ravaging of seaports by the enemy—those on the south coast being special sufferers [1]—the country's shipping was continually being diverted from its normal purposes by the military requirements of the Sovereign. In his great invasion of France in 1415, Henry V sailed from Southampton with a vast fleet of 1,400 vessels, having previously impressed all the craft in the country of 20 tons and upwards, and obtained his crews largely by similar methods. Brilliant as the adventure was in its temporary achievements, one is apt to overlook the enormous strain it placed on the economic resources of the kingdom, and to forget such contemporary protests as the humble petition of Parliament representing that the conquest of France would be the ruin of England.

Furthermore, the almost continuous state of war, foreign and civil, intensified the lawlessness which had so long prevailed at sea. The complex problem presented by mediæval piracy baffled the efforts of even the most statesmanlike rulers. Sea-trading in those days was anything but a peaceful occupation. Professional pirates, whether individual ships or organised gangs like the Rovers of the Sea, whose activities at Scarborough anticipated the modern revival of unrestrained piracy, infested the Channel and the North Sea, adding their depredations to those of enemy craft; and these marauders carried their daring to the extent of harrying the coast and burning seaside towns. At one time, the Isle of Wight was virtually in the possession of a certain John of Newport, whose misdeeds and " riot kept uppon the see " were the theme of a plaintive petition to Parliament.

But apart from sheer plundering, though not always distinguishable from it, was the system of legalised privateering arising out of the issue of Letters of Marque. By the licence thus obtained from the Crown, a trader who had been the victim of foreign aggression, or who sought the means of collecting a difficult debt, was given the right of reprisals on the goods of the community or country to which the offender belonged. The first recorded instance of such a grant occurs in the reign of Edward I, though it cannot safely be assumed that none was issued earlier. It

[1] The activity of the Norman corsairs in the early years of Edward III's reign was so effective that an order was issued directing dwellers on the south coast to take refuge in fortresses and withdraw their goods a distance of four leagues from the sea. (*Pol. Hist. of England*, vol. iii, p. 334.)

was made in favour of the English owner of a ship which, while bringing fruit from Malaga, was piratically seized off the coast of Portugal and carried as a prize into Lisbon. In this case, the licence to seize the goods of the Portuguese to the extent of the loss sustained was limited to five years. The disadvantages of such a rough-and-ready method of adjusting differences need no great emphasis. In the first place, experience showed that licence for reprisals tended to degenerate into licence of a more general kind ; and, secondly, this method of making innocent Peter pay for guilty Paul often acted as a serious deterrent upon trading.

In the British Museum may be seen a gold noble coined by Edward III after the taking of Calais had given him the command of the Channel. On the reverse it depicts a ship and a sword, and it possesses a peculiar interest as the symbol of the first claim by an English King to the sovereignty of the sea. In formally adopting the title of Dominus Maris Anglicani Circumquaque, this clear-sighted ruler was laying claim to no empty formula, but to a real sovereignty involving a number of substantial rights— such as those of fishing, the levying of tolls for the use of the sea, free passage for ships-of-war, and, lastly, jurisdiction for crimes committed at sea. It was therefore by the active assertion of this claim that Edward sought to deal with the growing practice of piracy and give protection at sea. His practical measures included the granting to merchant vessels of letters of safe-conduct and the organising of fleets in convoy. Vessels bound for Gascony, for instance, were directed to assemble on the day of the Nativity of the Virgin outside Southampton Water,[1] sailing thence under the charge of Royal officials. The main effect, however, of the first-mentioned remedy seems, in later times, to have aggravated the evil, for under the Lancastrian Kings we get many complaints of the forging of such documents ; and, moreover, it was found by the men on the English coasts that the issue of letters of safe-conduct prevented them from getting redress for pillage by taking the matter into their own hands. In short, the efforts of Edward III had little or no effect in giving protection on the seas. So it was with his successors. In the next reign, letters of marque were granted more

[1] " Chalcheford " in the original, which, according to Dr. Cunningham, was probably Calshot Castle.

freely than ever, and it is recorded of one of the merchants of Dartmouth, a port which held a general privateering commission from the Crown, that with a fleet of his own he captured no fewer than thirty-three vessels with 1,500 tuns of Rochelle wine.

Apart from its more direct results, the long period of wars, by its consumption of the national energies, offered an opportunity to foreign rivals which they were quick to seize. The Hanseatic League had become the most important commercial association of the world at the beginning of the fourteenth century; Bruges and Antwerp had established themselves as the great entrepôts of Northern Europe, and the merchant vessels of the Italian Republics were frequenting the markets of the Netherlands. To these several rivals fell, during the war, the bulk of the English carrying trade. Another cause operating against the interests of the English shipper was the commercial policy carried out by Edward III. His broad aims may be summed up as a combination of cheap imports for the benefit of the consumer, with high prices for exports as a means of providing revenue through the Customs; and those aims were apparent in the regulations affecting wool and wine, and the liberal provisions for encouraging the foreign trader. A few years after Edward's death saw the start of a reversal of this policy. The increased resentment of English merchants against the foreign trader, and the depressed condition of English shipping, found expression in the first of many Navigation Acts (1381), which provided that " to increase the Navy of England,[1] which is now greatly diminished, it is assented and accorded that none of the King's liege people do from henceforth ship any merchandise in going or coming within the realm of England in any port, but only in ships of the King's liegance." So diminished, indeed, was "the Navy" that in the following year the new ordinance had to be modified, owing to an insufficiency of shipping. Taken in conjunction with the new regulations for keeping bullion in the country, and the protective encouragement of tillage, not merely as a means of safeguarding the food-supply, but for the fostering of the country's military strength, the Navigation Act marks the beginning of a drastic change of mercantile policy—a change, in a happy

---

[1] That is to say, the general shipping of the kingdom.

phrase Bacon applies to the policy of the first Tudor King, "from consideration of plenty to consideration of power."

In spite, however, of the growth of national consciousness, an effective means of providing for the due protection of the country's coasts and shipping seemed for a time no nearer. It was the plundering of English vessels by a daring Scottish pirate early in the reign of Richard II, and the ravaging of Rye and other south coast towns by a French fleet, which induced Parliament, alarmed for the safety of the realm, to pass the first law levying dues on all merchant vessels (with a few exceptions) frequenting English ports, for the specific purpose of maintaining an efficient Royal Navy. But the fleet, no sooner created, was led by John of Gaunt on the wild enterprise of the Siege of St. Malo, instead of being employed in its proper service. And it was a squadron of sturdy merchant ships which, in the absence of the Royal fleet, and of its own initiative, repelled a French marauding expedition. The usurper of the following reign narrowly escaped capture by pirates when coming up the Thames to London, and he was so little able to achieve his aim of establishing a Royal Navy that for a period of over a year the entire guardianship of the coasts was entrusted to the country's merchantmen. By this plan, which illustrates the general system of protection by contract, the shipowners were required to maintain certain ships on the sea, and to two "fit persons" chosen from their body the King granted commissions to act as his Admirals, one for the north and one for the south. In recompense for these services they were empowered to take three shillings on every cask of imported wine, as well as certain dues on exports. It was the Crown's complaint, subsequently, that the merchantmen had failed to fulfil their part of the contract, and the scheme came to nothing. A similar plan was tried, with no better result, under Henry VI; in that case the Commissioners were the Earls of Salisbury, Shrewsbury, Worcester, and Wiltshire, and Lord Sturton, who were assigned the grant of tonnage and poundage on condition of "keeping the seas" for three years. The significance of the maritime efforts of Henry V's reign lies mainly in the improvements in shipbuilding. Three ships turned out at Southampton by the victor of Agincourt, on the models of three big Genoese merchantmen which traded with that port, excited the country's admiration; and examples of private enterprise are found in the great carack built by John Taverner, of Hull, and the fleet maintained by Bristol's merchant prince, William Canynges, among which was a vessel of 900 tons burden. It was owing to this advance in shipbuilding that, later in the century, Englishmen found themselves with vessels fit to take part in distant voyages of discovery.

It was in such conditions of turmoil as have been described that our merchantmen in the Middle Ages not only maintained and even extended their trade, but also, as we have seen, provided the only means for the defence and security of their country. In the light of their varied record we clearly perceive that the mariners who won wide renown in the days of Queen Elizabeth were but carrying a step forward in the dawn of a new age the traditions of their predecessors—" good felawes " of the type so vividly presented by Chaucer's shipman. The mariner of mediæval England was an example of the hardihood of his day. " Of nyce conscience took he no keep," the Prologue tells us. " If that he fought and hadde the hyer hond By water he sente hem hoom to every lond." But he was " hardy " and " wys to undertake," and again and again in the records of these centuries we get proofs of that endurance and tenacity, that native sea sense, that ready resource, which we have come to regard as the birthright of the English seaman. When in 1378, as already mentioned, the King's ships were busy besieging St. Malo, a squadron of French and Spanish galleys seized the opportunity of sailing up the Kentish coast and entering the mouth of the Thames, burning the towns and villages on its banks as far as Gravesend. On returning by the Channel, however, intent on further destruction, the marauders were met by a fleet of West Country merchantmen and valiantly repulsed. The English ships were of less tonnage than those of the enemy, but boldness of attack and better seamanship prevailed, as they have on so many historic occasions since. And in the fifteenth century, in spite of conditions which often approached to social anarchy, we get evidence of the slow but real progress of maritime commerce fostered by the new mercantile policy, which was still further developed under the Tudor kings. The reign of Henry IV saw the establishment of the Merchant Adventurers and similar organisations of English merchants, trading to the Baltic and to Prussia; commercial treaties were common from the reign of Edward IV onwards; in 1480, the year of the birth of the great Magellan, Bristol—then the most enterprising seaport of England, its fishermen making regular voyages to Iceland—dispatched an exploring expedition in search of the "Island of Brazil"; a score of years later John Cabot, sailing from the same port, had made two memorable voyages to the coast of Labrador, and though he found no precious metals, reported, what was far more significant, an abundance of cod-fish; in 1485 there appeared at Pisa the first English Consul to be appointed in the Mediterranean; and the decline in power of the Hanseatic League in this country, destined to be extinguished finally under Queen Elizabeth, was rapidly hastened. By the new consistency in her mercantile policy, based on national consciousness, England was steadily preparing to gather, by means of her merchantmen of a later day, the fruits of the Age of Discovery.

When men were bidden by law to eat fish twice a week, and throughout the whole of Lent, they were obeying an obligation which it was believed the political needs of the country imposed. Fish was, of course, an article of diet of national importance, apart from the religious considerations which entered into the matter. But the real significance of the act was political. The buying of fish stimulated the fishing industry, the fishing industry was the best school for seamen, and seamen and shipping were necessary for strengthening the country's power against its rivals. Another essential of the national ambition was wealth, and one avenue to wealth was already being indicated by the great explorations of the last decades of the century. The effects of the discovery of America, of the rounding of the Cape by Vasco da Gama, and later the accident of storm which gave Brazil to Portugal, were as swift as revolutionary. The Levantine trade with the East was ruined. For a time the Portuguese became the first maritime Power. Lisbon established itself as the great commercial depot for Western Europe. In their desire for wealth, as a means of national power, Tudor Englishmen turned their eyes to the New World and to the looked-for promise of a north-west route to Far Cathay. This sentiment found expression in 1511, in the protest made by certain members of King Henry VIII's Council against Continental conquest.[1] If we would enlarge ourselves, these statesmen argued,[2] "let it be that way we can, and to which it seems the eternal Providence hath destined us, which is the sea. The Indies are discovered, and vast treasure brought from thence every day. Let us, therefore, bend our Endeavours thitherward, and if the Spaniards or Portuguese suffer us not to join with them, there will be yet region enough for all to enjoy."

Henry VIII himself gave effect to the prevalent ideas of the time by endowing the country with its first Royal Navy on an organised basis. But his establishment of the Royal Navy as a regular department of the State was also in accordance with the Tudor dynasty's principle of personal power, and in idea it may be compared with the tendency towards standing armies on the Continent. The importance of Henry VIII's policy must be emphasised, for here we have the beginnings of the differentiation between the naval and mercantile services. A skilled amateur in many arts and crafts, the King concerned himself personally with improvement in construction, and his famous ship, the GREAT HARRY, of at least 1,000 tons, was the largest vessel then known. The first fleet which he secretly fitted out at Portsmouth, small but admirably equipped, was specially designed to deal with the French buccaneers who infested the Channel, and it successfully disposed of a squadron of marauders which had been plundering merchant craft in Mounts Bay. The great fleet, assembled at Spithead in his last war with France, was formed, as in the old days, on a nucleus of the ships flying the Royal Standard, but that nucleus organised, as indicated above, on definite lines. Privateers joined the Admiral chiefly from the West Country ports. At his death Henry left a fleet of over seventy vessels; but more important than that, he had applied a new principle to national defence. Nor did his scheme of organisation end with the provision of a Royal fleet and its crews. As a means of protecting London from pirates, he established two ports on the river at, and opposite to, Gravesend, so that Londoners enjoyed an

---

[1] This, it may be noted, was eight years after the Portuguese had tapped the sources of the Venetians' Eastern trade and had brought their first cargo of pepper to England.

[2] Recorded in Lord Herbert of Cherbury's *History*.

hitherto unknown security; he founded a Naval Arsenal at Deptford; and there also he established the Fraternity of the Holy Trinity, that since-famous body whose Tudor Charter empowered it to frame " all and singular articles in any wise concerning the science or art of mariners," and to make ordinances " for the relief, increase, and augmentation of this our Realm of England." Nor could we find clearer evidence of Parliament's recognition of the national importance of the Mercantile Marine than in the preamble of the Act passed in 1540 for the " maintenance of the Navy." The dual purpose of the " Navy or multitude of ships of this Realm " (the sense in which we now use the word Navy has, of course, become more specialised) is explicitly set forth—that is to say, first: " for the intercourse and concourse of merchants, transporting and conveying their wares and merchandise "; and, secondly, for " a great defence and surety of this Realm in time of war, and also the maintenance of many master mariners and seamen." It went on to complain of the infringement of the existing laws against importing in foreign ships, re-enacted the old Navigation Laws, and, among other provisions, arranged for the publication in Lombard Street of notice of the sailings of ships. Eight years later, Parliament passed the statute imposing the sumptuary regulations as to the eating of fish, to which allusion has already been made.

A significant event which followed the death of Henry VIII was the return to Bristol of Sebastian Cabot, who—whether or not he became, as Hakluyt says, " Grand Pilot " of England—received, at any rate, the recognition of a pension of 250 marks from Henry's youthful son and successor, who was himself a keen student of geography. It was Cabot who revived interest in the idea of a northeast passage to China, and, having formed the Company of Merchant Venturers to promote the scheme, he fitted out an expedition under the command of Sir Hugh Willoughby, with Richard Chancellor as Pilot-Major, which left the Thames on the first organised voyage of Polar discovery in 1553. All the famous explorer's skill and experience lent themselves to the preparations for this great voyage. Hakluyt tells us that " strong and well-seasoned planks for the building of the requisite ships were provided," and as a protection against the depredations of the worms which " pearceth and eateth through the strongest oak," parts of the keels of the ship were covered "with thin sheets of lead," which seems to be the first-recorded instance of such sheathing in this country. The little flotilla bore Royal Letters of Safe-Conduct, and the elaborate instructions drawn up for its government—an admirable document characteristic of the period—suggest the sagacity and ripe experience of Sebastian Cabot. The contemporary fame of the voyage may be judged from the large concourse which, amid the shooting-off of the ship's ordnance, bade the expedition farewell on the river-shores of Greenwich.

The auspicious start—"a very triumph," says the chronicler—was belied by speedy disaster. Violent storms separated the ships, and Willoughby, with two vessels, beaten out of his course and unable to make the appointed rendezvous, remained to winter in Lapland; there, from cold, famine, and disease, he and all his men miserably perished. Chancellor was more successful. After waiting a few days at the rendezvous, he at length passed through the uncharted seas to the Bay of St. Nicholas, and landed at the spot near where the town of Archangel now stands. He entered into friendly relations with the natives, who were indeed "amazed at the strange greatnesse of the shippe," and then, after gaining a smattering of the language, this astonishing seaman started on a tour of the interior, which brought him finally to Moscow, where Ivan the Terrible gave him a kindly reception. A couple of years later, after vainly attempting to rescue his missing companions, Chancellor returned to Moscow, and succeeded so well in his negotiations that a Russian Ambassador accompanied him on the return voyage, to negotiate a treaty on liberal terms with the Association of Merchant Venturers. His ship was wrecked in a gale off the north of Scotland, and Chancellor lost his life in an effort to save the Russian Ambassador. That functionary, at any rate, escaped, and received an enthusiastic welcome in London. Though a north-east passage to Far Cathay[1] remained as much a dream as ever, Chancellor's enterprise laid the foundations of British commerce in Russia and the East. The new opening for overseas trade was speedily followed up. Another merchant (Captain

[1] The north-eastern passage from Europe to the Indies was not achieved till the nineteenth century. In 1878–80 the VEGA doubled the most northern promontory of Asia, and made her celebrated circumnavigation of the two continents of the Old World.

Anthony Jenkinson) pushed into Asia by way of the Volga and the Caspian Sea in 1558, and two years later was dispatched on a commercial mission to the Sophi of Persia. These beginnings led to considerable developments of England's Baltic trade during the next decade.

But it was westward, not eastward, that English seamen's eyes were chiefly turned; the treasure of the Spanish Main, not the merchandise of Tiflis and Samarcand, called aloud to the adventurous spirit of the nation of islanders. With the accession of Elizabeth we enter upon a new phase of national development. The bonfires which blazed up on the death of Mary symbolised the new expansive spirit of a nation which, though by no means completely united, was moved to the pursuit of aggressive aims; and the challenge to the domination by Spain and Portugal of the New Hemisphere rang out clearer and clearer with England's growing consciousness of power upon the seas. The Pope's decree, by which the New World had been divided between the two Catholic Sovereigns, was not at once actively defied either by England or France. Neither country, in fact, was in a state to do so at the end of the fifteenth century, nor had the new religion sprung into vigorous birth. But half a dozen decades had brought sweeping changes. Catholic England had become a Protestant State, and a long period of peace had fostered the growth of national self-consciousness. The almost submissive tone of Henry VIII's Council—"if the Spaniards or Portuguese suffer us not to join them"[1]—is replaced with a very different note. In the third year of Elizabeth's reign even the cautious Cecil bluntly tells the Spanish Ambassador that the Pope had no right to partition the world. It was, however, England's seamen—rough merchant sailors—rather than her statesmen, who were challenging the pretensions and the colonial regulations of the Catholic Powers. The English, freed from the last trace of Continental entanglements—even Calais had just been lost to them—were embracing more and more effectually their birthright on the sea. In other ways they were favourably placed for extracting full advantage from the new conditions. Geographically, the kingdom lay between the King of Spain's southern dominions and his rich and prosperous province of Flanders—a strategic

[1] *Vide ante*, p. 20.

position the value of which was illustrated by the frequent success of the reprisals at sea that marked Elizabeth's foreign policy. The staunch mercantile class, with which so much real power rested, were developing overseas trade at a rapid rate; and the experiences gained from many a stormy voyage in the northern latitudes were applied to good purpose in the shipbuilding yards, which were beginning to turn out swifter and more weatherly ships than those of any other nation. The day of the oared galley was already passing; its last great sea-fight was to come in 1571 in the Bay of Lepanto, a short-lived triumph for the decaying Spanish sea power. Hitherto, sea power had been, in a modern historian's happy phrase,[1] " pelagic not oceanic " ; now oars, the means of propulsion by which the mastery of the Mediterranean had been maintained for centuries, had yielded precedence to sails, the instrument of supremacy on the ocean. It was English merchant vessels and English seamen who were to prove the full significance of that revolution in the type of ocean-going ships which the age of discovery had inaugurated.

After his marriage with Mary Tudor, Philip of Spain sought for his own purposes to encourage the increase of the English Navy. But the unpopularity of the marriage was deepened by the persecuting zeal of the fanatical Queen, and before the end of the short reign the new religion had given many recruits—particularly from among the West Country families of good blood and with sea associations—to the ranks of the privateers. Without entering into the religious aspect of the matter, it may be noted how truly the rising Protestant States drew their strength from the sea. Persecution in France turned many Huguenots into sea adventurers, preying on the traffic of the Catholic nations, and even attempting settlements in Spanish America ; the dreaded " Sea Beggars " were a later creation of the burnings and slaughterings of Alva in the Netherlands.

England's national spirit, then, found its fullest and fittest expression in the deeds of the sea adventurers, and Elizabeth, of whom the Spanish Ambassador Feria told his master that " she is very much wedded to her people and thinks as they do," adapted this formidable weapon

[1] A. F. Pollard (*Pol. Hist. of England*, vol. vi, p. 309).

to the main purpose of her policy—namely, the unity of the nation and the preservation of the realm from foreign intervention. It was a policy that combined bold strategy with circumspect tactics. The privateers, with their often dubious letters of marque, found in their Sovereign a tacit ally. The Queen might, and as the reign advanced often did, take a private share in the expeditions to the West, or even lend a Royal ship to stiffen a squadron of merchantmen bound for the Indies. But it was clearly understood that officially she had no responsibility for any deeds that might be called in question, or for any unlucky miscarriages; and if any freebooters were caught red-handed, they knew they must abide their fate without appeal to their Queen. In fine, "it was Elizabeth's privilege to reap the fruits of public peace, while her subjects gleaned the spoils of private war."

This line of policy was, indeed, almost dictated by the conditions with which the reign opened. The Exchequer was impoverished, and the letters of Sir Thomas Gresham, the City magnate and Elizabeth's first Ambassador at Antwerp, plainly indicate two facts—the difficulty of maintaining the English Queen's credit, and the country's dependence for gunpowder on supplies from abroad. As to the Royal Navy proper, the imposing fleet which Henry VIII had assembled was represented at the accession of his daughter by a total of only twenty-two "great ships." These and other signs of weakness due to religious and political causes deceived some Spanish observers. Feria, bred up in the tradition of Spain's military strength on land, went so far as to describe England in a phrase which has become familiar in our own day as "the sick man of Europe," and recommended Philip to land an army promptly and turn the island into a Spanish province. Philip, probably, had a better idea of the latent strength beneath the apparent weakness. Elizabeth's difficulties and problems were, in truth, real enough; but a dozen years of her statesmanlike handling of affairs and of English enterprise on the seas were enough to give to Feria's words an echo of mocking irony. As to certain elements of our naval strength, some Spaniards remained deceived even after the defeat of the Armada, but there was little self-illusion in the letter written by Feria's successor, Guerau, in 1570. " The whole channel," he said, "from Falmouth to the Downs is infested. . . . They assail every ship that passes, of whatever nation, and after capturing them, equip them for their own purposes, by this means continually increasing their fleet, with the intention on the part of the queen thus to make war on his Majesty through these pirates without its costing her anything, and under the specious pretence that she is not responsible, since the pirates carry authority from Chatillon, Vendôme, and Orange."

That is a vivid glimpse of the unofficial war carried on in the Narrow Seas by the English seamen. Nor can it be regarded as too highly coloured a picture of a time when the Mayor and principal inhabitants of a port like Dover were among the most active of the Rovers, and when even English vessels engaged in the Antwerp trade and the very fishermen on the coast often fell victims to the more reckless type of pirate. But already greater deeds were being accomplished in the waters of the New World—deeds in which it is sometimes hard to distinguish the different elements of trading—legitimate enough according to the ideas of the time—exploring, and sheer piracy; yet which, by their daring, skill, and hardihood, have justly won a classic place in maritime history. The early slave-trading voyages of John Hawkins are of special interest as a definite attempt to break down the Spanish commercial monopoly in the New World. Modern ideas of slavery have cast an unjust opprobrium on the name of one of the greatest Elizabethan seamen. Hawkins was no better or worse than his time, and no " guilt " attached to slave-owning or slave-dealing in the sixteenth century. It was not in any case the nature of the cargo that gave special significance to this expedition of a seafaring merchant; its importance lay in its overt challenge to Spain. Hawkins, doubtless, spoke for a section of English mercantile opinion when he claimed the right, under treaties dating back to the first Tudor reign, to trade with the Spanish Colonies. Yet the challenge was a bold and new departure. French pirates, mostly Huguenots, had for thirty years been harrying Spain's trade routes in the West, and only ten years before a bold French corsair, with a single ship, had, with the help of escaped slaves, laid waste some of the chief settlements of the Spanish Main, and even sacked Havana itself. But no English squadron had yet navigated the waters of the Spanish Indies. And though Hawkins and other traders had flouted Portuguese pretensions, based on the papal decree already referred to, and had freely traded with the Guinea coasts, and even with Brazil, no similar invasion of Spanish claims had hitherto been attempted.

It was while trading to the Canary Islands that Hawkins learnt[1] that "negroes were very good merchandise to Hispaniola, and that store of them might easily be had upon the coast of Guinea"; and in 1562, with three small vessels, whose tonnage would make a Solent yachtsman smile, he sailed from Plymouth for Sierra Leone. There he collected two hundred negroes, "partly by the sword"—it is a rough story of rough times, which are not to be judged by the ordinary standards of the twentieth century—crossed the Atlantic, disposed of his human goods with much profit and little difficulty to the planters of Hispaniola, where the shortage of labour was severely felt, and returned home "with prosperous success and much gain to himself and the aforesaid Adventurers." In what seems to have been an honest belief in the legitimacy of his proceedings, Hawkins, on the return voyage, had dispatched two vessels chartered in the West Indies with a portion of his goods to a Spanish port. Philip left no doubt as to his view of the voyage. He seized the cargoes on their arrival, and dispatched peremptory orders to the Colonies forbidding all trading intercourse with English vessels. The Adventurers who had planned and financed the voyage, the Lord Mayor of London being of their number, sought in vain to obtain redress for what they regarded as an illegal seizure. While in American waters Hawkins had acted with the circumspection of an astute and experienced trader. He obtained the requisite licence to trade from the Governor at the ports of Hispaniola at which he had called; he paid the local customs dues, or left security for any sums in dispute; he even obtained from the authorities written evidence of his good conduct during his sojourn. These points were urged without avail; nor, indeed, did they touch the main issue. Philip's insistence on his exclusive policy showed clearly enough his recognition of a threat to his sea dominion more for-

[1] Hakluyt is our authority for this, as for the other great Elizabethan voyages.

midable than that of the French pirates, and his determination to resist it to the uttermost. If one were to compile a list of single voyages which have marked the opening of great commercial or political epochs, the little squadron with which John Hawkins made his first expedition might well claim its place therein.

Hawkins's second voyage, 1565, was a repetition of the first on a rather larger scale, and not only brought him and his fellow-adventurers a handsome profit of 60 per cent., but established his renown among his countrymen, particularly as a seaman. In this instance he had carried his negroes to the Spanish Main itself, and, confronted by the Viceroy's order forbidding any dealings with him, had to back his negotiations with a show of force before the necessary licence to trade was forthcoming from the authorities. He was careful to follow his usual custom of obtaining certificates for good conduct. The success of the voyage, while it excited feverish anticipations and hopes, and strengthened the growing consciousness of the superiority of English sea power, awoke the liveliest alarm in Spain, and fears for the two great treasure fleets which annually made the voyage between the West Indies and Spain now found expression in the Spanish Ambassador's correspondence with Philip.

Hawkins lost no time preparing for another expedition, and at the same time Thomas Fenner, one of the Chichester Fenners, was busy fitting out a trading expedition to the Guinea coast. Political reasons were, at the moment, giving a conciliatory turn to the Queen's foreign policy, and De Silva's remonstrances resulted in both seamen being required to find heavy security that they would not go to the Indies. Hawkins, therefore, temporarily abandoned his scheme, but Fenner, having no intention, apparently, of going farther than the Guinea coast, sailed in the *Castle of Comfort*, with one other small vessel. The voyage was to prove a memorable one, and to open many eyes to the fighting quality of the English merchantman of the day. At the Cape Verde Islands Fenner found all his attempts at peaceable trade prevented by the open hostility of the Portuguese authorities, and at the Azores, when separated from his consort, he was caught by a Portuguese squadron, consisting of a 400-ton galleon and two caravels. Three times that day the *Castle of Com-*

fort beat off her assailants. The next day, the Portuguese commander, reinforced by four more caravels, again attacked, but so gallantly did Fenner fight his ship that at nightfall the powerful squadron drew off and he escaped. English seamen already enjoyed a wide reputation for skill and hard fighting on the high seas. But Fenner's splendid combat against heavy odds went far to establish also the technical superiority of English gunnery. The incident is the more noteworthy since, only a decade earlier, the Portuguese had again and again proved themselves more than a match for English and French gold-dust traders in conflicts off the Guinea coast.

The third and most important expedition of Hawkins left Plymouth in October 1567, its unacknowledged destination, privily approved by the Queen,[1] being the Spanish Indies. The squadron of six vessels included two " great ships " of the Royal Navy, a fact in accordance with the universal custom of the day, by which ships-of-war were employed in commerce in times of peace. These ships were the JESUS OF LUBECK, of 700 tons, a sturdy survivor of Henry VIII's fleet, and the MINION, 300–350 tons. Of the remaining four vessels, the *Judith*, a little barque of 50 tons, was commanded by Hawkins's young kinsman, Francis Drake, now twenty-two years of age, and already burning with a grievance against treacherous treatment at Rio de la Hacha, and destined, as a result of his voyage, to become the terror of the Spanish Main. The presence of Her Majesty's ships had a political significance beyond the Royal desire to take a share in what promised to be a highly profitable enterprise. The squadron was armed and organised on the lines of the Royal Navy; its complement of 500 men included several gentlemen of good houses, whose swords were at the disposal of the Captain of Soldiers ; and Hawkins, who at this period might fairly be ranked among the merchant princes of his time, and who described himself in his letter to Cecil as an " orderly person " who had " always hated folly," who, moreover, as Hakluyt's pages proved, wielded an able pen—Hawkins himself kept the state of one of Her Majesty's Admirals at the Seas. A man, in

[1] Sir Julian Corbett thinks it " hardly doubtful " that the agent who brought Hawkins a letter from Cecil, warning him to avoid damages to Spaniards, also conveyed the secret consent of Elizabeth to the purpose of the voyage. (*Drake and the Tudor Navy*, vol. i, p. 99.)

short, worthy of the rôle with which he regarded himself as entrusted—that of vindicating, by force if need were, the legitimate aspirations of English commerce! Acts of illegality—judged by modern standards—were undoubtedly committed on this memorable voyage, but none of the great figures in the new school of adventure which was now arising, and Hawkins least of all, is to be classed with those cosmopolitan buccaneers of a later century, whose criminal deeds and reckless careers have surrounded the very name of the Spanish Main with an irresistible if sinister glamour of romance. Romance was far from wanting to the deeds of these Elizabethan mariners, but what gives those deeds their epic quality, as enshrined in the immortal pages of Hakluyt, is the national spirit and national purpose which inspired them.

The course of the voyage of the JESUS OF LUBECK and her consorts may be followed in the Admiral's own narrative as recorded by that chronicler. Reprisals on the Portuguese, as well as the usual hunting for negroes, marked the weeks spent on the African coast; and when the Atlantic had been crossed, the ship sailed from place to place, " making traffic " with the Spaniards—" somewhat hardly, because the King had steadily commanded all his Governors in those parts by no means to suffer any trade to be made with us." Nevertheless, they met on the whole with " courteous entertainment," save at Rio de la Hacha, the depot for the pearl trade, and a place of disagreeable memories for Francis Drake. Carthagena, which was to have been the last port of call, also proved officially obdurate, and then, some days later, arose the " extreme storm " which drove the ships out of their course, and ultimately involved them in the disastrous incident of San Juan de Ulua. Into this roadstead, the haven of the town of Vera Cruz, the battered squadron came to refit and revictual, and no doubt to force a market for the negroes that remained unsold. The consternation of the Spaniards was great when they recognised their formidable visitors, for lying at moorings were the treasure-ships with over a million on board, awaiting the annual fleet of New Spain and its escorts for the combined homeward voyage. A huge prize, in fact, lay at the Englishman's mercy. If Hawkins had been a mere pirate he would have seized it out of hand, and he proved himself the " orderly " trader

THE FIGHT IN THE HARBOUR

he had always claimed to be by ignoring the treasure. He took certain measures of defence against treachery, and sent a formal message to the city authorities for permission to refit and obtain requisite supplies, with the further request that action should be taken to prevent any conflict between him and the expected Mexico fleet. The very next morning the "flota" appeared at the mouth of the Haven, headed by a Royal galleon.

Of the dramatic events which followed, Sir Julian Corbett has given a singularly clear and unbiassed account, based on both English and Spanish authorities.[1] Passing over the details, one may state the facts broadly thus: Hawkins, with a couple of batteries mounted ashore for his protection, was strong enough to have prevented the entry of a newly-arrived fleet, and to have accomplished its destruction. But he was fully aware that an overt act of war would have been displeasing to the Queen, and he gave fresh evidence of his discretion and sense of responsibility by entering into negotiations with the Viceroy and the Admiral of the Fleet. Under the terms arranged after a good deal of disputation, the two fleets moored side by side within the protection of the breakwater, the English were permitted to continue their refitting, and hostages were exchanged. The sequel to this formal military convention was a carefully matured plot on the part of the Spaniards. Secret reinforcements were smuggled on board the ships, and the signal for a cowardly attack was given with the sudden stabbing of several English sailors who had been drinking and fraternising with the Spaniards ashore. Taken unawares and at a complete disadvantage, Hawkins fought a fierce action, in which his superior gunnery silenced the enemy's fire and sank at least two galleons; but discharges from the shore batteries, treacherously captured at the first signal, had sunk one of his own vessels and disabled another, and when the Spaniards loosed a couple of fire-ships at night, the badly crippled JESUS had to be abandoned to her fate, and Hawkins himself barely escaped by boarding the MINION just as her sails were filling. The only other vessel to get away was the *Judith*, Drake having worked out of the harbour. In the northerly gale which immediately afterwards sprang up the two ships were separated, and the little barque was the first to arrive home; but

[1] *Drake and the Tudor Navy* (Corbett), vol. i, p. 111 *et seq.*

there seems no evidence for Hawkins's complaint of desertion against his kinsman.[1]

It was a tragic and disastrous story, that lost nothing in its effect when told to English ears. It came at a time when the hostility of Spain and the activity of the counter-reformation were becoming more and more menacing, and when Catholic plots were on foot at home against Elizabeth's life and throne. "The military and seafaring men all over England," says Camden, of the San Juan de Ulua affair, "fretted and demanded war against the Spaniards." Cautious as ever, Elizabeth remained true to her principle "No war, my lords," but her help to the Huguenots and to the rebellious subjects of Philip in the Netherlands became more active. Finally, in 1572, came the exposure of the foreign plot to assassinate Elizabeth, which led to the dismissal of the Spanish Ambassador and brought the two countries to the verge of open war. It was in that same year that Francis Drake fitted out the expedition which was to achieve one of the greatest adventures in our maritime annals.

The incident of San Juan de Ulua had created in the minds of Hawkins and Drake a feeling of bitter resentment and irreconcilable hostility towards Spain. Hawkins, whose energies were soon to become absorbed in the official work of the Royal Navy, had secured the release of his abandoned crews, as well as heavy compensation, by the characteristic method of a sham intrigue in which he completely outwitted the Spanish Ambassador. Drake sought another way by taking out letters of reprisal, armed with which commission he joined in two voyages to the Spanish Indies. On the second occasion he captured at least one valuable prize. More important still, he effected a valuable reconnaissance in the Gulf of Darien, established friendly relations with the Maroons (the escaped negroes of the Panama Isthmus), and even set up a regular base for future operations. For Drake was taking up the work of Hawkins, and, by infusing into it a new spirit of daring and a contempt for tradition, bettering the instruction of his master. So now he sailed out of Plymouth Sound on the famous voyage of Nombre de Dios, bent on reprisals in the form of a piratical adventure, but, we cannot doubt, with a perfectly clear conscience, convinced, as

[1] "So," runs Hawkins's narrative in Hakluyt, "with the MINION only and the *Judith*, the small barque of ten ton, we escaped; which barque the same night forsook us in our great misery."

all his Protestant countrymen were convinced, of the absolute justice of the proceedings. The voyage may be said to mark a new departure in sea-going expeditions—a change in effect from armed trading to privateering.

The little squadron consisted of two vessels only—the *Pascha*, of 70 tons, and the *Swan*, of which his brother, John Drake, was captain, of only 25 tons. But small as it was, its equipment was as perfect as the military science of the day could make it. Crossing the Atlantic in twenty-five days, Drake anchored to water his ships off the American coast, and then made the secret harbour where on his previous voyage he had improvised a base. To his chagrin, he found that the Spaniards had discovered and plundered his stores. While at this spot he fell in with another English adventurer, Captain Ranse, carrying two Spanish prizes along with him. To the new-comer Drake revealed his plans; he meant to seize Nombre de Dios, the renowned depot of the Spanish traffic from Peru—to seize it while the treasure-houses were still full. Articles of partnership were agreed on; and after setting up the pinnaces which Drake had brought with him, the combined squadron sailed north-west along the coast to the Pine Islands, where Ranse remained with the three ships and the prize caravel, while Drake continued the voyage with the pinnaces and the remaining prizes and a force of seventy-three men.

In a few days the little expedition reached the entrance to Nombre de Dios Bay, and an hour before dawn dashed in to the attack by the light of the moon. While the Englishmen were forming up on the sand after surprising the shore battery, the church bell was frantically pealing its alarm in the ears of the terrified inhabitants. For his assault on the town Drake divided his men into two forces, and after a brief resistance the Spaniards, caught between the double fusilade and over-estimating the strength of their assailants, broke and fled, casting away their arms as the sailors, with broad West Country cheers, chased them through the Panama gate. With the *plaza* held, the hunt for treasure began. In the Governor's house were found bars of silver piled high, 350 tons in all, awaiting the arrival of the flota of Tierra Firme—the treasure fleet of the Spanish Main. But it was gold and jewels, not merely silver, that Drake was in search of, and these were stored within the solid masonry of the King's Treasure-House, down by the water. It was then that the first check occurred to damp the ardour of these amazing men of the sea. A tropical downpour of rain necessitated their seeking shelter for the sake of bow-strings and powder, and the consequent abandonment of their post in the *plaza*, and the stout walls of the treasure-house resisted all efforts to break in. Rumours of Spanish reinforcements produced something like a panic, and how natural was the feeling can easily be imagined. For never before had these simple though daring merchant seamen engaged in such an extreme adventure as this of Drake's—the deliberately-planned attack by a diminutive, if well-found, land force, upon a town of such size that the men of Devon could only compare it with their well-loved port of Plymouth.

The rain, however, ceased, and Drake controlled the panic with characteristic resource and courage. A detachment was sent round to break in the doors of the treasure-house, and the wildest dreams of the seamen might well have been realised but for another unlucky stroke of fate. Their indomitable leader had concealed a wound received in the first Spanish volley, and now at the critical moment he suddenly fell in a swoon. That ended the matter. The men, vowing their captain's life more valuable than all the treasure of the Indies, bore him to the boats, and picking up on the way out, with a coolness that provokes a smile, a solitary wine-ship newly arrived at its moorings in the harbour, they installed themselves and their wounded on the town's victualling island just outside the bay. Hither in due time came, on a spying errand and under a flag of truce, an officer bearing a message from the Governor couched in terms of true Spanish politeness, and paying tribute to the humanity shown by Drake on his previous expeditions. The visitor was finally dismissed with a flow of equally impressive compliments, but with the plain assurance that Captain Drake, ere he departed, meant to reap some of the harvest of that commodity which alone would satisfy his company. The story of this interview, the substantial truth of which seems indubitable, reads like a page from some stirring romance. It is of special interest, also, as illustrating those qualities in the young commander which consistently marked his future career—a strong regard for humane dealing, and a love of ceremonial and display befitting the dignity of a great sea-captain.

For the present, however, the stroke so daringly conceived and so energetically executed had failed. Yet the fact remained that Nombre de Dios, the very gate of the Peruvian Treasure-House, had been actually taken and for awhile held, and Drake returned to the waiting ships evolving new schemes in his restless brain. These plans, based on the information of a runaway slave called Diego, did not commend themselves to Ranse, who parted company with the bolder man, arguing, with reason enough, that the affair of Nombre de Dios would have given the alarm to all the coast settlements. So, indeed, the event proved when Drake turned to his next incredible adventure —an attempt on the capital of the Spanish Main itself. Carthagena, like the rest of the ports, was on the alert, and though he took three prizes in the bay, including a well-laden Seville ship, he quickly saw that some new plan must be evolved. What he finally decided on was a novel and characteristic departure from the general method of harrying the coast—nothing less than a raid into the interior. And his purpose was to seize, in co-operation with the Maroons, the mule-train which would bring the treasure of Peru from Panama across the Isthmus to Nombre de Dios for shipment to Spain. In order to man the pinnaces, which would be essential to the enterprise, it was necessary to sacrifice one of his ships, and the secret scuttling of the *Swan*, his own vessel and a particularly good sailer, is one of those incidents which cast a flood of light on the masterful and fearless character of this born leader of men. Back in the Gulf of Darien a new headquarters was established, and then passed months of waiting for the great attempt—months full of the most diversified incidents which are none the less astonishing for the simplicity and directness with which the Narrative sets them forth. It is a wonderful tale of privation, extremity of tempest, daring defiance of Spanish authority, threatened desertion, desperate fighting, decimating sickness—a succession of vicissitudes such as might have broken the stanchness of the bravest, and seemed only to stimulate the great sea-captain to fresh feats of resource and daring.

At length the march inland began, with the negro allies as guides, and on the fourth day this devoted band of English seamen reached the highest ridge of the Cordilleras, at a point where the faithful Diego had promised his white master that he should set eyes on the South Sea. Pizarro and Cortez and Balboa had been there before him, but can our maritime history conjure a more dramatic scene than was enacted on this spot in the vast mountain forest ? The Maroons led Drake to a " goodly and great tree," notched with steps for climbing, and promised him that from its top he might see the two oceans at once. So the mightiest of our mariners ascended, and having beheld—with what pure passion of the explorer surging in his heart !—" that sea of which he had heard such golden reports," made his memorable vow, beseeching " Almighty God of His goodness to give him life and leave to sail once in an English ship in that sea." And another contemporary chronicler (Camden) adds, " From that time forward his mind was pricked on continually night and day to perform his vow." Not long after his first sight of the Southern Sea, Drake had accomplished the crowning feat of his daring raid, by the capture of the mule treasure-train on its way across the Panama Isthmus.

It was not till November 1577 that Drake sailed from Plymouth on the immortal voyage of circumnavigation which was to accomplish his vow. The fame of his past exploits brought a throng of volunteers to his service, and the expedition was a considerable one for the time, consisting of the *Pelican* (Admiral), of 100 tons, and four smaller vessels, all well armed and equipped. To follow the course of one of the most famous voyages in history is beyond our scope, and excellent contemporary narratives have made its details familiar. Drake's purpose was to reach the Pacific, by way of the passage discovered by Magellan in his last fatal voyage; and so, having crossed the Atlantic, he took a south-westerly course along the South American coast. Every sort of misfortune seemed to dog his way; the fleet was scattered by storm, and one of the smaller vessels foundered; dissensions occurred between the sea officers and the gentlemen volunteers; and the extraordinary episode in which Thomas Doughty played the leading rôle ended with the execution of that officer in the little port of St. Julian. In the buffetings which befell the ships on rounding the American continent Drake discovered the open sea-passage south of Magellan's Straits, and it was during these terrible months of almost ceaseless tempests, contrary winds, and incipient mutiny, that the *Elizabeth*, Wynter's ship (Vice-Admiral), was separated from her consort in a fearful storm, and, giving up the struggle, made the best of her way home.

Thus it was left to Drake in the *Golden Hind* (as the *Pelican* had been rechristened on entering the Southern Seas) to accomplish the voyage alone. And everyone knows how magnificently he accomplished it, once he had burst into that sea which the Spaniards imagined to be their sole and secure domain. All along the Spanish settlements of Chili and Peru he spread amazed terror. Prize after prize was taken, generally with little resistance ; the port of the world-renowned Potosi Mine was coolly ransacked, though without much result ; and finally, despite her fortnight's start, a huge treasure-ship, " the great glory of the South Sea," was overhauled and captured before she could reach the shelter of Panama Harbour. So with £600,000 worth of treasure in his hold, literally ballasted with silver and gold and precious stones, Drake sailed north in a fruitless effort to make in reverse the north-west passage which Frobisher was supposed to have discovered in his famous voyage a few years earlier. Baffled by contrary gales and by conditions of Arctic severity, the *Golden Hind*, with the aid of a captured China pilot's chart, crossed the Pacific, reached the Moluccas (being nearly cast away in those perilous waters), and, having added a cargo of costly spices to her gold and silver, made her way home round the Cape of Good Hope.

So much for a bare outline of the voyage—the first circumnavigation of the world ever achieved by a sea-captain, and that captain a merchant seaman. Its political consequences were far-reaching. Drake became the hero of his fellow-countrymen, and the example of his great adventure, with its direct challenge to the pelagic empire of Spain, was a powerful incentive to national enterprise. The *Golden Hind's* reappearance in Plymouth Sound came at a critical moment to widen the breach already growing between England and Spain, and when the now-famous craft had been brought round in triumph to the Thames, and the Queen went down to knight its captain and to dine in state on board, the official recognition of the great raid was complete. After Philip's absorption of the kingdom of Portugal, with its immense maritime resources, open war became only a question of time, and no doubt existed as to the objects with which Philip was already beginning to prepare a great offensive fleet. So now we part company with Drake, the indomitable navigator and brilliant sea adventurer. Henceforth, it was largely to the work of national defence that Sir Francis Drake, as Admiral of Her Majesty's Navy, devoted himself in the interval that precedes the sailing of the Armada. It must suffice here to record that, after the discovery of Spanish complicity with Throgmorton's plot, Drake, with Frobisher as second-in-command, conducted a raid of reprisals on the Spanish Indies with a fleet of thirty sail, plundering, sacking, and ransoming, on a scale hitherto unattempted; and that, by his blockading operations off the Spanish coast two years later, he threw Santa Cruz's plans into utter confusion and delayed the sailing of the Armada by a twelvemonth.

The familiar story of that determined attempt at invasion need not be told here, beyond noting that this great fight in the Narrow Seas sheds lustre on the daring of the Elizabethan merchantmen, whether trading vessels or privateers, and on their crews. Her Majesty's ships formed only the nucleus of the fleet which gathered in the Channel under the flag of Lord Howard of Effingham, with Drake and Hawkins and Frobisher, as well as others scarcely less famous, as his vice-admirals and captains. The defeat of Medina Sidonia's vast and heterogeneous concourse of craft was conclusive evidence of the complete superiority of English ships, English gunnery, and English seamen of the Royal Navy, which was once more to assume importance. For not only were the English ships faster and more weatherly than the enemy's, but their crews were seamen and gunners too, capable equally of sailing their ships and fighting them, nor did they need to crowd their decks with soldiers as the Spanish did. Expressed briefly and broadly, the English sea tactic was naval in its origin, the Spanish military. In justice also to those fighting seamen of three centuries ago, one other point should be noticed. With some commentators it has been a habit to ascribe the defeat of the Armada to the storms which followed the battle off Gravelines. It is well, then, to record here the simple fact that the Armada was a beaten and utterly demoralised fleet before it turned northwards on its wild, storm-driven course round Scotland —beaten by the superior dash, gunnery, and seamanship of English sailors. The weather and the perils of those northern waters completed the work of the English guns. The bearing of this great fleet action on the further differentiation between the naval and mercantile services may conveniently be referred to later.

Drake's burst into the Southern Seas stimulated, as we have said, the national spirit of adventure, and, in particular, the minds of British merchant seamen were more than ever bent on the ambition of reaching the land of spices and precious stones, so long the close preserve of the Portuguese. Frobisher's great voyages to the north-west early in the reign were originally inspired by the desire to find a north-west passage to India, and they degenerated into a fruitless quest for gold-yielding ore. In the years between Drake's voyage of circumnavigation and the coming of the Armada, John Davis, one of the most scientific of Elizabethan navigators, followed in Frobisher's track in three successive years in the hope of reaching India; and in the same decade Thomas Candish, taking Drake's old route by way of the Magellan Straits, so far realised his ambitions as to reach China and the East Indies, and ended by sailing round the world. Sir Humphrey Gilbert's disastrous expedition to Newfoundland of 1583 is to be noted as one of those early attempts at British colonisation which seemed so fruitless in their immediate results; and in the following year Sir Walter Raleigh obtained his letters patent "for the planting of new lands on the coast of America," the first step to the successful foundation of Virginia, the original seat of the Anglo-American race.

It is, however, with the rise and prosperity of the East India Company that the history of the Merchant Marine in the seventeenth and eighteenth centuries is chiefly associated. The defeat of the Armada provided a new incentive to Englishmen to share in the coveted trade with India. Candish, who returned from his great voyage just in time to hear of his countrymen's triumph, brought home detailed observations of the greatest value to British seamen and British merchants. So in the following year we find a significant decision taken by the syndicate concerned in dispatching John Davis on his north-west voyages. Abandoning this long-cherished hope, they sent out yet another expedition under the great navigator, but this time by way of the Cape of Good Hope. It proved the first of a series of voyages which only ceased with the death of this fine seaman, who was killed by pirates off the coast of Malacca. More significant, however, than Davis's voyage of 1589 was the action taken in that year by certain English merchants in petitioning the Queen for licence and encouragement to open a trade with the East Indies. In support of their memorial, they urged that such trade would, as the example of Portugal had shown, tend to the increase of the strength of the Royal Navy. Elizabeth characteristically toyed with the proposal, but in the end granted the necessary authority, and in April 1591 " three tall ships "—the *Penelope, Marchant Royall*, and *Edward Bonaventure*—sailed out of Plymouth Sound under James Lancaster. Hakluyt's narrative of the voyage [1] shows that from Table Bay the *Marchant Royall* was sent back owing to the ravages of scurvy, and that the *Penelope* foundered in a " mighty storme " soon after rounding the Cape. With a stricken crew and a partially disabled ship, Lancaster kept steadfastly on his way through hurricanes and " electric storms," and with the further loss of his master and sixteen men treacherously slain at Comoro Islands, to Zanzibar. Here the mariners had their first taste of the acute jealousy with which the Portuguese regarded all rivals in the rich trade of the East. After some months on the African coast, Lancaster got a favourable wind to take him across the Indian Ocean, doubled Cape Comorin, missed the Nicobar Islands " through our master's default for want of due observation of the South Starre," and reached one of the small islands to the north of Sumatra. In spite of the weakness of a crew now reduced to thirty-three men and a boy, the *Edward* picked up two small prizes, and then, while lying in wait in the Malacca Straits, this resolute little fighter attacked and captured a Portuguese trader of 250 tons, and later on a ship of 750 tons with a cargo of great variety and value. In fact, profit was looked for from what was considered a legitimate form of piracy rather than from trade, and but for a run of ill-luck of all kinds, Lancaster would have remained lurking in the Nicobar Islands, whither he returned on the homeward voyage, in the

[1] He obtained his story from Lancaster's lieutenant, Edmund Barker.

knowledge that many a rich merchantman from Bengal and Siam would be sure to pass that way on the first stage of the voyage to Lisbon. A mutinous spirit among his men, damage by storm, contrary gales, shortness of provisions so that off Porto Rico they were reduced to eating hides, culminated in the loss of the ship herself while the majority of the company were ashore. Finally, Lancaster and his companions obtained a passage home on board a Dieppe ship, and crossed to Rye in May 1594. In a sense, the voyage had been disastrous. But Lancaster's misfortunes had purchased a fruitful experience and a fund of valuable information, and offered English merchants and seamen a great and convincing proof that the treasure-house of the East lay open before them.

Meanwhile, the Dutch were beginning to establish that trade with the Orient which was soon to enable them to supplant the Portuguese as our chief rivals, and their enterprise spurred London merchants to new action. In 1599, a number of them, chiefly associated with the Levant Company, which held a charter for overland trading to India, petitioned for a monopoly of trade with the East Indies. The Queen gave her assent to the petition at the end of the following year, the trading privilege being granted for a period of fifteen years, and thus came into existence the first East India Company—the progenitor of that " John Company " which was to be the means of adding India to the British Empire. No time was lost in dispatching the first expedition of these " Adventurers for the Discoverie of the Trade for the East Indies." The fleet of four vessels—of tonnage ranging from 300 to 130, with crews to the number of 480 men—left Woolwich in February 1601. A fitting " generall of the Fleet " was found in James Lancaster, who in his recent voyage had given such plain proof of indomitable courage and resourceful leadership, and with him as Vice-Admiral went John Middleton, and as Pilot-Major, the famous John Davis. The voyage was a complete success. Lancaster put his merchants ashore to trade, and established factories in Java and elsewhere, and while this more legitimate business was going on, himself got across the trade route and presently captured a rich carack of 900 tons. On the voyage home, this gallant seaman proved his rare qualities afresh by saving his ship in well-nigh desperate circumstances, such as would have tested the nerve and endurance of the bravest. The little fleet returned in the early months of James I's reign, laden with cargoes that included over a million pounds of pepper, and those who had invested their money received 95 per cent. on their capital. The same four vessels made the company's second voyage in the following year, with a resulting profit of nearly 100 per cent., to which, as before, extensive privateering had largely contributed; and in 1607 a third expedition set out, remarkable for the fact that now, for the first time, the company's ships entered a port of the Indian subcontinent itself. This port was Surat, just above Bombay, and an agent was landed to convey to the Great Mogul at Agra a letter of recommendation from King James I. A little later that Sovereign extended the Company's Charter, and in the same year (1609) was present at the launching of the largest contemporary East Indiaman, the *Trade's Increase*, one of the first two vessels built in the company's own yard at Deptford. A ship of 1,100 tons, she was one of the sensations of the early seventeenth century, but she proved clumsy and unhandy, and came to a tragic end after a brief and adventurous career. She may be taken as a fitting illustration of the rule of thumb methods of ship construction then prevailing, and it may be noted here that it was not until after the Stuart period that English shipbuilding began to establish itself on a scientific basis, largely as the result of the example of French naval models.

At this early period in its history, the East India Company is seen firmly established as well as earning handsome dividends for its shareholders, its ships built in its own yard (although this practice was changed at a later date) and victualled from its own stores, and enjoying the enormous advantage of a hydrographical department of its own, based on the journals and observations compulsorily contributed at the end of each voyage by the masters of its fleet. Developments in India came swiftly. Sailing with two vessels from Gravesend in 1612, Captain Best encountered the Portuguese traders in Surat Roadstead, and beat them in a skilfully-conducted action. It was a small if decisive affair; but its effects were immediate and far-reaching. For the prestige of the Portuguese in the East was sharply lowered, and the Grand Mogul hastened to confer trading privileges, hitherto denied it, upon the new Power in the East. Factories were set going at Surat and elsewhere, Sir Thomas Row came out three years later as an Ambassador to the Grand Mogul in order to ratify the new treaty, and by the same date the Indian Marine, initiated by the Corporation as a means of protection from pirates and Portuguese alike and manned by British seamen, had reached the total of ten local vessels. Forty years later Cromwell, in pursuance of that policy which is so well expressed in his Navigation Act, dealt the last blow to Portugal's pride and sea dominance by extorting a treaty giving to English ships the right to trade in all the Portuguese possessions in the East.

The Navigation Acts of the seventeenth century, however, were mainly directed against the Dutch, for Holland succeeded Portugal as our supreme rival on the seas. The struggle with that stubborn sea-going race continued almost ceaselessly for twenty-five years, and, while it nearly exhausted the Dutch, left England buoyantly ready to meet the more powerful rivalry of the French. In the great expansion of England's sea power which followed, the East India Company played a conspicuous part, and before the end of the eighteenth century it stood virtually alone as the one surviving trading Power in the Orient, its operations embracing China as well as India. Moreover, these strongly built, well-armed East Indiamen, with their fine crews of seasoned sailors, did yeoman service for the country in the long series of wars which culminated in the Napoleonic struggle. For they constituted the chief element in that large commercial marine which our mercantile policy created as a reserve from which the Royal Navy could be almost indefinitely increased.

It is convenient here to note one aspect of the significance of the Armada campaign for its effect on the movement towards that differentiation between the naval and mercantile services which, as we have seen, was initiated by the second Tudor king. Gallantly as the merchantmen fought in single-ship combats, the naval battle in the Channel showed how inadequate they were to the needs of a great fleet action, and from the clear perception of that fact sprang a strong impulse to specialisation and a widening of the breach between professional and amateur warfare at sea. The institution of Ship Money in the next century marked a further step in the same direction.

The policy of Charles I expressed in that levy was to substitute a system of money contributions as a means of forming a regular fleet for the mediæval plan of contributions of ships. A few years later, Cromwell's policy secured, under the professional soldier-admiral of the Blake type, an increased specialisation, which by the end of the century led to the practical disappearance of the merchantman as a fleet ship.

II

The Merchant Navy in the Revolutionary and Napoleonic Wars

In that period of almost continuous war which began with the struggle with Revolutionary France in 1793, and ended with the downfall and exile of Napoleon in 1815, the strength of France on the seas was devoted to the destruction of British commerce, and never with more determined persistency than in the ten years which succeeded the victory at Trafalgar. The conflict was maintained with all the resources which France, ruled by despotism, was able to throw into the scales, with the support of the resources of allies whom she made her vassals. Yet this result is clearly shown: that from the outbreak of hostilities the strength of the British mercantile fleet ever grew larger and larger, despite the unceasing onslaught which was maintained against it, and despite the heavy losses which such protracted warfare necessarily involved.

Eleven thousand British merchant ships passed out of the Service by capture as prizes during the French wars.[1] Some compensation was found in the numbers of enemy ships taken and transferred to our flag; but the activity in British shipyards was so well sustained that in 1815 this country possessed more ships and a greater volume of tonnage than at the opening of the Anglo-French struggle. On the other hand, French trade in a few years was almost swept from the seas by the British naval superiority, and opportunities of prize-taking by our cruisers were

[1] "Roll of English merchant vessels captured by the French during the war, 1793–1815"—Norman's *Corsairs of France*.

necessarily smaller. France maintained a coastal trade in the Mediterranean, but little more.

Fortunately for the world, at the outbreak of hostilities in February 1793 England found herself complete mistress of the seas. So early as 1795 the enemy had abandoned all pretence of opposing fleet to fleet, and entered upon an unrestricted *guerre de course*. France, the spirit of her navy having suffered during the Revolution, turned to her mercantile fleet to supply its place. The object of Revolutionary France was frankly stated by Citizen Boyer Fonfrède in the Convention: " We have now " (he said) " to wage a war of iron against gold. We must ruin the commerce of our enemies, and in order to remove all opportunity of reprisals we must suspend our own commerce. Our shipbuilding yards must build nothing but corsairs, and our manufactories turn out nothing but munitions of war." British seamen, on their part, responded with the audacity expected of them. Not only were our frigates and sloops engaged in constantly harrying the enemy and capturing his ships wherever they showed the flag, but our forces afloat were reinforced by hundreds of vessels, manned by British merchant seamen, which sailed from British ports under letters of marque. Liverpool alone had sixty-seven privateers armed and manned, at sea or ready for sea, four months after the outbreak of war.[1] Numbers were fitted out afterwards in the Thames and at east and south coast ports, and operated in the North Sea and on more distant cruising grounds. The significant admission was made by the enemy, after six years of war, that " not a single merchant vessel sailed under the French flag." [2]

The challenge made to our predominance at sea by the French Navy, revived under Napoleon, does not call for consideration here, but the circumstances of the two rival Powers at the outset coloured the whole conditions of the war. If unable to fight a fleet action, France, by reason of her geographical position, her long coasts, with so many favourably-placed sally ports, and her large maritime population, was more favourably situated than any other Power in the world to conduct a campaign against British maritime commerce. Those of her peaceful trading ships

---

[1] Gomer Williams, *The Liverpool Privateers*.
[2] Message to the Directory, January 1799.

which escaped capture by British cruisers, or in close pursuit were driven into her ports, effected a quick transformation. France had in the sturdy Norman and Breton populations of her coasts, inured to the hardships of life at sea and already made familiar with war, a striking force ready to be used, and they were not content to remain idle while rich rewards were within their grasp. In hundreds French merchant ships were armed and transformed into privateers, new craft specially designed for speed were laid down in the yards, and, sailing with letters of marque, they harried the long lines of British ships beating up the English channel or traversing the North Sea routes. Into the single port of Dunkirk thirty-six English prizes were brought within three months of the outbreak of war. No fewer than 407 English prizes were sold in that port alone before the Peace of Amiens brought the first pause in the war. The enterprise or greed of profit by owners was seconded by public subscriptions. A club at Strasburg fitted out a corsair, the *Jacobin*, which effectively raided British trade. The municipality of Bordeaux equipped three corsairs, one of which, the *Général Dumourier*, in her first cruise, returned with prizes valued at £240,000. Blank letters of marque were issued to the Commissionaires of Marine in every port of France, and from Dunkirk to St. Jean de Luz the coast was studded with companies whose sole aim and object was the destruction of English commerce.[1]

The more venturesome French corsairs, better equipped and fitted, and commanded by men whose daring won for them a warm place in the hearts of their countrymen, lay in wait for the valuable cargoes passing to and from India and the East, and the highly important trade carried on between England and the West Indies. France brought into this service swift sailing ships, powerfully armed. One of these privateers, the *Bordelais*, captured in 1799, had operated at no greater distance than Tory Island, about which she had done great damage in the previous summer. Her keel was as long as that of our 38-gun frigates, she was pierced for twenty-two guns on deck, had twenty-four brass 12-pounders mounted, and carried a crew numbering 222 men. The *Bordelais* was conducted into Cork by His Majesty's ship REVOLUTIONNAIRE, after having

---

[1] Norman, *The Corsairs of France*, p. 292.

been chased 129 miles in nine and a half hours, being finally overhauled in a gale of wind.[1]

As often before in her history, England at the outbreak of war was unready. Nearly six months passed before the Channel Fleet, under Lord Howe, got to sea. Near home, in the early days of the struggle, it was believed that British merchant shipping was best protected by the concentration of a main fleet in the vicinity of Torbay, with a reserve fleet off the Isle of Wight. Frigates watched Brest and other French ports, and a constant patrol was maintained. This disposition was afterwards varied, the blockade of Brest being made still closer, and two separate squadrons were formed, with bases at Spithead and the North Sea. The sealing of French outlets could rarely, however, as experience showed, be made effective against raiding craft.

The configuration of the opposing coasts of France and England and the small distances to be traversed by fast-sailing raiders added greatly to the perplexity of the problem confronting the British Admiralty. The English Channel has nowhere a greater width than one hundred miles, and at the neck narrows to twenty miles; and though the North Sea offered a broader expanse, the English coast was quickly reached from the northern ports of France and the Netherlands. The English south coast is poorly provided with natural havens, and in certain winds no shelter was to be obtained between Portsmouth on the one hand and the Downs on the other. Newhaven had not been developed into a port, nor had even a light been placed there. Opposite were the French ports of Cherbourg and Havre, with St. Malo, Boulogne, Calais, and Dunkirk, all within easy access of the trade routes; all offered admirable shelter to the French privateer able to wait a favourable wind and opportunity. The concavity of the English land-line, especially the long stretch from Selsey Bill to Beachy Head, the dangerous shore, the impossibility of weathering a southerly gale upon it at anchor, and the great want of lights and of convenient harbourage, all added to the perils to which British ships congregating there were exposed. If making a large offing to escape the bay, they ran imminent risks from privateers which sallied out from the ports of Normandy. Levillé, of

[1] *Naval Chronicle*, ii, 535.

Dunkirk, one of the most daring of these commanders, cruising in the Channel in the privateer *Vengeance*, and eluding British warships on watch, in five weeks of the autumn of 1795 made no fewer than twenty English prizes.

The most urgent call for naval ships being about the British coasts and in the West Indies, the Indian seas were left unprotected. When Admiral Cornwallis sailed for Europe with his small squadron in September 1793, a single sloop-of-war remained to protect the vast expanse of ocean covered by the commerce of the East India Company [1]; his successor did not reach the station till a year later. In such circumstances severe losses were inevitable. They were, however, less severe than might have been expected. The Indiamen of a century ago were the monarchs of the seas, stout ships of 800 to 1,200 tons, some reaching 1,500 tons, fast sailers, better armed and manned than any others flying the mercantile flag, and capable of giving a good account of themselves in an encounter with any interfering craft short of an enemy frigate. The East India Company, too, fitted out several heavily-armed ships to cruise for the protection of trade. The fleets engaged in the commerce carried on with the West Indies in sugar, coffee, rum, and other colonial produce—and in this connection slaves must not be omitted—offered an easier prey for the larger class of French privateer fitted for long voyages and ocean service, and facilitated raids upon the traffic to and from the West Indies, varied with irruptions upon the routes to India. To such attacks on commerce, the more daring of the French corsairs—men like the famous Robert Surcouf, of St. Malo—devoted their restless energies.

The fine spirit in which these attacks were met by British merchant seamen is manifested in the records of a hundred actions fought about the islands out in the Atlantic. This one is typical. The British ship *Planter*, in the year 1799, was overhauled by a fast sailer. Captain John Watts, her commander, backed his mainsail and laid by for the enemy, all hands giving three cheers. "We found her," he says, "to be a privateer of twenty-two guns, twelves, nines, and sixes, with small arms in the tops, and full of men. We poured in our lagrische, and used grape-shot with great success." The privateer sheered off to

---

[1] Brenton's *Naval History*, i, 346.

repair damage. The action recommenced, and was fought with great gallantry throughout the afternoon till the light waned. Captain Watts adds in a letter to his owners :

" At last he found we would not give out, and night coming on, sheered off and stood to the south-west. Our fire must have done great execution. My ship's company acted with a degree of courage which does credit to the flag. I cannot help mentioning the good conduct of my passengers during the action : Mr. McKennon and Mr. Hodgson, with small arms, stood to their quarters with a degree of noble spirit ; my two lady passengers, Mrs. McDowell and Miss Mary Hartley, kept conveying the cartridges from the magazine to the deck, and were very attentive to the wounded, both during and after the action, in dressing their wounds and administering every comfort the ship could afford, in which we were not deficient for a merchant ship. When he sheered off we saw him heaving dead bodies overboard in abundance. We had four killed, eight wounded. The force of the *Planter* was twelve 9-pounders and six 6-pounders—forty-three men." [1]

It was the common object of a privateer-captain wherever possible to effect a boarding. The advantage lay with him in his superior numbers of men, trained in the use of arms and excited by the prospect of a prize, while the merchantman's crew was generally weaker, and many a bloody fight was waged on the narrow decks. A letter from Barbadoes of December 1st, 1798, describes such an action, fought most gallantly, and in this instance successfully, by the Liverpool ship *Barton* (Captain Cutler), after being overhauled twenty leagues to windward by a French privateer mounting eighteen guns, 9-pounders and 6-pounders. The chase lasted two and a half hours, the privateer repeatedly altering her course to board, but the heavy and well-directed fire from the British ship prevented her from getting near enough to effect her purpose. Dismantled in her rigging, the enemy sheered off.

" But having refitted, commenced a second attack at noon, with a most sanguinary design of boarding, and notwith-

[1] *Naval Chronicle*, ii, 250.

standing the incessant cannonading from the ship, ran plump on board, and endeavoured to throw her men into her, but found her well prepared to receive the enemy, the whole of *Barton's* crew being assembled on the quarter-deck, and headed by their gallant commander, who was spiritedly seconded by his passengers. An attack, sword in hand, commenced, and the enemy were driven back with considerable loss, many of them being spiked from the netting and shrouds of the ship, while by a well-directed fire from the cabin guns, numbers were swept from their own deck; and a great part of her rigging being cut away she dropped astern and gave over the contest, amidst the victorious huzzahs of the British tars, whose bold commander, calling from his quarter-deck, defied the vanquished Republicans to return to the attack. His passengers bear a proportionate share of the honour with the captain."[1]

After such adventures in the open sea many a stout merchantman returned to port, badly mauled, for repairs, but ship and cargo saved by the dauntless conduct of officers and crew.

The geographical position of the French West India Islands favoured the operations of the raiders, affording bases into which prizes could be taken, and from which cruisers and privateers could sally out quickly upon the trade routes, besides offering shelter and opportunity for refitting. Around these islands the war on commerce was carried on with ever-increasing British losses, and the necessity of protecting this trade involved the detachment of large numbers of frigates and sloops which were badly needed for service elsewhere. The seizure one after another of all the French islands eventually checked the depredations, though it was found impossible to stop them altogether. Driven from their own lairs, French privateers fitted out in American ports, whence they sailed under a thin disguise to resume their predatory warfare upon British merchantmen.

The guarding of the long ocean routes to India and China offered far greater perplexities to the British Admiralty. As the years went on, the French made ever more determined efforts to cut our trading connections, strengthening

[1] *Naval Chronicle*, i, 437.

their already powerful patrols of cruising frigates and sloops with ships of the line. The concentration of a considerable fleet under Rear-Admiral Sir Edward Pellew, afterwards Lord Exmouth, resulted in the losses being kept within bounds, but throughout the long war the Eastern trade routes were the scenes of some of the most desperately contested actions between British and French frigates and our armed merchantmen and raiding privateers. The need for protection of the large British trade with the Baltic and that with America were other causes which made necessary the dissipation of British naval strength over many distant seas.

When all has been said, however, the area of the gravest peril was the waters about our own coasts, for there the greatest part of our commerce borne by the merchant fleets necessarily congregated. Mahan has drawn in lively fashion a picture of the seas in Napoleonic times :

" Fast frigates and sloops-of-war, with a host of smaller vessels, were disseminated over the ocean, upon the tracks which commerce follows and to which the hostile cruisers were therefore constrained. To each was assigned his cruising-ground, the distribution being regulated by the comparative dangers, and by the necessary accumulation of merchant shipping in particular localities, as in the North Sea, the approach to the English Channel, and, generally, the centres to which the routes of commerce converge. The forces thus especially assigned to patrol duty, the ships ' on a cruise,' to use the technical expression, were casually increased by the large number of vessels going backward and forward between England and their respective stations, dispatch boats, ships going in for repairs or returning from them, so that the seas about Europe were alive with British cruisers ; each one of which was wide awake for prizes. To these, again, were added the many privateers, whose cruising-ground was not, indeed, assigned by the Government, but which were constrained in their choice by the same conditions that dictated at once the course of the trader and the lair of the commerce-destroyer. Through this cloud of friends and foes the unprotected merchantman had to run the gauntlet, trusting to his heels. If he were taken, all, indeed, was not lost, for there remained the chance of recapture by a friendly cruiser; but in that case the salvage made a large deduction from the profits of the voyage." [1]

The unprotected merchantman making his way over seas covered with friends and foes was a reality; but this was not the typical British commerce-bearer. Always there was the individual owner willing to take the greater risks in order to earn enhanced profits, trusting to speed and good luck to avoid capture by the enemy, and crews were ready for high wage to tempt Fortune on an adventure. Such vessels were the constant cause of attention by and anxiety to the patrols which the Admiralty found itself forced to maintain. But the bulk of British ocean-borne commerce was not left to the hazard of chance. Convoy was offered and accepted; and the merchantmen outward sailing or congregating near our coasts were mostly gathered in large fleets. Every such convoy involved delay in the assembling of the ships; the speed of the fastest craft sailing in the company was brought down to that of the slowest; and the simultaneous arrival of many ships in port threw large cargoes upon a choked market, thus tending to lower prices and reduce profits. It was the elimination of these effects in the balance-sheet that made the daring individual voyage so attractivè. The evasions of convoy, and the many losses of ships and seamen consequent upon them, led to the passing of the Convoy Acts in 1798 and 1803, which compelled ship-masters to take convoy and to pay a certain sum for the protection afforded. The beneficial results were at once apparent in the fall of insurance rates, and in, what was more important to the nation, fewer captures of ships and men.

British convoys during the Napoleonic Wars reached the most unwieldy dimensions, and the fine spectacle such as a cluster of sail made at sea was well calculated to rouse enthusiasm in every British heart. Admiral Sir William Parker, when a young midshipman in the ORION in 1794, in a letter to his mother says:

" We left Torbay on the 13th, Saturday, and the next day were off Plymouth, where the convoy came out to us. It was the grandest sight ever was, a convoy of six hundred sail, besides thirty-six line-of-battle ships. The wind was

Influence of Sea Power on the French Revolution, ii, 204–5.

CH. I] CONVOY OF A THOUSAND SHIPS 53

quite fair and a fine evening: as soon as the convoy was all out, it came on so fine a breeze that we went eight miles an hour, without a stitch of sail set; in fact, in three days, they were all so far to southward that they were out of all danger; and so we hauled off. . . . Captain Duckworth says if I live to be one of the oldest Admirals, it is ten thousand to one if I ever see so large a convoy carried so far to the westward, and without the least accident, and the wind fair enough to bring us back again in so short a time." [1]

A stupendous convoy of no fewer than a thousand ships was gathered in October of the same year in The Belt, when Admiral Sir James (afterwards Lord) de Saumarez, on board the VICTORY, sailed with it, homeward bound from Swedish waters. An eyewitness has described the vast assemblage in the following passage:

" A scene so novel conveyed some idea of the wealth and power of the British nation—a most beautiful and wonderful sight. The day was very fine; the fleet was anchored in a close compact body, with the VICTORY in the centre, bearing the Admiral's red flag at the fore, surrounded by six ships of the line and six frigates, and sloops disposed for the complete protection of the convoy. The yacht, with a Swedish flag, containing the Crown Prince passed through; the convoy soon after weighed anchor, when the Royal stranger had the pleasure of seeing them all under sail and proceeding to their destination, regardless of the enemies who occupied the adjacent shores." [2]

The congregation of so many ships in a single convoy and a scene like that above described convey a better idea of the importance of the British merchant fleets a century ago than any elaboration of figures. Small though the wooden sailing-ships were, their management required the signing on of large crews, and the population afloat was nearly three times as numerous as would be required to carry the same trade in days of steam-power and improved mechanical appliances.

[1] Phillimore, *Life of Admiral Sir William Parker*, i, 39–40.
[2] Ross, *Memoirs and Correspondence of Admiral Lord de Saumarez*, ii, 214–5.

The attack by the enemy was not only against ships and cargoes, but also against the seamen. Happily, the barbarities which attended submarine warfare, as practised by the Germans in the European War, were then unknown. Ships were not sunk at sight, and merchant sailors—often, as well, passengers, delicate women and helpless children—left adrift in open boats at the mercy of the ocean, the gale, and the biting frost, sometimes when hundreds of miles from land. *Spurlos versenken* as a policy of warfare had not been invented. But the merchant seaman of the Napoleonic Wars was liable to capture and confinement till the end of the war or exchange, and this peril was ever present with him when he went to sea. He knew the risk, and accepted it, as seamen of the Great War of the twentieth century faced without flinching the far more serious risks of loss of life by torpedo and shell-fire or drowning, or maiming by exposure to frost-bite. The practice of confining captured merchant seamen was adopted by both belligerents, for in days of simple armaments the trained merchant seaman was already more than half a fighting man, and his transformation into an efficient naval rating was quickly accomplished. The Royal Navy was largely manned by men recruited from the merchant ships, so the capture and detention of peaceful seamen by the enemy served him in a double purpose—by injuring British carrying trade and by withholding a potential source of strength from the Navy.

Mention has been made of the large size of the East India Company's ships, rising to 1,300 registered tonnage, and in a few exceptional instances to as much as 1,500 tons. Such vessels exceeded the dimensions of a first-class frigate, and were almost equivalent to a small ship of the line. Early in the war their armament was increased by the addition of 18-pounders, and they were able to put up a good fight with any raiding corsair. These were, however, exceptions in our carrying trade—a class by themselves. The traffic between America and Europe was mostly done in vessels not exceeding 300 tons. From Macpherson's tables, quoted by Admiral Mahan, it appears that the ships trading to the West Indies and the Baltic, between 1792 and 1800, averaged about 250 tons; to Germany, to Italy, and the Western Mediterranean, about 150 tons; to the Levant, 250 to 300 tons, with a few

TONNAGE OF BRITISH SHIPPING

of 500 tons. Even by throwing into the scale the East India Company's ships (averaging about 800 tons), the general average of British shipping is reduced to as low as 125 tons, owing partly to the small capacity of the large number of vessels engaged in the Irish trade. In 1796 there were 13,558 entries and clearances from English and Scottish ports for Ireland, and the average size of these ships was only 80 tons. A similar average is found from the returns of the Irish trade in 1806. Other indications in the naval literature of the time confirm the small size of both our own and enemy shipping. Thus Sir William Parker, when an active frigate captain commanding a single ship from the year 1801 to 1811, was in that period interested in fifty-two prizes, the average tonnage of which, excluding a ship of the line and a frigate, was 126 tons.[1] Vessels engaged in the British coastal traffic were still smaller; of 6,844 coasters which entered or left the port of London in the year 1798, excluding the colliers—which, as a class, were of larger build—the average size was only 73 tons.[2]

Such was the type of vessel dotted about the oceans of the world. The merchant seaman of the day was a much harried individual, living the life of a fugitive, dreading not only capture by the enemy, but almost as much capture by the ships of war of his own country. Ashore or afloat the trained seaman, so much sought after, was never free from the attentions of the press-gang, which was the ultimate method of enforcing compulsory service in the Fleet on those who tried to avoid it. In the street, in the tavern, in his own home, the merchant seaman was marked down for seizure. He had no redress; the appeal which was supposed to shield him against injustice existed only in the letter. At night he was dragged out of his bed, to be herded with a crowd of others, awaiting distribution among the King's ships. Close as was the man-hunt ashore, it was not less keen afloat. The sailors in the Merchant Service had to run the gauntlet for their liberty from one end of the world to the other. A British ship-of-war, falling in with a merchant vessel in any part of the globe, would unceremoniously take from her the best seamen, leaving her just enough hands to bring her home.

[1] *Life of Admiral Sir William Parker*, i, 412.
[2] Colquhoun's *Commerce of the Thames*, p. 13.

As the vessel approached the English shore our cruisers, hovering in all directions, would take the pick of the remainder. An old Liverpool sea-captain, in reminiscences of the closeness of the press in that port, has declared that such was the dread of the ever-active press-gangs ashore that homecoming seamen would often take to their boats on the other side of the Black Rock, that they might conceal themselves in Cheshire, and many a vessel had to be brought into Liverpool by a lot of riggers and carpenters, sent round by the owner for that purpose.[1]

Many a merchant seaman figuring as "volunteer" was a pressed man, so described to get him the bounty, and others, when the emergency arose, volunteered to assure themselves of the bounty, knowing that they were liable to be impressed, and that the chances of escape were remote. Many men hid from the press-gangs while waiting for the offer of a bounty, which followed after compulsion had done its best. The importance of impressment in the scheme for manning the Royal Navy can best be judged from the establishment which was kept up for this service alone. In 1793-4, the first year of the long French Wars, when impressment was by no means at its height, nor was the Royal Navy maintained at anything comparable to its subsequent strength, there were three flag officers, twenty-nine captains, fifty-four lieutenants, employed in the impress service, with over 4,000 men—and on occasions many more.[2]

The rigour which marked the impressment on some occasions when men were badly wanted for the Royal Navy—and the want was never satisfied—is sufficiently illustrated by two quotations from the newspapers of the day:

"The impress service, particularly in the metropolis, has proved uncommonly productive in the number of excellent seamen. The returns at the Admiralty of the seamen impressed on Tuesday night amounted to 1,080, of whom no less than two-thirds are considered prime hands. At Portsmouth, Portsea, Gosport, and Cowes, a general press took place the same night. Every merchant ship in the harbour and at Spithead was stripped of its

---

[1] Gomer Williams, *The Liverpool Privateers*, p. 320.
[2] *Steel's Navy List*, 1794.

CH. I] THE WAR AFTER TRAFALGAR 57

hands, and all the watermen deemed fit for His Majesty's service were carried off. Upwards of 600 seamen were collected in consequence of the promptitude of the measures adopted. . . . Government, we understand, relied upon increasing our naval force with 10,000 seamen, either volunteers or impressed men, in less than a fortnight, in consequence of the exertions which they are making in all the principal ports. . . . Several frigates and gun-brigs have sailed for the Islands of Jersey and Guernsey, with impress warrants." [1]

" The impress on the Thames on Saturday, both above and below the bridge, was the hottest that has been for some time; the boats belonging to the ships at Deptford were particularly active, and it is supposed they obtained upwards of 200 men. . . . The impressed men, for whom there was no room on board the ENTERPRIZE on Saturday, were put into the Tower, and the gates shut to prevent any of them effecting their escape." [2]

The epoch of fleet actions between the British and French navies closed with the victory of Trafalgar. England had, thanks to her isolation by sea and her naval supremacy, maintained her independence and enlarged her Empire, while on the Continent State after State was tumbling to ruin and vassalage. Yet the cost had been a heavy one. Her merchant shipping had undergone devastation, though, thanks to the activity of her shipyards and her own wealth, the losses were more than made good. In the struggle lasting over twelve and a half years, broken by one brief interval of peace, England had lost some 6,500 ships by capture. In the single year 1797 the statistics show 947 vessels captured—a number, happily, far higher than in any other year, and only approached in 1799, when the captures are returned at 730. In the single month of June 1797 no fewer than 106 ships were placed upon the lists of prizes taken from us.

Trafalgar signalised the beginning of a yet more intense attack upon Britain's ocean-borne commerce. Napoleon, defeated in his efforts to oppose British naval strength at sea, despoiled of all hopes of effecting such a naval concentration as should make the invasion of England a practicable task, sought other means to accom-

[1] *The Times,* March 11th, 1803. [2] *Ibid.,* May 9th, 1803.

plish the downfall of his chief adversary. The Berlin and Milan Decrees of 1806 and 1807 aimed to shut out from the Continent all British commerce, and, by causing widespread ruin at home, to undermine the strength of the great Power against which, on sea and land, he had fought in vain. The Emperor, unable to keep a ship at sea except for such a time as it could elude the stronger forces of his opponent, declared a blockade of Great Britain. The British Ministers retorted by the famous Orders in Council which forbade all neutral vessels to trade between the ports belonging to the enemy and his allies, and sought to divert the world's trade through England. From Trafalgar onwards the French fleets, though continually enlarged, never deliberately attacked, and at sea, as in the earlier Revolutionary period, the struggle again became that of a *guerre de course*.

It was conducted with the extraordinary thoroughness and vigour which Napoleon, enjoying complete mastery over France, was able to employ in all his schemes. Nothing was permitted to stand in his way. Under his impulse the French fleet soon became stronger in material than it had been since the opening of the war; and the new fleet was created with a single object.[1]

Nelson's one call throughout his commands had been for more frigates—always more frigates. The larger number of them were employed on the protection of trade, and the shortage of cruising-vessels with the battle fleets—whose eyes they were—due to this cause, had a marked influence on many of the most important engagements. With the disappearance of fleet actions, the smaller ships were able to give less divided attention to trade protection, but there still remained work for the larger vessels. The French, for instance, detached several ships of the line to support the determined attacks they made on the Indian trade routes, and our own squadrons had similarly to be reinforced. England, after Trafalgar, devoted her chief energies in shipbuilding to launching increasing numbers of frigates and sloops. This growth in the number of cruising-ships actually employed on sea service, whilst the number of ships of the line remained practically stationary, is shown in the following table:[2]

[1] Brenton's *Naval History*.
[2] *Journal of Royal United Service Institution*, April 1913.

	1804.	1805.	1806.	1807.	1808.	1809.	1810.	1811.	1812.	1813.	1814.
Ships of the Line	75	83	104	103	113	113	108	107	102	102	99
Cruisers	356	473	551	606	618	684	666	620	584	570	594

The disposition of naval ships for the protection of trade necessarily underwent considerable modification. Squadrons of large frigates were kept constantly at sea, ranging from Cherbourg to Finisterre; the coastal trade and the St. George's Channel were guarded by the smaller craft; and a string of cruisers kept up communication between Falmouth and Gibraltar. The work put the greatest strain upon our seamen, who for yet another ten years were called upon to maintain their untiring vigilance. Collingwood, having embarked at Plymouth on the last day of April 1805, and after Trafalgar assumed the command in the Mediterranean, never found opportunity again to set foot in his native country, to which he was brought home a corpse in 1810.

The story of fights by British merchant crews in defence of their ships during the fierce attack upon our trade after Trafalgar is told in hundreds of letters from captains to their owners. Many of them are addressed from ports which the ships had safely made, with riddled hull and shot-torn sails, and rigging telling of the perils safely passed. Not less frequently, it must be admitted, the letters bearing the ill news of capture came from some prisoners' camp. Enemy cruisers were constantly on the look-out for vessels detached from the large sailing convoys, and against a well-armed man-of-war the merchantman, with a lesser weight of metal and ill-trained crew, had small chance. An Homeric contest, waged successfully against overwhelming odds, was that between the British packet *Windsor Castle* and the French privateer schooner *Le Jeune Richard*. A passenger, writing from Barbadoes on October 3rd, 1807, gives the following account:

" We are just landed here after an unpleasant passage of thirty-seven days, and experiencing one of the most desperate actions which has been fought in this war, though, thank God, we have been victorious, and have cleared those seas of one of the fastest-sailing privateers out of Guadaloupe, which had in the last six weeks taken no less than six fine-running ships—viz., the *America* and *Clio* in company, the *Margaret*, the *Pope*, the *Portsea*, and another. When we met her she was six days on a fresh cruise, with eighty-six men, and six long sixes and one long 32-pounder gun. Our force consisted of six guns, short sixes, and thirty men, including three passengers. We lost three men killed and seven wounded, the first broadside; but I am happy to say that with the remainder, in an hour and forty minutes, such was their gallantry, that they carried the privateer, after killing twenty-six, wounding thirty, and making prisoners thirty not wounded, in all sixty prisoners, almost treble the number we had left for duty. I cannot enter into more detail by this opportunity, and can only say that if any man has deserved a token of merit from your Underwriters, Captain Rogers deserves it in the highest degree. He is a young man, his first voyage as Acting Captain (the Captain being left at home), and has therefore nothing but his merit to depend upon. He was left with only ten men about him for the last half-hour, rallying them to their duty, with a determination to carry the prize, which repeatedly endeavoured to clear from the packet, but was too fast lashed by her bowsprit to escape, and he boarded her at the head of four men, and charged her deck, with a gallantry never excelled and seldom equalled. The officers of the man-of-war here are astonished when they look at the two vessels and their crews, and instantly in the handsomest manner relinquished all claim to the prize." [1]

Instances of such actions fought by British merchantmen, when practically every ship was armed for its defence, might be recorded indefinitely. It must suffice to mention the gallantry, both in defence and attack, of the little Falmouth packet *Antelope*, when chased off the Cuban coast by the French privateer *Atlante*. The packet carried a crew of twenty-three men, and had no better armament than six 3-pounders, but she had several passengers on board, who assisted in loading the guns with grapeshot, buckled on cutlasses, and primed their muskets. The privateer's first broadside at close range killed the *Antelope's* captain and the first mate. Her second mate having

[1] Gomer Williams, *The Liverpool Privateers*, p. 410.

died of fever a few days before, she was left without a senior officer. John Pascoe, the boatswain, took command of the ship, and the French, having boarded, were attacked with such vigour that they were hurled back to their own ship, leaving their captain run through the body dead, and several of their crew killed or wounded. Again and again the privateersmen attempted to board, but at each trial they were driven back by the desperate defence. Realising that they had " caught a Tartar " and that the ship was too hot for them, the French endeavoured to cut the grapplings and make off, but the *Antelope* lashed her foreyard to the enemy's shrouds, and poured in grape and musket-ball at point-blank range. Pascoe, daring everything, then determined to carry his enemy, and had collected a boarding party, who raised lusty cheers preliminary to the assault, when to their surprise the *Atlante's* red flag at the mainmast and the ensign at her peak were hauled down. The British merchantmen made their prize, and safely brought both ships into port at Jamaica. The privateer had twenty-eight killed and nineteen wounded, more than the entire number of the *Antelope's* crew and passengers when she went into action.[1]

It fortunately was customary, both on the French and British side, that after a fight at sea the prisoners taken should be well treated. A privateer, unable to bring his prize into port, would at times hold a ship to ransom, accepting the captain's acknowledgment on the part of the owners, and such arrangements were honourably fulfilled. In one letter of complaint of ill-treatment a British captain declared that it was " disgraceful to a polite nation like the French." This compliment of being " a polite nation " was frequently paid to our determined enemy. The chivalry of the sea is illustrated by many instances in the long wars. The British ship *Sally*, having fought the French privateer *L'Amélie* off the entrance to the Bristol Channel, and having been carried by boarding, the crew were allowed to preserve the whole of their private property, and given such comforts as the privateer afforded. Captain Lacroix promised the English commander his liberty and the first ship of little value that he should take, and he was, in fact, sent home in a captured Dundee brig with all his men and the brig's crew and passengers, a

[1] James Rowe, *History of Flushing, Cornwall*, pp. 26-9.

bargain having been struck that he should obtain the exchange of an equal number of French prisoners-of-war, to be sent from England to France. The French captain further declared that if the exchange were honourably made he would set free on the first opportunity every Englishman whom the fortune of war should throw into his power.

No royal road to preventing losses among our shipping was ever found, and year after year, until peace in 1815 crowned the titanic efforts of a nation almost exhausted in the struggle, the tables of statistics tell their own certain tale. By immense effort, continuously sustained by a Royal Navy which increased each year in strength of fighting ships, in guns and in personnel, the losses of merchant ships, in the ten years after Trafalgar, were so checked that they were not greater than in the corresponding earlier period. And it must be recollected that for a year and a half during that period hostilities with the United States added a heavy quota to the depredations of French privateers. The British merchant ships were pygmies compared with the leviathans that cross the seas to-day. Individually their loss counted for much less, but the large numbers taken each year, in a war waged continuously for twenty years, placed a strain upon the trade and resources of the nation which only the gigantic edifice of Britain's world-wide commerce, built up upon solid foundations of individual enterprise and served by a stalwart, seafaring race, could have borne.

Our ocean-borne trade, attacked with untiring persistence throughout two decades of war, was the chief object sought out by the French naval ships and the larger privateers, but it by no means represented the whole body of British commerce exposed to sea peril. England was at the same time served by great numbers of small sailing-ships, which conducted the coastal trade round the British Isles and that between our island colonies; and these lines of shipping were peculiarly open to raids by the enemy. Many such vessels undoubtedly swell the lists of captures, and they have complicated the tables of contemporary statistics, vitiating the conclusions drawn from them, both by their presence there and by their absence; for a large proportion of the coastal ships figure on no return, and the vast bulk of commerce which they carried, and of which the enemy took toll, escaped observation, as the clearances made are but imperfectly recorded.

Any estimate of losses among the ships trading from port to port around the coasts can only be made by inference, but there are abundant indications that these losses were severe. In a southerly gale blowing along the English south coast, ships-of-war guarding the Channel found themselves compelled to run for Portsmouth or the Downs, leaving the slower-sailing merchantmen, heavily laden, without protection or without harbourage about the long stretch of dangerous shore, and open to attack by French privateers putting out from Cherbourg, Havre, and Dieppe. The Frenchmen, well aware of the system pursued by our cruisers, and enabled constantly to keep to windward of them, found the merchantmen an easy prey in these conditions. They came out in the wildest weather, in which, far too often for our welfare, they achieved their greatest successes.

Mixed with the ocean traders beating up-Channel was a not inconsiderable coastal trade, and at the Thames mouth this was joined by a still larger stream of small vessels making the journey along the east coasts of Scotland and England to London. There being no inland waterways, and the main roads being wholly insufficient to carry the burden of traffic, London received, not only the great exchange of commerce which made it the trading centre of the world, but also the bulk of its own supplies from the sea. At every hour of the day and night long lines of ships, numbered by thousands in all, stretched from Orfordness to the far north of Scotland, and from Selsey to Ramsgate. In the Thames estuary hundreds congregated at every tide, passing on their way or waiting to go up or down the river, or taking advantage of the shelter. Given a dark night, a fair wind, often a fog, and a daring enemy was rarely without an opportunity for attack, the quick seizure of a prize, and safe escape. Of such opportunities he made full use. "With a fleet surpassing the navy of the whole world," complained a writer in the year 1810, "and by which we are enabled to set so large a proportion of it at defiance, we cannot guard our coasts against insult."

In addition to the cruising frigates and warships watching the French shore, our own coasts swarmed with brigs, sloops, and cutters, kept ready for instant action in every harbour and inlet, whose duty it was to patrol and to protect the coastal traffic. So numerous were these that at one period there were 149 stationed between Southend and Orfordness; 181 between the Thames mouth and Hastings; 138 from Newhaven to Poole; 21 at Liverpool, Glasgow, and Greenock; 114 on the coast of Ireland; and the long stretch from Yarmouth to Leith was protected by 135 craft.[1] Yet in spite of the utmost vigilance the losses continued. The public indignation at raids effected within sight of our coasts was expressed in the letter of another writer, who declared that the audacity of French privateers occasioned universal indignation and regret. "Our merchantmen captured before our eyes—the national colours of our enemy floating, with gasconading insolence, along our shores, and effecting their escape with impunity, is, indeed, too much for an Englishman's reflection, accustomed as he is to behold the vanquished streamers of the foe waving in submission beneath his country's flag."[2]

The French privateers engaged in these depredations upon the coastal traffic were mostly the smaller vessels which swarmed in the harbours of Dunkirk, Calais, Boulogne, and Dieppe. Any craft could be made to serve, provided it had speed. The provision of a gun or two, a few hands collected from the desperate riff-raff of the ports, the very minimum of provisioning, and all was ready. Little was risked by the owners, whose craft was worth no more than the proceeds of one or two fortunate voyages. The crews, it was true, ran the chance of capture and of pining in an English prison, but the reward, quickly earned, was an ample incentive. Luggers, sloops, fishing-smacks, with a single gun placed on board, even open row-boats, played their part in the service; and though individual prizes might be of small value compared with those made by the ocean-going corsairs, together they amassed a very considerable sum. A privateer, stealing out at dusk before a long winter's night, might with fortune return with its prize before the next day's sun was high.

Naturally the headlands, such as Portland, Beachy Head, Dungeness, and others, were favourite places for attack, and not infrequently those watching from the shore

---

[1] Hannay's *Short History of the Royal Navy*, ii, 440.
[2] *Naval Chronicle*, xxiv, 460.

were witnesses of some smart bit of "cutting out" which the British naval forces were powerless to prevent. Utilising the British flag—a frequent ruse—and moving on the skirts of the assembled shipping, a daring raider in full daylight would make prizes and get clear away under the very eyes of watching seamen. But night was, of course, the most favourable time, and the very severe losses of trade in the winters immediately before and after Trafalgar led to the introduction of a system of watching, by appointed cruisers, each harbour and outlet on the French coast, thus blockading the privateers seeking to dash out from the ports between Cherbourg and Dunkirk; but, notwithstanding this vigilance, many continued to slip through the cordon, as the heavy losses among the British merchant ships from 1805 to 1810 testify. A complete chain of watching cruisers to be maintained all along the French coast was one of the means recommended by the shipowners to reduce the tale of losses.[1]

The French spirit made their men quick to adopt every ruse. A common peril besetting our coastal trade was found in innocent-looking fishing-boats, showing their half-dozen men busy at their work, which lay at anchor upon, or within, the lines joining headland to headland. Desperadoes out from Dunkirk or Calais, armed with nothing more effective than the short-range muskets of the day, watched the character and appearance of passing vessels. When night or other favourable opportunity came they pulled quickly alongside the unsuspecting merchant ship which, undermanned and unwatchful, from the scarcity of seamen, was first awakened to the danger by a volley of musketry, followed by the clambering of the enemy on the decks. The crews, few in number, poor in quality, and not paid for fighting, frequently could offer but slight resistance to an overpowering assault.[2] Typical of French daring was the capture of a West Indiaman, the *Benjamin and Elizabeth*, in 1799, four leagues off Dungeness, in a fog. She was hailed by a lugger, who, running under her quarter, asked her if she wanted a pilot. On being answered "No," a man on board the little craft who spoke good English called on

---
[1] Memorandum on the Protection of the Coasting Trade, presented by Mr. Greville, 1809.
[2] Mahan, *Influence of Sea Power on the French Revolution*, ii, 208.

the Indiaman to back her mainyard and surrender, following this demand with a volley of musketry, after which men, swarming on the lugger, boarded her on the quarter. A sharp fight resulted in the crew being overpowered, and the prize was headed for France. H.M.S. RACOON came up on the crossing, recovered the ship, and sank the lugger with a broadside, all on board going down.[1] Tales of the sort were the common talk in every sailors' tavern.

The total losses to which the British mercantile fleets and British commerce were subjected during the Revolutionary and Napoleonic Wars have been discussed by Commander (now Captain) K. G. B. Dewar, R.N.[2] It must be admitted that the material available is far from satisfactory, owing to various causes: the incomplete manner in which statistics were kept; their not infrequently conflicting nature; the complications introduced by the recapture of vessels taken by the French, and the additions of enemy prizes which were diverted to the British merchant fleets; and the uncertain evidence concerning clearances and times of voyages, which require an average to be assumed. Admiral Mahan estimated the total losses of British ships in round numbers at 11,000, an annual average of about $2\frac{1}{2}$ per cent.,[3] and held that the direct total loss to the nation by the operation of hostile cruisers did not exceed $2\frac{1}{2}$ per cent. of the commerce of the Empire.[4] The studies of the Naval War College have placed the losses at double that proportion—5 per cent.[5] Low as his estimate is, Mahan qualified and reduced it, adding:

"This loss was partially made good by the prize ships and merchandise taken by its (Great Britain's) own naval vessels and privateers. A partial, if not complete, compensation for her remaining loss is also to be found in the great expansion of her mercantile operations carried on under neutral flags: for, although this too was undoubtedly harassed by the enemy, yet to it almost entirely was due the volume of trade that poured through Great

---

[1] *Naval Chronicle*, ii, 162.
[2] "What is the Influence of Overseas Commerce in the Operations of War, etc." Printed in *Journal of the Royal United Service Institution*, April 1913.
[3] *Influence of Sea Power upon the French Revolution*, ii, 223.
[4] *Ibid.*, ii, 226.
[5] *Official Memorandum*, by Sir Julian Corbett.

Britain to and from the Continent of Europe, every ton of which left a part of its value to swell the bulk of British wealth. The writings of the period show that the injuries due to captured shipping passed unremarked amid the common incidents and misfortunes of life; neither their size nor their effects were great enough to attract public notice, amid the steady increase of national wealth and the activities concerned in amassing it." [1]

The duties levied upon cargoes of neutrals who were forced to enter our ports, by the Orders in Council framed as an answer to the Berlin and Milan Decrees, certainly assisted Great Britain in bearing the cost of the war; but it is straining the meaning of words to comprise such traffic within the ambit of British wealth. Mahan claimed, in particular, that the British returns of British losses at sea were larger than those made by the French, but that result is probably due to the very inefficient manner in which the French returns were compiled, and the omission of colonial captures.

Without entering into detailed examination of statistics on which there is ground for disagreement, we may cite the table (p. 68) compiled by Commander Dewar as affording an approximate indication of the intensity of the attack on trade during the war.

Neglecting the year 1793, the average column (IV) works out at 5·6 per cent. As, however, ships must on the average have cleared more than once a year, the number of ships must be considerably overestimated, and the percentage of captures in Column IV correspondingly underestimated. On the other hand, a large number of captures included ships engaged in the coastal trade, and if the tonnage of the coastal shipping were added to Column III, the percentage of captures would be decreased.

Returns of the coasting trade were not made until 1824. It was a vital part of our commerce in an epoch when the bulk of the distribution of merchandise throughout the British Isles was done by water, and the many hundreds of small sailing-ships continuously engaged in this traffic traded with a comparatively small number of ports. To

[1] *Influence of Sea Power upon the French Revolution*, ii, 227.

BRITISH MERCHANTMEN CAPTURED 1793–1812

By Commander K. G. B. Dewar, R.N., *Journal of the Royal United Service Institution*, vol. lvii, No. 422.

I Year.	II British Merchantmen captured.	III Clearance of British Shipping engaged in the Foreign Trade.	IV Percentage of Captures to British Ships engaged in Foreign Trade (assuming One Clearance a Year).
		Tons.	Per Cent.
1793	352	1,240,000	3·8
1794	644	1,382,000	6·2
1795	640	1,145,000	7·5
1796	489	1,254,000	5·2
1797	949	1,103,000	11·5
1798	688	1,139,000	6·9
1799	730	1,302,000	7·5
1800	666	1,445,000	6·1
1804	387	1,463,000	3·5
1805	507	1,495,000	4·6
1806	519	1,486,000	4·7
1807	559	1,424,000	5·2
1808	469	1,372,000	4·6
1809	571	1,531,000	5·0
1810	619	1,624,000	5·1
1811	470	1,507,000	4·3
1812	475	1,665,000	3·8

AUTHOR'S NOTE.—The accuracy of this table cannot be guaranteed, but it affords an accurate comparison between the various years. Columns II and III are taken from the *Cambridge Modern History*, vol. viii, pp. 485 and 486, vol. ix, pp. 241 and 242. The average tonnage of ships employed in the foreign trade in 1802 is taken as 134 tons (*Essays on Naval Defence*, by Vice-Admiral P. H. Colomb, p. 241). Assuming that each ship cleared once a year, the number of ships employed in the foreign trade is obtained by dividing Column III by 134.

ignore it, as too often has been the tendency, is to throw out all the calculations.

Insurance rates may be taken as affording some guidance. They fluctuated violently, and seem to have been highest in 1805, when two strong French fleets were at large in the Atlantic; but it is not without significance that the average rate of insurance during the long wars was more than 5 per cent.[1]

Although, with the materials available, anything beyond an approximate estimate is impossible, there appear to be sound reasons for the conclusion that the losses incurred by British commerce in the great struggle in which it was engaged a century ago were much nearer to 5 per cent. than $2\frac{1}{2}$ per cent., as suggested by Admiral Mahan. The wonder is, not that the proportion was so large, but that it was not larger, in view of the advantages which lay with the enemy, possessing many convenient ports and a large number of small craft.

A table showing the number of British-owned ships during the Revolutionary and Napoleonic Wars is appended. It reflects the steady growth of the British Mercantile Marine in spite of the losses sustained during the years of war. It will be seen that, mainly owing to activity of shipbuilding, the numbers increased from 16,329 to 24,860 between 1793 and 1815, the year when peace was concluded.

REGISTERED SHIPS BELONGING TO THE BRITISH EMPIRE DURING THE PERIOD OF THE NAPOLEONIC WARS

From the Appendix to Minutes taken before the Manning Committee, 1859.

Year.	No.	Year.	No.	Year.	No.
1793	16,329	1801	19,711	1809	23,070
1794	16,806	1802	20,568	1810	23,703
1795	16,728	1803	20,893	1811	24,106
1796	16,903	1804	21,774	1812	24,107
1797	16,903	1805	22,051	1813	23,640
1798	17,295	1806	22,182	1814	24,418
1799	17,879	1807	22,297	1815	24,860
1800	17,895	1808	22,646		

[1] *Cambridge Modern History*, i, 241.

III

The Development of the Merchant Navy, 1815–1914

The British people emerged from the Continental struggle victorious but exhausted. Famine is the offspring of war, and it seemed to contemporaries that, although the supremacy of the seas had been won, economic ruin confronted them. While wages had risen by about 60 per cent., the price of wheat had gone up by 130 per cent. Throughout the country the lower classes of the population had been reduced to a state of privation. In the rural districts, particularly in the south, the advent of the steam-engine, and the industrial movement northward, towards the coal-fields, in association with the economic effects of the war, had robbed prosperous little towns and hamlets of the means of livelihood. The conditions had become so grave that, in the absence of Parliamentary intervention, local justices felt compelled before the end of the century to grant allowances from the rates to supplement the low wages then ruling, the allowances being varied according to the price of corn. Rural England, largely owing to the extinction of village industries, was brought to a condition of misery which had not been known hitherto. The sufferings of the towns were even worse, and distress was widespread. The privations of the mass of people had seemed to reach a climax in 1811–12, when the harvest failed all over Europe. The evil was deep-rooted, and did not soon pass away. Riots, due in the main to the introduction of machinery at this period of economic disturbance from the effects of war, contributed to render the outlook so grave that men feared that industrial unrest would be followed by national ruin.

Contemporary opinion failed to realise that, in liberating Europe by the use of sea power, this country had created the foundations upon which it might build on the ruins of the war a new and better state of society. Not only had the supremacy of the seas been gained, but during the long period covered by hostilities an organisation had been created to enable the British people to take advantage of that success, constituting themselves in process of time the sea carriers of the world. Both the Royal Navy and the Merchant Navy were stronger when peace was signed than they had been when it was broken in 1793. The Merchant Navy had grown in spite of the heavy losses sustained at the hands of the enemy. In other words, as the conflict by sea drew to its close, British sea power, notwithstanding the risks to which it had been exposed over a period of two decades and the losses sustained, rose to a greater strength than it had before attained.

In the opening years of the nineteenth century, the British people were so impressed with the miseries which they attributed too exclusively to the war that they were blind to the promise of prosperity which their sea power assured them as an island people. They had, in fact, suffered less in consequence of the long-drawn struggle than any other people in Europe, owing to the policy consistently adopted by successive Governments. Ministers had refused, in spite of temptations, to embark upon a policy of military expansion which would have drawn tens of thousands of men away from productive employment, and in particular from the industries specially associated with the maintenance of the country's sea power. Foreign troops were subsidised, but the utmost reluctance was exhibited to take any step in opposition to the unadulterated maritime principles of defence and offence. Even in 1815, the year which was marked by the overthrow of Napoleon at Waterloo, the number of men voted for the British Army was only 275,392. The country reaped the full advantage of this adhesion to a maritime policy. While the war was still in progress, and the population of the British Isles was suffering economically, the work of industrial reconstruction was undertaken. The development of the steam-engine had directed attention to the vast wealth represented in the coal seams in the northern counties, and the opening years of the century witnessed the uprising of the great manufacturing centres which were to transform England from a country in the main agricultural into one distinguished by its industrial pre-eminence. The foundations on which the promise of the future rested was the supremacy of the Royal Navy and the strength of the Mercantile Marine.

Merchant shipping is not a basic industry : it produces nothing. It is, however, the conduit pipe of commerce from market to market. Leaders of public opinion in the early years of last century failed to realise that a new age was dawning, owing to the invention of the marine steam-engine, which was to contract the world and thus encourage ocean-borne trade. Yet events were to prove that this non-productive industry was the most essential element in the life of a people, living in a group of islands, drawing their raw materials, in large measure, from oversea, and relying upon oversea markets for customers to purchase their goods. British merchantmen became the shuttles in the great economic loom which was created in the years following the conclusion of peace by slow and painful stages and amid much political turmoil. As industry developed, the Merchant Navy supported it with an increasing strength that passed almost unnoticed. The shipping industry in those days owed little to the State; it was an individualistic movement, its inspiration and mobility due to far-sighted and resourceful business men in the great sea-ports, who devoted themselves to the creation, as a commercial enterprise, of a great carrying trade. So long as war continued they had maintained their sailings, in spite of the action of enemies and the interference of the press-gang. With the coming of peace, when the demands of the Royal Navy for men were no longer paramount, they devoted themselves without embarrassment to the management of the British Merchant Navy, which for a hundred years was to prove the lynch-pin of the industrial movement of the British Isles and the foundation of British economic strength, for a free sea and a healthy marine were the bases on which the Free Trade policy of the latter part of the Victorian Era rested.

Though the nation had preserved its Mercantile Marine in strength, that organisation was in anything but a healthy state. The old Navigation Laws—the expression of a traditional mercantile policy now outgrown and soon to be changed—were still in force. They confined the import trade to British ships or ships of the producing country, restricted to British ships the carriage of merchandise to the Colonies, and reserved the whole of the coasting trade to British vessels navigated by British masters, and manned by crews containing at least 75 per cent. of British subjects. The Navigation Laws limited competition at a moment when the marine steam-engine was making its appearance, and the nation was beginning to understand the advantages it possessed by reason of its coal-fields. It was apparent to far-seeing men that the iron ship was about to make its appearance. Even while the war was still going on, experiments had been made with iron for the construction of ships, and in 1819 the first vessel built entirely of iron was completed on the Clyde. She was intended for carrying coal on the Forth and Clyde Canal. In subsequent years other experiments were made. In view of the advent of the steam-engine and the possibility of employing iron in the shipyards in place of wood, shipbuilders thought it necessary to adopt a cautious policy. They could well afford to do so, since they were protected from the full brunt of foreign competition, at any rate so far as British and Imperial trade was concerned.[1] Between the signing of peace in 1815 and the close of the year 1830, the British Merchant Navy not only did not increase, but was thought to have declined slightly both in numbers and tonnage. The falling off, however, was more apparent than real. In 1823 Parliament began the task of repealing the Navigation Laws, but it was one beset with many difficulties. Further evidence of a national awakening to the importance of the Mercantile Marine was supplied in 1836, when a Committee was appointed to inquire into the causes of wrecks. It became apparent that all was not well. The Committee reported that the ships "were so faulty in design and as sailers so slow, that British shipowners feared free trade because they knew that successful competition on equal terms with foreign ships was impossible." The Committee's report contained the following significant passages:

"That the frequent incompetency of masters and officers appears to be admitted on all hands, this incompetency sometimes arising from want of skill and knowledge in seamanship, but more frequently from the want of an adequate knowledge of navigation, it being proved that some masters of merchant vessels have been appointed to command after a very short time at sea; that others have hardly known how to trace a ship's course on a chart, or how to ascertain the latitude by a meridian altitude of the sun; that many are unacquainted with the use of the chronometer, and that very few indeed are competent to

[1] The rule as to the employment of *English* ships for imports was relaxed in the case of America in 1796.

ascertain the longitude by lunar observations, while some are appointed to command merchant vessels at periods of such extreme youth (one instance is given of a boy of fourteen, all of whose apprentices were older than himself), and others so wholly destitute of maritime experience (another instance being given of a porter from a shipowner's warehouse who was made a captain of one of his ships), that vessels have been met with at sea which were out of their reckoning by several hundred miles; and others have been wrecked on coasts from which they believed themselves to have been hundreds of miles distant at the time.

"That drunkenness, either in the masters, officers, or men, is a frequent cause of ships being wrecked, leading often to improper and contradictory orders on the part of the officers; sleeping on look-out, or at the helm among the men, occasioning ships to run foul of each other at night, and one or both foundering; to vessels being taken aback or overpowered by sudden squalls, and sinking, upsetting, or getting dismasted, for want of timely vigilance in preparing for the danger, and to the steering of wrong courses so as to run upon dangers which might have otherwise been avoided.

"That the practice of taking large quantities of ardent spirits as part of the stores of ships, whether in the Navy or in the Merchant Service, and the habitual use of such spirits, even when diluted with water, and in what is ordinarily considered the moderate quantity served to each man at sea, is itself a very frequent cause of the loss of ships and crews. Ships frequently taking fire from the drawing off of spirits, which are always kept under hold: crews frequently getting access to the spirit casks, and becoming intoxicated, and almost all the cases of insubordination, insolence, disobedience of orders, and refusal to do duty, as well as the confinements and punishments enforced as correctives, both of which must for the time greatly lessen the efficiency of the crews, being clearly traceable to the intoxicating influence of the spirits used by the officers and men."

The maritime position of the country was unsound. Many harbours were so shallow that the bottoms of ships were specially constructed to take the ground. In

CH. I] CONDITION OF MERCANTILE MARINE 75

spite of the fact that some of the officers of the larger foreign-going ships were men of the highest attainments and of undoubted reputation, drunkenness and incompetency among officers of average type, as well as the seamen, were notorious. Ships were provided with inadequate charts even where any charts were supplied. The Mercantile Marine depended largely on pauper apprentices for its supply of seamen, and there was no examination of masters, mates, or engineers, to test their professional skill. Numerous lighthouses still remained the absolute property of individuals, or were leased to individuals for their personal benefit, and surplus light dues went to so-called charitable purposes and were dispersed through avenues entirely unconnected with shipping. Harbour dues, town dues, charity dues, and passing dues levied on ships were similarly diverted. There were no harbours which could be described as harbours of refuge, though a passing toll had to be paid by all ships off Whitby, Bridlington, Dover, or Ramsgate. The Tyne, Clyde, and Tees were navigable only by small vessels even at high-water, and many other ports now flourishing scarcely existed. "Freight was the mother of wages"; payment for salvage of life was unknown; ships did not carry side-lights; no international rule of the road at sea existed; neither reports of wrecks nor inquiries as to the cause of wrecks had been instituted; crimps preyed, and preyed unchecked, on British seamen; there was no system of recovering the wages or effects of deceased seamen; Parliament had not thought it necessary to make any practical statutory provision as to the supply of food, or as to the accommodation of seamen; there were no checks on the tyranny of masters at sea, and no provision for the proper execution of contracts between masters and seamen; a seaman could not raise any question as to the unseaworthiness of his ship, but could be sent to prison as a deserter if he went ashore to complain; there were no international or code signals.[1] That was the condition of the British merchant fleet at the time when a Committee was appointed to inquire into the

---

[1] This summarised statement of the condition of the Mercantile Marine is based on an address at the Mansion House, February 17th, 1887, by Mr. Thomas Gray, C.B., Assistant Secretary, Marine Department, Board of Trade.

causes of wrecks. The investigation showed that the maritime interests of the nation were suffering, to the injury of trade and the weakening of the Imperial system. The Committee emphasised many of the causes of the decline of the shipping industry which have already been summarised, and in particular remarked on the increasing competition with foreign shipowners, "who, from the many advantages enjoyed by them in the superior cheapness of the materials for building, equipping, and provisioning their vessels, are enabled to realise profits on terms of freight which would not even cover the expenses of English ships." The report of this inquiry went a long way to confirm the statements which had been made by Mr. Joseph Hume, who from his place in the House of Commons had declared that the British Merchant Navy was losing its place among the mercantile marines of the world, and that it was urgently necessary that Parliament should, in particular, direct attention to the administration of lighthouses around the coast and the provision of harbours.

The public attention which was attracted to the state of the Mercantile Marine at this period at last led Parliament to pass a succession of acts which, practically for the first time since the expansion of the country's maritime power,[1] recognised the principle that the State had a responsibility towards the shipping industry beyond that which reflected the broad economic policy of the country, and that it was, especially, bound to enforce regulations for the protection of the lives of passengers and seamen. Measures were passed regulating the conditions under which emigrants travelled, establishing a registry office for seamen, and transferring to Trinity House a number of lighthouses which formed part of the hereditary estate of the Crown, and steps were also taken to provide better harbours. In 1846 further progress was made to insure greater safety at sea. It was enacted that all iron steamers should be divided by watertight compartments into three divisions; that all sea-going vessels should be provided with boats in proportion to their tonnage; that steamers should pass to the port side of each other; that steamers when within twenty miles of the coast should carry lights to be prescribed by the Admiralty; that passenger steamers should be surveyed

[1] The essential fact seems to have been that shipping expanded so enormously as to render existing regulations out of date.

half-yearly by surveyors to be approved by the Board of Trade; that accidents to steamers should be reported to the Board of Trade, that department having power to inquire into the cause of the loss.[1]

In 1843 fresh light had been thrown upon the condition of the Merchant Navy owing to the action of Mr. James Murray, of the Foreign Office, who, at the request of the Admiralty, addressed a letter to British Consuls abroad asking them to supply him with information "respecting the character and conduct of British ship-masters and seamen." He added in his circular letter that his object was to show "the necessity for authoritative steps on the part of Her Majesty's Government to remedy what appears to be an evil detrimental to and seriously affecting the character of our commercial marine, and therefore advantageous to foreign rivals, whose merchant vessels are said to be exceedingly well manned and navigated."

At that time nine separate departments were concerned in administrating the laws affecting the Merchant Navy, and there was no central board to co-ordinate the work of these several authorities, each department being left to look merely to those interests committed to its charge and to its own convenience. The reports which were received fully confirmed the widespread anxiety which was entertained as to the decline of the character of the British Mercantile Marine. Mr. Murray summed up their general purport in the following statement:

" It is stated from various parts of the world that persons placed in command of British ships are so habitually addicted to drunkenness as to be unfitted for their position, and it will be seen that Her Majesty's Consuls allude specifically to the notorious and gross intemperance, and to the ignorance and brutality of British ship-masters, many of whom are totally void of education. In several reports it is stated that there are honourable exceptions to the unworthy class of masters, thus showing that among British masters frequenting foreign ports bad conduct and ignorance is the rule, and intelligence and ability the exception; that, on the other hand, foreign masters are

[1] This Act is of interest as marking the initiation of a new policy on the part of the State in its relation to the Mercantile Marine. It has since been modified.

educated, sober, intelligent men, capable of commanding their ships, and that foreign seamen are consequently more orderly."

Eventually Parliament took action on the lines suggested by Mr. Murray, and in 1850 the Marine Department of the Board of Trade was established. In the previous year the last remains of the Navigation Laws as to foreign trade had been repealed, to be followed five years later by the abolition of the restrictions on the coasting trade. Almost simultaneously, therefore, the protective system as applied to merchant shipping was abolished, and a special office created to administer the varied and often contradictory legislation with reference to the Mercantile Marine which had been passed since the opening years of Queen Victoria's reign. Henceforward the confusion which had hitherto existed with reference to the administration of the laws relating to shipping was mitigated, and there were many indications of increased public interest in the industry, particularly as affecting the safety of passengers and crews.

Mr. Samuel Plimsoll was largely responsible for the movement of public opinion which occurred in later years. He directed attention, in particular, to the number of vessels which put to sea in an unseaworthy condition and overloaded, having often been heavily insured by their owners, who thus stood to gain in case of disaster. Mr. Plimsoll's agitation against " coffin-ships " greatly exaggerated the extent of the evil, but the evil undoubtedly existed. His pertinacity led to the appointment of a Commission of Inquiry, and the publicity given to the scandal resulted in the passing of the Merchant Shipping Act of 1873, giving stringent powers of inspection to the Board of Trade, and legalising what is now known as the " Plimsoll Mark " as a protection against overloading. The evil was scotched but not killed, and the matter received further attention about ten years later, when Mr. Joseph Chamberlain, President of the Board of Trade, introduced into the House of Commons a Bill to provide for " greater security of life and property at sea." In moving the second reading of the Bill on May 19th, 1884, he reverted to the controversy which had arisen as to the responsibility of shipowners for the abuses which had undoubtedly existed over a long period. He made it clear

THE WORK OF REFORM

that he advanced no charge against shipowners generally, but was dealing only with a minority. He pointed out that, according to Mr. Hollams, a well-known lawyer, the law as it then stood declared to the shipowner, " buy your ship as cheaply as you can, equip her as poorly as you can, load her as fully as you can, and send her to sea. If she gets to the end of her voyage you will make a very good thing of it; if she goes to the bottom you will have made a very much better thing of it. . . ." Mr. Chamberlain, referring to the Report of the Commission, added :

" The Commissioners pointed out that ' the system of our marine insurance, while it protects shipowners against losses which would otherwise be ruinous, tends to render them less careful in the management of their ships. . . . The contract of marine insurance is, in its essence, a contract of indemnity, and the spirit of the contract is violated if the insured can make the occurrence of a loss a means of gain.' The Commissioners added that ' our whole system of insurance law requires complete revision, for not only does it allow the shipowner in some cases to receive more than the amount of the loss sustained by him, but it also, on the other hand, deprives him of an indemnity in cases in which he ought to be protected by his insurance.' "

Further important and far-reaching reforms were introduced towards the end of the nineteenth century, thus completing the task of revising and codifying the law relating to the Mercantile Marine which had been attempted with a large measure of success in 1854.

It may be profitable to turn from this survey of legislation to an examination of the progress of the Mercantile Marine during these years when British shipping, the Navigation Laws having been repealed, had to face world-competition, when some of the burdens imposed on British shipowners were lifted from them, and when Parliament intervened to enable the Board of Trade to insist upon the seaworthiness of ships and the safety of passengers and crews. In 1875, Sir Thomas Farrer,[1] then Secretary to the Board of Trade, prepared a memorandum with reference to the " state of British shipping

[1] Afterwards Lord Farrer.

and seamen." He pointed out that "the actual increase of our Merchant Navy is a most remarkable fact," and in order to illustrate the progress gave a series of figures (see below).

Commenting on those figures, the Secretary of the Board of Trade remarked that they gave a very imperfect reflection of the increase in the quality and quantity of the work done by the Merchant Navy. "The quantity of that work is to be measured by the number and length of voyages made and the nature of the freights carried. It is scarcely possible to get at this accurately, but some

PROGRESS OF BRITISH SHIPPING

Years.	Ships belonging to the British Empire at the End of Each Year.		Ships belonging to the United Kingdom at the End of Each Year.	
	No.	Tons.	No.	Tons.
1818	25,507	2,674,468	21,526	2,426,969
1820	25,374	2,648,593	21,473	2,412,804
1830	23,721	2,531,819	18,675	2,168,916
1835	25,511	2,783,761	19,737	2,320,667
1840	28,962	3,311,538	21,983	2,724,107
1842	30,815	3,619,850	23,207	2,990,849
1850	43,281	4,232,962	25,131	3,504,944
1852	34,402	4,424,392	25,228	3,698,004
1860	38,501	5,710,968	26,764	4,586,742
1862	39,427	6,041,358	27,525	4,860,191
1870	37,587	7,149,134	25,643	5,617,693
1872	36,804	7,213,829	25,083	5,681,963
1873	36,825	7,294,230	24,873	5,736,368
1874	36,935	7,533,492	24,828	5,912,314

notion of it may be found from the number of entrances and clearances. For the Foreign Trade of the United Kingdom we can give these. For the Coasting Trade we cannot, since a large proportion of coasting voyages do not appear in the Custom House books; nor can we give complete returns of the employment of British ships on the Foreign Trade of foreign countries." In order to make this point clear, quotation was made of the number and tonnage of British vessels entered and cleared in the foreign trade of the United Kingdom (with cargoes and in ballast) between 1818 and 1874. In the former year the number of ships was 24,448, with a tonnage of 3,601,960; in the latter year the number was 73,534 and the tonnage

30,089,683. It was remarked that, "if complete returns were available for the coasting trade and for the trade carried on between foreign ports by British ships, an even more remarkable indication of the progress of British shipping would have been possible, since the coasting trade has been carried on almost exclusively by British ships." From the statistics given it was evident that, whilst British tonnage nearly trebled between 1835 and 1874 and more than doubled between 1842 and 1874, the tonnage entrances and clearances of British ships in the foreign trade of the United Kingdom in 1872 were about six times what they were in 1835, and more than four times what they were in 1842. The explanation, it was pointed out, was to be found in the increase of steam-vessels, making many voyages where a sailing-vessel makes but one. Statistics were quoted by the Secretary to show the great growth of steam tonnage and the increase in the number of men, exclusive of masters, in spite of the introduction of labour-saving devices. The number of men in 1852 was 159,563, and in 1874, 203,806.

During the period when Parliament was turning its attention to the condition of the Mercantile Marine the United States was developing a great sea-carrying trade. The Americans had not only shown that they could build the finest and swiftest clipper ships, but in 1814 they launched their first steamship on the great waters of the Mississippi, and immediately proceeded to the development of their internal maritime communications which the new propulsive agent made possible. With a fine spirit of enterprise they cultivated their merchant navy by every practicable means, and by the middle of the nineteenth century were the most serious competitors of this country for sea power. By the early sixties the British lead amounted to little more than a quarter of a million tons. And then came the Civil War. The North possessed only a small fighting fleet, and in the emergency the authorities turned to the Mercantile Marine to supply the deficiencies in order that economic pressure, by means of a blockade of the numerous ports of the Confederacy, might be applied without delay. Warships were improvised, but at a terrible cost to the Merchant Marine. Prior to the Civil War, two-thirds of the foreign trade of the United States was carried in ships flying the Stars and Stripes. American shipping represented 5,250,000 tons. "The extraordinary character of the emergency demanded that much of this tonnage should be impressed into the naval and military services. One million eight hundred thousand tons were taken, and $100,000,000 withdrawn from the capital embarked in the shipping industry. The ALABAMA, the Confederate tiger of the sea, destroyed 100,000 tons of shipping, and caused the owners of vessels to seek foreign registries or tie their craft to the dock, rather than send them unprotected on voyages which were likely to end in the prize court or destruction by fire at sea. Foreign ships and foreign capital eagerly entered the industry which the United States was compelled to abandon.[1] From the damage inflicted upon our Merchant Marine during the Civil War there has been, as yet, no full recovery; and the stupendous increase in our foreign trade is the more remarkable in view of the fact that it has been effected in spite of the disadvantage of its conveyance in ships flying the flags of other nations than our own." [2]

The American Civil War, coming in the very midst of the transition from sails to steam, removed the most serious competitors with whom British shipowners had had to contend. When in 1875 the Secretary of the Board of Trade, continuing his examination of the state of British merchant shipping, investigated the progress of the British Mercantile Marine in relation to that of other countries, he was able to paint a gratifying picture. Whilst the British tonnage in the trade of the United Kingdom had increased from 65 per cent. of that trade in 1850 to 68 per cent. in 1870, United States tonnage, which had 60 per cent. of the trade of the United States in 1850, had only 38 per cent. of it in 1870. French tonnage, which had 41 per cent. of the trade of France in 1850, had only 31 per cent. in 1870. Dutch tonnage, which had 42 per cent. of the trade of Holland in 1850, had only 28 per cent. in 1870. Prussian tonnage, which had 49 per cent. of the trade of Prussia in 1850, had 46 per cent. in 1870. Swedish tonnage, which had 43 per cent. of the trade of Sweden in 1850, had only 32 per cent. in 1870. Even in the case of Norway, whose marine had grown rapidly,

[1] An interesting parallel is the blow to English merchant shipping as the result of the Wars of the Roses.
[2] *The New American Navy*, by the Hon. James Long, former Secretary of the Navy Dept., U.S.A. (1903).

Norwegian tonnage, which had 73 per cent. of the trade of Norway in 1850, had decreased to 70 per cent. in 1870. "It was, of course, to be expected," the Secretary to the Board of Trade remarked, "that when the foreign trades of the different countries were opened to foreign ships, the native ships of each country would do a smaller proportion of that trade, finding their compensation in the new trades between other countries thus opened to them. And so it happened in the case of all maritime countries, except Great Britain. But in her case, with a trade far exceeding that of any other country, and increasing more rapidly than that of most countries, her shipping has not only continued to do the same proportion of her own trade as it did before the trade was opened to other nations, but has increased that proportion. Nor is this all. The foreign trade of each foreign country has also increased very largely; and the native shipping of each foreign country no longer does the same proportion of her own trade as it formerly did. The proportion which native shipping no longer does must be done by ships of some other flag; and though we have no complete figures to show how much of the trade of each of these countries is done by the British and how much by other foreign flags, we have some evidence to show that the British flag comes in for the lion's share of it."

Summarising all the evidence which he had been able to collect, the Secretary of the Board of Trade came to the conclusion that "it is abundantly evident, not only that British merchant shipping has, in the twenty years succeeding the repeal of the Navigation Laws, enjoyed its due proportion of the increase in the trade of the world, which has followed on free trade and the use of steam, but that it has obtained much more than its due proportion, and has outdistanced many of its once-dreaded competitors. Having special advantages in the possession of coal and iron, and having the mechanical genius to turn these advantages to account, it has led the way, and secured itself, not only the largest share of the carrying trade of the world, but the most valuable part of that trade."

The legislation affecting shipping which was passed during the latter part of the nineteenth century was opposed to the political sentiments of the time. State interference with trade, either by land or by sea, was regarded with suspicion and distrust. It was felt that Parliament was treading dangerous ground in attempting to regulate industry. A powerful impulse from without was necessary in order to secure Parliamentary action, even to assure the safety of passengers and crews. Shipowners generally were no doubt guiltless of the gross charges which were levelled against them as a class by those who were stirred to action by the abuses which existed in some ships of the Mercantile Marine. The scandals may have been due to the neglect or criminality of the minority. Practically everyone who was concerned with financing and managing the Mercantile Marine opposed the earlier legislative measures, believing them to be harmful to an industry which had hitherto been individualistic. However exaggerated the statements may have been which were made by Mr. Joseph King, Mr. Samuel Plimsoll, and others—and most agitations are based on ex-parte and overcoloured assertions—it cannot be doubted that, had it not been for the intervention of such public-spirited men and the success with which they played on public sympathy, little would have been done by Parliament; or, at any rate, action would have been indefinitely postponed. On the other hand, the pressure of uninstructed public opinion in the country led to the passing of measures without due consideration of details, and a succession of amending and consolidating Shipping Acts was required to unravel the tangle created by the legislation carried in the years of agitation. The movement was not continuous, nor was it always wisely directed, but its general effect was good. Stage by stage, important powers were conferred on the Board of Trade. Its Marine Department is a modern development, created to meet modern needs; its duties, though numerous, are clearly defined and restricted. It is concerned mainly with the security of life and property at sea, and has had, directly, no share in the upbuilding of the Mercantile Marine. The strength of the Merchant Navy has always depended in the main upon the enterprise and business ability of the shipowning community in meeting the nation's needs without State subvention or State encouragement.

The passage of merchant shipping legislation between 1880 and 1885 was succeeded by a further period of great prosperity for British shipping. Freights, both homeward

BRITISH TONNAGE IN 1914

and outward, with some fluctuations, continued high, reaching their maxima in 1889. The prosperity of the industry was reflected in the output of new ships. At the turn of the century freights fell, pointing to over-production, and this was reflected in the orders placed in the shipbuilding yards. On the eve of the outbreak of war in 1914, the earning capacity of shipping had for six years shown a gradual but healthy improvement, with the result that fresh capital was invested in the industry. Even shipyards throughout the United Kingdom benefited from this recovery, and in 1913 were responsible for nearly two-thirds of the world's new construction in spite of the activity in Germany.

At the outbreak of war the British Mercantile Marine was the largest, the most up-to-date, and the most efficient, of all the merchant navies of the world.[1] It comprised nearly one-half of the world's steam tonnage (12,440,000 tons out of about 26,000,000 tons net), and was four times as large as its nearest and most formidable rival—the German Mercantile Marine. The tonnage owned by the principal maritime countries of the world on June 30th, 1914, is shown below:

STEAM-VESSELS

	Tons Net.	Per Cent.
British Empire:		
United Kingdom	11,538,000	44·4
Dominions and Colonies	902,000	3·5
Total	12,440,000	47·9
Germany	3,096,000	11·9
United States [2]	1,195,000	4·6
Norway	1,153,000	4·4
France	1,098,000	4·2
Japan	1,048,000	4·0
Netherlands	910,000	3·5
Italy	871,000	3·4
Other Countries	4,179,000	16·1
Total	25,990,000	100·0

NOTE.—This table was prepared for the Departmental Committee on Shipping and Shipbuilding, Cd. 9092. The steam tonnage of the three Scandinavian countries (Norway, Sweden, and Denmark) amounted together on June 30th, 1914, to 2,185,000 tons net, or to 8·4 per cent. of the world's steam tonnage.

[1] This review of the strength and development of the British Mercantile Marine is based, in large measure textually, on the Report of the Departmental Committee on Shipping and Shipbuilding, Cd. 9092.

[2] These figures do not include United States vessels engaged in trade on the Northern Lakes (1,693,000 tons).

The tonnage of the United Kingdom consisted mainly of vessels large enough for ocean voyages. If the dividing-line between ocean-going and other vessels is taken at 1,000 tons net (or 1,600 tons gross), it will be found that 90 per cent. of the tonnage of the United Kingdom was made up of vessels of the larger type. The number and net tonnage of steam-vessels (a) of less than 1,000 tons, and (b) of and above 1,000 tons, which were on the Register of the United Kingdom at the end of 1913 were as follows [1]:

	No.	Net Tons.
(a) Steam-vessels of less than 1,000 tons net	8,855	1,100,000
(b) Steam-vessels of and above 1,000 tons net	3,747	10,173,000
	12,602	11,273,000

It is thus evident that the nation was dependent for supplies and trade on a comparatively small number of vessels of great size—the secret of success in peace and danger in war. Vessels of large size are generally more economical than smaller vessels, but in war their loss is the more severely felt proportionately as their number is limited. The enemy's submarine warfare became vital the moment it began to attack the larger vessels on a great scale.

Before the war this country led the way in most matters of shipowning and shipbuilding; and not least in the building of merchant vessels of large size. Between the end of 1910 and the end of 1913 the average size of the

Steam-Vessels on the Register of the U.K. on December 31st.	1910		1913	
	No.	Net Tons.	No.	Net Tons.
Of 1,000 and under 2,000 tons net	1,370	2,138,000	1,134 [2]	1,751,000
Of 2,000 and under 3,000 tons net	1,569	3,878,000	1,599	4,001,000
Of 3,000 and under 5,000 tons net	630	2,324,000	804	2,975,000
Of 5,000 tons net and above	148	994,000	210	1,446,000
	3,717	9,334,000	3,747	10,173,000

[1] In the more detailed survey of the position of the British Mercantile Marine before the war, the shipping of the United Kingdom, which represented 93 per cent. of the Empire's shipping, is generally referred to, the reason being that detailed statistics were not always available for the remainder.

[2] The reduction in the number of ships of less than 2,000 tons exactly corresponded with the increase in the number of vessels of and above 3,000 tons.

TONNAGE AND SPEED

"ocean-going" steam-vessels on the register of the United Kingdom increased from 2,500 to 2,700 tons net, a significant movement.

It is not necessary to make any detailed comparison between the British and other mercantile marines as regards the size of vessels employed. The average size of steam-vessels of and above 100 tons gross (or about 60 tons net) is a rough index to the kind of trade in which the vessels of the respective countries were principally employed; and the average tonnage of such vessels which were on the Register on June 30th, 1914, is accordingly shown below:

	Net Tons.		Net Tons.
United Kingdom	1,350	France	1,100
Germany	1,500	Denmark	800
Italy	1,400	Norway	750
Japan	1,300	Russia	700
Netherlands	1,300	Sweden	600

The high average tonnage of German and Italian vessels indicated that their trades were almost wholly ocean, and indeed liner, trades. This was true also, though in a lesser degree, of Japan and Holland. The low average tonnage of Danish, Norwegian, Russian, and Swedish vessels was equally significant for the converse reason. This comparison, moreover, does less than justice to the United Kingdom, because British ocean-going tonnage alone was more than three times as large as the entire German Mercantile Marine.

The British carrying trade before the war was divided between the regular lines with scheduled sailings, which traded on defined routes, and owners of vessels engaged in general trade, or "tramp" owners, whose vessels were often chartered to third parties, and traded wherever a cargo might be found. It is impossible, however, to state how much tonnage was allocated at a given time as between "liners" and "tramps." The Lines ran passenger vessels and also cargo vessels, generally of a higher type and speed than ordinary tramp vessels, but there was always a class of vessel on the border-line between "liners" and "tramps" which might be of service in either capacity, as occasion required. The only available index of the importance of tramp tonnage is that afforded by the speed of the vessels. Particulars given in Lloyd's Register indicate that, of the steam tonnage owned by the British Empire on June 30th, 1914, 35 per cent. was capable of maintaining a sea speed of 12 knots or more; and probably all vessels of that speed were liners. It may be estimated roughly that, of the total tonnage of the United Kingdom before the war, 60 per cent. consisted of tramps and 40 per cent. of liners.

The importance of the tramp-owner in the shipping economy of the Empire cannot be too much emphasised. "Not only was he responsible for the larger part of our steam tonnage, but we were dependent on him for the import and export especially of what may be termed the rougher class of bulk cargoes, which are not as a rule suitable for liner business. It would be impossible for a country like the United Kingdom, with its enormous flow of trade, to depend wholly on regular lines with scheduled sailings."[1] It had been recognised for many years that it was essential that there should be a large amount of "loose" tonnage capable of supplementing the liner sailings, and prepared to trade at short notice to any part of the world. "Yet, precisely because of his ubiquitous presence, the tramp-owner's difficulties," the Committee on Shipping and Shipbuilding remarked, " were the least easily defined and met, and he was peculiarly susceptible to any serious modification of the conditions under which shipping is usually carried on."[2]

No account is taken of sailing tonnage. Its importance was small. The disadvantages of ships dependent on wind and weather had become obvious. Already the carrying-power of sailing-vessels of a given tonnage was incomparably lower than that of steam-vessels of equivalent tonnage; and the error due to the omission of sailing tonnage from any estimate of the world's carrying-power is almost negligible. In 1890 the United Kingdom possessed 3,000,000 tons of sailing-vessels; by 1900 the amount had declined to a little over 2,000,000 tons, and

---

[1] Committee on Shipping and Shipbuilding, Cd. 9092.
[2] The speed of vessels of foreign countries did not, on the whole, compare favourably with British vessels. The proportion of Norwegian vessels of 12 knots and above was insignificant, but the number of Norwegian liners was small. Only 23 per cent. of German steam tonnage was capable of maintaining a sea speed of 12 knots or more, and yet the German trades were pre-eminently liner trades, their tramp interests being small.

CH. I] THE WORLD'S ECONOMIC EXPANSION 89

by 1913 to 850,000 tons. A similar, though a somewhat less rapid, decline, due to the supersession of sailing craft by steam and other self-propelled vessels, occurred in the case also of other countries.

During the twenty-five years or so preceding the war there was an enormous expansion of the world's sea-borne commerce, and, consequently, of the world's tonnage, which trebled in volume. "In the twenty years up to the end of 1913 there were built some 25,000,000 tons of steam shipping, of which two-thirds was built in the United Kingdom and over one-half for the British flag. The world's shipbuilding had increased progressively from some 700,000 tons net in 1894 to an average of about 1,000,000 tons net a year in the period 1894—1903, to 1,500,000 tons net a year in the period 1904—1913, and to 2,000,000 tons net in 1913 itself. Those figures illustrate the growing demand for shipping that followed the world's economic expansion before the war."[1] In that period the steam tonnage of the United Kingdom was more than doubled; but, even so, its rate of increase was proportionately not so rapid as that of certain other countries—notably Germany—whose steam tonnage increased fourfold. The fact that the volume of British shipping did not grow at the same relative rate as that of some other countries was thus explained by the Committee on Shipping and Shipbuilding:

"(1) It was not to be expected that the United Kingdom could maintain its great *relative* preponderance in the world's carrying trade in face of the enormous economic expansion taking place in such countries as Germany and the United States, and the opening up of new markets in all parts of the world. It is not surprising that the smaller mercantile marines should have expanded more rapidly than the powerful Mercantile Marine of the United Kingdom, more especially in view of the maritime efforts of most countries in the period. It is noteworthy that, if *actual* as opposed to *relative* growth be considered, no foreign country even approximated to the United Kingdom.[2]

[1] Committee on Shipping and Shipbuilding, Cd. 9092.
[2] The growth of Germany's mercantile marine was proportionately much more rapid than that of the United Kingdom; but whilst between 1900 and June 1914 the United Kingdom added 4·3 million tons to its steam tonnage, Germany added only 1·75 million tons.

"(2) Great as was the expansion of the world's tonnage in the twenty-five years before the war, the expansion of the world's power of transportation was even greater, owing to the superiority, first of steam over sailing ships, and then of improved types of steamships over the older types. The carrying-power of the United Kingdom proportionately to the tonnage on the Register increased more rapidly than that of other countries. In any appreciation of the maritime position of this country before the war, this factor cannot be overlooked."

The world's shipping was undergoing a continual process of renewal and replacement in the years preceding the outbreak of war. Immediately before the war, the average annual rate of expansion of the world's steam tonnage as a whole was rather less than 5 per cent. of the tonnage on the Register. The output of new tonnage amounted to rather over 7 per cent. of the tonnage on the Register; and it may therefore be inferred that about 2 per cent. of the world's shipping was every year lost or broken up.

Nearly one-half of the world's shipping, as has been above indicated, was on the Register of the United Kingdom. If the Mercantile Marine of the United Kingdom be taken by itself, it will be seen that the process of development in its case was widely different. In the years immediately before the war the steam tonnage of the United Kingdom increased by not more than $2\frac{1}{2}$ per cent. annually. But it is significant that some 600,000 tons net, or nearly $5\frac{1}{2}$ per cent. of the total tonnage, was every year removed from the Register for one reason or another. Two-thirds, or 400,000 tons, was sold to foreign flags, the amount accounted for by vessels lost or broken up averaging only 150,000 tons. On the other hand, additions to the Register of the United Kingdom in the years 1911–13 averaged about 863,000 tons a year, of which 93 per cent. comprised vessels newly built.

This transfer of large numbers of older British vessels to foreign flags was of great importance in connexion with the development of the Mercantile Marine. Our shipowners were thus afforded a ready market for the disposal of vessels no longer satisfactory to them as a preliminary to the ordering of new vessels better suited to their

RENEWAL OF BRITISH SHIPPING

purpose, and the merchant tonnage of foreign countries, as a whole, was older, and therefore less efficient, than the tonnage of the British Mercantile Marine.

As a result of this process of sale and replacement, 85 per cent. of the tonnage on the Register of the United Kingdom at the end of 1913 had been built since 1895, including 68 per cent. built since 1900, and 44 per cent. built since 1905. The following table shows the distribution of our steam tonnage according to age at the end of 1913 [1]:

	Net Tons.	Per Cen
1890 and earlier	724,000	6·4
1891 to 1895	930,000	8·3
1896 to 1900	1,979,000	17·6
1901 to 1905	2,718,000	24·1
1906 to 1910	2,614,000	23·2
Since 1910	2,308,000	20·4
	11,273,000	100·0

In this short survey no account has been taken of those personal factors which, whilst an indispensable element of success, are the most difficult to appraise. "The initiative and enterprise of shipowners and shipbuilders were a vital element in the building up of the greatest carrying trade that the world has ever seen. A further element of success, on which it is impossible to lay too much stress, was the skill, efficiency, and seamanship of the officers and men who manned and navigated our vessels in peace, and who during the war have, by their courage and devotion, insured the maintenance of our sea-borne trade." [2]

A statistical basis for estimating the size and character of the target exposed to enemy attack on the outbreak of war in 1914 is supplied by the calculations on p. 92.

There is a discrepancy between these figures and the aggregate tonnage of the Mercantile Marine as recorded by the Board of Trade in its general statement of the strength of the Merchant Fleet. This is due to the exclusion from the table which follows of a large number of small vessels, yachts, and inland navigation vessels, which are all counted in the official enumeration of tonnage

---

[1] Statistics of the age of the merchant tonnage of other countries do not, on the whole, compare favourably with those for the United Kingdom.
[2] Cd. 9092.

over 100 tons net. The smaller tonnage—of sea-going trading-ships—was the asset which the nation had at its disposal when the Great War occurred. Even this reduced figure may be analysed with profit. The Annual Navigation Statement included, under the description of Home Trade, not only vessels employed in the coasting trade of

SAILING AND STEAM VESSELS EMPLOYED IN TRADING[1]

	In the Home Trade.		Partly in the Home and Partly in the Foreign Trade.		In the Foreign Trade.		Total.	
	Number of Vessels.	Tons Net.	Number of Vessels.	Tons Net.	Number of Vessels.	Tons Net.	Number of Vessels.	Tons Net.
Sail	1,867	143,335	37	4,783	177	275,414	2,081	423,532
Steam	2,038	495,619	326	599,615	3,791	9,650,401	6,155	10,745,635
Total	3,905	638,954	363	604,398	3,968	9,925,815	8,236	11,169,167

the United Kingdom, but also those trading with the Continent of Europe between the River Elbe and Brest inclusive, and it failed to distinguish between the vessels employed in these two trades. But the tables published in 1913, to show the progress of merchant shipping,[2] made this distinction, the number as on April 3rd, 1911, being :

Foreign Trade within Home limits	.	459	steamships
Coasting Trade .	. . . .	1,565	,,
		2,024	

The 2,024 steamships above referred to included only the vessels which on April 3rd, 1911, had crews on board, and if allowance be made for the ships which were not in commission on the given date, it is probable that in 1911 there were in all about 2,200 steamships employed in these two trades. The number of steamships so employed remained practically the same in 1913, being made up of 2,038 vessels described as employed in the Home Trade, and about one-third of the 326 vessels employed partly in the Home and partly in the Foreign Trade.

[1] Annual Statement of the Navigation and Shipping of the United Kingdom for the Year 1913, Cd. 7616.
[2] *Ibid.*, Cd. 7033.

The total number of steamships which on December 31st, 1913, were engaged in Foreign Trade was therefore about 4,500, made up as follows:

(1) In Foreign Trade outside of Home limits:
  Solely employed . . . . 3,791 steamships
  Partly employed, say . . . 209 ,,
  4,000 ,,

(2) Foreign Trade within Home Trade limits:
  say 500 steamships
  4,500 ,,

The matter may be carried a stage farther.[1] In the oversea trade the steamships of under 1,000 tons net were employed principally to trade with the Continent within Home Trade limits, ports on the western coast of France, and the Baltic ports; on ocean voyages the steamship of under 1,000 tons net is of little account. Of the 2,038 steam-vessels employed in 1913 in the Home Trade, only 54 were of over 1,000 tons net. Of the 326 steam-vessels employed in 1913, partly in the Home Trade and partly in Foreign Trade, 177 were of over 1,000 tons net. And of the 3,791 vessels employed in 1913 in the Foreign Trade, 3,444 were of over 1,000 tons. The total number of steam-vessels of over 1,000 tons net belonging to the United Kingdom on December 31st, 1913, was therefore 3,675, and the nature and employment of these vessels was as under:

STEAM-VESSELS OF OVER 1,000 TONS NET EMPLOYED IN TRADING

	Number.	Tonnage.
Home Trade	54	64,820
Partly Home and partly Foreign Trade .	177	529,204
Foreign Trade	3,444	9,443,838
	3,675 [2]	10,037,862

The number of vessels belonging to the United Kingdom had not increased on the date of the outbreak of war in August 1914, although the aggregate of the tonnage may have slightly increased since December 1913. Of the vessels of importance in the Ocean Oversea Trade, the number belonging to the United Kingdom was, therefore,

[1] Report by the Secretary of the Liverpool Steamship Owners' Association, October 1915.
[2] The average size of these vessels was 2,731 tons net.

on the outbreak of the war, 3,600 steam-vessels of over 1,000 tons net, their tonnage being 10,000,000 tons net. Those steamships were classified under two heads—first, the vessels trading in regular lines on fixed routes; and, secondly, the general traders going wherever cargo offered. The liners numbered about 1,200 and the general traders about 2,400. The average size of the liner was 3,500 tons net, representing about 5,800 tons gross; and that of the general trader about 2,400 tons net, or about 4,000 tons gross.

It would be an error to assume that before Parliament began to evince an interest in merchant shipping no control of any kind was exercised over the design and construction of vessels. Early in the seventeenth century Lloyd's Coffee-House had become the recognised headquarters of maritime business in London, and especially of marine insurance. "There, whether on the initiative of the proprietor or the frequenters, were kept certain records of shipping, termed 'ships' lists,' which contained an account of vessels which the underwriters who met at the house were likely to have offered to them for insurance." This coffee-house proved the foundation of a corporation which was to exercise a widespread and beneficial influence on the development of the industry. The Register became the guide to the insurer who was asked to risk his money, and shipowners who wanted to insure on advantageous terms found it to their advantage to meet the views of the underwriters when placing their orders for vessels to be built. In 1760 the underwriters established a society for their protection, and issued a register which came to be known as the *Green Book*. It was supported exclusively by underwriters, and was intended for their sole use. At the end of the eighteenth century the shipowners, who had long objected to the classification of their vessels at the uncontrolled discretion of the body of underwriters, started the *Red Book*, which was virtually a shipowners' register. Not until 1834 were the competing interests led to make an arrangement under which Lloyd's Registry of British and Foreign Shipping was established, a committee being appointed, consisting of eight merchants, eight underwriters, and eight shipowners, with the chairman of Lloyd's and of the General Shipowners' Society as ex-officio members. The general principle of classification on which the Registrar was to act was to assign characters which should be as nearly as possible " a correct indication of the real and intrinsic quality of the ship"; the practice of classing vessels according to place of build or the decision of the surveyors was to be abandoned, and all characters were to be granted only by the Committee " after due inspection of the report of the surveyors and the documents which may be submitted to them." It was not until several years later that Lloyd's Register obtained an assured position, and was able to exercise a compelling influence on ship-construction.

In the meantime, the industry was undergoing a revolution. First, the marine steam-engine had made its appearance; and, secondly, experiments in building ships of iron instead of wood gave rise to a controversy which divided the shipowning class into different camps, and interfered with the efficient discharge by the Registry of its responsibilities towards underwriters, merchants, and shipowners. Experience with the steam-engine had to be acquired and a new class of seamen educated. Later on, when the iron ship took the waters, a somewhat similar situation developed. During those years of transition the control exercised by Lloyd's Register was subject to fluctuations, and it was only gradually that a volume of experience was built up, enabling the Society to lay down definite rules calculated to protect the interests of those intimately associated with the industry and to satisfy the natural concern of the nation at large—particularly that part of it accustomed to travel by sea—for the safety of ocean-going vessels. Lloyd's Register, in process of time, became the supreme arbiter in ship-construction, not only in this country, but, to a large extent, abroad.[1] In the first instance, the plans of vessels and of boilers of steamers for which the Society's classification is sought are sent for approval. Clearly, if a vessel is in-

[1] Lloyd's Register is the oldest Society of this description in the world. Next to Lloyd's Register in point of antiquity comes the Bureau Veritas, of Paris, founded in 1828. The Norske Veritas, of Christiania, was founded in 1864; the Germanischer Lloyd, of Berlin, in 1867; the Record of American and Foreign Shipping, of New York, in the same year; the Registro Italiano, of Genoa, in 1870; the Veritas Austro-Ungarico, of Trieste, in 1858; and the British Corporation for the Survey and Registry of Shipping, with its headquarters at Glasgow, in 1890. In addition may be mentioned the Liverpool Underwriters' Registry for Iron Vessels, which was established in 1862 and amalgamated with Lloyd's Register in 1885.

tended for general trade, no class can be assigned unless she conforms to the standard of strength set up by the Rules as requisite for vessels intended to go anywhere and do anything—though how that strength is attained may be immaterial. If, however, a vessel is intended for a special trade, she can receive a class for that trade, if her scantlings and arrangements are considered suitable, quite irrespective of the Rules governing the classification of general traders. The construction of vessels, including the machinery and boilers of steamers, then proceeds from start to finish under the Society's inspection, no steel being used which has not been produced at approved works and tested at the manufactories by the surveyors to Lloyd's Register. For the examination of large forgings to be employed in the structure of the vessels the Society employs specially trained and experienced men, who carefully inspect them while in process of manufacture, in order to detect defects which could not be observed in their finished state after delivery. Similarly, all heavy steel castings are carefully tested before they are accepted for use in a classed vessel. The surveyors see that the equipment of anchors and chain cables corresponds with the Rules, and that they have been tested in accordance with statutory requirements at public proving-houses, all of which are under the superintendence of the Committee of Lloyd's Register. Beyond the statutory requirements, all cast-steel anchors are required to undergo special tests at the manufactory in the presence of the Society's surveyors. Finally, detailed reports are sent to headquarters, where they are examined by the technical staff, being submitted to the Committee with a view to classes being assigned.[1]

In any effort to indicate the progress of the British Mercantile Marine since the opening of the nineteenth century, it is impossible to ignore the influence which Lloyd's Register exercised during the critical period when the industry was undergoing a succession of revolutions owing to the application of physical science to ship propulsion, construction, and equipment. Lloyd's Register was the necessary counterpart to the responsibilities which were thrown by legislation on the Board of Trade. It

[1] "The Classification of Merchant Shipping," a paper read by Mr. H. J. Cornish, Chief Surveyor to Lloyd's Register, at the summer meeting of the Institution of Naval Architects, 1905.

may, indeed, be said that, if it had not been for Lloyd's Register, Parliament would have been unable to take effective steps to enforce its will. During the sixty years preceding the outbreak of war, the Board of Trade and Lloyd's Register, in association with other classification societies and the shipowners, shaped the valuable economic and warlike weapon which proved an essential element to victory when at last the Great War opened.

IV

THE MEN OF THE MERCHANT NAVY

WITH the introduction, in 1853, of a system of continuous service for the Royal Navy, the relations between the fighting service and the Mercantile Marine underwent a radical change. Hitherto, on the first whisper of war, the Admiralty had exercised its constitutional right to impress seamen for service in the Fleet. The established principle was that the Navy should normally be maintained on a peace footing, and that it should draw additional men from the Mercantile Marine in order to enable the men-of-war in reserve to be commissioned. Impressment was, in fact, the last remaining link in that connection between the two services the developments of which have already been outlined. The resources of the country were large, and down to the close of the Napoleonic War not only were these islands largely independent of overseas supplies for the necessaries of life, but means of inland transport were so defective that counties were in large measure self-contained economic units. The population of the country, in short, could exist in some measure of comfort even though ocean communications were arrested and the cumbersome means of conveying goods on land restricted. The naval authorities were able to exercise their power of impressment without serious injury to national interests. The Mercantile Marine was not at that time the loom of a great and essential world commerce, interference with which would mean starvation for the people of the British Isles and a complete dislocation of British industry. On the contrary, seaborne commerce at the time of the last Great War, which closed at the beginning of the nineteenth century, was desirable because it was the foundation of the country's internal commerce; but the British industrial machine could exist for a long period in spite of the laying up of large numbers of merchant ships. The naval authorities, from the earliest times down to the peace of 1815, continued, without injury to vital interests, to regard the Merchant Service as a reservoir upon which almost unlimited drafts could be made for men.

But from the period of the French Revolution onward the custom of impressing men of the Merchant Service for the Royal Navy became increasingly unpopular. For some years prior to the passing of the Reform Bill of 1832, a strong feeling existed in the country against the Royal Prerogative, and no sooner was the Reform Act in operation than expression was given to that feeling. Many Members were returned to the new Parliament pledged to do all in their power to procure the abolition of the press-gang, and the adoption of a system of recruiting for the Navy less at variance, it was claimed, with the spirit of the British Constitution. A Bill dealing with the Merchant Service was accordingly introduced into Parliament, in 1834, by the First Lord of the Admiralty, Sir James Graham. It was drawn up with a view to increasing the number of merchant seamen by improving their position, and to providing a system of registration which would secure the services of maritime persons generally in the event of an emergency. Their identity was to be established by means of a register ticket, " in conformity with an opinion expressed by Lord Nelson in a letter to Lord St. Vincent in 1803, that that system of registration was of great effect, and, in his opinion, indispensable."[1] The Bill as first drafted was not proceeded with; but in 1835, the Merchant Seamen's Act, 5 & 6 Will. IV, cap. 19, was passed, containing the provisions of the original measure, except that a register of the names of seamen was substituted for the personal register at first contemplated. The alteration was made after much deliberation; it being finally considered advisable not to attempt too much in that direction in the first instance. The full title was " An Act to amend and consolidate the Laws relating to the Merchant Seamen of the United Kingdom, and for forming and maintaining a Register of all the Men engaged in that Service."

[1] Evidence of Sir J. Graham before Manning Commission in 1858, p. 52.

In the same session was passed " An Act for the encouragement of voluntary enlistment of seamen, and to make regulations for the more effectual manning of His Majesty's Navy" (5 & 6 Will. IV, cap. 24). The Act reaffirmed the mediæval principle of compulsion by giving a " statutory sanction to the power of the King to call for the services of seafaring men in the event of an emergency." The policy of the Government, as enunciated by Sir James Graham, was to maintain the prerogative of impressment, but " to take every measure which might render the use of the power of impressment even in time of war an exception to the rule, based only upon urgent necessity." Provision was made for exempting from further impressment men who had once been pressed, and had served at sea for a period of five years. This Act was a measure of expediency and compromise, and the Government, doubtless, were justified for a time in feeling their way; but, seeing that the system of impressment was so widely condemned, a grave responsibility was incurred by those in authority in allowing a quarter of a century to elapse before another recognised system of providing seamen at short notice was substituted. Happily, no national emergency arose during the period; and, ultimately, the system of registry, with the necessary machinery, initiated by Sir James Graham's Act, resulted in bringing the sailor under official control, and afforded a means of securing his service when occasion required.

This legislation marked the beginning of the end of the system of impressment, but an old custom was slow to die. Senior officers of the Navy who had served throughout the Revolutionary and Napoleonic Wars were unwilling to agree to any weakening of the power of the Admiralty to make whatever claims it deemed fit upon the Merchant Service in time of war; and, in point of fact, the right of the Crown to call upon seamen to serve the State was never abandoned. What happened was that the introduction on February 14th, 1853, of a system of continuous service for seamen in the Navy—representing the last word in that process of specialisation which, as we have seen, dated from the reign of Henry VIII—gradually provided the fighting arm of the country with a well-trained personnel. Prior to this event, it had become apparent that the Royal Navy and the Merchant Navy were developing on different lines. The fighting service was responding to new demands arising from the application of physical science to naval warfare, while the Merchant Service was also undergoing a change in character. The growth of international commerce was leading to the foundation of great shipping companies, making regular sailings over prescribed routes at definite times, and it was dawning on the authorities that even in war the maintenance of these communications would be essential. Owing to the rapid industrialism of England and the consequent depression of agriculture, the population was becoming increasingly dependent on overseas supplies. In short, the former haphazard manner of manning the fighting service was unsuited to conditions at sea, which required that men of the Fleet should be carefully trained over a long period of years, in order to enable them to handle the increasingly complicated weapons of warfare which were being introduced, while the country was becoming so dependent on oversea supplies that the possibility of laying up any portion of the Merchant Navy in order to complete the manning of the Royal Navy suggested peril.

Before the introduction of long service in the Navy, attention had been directed to the deterioration of the personnel of the Merchant Fleet, and no doubt those revelations were not without their influence upon the course eventually taken by the Admiralty in providing the Royal Navy with a body of specially trained men who engaged to serve continuously, with the prospect of pension. Reference has already been made [1] to the circulars issued from the Foreign Office in 1848 to British Consuls abroad as to the manning of the Merchant Fleet. In order to obtain a correct view of the progress of the Merchant Service between the close of the last Great War and the opening of hostilities in 1914, it may, perhaps, be of interest to quote from some of the reports sent to the Foreign Office, which had their influence on the development of the two Services:

" Our merchant seamen are picked up as they may be found. On discharge no writing of character is given; on re-engagement, of course, no such certificate can be

[1] See p. 77.

required. How can the good or bad character of a man be known? Certificates may be false, incomplete, not well drawn up; but they have been useful in the Navy, and they might, I imagine, be tried in the Merchant Service. . . . Competition and low wages, in the maddest excess, are the order of the day, and, of course, vessels are worse manned and navigated than formerly."—*Gothenburg.*

" Another very material point to which more attention should be given is the, more frequent than otherwise, lamentable condition of apprentices in these small traders, many of them probably more neglected and ill-used than a West Indian slave formerly, the interest of the owner of the latter being more at stake. These forlorn objects (here again we must not forget exceptions) often seek relief from their Consul without his being able to afford it; for unless some glaring act of brutality is observable, the unhappy sufferer is sure to be in the wrong, and the treatment he receives is merely ' deserved wholesome correction!' which power is certainly desirable for masters to possess. No wonder such apprentices produce seamen disposed to all sorts of irregularities, and sometimes captains a very few degrees better. Boys ought not to be bound without first having been at school, to learn at least right from wrong, and the rudiments of education fitted for their station. When out of service they should be compelled to attend school, and by having their ambition awakened, they would thus be prepared for obtaining the petty officer's or mate's certificate. I know the Marine Society, Bishopsgate Street; such establishments, as to principle, should exist in every port in Britain."—*Danzig.*

" The conduct of British shipmasters and seamen in this port, in general, is very disorderly, specially those belonging to vessels proceeding from the northern ports—Sunderland, Newcastle, Shields, etc. It arises principally from the rough and uneducated character of both masters and men; their great tendency of intoxication; the facility of obtaining wine and spirits in this port; and the little restraint held over them by the local authorities or power of the Consulate, in case of misbehaviour, to exercise control over them.

" During the outward voyage both masters and men

become irritated against each other in consequence of harsh and violent conduct shown on one side, and discontent, ill-humour, and insubordination, on the other. Their mutual animosities are, however, in general, suppressed, and kept within certain bounds by necessity during the time they are at sea. On their arrival in port their first thought (too generally, of masters as well as men) seems to be to get drunk. All their animosities then break out with redoubled violence, and quarrelling, fighting, and other disgraceful scenes ensue, which bring discredit upon their country, equally with themselves. . . .

"Motives of economy are, amongst some, a source of disturbance. On arriving in British ports many masters discharge almost all their crew, in order not to be at the charge of maintaining and paying them while they are in port. They do not fill up their complements until they are just on the point of sailing again on their outward voyage; they are then obliged to take the first persons they can find, who frequently prove not to be seamen, or very inefficient men, and often turn out to be very bad characters, and cause a great deal of trouble."—*Constantinople.*

"In point of intelligence, address, and conduct, they—British masters—are the inferior to the American shipmasters, and, in consequence of their intemperance when in port, great dissatisfaction is expressed by their crews. What their knowledge of 'practical navigation and seamanship' may be, I am not competent to say, having always preferred, when visiting England, taking a passage in an American vessel; but I have observed that desertions very seldom occur, or only to a limited extent, from vessels commanded by superior men, while less efficient masters not infrequently lose their entire crews.

"I have in a former year ascertained the amount disbursed by every British and every American vessel frequenting this port, and the expenditure of the British was from 30 to 50 per cent. greater than the American. The British master seldom receives more than £10 per month whilst afloat, and consequently prefers a long to a short voyage. The wages of an American master, with his perquisites, are nearly treble that amount; he has, therefore, no inducement to dishonesty to support himself. The British masters, I have been credibly informed, run up longer bills with the different tradesmen, and after payment of them, and a receipt in full taken, many articles are sent back, and the cost of them, as charged in the bill, refunded to the master; the inference is, that the owners of the vessels never receive credit for the articles so returned."—*Savannah*.

"There does not appear to be the same encouragement extended to British masters as there is to American. The average wages per month (in this trade) paid to the former is £8 10s., together with the average of his proportion of the cabin freight, £2, is equal to say £10 10s. per month; while to the latter, including all his perquisites, say £20 per month. It is very usual for the American master to have an interest of an one-eighth to one-fourth in the vessel under his command, and owners of vessels, being so convinced that it is to their advantage that the master should be so interested, frequently give them a share on credit. As a proof that the character of British shipping has declined, I would instance the fact, that almost invariably, American ships not only obtain a decided preference over British ships, but generally a higher rate of freight."—*Norfolk, Virginia*.

"If I were to mention the names of those persons whom I deem unfitted for command, I fear I should include the whole of the remaining traders to this port. With the former exceptions (mentioned earlier in the report), I do not think that a British vessel arrives at Pernambuco without some complaint being made to me from the men, of brutality, starvation, insulting language, overwork, or want of sufficient hands. In nine cases out of ten, I am obliged to decide in favour of the men; and what is the consequence? Why, that armed with no specific powers, the master laughs at the decision which he himself has oftentimes invoked; even here, where the Commercial Treaty makes Her Majesty's Consuls arbitrators in the disputes of their countrymen, no powers of enforcing them are conferred."—*Pernambuco*.

Mr. James Murray, in a memorandum dated November 22nd, 1847, declared that "the condition of British Shipping, according to evidence from the ports of foreign States, may not unjustly be termed discreditable to this country. No sufficient efforts appear to have been made in Great Britain to remedy the existing evils; while pains have been taken by foreign Governments, and with success, to improve the condition of their Mercantile Marine."

We may turn from the evils so fully illustrated in these reports, and so clearly emphasised in Mr. James Murray's memorandum, based upon them, to the related question of the ineffective control by the State of the manning of the Mercantile Marine. Beyond the muster rolls required since 1747, by the Seamen's Relief Act (20th of Geo. II, cap. 38) and subsequent Statutes, to be kept on board merchant ships, and the duplicates to be rendered to the collectors of Customs, in connection with the Merchant Seamen's Fund,[1] no records of the crews of British vessels were in existence; and apparently no statistical use was made of the accounts so rendered. The only published figures in connection with the Merchant Service were contained in the Parliamentary Return, prepared by the Registrar-General of Seamen, subsequently of Shipping and Seamen, who was for many years an officer of the Admiralty, and afterwards of the Board of Trade, showing the number of vessels, with the amount of their tonnage, and *the aggregate number of men and boys usually employed in navigating them,* that belonged to the several ports of the British Empire on December 31st in each year. The Admiralty had thus but a vague knowledge of the source from which the Navy was partly manned in time of peace, and from which it would be recruited in time of war. In short, the constitution of the Mercantile Marine was a matter of surmise and assumption, offering no basis for a scheme by which the supply of seamen could be increased.

---

[1] This was a fund established with a view to granting pensions to seamen. All seamen were compelled to contribute to it. After a long period of mismanagement it became insolvent. By an Act introduced by Mr. Labouchere in 1851, the Government undertook to remove the great grievance to seamen by winding up the fund at the cost of the country. The principle adopted was to take all existing assets; to pay all existing pensions or claims to pension; and to allow existing contributors to continue their contributions with the prospect of a pension. The amount of future pensions was determined by taking the average of then existing pensions, which, besides being frequently withheld from want of funds, differed in amount at the different ports. The difference between assets and liabilities was paid out of the Public Exchequer. The winding up process cost the State about £1,500,000.

In those circumstances the nominal register of the seamen belonging to the United Kingdom, provided by Sir James Graham's Act—though, of course, it could be of no direct service in manning the Navy—was calculated to be of value statistically. The Act came into operation on July 31st, 1835; and, under it, masters of British ships were required to deposit with the Officers of Customs at the several ports of the United Kingdom returns of the names and description of their crews at the commencement and termination of voyages, in the case of foreign-going vessels; and half-yearly, in the case of Home Trade and fishing vessels. For the due supervision, scrutiny, and custody of these documents, sect. xix provided for the establishment of " The General Register Office of Merchant Seamen," under the control of the Admiralty. From the lists of crews forwarded to that office, the name of each seaman was entered alphabetically into a general register, with his age, place of birth, previous ship and latest voyage; a separate book was kept for apprentices. Besides affording the Admiralty useful and necessary information respecting the numbers, ages, ratings, and whereabouts of merchant seamen, this register proved itself of importance in bringing to light the fact that the law respecting the compulsory employment of apprentices was largely ignored.[1] It was found that only some 5,000 apprentices were registered, although the number to be maintained, according to the tonnage scale, was nearly 14,000. By the establishment of an office to insure that the laws for the Increase and Encouragement of Seamen were duly carried out, a material change was effected; in seven years from the coming into operation of Sir James Graham's Act, more than 40,000 apprentices were registered, being at the rate of over 5,000 per annum.

The legislation of 1835 was generally understood to be an instalment only. The Merchant Seamen's Act was useful, since under its operation there was a continual influx of young blood into the Service, but it did nothing directly towards obviating the necessity for impressment. In reply to awkward questions in Parliament as to what was to come of the registration, it was officially stated that " so many more thousand apprentices " served for a time; but, in view of promises given, uneasiness presently

[1] 4 Geo. IV, cap. 19.

prevailed at the Admiralty lest the necessity for issuing Press Warrants should arise before milder and wiser methods had been tried.

The Registrar-General of Seamen was, in consequence, called upon by the Admiralty, in October 1838, to state whether he was "prepared to recommend any measure to insure the power of procuring a certain number of men for filling up the ships at short notice." Captain Brown, R.N., the Registrar-General, at once submitted his views, setting forth, as the result of his experience, two remedies for forcible impressment:

"(1) A general personal registry of all mariners of every degree, taking minute individual description of each as to age, capacity, etc., and after rejecting the aged and incapable from the list, to draught or ballot a certain number at fixed periods; the names of men so drawn to be exhibited at every Custom House, with notice to come forward, under certain penalties for refusal or neglect, when called on by Proclamation.

"(2) To form a reserve of men either in one, two or three classes, which may be distinguished as the 'Naval Reserve.'"

He pointed out, however, many serious objections to the first plan, and warmly advocated the adoption of the second.

The matter remained in abeyance till 1842,[1] when, in connection with the Merchant Seamen's Fund, the question of establishing a test of identity for each British seaman was considered by a Parliamentary Committee appointed to inquire into the working of that Fund. It was at length resolved to amend the Merchant Seamen's Act, and to inaugurate a new system of registry, with a twofold object: first, to benefit seamen by affording them a ready means of establishing their claims for relief or support from the Merchant Seamen's Fund; and, secondly, to provide for the abstraction of classes of seamen from the general body, without resorting to indiscriminate impressment. A measure was accordingly prepared, which passed into law on September 5th, 1844, entitled, "An Act to

[1] This was the year in which the Foreign Office, at the request of the Admiralty, called for reports as to the manning of the Mercantile Marine.

amend and consolidate the Laws relating to Merchant Seamen, and for keeping a Register of Seamen" (7 & 8 Vict., cap. 112). The Act provided for the adoption of the register ticket, and Sir James Graham declared in the House of Commons, when the Bill was read a third time, that this provision formed part of his original intention. Under the new law, no person, except a master or surgeon, being a British subject, was to serve on board ship without a ticket bearing his name and description. This ticket each seaman was required to deposit with the master of the vessel in which he engaged when signing articles, and the master was required to return it to the seaman at the expiration of his agreement.

The Registrar-General of Seamen was deputed to carry the measure into effect, and it fell to the Officers of Customs at the several ports to issue the tickets. Each ticket was distinguished by a number from "1" upwards, and bore the stamp of the "General Register and Record Office of Seamen"—the words "and Record" having been added to the title by the new Act.[1] A numerical register was opened in that Office in which were recorded the particulars of the men to whom the register tickets were issued, and their subsequent movements were duly entered thereon, from the crew lists furnished as heretofore, with the addition of each man's especial number. To quote from a report by Captain Brown, dated November 24th, 1847, "the measure as carried into effect became popular with the seamen, who adopted the opinion that the ticket, being issued to British subjects only, would prevent foreigners from usurping their berths." At this time, and until 1853, no foreigners were allowed to serve in coasting vessels, and not more than 25 per cent. of the crew in foreign-going vessels. It also appears from the report that the measure was generally popular with the shipowners, "because they considered that the deposit of the ticket with the masters of vessels during the terms of a seaman's service gave them a lien upon him which would prevent desertion." Disappointment ensued, however, when it was found that

[1] A further addition to the title of the Office was made in 1872. Under the Merchant Shipping Act of that year, there was a transfer of registry work from the Customs, and the Registrar-General of Seamen became the Registrar-General of Shipping and Seamen. The office then assumed its present title of the "General Register and Record Office of Shipping and Seamen."

the machinery of the Register Office was not "to be brought to bear upon deserters to procure their conviction and punishment."

However good the system was on paper, it broke down in practice; mainly because there was no direct inducement for the men to take care of the tickets. The Merchant Seamen's Fund offered none, as it turned out. For some time in an insolvent state, owing to gross mismanagement, it was practically abolished, so far as nine-tenths of the Service was concerned, by the Winding-up Act of 1851. The majority of seamen had long looked upon the Fund with suspicion and disgust: money was stopped from their wages, and they understood not where the money went. Thus, having no palpable interest in safeguarding their identity, it is not surprising that the seamen resorted to an illegal traffic in tickets, in spite of cautions and penalties. With the strength of the Mercantile Marine then ranging from 160,000 to 170,000 British seamen (exclusive of masters), the issue of over half a million tickets in the course of six years pointed to the prevalence of abuses. Indeed, it was stated in evidence before the Lords Committee sitting in 1848 to inquire into the Navigation Laws "that in the Jews' shops at Shadwell, and in similar places at Bristol, sailors could purchase as many register tickets as they wanted, and for half the amount of the fine that would be asked of them if they went to the Custom House."

The repeal in 1853 of the Manning clauses of the old Navigation Laws, which excluded foreigners from serving in coasting vessels and limited the number to be employed in foreign-going vessels, made it no longer necessary to prove nationality at time of engagement, and so did away with what little value the ticket still possessed for a British seaman. In the circumstances, there was but one thing to be done. The functions and powers vested in the Admiralty under the Merchant Seamen's Act and the amending Act of 1844 [1] had been transferred to the Board of Trade by the Mercantile Marine Act of 1850 (13 & 14 Vict., cap. 93), with full powers to alter or dispense with the register-ticket system. Acting on these powers, the Board of Trade formally abolished the system by notice in the *London Gazette* of September 30th, 1853.

[1] Acts 5 & 6 Will. IV, cap. 19, and 7 & 8 Vict., cap. 112.

END OF THE TICKET SYSTEM

But the story of the ticket system was not thereby closed. It was originally framed with a view to restricted impressment (i.e., to calling out merchant seamen of certain ages for service in His Majesty's ships at short notice), and it was not till 1853 that an Act was passed empowering the Crown to call out seamen in classes, according to age, described in " their register tickets, or otherwise." There was a virtue in the " otherwise," seeing that register tickets were then no more. In the absence of the register ticket, resort was had to the certificate of discharge given to every seaman at the end of a voyage. It is more than doubtful whether the provisions of the Act in question, 16 & 17 Vict., cap. 69, could ever have been enforced by means of this test of identity; fortunately, like those of the earlier Proclamation Act, 5 & 6 Will. IV, cap. 24, they were allowed to remain inoperative.

Although proved to be unworkable as applied to the whole Mercantile Marine, the system of individual registration was not entirely discarded, but for " Fund " purposes was continued in operation as regards some 12,000 men, to whom special tickets were issued under the Winding-up Act, 14 & 15 Vict., cap. 102, and for over fifty years it has been worked with success in connection with the Royal Naval Reserve. The certificate R V 2, issued to each member of that force, corresponds to the old register ticket, with the difference that, whereas the majority of men had little or no interest in looking after the latter, the former is as important to a Naval Reserve man as a Savings Bank Book, guaranteeing to him so much money for so much drill performed.[1]

After 1853, however, no attempt was made to revive the maintenance of an individual or even nominal register of seamen, except as regards certificated officers, apprentices, and Naval Reserve men. The general body of seamen were dealt with in the Seamen's Registry Office, as mere numbers; they were noted in the registers of ships and their voyages, kept since 1857, and were periodically set

[1] A central indexed register of seamen employed in foreign-going vessels was started in October 1913, in the General Register and Record Office of Shipping and Seamen, and was found of great use. An Order in Council, dated August 2nd, 1918, provided that "the Shipping Controller, in conjunction with the Board of Trade, may make orders relative to the holding of a certificate of identity and service by every master, seaman, or apprentice employed on a British ship, and in relation to kindred matters."

forth in the Shipping and Navigation Returns under the head of "Persons Employed." In addition, the crew lists containing their signatures and descriptions were filed and were available for reference.[1]

The breakdown of the personal test system led to the consideration of Captain Brown's second plan for procuring men for the Navy at short notice—viz., the formation and maintenance of a voluntary Naval Reserve. In fact, money was voted in the Navy Estimates of 1852–3 for experimenting with the scheme to the extent of 5,000 men, but owing to a change of Government nothing was done. The Admiralty, however, were soon to experience the truth of Captain Brown's dictum that "the means of augmenting our naval force cannot be extemporised, but must be preorganised." According to the evidence of Rear-Admiral Milne and Sir James Graham before the Commissioners for manning the Navy, in 1858, immense difficulty was experienced in 1854 in fitting out the Baltic and Black Sea Fleets. The operation was slow in the extreme; small vessels had to be recalled from foreign stations, and their crews transferred as a nucleus to the larger ships. Most of the men sent out to the Baltic Fleet were "very young, and without experience"—landsmen, in fact. Well might Admiral Sir Charles Napier complain of the delay in getting his complement of men, and of the quality of those he did get. It was just the time when a reserve of seamen would have been invaluable had there been one. Sailors were urgently needed, and yet the situation was not sufficiently serious to warrant the issue of a proclamation, with all the inconveniences attending bounties and embargoes.[2] Even as it was, there was such a demand for seamen that wages increased nearly 40 per cent. With shipowners outbidding the Government, as

---

[1] The preparation of the statistics referred to in this paragraph calls for a few remarks. The first reliable figures were compiled in 1700, when the Registrars of Shipping in England were required to send in lists of the vessels on their registers, with the numbers of men usually required to man them. Registrars in Scotland and Ireland were brought into line later on. After a long period it was recognised that many vessels on the register were either laid up, employed inland, or out of existence, so since 1848, only those vessels employed at some time during the year in the Home or Foreign Trade or in Fishing have been included in the Annual Statistics. A more detailed analysis of ships and crews has been made in the quinquennial Census returns compiled since 1891.

[2] Cf. Sir James Graham's evidence before Manning Commission in 1858, p. 53.

THE ACT OF 1859

they would have done, wages must have gone up to a ruinous rate. The lesson then taught the authorities was not forgotten, and resulted in the appointment of a Royal Commission in 1858 to inquire into the best means of manning the Navy. The Commission, presided over by Lord Hardwicke, favoured Captain Brown's scheme of a voluntary Naval Reserve. They proposed in their Report the substitution " of a system of defence, voluntary and effective, for untrained compulsory service." They were of opinion that from the Merchant Service could be formed a force of "thorough seamen, trained in gunnery, and qualified for immediate service on board a ship of war." An Act was accordingly passed in August 1859 (22 & 23 Vict., cap. 40) giving the Admiralty power to raise "Royal Naval Volunteers, not to exceed 30,000 men." The machinery for the establishment of the Force was ready to hand in the General Register and Record Office of Seamen and the various shipping offices in the United Kingdom. Under the Mercantile Marine Act of 1850, which placed the management of matters relating to the British Mercantile Marine under the Board of Trade, Shipping Masters—since described as Superintendents of the Mercantile Marine Offices—had recently been appointed to superintend the registry, engagement, and discharge of seamen, etc., and their status and duties were further defined by the Merchant Shipping Act of 1854. These officers were necessarily in close touch with the seamen, and, acting under the direction of the Registrar-General of Seamen, were the best possible agents for procuring volunteers. It is interesting to note that as the first suggestion in modern times to raise an effective Naval Reserve originated in 1852 with Captain Brown, the original holder of the appointment of Registrar-General of Seamen, so when the scheme was adopted it was found that in that office, with its records and administrative machinery throughout the country, lay the hopes of success. Succeeding Registrars-General—notably Mr. J. J. Mayo, Mr. H. N. Malan, Mr. John Clark-Hall, and Mr. C. H. Jones—working in conjunction with the various Admirals Superintendent of Naval Reserves (after 1903 Admirals Commanding Coast Guard and Naval Reserves), succeeded in organising out of the personnel of the Mercantile Marine and the fishing industry a large, dependable, and readily available reserve force for the Royal Navy. Certain alternative proposals were brought forward or given a trial, and the Royal Naval Coast Volunteers, established in 1853, continued in existence for twenty years; but experience at last confirmed the wisdom of obtaining a sea-going force, thus giving effect to suggestions made by leading naval officers of the war period, including Nelson, who on several occasions urged on the naval authorities the advisability of fostering the Merchant Navy as the source of a supply of handy and experienced seamen for men-of-war in a time of sudden emergency.

The history of the Royal Naval Reserve has been a chequered one. Officers of the Naval Service who sat on the Board of Admiralty were apparently impressed increasingly, in process of time, by the wide divergence between the needs of the Royal Navy and those of the Merchant Service, as the former responded to the impulse of invention and developed a demand for men of special training—for signalling, gunnery, torpedo work, and other duties. At first the Royal Naval Reserve consisted only of lower-deck ratings, and there was considerable opposition to the proposal that officers of the Mercantile Marine should be included in the Force, but an Act was passed in 1861 providing for their appointment. It was repealed and fresh provisions were made by the Act of 1863 (26 & 27 Vict., cap. 69). Captain H. J. Challis, R.N., in his evidence before a General Committee of the Admiralty and Board of Trade in 1869, stated that he "objected altogether to the principle that officers of the Mercantile Marine be employed in the Naval Reserve," adding that he considered that there was "sufficiency of naval officers who are well fitted for the work." Captain Challis evidently reflected the general view of the Navy at the time.[1] For many years the training of the Force was neglected; officers and men were relegated to shore batteries provided only with muzzle-loading guns after the breech-loader had been adopted for service at sea. Generally the Service suffered from unintelligent discouragement. "In January 1889 . . . there was not (except on board the District Coastguard ships) a single breech-loading or machine-gun used in the instruction of the Reserve, but early in 1891 we find that fourteen 5-inch

---

[1] Even in 1879 Admiral Sir Augustus Phillimore urged that commissions "should be confined to a very limited number."

breech-loading guns, one 6-inch breech-loading gun, one Gatling, one Gardner, and sixty-seven Nordenfeldt machine-guns were so employed. Since then a certain number of quick-firing guns have been supplied, and, doubtless, something more has been effected in the direction of increasing the modern armament, although much remains to be done."[1] In spite, however, of inadequate official recognition, the Force continued to expand from year to year; Commander W. F. Caborne, C.B., R.N.R., and others, continually kept the subject before the public, and slowly the conditions of service were improved. At the beginning of the century the Force reached its maximum strength of ratings, 29,538 (1904). A few years previously the Admiralty had decided on establishing a reserve force of its own, to be known as the Royal Fleet Reserve. It consisted of men of good character who had served for a term in the Fleet, and who, in return for a retainer, agreed to keep themselves efficient for service afloat. Even so enthusiastic a supporter of the Royal Naval Reserve as Commander Caborne approved this step, though it threatened the force hitherto recognised. He admitted that " it is obvious, from what has gone before, that the Royal Fleet Reserve, consisting as it does of men who have seen long, or at any rate considerable, service in the Royal Navy and have been thoroughly trained in their respective duties—trained far better than any other auxiliary naval body can be in time of peace—must of necessity, so far as ratings are concerned, be our first and principal stand-by in time of war for service in the Fleet."

No doubt this was the view taken by the Admiralty, for in consequence of the success attending the formation of the Royal Fleet Reserve, and also looking at the fact that the numbers in the Royal Naval Reserve had reached probable requirements, recruiting for the latter body was suspended from December 1904 until October 1906. The formation of the Royal Fleet Reserve was part of a wide-sweeping movement for assuring a supply of well-trained seamen for the Fleet, and the training of the Naval Reserve was reconsidered. In his " Statement of Admiralty Policy " in 1905, the First Lord (Earl Cawdor) remarked:

[1] Lecture on the Royal Naval Reserve, by Commander W. F. Caborne, R.N.R., May 10th, 1895.

"The arrangements for the drill and training of men of the Royal Naval Reserve have been recently reviewed in order to improve the efficiency of this branch of the Reserves, and also to reduce its cost. Hitherto, Royal Naval Reserve men have been drilled on board the harbour drill-ships and batteries established round the coasts of the United Kingdom, and a certain number have undergone a period of naval training on board the sea-going drill-ships, or in ships of the Channel Fleet. This system is, however, no longer well adapted to the requirements of the Service, inasmuch as the greater part of the drill has been devoted to gunnery, a class of duty which is very unlikely to devolve upon Royal Naval Reserve men in war, and as (except, perhaps, the limited number of men who embark for nine months of naval training) they do not acquire and maintain sufficient knowledge of the general routine of a man-of-war. The establishment of the divisions of ships in commission in reserve has now given an opportunity for affording the Royal Naval Reserve the training in which they have hitherto been wanting. These ships have only a portion of their crews on board, and can therefore accommodate a considerable number of Reserve men, with advantage both to themselves and their crews. Although the ships only go to sea for cruises once a quarter, the general routine is much the same as when they are fully commissioned for sea service; and since they will change frequently, the Reserve men will have more facilities for becoming familiar with the internal economy of a modern man-of-war. It has accordingly been decided that from April 1st next, all drill at batteries and in harbour drill-ships shall cease, and the establishments will be closed, except in a few cases, where the present system will be continued a little longer. These exceptions are the drill-ships in London, Aberdeen, Bristol, and Liverpool, and the Royal Naval Reserve batteries at Penzance, Yarmouth, Wick, Stornoway, Lerwick, Greenock, Upper Cove, and Rosslare. Under this new system of training, the men will be expected to embark in the first year for three months, and thereafter for one month every alternate year."

The regulations for carrying into effect the foregoing policy were issued on March 29th, 1906; on March 31st five harbour drill-ships and five torpedo gunboats were paid off, and twenty-five Royal Naval Reserve batteries closed; and on April 1st, 1906, the new system of training came into force. Officers of the Royal Naval Reserve were given the option of drilling at the remaining drill-stations under the old system for five years from April 1st, 1906, but on promotion they were required to embrace the new system. Royal Naval Reserve men serving in the Force on April 1st, 1906, were given the option of carrying out their drills at the remaining harbour-ships or shore batteries during their current period of enrolment or of adopting the new system, but upon re-enrolment they were required to fall in with the new system. The remaining harbour drill-ships and Royal Naval Reserve batteries were finally paid off and closed on March 31st, 1911.

The effect of the formation of the Royal Fleet Reserve and the change in the system of training Naval Reservists reacted on the strength of the latter force, which, if it gained in efficiency, lost in numbers, since under the new system it was less convenient for merchant seamen to put in their training than was the case when they could go to a local battery and qualify. Experience confirmed the Admiralty in its opinion of the new scheme, and in 1910 the First Lord (Mr. Reginald McKenna) announced that " the training in the ships of the Home Fleet under the new system is very valuable, and will render the Royal Naval Reserve Force an efficient portion of the naval personnel," as time was to show. In 1910 a trawler section of the Royal Naval Reserve was formed, consisting of skippers, second hands, deck hands, and engine-room hands of trawlers.

The policy of the British Government, which has been traced in brief summary, was developed, in some confusion, on the following lines :

(1) To develop the Merchant Service by means of the Navigation Laws, which were repealed when it was decided that they were injurious.

(2) To ascertain the number of ships and men belonging to the Empire by means of the laws for registering ships.

(3) To establish suitable Reserves.

As to the third point, the chief object was to replace untrained merchant seamen by " gunners with sea-legs," which led to the formation in 1872 of the old Second-Class Reserve, recruited chiefly from the fishing industry.

Here we reach the final stage in the secular relations between the Navy and the Mercantile Marine. The nineteenth century saw the complete extinction of the mediæval system. Yet within a few years of its extinction it had begun to be revived on new lines by the formation of a Reserve drawn from the Merchant Service and in other ways. And the general conclusion to be noted is that long before the European War came upon us the Admiralty, so far from having forgotten the historic connection between the two Services, was endeavouring to rev ve it, though to a limited extent only, in a modern form.

As a result of these efforts, when the storm broke in August 1914, the Admiralty controlled a Naval Reserve of upwards of 18,000 trained officers and men of the Mercantile Marine and Fishing Industry, besides nearly 24,000 officers and men of the Royal Fleet Reserve. In addition, the nation benefited by the ameliorative measures affecting the personnel of the Merchant Navy, which had been carried out in the preceding fifty years. Whereas, during the Revolutionary and Napoleonic Wars, the constant preoccupation of the naval authorities was the manning of the Fleet, as was also the case at the time of the Crimean War, in the summer of 1914 the Admiralty had at its disposal, in addition to the regular personnel of the Royal Navy with its own reserve, not only 18,000 R.N.R. officers and men trained in war duties, but the whole reformed personnel of the Mercantile Marine, consisting of some 170,000 men of British birth, a larger number than at any previous date in British annals, together with some 100,000 fishermen. At the beginning of August 1914 the strength of Naval personnel was 147,667; in November 1918, when the Armistice was signed, it had been increased by some 200,000 officers and men, in addition to the making good of a wastage of some 80,000. It was largely from the 170,000 men of British birth belonging to the Mercantile Marine and the 100,000 men employed in fishing round the coasts of the United Kingdom that the required recruits had been obtained. The history of the Merchant Navy's part in the war reveals the manner in which these men acquitted themselves in face of dangers unprecedented in variety and character.

CHAPTER II

ON THE EVE OF WAR

THE position of the officers and men of the British Mercantile Marine on the outbreak of war was an unenviable one. They had entered the Service, the youngest as well as the oldest, without a thought that any circumstance could arise bringing them into conflict with the armed forces of an enemy in such a manner as to endanger their lives, although they must have been familiar with the possibility that their ships and the cargoes carried in them might in certain conditions be seized in war-time. They had regarded as adequate for the defence of their lives the generally accepted provisions of international law, and, for the rest, had placed their trust in the camaraderie of the sea and the spirit of mutual helpfulness which had grown up during the latter half of the nineteenth century to be embodied in regulations universally respected. The sea had to be fought, and their ships were built to enable them to wage that form of warfare which all British seamen have conducted with fine courage from age to age. But their ships, as they knew, were not constructed for the organised violence of war: they could not resist attack by gun or torpedo; and, for the most part, the merchantman of commerce possessed inadequate speed ever to permit of escape when pursued. The tramp, for instance, was designed to conform to economic conditions, and since coal is expensive, as little as was compatible with efficient service as a trader was used to attain a moderate rate of steaming. The sailing-ship was in a worse case. On the other hand, the leading liner companies owned ships capable of travelling at higher speeds, and there were a comparatively few large vessels, equipped for carrying passengers, with power enabling them to compete for the " blue ribbon of the Atlantic," to which route all such ocean greyhounds were confined. But when those distinctions between the various types of merchantmen have been admitted, it remains true that not one of the ships of the British Merchant Navy was capable of steaming as fast as the latest and swiftest cruisers of the national fighting fleets of the Great Powers, quite apart from the other disadvantages from which they suffered. In these circumstances, merchant officers and men confronted the new conditions, realising their defencelessness, but with confidence that no developments were probable during the course of war, when passions become excited, which would put their lives in danger as defenceless non-combatants.

The sense of security of merchant seamen had been strengthened by the discussions affecting the interpretation of maritime law which had taken place at The Hague, and later on during the Naval Conference in London. Certain provisions were accepted without controversy from any quarter. Wider recognition was given to the distinction between combatants and non-combatants, and it was affirmed that all the Powers concerned in these deliberations, though exhibiting differences in approaching some details, were united in their desire to spare as much as possible the unprotected merchant seamen, whether of enemy or neutral nationality, from the sufferings incidental to warfare in the past. An illustration of the attitude assumed towards seamen generally during the discussions is furnished by the remarks of Baron Marschall von Bieberstein when the subject of the laying of mines was under discussion at The Hague in 1907. Admiral Siegal, Germany's naval adviser, objected to a proposal intended to adjust the diversity of opinion which had been revealed in the Examining Committee. Sir Ernest Satow, on behalf of the British Government, followed, contending that the draft regulations were inadequate as a safeguard to legitimate neutrals. In effect, he urged amendments in line with the dictates of humanity. Baron Marschall von Bieberstein (Germany) intervened, disclaiming that Germany intended to demand unlimited liberty in the use of mines or had any desire to " sow mines in profusion in all the seas." The subject came up later on at the eighth plenary meeting of the Conference (October 9th, 1908), when he made the following amplified statement:

" A belligerent who lays mines assumes a very heavy responsibility towards neutrals and peaceful shipping.

On that point we are all agreed. No one will resort to such measures unless for military reasons of an absolutely urgent character. But military acts are not governed solely by principles of international law. There are other factors; conscience, good sense, and the sentiments of duty imposed by principles of humanity will be the surest guide for the conduct of sailors, and will constitute the most effective guarantee against abuse. The officers of the German Navy, I emphatically affirm (je le dis à voix haute), will always fulfil, in the strictest fashion, the duties which emanate from the unwritten law of humanity and civilisation.

"I have no need to tell you," he continued, "that I recognise entirely the importance of the codifications of rules to be followed in war. But it would be well not to issue rules the strict observance of which might be rendered impossible by the force of things. It is of the first importance that the international maritime law which we desire to create should only contain clauses the execution of which is possible from a military point of view, even in exceptional circumstances. Otherwise, the respect for law will be lessened and its authority undermined. Also it would seem to us to be preferable to preserve at present a certain reserve, in the expectation that five years hence it will be easier to find a solution which will be acceptable to the whole world. As to the sentiments of humanity and civilisation, I cannot admit that there is any Government or country which is superior in these sentiments to that which I have the honour to represent."[1]

That statement, one of many made by the representatives of Germany and other maritime Powers, encouraged merchant seamen to hope that when war came it would bear less hardly upon them than past conflicts by sea had done. Whatever may have been the merits or demerits of the Declaration of London, it did at least confirm the belief that hostilities would be conducted in future with less risk to innocent life.

On one matter, apart from mines, doubt existed as to the course which Germany would adopt. At the Second

[1] *Parl. Papers*, Misc., No. 4 (1908).

Conference at The Hague, as at the London Conference, she had stoutly opposed the British proposal, supported by Japan and the United States, which would have allowed the arming of merchant ships only in the national ports and territorial waters of the converting Power, or in ports and territorial waters occupied by that Power. Conversion on the high seas would have been prohibited in the case of all ships. Germany, on the other hand, stood for the utmost measure of freedom.[1]

Suspicions were subsequently aroused as to the course which Germany intended to pursue in the event of war. In 1912 the Admiralty, in view of information which had reached it, appointed a Committee to consider the advisability of defensively arming merchant ships. The Committee favoured a scheme of armament, and in November of the same year Rear-Admiral H. H. Campbell, C.V.O., was appointed to carry it out. It was agreed that the weapons should be mounted aft, so as to be available only when the ship was trying to escape. This officer determined that nothing should be done to affect the status of the ships provided with guns, and he decided to place the administration of the scheme at the three ports selected in the hands of officers of the Royal Naval Reserve who were already acquainted with the marine superintendents and other officers whose intimate knowledge of shipping matters would enable them to arrange the training of the guns' crews so as to cause the minimum of inconvenience and loss to the owners. Liverpool, London, and Southampton were chosen as bases for the trial of the scheme, because these ports were used by vessels bringing in frozen meat from the Plate and Australia.

Admiral Campbell at once got into touch with the leading shipowners, and attention was turned to the risk of complications abroad which might arise owing to this reversion to the old policy of the British Mercantile Marine. The Royal Mail Steam Packet Company was the first line to be approached. Sir Owen Philipps, the Chairman of that company, was so impressed by the situation that he agreed to fit guns in a number of the company's big steamers free of expense to the Admiralty, on condition that guns and ammunition were supplied. On April 25th, 1913, the *Aragon*, one of the vessels of the Royal Mail

[1] *The Hague Conference.* By A. Pearce Higgins.

Steam Packet Company, sailed for South America armed with two 4·7 inch guns. The patriotic lead given by Sir Owen Philipps, the Chairman of that line, was not without its influence on other shipowners, many of whom promptly took the same course, with the result that the work of arming a number of the principal food-carrying ships went forward smoothly and rapidly. In the following June the *Tainui*, also armed, left for Australia, and in July the new White Star liner *Ceramic*, which during construction had been given two 4·7 inch guns with shields, carried out successful firing trials. The Admiralty in the meantime had given to each of the companies a guarantee of indemnity against all loss and expense due to any restraint or detention of the vessels to which they might be put in time of peace owing to the ships being defensively armed.

The task of mounting the guns was carried out by the owners at their own cost in accordance with the advice given by the constructive staff of the Admiralty. A system of training guns' crews was also introduced, and short experience suggested that, if the higher ratings were trained in classes, the officers could efficiently train the remainder of the men at sea.

The whole scheme was making good progress when it received an impetus from the discovery that the *Kaiser Wilhelm II*, one of the North German Lloyd vessels, was provided with gun mountings. This German liner had had to put into Southampton for repairs after collision in the Channel, and evidence was thus obtained that some German ships, as had been suspected, were fitted to facilitate conversion on the outbreak of war. About this time, British visitors who had returned from Kiel stated that at that naval establishment they had seen storehouses with the names of German merchant ships painted over the doors. It was added that German officers had admitted that in those buildings armament was kept for a number of merchant ships. Other evidence pointing to a settled German policy in this respect was reluctantly received—reluctantly, because it pointed to a new danger on the trade routes calling for protective measures. On March 26th, 1913, Mr. Churchill, then First Lord of the Admiralty, made his annual statement of the Navy estimates, in the course of which he remarked:

" I turn to one aspect of trade protection which requires special reference. It was made clear at the Second Hague Conference and the London Conference, that certain of the Great Powers have reserved to themselves the right to convert merchant steamers into cruisers, not merely in national harbours, but, if necessary, on the high seas. There is now good reason to believe that a considerable number of foreign merchant steamers may be rapidly converted into armed ships by the mounting of guns. The sea-borne trade of the world follows well-marked routes, upon nearly all of which the tonnage of the British Mercantile Marine largely predominates. Our food-carrying liners and vessels carrying raw material following these trade routes would, in certain contingencies, meet foreign vessels armed and equipped in the manner described. If the British ships had no armament, they would be at the mercy of any foreign liner carrying one effective gun and a few rounds of ammunition. It would be obviously absurd to meet the contingency of considerable numbers of foreign armed merchant cruisers on the high seas by building an equal number of cruisers. That would expose this country to an expenditure of money to meet a particular danger altogether disproportionate to the expense caused to any foreign Power in creating that danger. Hostile cruisers, wherever they are found, will be covered and met by British ships of war, but the proper reply to an armed merchantman is another merchantman armed in her own defence.

" This is the position," Mr. Churchill added, " to which the Admiralty have felt it necessary to draw the attention of leading shipowners. We have felt justified in pointing out to them the danger to life and property which would be incurred if their vessels were totally incapable of offering any defence to an attack. The shipowners have responded to the Admiralty invitation with cordiality, and substantial progress has been made in the direction of meeting it, by preparing as a defensive measure to equip a number of first-class British liners to repel the attack of armed foreign merchant cruisers. Although these vessels have, of course, a wholly different status from that of the regularly commissioned cruisers, such as those we obtain under the Cunard agreement, the Admiralty have felt that the greater part of the cost of the necessary equipment should not fall

STATUS OF ARMED MERCHANTMEN

on the owners, and we have decided, therefore, to lend the necessary guns, to supply ammunition, and to provide for the training of the members of the ship's company to form the guns' crews. The owners, on their part, are paying the cost of the necessary structural conversion, which is not great. The British Mercantile Marine will, of course, have the protection of the British Navy under all possible circumstances, but it is obviously impossible to guarantee individual vessels from attack when they are scattered on their voyages all over the world. No one can pretend to view these measures without regret, or without hoping that the period of retrogression all over the world, which has rendered them necessary, may be succeeded by days of broader international confidence and agreement than those through which we are passing."[1]

This decision was welcomed generally in the House of Commons and in the country. It was declared by Lord Charles Beresford[2] to be "the most important scheme of all those announced by the Admiralty, even more important than building men-of-war," for, he added, "you cannot build any more than you are doing." Some doubt was subsequently expressed as to what the status of these vessels would be in the time of war. The First Lord of the Admiralty explained that merchant vessels carrying guns might belong to one or other of two different classes.

"The first class," he added, "is that of armed merchant cruisers, which on the outbreak of war would be commissioned under the White Ensign, and would then be indistinguishable in status and control from men-of-war. In this class belong the *Mauretania* and the *Lusitania*. The second class consist of merchant vessels which would (unless specially taken up by the Admiralty for any purpose) remain merchant vessels in war, without any change of status, but have been equipped by their owners, with Admiralty assistance, with a defensive armament in order to exercise their right of beating off an attack.

[1] *Hansard*, House of Commons, March 26th, 1913.
[2] Afterwards raised to the Peerage as Lord Beresford.

There is no rule that the master or chief officer must belong to the Royal Naval Reserve, and it will be clear, from what I have said, that no such rule is necessary. The Blue Ensign would only be flown if the vessel had received an Admiralty warrant. Before lending the guns, the Admiralty satisfies itself that the handling and firing of them will be carried out by men who have become conversant with these operations through drill."[1]

The Admiralty continued to pursue with renewed energy and in face of a good deal of adverse criticism the policy which it had adopted, and at the opening of the war thirty-nine vessels belonging to the following companies had been defensively armed, each having been provided with two 4·7 inch guns:

		Ships fitted.
1.	White Star Line	11
2.	Royal Mail Steam Packet Co.	10
3.	Federal Houlders Argentine Line	5
4.	G. Thompson & Co. Ltd.	3
5.	Wilson Line, Hull	3
6.	New Zealand Shipping Co., Ltd.	2
7.	Federal Steam S. Co., Ltd.	2
8.	Shaw, Savill & Albion, Ltd.	2
9.	Turnbull Martin & Co.	1
		39

In those circumstances the situation was full of unwelcome possibilities when at length war was declared. Germany possessed a large number of vessels which were capable of conversion. There were about twenty such ships in German ports, including the following: *Bremen* (15 knots); *Cap Finisterre* (17); *Cap Poloni* (18) (completing for sea); *Cleveland* (16); *Colva* (14·5); *Graf Waldersee* (13); *Imperator* (25); *Kaiserin Auguste Victoria* (17·5); *Kigoma* (15·5); *König Friedrich August* (15·5); *Königin Luise* (15); *Helsor* (12·5); *Pratonia* (13); *Prinz Ludwig* (15·5); *Scharnhorst* (14·5); and *Victoria Luise* (18). The menace which these ships suggested was limited by the knowledge that the Grand Fleet had taken up its

[1] *Hansard*, House of Commons, June 10th, 1913.

CH. II] GERMANY'S CONVERTIBLE SHIPS 125

station in the northern part of the North Sea, with cruiser squadrons at the focal points of the trade routes, and that the Straits of Dover were held by more or less adequate forces. Escape by the narrow route to the southward was unlikely in view of all the circumstances, but there was less certainty to the northward, for the distance from the North of Scotland to Iceland being 450 miles, and from Iceland to Greenland 160 miles, a line of over 600 miles required to be watched by the Northern Patrol. This Northern Patrol consisted eventually of twenty-four armed liners, known as the 10th Cruiser Squadron, or blockading squadron, under the command of Rear-Admiral Sir Dudley de Chair. The possibility of several of the swiftest of the German merchant vessels, their character disguised, breaking out in thick weather, and taking the fullest advantage of the period of darkness, was one that it was impossible to ignore. In the outer seas the danger was far greater, as there were distributed in neutral ports a large number of ships which could be converted into armed vessels for use on the trade routes. They included :

In North American Ports and North Atlantic:
Friedrich der Grosse (14·5 knots), at New York on August 4th.
Barbarossa (14 knots), at New York on August 4th.
Grosser Kurfurst (15·5 knots), at New York on August 4th.
Kronprinzessin (23·5 knots), at New York on August 4th.
Vaterland (26·75 knots), at New York on August 4th.
President Grant (14·5 knots), at New York on August 4th.
George Washington (19 knots), arrived New York, August 5th.
Kaiser Wilhelm II (23·5 knots), arrived New York, August 6th.
President Lincoln (14·5 knots), at New York on August 4th.
Pennsylvania (13·5 knots), at New York on August 4th.
Amerika (17·5 knots), at Boston on August 4th.
Cincinnati (16 knots), arrived Boston, August 8th.

Prinz Oskar (12·5 knots), arrived Philadelphia, August 5th.

Kronprinz Wilhelm (23 knots), sailed from New York, August 3rd, to meet the KARLSRUHE, by whom she was armed.

Spreewald (12·5 knots), at sea; captured by the BERWICK, September 12th.

Neckar (14 knots), at sea; arrived Baltimore, September 2nd.

Kaiser Wilhelm der Grosse (22·5 knots), on her way out from Germany into the Atlantic (movements unknown at the time).

Bethania (12 knots), on her way from Mediterranean to join the KAISER WILHELM DER GROSSE, captured by the ESSEX, September 7th.

In Spanish and Portuguese Ports :
  Westerwald (12·5 knots), at Lisbon on August 4th.
  Goeben (14·5 knots), at Vigo on August 4th.
  Bülow (14·5 knots), at Lisbon on August 4th.

In Mediterranean :
  König Albert (15 knots), at Genoa on August 4th.
  Moltke (16·5 knots), at Genoa on August 4th.

In Sea of Marmora :
  Corcovado (13·5 knots), at Panderma.

East of Suez :
  Sudmark (12·5 knots), at sea between Colombo and Aden; captured by the BLACK PRINCE, August 15th, in Red Sea.
  Zeiten (14·5 knots), at sea between Colombo and Aden, joined the KÖNIGSBERG. Arrived Mozambique, August 20th.
  Kleist (14·5 knots), sailed for Colombo, August 2nd; arrived Padang, August 7th.
  Tabora (14·5 knots), at Dar-es-Salaam. Blocked in port, August 8th.
  Yorck (14·5 knots), at Tsingtau. Sailed, August 4th, with supplies for Admiral Von Spee.
  Prinz Eitel Friedrich (15 knots), at Tsingtau, sailed (armed), August 6th.

GERMANY'S CONVERTIBLE SHIPS

Princess Alice (15·5 knots), arrived Manila, August 5th; moved about for some time around Philippines.
Seydlitz (14·5 knots), sailed for Sydney, August 3rd; arrived Valparaiso, August 20th.

In Suez Canal:
Derfflinger (14·5 knots), interned by Egyptian Government.

In South American Ports or Waters:
Cap Trafalgar (18 knots), at Buenos Ayres. Put to sea and armed from the EBER. Sunk by the CARMANIA, September 14th.
Blücher (16·5 knots), at Pernambuco on August 4th.

West Coast of Africa:
Max Brock (11 knots), at Duala. Captured by the CUMBERLAND in September.
Itolo (9 knots), sunk by French in Corisco Bay.

In British and Belgian Ports:
Gneisenau (14·5 knots), at Antwerp on August 4th. Seized by Belgians.
Prinz Adalbert (12·5 knots), seized at Falmouth, August 4th.

Some other ships, such as the *Prinz Heinrich* at Lisbon, were also suspected by the Admiralty of having been prepared for conversion.

In addition to these German merchantmen, the future use of which was open to suspicion, there were a number of Austrian ships. Moreover, Germany and Austria-Hungary had, in foreign waters, many other ships which were capable of employment for intelligence purposes, or might be used as store-ships or colliers.

Beyond all these elements of danger, which the Admiralty could not, and in fact did not, ignore, there was a powerful squadron of German men-of-war in the Pacific, and cruisers were known to be serving in other parts of the world.[1]

---

[1] Austria-Hungary had in foreign waters only one man-of-war of importance, the light cruiser KAISERIN ELIZABETH, 3,936 tons displacement; armed with eight 5·9-inch; fourteen 3-pounders; 1 machine-gun. Her sea speed was 17·2 knots. She was at Tsingtau.

The following list conveys some idea of the added menace arising from these vessels[1]:

	Displacement.	Sea Speed.	Armament.
	Tons.	Knots.	
Mediterranean:			
GOEBEN (1911) b.c.	24,640	22·8	10–11 in.; 12–5·9 in.; 12–22 pr.
BRESLAU (1911) l.c.	4,480	24·5	12–4·1 in.; 1–7 pr.; 2–m.
Far East:			
SCHARNHORST (1906) a.c.	11,420	20·5	8–8·2 in.; 6–5·9 in.; 18–22 pr.
GNEISENAU (1906) a.c.	11,420	20·5	8–8·2 in.; 6–5·9 in.; 18–22 pr.
EMDEN (1908) l.c.	3,592	21·8	10–4·1 in.; 1–7 pr.; 2–m.
ILTIS (1898) g.b.	885	14·0	4–15 pr.; 6–1 pr.; 2–m.
JAGUAR (1898) g.b.	885	14·0	4–15 pr.; 6–1 pr.; 2–m.
TIGER (1899) g.b.	885	14·0	2–4·1 in.; 6–1 pr.; 2–m.
LUCHS (1899) g.b.	885	14·0	2–4·1 in.; 6–1 pr.; 2m.
CORMORAN (1892) g.b.	1,602	16·0	8–4·1 in.; 5–1 pr.; 2–m.
TSINGTAU (1903) r.g.b.	220	13·0	1–4 pr.; 2–m.; 1–15 pr.
VATERLAND (1903) r.g.b.	220	13·0	1–4 pr.; 2–m.; 1–15 pr.
OTTER (1909) r.g.b.	265	15·0	2–4 pr.; 3–m.
TAKU (1898) t.b.d.	276	30·0	2–4 pr.
"S.90" (1899) t.b.d.	394	26·0	3–4 pr.; 2–m.
East Pacific:			
NÜRNBERG (1906) l.c.	3,400	21·5	10–4·1 in.; 1–7 pr.; 2–m.
LEIPZIG (1905) l.c.	3,200	20·0	10–4·1 in.; 1·7 pr.; 2–m.
Australian Waters:			
GEIER (1894) g.b.	1,590	16·0	8–4·1 in.; 5–1 pr.; 2–m.
PLANET (1905) s.v.	650	9·5	3–1 pr.; 2–m.
West Coast of Africa:			
EBER (1903) g.b.	984	14·0	2–4·1 in.; 6–1 pr.; 2–m.
East Coast of Africa:			
KÖNIGSBERG (1905) l.c.	3,350	21·3	10–4·1 in.; 1–7 pr.; 2–m.
West Atlantic:			
KARLSRUHE (1912) l.c.	5,500	27·25	12–4·1 in.; 2–m.
DRESDEN (1907) l.c.	4,520	24·0	10–4·1; in 2–m.

The sheet anchor of British merchant seamen, confronted by the unknown possibilities of war, was the increased regard which all the polite nations of the world had paid to international law for many years, and the anxiety which had been expressed by them to make their acts conform to the unwritten code—the dictates of humanity.

[1] b.c.—battle cruiser; a.c.—armoured cruiser; l.c.—light cruiser; g.b.—gunboat; r.g.b.—river gunboat; t.b.d.—torpedo-boat destroyer; s.v.—surveying vessel.

The evidence as to the German policy of arming merchant ships on a large scale on the outbreak of war was not confirmed by subsequent experience. Diplomatic documents since published suggest that Germany did not expect that the United Kingdom would intervene, and she was convinced that in any event the British Navy would not be mobilised rapidly, and that she would have ample time to carry out the scheme of conversion. The British Admiralty was ready for eventualities, with the result that the German Fleet was at once thrown back on the defensive, not only in the North Sea, but in every sea in which German men-of-war were stationed, and neither time nor opportunity permitted full advantage being taken of the large scheme for attacking British commerce. In February 1914, the Nautical Division of the Norddeutscher Lloyd issued instructions of a general character to all merchant vessels equipped with wireless installation. They were told that if war broke out they would be informed by wireless. This action suggested that preliminary arrangements were then being made by the German naval authorities for securing the safety of the general body of German merchant shipping and releasing other vessels for offensive operations. But towards the end of July of the same year, the only official instructions, so far as is known, which were issued, were to the effect that masters should make for the nearest neutral port. These orders were to the following effect:

" Although there are at present no reasons whatever to fear war complications with any other Power, still it appears desirable to us to issue the following instructions, which are to be strictly observed :

"(Unless Requisitioned)

" We hereby prescribe that, in case of war or complications threatening war, you, with the ship entrusted to you, when lying in a neutral port, will remain there or will immediately endeavour to reach the nearest neutral port or neutral territory. You will then await there the further course of things, and we shall then transmit to you further instructions direct or through our representatives."

Before declarations of war began to issue from the

capitals of Europe, German merchantmen were already running in all haste to safety. On the other hand, the German authorities, ignoring the precedent they set in 1870,[1] revealed by their acts that they intended to put every obstacle in the way of British merchant ships leaving German ports. In some cases the instructions may have been exceeded owing to the zeal of the local authorities, but it was subsequently established that the Imperial Government had intervened to stop sailings. On August 1st, Sir Edward Grey sent a dispatch to the British Ambassador at Berlin, in which he reported that information had reached the Foreign Office that the " authorities at Hamburg had forcibly detained a steamer belonging to the Great Central Railway Company and other British merchant ships." Surprise was expressed at this action, and Sir E. Goschen was asked to request the German Government to send immediate orders that vessels should be allowed to proceed without delay, it being added that " the effect on public opinion here would be deplorable unless this is done." An immediate reply was received from Berlin stating that " the Secretary of State, who expressed greatest surprise and annoyance, has promised to send orders at once to allow steamers to proceed without delay." In a subsequent telegram, Sir E. Goschen added that the " Secretary of State informs me that orders were sent last night to allow British ships in Hamburg to proceed on their way. He says that this must be regarded as a special favour of His Majesty's Government, as no other foreign ships have been allowed to leave. Reason of detention was that mines were being laid and other precautions being taken "—a mere cloak for illegality. On the same day (August 2nd) the Foreign Office sent to Berlin another telegram to the following effect: " I regret to learn that 100 tons of sugar were compulsorily unloaded from the British steamship *Sappho* at Hamburg, and detained. Similar action appears to have been taken with regard to other British vessels loaded with sugar. You should inform Secretary of State that, for reasons stated in my telegram of August 1st, I most earnestly trust that the orders already sent to Hamburg to allow the clearance of British ships covers also the release of their cargoes, the

---

[1] Days of grace, running to a period of six weeks, were extended to enemy merchant ships to enable them to leave German ports.

detention of which cannot be justified." Sir E. Goschen replied on the following day that "no information was available." On August 4th, Sir E. Grey sent another message to the British Ambassador at Berlin stating: "I continue to receive numerous complaints from British firms as to the detention of their ships at Hamburg, Cuxhaven, and other German ports. This action on the part of the German authorities is totally unjustifiable. It is in direct contravention of international law and of the assurances given to Your Excellency by the Imperial Chancellor. You should demand the release of all British ships, if such release has not yet been given."[1] On the same day the German Ambassador in London issued the following explanation, which, it will be seen, avoided the fact that a general policy of detention had been adopted: "The Wilson liner *Castro* was in Kiel Canal, and was ordered by the German authorities to proceed to Hamburg for military reasons, as it was not desirable that any commercial vessel should be in the canal at present. As regards the second case, the Government had purchased coal shipped for Germany to a private firm, and the order was given for the ship to proceed to Hamburg with her cargo. It was solely a matter of changing its destination. In both cases there was no intention whatever of interfering with the property of the vessels. It was simply a police measure." It was subsequently ascertained that in many of the German ports every possible obstacle had been put in the way of the British shipmasters to prevent them taking their ships to sea, before war had begun; in some cases guards were mounted while the two countries still maintained friendly relations, and threats were made to deter masters from communicating with their owners. Many of the merchantmen prisoners who for many weary months, some almost for the entire duration of the war, languished in German camps belonged to vessels which had thus been detained contrary to the recognised practice. The enemy treated these seamen with great harshness, as was revealed when their miserable experiences were subsequently recounted. Some of them were maimed for life, owing to injury inflicted upon them by their guards, and others never recovered from the effects of bad food, damp and exposure. The Germans detained no fewer than eighty

[1] Cd. 7860.

British ships.[1] Unfortunately, the action cannot be attributed to over-zeal of the officials of one port, for the detentions were enforced in practically all German ports.

This early indication of the contempt of the German Government for international law may be contrasted with the attitude of the officers of the German men-of-war during the first phase of the conflict. So far as is known, they received no special instructions as to the treatment of enemy merchantmen, but were left to act in accordance with the Naval Prize Code, based generally on the provisions of the Declaration of London. Under the first article it was laid down that [2] : " During a war the commanders of His Majesty's ships of war have the right to stop and search enemy and neutral merchant vessels, and to seize —and, in exceptional cases, to destroy—the same, together with the enemy and neutral goods found thereon." The limits to the right of capture were dealt with at length, and in describing the object of stoppage and search it was declared that—" The stoppage and search shall take place only if the commander deems that it will be successful." It was added : " All acts shall be done in such a manner—even against the enemy—as to be compatible with the honour of the German Empire, and with such regard towards neutrals as may be in conformity with the law of nations and the interests of Germany." The ships specifically mentioned as being free from capture included hospital ships and vessels engaged exclusively in coastwise fishery or in the small local shipping trade, so long as they did not in any manner participate in the hostilities. " Coastwise fishery is not confined to the territorial waters of a particular State. It is deemed to include all fishing, with the exception of what is clearly deep-sea fishing." Enemy merchant vessels which at the beginning of hostilities were on a voyage from a German port or the port of an Ally to their port of destination, or to such other port as might have been designated to them, and were in

[1] On August 4th, 1914, a proposal from Germany, made simultaneously to Great Britain, France, Russia, and Belgium, that days of grace should be recognised reciprocally, was received by the British Government. A counter-proposal, incorporated in the *London Gazette* of August 4th, was communicated to Germany, the offer expiring on the 7th. The suggestion was not received in Berlin until the 8th, and nothing came of the matter.

[2] The Prize Code of September 30th, 1909 ; Bulletin of Laws of August 3rd, 1914, amended to July 1st, 1915. (*German Prize Law*, Huberich and King. London : Stevens & Co.)

possession of a pass—provided, however, that they had not deviated from the course prescribed to them, unless they could explain such deviation in a satisfactory manner —were also exempt from capture.

The Prize Code set out the procedure to be followed in case of stoppage and capture, in accordance with international precedent, and several paragraphs were devoted to the treatment of crews and passengers of captured vessels. It was laid down that, if a vessel were captured while making armed resistance or participating in belligerent operations, " persons on board thereof not embodied in the armed forces, who have participated in the belligerent operations or offered armed resistance, are dealt with according to the usages of war. Other persons belonging to the crew are made prisoners of war." In the case of capture of an enemy vessel or a neutral vessel rendering unneutral service, "the master, officers, and crew, if subjects of an enemy State, are not to be made prisoners of war, providing they enter into a formal written engagement not to undertake any services connected with the belligerent operations of the enemy during the pendency of the war. Members of the crew who are subjects of a neutral State must be released without the imposition of any conditions. If the master and officers are subjects of a neutral State, they are to be released, provided they give a formal written promise not to accept service on board any enemy vessel during the pendency of the war." It was furthermore declared that " passengers on board captured vessels are not to be deprived of their liberty, and are to be released as soon as possible, unless required as witnesses." It was added that the treatment of prisoners of war should, so far as the circumstances of the naval warfare permit, be in conformity with Articles 4 to 20 of the Appendix to Convention IV of the Second Hague Conference. It was also provided that " the master and crew of a captured vessel, unless they are prisoners of war, shall continue to perform their former duties until they are released. So far as possible the use of force is to be avoided. In so far as the circumstances of the war permit, they remain in the enjoyment of their rights." It was further laid down that " the rights of the passengers on board captured vessels shall be restricted only in urgent cases—e.g., on account of unneutral acts." Persons on board a captured vessel might be placed on board another vessel, even the war-vessel, if the circumstances required such a course, remaining on board the war-vessel "only so long as this is absolutely necessary."

Other clauses of the Prize Code covered the method of dealing with captured vessels and seized cargoes. The commander, it was declared, "provides for bringing the vessel into a German port or the port of an Ally with all possible despatch and safety. A prize may be brought into a neutral port only if the neutral Power permits the bringing in of prizes. A prize may be taken into a neutral port on account of unseaworthiness, stress of weather, or lack of fuel or supplies. In the latter cases she must leave as soon as the cause justifying her entrance ceases to exist." The commander was instructed to give to the officer of the prize crew the necessary written instructions in regard to the voyage, and to make up the crew so as to enable the officer to bring in the vessel. It was added that, "before proceeding to the destruction of a vessel, the safety of all persons on board, and, so far as possible, their effects, is to be provided for, and all ship's papers and other evidentiary material, which, according to the views of the persons at interest, is of value for the formulation of the judgment of the Prize Court, are to be taken over by the commander." A section of the Prize Code was also devoted to the rights and duties of officers of a prize crew, it being added that "unnecessary measures of force are to be avoided."[1]

On June 22nd, 1914, the Chief of the Admiralty Staff of the German Navy addressed an order to the commanding officers and commanders in respect of their conduct when encountering armed merchant vessels during war. It was therein stated that:

"The exercise of the right of stoppage, search, and capture, as well as any attack made, by an armed merchant vessel against a German or neutral merchant vessel, is piracy. The crew are to be dealt with under the ordinance relating to extraordinary martial law.

"If an armed enemy merchant vessel offers armed

[1] Prize Code of the German Empire as in force July 1915 (London: Stevens & Co.).

AFTER A MINE EXPLOSION.

resistance against measures taken under the law of prize, such resistance is to be overcome with all means available. The enemy Government bears all responsibility for any damages to the vessel, cargo, and passengers. The crew are to be taken as prisoners of war. The passengers are to be left to go free, unless it appears that they participated in the resistance. In the latter case they may be proceeded against under extraordinary martial law."

It will thus be seen that on the eve of hostilities the enemy declared that the crews of merchant vessels were to be treated as prisoners of war if they resisted capture, and that the passengers, in case of resistance, might be proceeded against " under extraordinary martial law." That exposure of policy is the primary factor in the understanding of the German attitude, and an essential element in the due appreciation of the danger to which merchant seamen were exposed. Such was the position at sea when the war opened, which was to convert Europe into a vast battle-field and strew the seas with the bodies of defenceless men, weak women, and innocent children.

On a date preceding the British declaration of war, August 3rd, evidence was supplied that Germany had already completed measures for the defence of her ports. On August 3rd, the steamship *San Wilfrido* (6,458 tons) was in the River Elbe, about eight miles above Brunsbuttel, when orders were received that she might proceed on her voyage, calling at Cuxhaven. No pilot was available to take her through the minefield which had already been laid at Cuxhaven, so the *San Wilfrido* followed the usual channel. The men in charge of the harbour tugs, who were watching her progress, realised that the ship was in danger, and shouted to the master, who immediately attempted to go full speed astern. Before way was off the ship, she was caught by the strong ebb tide and drifted into the mine zone. Three explosions occurred, and then the steamship began to settle down by the stern, taking a heavy list to port. A German tug went alongside to take off the crew, and shortly afterwards the *San Wilfrido* was firmly aground. Two days later a somewhat similar incident occurred to the steamship *Craigforth* (2,900 tons), which had shipped a cargo of wheat at Ghenichesk consigned to Hamburg. She was proceeding on her voyage in the Bosphorus when she struck a mine. A patrol steamer came to her assistance, and the vessel was beached. While temporary repairs were being carried out the Turkish authorities seized the cargo. Within a week the *Craigforth* was refloated, and was about to resume her voyage to Hamburg when the master and crew were ordered by the British Consul to leave her. These two minor incidents, however, conveyed no suggestion of the experiences which were to befall British merchant seamen during the first phase of the enemy's operations against sea-borne commerce. Both ships had suffered injury in territorial waters. But, in the meantime, an event had occurred in the North Sea which indicated that the Germans intended to take the fullest advantage of a mining policy, the *Königin Luise* being caught off Aldeburgh, on the morning of August 5th, laying mines in the track of merchantmen. In spite of these developments, shipping in British waters was conducted for several weeks without mishap, except for the damage from a mine sustained by the *Oakby* off Seaham on August 30th; that vessel, however, succeeded in reaching the Tyne.

CHAPTER III

CRUISER ATTACKS ON SHIPPING

WITHIN less than two days of the outbreak of war an incident occurred off the Gulf of Aden which showed that enemy cruisers which were at large in the outer seas intended to make the best of what was to prove a comparatively short period of freedom from interference. For as soon as war was declared, the Admiralty put into operation the plans for the protection of merchant shipping which had been prepared in advance.

On July 23rd, the s.s. *City of Winchester* (6,601 tons), of the Hall Line, had left Calcutta with a general cargo for London and Dunkirk. The voyage was marked by no notable incident until the evening of August 5th, when the master (Mr. George R. Boyck) received news of the outbreak of war in a dramatic manner. At 8.30 p.m., when the vessel was steaming at full speed in the Gulf of Aden, a strange cruiser, afterwards recognised as the KÖNIGSBERG, drew towards her, making no signal and firing no gun. The significance of the movement was not missed by the captain of the British vessel. The warship's guns could be seen in the moonlight trained upon the defenceless merchant ship, and, when the signal was received to stop, Captain Boyck had no alternative but to comply. A boat was immediately sent off from the KÖNIGSBERG with an armed crew, and after the ship's papers had been seized, and the ship's wireless installation destroyed, orders were given for her to proceed in accordance with directions received from the KÖNIGSBERG, an officer and four men remaining on board to insure obedience. During the whole of that night and until the afternoon of the next day, the captain, the first British merchant officer on the high seas to experience the annoyances and delays of war, was directed to steam various courses, but always to the westward, until anchor was at last dropped in the bay of the small port of Makalla, about 200 miles from Aden on the Arabian coast. At this point the KÖNIGSBERG was joined by the Norddeutscher Lloyd steamship *Zieten*, and the *Ostmark*, of the Hamburg Amerika Line, acting as supply ships. A steam-pinnace, with an officer and a party of men, was then sent to the *City of Winchester*, and they took away all the charts and sailing directions. Another prize crew, consisting of two lieutenants and fifteen men, all well armed, was placed on board, and that evening the four ships put to sea with all lights out, the *Zieten* leading. After leaving the bay, the KÖNIGSBERG and *Ostmark* disappeared, and for the time nothing more was seen of them. For the next two days the *City of Winchester* continued to follow the *Zieten*, always making to the north-east, until anchor was cast in the north-east bay of Hallaniya, the largest island of the Khorya Morya group. On the following morning the *Zieten* went alongside the *City of Winchester* and commenced to take about 300 tons of her bunker coal, as well as her stores of food and drink. In the meantime the captain and the European crew, with the exception of the second officer, the third engineer, and the carpenter, were transferred to the German ship, and early on the following morning, the coaling being completed, the *Zieten* disappeared in the darkness. During the day the prize crew completed the task of seizing all the foodstuffs to be found in the cargo. The same afternoon the KÖNIGSBERG reappeared, and, making fast on the port side of the *City of Winchester*, took the remainder of the coal (about 250 tons), all the fresh water, and what was left of foodstuffs. Throughout the night, work continued with carefully screened lights. At 4.30 on the following morning, August 12th, the remaining officers and the lascar crew were ordered on board the cruiser with their personal belongings. While the third engineer, under compulsion, was pointing out to the German officer the steps which could be taken to flood the ship, the task of dismantling all that was portable of her equipment was completed by the enemy. In a short space measures were taken to insure the sinking of the vessel, and then the KÖNIGSBERG, having embarked the boarding-party, stood off, fired three shells into the abandoned vessel, and steamed away. Two hours later, the KÖNIGSBERG reached a bay

END OF THE "CITY OF WINCHESTER"

of Soda Island, where she met the German merchant ship *Goldenfels*, which was encountered at a convenient moment when homeward bound from Hankow; to her the second officer, the third engineer, the carpenter, and the lascars, were transferred. For some unexplained reason the *Goldenfels* then returned to the spot where the *City of Winchester* had been left in a sinking condition. It was the unhappy experience of the former officers and men of this ship to spend the remainder of the day watching her founder until only the black top of the funnel, the wireless mast, and part of the top of the mast remained in view. The elaborate and lengthy ritual had at last been completed after an interval of a week. " We were afterwards conveyed in the *Goldenfels* to Sabang, where," the second officer recorded in his report to the owners, " I safely arrived with all my men, and I have obtained a paper from the master of the *Goldenfels* certifying that he saw the ship sink ; it is witnessed by the commander of a Dutch gunboat." The *Zieten* reached Mozambique with her funnels disguised so as to represent a vessel of the British India Steam Navigation Company, and she hoisted the British red ensign on entering the port. In the meantime, the master and his companions had already been landed at Mozambique, leaving on record that he and his companions " were treated with every civility and respect by the Germans." [1]

While these adventures were befalling the officers and men of the *City of Winchester*, the German cruiser DRESDEN had begun her short career as a commerce destroyer, making her presence felt on the trade route from South America to the United States. Two days after the opening of the war, she fell in with three British vessels, the *Drumcliffe* (4,072 tons), the *Lynton Grange* (4,252 tons), and the *Hostilius* (3,325 tons). The first of these vessels had left Buenos Ayres in ballast on July 24th with instructions to call at Trinidad to replenish her bunkers for her voyage to New York. Captain Evans was unaware of the outbreak of war, and was proceeding on his

---

[1] The *City of Winchester* was the only capture of the KÖNIGSBERG. At the end of October 1914, this German cruiser was found to have taken refuge in the Rufigi River (German East Africa). There she was blockaded, and in the following July she was destroyed by British men-of-war.

course, unconcerned, when he was stopped by a strange man-of-war off the mouth of the Amazon. The warship proved to be the German light cruiser DRESDEN on her way round the Horn to the Pacific, possibly intending to join Admiral von Spee, commanding the German Pacific Squadron. The meeting was as unwelcome to her captain as it was to the master of the *Drumcliffe*, who had on board his wife and child. The British seaman had, of course, received no instructions from the Admiralty, while Captain Lüdecke found himself in a situation which had not been anticipated in his orders. A party was sent to the *Drumcliffe*, and it was at once reported that a woman and child were on board. Three courses were open to the German officer conversant with the humane sentiments expressed at The Hague Conference, and embodied in the German Naval Prize Code. He could either send the *Drumcliffe* with a prize crew into port, but none of a suitable character existed in the vicinity; he could order the ship to follow his movements; or he could release her on parole. He chose the last course. The vessel's wireless installation was dismantled, and the officers and crew were called upon to sign a declaration not to take service against Germany during the war. Captain Evans feared that a refusal to comply with this demand might jeopardise the safety of his wife and child, and he and his men gave the necessary undertaking. Within two hours or so the *Drumcliffe* was again under way. The troubles of the captain of the DRESDEN were not yet at an end. The *Drumcliffe* having been released at 3.40 on the afternoon of August 6th, it was his misfortune at 4.45 to fall in with the Houlder liner *Lynton Grange*, on passage from Rosario to Barbadoes. By signal from the DRESDEN, the master of the *Lynton Grange* (Mr. H. L. Simpson) learnt that a state of war existed between his country and Germany. While the signals were passing between the two ships, the Houston liner *Hostilius*, on her voyage from Montevideo to Cienfuegos, Cuba, via Barbadoes, came in view. She also had put to sea before the outbreak of war, and was proceeding in company with the *Lynton Grange*. The captain of the DRESDEN sent boarding-parties to both ships. In the case of the *Lynton Grange* the ship's papers were examined on board the cruiser, and then a naval officer returned

"HOSTILIUS" RELEASED WITHOUT PAROLE

and required that the British officers and men should sign a declaration to the following effect:

" We, the captain, officers, and crew of the s.s. *Lynton Grange*, declare formally that we will not do any service in the British Navy or Army, and will not give any assistance to the British Government against Germany during the present war."

A threat was made that, if the declaration was not signed, the officers and men would be taken on board the cruiser as prisoners of war, and the *Lynton Grange* sunk. If, on the other hand, the pledge were given and subsequently contraband were carried during the war, the crew, if caught, would be shot and their vessel destroyed. In the circumstances, the master and the other officers and the men decided to comply with the demand, and the vessel was released. In the case of the *Hostilius*, the boarding officer took the papers, which were in Spanish, back to the cruiser to be translated. He returned with them in about an hour, bringing with him the form of parole. The master (Mr. James Jones) conferred with his officers, and told them that he himself would not sign this document. It was then agreed to refuse unanimously to give the parole. The German boarding officer, on being informed of that decision, himself called the crew together and read the document to them. The men stated that they would stand by Captain Jones. A signal was then made to the DRESDEN, and, to the surprise of everyone on board, the ship was ordered to be released. Before the boarding officer left, however, he made the following entry in the chief officer's log book:

" *Hostilius*.

" Held up by S.M.S. DRESDEN: Commander-Frigate Captain Lüdecke.

" Lat. 1° 21″ N., long. 45° 1″ W. Held up, August 6th, 1914, 5.20 p.m.; let go, August 6th, 1914, 7.40 p.m.

" Let go because her destruction did not seem worth while.

"(*Signed*) FRIEDRICH BURCHART,
" *Lieut. Captain*."

The first ship to be sunk by the DRESDEN was the

s.s. *Hyades* (3,352 tons), which left Pernambuco on August 14th, the master having put into that port for instructions on his passage from Rosario to Rotterdam with a cargo of maize and foodstuffs shipped by a German firm. She was not fitted with wireless, but the master (Mr. John Morrison) had fallen in with the cruiser GLASGOW on August 8th, and, as a result of the warning given, put into Pernambuco on the 10th. The Vice-Consul at Pernambuco had taken some pains to ascertain the extent of the danger threatening British ships, having interrogated masters of three British vessels arriving from British or American ports. The reply in each case was identical: nothing had been seen of enemy cruisers. In the meantime the agent of the Houston Company, in reply to an inquiry, had received a telegram from the owners stating that, unless the British authorities specially detained the steamer, he was to instruct the master to proceed to Las Palmas, adding, " German cruisers allowing British steamers proceed unmolested, with exception removing wireless apparatus." The master was therefore directed to avoid the regular route. The ship was considerably to the eastward of the most easterly track to Brazilian ports and River Plate from the Canary Islands, when smoke was seen on the horizon off the port bow. The smoke, it was found, came from the German cruiser DRESDEN, which was accompanied by two tenders, the *Baden* and *Prussia*. As the DRESDEN approached, she was seen to be flying the French flag, a familiar decoy, but this was replaced by the German ensign when about a mile and a half distant. The *Hyades* continued on her course until signalled to stop. A boarding-party took the ship's papers, and Captain Morrison was told that it would be impossible for him to reach Rotterdam, as he would be diverted to a British port on entering the Channel. The officers and men were given an hour to leave the ship with their effects, and boats from the DRESDEN conveyed them to the *Prussia*. The *Hyades* was afterwards sunk by gunfire, explosives having been previously placed on board and the covers taken off the condensers. The *Prussia*, accompanied by the DRESDEN and *Baden*, then proceeded south. As the *Hyades* carried a cargo destined for Germany, the loss of the vessel, as the British Consul at Buenos Ayres remarked, was "not an unmixed evil." The gunnery of the DRESDEN, according to the master's statement, was "noticeably bad"; the sea at the time the *Hyades* was sunk was quite calm, the range was barely a quarter of a mile, yet it took the DRESDEN some forty minutes to sink her. The officers and crew of the *Hyades* were landed at Rio de Janeiro, the master leaving it on record that "he and his men were well and kindly treated while on board the s.s. *Prussia*."

Before the *Prussia* parted company with the DRESDEN, that cruiser met the s.s. *Siamese Prince* (4,847 tons), on her way from London to the River Plate with a neutral cargo. The vessel was stopped and boarded, but after a delay of two hours was allowed to proceed, this leniency being apparently due to the character of her cargo.

At this period in her career, the DRESDEN fell in with only two other British ships, the *Holmwood* (4,223 tons), outward bound form Newport with coal for Bahia Blanca, and the *Katharine Park* (4,854 tons), on passage from Santa Fé and Buenos Ayres to New York. Both ships were off the usual track in accordance with Admiralty instructions. The story of the experiences of these two ships became known when the *Katharine Park* (master, Mr. H. Paterson) put into Rio de Janeiro on August 30th for the purpose of landing the captain and crew of the *Holmwood*. It was then reported that the *Holmwood* (master, Mr. R. H. Hill) had put into Las Palmas and had met with no incident at sea on leaving that port until the morning of August 26th, when she encountered the DRESDEN. The German officer of the boarding-party which went on board ordered the captain and crew to collect their personal effects and to proceed on board the *Baden*, a tender which was standing by. After these instructions had been carried out and some provisions had been transferred to the DRESDEN, a mine which had been placed in the *Holmwood* was exploded and the vessel sunk. At the moment when this ship was being despatched, the *Katharine Park* arrived on the scene. The DRESDEN immediately sent a party on board, the ship's papers were examined, half an hour was given to the surprised master and crew to pack their belongings, and preparations were made to sink the ship. As an alternative, the captain was told he would be released if he and his men entered into the usual parole. The latter course was adopted, and forthwith the master and crew of the *Holmwood* were transferred to the *Katharine Park*, which owed her release to the fact that she carried an American cargo. The DRESDEN and her supply ship then made off.

The captain of the DRESDEN was denied a further success owing to the competency with which the Pacific Steam Navigation Company's s.s. *Ortega* (8,075 tons) was handled. She escaped capture and destruction in circumstances which later' on drew from the Admiralty, in a letter to the owners, a glowing appreciation " of the courageous conduct of the master, Capain Douglas R. Kinneir, in throwing off his pursuers by successfully navigating the uncharted and dangerous passage of Nelson's Strait." Three hundred Frenchmen were thus saved from becoming prisoners of war, and eventually joined the Army of our Ally. Nothing might have been known of this incident but for the action of His Majesty's Consul-General at Rio de Janeiro, who, learning the details, embodied them in a despatch to the Foreign Office. In this statement he recalled that the *Ortega* sailed from Valparaiso with some 300 French Reservists on board towards the close of September. These men were in considerable danger of falling into the hands of any enemy cruiser which sighted the *Ortega*, as the ship possessed a speed of only about 14 knots, whereas, as has been noted already, the Germans had at sea a number of ships of twenty or more knots. When the British vessel was close to the western entrance of the Magellan Straits, a German man-of-war, which was subsequently identified as the DRESDEN, appeared and gave chase. The *Ortega*, being the slower ship, ought speedily to have been captured, but, in fact, she made her escape in the manner narrated by the Consul-General at Rio de Janeiro:

" Under these circumstances the master of the *Ortega* took a heroic resolve. He called for volunteers to assist in stoking his vessel: that appeal met with hearty response: firemen, engineers, and volunteers, stripped to the waist, set to work with a will, and the master assured me that they actually succeeded in whacking the old ship (she was built in 1906) up to a good 18 knots: the master headed his ship straight for the entrance of a passage known as Nelson's Strait; and he made for the Strait at full speed, hotly pursued by the German cruiser, which kept firing at him with two heavy bow guns. Luckily none of the shot took effect, and the *Ortega* succeeded in entering Nelson's Strait, where the German cruiser did not dare to follow her.

" In order to realise the hardihood of this action upon the part of the master of the *Ortega*, it must be remembered that Nelson's Strait is entirely uncharted, and that the narrow, tortuous passage in question constitutes a veritable nightmare for navigators, bristling as it does with reefs and pinnacle rock, swept by fierce currents and tide-rips, and with the cliffs on either side sheer-to, without any anchorage. I can speak from personal experience as to the terrifying nature of the navigation of Nelson's Strait, having once passed through it many years ago in a small sealing schooner.

" However, the master of the *Ortega* managed to get his vessel safely through this dangerous passage, employing the device of sending boats ahead, to sound every yard of the passage. Eventually, by a miracle of luck and good seamanship, he worked his way into Smyth's Channel, without having sustained even a scratch to his plates, and finally brought his vessel to this port."

It will be admitted that to take an 8,000-ton steamer safely through so perilous a passage constituted a most notable feat of pluck and skilful seamanship. Captain Kinneir, confronted with the possibility of falling the victim of an enemy cruiser, had exhibited once more the resourcefulness, daring, and skill which British seamen have so frequently displayed, to the admiration of the world. The publication of the story of his escape raised the spirits of the nation at a moment when, unaccustomed to the hazards of naval warfare, it was inclined to wonder what further misfortune was to happen, while at the same time it inspired the whole Merchant Navy with a high pride in its mission.

Before her career ended, the DRESDEN encountered two other British ships, the s.s. *North Wales* (3,661 tons; master, Mr. G. Owen); and the *Conway Castle* (1,694 tons; master, Mr. J. Williams). The former vessel was on passage from Juan Fernandez Island, on charter by the Admiralty, with 704 tons of coal for the Falkland Islands, when she was captured by the DRESDEN on the morning of

November 16th, in lat. 37° 30′ S., long. 77° 0′ W. The day had just dawned when the lookout of the *North Wales* noticed what he took to be two war-vessels on the starboard bow, distant about nine miles. The British vessel immediately altered course, hoping to avoid being seen by the two strange ships, which, in fact, kept on their course until about 6.30 a.m., as though not noticing the merchantman, when one of them, which proved to be the DRESDEN, turned towards the *North Wales*. An hour later she signalled to her to stop. The order was obeyed, and the British ensign was hoisted under the impression that the strange ship was a Japanese cruiser. As the master had been observing the Admiralty's instructions, steering a course which took him well clear of the trade route, the encounter with the DRESDEN was an unfortunate sequel to his well-directed efforts to avoid enemy ships. As soon as the German boarding-party had examined the ship's papers, the master was informed that the vessel would be sunk, time being allowed for the officers and men to collect their clothes and personal effects. Half an hour later the *North Wales* was sunk, and on the following day the crew were transferred to the German s.s. *Rhakotis*, which was in company with the DRESDEN. Several days later an officer from the DRESDEN demanded that the master and men should sign a formal declaration to take no part in the war, and they were subsequently landed by the *Rhakotis* at Callao on December 14th. The master of the *North Wales*, putting a strict interpretation on the parole into which he had entered, refused to give any information to the British Consul at the port as to what had happened on board the *Rhakotis* during the intervening weeks since the capture of his ship, beyond stating that " during our whole time on board the s.s. *Rhakotis* we were very well treated."

The last vessel to be captured by the DRESDEN was the sailing-vessel *Conway Castle*, which had left Valparaiso on February 17th, 1915, for Queenstown, with a cargo of barley. All went well for ten days. In lat. 37° 21′ S., long. 81° 58′ W., the DRESDEN appeared, and when still three miles distant exchanged signals, ordering the ship to stop. The boarding-party then proceeded on board, and after the ship's stores and provisions had been transferred to the DRESDEN, to which the crew had been ordered to row

THE SINKING OF A MERCHANT SHIP.

in their own boat, the *Conway Castle* was sunk. On March 7th, master (Mr. John Williams) and men were transferred to the Peruvian barque LORTON, and reached Valparaiso five days later. This proved to be the last exploit of the DRESDEN, which was sunk at Juan Fernandez Island on March 14th by British cruisers. The narrative of the experiences of British shipmasters shows that the captain of the DRESDEN had a proper appreciation of the mandates of humanity, and respected them in his dealings with the unfortunate officers and men of British merchant ships which he encountered during his cruise as a corsair.

Nor does the story of the career of the armed merchant cruiser KAISER WILHELM DER GROSSE reveal any less respect for the laws of the brotherhood of the sea which had obtained general acceptance throughout the world before the outbreak of war. Of the swift merchant ships in German ports which were capable of offensive use on the trade routes, this was the only one to put to sea in the early days of the war. It is probable that she was despatched in order to test the efficiency of the British control of the seas. She must have moved up the Norwegian coast at full speed, taking the fullest advantage of the darkness, and proceeded on an extreme northerly route, since at 7 o'clock on the evening of August 7th she came upon the British steam trawler *Tubal Cain* (227 tons). A heavy sea was running, and the skipper of the *Tubal Cain* (Mr. Charles Smith) had just got his gear on board and was preparing to light a buoy near which he intended to " dodge," when the KAISER WILHELM DER GROSSE appeared. The scene of the incident was about fifty miles west-north-west from Staalbierghuk, on the west coast of Iceland. The German vessel put out a boat, and two officers boarded the *Tubal Cain*. They asked the skipper if he had heard that war had broken out between Germany and England. The reply was in the affirmative, as he had heard it two days ago, although the ketch had left Grimsby on July 25th. A demand was made for the ship's papers, and the crew of fourteen hands was directed to get into the trawler's small boat and proceed on board the KAISER WILHELM DER GROSSE. As there was a heavy sea running with a strong wind, two journeys had to be made, but by 9 o'clock the transfer had been completed, and then the KAISER

WILHELM DER GROSSE moved a short distance from the *Tubal Cain* and began firing. Altogether forty-eight shots were fired before the vessel was sunk. The firing officer remarked to the skipper by way of apology for the bad gunnery, that "the trawler, being British, took a lot of sinking." The skipper and the chief engineer were taken to the officers' quarters, an act of consideration which was appreciated, but the rest of the crew were sent below.

In those circumstances the KAISER WILHELM DER GROSSE began her career, in the course of which she was attended from time to time by at least four supply ships, and sank only two British merchantmen. On August 15th she fell in with the Union Castle liner *Galician* (6,762 tons), which had left Table Bay on July 28th for London. The *Galician* was in lat. 27° 30′ N., long. 18° W., being about sixty miles off the usual track from South Africa to Tenerife, when the KAISER WILHELM DER GROSSE overhauled her. According to the German officers, the presence of the liner had been revealed by a wireless message which she had sent. The narrative of events can best be given in the words of Captain E. M. Day, the master of the *Galician* :

" On August 15th, at 2.45 p.m. in lat. 27° 30′ N., long. 18° W., we were overhauled by the German armed cruiser KAISER WILHELM DER GROSSE, who signalled, ' If you communicate by wireless I will sink you.' He then ordered us to lower our aerial and to follow him at full speed. At 3.15 p.m. we were ordered to stop. The cruiser then sent a boat manned by two officers and men who destroyed the wireless, inspected the ship's papers, and mustered and inspected all passengers and crew. At 5.30 p.m. the Germans left the ship, taking with them Lieutenant Deane, first-class passenger, and C. Sheerman (gunner), third-class passenger, also all ship's papers and documents, etc. At 5.40 p.m. we were ordered to precede cruiser at full speed and to steer S. 25° W. (magnetic). At 6 p.m. we received orders to keep all lights extinguished, and to have all effects belonging to passengers and crew ready on deck, to provision all boats, and to have everything in order for leaving the ship at daylight. At 8.30 we were ordered to alter course to S. 17° E. (magnetic), on which course we continued until 3.40, August 16th, when we received orders to steer S. 45° W. (magnetic), the cruiser throughout following closely in our wake. At 5 a.m. the cruiser sent the following message: 'To Captain Day: I will not destroy your ship on account of the women and children on board—you are dismissed —good-bye.' To which the following reply was sent: 'To German Captain—Most grateful thanks from passengers and crew—good-bye.' Lat. 25° 25′ N., long. 17° 20′ W. The cruiser then left us at full speed, and we turned ship and shaped a course for Tenerife."

A further statement was made by Captain Day in the following terms:

"Having made a verbal report this forenoon at the Admiralty, I now beg to add the following observations regarding the points with which I was then desired by Captain Webb[1] to deal specially in my formal report:

"*Courses.*—The KAISER WILHELM DER GROSSE did not approach the *Galician* directly, but at first kept wide of us on a parallel course, *flying no colours*, and it was only when turning in towards us that she hoisted the German ensign. I then ran up the Red Ensign, and it was at this time the German cruiser threatened to sink me unless I stopped wireless communication. The commander of the cruiser then ordered me to follow him, and ultimately to come alongside on his starboard side.

"As will be seen from my report above, after the German officer had taken away my papers, we were ordered to alter our courses from time to time, at a speed of 12 knots, in such a way that we steered three triangular courses, obviously as if the cruiser were looking out for some other vessels, and it was possibly owing to failing in this attempt that he at last dismissed my ship and allowed me to proceed on my voyage.

"*Wireless Apparatus.*—The manner in which I was boarded has already been dealt with, but I may now say that, after my aerials had been sent down, the wireless installation was broken up by the Germans. I am pleased to add that, as our aerials had not been thrown overboard, the Senior Marconi Operator of my ship went ashore,

[1] Director of the Trade Division of the War Staff, now Rear-Admiral Sir Richard Webb, K.C.M.G., C.B.

upon our arrival at Tenerife, and obtained some spare parts which enabled him to fit up an emergency apparatus of moderate power. When this had been done, I instructed him that, while he should take every opportunity of receiving messages, he was on no account to transmit any messages or to communicate with other ships until we reached the English Channel. The fitting of this temporary apparatus enabled me later on to communicate with my owners. In my opinion great credit is due to the operator for the steps he took to enable me thus to maintain communication, and I have every reason to believe, not only that he strictly carried out my orders in listening for messages, as we afterwards received several, but that he also avoided sending any messages without my authority.

"*Tobacco.*—Having heard that some of the German boatmen were trying to purchase cigars and cigarettes from our men on the lower deck, I passed along word that there must be no trading with this German ship, and this I believe was also done by the German officer who was then in my cabin. After the mustering of the crew and passengers, and the examination and removal of the ship's papers, I asked the German officer if he would take a cigar, and he laughingly observed, 'Yes, we have no cigars left.' This I felt to be a convenient opportunity for showing my sense of the courtesy with which this individual officer had treated myself and my ship, and I said to him, 'If you will have a few cigars or cigarettes, I shall be very pleased.' I then sent a steward to fetch 300 cigars and 1,200 cigarettes, which I asked the officer to accept, and he expressed his thanks for this act of courtesy.

"In this connection I may add that, after the German cruiser had left us, I was told by several of my first-class passengers that the men in the German boat did not appear to relish their task, and that when asking for cigarettes and tobacco they said, in what appeared almost a state of trembling anxiety: 'We do not want to fight; we have no grudge against your English ships.'

"*Medical Stores.*—From casual conversation afterwards with passengers, I learned that some of them had been told by the men in the German boat alongside that the KAISER WILHELM DER GROSSE had a crew of about 450 men, very largely R.N.R. men, and it is significant of the possibility of a considerable amount of sickness being on board that the German officer in charge of the boat's crew took away all the quinine from the surgery of my ship."[1]

Early on the morning of August 16th, when the New Zealand Shipping Company's s.s. *Kaipara* (7,392 tons) was on passage to England from Montevideo with a large cargo, the KAISER WILHELM DER GROSSE, which had just released the *Galician*, appeared, making signals which the master (Mr. H. Makepeace) "could not understand." He realised, however, that he was in danger. He was sending wireless messages for assistance when the KAISER WILHELM DER GROSSE steamed up and hailed him through a megaphone: "Stop your wireless or I will sink you." A boarding-party then went on board, threw several parts of the wireless apparatus overboard, examined the ship's papers, and, sending the officers and men on board the merchant cruiser, sank the British vessel. A charge of gun-cotton was put in the stokehole, the condenser doors were opened, and then fifty-three shots were fired.

On the following day the Royal Mail Steam Packet Company's liner *Arlanza* (15,044 tons) was intercepted on her voyage from Buenos Ayres to Southampton. She had left the former port on July 31st, and was in lat. 24° 40′ N., long. 17° 14′ W. The procedure in the case of the *Galician* was repeated. The *Arlanza* first received a signal, "Heave to, or I will fire into you." When that order had been complied with, the enemy vessel, which was then within 200 or 300 yards, sent another signal: "Lower away and throw overboard all your wireless installation." A later inquiry elicited the fact that the *Arlanza* was carrying a number of passengers. That was followed by the welcome notification: "Dismissed on account of your having women and children on board." That signal was twice repeated. Then came the final message: "I have no further commands for your captain." Commander C. E. Down, in a report to his owners, stated that his passengers were naturally rather excited during the exchange

[1] In his report to the Union Castle Steamship Company, Captain Day recorded that "the German officers were most courteous throughout." The Admiralty sent through the Union Castle Mail Steamship Company a special message of commendation to Captain Day and the wireless operator of the *Galician* : "To the former for the tact which he had displayed in difficult circumstances, and to the latter for the promptitude and resource with which he replaced the wireless installation."

of signals, wondering what their fate would be; " but there was no panic or noise, and the relief was very marked when they heard the verdict that we could proceed." The *Arlanza* reached Las Palmas at 7 a.m. on the following morning, having by 8 p.m. on the preceding night, or six hours after the arrest, fitted up and put in working order the ship's duplicate wireless set and sent warning messages to the cruiser CORNWALL, which was known to be cruising in the neighbourhood of the Canary Islands, and that vessel passed them on to the CUMBERLAND.

The KAISER WILHELM DER GROSSE next fell in with the Elder liner *Nyanga* (3,066 tons). That vessel had sailed from Calabar, on the West Coast of Africa, on July 28th with a cargo of African produce for Hamburg; but on arrival at Sierra Leone, the master (Mr. C. H. Jones) received orders to proceed to Liverpool, war having broken out. The *Nyanga* was about 230 miles south-west of Cape Blanco, being to the eastward of the usual track, when the German cruiser was reported about seven miles on her port bow, drawing in. A short time afterwards the *Nyanga* was ordered to stop, and, after the preliminary inquiries had been answered by signal, a boarding-party instructed the officers and crew to collect their belongings and proceed on board the KAISER WILHELM DER GROSSE. The sea-cocks were opened, the condenser covers removed, and the *Nyanga* was then sunk by means of a dynamite charge, which blew the ship's side out.[1]

While the KAISER WILHELM DER GROSSE was operating, with small results, in the south-east Atlantic, the German cruiser KARLSRUHE, the whereabouts of which had been for some time the subject of anxiety to the Admiralty, was busy in the neighbourhood of the West Indies, afterwards reaching out to South American waters. Elaborate arrangements had been made to insure adequate supplies of coal and stores, tenders being placed under orders to meet the warship as directed from time to time. The cruise of the ḰARLSRUHE stands out from the history of the warfare on commerce as a notable success achieved by a weak sea power in face of superior force. After

---

[1] The crews of the *Kaipara* and *Nyanga* were sent off in the German tender *Arucas* before the action with the HIGHFLYER and landed at Las Palmas on August 28th.

escaping from Rear-Admiral Cradock's squadron in the West Indies on August 6th, she revealed her presence to the east of Barbadoes on August 18th. The steamship *Bowes Castle* (4,650 tons), of the Lancashire Shipping Company, had left Montevideo for New York on the very day war was declared. Three days later the ship was stopped by the British cruiser GLASGOW and warned that, as war had broken out, she should proceed direct to New York, avoiding the usual course and screening lights. On noticing a warship of unknown nationality at sea, about ten miles away on the port bow, the master of the *Bowes Castle* (Mr. E. Howe) apparently thought little of the incident, and proceeded on his course. The strange ship, however, gradually drew in, and at length fired a shot as a warning to the *Bowes Castle* to stop. This signal was immediately complied with, and it was then found that the stranger was the KARLSRUHE. The usual routine with which other masters had already become familiar was then followed. The crew was sent on board the supply ship *Patagonia*, and the *Bowes Castle* was sunk by explosive charges. The *Patagonia*, with her involuntary passengers, subsequently followed the movements of the KARLSRUHE, and on the 21st the two ships anchored off Maraca Island, at the mouth of the River Amazon, and the cruiser proceeded to coal from the *Patagonia*. Six days later the British seamen were transferred to another of the KARLSRUHE's attendant ships, the collier *Stadt Schleswig*, and were eventually landed at Maranham on September 2nd.

The German cruiser's bunkers having been filled, she resumed her career of commerce destruction. On the evening of August 31st, at 5 p.m., she fell in with the steamship *Strathroy* (4,336 tons) 120 miles N.N.E. of Cape St. Roque. This Glasgow-owned vessel was a valuable prize, as she was carrying a large cargo of coal from Norfolk, Virginia, to Rio de Janeiro. She left the former port on August 15th. The *Strathroy* was overhauled by the warship and ordered to follow her to the lee side of Rocas Island, where anchor was cast about three-quarters of a mile from the shore. An armed guard then proceeded on board the *Strathroy* and took possession of her, in spite of the protests of the master (Mr. J. Mason), who urged that the ship was in neutral waters. The officer in command of the guard disregarded this plea. Possibly in a spirit of bluff, he explained that the enemy had learnt of the ship's departure from Norfolk, and that her coal was badly needed, adding that he could not let legal trifles stand in his way when the success of the cruiser's operations was at stake. All the crew, with the exception of some Chinamen, who were retained to transfer a portion of the coal to the KARLSRUHE, were ordered to leave the ship, which was taken away and sunk some days later when she had served the enemy's purpose.

Her bunkers replenished, the KARLSRUHE again put to sea and overhauled the s.s. *Maple Branch* (4,888 tons), on passage from Liverpool to Punta Arenas, Chile. Although the *Maple Branch* carried a valuable cargo of 2,000 tons and prize cattle stated to be worth £4,000, the ship was destroyed without compunction, the master and crew being removed to the *Crefeld*, of Bremen, which was in company with the KARLSRUHE. For service as scouts, the captain of the KARLSRUHE kept in attendance on him two other vessels, the *Rio Negro* and *Asuncion*, both being fitted with wireless, thus facilitating their use for intelligence purposes. Provided with eyes and ears, the KARLSRUHE remained in the neighbourhood of Pernambuco, where she had already done so well, and in the second fortnight of September added four more large ships to her list of captures—the *Highland Hope* (5,150 tons), the *Indrani* (5,706 tons); the *Cornish City* (3,816 tons); and the *Rio Iguassu* (3,817 tons). All these ships, except the *Indrani*, which, under the name of *Hoffnung*, joined the KARLSRUHE's force of supply ships, were sunk.

When the Germans boarded the *Highland Hope*, Lieutenant Shrovder, with his armed party standing behind him, confronted the British captain in his cabin. He demanded in a peremptory manner why the *Highland Hope* had not stopped when requested to do so; his displeasure probably was not lessened by an arresting caricature of the Kaiser which could hardly have escaped his notice. He was so incensed that he threatened to have the master (Mr. J. B. Thompson) taken to the cruiser and put in irons. This intention was not, however, carried out, but officers and men were directed to get their personal belongings together, and in the meantime the German seamen rummaged the ship, eating anything they could lay their hands on. The transfer to the *Crefeld* was not effected without difficulty, and the engineer, weighing about seventeen stone, in climbing up the rope ladder while the ship was rising and falling in the swell, fell back on the captain, who was attempting to help him. The British seamen joined on board this German vessel the captured crews of the *Strathroy* and the *Maple Branch*. The men fairly took charge of the ship, all hands singing, " It's a long way to Tipperary." Thus these brothers in misfortune began their enforced cruise in the *Crefeld*. The cruiser remained stationary while the *Crefeld* steamed to the west and the *Rio Negro* steamed to the east, at distances enabling them to keep in visual touch with the cruiser. Owing to the clear atmosphere and the crow's nests at the mastheads, the enemy covered a field with a front of about 140 miles. On the 17th the *Indrani* [1] was captured, and then the scouting was resumed. On the 21st the Dutch steamer *Maria*, laden with wheat, from Portland, Oregon, for Belfast and Dublin, was captured.[2] The crew, consisting of a motley crowd of Greeks, Chilians, and Arabs, had little time to make their final preparations; some of them arrived on board the *Crefeld* in hard hats and wearing their best suits; others had no shirts or singlets, and were without stockings. Some of the firemen had been called straight from the stokehold, and were black with grime. These men, like those of the *Indrani*, were greeted on board with the singing of " It's a long way to Tipperary," and were then submitted to close questioning to learn the latest news of the progress of the war.

A further interesting sidelight on the procedure followed by the KARLSRUHE is furnished by the master of the *Cornish City* (Mr. J. Bethke), who, together with his crew, was taken on board the *Rio Negro*, where they were " received with all friendliness" :

" By this time the cruiser's crew were busy connecting fuses, etc., from the ship to the cruiser ready for blowing up the *Cornish City*. The sea-cocks had already been

[1] Master, Mr. N. B. Pilcher.
[2] The *Maria* left Punta Arenas with a cargo of wheat for Belfast and Dublin. She was sailing under the Dutch flag, and was subsequently condemned by the German Prize Court on the plea that Belfast, the first port of destination, had been declared a naval harbour on August 14th.

opened, and already the steamer could be seen to settle down slowly. About this time we were joined by another German steamer, the *Crefeld*, who, we were told, had already on board five British crews of steamers that had been captured and sunk. Only the same morning she had taken a crew off a steamer which was found to be carrying contraband, and therefore sunk. All our crew were standing about the deck waiting to see the last of the *Cornish City*, but only a small hole two feet square had been blown into her, and she took a long time to sink, and when she did finally take her last dive it was too dark to see anything of her. She sank at 7.35 p.m. At 9 p.m. the cruiser KARLSRUHE proceeded again, followed by the *Crefeld* and the *Rio Negro*, steaming to the southward. As I have already said, we were received with the utmost kindness on board the *Rio Negro* and made as comfortable as possible. This steamer is a passenger boat fitted to carry 60 first-class and 200 second-class passengers. We were all given first-class berths, with the exception of the sailors and firemen, who were put into the third-class. Far from being regarded as prisoners of war, we were treated like first-class passengers throughout, everybody on board combining to make us comfortable.

"*September 22nd.*—On this day, at 5 a.m., the cruisers stopped an Italian and an Austrian steamer, but, after being examined, they were allowed to proceed. At 7 a.m. another steamer was sighted; this turned out to be the *Rio Iguassu*,[1] a British steamer loaded with coal. She was stopped and examined and the crew told to clear out. But just then a Swedish steamer came along, and she must have given the cruiser some information about a British cruiser, for a few minutes later we were all under way again, followed by the *Rio Iguassu*, and steering due west to get clear of the track. As in the case of the *Cornish City*, these steamers were held up right in the usual shipping track, where at any moment a British cruiser might have turned up. We steamed west until 1 p.m., when a stop was made and the cruiser went alongside the *Rio Iguassu* to bunker. Owing to the heavy swell, she found this to be impossible, and she cast off again at 2 p.m., after which a crowd of marines were sent on board to take off any provisions. Several boat-loads were taken away, and then

[1] Master, Mr. George Johnstone.

she too was made ready to be blown up. The crew were transferred to the *Crefeld.* Her sea-cocks were opened, and at 5 p.m. she began to settle down by the stern. At 5.30 p.m. a hole was blown in her, and now she seemed to be heeling over to port rapidly. We had a good view of this steamer, and could see her going over all the time. At 6 p.m. she suddenly turned right over on her beam ends, and then, with a noise like a last groan, disappeared beneath the water head first. It was a pitiful sight to see a good ship like that destroyed, and it made us wish that a British cruiser would come along and put a stop to this ruthless and absolutely useless destruction of British merchant ships. However, we were helpless in this matter, and must put up with it. This evening we passed in the saloon playing cards, draughts, and chess, with the officers of this steamer, and we had a very pleasant time. We are now beginning to wonder what they intend to do with us, and when and where we are likely to be landed. The worst trouble is that there is no means of letting our families know what has happened, and we are afraid that if we do not arrive at Rio by next Monday or Tuesday they will begin to wonder, and of course at once imagine the worst. We hope now that the *Crefeld,* having six crews on board, must be nearly full, and that they will therefore transfer us to her and send us in to one of the Brazilian ports.

" *September* 23rd.—Nothing of any consequence occurred to-day. The cruiser and her two consorts are cruising about all day looking for any foreign steamers, but none are to be seen. A masthead lookout is being kept on board the steamer continuously day and night. We are hoping a British cruiser will come along soon, but it looks as if we were fixed here for some time to come. We are passing our time playing shuffleboard on deck in daytime, and cards or chess in the cabin at nights. The captain and the second mate are the only deck officers left on board here now, and they are keeping an hour watch, as the chief mate and the third mate were left in charge of a British steamer in some port on the African coast, where they are waiting ready to coal the cruiser if she should run short of bunkers. I can't find out the name of this steamer, but I have heard it is one of the Wilson liners. The crew of her are on board the *Crefeld.*

" *September* 24th.—Everybody is beginning to feel pretty

sick at being held up like this, as there seems no chance of our being set ashore anywhere for some time. We are still being treated as well as we could wish, but the time hangs heavily on our hands, and we want to be on our way home again. Even this steamer's crew wish a British cruiser would come along and capture us, as they have been out here cruising around for the last seven weeks, and they begin to get tired of it, and they think, if a British cruiser would capture us, she would send them all home. This afternoon the news got around that the KARLSRUHE is only looking for one more capture before sending us all to Para, and nothing would suit us better if it were only true. But I am afraid things will be pretty bad at Para too, and we shall have a good deal of trouble to get home from there. Well, we are hoping for the best, and if we have to stay here for a month or so we shall be half dead with ennui.

"*September 25th.*—This seems to be a day of rest, as the cruiser and her two escorts are lying still and not moving through the water for once. It appears that the former is cleaning out some of her boilers. Our boats have been over to her several times to-day taking provisions, such as flour, beef, and sugar, and have brought back an injured sailor for attendance by the doctor. Of course, they have a surgeon on board the cruiser, but I take it they wish to keep their hospitals clear, and have no sick people on board, in case they should have to fight.

"*September 26th.*—The three of us are still lying motionless in the same place, apparently while the cruiser is executing repairs. I wish I could find out our whereabouts, but the movements are kept very close. I think we should be very near the Rocas and to the westward of them, as we have been steering to the westward since we left the track. The time passes very slowly with us all, and we shall be glad when they land us.

"*Sunday, September 27th.*—This is the first Sunday we have spent as prisoners of war, and we earnestly hope it will be the last, and that before next Sunday we shall all have been landed at some port where we shall be able to get a steamer for home. We have been lying idle all the morning again, but at 2 p.m. we commenced to steam again, taking a course to the southward. I heard there was a steamer in some port on the South American coast, or rather in some unfrequented bay, where we are to go to coal the cruiser. This may be true or not; we hear so many tales that we can't tell which to believe. If it is true, we should reach the coast some time to-morrow—that is, if I am right in my approximate position of the ship. We are now twenty-four days out from home, and to-morrow the owners will be expecting to hear of our arrival at Rio de Janeiro. It's not likely they will have heard of our capture, but if they don't hear by Wednesday they will probably imagine something of the sort. I wish it were possible to let them know about our being safe, because our people will be sure to begin inquiring of the owners, and if they can't hear anything definite about us they will begin to worry about our safety. But we must wait until we get to some port from where I can cable home. Let's hope that it won't be too long to wait.

"*September* 28*th.*—We kept steaming all this morning to the southward, and at 10 a.m. stopped, and the three ships spread out so that each ship was just within sight of one of the others. This looked as if we were looking for something, and sure enough, at 2 a.m., we met another German steamer, the *Asuncion*, of this same company. Until 5 p.m. she kept in constant communication with the cruiser and the *Crefeld*, and then she again steamed away the same way she had come. We then remained stationary for the remainder of the day and part of the night.

"*September* 29*th.*—In the early morning of this day we again began to steam, but this time to the south-east, and proceeded until 2 p.m., when we were again joined by two other steamers. One of these steamers had the prize crew of the *Strathroy* on board. She (the KARLSRUHE) had taken the last of the coal out of her, and then, after taking the prize crew off, had scuttled her. The *Strathroy* is another British steamer the Germans had captured and hid away in one of the many unfrequented bays on the North Brazilian coast, to wait until her cargo of coal would be wanted. Her original crew is on the *Crefeld* now. At 3 p.m. the cruiser and the two strangers steamed away, leaving the *Crefeld* and ourselves here to wait for orders.

"*September* 30*th.*—This day has been a very gloomy one for everyone on board, and has left everyone feeling pretty miserable. At 7 o'clock this morning, whilst some beef and potatoes were being sent over from our ship to the *Crefeld*, the boat capsized and all the provisions were spilt into the sea. This happened while the boat was being lowered into the water, so that, luckily, no men were in her and no lives were lost. At 10 a.m. the ship's doctor was found dead in his room next to mine. He had been complaining for a long time about a severe pain in his chest, but no one dreamt that he was seriously ill, because he always used to be about joking and playing with everyone. It appears, however, that he had been unable to sleep at nights for some time, and was in the habit of taking morphia to induce sleep, and, his heart being weak, it was unable to stand it. When he was found he had not been dead for more than half an hour or so, but although the doctor from the *Crefeld* came over at once, he was not able to do anything. We buried him at 5 p.m., his body being laid in a teakwood coffin and, covered with a German flag, lowered into the sea. We feel awfully sorry for him, because he was a well-to-do man who only came to sea for the benefit of his health, and was kept at sea owing to the war.

" *October 1st.*—At daylight we were joined again by the *Asuncion*, and she remained with us all day. We were continually steaming at about half-speed all day, waiting for the cruiser to return, but all we saw were one or two merchant vessels, who got away all right, as there was no one to chase them. We are all longing to hear some news from home, and how the war is getting on. Yesterday the doctor and the mate of the *Crefeld* told us that the Germans had taken Paris and had driven the Russians out of East Prussia altogether, but, of course, we don't know how much of this is true.

" *October 2nd.*—At 9 o'clock this morning we sighted the cruiser, accompanied by another large steamer, coming towards us. This steamer turned out to be the *Indrani*, of Liverpool. She is a large cargo steamer, and was captured by these people some weeks ago. Laden with coal, she had been kept out of the way somewhere as a collier for the cruiser, and a new name painted on her bows, the *Hoffnung*. I suppose, after bunkering out of her, the cruiser brought her back to act as a kind of scout for us, for after getting under way for the track again,

"A KIND OF HOTEL LIFE"

about noon, the *Asuncion* steamed away to the northward, while the *Indrani* went to the southward, both steamers keeping just within sight on the horizon. To-day we heard that a big battle has been won by the Germans against the British Fleet, where the former are supposed to have lost twenty-five torpedo-boats, while the losses of the British were ninety torpedo-boats and six Dreadnoughts and cruisers. I suspect these news are like all the war news we get here, specially got up to cheer the hearts of the Germans, and we don't take much notice of them. We are now cruising around looking for other harmless merchant vessels to sink; wish we could run against the GLASGOW or some other British cruiser, to put an end to this destruction of British ships and send us home. There has been no more talk as to when we are likely to be transferred and sent into a neutral port, so we have to just sit and wait.

"*October 3rd.*—Nothing of any consequence occurred to-day. The cruiser and her consorts were steaming due east again until 5 p.m., when she stopped for the night, apparently near the track. Of the *Asuncion* and the *Hoffnung* we have seen nothing all day; they have probably gone back to shelter.

"*October 4th.*—This is the second Sunday since we came on board here, and everyone wishes they were at home instead. As far as comfort is concerned, we have nothing to complain about; we have first-class cabins and are having splendid food; in fact, are living a kind of hotel life, with nothing to do save eat, sleep, and drink. There is no doubt we are a jolly sight better off than the crews on board the *Crefeld*. Exclusive of her own crew, there are now six other crews, of steamers that have been sunk, on board her, in all about 200 people. She is so crowded that we have heard the captains and officers have to have their meals on deck; and as she is only fitted out for forty first-class passengers, a good few of them have to sleep in the steerage. Besides this, she has no refrigerating machinery, being a much older ship than this, so that they have to live on salt provisions practically. Once or twice a week we send some fresh beef over to her from this ship, and a few potatoes, but that is all. Now we are getting everything of the very best—fresh provisions and fresh fruit every day, and can have as much beer as we want. So we really have nothing much to complain about; but we wish to get home, and even good living does not make up for that. We are in the track again now looking for ships, but there do not seem to be any about. The three ships are lying scattered all day, but before dark they are all close together and lie all night. The weather is keeping very warm and fine.

"*October 5th.*—Still lying scattered looking for ships, the three ships just within sight of one another. At 4 p.m. the cruiser sighted something, for she was off in chase of some steamer, ourselves following at full speed. At 6 o'clock the cruiser caught her quarry and stopped her, but we did not get up to her until 7 p.m., and by this time it was too dark to see who the steamer was. She seemed a large boat, and must have been either English or French, but the crew was transferred to the *Crefeld* and a prize crew put on board to take charge. We heard she was laden with coal, so they probably intend to keep her for bunkering purposes like the *Indrani*. At midnight she steamed away, leaving the cruiser and her two escorts behind, and we stopped where we were all night. I wonder if they will transfer us now and send us in to be landed; as I mentioned some time ago, there has been some talk of the *Crefeld* being nearly full of prisoners, and that as soon as one more steamer was caught and captured, we should be transferred to her and the lot of us sent to be landed at a South American port. I only hope it will turn out to be true.

"*October 6th.*—This morning we heard that the steamer caught last night was the *Farn*,[1] outward bound from Cardiff. We had expected that she might have some news about the war, but if she had it has been suppressed, and we have heard nothing. The crew may have been able to tell us something, but, as I have said, they have been sent to the *Crefeld*. We were cruising around again this morning looking for steamers, and at 3 p.m. one was sighted

[1] After her capture the *Farn* (4,393 tons; master, Mr. G. T. Alleyne) put into San Juan (Porto Rico) on January 11th, 1915, under the command of a lieutenant taken out of the cruiser KARLSRUHE, her mission being to obtain provisions. The State Department at Washington declared that she was to be regarded as a naval tender, and twenty-four hours were given for her to leave. At the end of that period the vessel was interned.

steering to the north-eastwards. She turned out to be the *Niceto de Larrinaga*,[1] of Liverpool, homeward bound from the River Plate with a cargo of foodstuffs. She was sighted from this ship first, and the signal given to the cruiser, who at once set off in chase. At 5 p.m. we came up with her, a boat from the cruiser boarded her, and a little afterwards we could see all the crew getting ready to leave the ship. She is a fine steamer and looked nearly new, but of course, being laden with grain, she was of no use to the cruiser, and had to be sunk. It is a shame to see so many fine steamers sunk, but so long as no British cruisers come here to put a stop to it, they will no doubt continue. A lot of time was taken up taking stores out of the ship for the cruiser, especially potatoes, of which these ships are running short. At 9 p.m. the steamer began to settle, but the hole blown into her must have been very small, for she was a long time going down, taking a list first one way and then the other. She settled down bodily until her engine-room skylight was awash, after which she went down by the head. I suppose her cargo helped to keep her afloat, because it was 2 p.m. when at last she took her last dive.

" *October 7th.*—This morning we could still see a lot of wreckage floating around belonging to the steamer sunk last night, such as boats, spars, and boxes. At 8 a.m. two other steamers were seen, and the cruiser set off after one of them, ourselves following him. The other steamer, of course, managed to get away, so she had something to be thankful for, because if the two of them had not happened to be seen together, at the same time, both of them would have been caught. The one we followed was the *Lynrowan*,[2] of Liverpool, also homeward bound from the River Plate, and laden with sugar, oats, etc. She also was condemned and the crew transferred to the *Crefeld*, like the crew of the steamer caught last night. Among her crew were two ladies, and I was surprised they were taken to the *Crefeld*, because that steamer must be getting pretty overcrowded with all her ' prisoners of war.' She must have at least 300 on board now, and, seeing that this steamer is bigger and better than she is, it seems strange that they should overcrowd her like that and leave this

---

[1] *Niceto de Larrinaga* (5,018 tons; master, Mr. R. F. Nagle).
[2] *Lynrowan* (3,384 tons; master, Mr. Arthur Jones).

steamer with only one ship's crew on board. As far as we are concerned, we should welcome some new arrivals, for we may get some fresh news from them, but I suppose they have their reasons for putting all the people on board there. Each of the three steamers took a couple of boat-loads of sugar out of the ship, and at 11 a.m. all the crew were away and the ship ready for sinking. We did not get a chance to see her sink at close quarters, because both the *Crefeld* and the *Rio Negro*—that is, ourselves—were ordered away to look for other steamers. However, we could see from a distance that the cruiser was using her for target practice, and was shooting at her. She sank at 2 p.m.—this is now two ships sunk within three days, and another one captured and detained, and it seems strange to us that this should be allowed to go on. Surely long before this the news must have reached home, if not definitely, still, so many ships being so long overdue must have given them some idea of what is going on here. And yet the track is said to be clear—clear of British shipping; it will be before long if this goes on much longer. We hear that there are some British cruisers on the South American coast, and indeed there must be, for so many ships to get as far as this in safety only to be caught here; but it is sure enough there is no British cruiser anywhere around here, or it could not help spotting us, for we seldom go far off the track.

"*October 8th.*—At 6 a.m. a steamer was sighted, and the cruiser set off in chase of her, bringing her up about 8 a.m. She turned out to be the s.s. *Cervantes*,[1] of Liverpool, bound from the West Coast to Liverpool. Crew was ordered off the ship; the cruiser took a lot of provisions off, and a hole was blown into her. At 11 a.m. she began to sink. We were then ordered away to scout, and at 12.40 p.m. saw her disappear stern first. At 1 p.m. our crew received orders to hold ourselves in readiness to be transferred to the s.s. *Crefeld.* All this afternoon the *Rio Negro* was away scouting, while the cruiser and the *Crefeld* kept close together. At 6 p.m. closed up for the night.

"*October 9th.*—At 1 a.m. another steamer was sighted, and stopped by a shot across her bows, turning out to be the s.s. *Pruth*,[2] of London, on a voyage from the West

---

[1] *Cervantes* (4,635 tons; master, Mr. E. J. Holton).
[2] *Pruth* (4,408 tons; master, Mr. J. Evans).

Coast to St. Vincent for orders, with a cargo of nitrate. Crew ordered to leave : at 6 a.m. crew transferred to the s.s. *Crefeld*, and at 8 a.m. ourselves were ordered to be sent across to the same steamer. By the time we came on board, the *Pruth* was abandoned, and fuses fixed. Two explosions occurred, one at 10.30 a.m. and the second at 10.45, in the after part of the ship. She then began to settle down rapidly, and at 11.20 sank stern first. 1 p.m., steaming to westward for scouting purposes. At 4 p.m. turned to east-south-east. 7.30 p.m. we joined the cruiser for the night. (3 p.m., stopped a large Spanish steamer and examined her, but she was allowed to proceed homeward.)

"*October* 10*th*.—At 3 a.m. the cruiser stopped and examined an Italian steamer, allowing her to proceed at 4 a.m.; 9.30 a.m. the *Crefeld* steamed away for scouting purposes; 5.45 rejoined the cruiser and the s.s. *Rio Negro* and set a westerly course. Continued steaming all night, apparently for the Rocas Islands to bunker the cruiser.

"*October* 11*th*.—Still steaming to westward at full speed, about twelve miles per hour. We are finding a great difference in the food and quarters to those we had on the *Rio Negro*, but this is probably due to the great number of prisoners of war and the fact that there is no refrigerating machinery on board here. There are now about 389 people on board here, prisoners of war, besides the crew belonging to this steamer, so it can be imagined that the ship is pretty crowded. 5 p.m. we came up to the *Farn*. She was lying in company with a British steamer, the *Condor*,[1] bound from New York to the West Coast with a general cargo. It appears that she found the *Farn* flying the British flag, and signalled, asking the *Condor* to stand by her, as she had trouble with her machinery. The *Farn* is, of course, a British steamer of that name, which was captured on October 5th and put under

---

[1] The s.s. *Condor* (3,053 tons; master, Mr. S. Purdy) constituted somewhat of a problem for the captain of the KARLSRUHE, as she carried a general cargo of about 4,000 tons belonging to neutrals. At first it was decided that, in view of the ownership of the cargo, the ship should not be sunk. In the meantime, the work of discharging such goods as the KARLSRUHE required went on by day and by night on October 12th and 13th. The captain of the KARLSRUHE took the master and crew out of the ship later on, and on the 13th they left in the *Crefeld*, in company with the other British seamen, for Tenerife.

the German flag. She knew that the cruiser was due to arrive here, and tried to detain the *Condor* so that she would be captured. Anyway, the ruse succeeded, and then the cruiser came on the scene just in time. She then boarded her, and the crew was ordered to leave her. She was abandoned at 8 p.m., and the steamer kept till the morning, to allow the crew of the cruiser to get at some of the cargo.

" *October 12th.*—The cruiser is busy all this morning getting some of the cargo out of the *Condor*. She has a lot of oils and milk among her cargo, and this is just what the cruiser and her escorts need. Our boats are helping her, so there seems no chance of getting away to-day.

" *October 13th.*—Boats still busy this morning getting cargo from the *Condor*. 11.30 a.m., heard that we are to leave at 4 o'clock this afternoon. 4 p.m., cruiser hoisted signals L E X & T D L, which meant ' Dismissed; wish you a pleasant voyage.' Began our homeward journey at 4.30 p.m., steering to the north-eastward, bound for Tenerife."

The cruise of the KARLSRUHE was nearing its end. Reports of the destruction she was spreading had already led to the necessary measures being taken by the British naval authorities to put a stop to her career. But before the end came she effected three more captures—the *Glanton* (3,021 tons) on October 18th; the *Hurstdale* (2,752 tons) on the 23rd; and the *Vandyck* (10,328 tons) on the 26th, the last-named being captured 410 miles from Cape St. Roque. The *Glanton* (master, Mr. George Arthur) had shipped a cargo of coal and general merchandise from Barry to Montevideo. When she was overhauled by the KARLSRUHE, at 10 a.m. on October 18th, the vessel was on the usual trade route between Cape Verde Islands and Fernando Noronha. After the master and crew had been taken off, and everything in the shape of oil, stores, rope, etc., had been commandeered, the *Glanton* was sunk by explosive charges. The KARLSRUHE then resumed her cruise, and five days later fell in with the *Hurstdale* (master, Mr. John Williams), which was on passage from Rosario to Bristol with maize; and three days afterwards she came across the *Vandyck* (master, Mr. Anthony Cadogan), which was proceeding to New York. She shared the same fate

CH. III] THE "KARLSRUHE'S" LAST PRIZE 167

as the other ships. If it were only because the *Vandyck* was the KARLSRUHE'S last success, her fate and the experiences of those on board would be of interest; and it happens that in this instance some notes are available of an American citizen who was travelling on board this British ship at the time:

" Our ship *Vandyck*, captured October 26th, lat. 1° 14′ S. and long. 40° 42′ W., by the German cruiser KARLSRUHE.

" All on board the *Vandyck* were transferred to the old (1895) Hamburg South American cargo-boat *Ascuncion*.

" If you refer to Register of Shipping, you will appreciate the conditions confronting our passengers and crew of 410 souls, added to fifty-one officers and crew of two previously captured British cargo steamers, together with fifty officers and crew of the said *Asuncion*.

" Under stress, men alone usually fear for themselves and say little about it, but when you realise that more than fifty of the people sent on board the old *Asuncion* were women and children, most of them ladies unaccustomed to those roughest of conditions, you will understand the intolerable state of affairs that met them when the transfer was made from the *Vandyck* to the *Asuncion*. The nearest port—Para—could have been reached in thirty hours; instead of which the *Asuncion* was kept going at about 2 knots per hour, on longitude (more or less) 45° W., just above the Equator, until our days of probation were ended, and we were landed at Para, November 2nd.

" The women behaved remarkably well from the first shock of being under the guns of the man-of-war until the end, relying on the men who surrounded them—and their faith was not misplaced.

" Once on board the *Asuncion*, the women and children were packed in the few cabins on board, including the officers' quarters, and the men slept on the decks and anywhere they could find stowage place.

" Food was brought on board from the *Vandyck* and cooked as best might be, and served by the volunteer cooks and stewards of our English crew—all praise be given to them for the fact!

" The officers of the KARLSRUHE, as well as of the *Asuncion*, were courteous—but then, Navy men and sailors are gentlemen all over the world, and live up to the standard, particularly where ladies are concerned. . . .

" When captured we were on the accustomed route from Cape St. Roque to Trinidad, and had steamed all our voyage in darkness at night—all to no avail, as we were captured in full daylight, 11.30 a.m.

" The five merchant steamers (captured or otherwise) spread out, and scouting in zigzag, in touch by wireless with the KARLSRUHE, formed a net impossible to evade, no matter what course we might have made.

" KARLSRUHE has no intention of fighting, her mission is to destroy shipping. She can easily escape anything so far sent after her. From horizon to being under her guns she was twenty-six minutes. She came down on us at the rate of 28 knots. They *say* she can do 30—despite her months in commission and consequent fouling.

" She has captured, up to October 24th, sixteen British cargo steamers, having sunk all but three. *Vandyck* was number seventeen—October 26th.

" The weather was good during our cruise about the Equator—fortunately so, as the old *Asuncion* was flying light, very little coal, no ballast excepting some hardwood beams (for gun mounting) on the main deck just where they would do the most damage in case of bad weather. As much as was possible we were kept in ignorance of our ship's position, probable port of landing and date of same, until the night of October 31st, when we bore away to the westward—for Para—and finally landed there on November 2nd. Two hotels were presented for our passengers, and the good people on shore lent every assistance. It was a new lease of life to all of us. Some of the ladies collapsed when relieved of the greater strain, but finally they recovered.

" Six days more of waiting cheerfully passed, despite the great heat, and on November 8th, the Brazilian steamer *San Paulo* took on board all of the ladies and chilren (excepting four couples who chose to remain for the next boat), together with the men to the extent of fifty more than the *San Paulo's* passenger certificate as arranged officially. The men continued to sleep on the deck and in the passages.

" We arrived New York, November 19th, and were thankful. S.s. *Byron* and s.s. *Sceptre* bring on remainder of

CH. III] HOW "ROYAL SCEPTRE" WAS SAVED 169

our passengers, crews, and third class—all of whom were comfortably cared for in the meantime.

"A tribute is certainly due to our English officers and crew of the *Vandyck*, also to the owners, Lamport & Holt, who, although there was no legal obligation whatever to do so, paid our ordinary hotel expenses at Para and our passage to New York."

Before she was at length forced to abandon her career, the KARLSRUHE came across the steamer *Royal Sceptre* (3,888 tons) on passage from Santos, Brazil, to New York, with a cargo of coffee valued at £230,000. The master (Mr. W. H. Estill) was successful in saving not only the ship, but the cargo. He was proceeding on his course on the night of October 27th when, under the light of the moon, a four-funnelled warship, accompanied by three steamers, was noticed. They appeared to be stopped and showed no lights. "I suspected," the master afterwards stated, "that the former was a German vessel; but thinking any attempt on my part to elude it was only the more likely to cause suspicion, I decided to keep on my course. On getting closer, my suspicions were confirmed, and when abeam of her at 11.30 p.m. I was ordered to stop. An officer and an armed guard were put on board, the former informing me I was stopped by the German cruiser KARLSRUHE." And then the master gave particulars of how he outwitted the enemy: "Previous to this, I must state, I had taken the precaution to hide my seventy-five Bills of Lading and other papers relating to the cargo, relying for examination on my Brazilian clearance, Brazilian and American Bills of Health, detailed manifest of cargo for Customs New York Register, and Articles. Seeing that 60,025 bags of coffee were via New York in transit for Toronto, Canada, and were specified to this effect on Bills of Lading, I felt sure it would be disastrous to the ship if they were seen by the Germans; hence my reason for this action. On being asked by the officer for my papers, etc., I produced the aforementioned, and after replying to the numerous questions *re* cargo, etc., in a way I thought suitable for the occasion, and, if not altogether truthful, quite in order considering the serious position I was in, he appeared satisfied that the cargo was for New York only, and eventually conveyed the necessary information to the captain of the KARLSRUHE. At 12.30 a.m. on October 28th, I was informed I could proceed, and at once ran full speed ahead again, thinking I was very lucky, which was the last remark the officer made as he left me."

The cruiser was fortunate in intercepting a number of large coal cargoes, and the captain obtained, in all, nearly 20,000 tons of coal from his prizes. Similarly, from all the ships which were intercepted, stores, foodstuffs, and wines were abstracted in order to replenish the cruiser's supplies, as well as any plate or crockery which took the fancy of the boarding-parties. The Germans, as has been indicated, treated the captured crews generally with courtesy, and returned to the merchant officers all their private property, including their revolvers and guns.

Before passing on to describe the memorable exploits of the German cruiser EMDEN, some reference must be made to another corsair, the armed merchant cruiser KRONPRINZ WILHELM. On the outbreak of war the Norddeutscher liner KRONPRINZ WILHELM was one of the large German ships in New York Harbour which caused the Admiralty a good deal of anxiety in view of the reports that they were being armed and might put to sea at any moment. These rumours had various sources, and they seemed to fit in with the theories which had inspired Germany's action at The Hague Conference, and later on at the Naval Conference at London. The KRONPRINZ WILHELM, however, was the only one of the enemy ships which got to sea from New York, and she broke out on the eve of the British declaration of war, before the American authorities had perfected their arrangements for watching enemy shipping. This liner, indeed, left as though she had no belligerent purpose. All doubts, however, as to her mission were set at rest on August 6th, when Rear-Admiral Christopher Cradock, with his flag in the cruiser SUFFOLK, came upon the KRONPRINZ WILHELM, about 120 miles north-east of Watling Island, in the West Indies, in company with the cruiser KARLSRUHE. Guns and guns' crews were being transferred when the SUFFOLK, in company with the light cruiser BRISTOL, appeared. The KRONPRINZ WILHELM made off in one direction, and her consort in the other. The British Admiral had to make choice of his quarry, and he selected the man-of-war, sending the BRISTOL on ahead at full speed, and at the same time calling up by wireless the armoured cruiser BERWICK. Neither of the British ships equalled the speed of the German cruiser, which was consequently able to elude capture, though she nearly fell to the BERWICK, as subsequently appeared. The KRONPRINZ WILHELM seems then to have coaled from the *Walhalla* off the Azores, and on September 19th took her first prize—the s.s. *Indian Prince* (2,846 tons). The capture took place 210 miles east of Pernambuco, indicating that the liner was operating in the same waters as the KARLSRUHE. The *Indian Prince* left the port of Bahia, Brazil, on September 2nd, for New York. On the evening of September 4th, when the *Indian Prince* was well off the usual trade route, in accordance with Admiralty instructions, the KRONPRINZ WILHELM was sighted. No resistance to capture was made, the British vessel steaming ahead of the German auxiliary cruiser throughout the night. The following day two German naval officers boarded the *Indian Prince* and took away with them her papers, as well as all charts, chronometers, binoculars, rockets, blue lights, and the British Ensign. In accordance with orders from the KRONPRINZ WILHELM, the British vessel steered on various courses until September 8th, when she was directed to stop in mid-ocean and the German auxiliary cruiser came alongside. An officer, accompanied by an armed guard, proceeded on board, and handed the master (Mr. J. R. Gray) a notification in German, accompanied by an English translation, as follows:

" I hereby give you the official proclamation:
" 1. Your ship is hostile.
" 2. The cargo of your ship are hostile goods.
" 3. You must immediately go with all your crew on board of the auxiliary. Personal goods may be taken along.
" 4. Resistance will result compulsion (*sic*).
"(*Signed*) THIERFELDER,
"*Lieutenant Commander.*"

The crew, passengers, and effects having been transferred to the KRONPRINZ WILHELM, the work of looting the ship was begun, and continued throughout the night, all the stores and coal being transferred to the KRONPRINZ WILHELM. Finally the British vessel was sunk.

More than a month elapsed before this German auxiliary cruiser captured another British vessel. The s.s. *La Correntina* (8,529 tons), the Vice-Consul at La Plata having stated that no local danger had been reported, was on her way to Liverpool with a cargo of frozen meat weighing 3,500 tons, the property of the British military authorities, when the KRONPRINZ WILHELM was sighted early on the morning of October 7th. "I then kept the ship away to the eastward," the master (Mr. A. Murrison) subsequently recorded, "to see if the vessel would follow. He still kept end on and appeared to be steaming slowly towards us, allowing us to pass. Consequently I took him to be a British or French auxiliary cruiser. But when well astern on our port quarter he came rushing on at full speed and, when half a mile off, he opened out his starboard side, and at the same time signalled to us to stop instantly. He also hoisted his ensign, and then we found he was a German. I complied and stopped our ship, and he came alongside our port side (about fifty yards), and I then found that he had about 200 men with rifles, and other men stationed at two 12-pounders on his forecastle head, covering our ship fore and aft." The wireless operator of the *La Correntina* sent out a signal for help, but no reply was received. The ship was subsequently ordered to be abandoned, the passengers and crew being transferred, with their personal belongings, to the KRONPRINZ WILHELM, as the ship, so it was stated, would be sunk in an hour. However, they did not sink her as threatened. "In the meantime the cruiser backed astern and came up on our starboard side, smashing our boats and davits and bridge deck, and her men swarmed on board and took charge of the bridge, engine-room, and the ship generally. Then a gangway was put out between the vessels, and passengers and crew and their baggage were transferred to the cruiser, after which the ships parted and steamed away to the eastward in company."[1] The British vessel was sunk on

[1] The crew and passengers of *La Correntina* were transferred about a week later to the supply ship *Sierra Cordoba*, which met the KRONPRINZ WILHELM at a rendezvous with a quantity of coal, but it was not until November 9th that the two vessels parted company, the *Sierra Cordoba* eventually landing her British passengers at Montevideo on the 22nd.

October 14th, after being stripped of all the stores and a good deal of coal, besides some deck gear, provisions, and guns.

This vessel was one of the ships embraced in the Admiralty scheme of defensive armament. When she left Liverpool on her voyage to La Plata, she mounted two 4·7-inch guns aft, and was provided with complete gun crews; but, having sailed before the outbreak of war, she had no ammunition on board. This was an unfortunate circumstance, as the KRONPRINZ WILHELM had only a light armament. In his report the master stated that, "owing to the suddenness of the attack, the two 4·7-inch guns fell into the enemy's hands complete, as we had no time to disable them." A bag of dispatches from the British Legation was, however, weighted and thrown overboard in accordance with instructions received from the Consul-General of Buenos Ayres. After the British ship had been sunk, the KRONPRINZ WILHELM steamed north-westward, making for Cape Frio, off which she arrived about midnight on October 16th. She was apparently on the lookout for another vessel. From statements made by the captain of the s.s. *Niceto de Larranaga*, the suspicion was strengthened that the German ships operating in the neighbourhood of Pernambuco were kept closely informed of the names of steamers traversing the American and English tracks to and from the River Plate, learning their dates of departure as well as the character of their cargoes. The enemy, it was alleged, was aware that the s.s. *La Correntina* had no ammunition on board.[1]

The KRONPRINZ WILHELM did not capture another British ship until December 4th. She then met the *Bellevue* (3,814 tons). This vessel was well laden with a coal and general cargo, and was on her way from Glasgow to Montevideo. The *Bellevue* (master, Mr. Iver Iversen) was about forty-six miles east-north-east of Pernambuco when the German merchant cruiser overtook her at full speed in the early morning. The usual routine was followed, the crew was transferred

---

[1] On August 4th, as soon as war was declared, Messrs. Houlder Bros., the owners of the *La Correntina* and other ships of the same line, wrote to the Admiralty suggesting that the ammunition for *La Correntina* should be sent to Buenos Ayres by their *La Roserina*, leaving Liverpool on August 8th and due at Buenos Ayres on August 30th. This arrangement was approved, but the ammunition on board the *La Roserina* was unshipped in the belief that she would not reach the Plate before the sailing of the *La Correntina*.

to the KRONPRINZ WILHELM, and the British ship, navigated by a prize crew, was taken to the westward, when the work of transhipping the cargo and stores to the cruiser was begun. This operation lasted from December 8th to 20th, when the *Bellevue* was sunk. In this case, the ship had been kept well off the usual trade route, and the master was complimented by the Admiralty on the manner in which he had conformed to Admiralty instructions. The KRONPRINZ WILHELM rounded off the month with another capture not far from the scene of her meeting with the *Bellevue*. The *Hemisphere* (3,486 tons; master, Mr. Richard Jones) was on passage from Hull to Buenos Ayres with coal when the KRONPRINZ WILHELM headed for her on the 28th. After the capture had been effected, both vessels steamed away to the eastward until early in the morning of December 30th, when the *Hemisphere* was brought alongside the cruiser and her cargo, stores, and most useful fittings were taken on board the KRONPRINZ WILHELM. In this case, as in others, the master and crew were called upon to sign a declaration undertaking not to take up arms against the German Empire during the war. The German vessel was joined by her tender, the s.s. *Holger*, to which the *Hemisphere's* officers and men were transferred, after which the KRONPRINZ WILHELM steamed away to the northward.

About this time the Royal Mail Steamship Company's s.s. *Potaro* (4,419 tons), which had left Liverpool in ballast on December 25th, was on her way to Montevideo. Half an hour after midnight on January 10th, she sighted, at a distance of about three miles, a large steamer, which turned out to be the KRONPRINZ WILHELM. The British master's attempt to escape failed, and after an hour's chase the *Potaro* was captured. A call for help was sent out three times during the pursuit, but the wireless operator of the German ship jambed all messages. A prize crew having been placed on board, the two vessels proceeded in a south-easterly direction, and the same afternoon the master and crew were transferred to the KRONPRINZ WILHELM. The *Potaro* then steamed away, and according to the master (Mr. Henry J. Bennett) was not seen again till January 19th. Then she appeared with everything painted man-of-war colour and with extra aerials aloft. In the meantime the

German ship had secured two more prizes—the s.s. *Highland Brae* (7,634 tons; master, Mr. R. R. Pond), which was on passage from Gravesend to Buenos Ayres, and the sailing-ship *Wilfrid M.* (258 tons; master, Mr. C. W. Parks), proceeding to Bahia from St. John's, Newfoundland. The former ship was taken by surprise. She was well off the usual track, in obedience to Admiralty instructions, when the KRONPRINZ WILHELM appeared " keeping end on and enveloped in smoke, so that we were unable to distinguish whether she was British or German until within half or three-quarters of a mile off, when she hoisted the German ensign, fired a gun, and signalled to us to stop." Subsequently a prize crew was put on board, and the two steamers proceeded in company until the *Wilfrid M.* was sighted. The captain of the German ship could not resist the temptation to intercept this vessel, small as she was, but later on he probably regretted his decision. She was carrying a cargo of dried fish. The gunners of the German ship had already proved, by demonstration, their inefficiency, and there was a shortage of ammunition. At any rate, it was decided to ram the small wooden vessel. Probably the subsequent course of events constitutes one of the most curious incidents in this war. After the crew had been taken on board, the great German liner proceeded to ram the *Wilfrid M.* Four times in succession the bow of the KRONPRINZ WILHELM was driven into the little ship, and even then she was not sunk. At the end of April 1915, the General Registrar of Shipping at Grenada reported to the Board of Trade that "a large portion of a derelict ship was seen drifting off the south coast of the Island of Carriacou, a dependency of the Government of this island, which finally settled off the reef of Dumfries Bay, about 600 yards from shore." On examination it was found to be the remains of the *Wilfrid M.*, which the German liner, in spite of all her efforts, had failed to sink.

During the rest of January the Germans were busy looting the *Highland Brae*, and afterwards the *Potaro* was dealt with in the same way. Early in February the four-masted Norwegian barque *Semantha*, carrying grain from Portland, Oregon, to Falmouth or Queenstown for orders, was captured and afterwards sunk, the crew having been transferred to the German vessel. In this instance again the gunners of the KRONPRINZ WILHELM showed a lack of practice, since, of the thirteen shots which were fired at the barque, only one took effect. The looting of the *Potaro* was then resumed, and on February 12th the tender *Holger* was brought alongside; a high sea was running, and the two ships bumped heavily as the transfer of passengers took place. The transhipment proved a dangerous task, but was at last completed, and then the *Holger* parted company, landing her passengers, on February 18th, at Buenos Ayres, where she was interned.

The KRONPRINZ WILHELM met with no further success until February 22nd, when the British s.s. *Chasehill* (4,583 tons) was intercepted on her passage from Newport News to Zarate, La Plata, with coal. The master (Mr. R. H. Kidd) and the crew were transferred to the KRONPRINZ WILHELM, and a prize crew was put on board the *Chasehill*. The German vessel then took out of the British ship practically all the coal. On March 9th the crew were retransferred to the *Chasehill*, together with the crew and passengers of the French mail steamer *Guadaloupe*, which the KRONPRINZ WILHELM had captured some days before, to find that their ship had been much damaged during the process of transhipping the coal. The *Chasehill*, with her French passengers and seamen, reached Pernambuco early on the morning of March 12th.

It appeared later on that the KRONPRINZ WILHELM, though she had obtained considerable quantities of coal and general stores which would have enabled her to seek fresh scenes of activity, still continued her depredations on the trade route which had already proved so fruitful. On March 24th, the Royal Mail Steam Packet Company's s.s. *Tamar* (3,207 tons), with a large cargo of coffee, from Santos to Havre, was captured. On sailing, the master (Mr. F. S. Hannan) was warned to stand to the eastward, and was attempting to avoid danger when he was overhauled by the German raider. As usual, the British crew were transferred, and then the *Tamar* was sunk by gunfire. A declaration of neutrality during the war was required from the crew and passengers. The KRONPRINZ WILHELM then resumed her course, and on the 27th fell in with the British s.s. *Coleby* (3,824 tons), which was bound from Rosario with a cargo of wheat. By this time, according to the master of the *Tamar*, the KRONPRINZ WILHELM showed signs of damage through having several vessels lashed alongside of her, and practically every plate on the port side was standing out throughout her length. In this case also the capture was due to mischance, as the master of the *Coleby* (Mr. William Crighton) was well off the usual track. With the sinking of this vessel the active career of the KRONPRINZ WILHELM came to an end. Her captain, in view of her condition, including shortage of coal and stores, decided to abandon his depredations. The cruiser cast anchor in Hampden Roads on April 11th, after a cruise covering a period of over eight months. A fortnight later she was interned at Newport News.[1]

The only other German liner which engaged in commerce-destruction was the PRINZ EITEL FRIEDRICH, which got out of Tsingtau on the outbreak of war, and finally reached Newport News, Virginia, on March 11th, 1915, after a cruise of seven months, during which she sank five British merchant ships, and in addition excited American public opinion by destroying the United States' *William P. Frye*. The PRINZ EITEL FRIEDRICH was homeward bound at the end of July when she was recalled to Tsingtau, and, mails and passengers having been disembarked, she was filled up with coal, armed with guns taken from the gunboats LUCHS and TIGER, repainted, and sent to sea, proceeding to the Mariana Islands, where she joined the SCHARNHORST, GNEISENAU, and other German men-of-war. Her subsequent career was, in the main, disappointing to the Germans. She joined von Spee at the Marshall Islands, and was detached by him in company with the CORMORAN (ex RIASAN), a Russian capture made by the EMDEN and armed at Tsingtau, for commerce-destruction. After an unsuccessful cruise she went to look for coal among the German Pacific Islands, and finally obtained some at Malekula (Pelew Islands). Then she rejoined von Spee off Valparaiso, but parted from him before the Falklands action. Though she had chased the British s.s. *Colusa* on November 1st, it was not until December 5th that the PRINZ EITEL FRIEDRICH made her first capture.

[1] In order to enable a good lookout to be kept, the captain of the KRONPRINZ WILHELM had a barrel lashed to the mast about 200 feet above sea-level, and later on another barrel was lashed to the mainmast, and thus a double lookout was kept by men provided with powerful glasses. According to the master of the *Bellevue*, an officer of the KRONPRINZ WILHELM stated that British cruisers had been seen on several occasions, but the German corsair had not been observed by them, and had had time to run away.

She was cruising about seventy miles south of Valparaiso, in a fog, when she came upon the British s.s. *Charcas* (5,067 tons), steaming from Corral to Guayacan, Chile, en route to New York, with a small load of nitrate of soda. The master (Mr. A. C. Norris) was hugging the shore as closely as possible when the PRINZ EITEL FRIEDRICH intercepted her, following the same routine as in the case of the other raiders. On December 12th the German ship fell in with the sailing-vessel *Kildalton*, on passage from Liverpool to Callao. Before the ship was sunk, the master (Mr. W. Sharp) and crew were taken on board the cruiser and eventually landed at Easter Island. There they remained marooned from the last day of the year which had seen the outbreak of the war till February 26th, when they were taken off by a Swedish steamer and landed at Panama on March 12th.

Exactly two months elapsed before the PRINZ EITEL FRIEDRICH had another success, and again her capture was a small ship—the s.v. *Invercoe* (1,421 tons), which was carrying wheat from Portland, Oregon, to a British port. This proved an easy capture, and after the master (Mr. Wm. J. King) and crew had been transferred, she was sunk. Less than a week later the PRINZ EITEL FRIEDRICH had better fortune. When off Pernambuco, in the area in which the KARLSRUHE and the KRONPRINZ WILHELM had operated with such effect, she fell in with the s.s. *Mary Ada Short* (3,605 tons; master, Mr. A. E. Dobbing) on February 18th. This ship, loaded with maize, was proceeding from Rosario and St. Nicholas (St. Vincent) for orders, when the PRINZ EITEL FRIEDRICH was sighted. After provisions had been removed, a dynamite charge was placed in the engine-room, and, as this proved ineffective, two shots were fired into the hull, and the vessel then disappeared. Two days later it was the ill-fortune of the s.s. *Willerby* (3,630 tons) to be encountered by the German merchant cruiser while proceeding from Marseilles to Buenos Ayres in water ballast. All went well until February 20th, when the master (Mr. J. Wedgwood) was ordered by the PRINZ EITEL FRIEDRICH to stop. He ignored the signal, but three-quarters of an hour later was overhauled. On March 11th, the PRINZ EITEL FRIEDRICH, whose cruise had been barren since the capture of the *Willerby*, put into Newport News for repairs. On arrival the captain found he had gravely prejudiced himself in the eyes of the American public by sinking the American s.s. *William P. Frye*, which had on board wheat consigned to a British port. The story of the destruction of this ship, though she was not of British nationality, is of such historical importance from many points of view that it may be of interest to give the statement made by her captain (Mr. H. H. Kiehne) after he had been landed by the PRINZ EITEL FRIEDRICH at Newport News.

On January 27th he was approached by the PRINZ EITEL FRIEDRICH in the South Atlantic. Having made the usual inquiries, the German captain told him that he deemed his cargo contraband, and proposed to destroy it. Captain Kiehne protested, but German officers and men came on board and began to jettison the grain. The PRINZ EITEL FRIEDRICH then disappeared after another ship, and when she reappeared, to use Captain Kiehne's words, "evidently the grain was not being thrown overboard fast enough to suit the German skipper, for he sent half a hundred men aboard soon afterwards, and the work went on for hours without interruption. However, it was slow at the best, and I was informed the next morning that my ship would be sent to the bottom. It was originally the intention of the German captain to leave enough cargo in the hold of the ship for ballast. That part of the grain was to be rendered useless by salt water. As soon as I was informed that my ship was to be sent to the bottom, I and my wife, with our two boys and the crew, made for the German steamer in our own boats. We were taken on board and shown every courtesy throughout the remainder of the voyage."

Investigation after her arrival at Newport News showed that the PRINZ EITEL FRIEDRICH required new boilers, and on April 8th she was interned on the application of her captain, who handed to the collector of the port the following statement:

" I inform you that I intend to intern S.M.S. PRINZ EITEL FRIEDRICH. The relief I expected appear not to arrive in time, so number and force of enemy cruisers watching the entrance of the bay makes to me impossible the dash for the open sea with any hope of success. I have decided not to deliver the crew and the ship to fruitless and certain destruction. Being obliged for the courtesy shown by all the United States authorities, I am expecting your orders. I have sent same information to Rear-Admiral Helm, of the United States ship ALABAMA."

Another commerce-destroyer was the cruiser LEIPZIG, a vessel of small tonnage which formed one of the units under the command of Admiral von Spee. Within about six weeks of the opening of the war, the LEIPZIG made her first capture. On September 11th the s.s. *Elsinore* (6,542 tons) was on her passage from Corinto to San Luis Obispo, California, in ballast, when she was encountered by the LEIPZIG, a warning shot announcing that the stranger was a foreign cruiser. In this case the master (Mr. J. Roberts) was taken on board the German ship, and received orders to return and navigate his vessel in accordance with instructions received from the German commander. Various courses were then steered, the German s.s. *Marie* being at that time in company with the LEIPZIG. Captain Roberts made the following statement as to his experience, which indicates the course pursued by the commander of the LEIPZIG in his efforts to intercept British merchantmen:

"*September 11th.*—At 4.10 a.m. I arrived on board of my own vessel, and set the engines at full speed and course was set N. 62° E.

"5.20 a.m. I was signalled by Morse to alter my course to S. 15° E., and again at 9.25 a.m. was signalled to steer S. 45° E.; then I began to get anxious wondering when we were to leave (the ship), as I was at this time fifty miles from the land.

"At 10.10 a.m. I was signalled to make the best possible speed, and at 10.30 a.m. we sighted a cargo steamer ahead which proved to be a German ship named the *Marie*, but which at first I thought to be a poor unfortunate like myself owing to his movements, but I afterwards found out that he was only obeying orders from the LEIPZIG, and that the meeting was prearranged, and that the *Marie* was in company with the LEIPZIG, supplying her with coal and stores.

"At 11.15 a.m. I was again signalled to heave to and to

proceed on board of the *Marie*, taking sufficient stores for eight days, and they allowed us two hours to be out of the vessel, so I immediately proceeded to carry out these orders; in the meantime a number of armed officers and men from the LEIPZIG came on board and commenced ransacking the ship, taking all stores and articles which were of any use to them, and they also took our boats and hoisted them up in the davits of the *Marie*; our position at this time was 19° 31′ 00″ N., and 105° 56′ 00″ W.

"At 12.30 p.m. myself and crew boarded the *Marie*, and at 1.10 p.m. the cruiser commenced firing upon the *Elsinore* at about a mile distant; the sight was too heartbreaking for me to witness, so I kept to my room, but my officers afterwards informed me that (they) put twelve shots into her and she became ablaze, and that she sank stern first; before my vessel sank the captain of the *Marie* was ordered to go full speed on a south-easterly course; and so came the end of one of the finest oil-steamers on the Pacific Coast.

"When first taken prisoner by the Germans, the commander promised to cast me off a few miles from Cape Corrientes, which he afterwards failed to do, and I think the reason was that he was rather anxious for his own safety.

"*September 12th.*—The *Marie* proceeding on the same course S.E., and during the day the cruiser would lead ahead at about three miles distant, and by night about the same distance astern. There was an armed crew of about fourteen men placed on board the *Marie* from the cruiser to guard my men. The commander of the cruiser signalled to the officer in charge to treat my men as well as possible.

"*September 13th.*—Ordered to stop by the cruiser, when they passed several hundred coal-bags on board to be filled by my men, whom they would pay their usual rate of wages. Both ships proceeding same course and direction.

"*September 14th.*—Again stopped by cruiser, and more coal-bags passed on board to be filled by my men: ship's course the same and convoyed by the cruiser.

"*September 15th and 16th.*—Proceeding same and position of ship the same; we are steering for the Galapagos Islands.

"*September 17th.*—Sighted Galapagos Islands, 7 a.m.;

came to anchor in Tagus Cove, Atternave Island, and at 11.30 p.m. the cruiser came alongside and commenced to bunker. 7 p.m., owing to cove being so small, the cruiser cast off and went to a safer anchorage. Previous to her going away the commander sent for me to come on board ; he then told me that he would faithfully land us all safe at Callao, and how sorry he felt for me in such a position, and, being a sailor himself, he was sorry that he had been obliged to destroy such a fine ship. Then I informed him that I had a bag of mail on board from the American cruiser DENVER for San Francisco, which he promised he would safely deliver.

"*September* 18*th*.—The cruiser came alongside at 6 a.m., and again commenced to bunker, and at 9 a.m. completed 500 tons. At 11.30 a.m. both ships got under weigh and proceeded out of the cove at full speed, and course was set south.

"*September* 19*th*.—Came to anchor off Hood Island, Galapagos, at 8.30 a.m., and the cruiser left and proceeded for Chatham Island for fresh provisions, which I still believe was not necessary, as he had more important business in view.

"*September* 20*th*.—Ship still at anchor off Hood Island, and at 6 p.m. I am positive I saw two distinct smokes from steamers in the direction of Chatham Island, and this proved to be correct, as the cruiser had another steamer awaiting with her stores, etc., and equipped with wireless.

"At 6 p.m. the cruiser returned and anchored close to, and signalled that the commander would send his boat to take me on board, as he wished to speak to me. On arrival on board of the cruiser, he informed me that, owing to information he had received, he was unable to fulfil his promise to land me at Callao, but he had made arrangements at Chatham Island for our board, etc., and that after fourteen days a vessel would take us off for Guayaquil, and I was to prepare to leave at 8.30 the following morning. The commander now seemed to be working in some mysterious way as if he were anxious to get clear of us. He invited me to take dinner with him, but I was obliged to refuse, owing to being so depressed to find the precarious position that Fate had placed both my crew and myself in, so I came back on board and called my officers together and told them the exact words the commander of the

LEIPZIG had said; and when the crew were informed they became very dissatisfied, which caused the cruiser's people to double up the armed guard, but, however, the night passed quietly.

"*September* 21*st*.—At 3 a.m. both ships got under way and proceeded towards Chatham Island, and at 7 a.m. came to anchor in the roadstead.

"At 8 a.m. we all embarked in the cruiser's boats with our remaining effects and small amount of provisions, and at 9 a.m. we landed on Chatham Island, with only two houses in sight and a large store shed, in which place the crew were lodged. (This island belongs to Ecuador, and is used as a convict station.)

"I arranged for two officers to remain with the crew to keep order, and taking the chief officer, chief signaller, and second engineer, we rode on horseback to the settlement six miles inland (a sugar and coffee plantation), and even here we fared very badly with regard to food and beds; but the crew fared very bad, as the provisions were very scarce and had to be carefully rationed.

"*September* 22*nd*.—This day passed away after many troubles regarding sleeping accommodation, etc., but my crew seemed to be getting very dissatisfied, though up to the present they had borne the hardships bravely.

"*September* 24*th*.—To-day I made arrangements with the Governor of the Island, a Mr. Araz, to take me and half of the crew to Ecuador, as this was the only means of getting into communication and reporting the loss of my ship; and he arranged to send us away in a small sloop of fifty tons, the distance to Guayaquil being about 670 miles, so he provisioned her accordingly, she being about half loaded with a cargo of dried fish and hides, and ordinarily would not have sailed for another ten days.

"The commander of the LEIPZIG's intention was to detain me on the island as long as possible, so as to prevent me communicating with the authorities and spoiling his chances of sinking merchant vessels, for when the Governor of the island offered to assist me, one of the German officers remaining on the island strongly objected; but the Governor insisted on our leaving owing to the scarcity of food, there not being sufficient to keep all the men for any length of time, and also owing to his good feeling towards us.

"So, after some considerable trouble, I picked out half of the crew that was to accompany me on what turned out to be one of the most monotonous and hardest five days at sea I ever experienced. The accommodation for the crew was in the hold, where they slept on the hides and dried fish, and the smell at times was something terrible.

"So at 3 p.m., after saying good-bye to the remaining crew, we boarded our small craft, lifted anchor and set sail for Guayaquil. I may mention that this is the most isolated and unfrequented stretch of water in the world.

"Mr. Araz, the Governor, accompanied us, and we occupied the cabin together, and he was most kind and considerate to us all right through the trip and did all possible for our comfort.

"*October 1st.*—This day we arrived at Guayaquil, after a most eventful trip in many ways; the total number of persons on board the small craft was twenty-nine, so our comfort and living can be better imagined than described."[1]

As soon as the *Elsinore* had been dispatched, the LEIPZIG again got to work, and in the Gulf of Guayaquil, on September 25th, she met the s.s. *Bankfields* (3,763 tons; master, Mr. John Ingham) just out of Eten bound for a British port with a cargo of sugar and copper ore. Rumours had already reached Callao that a German cruiser was off the Peruvian coast, but the warning, which was immediately issued, did not reach Eten until some hours after the *Bankfields* had left, the official telegram being delayed in transit. Thus it happened that this fine British ship fell an easy prey to the LEIPZIG, by whom she was forthwith sunk. The rather unprofitable career of the LEIPZIG was next varied by the capture of the sailing-vessel *Drummuir* (1,844 tons), on December 2nd, when off Staten Island near Cape Horn. She was carrying a cargo of anthracite coal, which was too valuable to be sunk, so she was taken to the east side of Picton Island, about one mile from the shore.

---

[1] The remainder of the crew of the *Elsinore* left Chatham Island a few days after the departure of the master; they were conveyed to Panama in the s.s. *Ecuador*, and proceeded thence to Colon, arriving in London on November 25th by the Royal Mail Steam Packet Company's *Danube*.

The coal transports *Baden* and *Santa Isabel*, which were in attendance upon the German cruiser, were placed one on each side of the *Drummuir*, and the cargo of coal was discharged. The ship was then ransacked for food, stores, and other things which might be of use to the Germans, and was sunk four days after her seizure, the master (Mr. J. C. Eagles) and crew having in the meantime been transferred to the Norddeutscher Lloyd s.s. *Seydlitz*, which was in company with the LEIPZIG. The capture had been effected on the very eve of what was to prove one of the most decisive events of the war by sea, for two days after the *Drummuir* was sunk the battle of the Falkland Islands occurred, the LEIPZIG sharing the fate of all the other ships under Admiral von Spee's flag, except the DRESDEN, which, as has already been noted, came to her end early in the following year. The *Baden* and *Santa Isabel* were sunk by the cruiser BRISTOL, but the *Seydlitz* managed to escape, and on December 18th she arrived with British seamen at San Antonio, Patagonia. According to the master of the *Drummuir*, the loss of that vessel prevented the Germans capturing the Falkland Islands, as the days which were occupied in looting the ship gave Admiral Sturdee time to reach the islands. " I understand," the captain declared in a subsequent statement, " that there were men armed ready to occupy the islands as soon as they had been taken by the fleet, and if this is the case, the loss of the *Drummuir* was a providential act."

CHAPTER IV

THE EXPLOITS OF THE "EMDEN"

THE story of the raids on British shipping by the German cruiser EMDEN still remains to be told. It is perhaps an advantage that the experiences of merchant seamen at the hands of other enemy vessels should have already been described. A standard had thus been afforded by which the ingenuity, resourcefulness, and humanity of Captain von Müller of the EMDEN can be measured. When brief particulars of his exploits were first published in England, there was a tendency to regard this German naval officer's consideration towards the passengers and crews of captured merchant ships as quite exceptional. The legend also grew up that the EMDEN alone among the German ships had succeeded in carrying on commerce-destruction with any considerable degree of success. In the light of the fuller revelation of the operations of German men-of-war and converted merchantmen, we are able to correct the somewhat exaggerated estimate which was formed by contemporary British opinion of the resource and seamanship of Captain von Müller. He did better than his compeers, but will hold no such place in the history of this war as was accorded to Captain Semmes in the American Civil War, and to Captain Paul Jones in the War of Independence.

Captain von Müller struck where he could produce the maximum effects, political and commercial, though he profited by an element of luck. Moreover, he, like the officers who commanded other German men-of-war during the period when attack was being made on British merchant shipping by surface ships, besmirched his reputation with no act contrary to the principles of the brotherhood of the sea, or opposed to the dictates of human-

… IN THE BAY OF BENGAL …

ity. The day was to come when German naval officers and men were to earn the contempt of other seamen owing to the callousness and inhumanity which many of them exhibited. During the opening phase of the war the world welcomed many indications of an intention, so far as naval hostilities were concerned, to fulfil the undertakings which Germany's representatives had given at The Hague and at London, when the rules governing the conduct of war were discussed.

In the course of her career, the EMDEN captured and sank fifteen merchant ships, the same number as the KARLSRUHE: she overhauled seven other vessels, of which one escaped, two were captured and utilised, and the other four were released. The story of the EMDEN's operations, therefore, resolves itself into the narrative of the experiences of the officers and men of twenty-two British merchant ships. From the time when the cruiser, on the eve of the war, was reported to be at Tsingtau until she appeared dramatically in the Bay of Bengal, little or no authentic information had reached the British Admiralty as to her whereabouts. The war had run its course for a period of over a month before the Indian Government was suddenly forced to admit that it was confronted with a situation which had not been foreseen, and against which no adequate precautions had been taken. Reviewing the depredations of the EMDEN in the light of the subsequent attack on ocean-borne commerce as waged by the enemy, and the heavy losses inflicted, the widespread irritation which she occasioned both in the Eastern and Western world is notable. The first full and authentic news of the character of the EMDEN's operations in the Bay of Bengal to reach England was a message to the *Morning Post* of September 19th. The Colombo correspondent of that journal related an interview which he had had with a passenger in the s.s. *Diplomat* (7,615 tons), which had sailed from that port on the previous Friday. Squally weather had been experienced in the Bay of Bengal for some weeks before the EMDEN appeared, and that condition contributed to the enemy's success. " From the morning when we left the Sand Heads and dropped our pilot until the moment when, eighteen hours later, the EMDEN captured us by Puri, there were intermittent rain showers, when it was impossible to see fifty yards ahead. On the Saturday night we never troubled to extinguish lights, so confident were we, although we subsequently learnt that three British ships—the *Indus, Lovat,* and *Killin*—had already been sunk." Continuing his narrative, this passenger stated that: " About noon on Sunday we saw ahead a group of four vessels, in the centre of which was a warship, which the first officer on our bridge supposed to be British, with convoys. The manner in which the supposed convoys were lying raised our suspicions, however, and these were subsequently confirmed by the sight of the Prussian Eagle on the EMDEN's bows, and the shell which whistled across our bows. An officer, late of the Hamburg-Amerika Line, who was serving his two months' annual reserve training when war broke out, was deputed to board us. The boat's crew carried Mausers and side-arms. The first act was to hoist the German flag in the *Diplomat,* and the next to smash our wireless. Otherwise every courtesy was shown, and we were allowed to take our personal effects on board the previously-captured *Kabinga,* which subsequently brought us back. The EMDEN was in a dreadfully dirty condition, having been seven weeks at sea without touching port."

Some time elapsed before it was possible to piece together the story of the EMDEN's attack upon British shipping in the Bay of Bengal. An account of her experiences, the general accuracy of which was subsequently confirmed, was obtained later on from the diary of a German petty officer of the EMDEN who became a prisoner of war. The EMDEN was ordered to prepare for war on July 28th; she was then lying at Tsingtau. Thirty-six hours later, in the evening, she put to sea with all lights out. The early days of August, when the German cruiser was moving in Japanese waters, were comparatively uneventful. The only variation of the monotony was the capture of the Russian volunteer ship RIASAN,[1] which, being without guns or ammunition, became an easy prize, and was taken back to Tsingtau. War with England having been declared, the EMDEN again put to sea, on the evening of August 6th, in company with the collier *Markomannia,* loaded with 6,000 tons of coal and 1,000 tons of provisions. Evening was chosen as the time for departure,

[1] Renamed CORMORAN and utilised. See p. 177.

and the ships showed no lights as they crept out of the harbour. During subsequent days the EMDEN was intent upon avoiding the British China Squadron, and passage was made into the Bay of Bengal by a circuitous route, so as to cut across the network of converging trade routes. The Indian port authorities had no suspicion of the danger which threatened shipping, and consequently British vessels in those waters received no special warning, and proceeded on their voyages in a false sense of security. Captain von Müller was favoured in this, as in other respects. The first vessel he met was the Greek steamer *Pontoporos*, which was on her way from Calcutta to Karachi with a cargo of Bengal coal. The ship was retained, and shortly afterwards the British steamer *Indus* (3,893 tons; master, Mr. H. S. Smaridge) hove in sight. She had left Calcutta on September 7th for Bombay, in ballast, and was three days out when a man-of-war was sighted. Captain Smaridge, convinced that she was of British nationality, made no attempt to escape until it was too late, and thus he fell an unresisting victim to the enemy, who dismantled the wireless, transhipped several cases of soap, put the crew on board the *Markomannia*, and then sank the ship, after firing ten shots. On the following afternoon the EMDEN had a further success in similar circumstances. The *Lovat* (6,102 tons) had left Calcutta for Bombay two days after the *Indus*. She had, like the *Indus*, been fitted up as a transport. Late in the afternoon the man-of-war, accompanied by two steamers, was sighted, and the master of the *Lovat* (Mr. Robert Clegg) also assumed that the stranger was British, and that the two steamers formed part of a convoy which he should join. Unsuspectingly, therefore, he continued on his course. As the unknown cruiser drew in, however, the German ensign was run up, a signal to stop was broken, and a blank shot fired across the bows of the *Lovat*. Within a short time the crew had been transferred to the *Markomannia*, with the exception of six Indian firemen, who were sent to the *Pontoporos*, and the *Lovat* was sunk by gunfire.

The EMDEN then resumed her cruise. She steamed in the centre, with the *Markomannia* on one side and the *Pontoporos* on the other at a considerable distance, but within signalling range. Captain von Müller was convinced that he was in a good position for reaping a rich harvest, and his judgment was confirmed on the following night—September 12th—when he captured the *Kabinga* (4,657 tons). This ship had left Calcutta for Colombo the previous day, and was almost on the usual track, steering a south-south-westerly course from the Sand Heads with lights burning, when at 11 o'clock the EMDEN appeared. At the time the *Kabinga* put to sea there was still no suspicion at Calcutta of the EMDEN's presence in the Bay of Bengal, so her captain had no idea that he was running any particular danger. Suddenly the flash of gunfire pierced the darkness and a cruiser was observed on the port quarter, signalling to the merchantman to stop instantly and not to use her wireless. Shortly afterwards a boarding-party reached the *Kabinga*, her wireless installation was damaged, and orders were given to the officers and men to leave the ship in two hours, as it was intended to sink her. The weather was bad at the time. The crew was forthwith mustered in readiness to take to the boats. The boarding officer then discovered that the captain (Mr. Thomas Robinson) had his wife and child on board. A signal was at once made to the EMDEN, and a reply received that the transfer would not be made that night in consideration of the rough sea and the hardship which the woman and child would suffer. It was, however, anticipated that the order to destroy the ship would be carried out on the following morning, but in the early hours of the morning the Glasgow steamer *Killin* (3,544 tons; master, Mr. J. K. Wilson), which was on her way from Calcutta to Colombo, loomed out of the darkness and nearly ran into the EMDEN. She was carrying 4,980 tons of Bengal coal. At the moment the EMDEN was well supplied with fuel, so the *Kabinga* was ordered to receive the *Killin's* crew on board, and the latter ship was sunk. Accompanied by her two improvised tenders and the *Kabinga*, the EMDEN cruised until noon, when the Harrison liner *Diplomat* (7,615 tons) was captured on her way from Colombo to London with a valuable consignment of tea. When she left the former port on the evening of September 12th, the master (Mr. R. J. Thompson) had seen an official message from Simla in the office of the Calcutta agent of his firm to the effect that navigation in the Bay of Bengal was reasonably safe. Captain Thompson, like other masters, appears to have accepted this assurance as a guarantee of security,

CH. IV] MISTAKEN FOR A BRITISH CRUISER

which was not the meaning it really bore. When shortly before noon on September 13th a cruiser, followed by three merchant ships, came in sight, he at once assumed that the man-of-war was British and that she was bringing in three German prizes. He was supported in this belief by a report which had reached Calcutta before he had left. He was more or less on the trade route when the EMDEN appeared on the *Diplomat's* starboard quarter, fired a warning shot, and at the same time hoisted the German ensign. On the boarding-party reaching the *Diplomat*, the officer in command informed the master that the British vessel was an hour late. The crew were permitted to collect some clothes and were then taken on board the *Kabinga*, and the *Diplomat* was sunk. The *Trabboch* (4,014 tons) was the next British ship to fall a victim to the raider. She was proceeding in ballast from Negapatam to Calcutta. At 6 p.m. on September 14th she came out of a rain squall and the chief officer reported land on the port bow, but, to his unspeakable surprise, " the land " proved to be a cruiser in company with three other ships. The master (Mr. W. H. Ross) of the *Trabboch* made the same error as other masters in thinking that he had fallen in with a British cruiser with prizes bound for Colombo. When the unrecognised man-of-war was about three-quarters of a mile distant, she fired a shot, ran up the German ensign, made a signal to stop, and the *Trabboch* was then rounded up close to the other strange ships. In this manner another success was achieved by the EMDEN, more by luck than judgment, and, the crew of the merchantman having been transferred to the *Kabinga*, which was already crowded, the *Trabboch* was sunk.

Just before this the Italian steamer *Loredano* had appeared. Captain von Müller asked the master, Captain Giacopolo, to take off all the crews now assembled on board the *Kabinga*, and stated that he was about to sink that vessel. The captain of the *Loredano* refused to comply with the request, pleading that he had insufficient room on board his ship. In the circumstances, therefore, Captain von Müller had no alternative but to release this neutral vessel, which proceeded on her voyage and, in fact, conveyed to the Indian Port authorities information of the EMDEN's activities, enabling them to take precautionary measures which resulted in the saving of a considerable

volume of tonnage from capture.¹ The captain of the
EMDEN apparently realised that he could not much longer
keep his movements secret, since it was essential that the
Kabinga, with the captured crews on board, should be
sent into a neighbouring port. He doubtless regarded any
action taken by the Italian merchant officer as of little
importance. At any rate, the crews of the *Indus* and
Lovat, who had been on board the *Markomannia*, were
transferred to the *Kabinga*, and that ship was released to
proceed to Calcutta; her captain ² was warned to " take
care when approaching Sand Heads, as the lights are
out." That caution was typical of the consideration
which Captain von Müller exhibited throughout his raiding
cruise.

Just after the *Kabinga* had been released, the EMDEN
sighted the *Clan Matheson* (4,775 tons) coming up to the
eastward. When she left Madras on September 12th,
the Bay of Bengal was still believed to be fairly safe.
Captain William Harris, in an interview with Lloyd's
agent at Rangoon, subsequently gave the following details
of the circumstances in which he was captured:

" The steamer was bound from Madras to Calcutta.
On Monday, the 14th, the third officer called me and reported that a steamer on the port beam had shown a red
flare. I went out on deck and saw a steamer on the port
beam, some distance away, with two masthead lights
showing clearly. There was a steamer on the port bow
with all lights showing, both at the masthead and on
deck. It was about four miles distant. Both vessels
were apparently heading the same course as ourselves.
About 11.30 I perceived some signals from a point on the
port quarter, but the midshipman on watch could not
read them, as they seemed to say ' Do as,' repeated again
and again. At 11.40 there was a gunshot on the port

---

¹ Captain Giacopolo, of the *Loredano*, made every effort to warn British
shipping of the danger, and he succeeded in stopping the *City of Rangoon*.
His information was passed on to other vessels, and gave sufficient warning
to prevent the *Itonus*, *Lotusmere*, and *Rajput* from falling into the enemy's
hands. This Italian captain's action also enabled the port officer at Calcutta to withdraw the pilot vessel, to extinguish the trading lights in
channels, and to warn Akyab, Chittagong, False Point, Vizagapatam,
and Cocanada.

² Captain Robinson and the wireless operator (Mr. A. Weselly) of the
Kabinga showed considerable enterprise and ingenuity in restoring the
wireless installation, enabling messages to be sent to Calcutta.

CH. IV]   THE "CLAN MATHESON'S" FATE   193

quarter, apparently aimed at the steamer. A few minutes later a second shot came from the same position. I rang 'Stand by,' and after another short interval a third gun was fired, the shot passing across the steamer's bows. A few minutes later a large three-funnelled cruiser ranged up alongside with all lights out, signalling by Morse, 'Stop at once; do not use wireless; I will send a boat.' An armed boat with three lieutenants and some fifteen or twenty men came alongside, but not until that moment did we realise that the vessel was a German cruiser. The senior officer inspected the ship's papers and signalled to the warship, thereafter announcing to me that the crew would be transferred to a German transport immediately and the ship sunk. I was informed that the crew would be allowed to take part of their effects, personal property only. The whole of the steamer's crew, with such of their effects as they wanted most, were then transferred to the s.s. *Markomannia* in the boats of the EMDEN. This was at 2 a.m. on September 15th. In the meantime dynamite charges were placed in several positions in the steamer's hold, and these were fired, and the ship not sinking sufficiently quickly for the Germans' purposes, the vessel was fired upon by the cruiser four times, their searchlight playing upon her meanwhile. Thereafter the steamer sank by the head, and finally, at 2.35 a.m., all lights went out and the vessel disappeared.

"At 4 p.m. on September 17th steamer's smoke was sighted on the eastern horizon, and the course was altered to cut her off. At 6 p.m. the cruiser stopped the Norwegian s.s. *Dovre*, and signalled the *Markomannia* to ship the *Clan Matheson's* crew, which work was started at 7.15 and finished at 8 p.m. The whole seventy men were carried in the EMDEN's boats. The *Dovre* arrived at Rangoon on the morning of September 19th."

On September 15th the EMDEN still continued her northward cruise, steaming to within forty miles of Calcutta. She then turned south-east in the direction of Rangoon. By this time the captain of the EMDEN appears to have conjectured that he might be interrupted by British cruisers. He determined, however, to carry out a dramatic *coup* intended to produce psychological effects along the Indian coast. At the entrance to Madras Harbour there were a number of oil-tanks; Captain von Müller decided to fire into them. At 9.30 on the evening of September 22nd, the cruiser therefore crept in towards the harbour, and, playing her searchlights on the tanks, fired some preliminary shots in order to get the range. The searchlights were then turned off, leaving the cruiser in darkness, and the EMDEN poured in a series of broadsides, altogether 125 shells. Within a short time the harbour was lighted up by the fierce flames of the burning oil. The British s.s. *Chupra* was among the vessels in harbour which suffered damage by gunfire. Her dramatic purpose achieved, the German cruiser then steamed away at full speed in a north-easterly direction, the forts on shore opening fire without effect. The intention of Captain von Müller was to suggest that he was proceeding towards Calcutta, but when well out of touch with land he turned south, sailing round the east coast of Ceylon. At the same time the *Pontoporos* was sent away to a rendezvous. Good fortune again attended his cruise, for the EMDEN encountered the *King Lud* (3,650 tons), on passage from Alexandria for Calcutta. The ship was on time charter, and, at Perim, Lloyd's signal-station signalled that the *King Lud* was to proceed as fast as possible to Calcutta, in order to reach that port on September 30th. Captain David Harris subsequently stated that he understood that "the road was reasonably safe." He met with no incident until he arrived off Point de Galle, Ceylon, when the EMDEN hove in sight, flying no flag, and ordered the British merchant ship to stop. The usual routine was followed, the *King Lud* being sunk after the removal of her officers and men to the German tender *Markomannia*, where, according to Captain Harris, " we were all well treated."

Off Colombo the following day (September 25th) the EMDEN saw the British steamer *Tymeric* (3,314 tons) just coming out of harbour and followed her to about forty miles west. The *Tymeric* was carrying a cargo of sugar from Java to England, with orders to call at Falmouth for orders. The master (Mr. T. T. Tulloch) was taken by surprise, as he had not anticipated trouble. He was continuing his course to Minikoi when, shortly before midnight, he saw a vessel, showing no lights, coming up on the port quarter, only two or three miles distant. The

THE "GRYFEVALE'S" ADVENTURE

stranger, which proved to be the German cruiser, drew in and then sent the familiar signal. An armed party from the EMDEN afterwards took possession of the merchantman, and Captain Tulloch was instructed to follow the EMDEN. This he refused to do, saying that his captors must navigate the ship themselves. An exchange of signals took place. The captain of the EMDEN decided to sink the *Tymeric* as soon as the officers and men had been removed to the *Markomannia*, the captain himself being taken on board the EMDEN, from whose quarter-deck he watched his ship settle down. On the following day the German cruiser met the *Gryfevale* (4,424 tons), which was proceeding from Bombay to Colombo in ballast. The *Gryfevale* had been detained in Bombay owing to reports of the presence of an enemy cruiser in the Bay of Bengal; on September 22nd, however, clearance was given as far as Colombo. The ship, therefore, put to sea on the 23rd; a good lookout was kept, and no lights were shown at night. At midday on the 26th, when about thirty-five miles to the south-east of Cape Comorin, a man-of-war was sighted, and an hour later a signal to stop was received. In these circumstances the EMDEN made another capture. Captain Steel was told that he might either follow the cruiser or have his ship sunk. He accepted the former alternative.

"We steamed out to the westward until 1 a.m.," he stated in a subsequent report to his owners, "when lights were sighted, and shortly afterwards the Admiralty-chartered collier *Buresk* was stopped.[1] This was a valuable prize for the Germans. The crew, with the exception of the captain, chief officer, chief and second engineers, steward and cook, were sent on board us, and at the same time the prisoners from the *Markomannia* were sent on board; they consisted of the crew of the *King Lud* (sunk on the 25th off Galle, Ceylon) and part of the crew of the *Tymeric* (sunk outside Colombo at midnight on the 25th), third officer, fourth engineer, and carpenter; the captain and chief engineer were prisoners on board the EMDEN, and the

[1] The *Buresk* (4,337 tons) was on passage from Barry to Hong Kong with coal. She was utilised by the captain of the EMDEN during the remainder of his cruise, and was eventually sunk on November 9th, 1914, off North Keeling Island, Cocos Islands, when the Australian cruiser SYDNEY defeated and sank the EMDEN. Such of the officers and men as had not already been landed by the Germans were rescued by the SYDNEY.

Chinese crew were transferred to the *Buresk*. It appears that the captain and chief engineer of the *Tymeric* had refused to follow the EMDEN; they were given ten minutes to get their boats out and leave the ship; the ship was sunk at once. In all other cases where the crews made no trouble, but submitted to the orders given, the crews were allowed from one to three hours to pack up their effects and leave the ship. About 4 a.m. we steamed out to the westward, the *Buresk* accompanying us. Shortly after daylight the *Ribera*[1] in ballast was stopped, the crew transferred to us, and the ship sunk by shell fire. The course was again set to the westward, it evidently being the intention to get us as far as possible from Colombo before releasing us. Before dark another vessel, which proved to be the *Foyle*,[2] from Malta to Rangoon, light, was stopped, the crew transhipped to us, and the vessel sunk. At 10 o'clock—much to my relief, you may be sure —I was told that we were free to resume our voyage. I wish here to say that I appreciate very much the courtesy shown to us by the officer in charge of the prize crew, and also the good behaviour of the men; they one and all performed their duties with every consideration for everyone on board."

Interesting sidelights on the proceedings of the EMDEN in her attacks upon commerce were afterwards furnished by a diary which was kept by the master of the *Buresk* (Mr. F. G. Taylor), in which he recounted his remarkable experiences during the period when he was compelled to accompany the EMDEN:

"*September 27th.*—1 a.m. stopped by German cruiser EMDEN; officers came aboard and told crew to go on board *Gryfevale*. 2 a.m. proceeded full speed after EMDEN; 9 a.m. sank *Ribera*, proceeded west towards Minikoi.

[1] The *Ribera* (3,500 tons; master, Mr. John Isdale) was proceeding in ballast from Glasgow to Batavia when she encountered the EMDEN, north-west of Colombo.

[2] The *Foyle* (4,147 tons) was on passage from Dunstan-on-Tyne to Colombo and Rangoon in water ballast. According to Captain W. H. Gibson, he was informed at the Admiral Superintendent's office at Malta that "the eastern route was all clear," and, calling at Port Said, he received no instructions, and sailed on September 11th "with every confidence that the route was clear, having received no information to the contrary." The normal conditions in the Arabian Sea contributed to a false sense of safety.

9 p.m. sank *Foyle*; 10 p.m. released *Gryfevale*; EMDEN proceeded south full speed, *Buresk* and *Markomannia* following.

"*September* 28*th.*—Proceeding south full speed.

"*September* 29*th.*—Arrived off group Maldive Islands; 9 a.m. EMDEN took coal from *Markomannia*; 9 p.m. stopped coaling and proceeded south.

"*September* 30*th.*—Stopped off Maldive group; *Markomannia* came alongside *Buresk* with engine-oil and water for boilers; 1 p.m. *Markomannia* went alongside EMDEN to coal; 9 p.m. *Markomannia* left EMDEN and proceeded east; EMDEN proceeded south.

"*October* 1*st.*—Steaming south to Australian route.

"*October* 2*nd.*—Steaming south; EMDEN receiving wireless that trade route from Aden to Colombo was clear for commerce.

"*October* 3*rd.*—EMDEN steering on route from Aden to Cape Lemvin, south of Chagos Islands.

"*October* 4*th.*—Steaming on route, having big gun practice in the afternoon.

"*October* 5*th.*—Steaming slow all day on trade route, first north-west and then south-west, having rifle practice, etc.; also in wireless communication with KÖNIGSBERG.

"*October* 6*th.*—Steaming zigzag on trade route.

"*October* 7*th.*—Steaming zigzag on trade route, having target practice with big guns; shooting good and quick.

"*October* 8*th.*—Still cruising on trade route.

"*October* 9*th.*—Arrived in Diego Garcia at 7 a.m.; anchored; EMDEN scrubbed bottom and painted boot topping with paint taken from *Buresk*; at 2 p.m. finished painting, came alongside *Buresk* and took coal on board; 10 p.m. stopped coaling for the night.

"*October* 10*th.*—Coaling continued; noon, completed coaling, 1,300 tons coal on board; hove up anchors and proceeded north full speed.

"*October* 11*th.*—Proceeding north full speed, fresh wind and rain.

"*October* 12*th.*—Steering north full speed, crossed the line 6 p.m. Heavy rain and strong winds.

"*October* 13*th.*—Similar conditions, still steaming north.

"*October* 14*th.*—Steaming for the north group of the

Maldives to coal; received wireless that HAMPSHIRE was 500 miles off, also cruisers DUKE OF EDINBURGH, CHATHAM, WEYMOUTH were searching for them but knew their positions; also got wireless that Antwerp had fallen and Russians driven back to Warsaw.

"*October 15th.*—Arrived in the north group of Maldives to coal at 8 a.m.; left at 4 p.m. and steered for Minikoi Light.

"*October 16th.*—Captured at 1 a.m. the *Clan Grant* [1] and dredger *Ponrabbel*,[2] also *Benmohr* [3] at 10 a.m. All sunk same day.

"*October 17th.*—Cruising round Minikoi Light.

"*October 18th.*—Noon, received wireless that steamers were steering sixty miles north of track; EMDEN proceeded north and captured *Troilus* [4] at 8 p.m., and *St. Egbert* at 9 p.m.

"*October 19th.*—1 a.m. captured *Exford*; sank *Troilus* and *Chilkana* [5] at 4 p.m.; released *St. Egbert* at 6 p.m."

Another first-hand story of the EMDEN is that of Mr. Somers Ellis, who was one of the seven passengers on

[1] The *Clan Grant* (3,948 tons; master, Mr. N. Leslie) was on the track Minikoi to Colombo when captured, shortly after midnight on October 16th. She was proceeding from Glasgow to Liverpool to Colombo with a general cargo.

[2] The dredger *Ponrabbel* (473 tons; master, Mr. E. G. Gare) left Barry Dock on August 23rd, and was captured when eighteen miles north-west of Minikoi Lighthouse.

[3] The *Benmohr* (4,806 tons) left Leith on September 4th for Yokohama. The EMDEN, showing no lights, was indistinguishable in the darkness, when the British vessel was hailed. It was not until the boarding-party had examined the ship's papers and asked a number of questions in perfect English that the identity of the raider was revealed. Captain J. B. Sarchet, in reporting his experiences, subsequently stated: "I steered the usual track from Suez to Guardafui. From there I shaped my course to pass about thirty-five miles north of Minikoi. I inquired at the British Consul, Port Said, if they had any instructions to give me; they told me 'No,' but I was to signal at Perim or Aden for instructions. I stopped at Perim in the afternoon and signalled, asking if they had any instructions to give; their reply was 'No.' I then asked if there was any war news; they also replied 'No.' My intention was to ask at Colombo or Point de Galle for instructions. In all previous voyages I have always shaped my course, after passing Guardafui, to pass five miles south of Minikoi. I calculate I was about forty miles to the north of my usual track when the *Benmohr* was captured."

[4] The *Troilus* (7,562 tons) cleared Colombo on October 17th for London with a general cargo. The master affirmed that he was carrying out the instructions received from the Intelligence Officer at Colombo when he met the EMDEN.

[5] The *Chilkana* (3,244 tons; master, Mr. L. N. Archdeacon) was making for Calcutta when she encountered the EMDEN off Minikoi and was sunk.

board the *Troilus*, and was accompanied by his wife. According to Mr. Ellis :

"Captain Long called on the Naval Intelligence Officer twice while at Colombo—the last time just before leaving —and was told that the route to Aden was clear and safe, but that, as an additional precaution, it would be well for him to go about forty miles north of the usual track by Minikoi, first passing near Cape Comorin, and then setting a course parallel to the regular route. Captain Long carried out these instructions exactly, and informed me on Sunday morning that he had sighted the light on Cape Comorin during the night, and was then about forty miles north of the direct track from Colombo to Minikoi.

"Sunday, the 18th instant, was a brilliantly clear day after rain at early morning. At about 2 p.m. Captain Long said to me that a suspicious-looking vessel was approaching from the south; and after a short time we were able to identify it as a German cruiser of the EMDEN type. A little behind her was a merchant vessel, afterwards found to be the British coal transport steamer *Buresk*. The EMDEN rapidly came on, in a direction calculated to cut us off (an officer afterwards told me that they were steaming at 19 knots), and when between one and two miles away hoisted signal flags, which we could not at once identify. We were afterwards told that they signified 'Don't use your wireless,' and then 'Stop.' The EMDEN then fired a blank shot, and the engines of the *Troilus* were promptly stopped, at about 2.40 p.m. When about a quarter of a mile away, the EMDEN lowered a boat and we were boarded by a lieutenant, a petty officer, and (I think) twelve men, including artificers, who took charge of the engine-room. I did not hear the instructions given, but a commencement was at once made to swing out six boats and lower them to the level of the upper deck, where they were left hanging from the davits and lashed to prevent swinging. This operation was carried out smartly and well. We passengers were told to prepare all our private effects for transhipment to another vessel. Towards evening the German officer in command told us that the captured collier in attendance on the EMDEN had already several crews on board, and that the accommodation was very poor, so that we might remain on the *Troilus* that night.

He said that they expected another vessel that evening with better accommodation, and that we should probably be moved to her in the morning. This officer, a Naval Reserve lieutenant, Lauterbach by name, had been for some years in command of Hamburg-Amerika coasting steamers running between Shanghai and Tientsin, and knew both Captain Long (of the s.s. *Troilus*) and myself by name.

"They obviously expected the *Troilus*, and as obviously knew the course we (and other ships) were likely to take if not on the direct run to Minikoi.

"Immediately the boarding-party had taken charge, the head of the *Troilus* was turned round to a little south of east, and we proceeded at half speed for nearly six hours (say from 2.50 to 8.50 p.m.) in nearly the same direction in company with the EMDEN and *Buresk*. At about 8.30 p.m. a light was seen on the horizon to eastward, and the *Troilus* and *Buresk* were shortly afterwards stopped (we had all lights out), while the EMDEN went forward and captured the expected vessel, the *St. Egbert*, bound (last) from Colombo for Aden and New York. We all then went about south-south-east, slow, and at about 1 a.m. next morning the British collier *Exford*,[1] outward bound with 6,000 tons Welsh coal, was captured. . . .

"At 6 a.m. on the 19th we commenced to load the boats with baggage, and at about 7 a.m. we transferred therein to the *St. Egbert*, and met with the most kind attention from her commander, Captain Barr.

"The sea was smooth, with a south-east swell, and a gangway was lowered on both boats for my wife's use. Previous to our leaving the *Troilus*, twelve Chinese firemen and a Chinese steward were sent to the *Buresk* by the German officer's orders, and twelve other firemen were afterwards sent to the *Exford*. These men were promised the same pay as before.

"At about 7.30 a.m. smoke was seen on the horizon, and the EMDEN went away to welcome the British India boat *Chilkana*, a new ship of 6,000 tons,[2] outward bound.

"We soon afterwards received her captain, twelve

---

[1] The *Exford* (4,542 tons; master, Mr. W. C. Donovan) was on passage from Cardiff to Hong Kong under Admiralty sealed orders. The vessel was presumably expected by the enemy; at any rate, her commander was greeted by name by the EMDEN's officer who boarded her.

[2] The s.s. *Chilkana* (3,244 gross tons) was sunk by gun-fire, 110 miles E.N.E. from Minikoi.

passengers (all company's employees) and crew on the *St. Egbert*, and afterwards the captains and crews of the *Buresk* and of the *Benmohr, Clan Grant*, and a Tasmanian dredger, all of whom were on the *Buresk*.

"At 10.40 a.m. (on the 19th) the EMDEN fired three shells at the water-line of the *Troilus*, all forward (I think) of the bridge. She sank very slowly, and at 1.30 the EMDEN fired another shell or two forward, and one aft; all shots were on the port side. At 2.40 p.m. the *Troilus* sank, after listing heavily and then rolling over to her port side and diving stem first. It was a most distressing sight. The B.I. steamer *Chilkana* was sunk (in half an hour after being fired on) just before sunset. At about 7 p.m. the captain of the *St. Egbert* was told to set a course for the Indian Ocean between Calicut and Tuticorin, and we reached Cochin at 6 p.m. on the 20th instant. The *Buresk* and *Exford* were kept with the EMDEN, each having about 6,000 tons of coal on board. The *St. Egbert* was spared owing to her cargo being for the U.S.A." Mr. Ellis added that: "We have met with the utmost kindness and consideration from all concerned, including the officers of the EMDEN."

The experience of the *St. Egbert* (5,596 tons), mentioned in Mr. Ellis's statement, was exceptional. The ship had a neutral cargo for American consignees, and was on her passage from Yokohama to New York. She left the former port on July 18th, and therefore before the declaration of war, and, calling at Colombo, sailed thence on October 17th. Captain Barr learnt at Colombo that the route was reasonably safe, and was advised to keep close to Cape Comorin, and from thence to shape a course to pass forty miles north of Minikoi Island. The *St. Egbert* steered the course recommended, but at 9.30 p.m. on the following day the EMDEN stopped and boarded her. In the course of conversation with Captain Barr, the lieutenant who was in charge of the prize crew stated that the Germans had learnt of his departure from Colombo on the previous day, and were aware that he had received orders "to proceed on a more northerly track than usual," adding that he had been informed that the British cruiser HAMPSHIRE had arrived at Colombo that morning, and that her crew were ashore playing football. This embroidery, as in so many similar instances, was probably mere bluff. The next morning the EMDEN rounded up the captured vessels, and all the passengers and crews of the steamers *Benmohr, Clan Grant, Buresk, Troilus, Exford, Chilkana,* and *Ponrabbel,* were sent on board the *St. Egbert,* which was released on October 19th with orders to proceed to Aden. In view of the large number of persons on board and consequent restricted accommodation and food-supplies, Captain Barr was subsequently permitted to make for Cochin, where he arrived on the morning of October 20th.

The month of October was drawing to its close, and the captain of the EMDEN suspected that news of his captures must have become known on shore, and suitable measures taken by the British naval authorities to arrest his career of destruction. He determined to pay a visit to Penang and see what mischief he could do there. The EMDEN, as on the occasion of the Madras raid, erected a dummy funnel made of canvas, in the hope that she might be mistaken for one of the British cruisers which Captain von Müller thought to be in the vicinity of Penang. It is beyond the scope of this book to describe in detail the torpedoing of the Russian cruiser ZHEMCHUG, which was lying in the harbour. The EMDEN, having completed that task, turned and steamed out of the harbour at full speed. Outside she encountered the *Glenturret* (4,696 tons), which had left London on September 23rd for Yokohama, calling at Penang, Singapore, and Hong Kong. She was loaded with Government munitions and explosives, and would have proved a valuable capture for the Germans. On the night of October 26th, when in the neighbourhood of Sabang, the *Glenturret* sent a wireless signal that she would arrive at Penang on October 28th, and asking that a lighter should be provided to take off twenty tons of explosives. Arriving off the entrance to Penang Harbour in the early hours of the morning of the 27th, the *Glenturret* stopped, the master (Mr. H. Jones) deciding to wait until daylight before entering. She was on her way into the harbour later in the morning, with the B flag (explosives) flying, when the EMDEN ranged alongside her, being only about thirty feet distant. Captain Jones was hailed in English and asked his reasons for flying the

THE WHITE STAR LINER "OLYMPIC" (FROM THE AIR).

B flag. He replied that the *Glenturret* was carrying paraffin. The EMDEN then lowered a boat for the purpose of boarding her, when the French destroyer MOUSQUET, which had been in Penang Harbour, appeared. In the circumstances the captain of the EMDEN had no further interest in the *Glenturret*, but immediately made off to ascertain the identity of the strange destroyer on the horizon. Captain von Müller did not know what to make of the intruder, for at 6,000 yards the strange man-of-war appeared much larger than she really was, owing to the mirage of the early morning. As the EMDEN closed in to about 4,800 yards, she was recognised as the French torpedo-boat destroyer MOUSQUET. The subsequent fight was an unequal one. As the destroyer sank, the EMDEN rescued the crew, numbering in all thirty-six, three of whom afterwards died in the EMDEN owing to the severity of their wounds. The EMDEN had lost much time in dealing with the MOUSQUET, and now saw a torpedo-boat approaching her from Penang, so she at once steamed for the Indian Ocean at full speed with the torpedo-boat in chase. After being pursued for four hours, she lost sight of the torpedo-boat in heavy rain, and was free to proceed to her collier.

In the meantime the *Glenturret* had made her escape, but on the following day the EMDEN came across the s.s. *Newburn* (3,554 tons; master, Mr. J. R. Matthews), on passage from the Tyne to Singapore and Samarang. She was carrying a neutral cargo, so the captain of the EMDEN decided to release her. Before doing so, however, he put the survivors of the MOUSQUET on board, and the *Newburn* reached Penang on October 31st.

The cruise of the EMDEN was now nearing its close. Captain von Müller, suspecting that a hue and cry had been raised, decided that he would do well to change the scene of his activities. With the idea of cutting the cable, he steamed for Cocos Islands, which were reached on Sunday evening, November 8th. The German cruiser sailed round the islands in order to see that everything was clear, and then proceeded towards Direction Island, the dummy funnel being again in place, and landed a party of fifty men with instructions to destroy the wireless station and cut the cable. In the meantime, the wireless station had sent out an urgent message for help; it was picked up by the Allied men-of-war on convoy duty with the First Australian Contingent. On instructions from the senior officer, H.M.A.S. SYDNEY raised steam for full speed and proceeded to Direction Island. The story of the destruction of the EMDEN does not come within the scope of this history: it is sufficient to add that the German cruiser's career was brought to an end, the men on board the *Buresk* being rescued. When Captain Glossop reached this ship, he found that she was sinking, as the Kingston had been " knocked out and damaged to prevent repairing."

The story of the first phase of the attack on British commerce would be incomplete were no reference made to the circumstances in which the gunboat GEIER captured the s.s. *Southport* (3,588 tons). The adventurous story, which afterwards moved the Admiralty to express their approbation of the action of Captain A. Clopet and the officers and men, cannot be better told than in the form of a paraphrase of the narrative as related by the first-named.

The s.s. *Southport* left Auckland, New Zealand, on June 12th, to load a cargo of phosphates for the Pacific Phosphate Company at Nauru, calling at Ocean Island for orders. The voyage was uneventful. Off Nauru, information was sent by the manager of the Phosphate Company that loading had been delayed, owing to dangerous weather, strong currents, and the exposed position of the island, and that, in consequence of tonnage having precedence over the *Southport*, that vessel need not present herself for loading for some time. Captain Clopet decided to follow the example of other captains placed in similar circumstances, and wait at Tarawa (Gilbert Islands), where further orders could be conveyed to him, in preference to steaming round the island against the strong prevailing easterly current. The *Southport* returned to Nauru on July 28th. The captain found that only some 450 tons of phosphates had been loaded, and there was still a balance of 13,000 tons to be shipped before the *Southport* would be required. In order to save coal, he decided to bear up for Kusaie, the most easterly island in the Caroline group (German), where the conditions appeared to be better than at Taraiva. It was also arranged that the manager at Nauru should forward loading

CH. IV] CAPTURE OF THE "SOUTHPORT" 205

orders by the steamer *Germania*, due at Kusaie on August 28th. The *Southport* arrived at Kusaie on August 4th, and remained there awaiting instructions. The non-arrival of the *Germania* on the stipulated date caused surprise, owing to the regularity of her previous voyages. No news being forthcoming, it was decided to sail for Nauru on September 6th. On the 4th, the captain being ashore at the time, the German gunboat GEIER and the transport *Tsintau*, of Bremen, came to anchor in the harbour, and a boat full of armed officers and sailors put off from the GEIER and boarded the British ship. Captain Clopet, on returning on board his ship shortly afterwards, was informed by the German officers that, " war having been declared by England on Germany," they demanded that all the ship's papers, register, ship's articles, load-line, etc., be handed over. It was explained that the ship was chartered to load phosphates at Nauru for Stettin. The engineers of the warship then came on board and began disabling the vessel, principally by removing the four eccentrics of the L.P. and H.P. engines and other connected parts, as well as the intermediate stop valve. The following day the transport *Tsintau* proceeded alongside and started transhipping the *Southport's* coal into her bunkers, the work continuing until 6 a.m. on August 7th (Monday). The same day at 10 a.m. a boat full of armed officers and men boarded the *Southport* and came on the lower bridge, when a formal act of seizure was read over to the captain by the officer in charge, appropriating the vessel to the Imperial German Government. The armed sailors were lined up on one side of the lower bridge, and, the British ensign having been previously hauled down, the German naval ensign was hoisted on the flagstaff, the German officers and sailors saluting their flag. Everything was done in the most formal manner, as though the scene were being enacted on the stage before an appreciative audience. Captain Clopet was subsequently informed that he would remain in charge of the ship and responsible for it, as well as for the discipline of the crew, pending any future action on the part of the German Government. It should be mentioned that the commander of the GEIER at first decided to sink the *Southport*. He learnt afterwards that, owing to the non-arrival of the *Germania* with provisions, the

Southport was exceedingly short of food, and he was told that the crew would be faced with starvation unless the situation was relieved. The German officer was not unsympathetic, but urged that he could not send provisions, having himself an insufficient supply. Ultimately he did in fact send four loaves of bread, which were accepted. But his more effective aid took the form of an order on the King of Kusaie, in the name of the Imperial German Government, to supply the ship with such food as the island produced.

The GEIER and *Tsintau* left on the afternoon of the 7th, the Germans apparently satisfied that the *Southport* could not move; they disappeared in a south-easterly direction. After their departure, the captain consulted the chief engineer (Mr. J. C. Dodd) as to the possibility of repairing the engines in such a manner as to enable the *Southport* to put to sea. Mr. Dodd, nothing daunted by the damage which had been done, decided that the position was not hopeless. His confidence was justified. The work of repair was carried on from day to day until September 15th, when Captain Clopet had the satisfaction of learning that the engines were ready. Steam was raised and orders were given for a trial that night. The trial began shortly after midnight, the captain being present in the engine-room in order to judge the reliability of the engines. After two attempts the engines started. They were stopped after a few revolutions, the chief engineer stating that he was confident that everything was as satisfactory as could be expected. A statement was handed to the captain in confirmation of this opinion. The following evening, Captain Clopet called the officers and engineers of the ship to the cabin, and then told them that he intended to make an attempt to *recapture* the steamer and take her into Australian waters, Brisbane being the nearest port. As an alternative, it was suggested that the vessel might remain in Kusaie until the end of hostilities, when in all probability an exchange of vessels would take place between England and Germany. Captain Clopet pointed out, however, that the value represented by the *Southport* was at stake, and that at that moment, to all intents and purposes, the ship was the property of the German Government; if the attempt to bring the vessel to a safe Australian port was successful, the money represented in the ship would revert to the original flag. The captain's decision was unanimously accepted by the officers present, and on the following morning the crew gave their support. In anticipation of the voyage, since there was a shortage of provisions, the captain obtained from the shore some 400 pounds of roots, which are used by the natives only when on the verge of starvation, besides about 350 cocoanuts, the latter being provided by the King of Kusaie, who was by this time aware that an attempt to escape was to be made. Though other provisions were taken on board as a precautionary measure, the voyage was begun on straitened rations.

A word may be added as to the manner in which the engines were repaired. The German engineers had left the two eccentric rods for the L.P. engines; one of these was put on the ahead sheave of the H.P. engine, the other rod being kept in place on the ahead sheave of the L.P. engine. Thus the engineers were able to work the engines subject to the disadvantage that they could move only in one direction, i.e., ahead; it was impossible to reverse the engines, however great the need. There was also some difficulty in restarting the engines once they were stopped. These circumstances rendered the task of handling the ship difficult. The attempt to move the *Southport* was made early on the morning of September 8th. The harbour of Kusaie is very small, having on one side land and on the other a coral reef. It provided barely sufficient room for the steamer to swing, and at the time of starting, Captain Clopet swung her stem towards the entrance, the channel having been buoyed by his orders previous to heaving up the anchor. With the assistance of warps, the steamer's stern was brought into the wind, the anchor hove barely clear of the bottom, and her head started to pay off with the wind towards the entrance. When nearly square in the channel, the telegraph was rung " Full ahead," and the last rope was let go as soon as the engines started.

The voyage was uneventful; lights were carefully screened up to 9 p.m., when they were put out. The steamer passed to the westward of San Christoval (Solomon Islands) on September 23rd, and arrived to the north-east of Sandy Cape on September 28th—when, in reply to inquiries, the s.s. *Westminster* reported the coast clear of enemy ships. A course was then shaped towards Brisbane.

On the same day the *Southport* observed the Dutch steamer *Tasman*, of Batavia, altering her course towards the coast, and shortly afterwards a steamer ashore at right angles to the beach was observed. The *Southport* also turned towards the steamer, which was flying the International Distress Signal N.C. ("Want immediate assistance"). The vessel was the s.s. *Marlvo*. As the first impression conveyed by the steamer's position was that she must have gone ashore during the night, the captain of the *Southport* decided to come to anchor in a position to render help. It was a characteristic act on the part of a British seaman who had so recently been himself in trouble. The *Southport* drew in between the *Tasman* and the stranded vessel. Assistance had unfortunately come too late, for the *Marlvo* already had her after compartments full of water, through striking some obstruction off Sandy Cape. Her passengers were transferred to the *Tasman*, and the *Southport* proceeded on her voyage to Brisbane. She completed the passage without further incident. In these circumstances the GEIER was deprived of the only prize which she made during her career as a commerce-destroyer.

Though the enemy's attack on merchant shipping in the early days of the war was conducted on a much smaller scale than had been anticipated by many students of German naval policy in pre-war days, the measure of success which was attained made a deep impression on the public mind unaccustomed to the vicissitudes of naval warfare. The injury inflicted was, however, slight when studied in relation to the experiences of British shipping during the Revolutionary and Napoleonic Wars, the varied resources of the German Navy, or the size of the target offered by the British Mercantile Marine, comprising 44·4 per cent. of sea-going steam-vessels of the world, or 47·9 per cent. if the tonnage of the Dominions be included. At the end of the first quarter of 1915 the volume of British tonnage which had been lost through the agency of enemy vessels and mines since the opening of the war was only 232,824 gross tons,[1] a very small percentage of the tonnage afloat. Seventy-two vessels [2]

---

[1] Merchant Shipping (Losses), 199.
[2] Excluding the small sailing-vessels *Frau Minna Petersen* (captured by a torpedo-boat on August 7th) and *Ayesha* (captured November 9th).

were captured by enemy cruisers and armed merchantmen, including the *Glenturret*, which was not actually boarded, and the *Southport*, which escaped. The depredations were inflicted upon the Merchant Navy without the sacrifice of a single life. More than that, officers and men of the German ships, whether men-of-war or auxiliary cruisers, exhibited a high respect for the dictates of humanity, and showed to passengers and crews a consideration and a courtesy which, in view of later events, deserve to be recorded.

Name of Vessel.	Sunk.	Released.	Escaped.	Utilised.	TOTAL.	Remarks.
EMDEN	15[1]	4	1	2[2]	22	[1] The total excludes the small sailing-vessel *Ayesha*, captured by the EMDEN's landing-party. [2] The *Exford* was recaptured.
KÖNIGSBERG	1	—	—	—	1	
GEIER	—	—	1	—	1	
KARLSRUHE	15[1]	1	—	1	17	[1] The *Indrani* was utilised and subsequently sunk.
KRONPRINZ WILHELM	9[1]	1	—	—	10	[1] The *Potara* was utilised and subsequently sunk.
PRINZ EITEL	5	—	—	—	5	
DRESDEN	4	5	—	—	9	
LEIPZIG	3	—	—	—	3	
KAISER WILHELM	2	2	—	—	4	
	54	13	2	3	72	

CHAPTER V

THE PROTECTION OF MERCHANT SHIPPING

THE opening phase of the war by sea was marked by an attack by German cruisers and armed merchant ships upon British shipping. The effects of that campaign have already been described. It would be unfair to leave the records of the sinkings of British merchant tonnage during these early days without some reference to the steps taken by the Admiralty and other departments to afford protection to the Mercantile Marine. Strategical and tactical considerations are dealt with elsewhere,[1] but it is appropriate to an account of the part taken by the Merchant Navy in the war to examine the bases of national policy as determined before the outbreak of hostilities.

I. STRATEGIC POLICY

Time and again the subject of the relation of the Royal and Merchant Navies was considered, either directly or indirectly, by Royal Commissions and Select Committees. In particular, the responsibility of the Navy for the security of British ocean-borne commerce came under examination by the Royal Commission on the Supply of Food and Raw Material in Time of War, which was appointed on April 27th, 1903. The trading community was largely represented, and among the members were Vice-Admiral—afterwards Admiral—Sir Gerard H. U. Noel (who was succeeded in January 1904 by Admiral Sir Day Hort Bosanquet) and Sir John C. R. Colomb, M.P., who had devoted great attention to the matters with which the Commission was instructed to deal. The Commissioners were in constant communication with the Admiralty, and examined a number of naval officers of standing, including Captain

---

[1] Cf. *Naval Operations*, by Sir Julian Corbett.

Prince Louis of Battenberg—later Admiral the Marquis of Milford Haven—who was then Director of Naval Intelligence, Admiral Sir John O. Hopkins, who had held the command of the Mediterranean Fleet, and Admiral Sir Cyprian A. G. Bridge, a former Director of Naval Intelligence, who was in command of His Majesty's ships in the China Seas at the time of the outbreak of war between Russia and Japan.

The Report of the Commission was issued in 1905, and it is of interest in that it provides evidence of the attention which was then being given by the naval authorities to the protection of the Mercantile Marine. The Commission was appointed to inquire into the supplies of food and raw material in time of war and, *inter alia*, "to advise whether it is desirable to adopt any measures, in addition to the maintenance of a strong fleet, by which such supplies can be better secured and violent fluctuations avoided." It was assumed by the Commissioners that the term "a strong fleet" might be taken to imply the maintenance of the fleet at such a level of strength, compared with that of other nations, that there was no reasonable prospect of this country's maritime supremacy in time of war being seriously in danger. It was on that assumption that the inquiry was conducted.

At the very outset, the Commissioners were at pains to explain, after hearing a considerable body of expert evidence, the standpoint from which they approached this particular branch of their investigation. "We do not fail to take into account," they declared, "that a little time might elapse after the outbreak of war before our Navy was able to assert its supremacy, nor that at a later date some reverse might take place. However great our confidence in the Navy may be, such a contingency as a reverse is not impossible; but it is necessary to define very carefully what we mean by the term. A reverse may be of varying degrees of importance; it may affect a particular fleet or only a detached squadron; but broadly, for our purpose, it is only necessary to distinguish between a reverse that would cost us the command of the sea, and one which would not. The former, which would place our whole maritime trade at the mercy of an enemy, would be a disaster of the gravest possible character. Any lesser calamity, from the very fact that it would not cost us the command of the sea, would not produce a set of circumstances so far different from those with which we are now about to deal as to require separate consideration."

The report emphasised the fact that the Admiralty had constantly, and with ever-increasing solicitude, considered the steps to be taken to afford adequate protection to the Merchant Service. In this connection the Commissioners remarked that there was a certain degree of misconception in some quarters as to the nature of the protection which could be afforded by the Navy, or rather in respect to the methods by which it could be given. " It has sometimes been assumed that such protection can only be given either by sending a number of cruisers to protect the trade routes or by a system of convoy." The Commissioners, having had the advantage of consulting with the Admiralty, made a comment which, in the light of war experience, was significant. In their opinion protection of commerce could often be more adequately given in other ways. They were impressed by the knowledge that the supplies of food and raw material on passage to the United Kingdom were distributed among many ships rather than concentrated in a few, and that the trade itself was conducted in a fairly constant stream, and was not confined either to one period of the year or to a single route. " These facts, especially when taken in conjunction with the power afforded by steam of varying the routes according to the necessities of any given period, make the conditions of the chief trade routes an extremely favourable one for successful defence." The possibility of an effective blockade of the United Kingdom was dismissed; at that time the submarine had only recently appeared on the naval horizon, the small vessels of the type being always accompanied by "parent ships," and possessing only limited radius of action and low speed.

This conclusion having been reached, the ground was cleared for an investigation of the important problem— the protection which could be afforded to the Mercantile Marine on the trade routes. Two general principles were accepted. The first was that the command of the sea is essential for the successful attack or defence of commerce, and should, therefore, be the primary aim. The second was that the attack on, or defence of, commerce is best effected by concentration of force, and that a dispersion of strength for either of those objects is the strategy of the weak, and cannot materially influence the ultimate results of the war. They remarked that "best opinions all tend in the direction that the first and principal object on both sides, in case of future maritime war, will be to obtain command of the sea."

Reviewing the volume of authoritative evidence submitted to them, the Commissioners reached the following conclusion: "It follows from this that concentration of our forces will be the most effective protection that can be given to our trade from attack by the regular men-of-war of the enemy during, at any rate, the initial stages of a maritime contest, and that the policy of an organised attack on our commerce, if adopted, is not likely to meet with any great measure of success. The enemy, in fact, would find himself in this dilemma: on the one hand, if he should endeavour to organise an extensive attack on our trade, the inevitable result would be the serious weakening of his fleet in the contest for the really decisive factor—namely, the command of the seas: on the other, if he should merely detach one or two cruisers for harassing our commerce, and if these cruisers should escape from the surveillance of our squadrons, the Admiralty have pointed out ... that we could always spare a superior number of vessels to follow them. No doubt a considerable number of ships might be required to effect the actual capture of a single hostile commerce-destroyer, so long at least as her coal lasted; but it has been explained to us by Sir Cyprian Bridge that, even if only one of our cruisers were in pursuit, it could be made too dangerous for a hostile cruiser to remain on or about a trade route. Obviously, under these circumstances, her freedom of action would be much hampered, and the damage she would be able to inflict would be limited. It is, however, right to mention that Sir Cyprian Bridge pointed out that it is possible to overdo concentration, and he instanced the mistaken policy of the Federal States in allowing the ALABAMA to remain at sea practically unmolested. His view was that protection can be best assured by having sufficient cruisers to keep the enemy's commerce-destroyers continually on the lookout for their own safety, while concentrating the main force in the right place from a purely strategic point of view."

Some members of the Royal Commission were still in doubt as to the ability of the Fleet to fulfil its mission of protection, assuming the country to be at war with any two of the great maritime Powers. So a communication was made to the Admiralty, in reply to which the Admiralty stated that no guarantee could be given that no capture whatever could be made by the enemy—" a position impossible to maintain in argument "—but it was believed that there would be no material diminution in the supply of wheat and flour reaching the United Kingdom. Finally, in commenting upon the apprehension that the disposition of the British Fleet, squadrons, or ships might be adversely affected and the free action of the Admiralty impaired by popular pressure, exercised through Parliament upon the Government, thus influencing the Admiralty instructions to the admirals, it was remarked that the Admiralty could never allow their action to be influenced by any pressure, and yet consent to remain responsible for the conduct of war.

The Commissioners afterwards turned to another aspect of the question—viz., the policy which would most likely be adopted by shipowners either voluntarily or by stress of circumstances during a naval war. The evidence submitted on this question showed conclusively that any general laying-up of steamers, either liners or tramps, need not be expected, although a general rise in freights would occur. Assuming, as the Commissioners generally assumed, that shipowners would do their best to keep their vessels running, attention was then directed to the influence of steam on the enemy's operations against merchantmen. This section of the report reflected the best naval opinion of the day, and it is instructive, in the light of actual war experience, to recall the views which were expressed : " It is an interesting subject for conjecture, whether the change from sails to steam will or will not tell in favour of the chances of capture of merchant vessels at sea. If it stood alone, it is probable that the balance of evidence would tell in the direction of greater immunity from capture. A steamer has freedom to choose the least dangerous route, and to enter at the least dangerous time upon the area of the sea most likely to be infested with hostile cruisers; and, moreover, when such an area is entered, it can be passed through with greater rapidity and certainty than was ever possible in the case of a sailing-vessel. It seems also obvious that a steamer is exposed to less danger than a sailing-vessel, which was always at the mercy of winds and currents, and whose escape was always barred for twelve points out of the thirty-two of the compass. Moreover, the merchant vessel can now change her course at will, and, by leaving directly astern any possible pursuer so soon as sighted, can lengthen the chase to the utmost possible limit.

"These considerations," it was added, "tell powerfully in favour of the merchant vessel, though it may be said that, if flight can be taken in any direction, attack may now also come from any quarter so far as weather is concerned. On the other hand, the telegraph is a powerful ally to the attacking force, because it is now much less possible to conceal the movements of important merchant vessels. Without doubt, the telegraph will also to a certain extent disclose the movements of the attacking force, but we think the balance of advantage will be against the private owners. In any case, the existence of submarine telegraphy has probably put an end to the old system of collecting merchant vessels together for the purpose of giving them protection under the convoy of men-of-war. No assembly of vessels for convoy can be kept secret, and the enemy would, therefore, have an excellent chance of preparing an attack. The Admiralty pointed out to us that a mass of smoke by day, and even at times by night, would attract any hostile cruiser that might be about. It may be added that for commercial reasons the convoy system would not now be of advantage, owing to the loss of time involved in waiting for an escort, as well as to the fact that the speed of the whole convoy would have to be regulated to suit that of the slowest vessel."

Attention was also directed to another consideration. "Engines and machinery have reduced the space available for the personnel of warships as compared to that available in the days of sailing-ships. A modern warship could only to a very limited extent furnish prize crews, and she would impair her fighting and steaming efficiency by so doing." The restricted accommodation available for the crews of captured merchantmen was also commented on.

It was declared that " modern conditions tend to limit the capturing-power of regular war cruisers, it being remarked that these observations do not, however, apply to ocean-trading steamers converted and armed for the purpose of attacking commerce." It was added that torpedo-craft (i.e. destroyers and torpedo-boats) can neither spare prize crews nor accommodate anyone above their complement numbers. " If, therefore, employed against commerce, for which they were never intended, such craft could only compel merchant ships to follow them into port under threat of being torpedoed. Moreover, these craft can only operate within a comparatively short distance of their shore bases."

After noting that the Admiralty had in process of formation an organisation for keeping in touch with, and giving advice to, the Mercantile Marine in the event of an outbreak of hostilities, and urging that the matter " should receive the earnest attention of those in authority, as well on the part of the civil community as the Admiralty," the Commissioners proceeded to sum up their conclusions. They remarked that—"It must not be thought from anything we have said that we are of opinion that there will be no capture of British ships engaged in the carrying trade. Whatever our naval strength might be, some captures, as has already been pointed out, would certainly take place. But with a strong fleet ,we find no reason to fear such an interruption of our supplies as would lead to the starvation of our people, nor do we see any evidence that there is likely to be any serious shortage." [1] At that time the submarine was as yet in its infancy, and few craft of this type had been built by any country, though in the year in which the Commission reported Germany launched an experimental submarine from the Germania Yard, Kiel.

II. Pre-War Arrangements

During the nine years which intervened between the publication of the Report of the Royal Commission on Supply of Food and Raw Material in Time of War and the

[1] Minority reports were issued : the quotations given are from the main report of the Royal Commission.

actual outbreak of hostilities, in August 1914, considerable attention was devoted to the measures to be taken to safeguard merchant shipping. In particular, the Committee of Imperial Defence dealt with the matter in the course of the elaboration of steps to be adopted to protect British interests overseas. On May 19th, 1896, the Colonial Defence Committee, which subsequently became a subordinate branch of the Committee of Imperial Defence, had laid down the principle that—" The maintenance of sea supremacy has been assumed as the basis of the system of Imperial Defence against attack from over the sea. This is the determinating factor in shaping the whole defensive policy of the Empire, and is fully recognised by the Admiralty, who have accepted the responsibility of protecting all British territory abroad against organised invasion from the sea. To fulfil this great charge, they claim the absolute power of disposing of their forces in the manner they consider most certain to secure success, and object to limit the action of any part of them to the immediate neighbourhood of places which they consider may be more effectively protected by operations at a distance."

That principle became the foundation upon which all questions affecting the Mercantile Marine were considered. As a consequence, the scale of defence to be provided at oversea ports of the British Empire, which might be used by merchant ships as well as men-of-war, was considered in the light of that primary understanding. At the same time, it was recognised that His Majesty's ships engaged in seeking out and destroying the squadrons of an enemy might not be in a position to prevent predatory raids on British ports by hostile cruisers, which might temporarily have succeeded in eluding their vigilance, and that the capture of British shipping had also to be provided against. It was also essential that the squadrons of His Majesty's ships engaged in defending the trade routes against such raids should have adequately defended bases. "The object of the coast defences," it was declared, "is to deter attack by a hostile fleet not supreme at sea, and therefore not in a position to risk serious loss of fighting efficiency. Such defences must, therefore, be strong enough to be able to inflict substantial damage upon a squadron suddenly attacking them; but they are not required to sustain a deliberate duel between forts and ships for a prolonged period."

The whole subject of oversea port defence was reconsidered by the Colonial Defence Committee in 1910. The assurance was then given that the Admiralty were of the opinion that, so long as the then existing standard of naval strength was maintained, British fleets would be in a position effectually to frustrate any movements of enemy ships on a large scale within a comparatively brief period of their commencement, and it was assumed that any movement of enemy ships on a large scale would be followed up by a British force with the least possible delay. It was added in this connection that "the decisive advantages accruing to the belligerent who succeeds in establishing sea supremacy over his opponent are now well understood; and it is to be expected that any naval Powers hoping to inflict serious injury upon us will, on the outbreak of war, attempt to neutralise our naval superiority, and, if possible, wrest from us the command of the sea. This object can only be attained as the result of great naval battles, in which the main fleets of the contending Powers are concentrated for decisive encounters. It is immaterial where the great battles are fought. In whatever waters they may take place, the result will be felt throughout the world; for after having disposed of the battle squadrons of the enemy, the victor will be able to spread his force with a view to capturing or destroying any detached force of the enemy that may remain at sea. He will then be in a position to gather the fruits of victory, in the shape of the enemy's outlying possessions and his shipping and commerce, or to prosecute an overseas campaign."

In the succeeding paragraph of the Committee's report, attention was directed to a danger which the public, in the early period of the war which was to break out in the summer of 1914, was inclined to overlook. It was remarked that, with a view to impairing the measures of concentration in war and inducing a weakening of the main fleets, an enemy might endeavour to create a widespread feeling of insecurity and alarm throughout the Empire by utilising such classes of vessels as were unfitted for taking part in the decisive actions in raiding British sea-borne trade and threatening distant portions of the Empire. It was recognised that in themselves such raiding operations would be of only secondary importance, since the ultimate issue of a naval war must depend on the result of the fleet actions. It would, however, be necessary, it was admitted, to take a vigorous offensive against all such outlying raiding vessels in order to prevent the demoralisation and disturbance of trade due to their depredations.

The intelligence organisation which was maintained in time of peace would, it was believed, enable the Admiralty to learn the distribution at any moment of foreign navies, and of all foreign merchant vessels likely to be employed as armed auxiliaries. During the period of strained relations preceding the outbreak of hostilities every effort would be made, it was assumed, to keep the ships of the prospective enemy under observation. The great increase in the rapidity and certainty of transmission of intelligence consequent upon the development of submarine cables and radio-telegraphy were held to add to the difficulties of raiding operations, depending for success, as they would, on tactics of evasion and surprise. "Having regard to our present naval strength and dispositions, attacks on floating trade in distant seas will offer to an enemy but slight prospect of any but transitory successes."

The policy elaborated by the Colonial Defence Committee, and endorsed by the Committee of Imperial Defence, was accepted by the Government of the day for its guidance in framing the general defence policy not only of the Empire, but of the Merchant Navy, its life-line. Emphasis was laid upon the false strategy which might lead to the premature dispatch of reinforcements to distant seas, instead of delaying till a force could be sent so superior to the squadrons of the enemy that there would be practical certainty of engaging them with success. In order to avoid exposing fleets to the risk of suffering defeat in detail, naval action in remote waters, it was admitted, might have to be postponed until, by the clearing of the situation in home waters, adequate naval force could be brought to bear.

Attention was devoted to local defences both by naval and military forces, and to the necessity which might arise for establishing temporary naval bases, and the requirements in the matter of defence of commercial ports were also considered. In this connection the conclusions of the

Committee, endorsed at the time by naval and military opinion, have a peculiar interest in view of the course adopted by the enemy after the declaration of war. "An enemy possessing a powerful battle fleet is unlikely to undertake organised attacks on commerce in commercial ports until an attempt at least has been made to cripple our naval power, for which purpose his cruisers are likely to be required, in the first instance, to act in conjunction with his battleships. Isolated attacks on merchant vessels met during the progress of some strategic movements may indeed occur, but regular attacks on commerce in distant waters, if they take place at all at the beginning of a war, are more likely to be carried out by armed merchant vessels than by hostile cruisers, which are not likely, at that stage, to be available for such service. In view of the supreme value of armoured vessels in war, and of their great cost and consequent small numbers, it is improbable that a squadron would undertake a subsidiary operation such as the attack on a commercial port, if the defence were of such a nature that the attackers would run the risk of losing even one of their number, or of receiving such injuries as to involve risk of capture or immediate return to a base. Of recent years, foreign naval Powers have almost without exception ceased to lay down any but small unarmoured cruisers, and the armoured cruisers now under construction approximate to the battleship type. The great value of such armoured vessels as adjuncts to the battle fleet renders it improbable that they would be detached for attacks on commerce or on commerical ports until the struggle for the command of the sea has been decided. The older types of armoured cruisers may, however, become available in the future for subsidiary operations of this nature."

An attempt was made to forecast the probable policy of the enemy with a view to suggesting the measures which should be taken by the British Government to frustrate attempts to interfere with merchant shipping. The British naval reply to attacks on commerce, it was remarked, would probably involve extended operations with cruiser squadrons and single ships, taking full advantage of the facilities afforded by our numerous commercial ports as coaling places and as centres for the collection and distribution of intelligence relating to the movements of the enemy. In the circumstances anticipated, it was decided that certain fortified commercial ports on frequented trade routes would be useful as coaling-stations and harbours of refuge, where merchant vessels could, in case of need, seek protection from capture or molestation, and await a favourable opportunity of proceeding on their voyages. The need for fixed defence at certain great commercial ports was also admitted. The measure of protection, it was suggested, should be such as would "involve such risk of injury to the attacking cruiser as would not, in the opinion of a naval commander, be justified by the possible advantages to be obtained."

These statements are of interest as an indication that long before the probability of war was realised by the nation generally, and certainly before public attention had been directed to the dangers which would threaten merchant shipping at the outbreak of hostilities, the Government of the day, acting through the Committee of Imperial Defence, had been studying all the associated problems with a view of proper action being taken to support the influence exercised by the Fleet.

Furthermore, the Committee of Imperial Defence set up a number of Sub-committees which considered the responsibilities which would be thrown upon the various departments of the Government at the outbreak of war. With the assistance of these bodies, upon which the Admiralty, the Board of Trade, and the Post Office were represented, as well as the shipping industry, the Standing Sub-committee of the Committee of Imperial Defence gradually built up what afterwards came to be known as the "War-Book." The object was to co-ordinate departmental action on the occurrence of (*a*) strained relations and (*b*) the outbreak of war. The volume covered a wide field. But the present purpose is merely to refer to that portion which dealt with British Merchant Shipping. It is not necessary to consider in detail the large number of orders which had been prepared in advance in order to protect merchantmen cruising in distant waters, but it is of interest to recall that provision was made for appropriate action. On receipt of the notification of the outbreak of war, His Majesty's diplomatic representatives abroad had instructions to telegraph to every consular officer stationed at a port in the country in which he resided or its colonial possessions, directing warnings to be given to British merchant ships not to proceed to or enter enemy ports. Similar provision was made for the warning of vessels in ports of British possessions abroad. Steps were also taken for instructing representatives abroad in the responsibilities with reference to merchant shipping which would devolve upon them as soon as war was declared, with a view to safeguarding British merchant ships.

In the view of the Committee of Imperial Defence, the main security to the Mercantile Marine was to be found in the general naval arrangements made by the Admiralty in the years preceding the outbreak of war. In reply to Germany's policy of naval concentration, the Grand Fleet, as it was subsequently described, came into existence, changing the whole character of the problem of providing for the safety of British merchant shipping. The aim of the naval authorities was not to blockade the enemy fleet—an intention which Nelson always disclaimed—but to make such a disposition of the main forces of the country as to reduce to a minimum the probability of cruisers concentrated in the North Sea or Baltic ports of Germany escaping on to the trade routes. That object became in the course of time the decisive principle of Admiralty policy. Admiral Sir Arthur Wilson, who succeeded Lord Fisher as First Sea Lord, was led to give an exposition of the views of the Admiralty when the question of the possibility of invasion by the enemy was agitating the public mind. In a memorandum which he prepared for the Army Council in November 1910, he declared that " the really serious danger that this country has to guard against in war is not invasion, but interruption of our trade and the destruction of our merchant shipping." In the light of that conclusion, which reinforced the views of previous Boards of Admiralty, he remarked that " the strength of our fleet is determined by what is necessary to protect our trade, and, if it is sufficient for that, it will be almost necessarily sufficient to prevent invasion, since the same disposition of the ships to a great extent answers both purposes." That exposition of policy showed that, even four years before the outbreak of war, the Admiralty possessed what events were to show to be a correct perception of the main duty which, in the event of war, would devolve upon the fleet of a sea-dependent country, itself the centre of a maritime empire.

The adoption of the principle of concentration of naval force in the main theatre of war reduced the proportions of the problem of protecting merchant shipping, but it did not eliminate that problem. The Admiralty provided for squadrons to be stationed in the outer seas under peace conditions. Plans were also drawn up for commissioning special squadrons which on the outbreak of war would be dispatched for the patrol of the areas where the great trade routes, in turning in towards the British Isles, converge. The accompanying charts give a general idea of the distribution of naval force on the outbreak of war, and carry a reminder of the vast area of the sea, water covering nearly three-quarters of the earth's surface, and of the limited influence exerted by the restricted number of cruisers available after provision had been made for the needs of the Grand Fleet. Reference to those charts supplies the necessary corrective to any opinion unfavourable to the naval authorities which the narrative of the capture of British shipping during the early period of hostilities may have suggested. As has been indicated, both from the declaration of policy made by the Admiralty to the Royal Commission on Supply of Food and Raw Material in time of War, and from the reports of the Committee of Imperial Defence which have already been quoted, the naval authorities gave no guarantee, and believed that no guarantee could be given, that British merchant shipping would not suffer loss before enemy cruisers in distant seas could be rounded up and destroyed. It was foreseen that a considerable period might elapse before this object could be achieved, since the enemy would operate with many advantages in a trackless waste, and the Admiralty also foresaw that ships engaged in raiding British ocean-borne commerce might extend their careers by living upon merchant shipping captured, taking from such vessels coal, food, and stores, and then destroying the hulls.

III. The Creation of the Trade Division of the War Staff

During the proceedings of the Royal Commission on Supply of Food and Raw Materials in Time of War, attention was drawn to the need of an organisation at the Admiralty to receive from the shipping community information as to the movements of merchant ships, and to give advice to shipowners, in the event of an outbreak of hostilities, as to the voyages which their vessels might undertake with comparative safety, with more special reference to those points at which such vessels might expect to find protection. It was then stated by the Admiralty —that is, ten years before the opening of the war—that " an organisation of the kind is now in process of formation." The Commissioners stated that they were not satisfied that the means of communication between the Royal Navy and the Mercantile Fleet would on the outbreak of war be found sufficient to enable information to be conveyed to merchant vessels at sea, or that the orders of the Admiralty conveyed through the admirals by His Majesty's ships to merchant vessels would be understood. In the main report of the Commission a strong recommendation was made that " this matter should receive the early attention of those in authority, as well on the part of the shipping community as on the part of the Admiralty."

The problem of the best means of protecting trade continued under almost uninterrupted consideration by successive Directors of the Naval Intelligence Department. The matter was one which fell specially within the province of the Trade Division of that Department. During the early phases of the investigation, Captain Inglefield, Captain Harry Jones, and Captain Scott were concerned in the matter. In August 1906, Captain Henry Campbell was appointed to the Trade Division, and he at once began a very thorough investigation of the whole subject, Captain Charles Ottley having become Director of Naval Intelligence. Some progress was made, but it was not until Captain Edmond Slade became Director of Naval Intelligence that a practicable scheme began to take shape. In March 1908, Captain Campbell submitted a memorandum consisting of a complete and detailed examination of the problem. He received orders from the Director to amplify his arguments in favour of a system of advice, assistance, and decentralisation, in association with an intelligence scheme on the main trade routes. Captain Campbell suggested that " by leaving the owners in charge of their own ships, the control would be sectional; every vessel would have its own brain, so to speak, working out its own safety." He urged that under war conditions the owners, captains, and crews of merchant ships would be all personally interested in the safe arrivals of the vessels. " If they could be given some idea of what and where the dangers awaiting them were . . . they would be perfectly capable of avoiding and running through those dangers, for that is, after all, what their ordinary life is daily fitting them to do. And they would know, too, not only what was the best method of getting home, but also probably the quickest, and each would do this for his own individual case, and never bother with generalities." The purpose of this intelligence scheme was to obtain information, both positive and negative, from as wide an area as possible in order to make the best use of the protective force available and give advice to shipping. The aim was to provide the nucleus of an organisation, practised and developed in peace-time, which would combine all the facilities for receiving and disseminating intelligence through various channels—naval, diplomatic, Indian, Colonial, Customs, Lloyd's and other commercial organisations—and it was proposed to operate it by appointing officers at the principal commercial ports throughout the world, who would form a complete system of information bureaux. It is not too much to say that the action taken in this direction before the opening of the war saved the country from heavy loss, and at the same time enabled the trade routes to be kept open.

The nucleus of an organisation having been formed, the Trade Division was abolished in October 1909 and not resuscitated until August 1913, when it was re-formed as the Trade Branch of the Operations Division of the recently formed War Staff, being placed under Captain Richard Webb, assisted by a small staff. The reconstitution of this branch of the War Staff indicated that the naval authorities had finally come to the conclusion that special provision was necessary for dealing with matters affecting merchant shipping when war occurred, but the smallness of the personnel might have suggested that there was an inadequate appreciation of the number and complexity of the problems which war would raise in an acute form. On the other hand, such an organisation under peace conditions was necessarily on a modest scale, as its duty consisted merely in laying the foundations for action after hostilities had broken out; it formed the nucleus upon which an adequately-staffed branch of the War Staff could be built up when the necessity arose. Before the end of August 1914 it was, however, found necessary to expand this branch of the Operations Division into a separate division of the War Staff, known as the Trade Division. As the war progressed, its personnel was gradually increased in order to enable it to deal with this aspect of the war, and, in particular, to meet the requirements of the Mercantile Marine, the fishing industry, and the blockade of the enemy. As the organisation grew, the division was split up into separate sections to deal with various phases of the work, and, owing to the decision to institute a general system of Convoys which had been arrived at in June 1917, the Route-giving Section of the Trade Division was, at the end of September 1917, placed under Captain Frederic A. Whitehead as Director of Mercantile Movements, as was also the Convoy organisation for which Paymaster-Captain H. Eldon Manisty had been directly responsible since his appointment as Organising Manager of Convoys on June 25th, 1917. Under Captain Alan Hotham, who at the same time succeeded Captain Webb, the duties of the Trade Division were grouped into three main sections, each under a Captain R.N., to deal with (*a*) Trade and Blockade; (*b*) Equipment of Ships and Instruction of Personnel; (*c*) Shipping Intelligence, Casualties, etc. No department of the Admiralty responded more efficiently to the urgent demands of war than the Trade Division of the War Staff in the early phase of the operations at sea and during its subsequent course. Step by step, as the necessity demanded, the organisation was strengthened, until it became in time one of the most important divisions of the War Staff.

Previous to the outbreak of the war, with the exception

CH. V] THE MERCHANT NAVY'S PERSONNEL 227

of R.N.R. officers and naval chief petty officers appointed for duties with defensively armed merchant vessels at the ports of London, Liverpool, and Southampton, no direct link existed between the Admiralty and the Mercantile Marine; officers and men of the Royal Naval Reserve came, of course, under Admiralty instructions when under training, and when called up for war service, but the Mercantile Marine itself carried out its operations without naval control or jurisdiction. It was subject only to the Board of Trade, and the duties of that department, as has already been stated, were confined generally to enforcing provision for the safety of life and the proper treatment of seamen. The Merchant Service was regarded as a trade organisation, and the influence of legislation for some years previous to the opening of the war had been in the direction of weakening the disciplinary authority of masters over their crews. In a military sense, the Merchant Navy was an undisciplined force. While the great shipping firms maintained a regular body of officers, they drew upon the labour market as necessary for manning the ships, men in the oversea trade signing on for the voyage and then being discharged.

The occurrence of war revealed the rather unsatisfactory character of the limited control exercised over the personnel of the Merchant Navy. The Admiralty had at once to take up a large number of ships for fleet purposes, apart from the vessels required as transports, and the naval authorities had also to accept responsibility for the safety of about half the mercantile shipping of the world, which was at once exposed to enemy attack. Ten years previously the Admiralty had stated that " the number of British merchant steamers which would be taken up by the Government in war-time is so small, compared to the total number available, that it is not believed that the British carrying trade could be seriously interfered with." [1] At that time the Grand Fleet did not exist, and the Expeditionary Force had not been organised. The naval and military conditions affecting shipping had undergone a radical change by the time hostilities opened. In addition, Germany had revealed herself as the probable enemy in the event of war, and she had gradually increased

[1] *Report of the Royal Commission on Supply of Food and Raw Material in Time of War*, vol. i, Annex A.

her naval representation in foreign waters. The menace to the British Mercantile Marine from German men-of-war had consequently increased by 1914, apart from the threat which the Austro-Hungarian Fleet offered in the Mediterranean.

IV. THE WAR INSURANCE SCHEMES

The Admiralty's admission that a guarantee could not be given that no merchant ships would be sunk by an enemy brought home to the Government and the shipping industry a clearer apprehension of the conditions which would exist in the event of war. The Royal Commission on Supply of Food and Raw Material in Time of War had expressed the belief that a guarded and well-considered scheme of national indemnity would act as a powerful addition to our resources, but a Treasury Committee, appointed in 1907 with Mr. Austen Chamberlain as Chairman, declined to recommend the adoption of any form of national guarantee against the war risks of shipping and maritime trade "except that which is provided by the maintenance of a powerful navy." While Sir Frederick Bolton, of Lloyd's, was quietly working on the problem at the Admiralty, shipowners, in order to meet the situation which they feared would be created on the outbreak of war, determined to organise themselves, following the example already set by the North of England Association. On the outbreak of war nearly three-fourths of the British steamship tonnage employed in the overseas trade was embraced in the various War Risks Insurance Clubs or Associations.

In May 1913 the Prime Minister formed a Sub-committee of the Committee of Imperial Defence " to consider the insurance of British ships in time of war." This Committee consisted of the Right Honourable F. Huth Jackson, Lord Inchcape, Sir Norman Hill, Secretary of the Liverpool Steamship Owners' Association, Sir Raymond Beck, Deputy Chairman of Lloyd's, and Mr. Arthur Lindley, with Captain Maurice Hankey[1] as Secretary.

[1] Now Lieut.-Col. Sir M. P. A. Hankey, G.C.B.

BASIS OF THE PROBLEM

It adopted a series of general principles in the following terms:

(1) As laid down in the terms of reference, the scheme must be on the basis of reasonable contributions being paid by the owners of ships and cargoes towards the cost of insurance.

(2) The main object of the State is to keep the trade of the country going, and not to make a profit.

(3) Nevertheless, it is necessary to safeguard the State against incalculable financial liabilities, and more particularly against fraud.

(4) If the scheme is to have any prospect of success, it is essential to avoid the hostility of any of the interests concerned. It is, therefore, necessary to avoid any step prejudicial to the legitimate business of shipowners, insurance brokers, underwriters, merchants, or bankers.

(5) The scheme should avoid the appearance of a gratuitous gift from the State to a particular trade, at a time when all branches of trade will be very much hampered, and every class of the population will be subject to unforeseen and incalculable risks of loss.

(6) It should, on the other hand, avoid disclosing to the enemy the real conditions prevailing at any moment, by the quotation of official rates of insurance corresponding to the actual risks as known to the Admiralty.

(7) It should avoid or minimise, as far as possible, the administrative difficulties which will fall upon the State—e.g., of valuation, avoidance of fraud, congestion of business, etc.

At the outset it was apparent that the formation of the mutual insurance associations, or clubs, had eliminated some of the difficulties which had hindered action in the past. The North of England Protecting and Indemnity Association comprised, in its war risks class, steamers of a value of about £30,000,000. The London group of War Risks Associations had steamers of a value of £27,000,000 on its books. The London and Liverpool War Risks Insurance Association (Limited) comprised steamers of a value of about £30,000,000. Thus the total values insured in these three associations amounted to about £87,000,000, while the total steamer tonnage of the United Kingdom engaged in foreign trade was valued in 1911 at £127,000,000. The risks covered by these associations differed somewhat in detail, but the main principles embodied in their insurance were the same. They covered fully the risks incident to a war, so long as the United Kingdom was neutral, but the risks covered incident to a war in which this country was a party were strictly limited.

In its report, this Sub-committee of the Committee of Imperial Defence pointed out that " the losses and claims to meet which these Insurance Clubs were formed are those which are excluded from the ordinary marine insurance policy by the following, or similar clause : ' Warranted free from capture, seizure, and detention, and the consequences thereof, or any attempt thereat, barratry, piracy, riots, and civil commotions excepted, and also from all consequences of hostilities or warlike operations, whether before or after declaration of war.' " This cover applied both in the case of war between two foreign nations, and also when Great Britain was one of the belligerents; but when Great Britain was at war the cover was limited in the case of vessels actually at sea, or in any enemy port, on the declaration of war or the outbreak of hostilities, until the time of first arrival at a British or neutral port which was a safe port for the ship to lie in. The period of cover while in such safe places varied. In one Club it was limited to ten days, in another to thirty days, while in a third it extended to the date of expiry of the policy. Vessels which were not at sea on the outbreak of hostilities, but were in a safe port, were held insured while they remained there, for a similar period. Every vessel was deemed to be insured against all perils covered by an ordinary marine insurance policy, so long, of course, as it sailed under the British flag. There were a number of other conditions which it is not necessary to mention in detail. Only a nominal initial premium, amounting to a few pence per cent. on the value entered, was charged to cover the expenses of management, but the members shared all losses on the basis of the insured values. The Club insurances were effected on February 20th in each year, running until the same date in the following year, when, in ordinary circumstances, the policies were automatically renewed for another year. One essential fact emphasised by the Sub-committee was this—that it might happen that, " within a very short period after the outbreak of war in which we were one of the belligerents, the movements of practically the whole of the shipping under the British flag would be arrested, except, perhaps, in such areas (if any) as were outside the possibility of interference by the enemy."

The first point, then, to claim the Sub-committee's attention was the provision for the completion of voyages current at the outbreak of war, which would be automatically interrupted under the mutual insurance arrangements. Sir Norman Hill, the Secretary of the Liverpool and London War Risks Insurance Association, suggested that the Associations might be induced to run a maximum of 20 per cent. of the total King's enemy risks on current voyages, on condition that the State undertook the remaining 80 per cent. of these risks. He was quite convinced that shipowners would not be prepared to pay any premium to cover these additional risks which they would be under no obligation to incur at a time when, for the most part, they would be running at peace freights. Under the conditions of many bills of lading, they could, on the outbreak of war, discharge their cargo at a safe port, and start on a new voyage, at war rates of freight, as soon as insurance could be arranged. Failing this, it would probably suit them better, it was added, to lay up their ships for six or twelve months—a policy which some firms had adopted in recent years when they had been unable to obtain remunerative freights. The Sub-committee were informed that " managers of shipping companies might consider themselves under an obligation to their shareholders not to send ships to sea without war risk insurance, and that every mortgage deed or debenture bond had a stipulation of some kind that the vessel shall be amply insured."

Passing on to a closer examination of the problem, the Sub-committee thought it desirable to consider whether any scheme was possible which would avoid publicity before the outbreak of war. The plan that suggested itself was that the State should, immediately on the opening of war, make a public announcement that it was willing to accept 80 per cent. of the King's enemy risks for the completion of all current voyages from the time when the cover provided by the Club policies ceased. The difficulties which this scheme raised were weighed by the Sub-committee, and eventually it was decided to propose that the existing standard form of policy of the Associations should be altered so as to include the additional risks involved. This new form of policy would run from year to year as was at the time the case, a list of the policies issued by each Club being given to the State every year. The State would enter into a general agreement with each Association, accepting responsibility for 80 per cent. of the King's enemy losses incurred under these policies in the case of a war in which we were one of the belligerents. The insurance would remain in force for ten clear days following the arrival of the ship at her port of destination. The war risks, other than King's enemy risks, would be covered under the same Club policy, but for these the Club would alone be responsible.

Going a step further, the Sub-committee agreed that words should be introduced into the new policies providing a warranty that after the outbreak of war ships should, as far as possible, carry out any orders that the Admiralty might give in regard to routes, ports of call, and stoppages. If they failed to carry out the orders, it was provided that they should lose the benefit of insurance, unless the insured could satisfy the Committee of the Club that the breach of orders happened without the fault or privity of the assured and of the owners and of the managers of the ship. Even in those circumstances, it was thought that the shipowners should be liable to some penalty, and it was suggested that the State should require that the rules of every approved Club should contain provision for an appropriate penalty, taking the form of a levy of an extra premium payable by the member to the Club on the insured value of the ship in which the breach had taken place, or of a deduction in the settlement of a claim of an amount to be fixed, within reasonable limits, by the Committee of the Club. In extreme cases, the Committee, it was suggested, might have the power of expelling a member from the Club.

The Sub-committee, in its recommendations relating to ships afloat at the time of the outbreak of war, considered that the fact that the Clubs, and through them the ship-

INSURANCE OF NEW VOYAGES

owners, would retain 20 per cent. of the risks involved, and pay the whole cost of administration, might be looked upon as a "reasonable contribution towards the cost of insurance." The managers of the Clubs stated that some arrangement for the completion of the current voyages without payment of premium would probably be necessary as an inducement to the members of the Clubs to accept the proposals for covering the insurance of vessels starting after the outbreak of war. It was calculated that the scheme would involve a State liability of £3,000,000. In explanation of its recommendations, the Sub-committee added: "It may be argued that, even if our suggestions are adopted, they will not compel any ship to complete its voyage after the outbreak of war. It will still be optional for the shipowner to give directions that his ship is to go to a safe port and remain there until the war is over. We admit that, if this policy were generally adopted, our scheme would fail in its main object; but we think that few, if any, shipowners are likely to adopt this policy. In the first place, the vessels on voyages current at the outbreak of war will only be earning peace freights, and it will be a strong inducement to the owner to get his present voyage completed, so that he may be able to take advantage of the higher freights for new voyages which would presumably be offered after the outbreak of war. And, further, the shipowner would realise that, even if he laid up his ship, he would not thereby escape his liability to contribute *pro rata* to the loss of other ships insured in his Club which had run the risks he was afraid of."

Turning to the insurance of hulls of ships on voyages commenced after the outbreak of hostilities, it was proposed that these should be similarly insured by the Associations, and reinsured by the State to the extent of 80 per cent. of such risks. The premiums would be collected by the Associations when issuing their policies, and 80 per cent. of them would be accounted for to the State in consideration of its taking 80 per cent. of the risks insured under the Club policies, " a warranty being inserted that ships will not sail when ordered by His Majesty's Government not to do so." The Sub-committee proposed that the rates of premium for such new voyages should be fixed by the State, varied from time to time, and it was added: " It will, in our opinion, be necessary to have

different rates of premium for different zones, and it may be
found advisable, during the course of the war, to change the
rates for certain of these zones. But we are strongly of
opinion that the different rates should be as few as possible,
and also that the changes in these rates should be as in-
frequent as possible. It is admitted that the State is
not undertaking this business with a view to making a
profit out of it, but solely with the object of preventing
the interruption of our overseas commerce in time of war,
owing to inability to insure against war risks through the
usual channels. The rates charged by the State must not,
therefore, be so low as to compete with the rates that the
insurance market may be willing to quote, nor must they
be so high as to be prohibitive, or materially to affect
the cost of the food or other merchandise being brought
to or carried from these shores. At the same time, it
would be obviously unfair to the State's partners in this
business—the individual shipowners in the Clubs—that
they should be called upon either to pay premiums out of all
proportion to the risks of the voyages undertaken, or to
bear their share of losses in respect of voyages insured at
much too low a premium. It is for this reason that we
recommend that the premium charged should to some
extent depend upon the risks involved. But we should
like to suggest that the maximum rate for any voyage
should be 5 per cent., and the minimum rate 1 per cent.,
and that any rate accepted for a particular voyage shall
hold good, provided that the ship starts within fourteen
days after acceptance of the risk."

Provision was suggested for representation of the State
on the Committee of each Club or Association : the claims,
it was added, would be dealt with by the Committee of the
Club. Some difference of opinion was expressed as to when
and how payment of claims should be made. On this
matter the Sub-committee reported that " the general
principle underlying the proposed arrangements between
the State and the Clubs is that the Clubs take the whole
of the risks, and reinsure 80 per cent. of them with the
State. A Club would, therefore, be primarily liable for
the settlement of the amount involved." The conclusion
was reached that " the State had no concern with the internal arrangements of the Clubs with regard to the
collection of the contributions from their members to an

ascertained loss. Even if the Club were unable to collect from its members the whole amount required, this would not affect the State's liability to pay over its 80 per cent. of an agreed claim to the Club." The rules of all the Clubs then existing provided that if a ship were captured, seized, or detained, the owner should have no claim for total loss unless the capture, seizure, or detention, should have continued for a certain period. This period varied in the different Clubs from one month to six months. The Sub-committee proposed that, under the arrangement with the State, the Clubs should not be bound to pay a total loss if the ship were recaptured, released, or restored to the owner within six months of the date of capture; but if the vessel was restored, the Club should pay the cost of repair or damage to and expenses incurred by the ship by reason of such capture, together with a sum equal to 10 per cent. per annum on the insured value from the date of capture. Also, in the event of loss by destruction, it was decided that no payment should be made within a period of six months of the loss. It followed, therefore, that the earliest time of payment by the State for a total loss or capture would be six months after the event. In those circumstances, the Sub-committee recommended that the liability of the State should be discharged in three equal instalments: at six, nine, and twelve months from the date of loss or capture, with interest at the rate of 4 per cent. per annum. One of the principal objects in suggesting deferred payments was to relieve the State as far as possible from immediate and, perhaps, heavy calls on its resources to meet these losses, at a time when its revenue would be strained to the utmost to meet the expense of carrying on the war.

Turning to the basis of the value of shipping for the purpose of war risks insurance which should be accepted, the Sub-committee found that the practice of the various Associations differed in this respect. "We suggest that, for the purposes of this arrangement, the basis of values should be the first cost of the vessel, without allowance for the cost of alterations or additions, less depreciation at the rate of 4 per cent. per annum, but without any minimum limit per ton. This is the basis accepted for income-tax purposes, and we consider it a reasonable one; but we think the Committee of each Club should have the right, at its discretion, to refuse to accept a vessel for insurance on this basis, if they are of opinion that the value thus arrived at is excessive. The agreement for valuation on this basis will be provided for in the articles of association or rules of the Club which will, in accordance with the practice of the Clubs, be incorporated in the policies."

It is unnecessary in this connection to deal at length with the proposals for the insurance of cargoes.[1] The Sub-committee, in the concluding remarks in its Report, dated April 30th, 1914, suggested that, if its proposals were approved, they should be made public as soon as possible. It was urged that the earliest possible publicity was essential, "not only in order that the necessary changes in the present arrangements for mutual insurance of hulls should be made by the Clubs, but also in order that the details of our proposals for insuring cargoes may be carefully prepared and periodically revised by the Board of Advisers which we recommend should be appointed for the purpose." While admitting that, in the absence of experience of the effect of naval warfare on British overseas trade, it was impossible to form any reliable estimate of the State's liability, it was estimated that "the total losses on hulls insured against premiums would be £6,133,750, and the State's share of those losses would be £4,907,000." "We estimate the value of the steamship tonnage remaining available for foreign trade during the six months following the outbreak of war at £122,675,000. Under normal conditions each vessel in that part of our foreign trade which is with the United Kingdom makes, on the average, ten voyages each year, counting each outward and inward voyage as a separate voyage. If that average can be taken as generally applicable, and if the number of voyages be maintained after the outbreak of war, premiums at the average rate of 1 per cent. per voyage on the new voyages would in six months be sufficient to cover the whole of the losses on hulls insured against premiums." The difficulty of estimating the total value of cargoes carried in British steamships in foreign trade during the six months following the outbreak of war was greater. In the circumstances, the Sub-committee accepted, as a basis for its calculations,

[1] Cf. *Seaborne Trade*, by Mr. C. E. Fayle.

that the values would be £800,000,000. If the whole of these cargoes were insured with the State Office, the assumed loss would be covered by premiums at the rate of 1 per cent. per voyage. It was added that, " It is probable that at average premiums of 1 per cent. per voyage the greater part of the hulls would, through the Clubs, be insured with the State, but the amount of cargo so insured, and therefore the amount of cargo at the risk of the State, would depend largely on the facilities offered by the insurance market." Finally, it was remarked that, " when every allowance is made, it will be seen that, even on an assumed loss of nearly 10 per cent. of all British steamers employed in our foreign trade, which on the outbreak of war, and for six months thereafter, are at risk, the claim on the State in respect of hulls and cargo would be but a very small percentage on the total volume of our trade."

In concluding its report, the Sub-committee submitted that they had prepared " an administratively practicable scheme." " We believe that it will secure that, in case of war, British steamships will not be generally laid up, and that oversea commerce will not be interrupted, by reason of the inability to cover the war risks of ships and cargoes by insurance. Even if the maximum premium of 5 per cent. on ships and of 5 per cent. on cargoes is charged for all voyages, and the whole of this premium is borne by cargoes, the total increased cost of such cargoes, on account of war risk insurance, will not be excessive, and will not, in our opinion, approach the extreme fluctuation in prices of many articles, especially of articles of food, in recent years."

It was a fortunate circumstance that the subject of war risk insurance had been considered, and a practical scheme dealing with hulls and cargoes drawn up, before the shadow of war was thrown across the country. As the report of the Sub-committee had not been published, the nation generally was in ignorance of the steps which had been taken to grapple with the situation which rapidly developed towards the end of July 1914. The Board of Trade kept itself informed of the trend of events, and during the days of uncertainty as to the issue of the action which diplomatists were taking, it was in constant communication with the managers of the three Clubs to which reference has been made. On Saturday, July 31st, Sir H. Llewelyn Smith, the Secretary of the Board of Trade, informed them that the Government had determined to adopt the scheme of the reinsurance of hulls, and requested them to arrange at once for the issue of revised forms of policy. This was done with the utmost dispatch. As an illustration, it may be added that on August 4th, when the British declaration of war expired, Sir Norman Hill addressed a circular to the members of the Liverpool Association explaining the Government scheme, and stating that his Committee had decided to bring the new forms of insurance into operation "without waiting for completion of legal formalities as to the actual issue of the new form of policies." He added that, "pending the completion of all such formalities, an undertaking had been given on behalf of the Government that the State will hold itself bound as if the reinsurance had been given."

The prompt action of the Government, in association with a certain feeling of nervousness, led many large firms who had previously effected their own insurances to join the Clubs. In this way, practically the whole work of reinsurance of steamships under the Government scheme was conducted from the first by the three Associations. Forms of policy were immediately drawn up by the Clubs for issue to their members for current and new voyages, together with a form of reinsurance in regard to each such policy as between the Board of Trade and the Associations. In illustration of the celerity with which the scheme was put into operation, it may be added that the agreement between the Board of Trade and the Associations was dated August 14th, 1914, although some of its details were not completed until a few weeks later. This delay did not interfere with the operations of the scheme, which from the first centred in the Marine Department of the Board of Trade. The managers of the various Associations rendered the most efficient help in this department. Sir Maurice Hill, K.C., placed his services at the disposal of the Board as a legal adviser, and gave valuable assistance both in drafting and in interpreting. From the very outset the relations between the central department and the Associations were placed on a satisfactory footing, with the result that the scheme worked smoothly and the dangerous dislocation of ocean-borne commerce which the enemy no doubt hoped to produce was averted. As to cargoes, it need only be added that the Sub-committee's recommendations were also adopted, the Advisory Committee for the National Insurance of British Shipping, with Mr. (afterwards Sir) Douglas Owen as Chairman, holding its first meeting on August 5th, and a War Risks Insurance Office was opened forthwith at Cannon Street Hotel, to be moved later on to 33–35 King William Street.

The precautionary measures adopted by the Admiralty, and the prompt action of the Board of Trade, saved the situation. Shipowners, charterers, masters and men were given confidence at a moment when there was a possibility of panic, and from the first day of hostilities the British Mercantile Marine continued its sailings under Admiralty advice with almost the same freedom as under the conditions of peace.

V. ADMIRALTY DIRECTIONS TO SHIPPING

The imminence of hostilities in July 1914 prompted the Admiralty to get into direct touch with the shipping community as soon as possible. In the emergency, the Customs, Lloyd's, and the War Risks Clubs, as well as the Brethren of Trinity House, rendered invaluable aid; all their resources were placed unreservedly at the disposal of the Admiralty. The officers at Whitehall dealing with trade matters were thus enabled to get at once into communication with ships and shipowners more quickly and with more satisfactory results than would otherwise have been the case. It is impossible to lay too much stress on the salutary influence of the close relations between the naval authorities and the shipping industry which came into existence in the summer of 1914. The Consular and Colonial services also gave great assistance, and the Foreign, Colonial, and Indian Offices promptly transmitted Admiralty instructions to their officials for the information of ships in distant waters, through the medium of the Intelligence Scheme already described, thus enabling the Admiralty to establish a very complete chain of communications all over the world. That intelligence service, varied in character and efficient in operation, proved of incalculable value.

The first and most urgent necessity which confronted

the Admiralty was to convey to the British Mercantile Marine, distributed in all the seas, short and comprehensive instructions embodying the policy of the naval authorities in relation to the protection of trade. Orders to His Majesty's ships operating in and about the trade routes had been in existence for some time, and they formed the basis on which the early directions to merchant shipping were framed. As a normal matter of peace routine, commanders-in-chief and senior officers of British naval forces had received instructions from the Admiralty as to the action to be taken in the event of war in order to afford protection to merchant shipping. These orders were based upon the well-established principle that the surest way of striking an effective blow at the enemy, and at the same time safeguarding tonnage and territory, was a prompt attack upon the enemy's fighting-ships. That principle had guided British policy for centuries. The primary object—the annihilation of the enemy's forces—included the secondary, the security of British ocean-borne commerce. Subsidiary to both those objects was the capture of enemy merchant vessels with the object of stopping his trade and all contraband destined for his use. It was suggested by the Admiralty, in its earliest orders, that the patrolling of areas or routes on the chance of meeting an enemy on them was not feasible, and the allotting of single vessels along the routes was also condemned. It was declared that the salient points and the confluences of the various ocean routes used by the British Merchant Marine were the most profitable places for its destruction by enemy vessels, and if those points were in W.T. communication with British W.T. stations, they were the best positions in which to work and await intelligence of the enemy's movements. It was added that the forces employed in company should be of such a strength as to afford reasonable prospects of searching for and engaging the enemy with success. Those instructions embodied rudimentary principles. Their restatement was necessary in view of the tendency to confusion of thought which had occurred since the steam-engine made its appearance, suggesting that the character of the menace offered by enemy ships, and the best means of combating that menace, had undergone changes deep, permanent, and revolutionary. However widespread those opinions may have been during the Victorian period, the clouds of doubt had been dispersed long before the opening of hostilities. It is apparent, from the action of Admirals and other senior officers during the opening phase of the war, that the naval authorities had reached a right conclusion as to the policy to be adopted by a supreme navy in protecting the Mercantile Marine under its national flag.

Although the possibility that the enemy might employ submarines to prey on commerce could not be ignored after the sinking of the HOGUE, CRESSY, and ABOUKIR on September 22nd, 1914, and the destruction of the merchant ship *Glitra* in the following October, the primary concern of the Admiralty during the early phase of the war was for the safety of vessels, both naval and mercantile, attacked by enemy cruisers. The naval authorities had always admitted that, if sailings were maintained during the first few weeks of war, some losses were inevitable. It had been suggested in some quarters that it might be advisable for all ships, on the outbreak of war, to be warned to put into the nearest friendly port, and remain there until a guarantee of safety could be given by the Admiralty. That policy would have freed the naval authorities from a heavy responsibility, while attention was devoted exclusively to hunting down enemy cruisers and providing escort for the transports which were on passage from India, the Dominions, the Crown Colonies, and the Dependencies. These counsels were, however, rejected. The bold policy was adopted of urging merchant shipping to continue its operations. In these circumstances, the Admiralty had to choose between three courses. The first was the concentration of trade on definite fixed routes, these routes being closely patrolled by British cruisers; the second, a dispersal of trade away from the usual routes, thus taking advantage of the vast tracts of ocean as a means of protection, and leaving British cruisers free to hunt down enemy warships. The third course consisted of either of the alternatives mentioned in association with convoy. That policy, however, would have involved a weakening of the offensive action against the enemy in order to provide direct protection to shipping. Shipowners and masters were generally opposed to a system of convoys, while naval opinion as to its wisdom was divided. Reviewing the situation broadly, and having regard to the limited number of cruisers available for trade protection, the Admiralty decided upon as wide a dispersal of ships as possible during the period when enemy cruisers were being tracked down. Orders were promulgated to the Mercantile Marine in accordance with this decision through the channels of communication then available at home and abroad.

In order to convey to the Mercantile Shipping the Instructions, Route Orders, and Advice necessary to enable vessels to navigate with the least possible risk, both from direct enemy action and also from mines, a number of Shipping Intelligence Officers were appointed at the principal commercial home ports, and the system was gradually extended to other ports in the United Kingdom. These officers were in direct touch with the Admiralty (Trade Division), and received instructions from time to time as to routes to be followed, etc., while somewhat similar arrangements were made at ports abroad so that masters could obtain the latest Admiralty instructions as to their routes from reporting officers, who were usually Consular or Colonial officers. As has already been pointed out, Lloyd's and the War Risks Clubs were also used as channels of communication where this was the most convenient means, the existing channels being gradually co-ordinated to form a rapid means of communication between the Admiralty and the Mercantile Marine. The Board of Customs and Excise likewise placed their entire organisations at the disposal of the Admiralty, and throughout the war rendered invaluable assistance in the dissemination of "Traffic Instructions" to merchant vessels. These Traffic Instructions consisted principally of directions for coastal voyages, which every vessel had to obtain from the Customs Authorities at the port of departure immediately before sailing. It is impossible to speak too highly of the cordial support and co-operation received by the Admiralty from the Board of Customs and Excise.

Except on special short sea and coastal routes where concentration of naval forces was possible, the convoy system was not employed for merchant ships in the early part of the war; this was due partly to delays regarded as inevitable with any system of convoy, and partly to the congestion which it was considered would have been caused in British ports by the sudden entry of large convoys; but the chief obstacle, as already indicated, was the lack of protective vessels. When the Admiralty found themselves in a position to spare destroyers and cruisers for convoy work, due to the increased output of destroyers and the advent of the United States of America into the war, the convoy system for overseas trade was adopted, and gradually increased to include practically all vessels trading to and from the United Kingdom. After the system had become properly organised it was found that delays in the voyages of ships were not in fact greater than had been experienced by ships sailing individually under war conditions, which entailed the periodical suspension of sailings in certain areas owing to enemy activity, and the lengthening of voyages due to diversion and the necessity for observance of Admiralty instructions for the protection of merchant ships in the danger area. Partly for the same reason, but mainly due to the sailing of convoys at more frequent intervals as a greater number of escort vessels became available, no appreciable difference was experienced in the conditions obtaining at the principal commercial ports for dealing with the cargoes of the ships as they arrived.

In conformity with the Admiralty decision to adopt the policy of dispersal, the Trade Division, on August 3rd, sent out an instruction to Lloyd's and the War Risks Clubs in the following terms:

"Advise British shipping to abandon regular tracks. Complete voyages without bunkering, if possible; reduce brilliancy of lights. Make use of territorial waters when possible. Homeward-bound vessels call for orders at any Signal-station on South coast of Devon or Cornwall, or on South or North or West coasts of Ireland. Pass this as far as possible to all British ships."

On the following day a short message in the same sense was dispatched by cable or wireless telegraph to Lloyd's agents in all parts of the world, numbering 265. Orders of a somewhat more detailed character were issued simultaneously to all Intelligence Officers and Reporting Officers to the following effect:

"Advise British shipping to steer course parallel to and from 80 to 150 miles distant from regular track. Endeavour to fill up sufficiently with coal to avoid bunkering on passage. Reduce brilliancy of lights. When obliged to pass through localities where traffic is most congested, endeavour to do so at night. Use neutral territorial waters when possible. Homeward-bound vessels call for orders at any Signal-station on South coast of Devon or Cornwall, or on South, North, or West coasts of Ireland. Pass this secretly by visual to any British ships met with."

During the succeeding week it became apparent that, in spite of the action of the naval authorities and the cover provided under the War Insurance scheme, some ships were being held up. Further instructions to check this development were decided upon on August 13th, and communicated to all British possessions and to His Majesty's representatives and others throughout the world. After recommending that navigation lights should be extinguished only when an immediate attack was apprehended, and that, the danger passed, they should be relighted, the Admiralty added that it was most important that British trade should be interrupted as little as possible, and that "British vessels should not be held up nor advised to remain in port unless such a course should be deemed absolutely necessary." A week later, an enemy armed merchant cruiser having interfered with vessels south of the Canaries, it was suggested to Lines using this route that, under the circumstances then existing, vessels should be directed where possible to avoid passing the Canaries, and that in other cases they should go well clear to the westward of those islands, the exact distance depending upon the importance of the voyage, the amount of coal available, and other special considerations. "If ships are so diverted," it was added, "it is considered that the chance of capture will be considerably modified."

In spite of the action which the Admiralty had taken, a feeling of nervousness in commercial circles still existed owing to news of captures by the KÖNIGSBERG, DRESDEN, KARLSRUHE, and KAISER WILHELM DER GROSSE. In order to arrest anything approaching a feeling of panic as to the danger on the trade routes, fresh instructions were issued to the Intelligence Officers on August 29th, advising them not to hold up British shipping except for good reasons, it being added that "the Government Insurance Scheme provides for a small percentage of loss, and it is most important to keep the trade moving, even if slight loss is incurred." In further reference to the same tendency to check the flow of shipping, and therefore of trade, another telegram was dispatched on the following day to all Naval, Indian, and Colonial authorities in the East. Reference was made in that message to the continual complaints received from shipowners as to their vessels being detained, " especially in Far Eastern and Australian waters," and it was added that the " essential trade of the Empire should continue uninterrupted." The telegram added that, " If vessels sail after dark, make good offing, avoid regular tracks, danger of capture small. Most essential impress this on all concerned. No ships should ever be detained unless definite news of presence enemy's cruisers in immediate vicinity." In order that commercial communities throughout the Empire should be in no doubt as to the policy which was being pursued by the naval authorities, a statement was drawn up headed " Sea is free to all." It appeared in the newspapers on September 3rd :

" There appears to be an impression in shipping circles that the Admiralty have prohibited the use of certain trade routes for mercantile shipping. This is quite erroneous. The Admiralty policy is that the sea is free to all. Any limitations which the Admiralty may advise are intended solely to assist shipowners in safeguarding their vessels, and no routes are prohibited.

" Owing to the German policy of laying mines in waters principally frequented by peaceful trading vessels, and other threats to the safety of shipping, the Admiralty have, in some cases, considered it advisable to warn shipowners that certain routes are exceptionally dangerous, and are, therefore, not covered by the War Risks Insurance scheme. But should the shipowners decide to use those routes, there is no desire on the part of the Admiralty to interfere with the shipowners' absolute discretion in the matter."

By the following day the Trade Division was able to

modify the advice previously given with reference to the Canary Islands, since its information suggested that the danger was not for the time so acute as formerly. Shipowners desirous of sending their vessels to the Canaries were therefore informed that they could do so without undue risk. Knowledge of the activities of the KARLSRUHE led the Trade Division to issue an instruction to the effect that, in the absence of definite news of the presence of enemy cruisers in the vicinity of ports, ships should not be detained.

By these measures the Trade Division endeavoured to give shipowners confidence to continue running their vessels in order that the maritime trade of the Empire might not be endangered during the critical period of the transition from the conditions of peace to the conditions of war. By the end of September, although in the meantime the EMDEN had made her appearance off Madras, the War Staff was encouraged to issue a further instruction to His Majesty's representatives abroad. They were advised that the experience of the first two months of the war had shown that " no increase in the loss of merchant shipping will be incurred by always keeping trade routes open. When a hostile cruiser makes her presence known by sending crews or prizes into port, she is unlikely to remain on the same route; short of closing all routes for indefinite time, there is no remedy, as next point of attack is matter for conjecture." It was also pointed out that " the detention of insured vessels in port was extremely costly to owners and merchants, and if continued defeats the object of Government Insurance Scheme." That British representatives abroad might have confidence, they were reminded that " vessels sailing after dark and making good offing with dimmed lights run little chance of capture." So insistent was the Trade Division on the absolute necessity of checking any nervous action on the part of British representatives abroad, that instructions were issued " that any detention of shipping should at once be reported by cable." That instruction conveyed to His Majesty's representatives an intimation that detention of shipping was to be regarded as justified only in very exceptional circumstances, and that the policy should not be adopted unless it became imperatively necessary owing to local conditions. Similar warning notices were sent through the Colonial Office to all self-governing Dominions and to the principal Crown Colonies.

In the meantime, the Trade Division had drawn up a Memorandum in which it set forth the conclusions which had been reached as to the best course to be adopted for securing the safety of British shipping :

"The experience gained during the first two months of war clearly proves that the most effective manner of evading capture is by a complete abandonment of the regular tracks. Closely associated with this is the necessity for reducing the number of lights carried by vessels at night to a minimum, and for dimming their brilliancy as much as possible consistent with safety of navigation.

"Vessels should always endeavour to pass through focal areas at night.

"When leaving a port in the vicinity of which an enemy cruiser is suspected of operating, the departure should be made soon after dark, the intention to sail being kept as secret as possible. A good offing should be made during the night, care being taken to be well off the usual route at daylight.

"Similarly, it is advisable to make a port at or just before daylight, thus insuring that the usual route is only approached in the dark, and at the latest possible moment.

"Masters should be warned, when abandoning a track, to make sure that such deviation does not place them on other routes. Neglect of this precaution has been the immediate cause of at least three captures in the Atlantic.

"In the case of the EMDEN's recent captures in Indian waters, two main features present themselves :

"(1) So far as can be ascertained at present, the vessels themselves, when captured, were adhering very closely to the usual trade routes.

"(2) No attempt seems to have been made by the vessels in the way of obscuring lights, or of otherwise avoiding capture.

"(The only exception seems to have been the *Gryfevale*, which made a practice of putting out her lights. This vessel, however, was captured during daylight, but it is satisfactory to know that she was released.)

"The EMDEN was thus enabled to effect more captures in Indian waters in the space of a few days than all the German cruisers in the Atlantic have hitherto made.

"Trade routes in the Indian Ocean are admittedly somewhat more constricted than in the Atlantic, but a divergence of 100 miles from the normal course would have probably ensured safety, except in the case of three vessels captured near ports.

"Several reports which have reached the Admiralty of late point to the fact that the comparatively small number of captures is inducing some masters to return more nearly to the usual trade routes.

"Masters should be constantly reminded that the farther from the trade routes, the greater will be the safety; this will continue throughout the war.

"Wireless communication should be reduced to a minimum, and the vessel's position and future movements should always be kept secret.

"It is assumed that no vessel carries any enemy subject as part of her crew, and that no enemy subjects are employed in any capacity by owners whose vessels are covered by the Government Insurance Scheme.

"It is pointed out that even one spy in a vessel would most seriously compromise the secrecy of instructions upon which the safety of British shipping so largely depends."

This Memorandum was immediately given wide circulation among His Majesty's diplomatic representatives and Reporting Officers in British Dominions, Colonies, and Protectorates.

The Trade Division, in spite of all the action which had been taken, was still not fully satisfied, in view of the day-to-day reports which reached it, that its policy was clearly understood. So, on October 26th, further instructions were issued all over the world as to the necessity of keeping open the trade routes. At that time the KARLSRUHE and EMDEN were busy, the former off Pernambuco and the latter off Minikoi. "It is undesirable," it was remarked, "that vessels on passage should be directed to converge on focal points such as Colombo or Singapore merely for orders, and unless absolutely necessary. Shipping must be more scattered off the routes, and where a choice of passages exists, this should be taken full advantage of. As enemy is evidently aware of present scattering limits, substitute general order that vessels must scatter widely both sides of usual track, so that distribution of shipping shall be as effective as possible. Instructions by Reporting or Intelligence Officers should, wherever possible, be handed to the masters in writing, and a record of such instructions should be kept. Masters must be warned to destroy these instructions if in danger of capture. Colours are no indication of nationality until the vessel opens fire. It must, therefore, be impressed on all masters that measures should be taken to avoid vessels directly they, or their smoke, are sighted. All lights except Navigation Lights should be hidden, and Navigation Lights should not exceed brilliancy laid down in Rules for Prevention of Collisions at Sea. The second masthead light is unnecessary." On the following day instructions of a very similar character were issued to His Majesty's representatives in the areas chiefly affected by the operations of enemy ships. An additional paragraph suggested that an endeavour should be made to advise British shipping secretly of the best measures of evading capture by hostile vessels.

At the opening of the new year the naval situation changed for the better, the KRONPRINZ WILHELM, PRINZ EITEL FRIEDRICH, and the DRESDEN being the only enemy vessels known then to be at large. In the meantime, shipowners had made complaints that merchant vessels had been captured very shortly after official advice had been given that certain routes were " safe " or " clear." In a telegram to Intelligence Officers at the ports most affected, the Trade Division remarked that such statements could only be personal opinions, which might be formed on unavoidably imperfect information. " These and similar expressions should never be used by anyone giving advice or instructions as to routes. They imply assurances of security which are obviously impossible in war-time; this tends to discredit the value of Admiralty advice. Events have proved that such statements may be misleading, may cause relaxation of the vigilance which is so essential, and may cause serious disaster. Advice should be confined to statement of facts as to course to steer and similar matters. Any helpful information should be given which does not disclose our plans or the position of our own war-vessels."

While the Trade Division was advising and shepherding the Merchant Navy during these early days of the war, the Operations Division of the War Staff, under Rear-Admiral Arthur C. Leveson, was also busy in its own particular sphere. The Operations Division was charged with taking a wide survey of the naval situation, and close touch was maintained between it and the Intelligence and Trade Divisions. From August 5th onwards, the Trade Division was in a position to issue daily voyage notices,[1] specifying the passages forbidden under the War Insurance Scheme in view of the Admiralty's knowledge of the enemy's actions and probable plans. The character of the services which this branch of the War Staff rendered in this respect may best be illustrated by the " daily voyage notice " of August 5th, in which passages were forbidden to the Baltic, to the North Sea Continental ports east and north of Dunkirk, the North Atlantic, from Canadian ports and ports of the United States as far south as, but not including, Philadelphia, and trade on the North Pacific coast. It would be tedious and unnecessary to trace the gradual development of this work during succeeding months as the British naval authorities gained a fuller appreciation of the situation. It may be of interest, however, to give by way of contrast the daily voyage notice which was issued on the last day of 1914:

" For the purposes of the Government War Insurance scheme, the Admiralty consider all voyages may be undertaken subject to local conditions, except the following:

"(1) All ports in Belgium, Holland, Denmark, and Germany.
"(2) All ports in Sweden, except Gothenburg.
"(3) All Russian Baltic ports.
"(4) Adriatic, North of Viesti.
"(5) All Black Sea and Turkish ports.
"*Note* 1.—Vessels from the Atlantic bound to Gothenburg or Norwegian ports are required to call at a port in the United Kingdom for orders, before proceeding to destination.
"*Note* 2.—Owners whose ships are trading to and from

[1] The daily voyage notices subsequently became known as " Standing Orders under the Government War Insurance Scheme."

Norwegian ports or Gothenburg should send a representative to the Trade Division, Admiralty, for special instructions.

"*Note 3.*—A mine area exists between lat. 51° 15′ N. and 51° 40′ N., and between long. 1° 35′ E. and 3° E.

"*Note 4.*—Vessels trading to Gothenburg and Norwegian ports are warned that it is unlawful to carry goods that are contraband of war or the export of which is prohibited, unless they have a licence from the Privy Council to do so. Very serious consequences may ensue if vessels knowingly carry such cargo.

"*Note 5.*—The route along the East Coast is now open. When passing coast between Filey Brig and Scarborough, vessels must do so during daylight only. They must keep as close to the shore as possible, and must pass to the westward of the position 1½ miles E. by S. Scarborough Rock and 1 mile N.E. ½ E. Filey Brig Buoy.

"*Note 6.*—No Atlantic traffic is to pass round North of Ireland until further orders."

With the rounding up of the enemy's cruisers and armed merchantmen, a feeling of security began to influence shipowners and masters. It was assumed by some of them that no further trouble was to be apprehended, and that the precautions hitherto observed might therefore be disregarded. The Trade Division considered it desirable to check without delay the growth of any such idea. They let it be known that "the suggestion that certain routes are now safe, and that vessels can safely follow the usual route, is a most dangerous one, and should be combated whenever it is mooted, either formally or in conversation." It was pointed out that it would never be known from day to day when German vessels might break out through the North Sea and appear suddenly upon the great trade routes. The shipping interest was reminded that the surest way of encouraging such raids was to let it be generally known that precautions had been relaxed : "If precautions are in any way relaxed, enormous losses might be inflicted on trade in a few days before we were even aware that raiders had escaped."

Wise as these precautions were, experience was to show that the Admiralty credited the enemy with a greater degree of enterprise than he had, in fact, any intention of exhibiting. During the whole of March, only two vessels were destroyed by enemy surface vessels—the *Tamar* (3,207 tons) on the 25th, and the *Coleby* (3,824 tons) two days later, both by the KRONPRINZ WILHELM and both off Pernambuco. These two incidents marked the end of the enemy's cruiser warfare, and in subsequent months the Admiralty's main preoccupation was the protection of merchant shipping against submarine attacks.

CHAPTER VI

THE ORGANISATION OF THE AUXILIARY PATROL

IT may be said of the Admiralties of the world, even those responsible for ocean commerce on a large scale, that none foresaw the course which the war by sea would take, and consequently there was a good deal of hasty improvisation to meet its needs, particularly on the part of the Entente navies, which had to keep open the maritime communications of armies and peoples. For ten years or more attention had been directed almost exclusively to the building of big men-of-war, battleships, and battle cruisers; and in 1914 the number of small craft—light cruisers, destroyers, and torpedo-boats—possessed by the Great Powers, not excluding Germany and Austria-Hungary, was relatively small. That was a matter of slight importance to the enemy, because he relinquished, almost from the first, all attempt to use the sea for military or economic purposes; but it would have proved a grave embarrassment to the Entente Powers if they had not had a reserve, to be called upon as required, consisting of the unconsidered and uncatalogued latent elements of naval power possessed by the British people with ancient sea traditions. Because it was responsible for protecting about half the ocean tonnage of the world, and was better provided with small craft than the French or Italian navies, the burden of sea command bore mainly on the British Fleet throughout the war. It had not been foreseen that it would be necessary to organise what at length reached the proportions of a second fleet under Admiralty control, consisting of craft which were never intended for the violence of warfare, but when the need arose it was met with complete success.

There had been no intention of making heavy demands upon the ships or men of the Mercantile Marine, though the Admiralty was prepared to take up a limited number of steamships for use as store, ammunition, and hospital ships, while other vessels were held available for employment as auxiliary cruisers and transports. The necessity for organising a great auxiliary fleet would not have arisen, or, at any rate, it would not have assumed such large proportions as it did assume, had it not been for the enemy's decision to dispatch submarines to attack merchant shipping. That policy was an afterthought. It is hardly too much to say that before the outbreak of war no naval officer, whatever his nationality, seriously contemplated the possibility of vessels being used for attacking ocean-borne commerce which could not supply prize crews or make provision, in case the prize was destroyed, for the safety of the crew as well as passengers, if passengers were carried. For a number of years torpedo-boats, swift and carrying guns as well as torpedoes, had been in commission, but it had never been suggested that these small vessels, the forerunners of the submarines, should be pressed into such service, because it was realised that such a departure involved the infraction of the generally-accepted law of nations, and, if human life was lost, the flouting of the dictates of humanity. The Germans themselves entertained no such proposal. When the submarine appeared and proved its efficiency, no idea was held of converting it into an instrument for attacking commerce, as is proved by the fact that in the summer of 1914 the enemy possessed only twenty-eight completed vessels of this type. If any such scheme had been determined upon as part of the war plans of the Germans, many more submarines would certainly have been in readiness to be thrown into the war when the struggle by sea opened. It was not until after the British cruisers HOGUE, CRESSY, and ABOUKIR had been sunk by U9, and the German flag had been banished from the outer seas, that the idea was conceived that, if men-of-war, armed and armoured and with highly trained crews, could be so easily destroyed as experience had shown, submarines should be employed against unarmed merchantmen, manned by crews unfamiliar with war conditions.

That determination on the part of the enemy, reached in the late autumn of 1914, vitally affected the naval situation as it had been studied by the British naval

A SUPPLEMENTARY FLEET

authorities in pre-war days. It forced them to assume an added responsibility, as unexpected as it was embarrassing. The Fleet had been organised to take its part in surface warfare; within a few months it had to adapt itself to a new form of warfare, pursued by the enemy with determination, with vessels capable of operating below the surface.

In conjunction with the appearance of the submarine the enemy's resort to indiscriminate mining changed the character of the British naval problem, and thus it came about that gradually a supplementary fleet was evolved—the Auxiliary Patrol. It eventually consisted of a great assemblage of small vessels of varied types—trawlers, whalers, drifters, steam-yachts, paddle-steamers, motor-launches, and motor-boats. Those vessels were manned by merchant seamen, fishermen, yachtsmen, and naval enthusiasts drawn promiscuously from the coast and inland towns and villages, from counting-house and shop and factory. Few persons before the war imagined that the stately white enamelled yachts seen in the Solent during Cowes Week would one day be painted grey, and, mounting guns fore and aft, would be commissioned under the White Ensign to hunt German submarines and assist in patrolling the ocean highways. Certainly the fishermen of the North Sea, the Irish Sea, and the English Channel did not foresee that they would spend several of the best years of their lives in sweeping up German mines and assuring the safety of merchant shipping from a deadly peril, besides assisting to bring to the British Isles the food and raw material required by the crowded population. Similarly, none of the yachtsmen who sought service under the Admiralty later dreamed that the summer cruises which they had been accustomed to make would furnish sea training and sea experience to fit them to take a foremost part in the world war. And yet, owing to the force of circumstances, this apparently miscellaneous collection of ships and men was to be welded together into a great disciplined force which bore no mean share of the burden of the war by sea during the whole of the long period covered by hostilities.

It was because the Royal Navy was so powerful that it needed these small ships, claiming them as necessary auxiliaries, arming them and sending them to sea in all weathers to fight the enemy and to assist in protecting the supreme weapon—the Grand Fleet—on which the fortunes of war mainly depended. Owing to the preponderating strength of the Grand Fleet over the High Sea Fleet, the enemy, thrown back on the defensive, decided to rely almost exclusively on two methods of offence, the mine and, afterwards, the submarine. They constituted deadly perils, not only to ships of commerce, but to men-of-war, and it was realised from the first that battleships, battle cruisers, and light cruisers were unsuited to offer an adequate defence against such instruments of warfare. A battleship or cruiser carries too many lives in her vulnerable hull, is too costly to build, is too difficult to replace, and has too great a turning circle, to engage in harrying, chasing, and sinking submarines. Destroyers were admirably suited to the work, but they were required as screens for the battle and cruiser squadrons, and the British Navy, in common with the other Allied navies, was short of these small craft. It soon became apparent that the Navy must have assistance, and, once the need was recognised, it was met by one of the most remarkable voluntary movements for which the war was responsible.

The unexpected development of the enemy's naval policy suggested the employment in this service of the steam-yacht, the paddle-steamer with its moderate draught, the motor-vessel, the drifter, and the trawler, thus utilising in fighting at sea the tonnage of the country which in normal times was used either in the pursuit of pleasure or in the fisheries. Fishing vessels were admirably adapted to meet the Navy's urgent requirements, carrying small crews, being handy in a seaway, drawing little water, and being cheap to build. These were the ships which were consequently taken up soon after the outbreak of war, fitted out, and placed on duty in the waters surrounding the British Isles. On these vessels devolved the duty of examining and controlling millions of tons of shipping passing through the narrow seas; day by day they swept channels of safety, destroying thousands of mines in the process; they encircled the British Isles with their ever-vigilant patrol, in fog and in storm, in summer and in winter; they escorted merchant ships, warning them from dangerous areas; they towed torpedoed vessels into safety; they sent enemy submarines to their doom by ramming, shelling, dropping explosives, or

CH. VI] MINE-SWEEPING EXPERIMENTS

other means. These auxiliary craft proved the salvation of the Royal Navy as of the Merchant Fleet. Gradually the sphere of operations of the Auxiliary Patrol was extended as far north as the White Sea, as far south as the Mediterranean and Ægean, and as far west as the West Indies. Wherever these vessels were employed, their officers and men performed redoubtable service in the common cause. They were the heroes of some of the most gallant exploits in naval history, as was attested by the long list of decorations won in unequal contests against the mine and submarine. The story of the part taken in the naval war by the Auxiliary Patrol, consisting of nearly 4,000 vessels and manned by nearly 50,000 officers and men, constitutes a chapter in our naval annals of imperishable renown. It is a story which proves that the British seaman, even in the days of highly developed mechanically-driven ships, has nothing to fear by comparison with the standards of the golden age of the sailing-ship. Side by side with the personal achievements of the seamen, an endeavour will be made to show how a fortuitous and unorganised assemblage of shipping, with crews undisciplined to the demands of war, developed into what was in effect a supplementary navy.

When the war broke out in August 1914, a modest organisation was already in existence for the employment of fishing craft under the White Ensign, which enabled trawlers to be dispatched within a few hours to sweep up the first minefield laid by the enemy off our coast.

In 1907 Admiral Lord Charles Beresford was Commander-in-Chief of the Channel Fleet, with his flag in the KING EDWARD VII. For some time past he had been concerned with the best method of clearing a channel for a battle-fleet leaving harbour during strained relations or in time of war. When earlier he had been Commander-in-Chief of the Mediterranean Fleet he had tried sweeping experiments with tugs and destroyers, but both classes of vessels were found to be unsuitable. Whilst on a visit to Grimsby he saw about 800 trawlers congregated in the harbour. He inspected some of them, and talked with the skippers. Here were men accustomed to deal with trawl-ropes and trawls, the equivalent to mine-sweeps. These fishermen were so expert at their work that they never fouled their screws with the wire ropes, and their ships were fitted with steam winches and all the necessary gear required for sweeping. What could be more suitable than these ships and men for mine-sweeping? In July 1907 he therefore suggested to the Admiralty that a trial should be made with these craft, and, further, that, if successful, a certain number of trawlers should be requisitioned for the different ports so as to be ready for service when the period of strained relations with a foreign Power arrived.

In response to this suggestion, the Admiralty approved of Lord Charles making a practical test. At the beginning of the following year, Commander E. L. Booty of the KING EDWARD VII was sent to Grimsby, where he selected two typical steam trawlers, the *Andes* and *Algoma*. They reached Portland on February 5th, with their skippers and crews of nine apiece; and for the next eight days they proceeded to sweep up dummy mines. The trials were carried out under the supervision of a Channel Fleet Mining Committee, of which Captain F. C. D. Sturdee,[1] then commanding officer of the NEW ZEALAND, was President. Associated with him were Captain R. F. Phillimore and two torpedo lieutenants, together with a mining expert from the VERNON. The Committee reported that the experiments had proved sufficiently satisfactory to justify the taking up of trawlers for service in war, to assist in keeping clear the approaches to harbours that were likely to be mined. Lord Charles Beresford stated in his report that the trawlers would prove invaluable for sweeping duties, as the crews had been accustomed to earning their livelihood by this class of work. Skippers and crews had entered into the trials with both enthusiasm and delight; as to the trawlers themselves, their shape and build rendered sweeping easy, and practically no additional gear was required. In other words, a trawler with its crew, when ready to proceed to the fishing-grounds, was equally prepared for mine-sweeping.

As these trials actually brought about the creation of the mine-sweeping service, which rendered such gallant assistance throughout the war, it may be not out of place to set down the details of the *Andes* and *Algoma*. They measured 105 feet in length, 21 feet beam, with a draught of 13 feet aft and about 9 feet forward. Their speed was 8½ knots; i.h.p. 240, and they carried 80 tons of coal,

[1] Afterwards Admiral Sir Doveton Sturdee.

having an expenditure of five to six tons a day. Each trawl warp consisted of 250 fathoms of 3-inch wire, and at first the trawlers' own otter-boards were used as kites, though later, after further experiments, the right size and type of kite for mine-sweeping was evolved. The crew in each case consisted of skipper, mate, third hand, two deck hands, steward, chief engineer, second engineer, and trimmer. After the outbreak of war, when fishing trawlers became His Majesty's ships, the Admiralty made the fewest possible modifications in the personnel and the running of these vessels.

The result of the experiments at Portland was to convince the Admiralty that trawlers could be depended on to clear a channel with practically only their own resources. One distinguished officer, Captain Bernard Currey (afterwards Director of Naval Ordnance), pointed out that they would be indispensable in war-time as an Auxiliary Sweeping Service, and suggested the desirability of preparing a contract with the trawler-owners so as to enable a number of these craft to be taken up on the approach of war. With this suggestion Captain E. J. W. Slade,[1] then Director of Naval Intelligence, concurred, and he further emphasised the fact that trawls were obviously more efficiently worked by men accustomed to their use than by untrained crews. The solution of the manning problem, therefore, appeared to lie in employing Royal Naval Reserve men, of whom a large number were fishermen. The proposal was approved by Admiral Sir John Fisher, the First Sea Lord.

On August 1st, 1908, five months afterwards, an important Mining Committee was formed at the Admiralty under the presidency of Rear-Admiral G. A. Callaghan to consider the general question of mine-laying and mine-clearing. It was evident to anyone able to read the signs of the times that war with Germany was sooner or later possible, and that mines might play no inconsiderable part in the enemy's operations. Hitherto the method of destroying a minefield was to countermine. But after going into the matter very carefully, the Committee recommended that a mine-sweeping service should be instituted in lieu of countermining; that the wire-sweep should be adopted; that 6-foot kites should be used for small craft,

[1] Afterwards Admiral Sir Edmond J. W. Slade.

and 9-foot kites, or even 12-foot, for larger craft. They further suggested that six trawlers should be purchased immediately for experimental and instructional service, and that trawler-owners should be approached by the Admiralty to ascertain if they could provide crews in peacetime for instruction, as well as in war-time for sweeping mines.

Little time was wasted, for by the middle of August both Sir John Fisher and the First Lord, Mr. Reginald McKenna, had approved of six trawlers being obtained (two for each of the three Torpedo Schools) in order to enable instruction in mine-sweeping to proceed without delay. There was still much to be learnt in regard to the best types of kites and the most suitable wires, and, furthermore, officers and men required a certain amount of instruction. The urgency of the matter arose from the fact that foreign Powers were known to be increasing the numbers of their blockade mines. There was the consequential danger that at the outbreak of war the British Fleet might be taken by surprise, blockaded by minefields, and unable to emerge from its bases.

In spite of the urgency of the matter, there followed some delay in obtaining financial sanction for the purchase of these trawlers; but in the Naval Estimates for 1909–10 this was provided for. In March 1910 Mr. McKenna stated that during the year great attention had been paid to mine-sweeping, and that six trawlers had been bought for "subsidiary services." More than this was not revealed publicly, as there was a desire to keep all mine-sweeping details secret. The first four trawlers were purchased in April 1909, their names being the *Spider*, *Sparrow*, *Seaflower*, and *Seamew*. From this date practice and experimental work in mine-sweeping were carried out continuously, and the results were eminently satisfactory. In December it was decided to allocate the *Sparrow* and *Spider* to the VERNON at Portsmouth, the *Seamew* and *Seaflower* to the ACTÆON at the Nore, whilst the two others still to be bought were to be attached to the DEFIANCE at Devonport. But from June to the end of September every year these six trawlers were to be used for visiting the fishing ports and training ratings.

The Admiralty having obtained these trawlers, the next step was to secure the personnel. It was necessary to detail naval officers to take charge of the units of trawlers when sweeping, but a difficulty arose. In the first place there were very few officers who had experience of sweeping, and it was clear that in time of war every available officer on the active list would be required for service in the Royal Navy. The difficulty was met when it was decided, early in 1910, to detail and train certain officers on the emergency and retired lists for this special purpose. At the outset twenty-two lieutenants or commanders were required, each of whom in time of war would command a unit consisting of six trawlers. Of those who were invited, about twenty commanders and lieutenants accepted the call and underwent a fourteen days' course in the VERNON. This was soon followed by another course for an additional number, and thus a fairly big nucleus of trained officers became available. These details of organisation were arranged none too early. Since the year 1906, Germany had been expending large sums of money on the construction of mine-layers, the manufacture of mines, and the training of officers and men in mine-laying. The Russo-Japanese War had shown the value of mines, for no fewer than thirty-seven craft, from battleships to picket-boats, had struck mines, and there were also losses to merchant shipping.

Officers for the units having been obtained, the next step was to get together a special section of the Royal Naval Reserve, to be known as the Trawler Section, which would man these craft. Men were not to be drawn from the existing Royal Naval Reserve, as obviously such a step would interfere with the manning of some of the bigger ships in time of war. The regulations for this Trawler Section were drawn up in October 1910. It was decided to retain for the men their existing titles of ranks and ratings—" Skipper," " Second-hand," and so on. The pay was based on the wages normally obtaining in the trawling industry, but about 20 per cent. lower. The skipper was to be given the rank of a warrant officer; it was determined that he must have commanded a trawler for at least two years, possess a Board of Trade certificate, and before receiving the Admiralty warrant must undergo eight days' training in one of His Majesty's steam trawlers.

The slack season in the trawling trade occurs immediately after Lent, especially between June and September, and the decision was made that the training season should coincide with the slack season as far as possible. The first enrolment of fishermen for the Royal Naval Reserve (T.) was postponed until the beginning of 1911, when the Admiralty endeavoured to obtain fifty skippers and fifty second-hands. The training was to be carried out on board the six trawlers now attached to the Torpedo Schools, the names of the recently-added pair being the *Rose* and *Driver*, attached to Devonport. For the commencement of this training Aberdeen was selected, and there the six Admiralty trawlers were to assemble, together with H.M.S. JASON and CIRCE, those two gunboats having been selected by reason of the training and experience of their commanding officers in mine-sweeping. The first course at Aberdeen began on January 30, 1911, and ended by the middle of April, during which time twenty-eight skippers, twenty-seven second-hands, twenty deck-hands, twenty-one engineers, and twenty trimmers, had been recruited and trained. Thus the first batch of the Trawler Reserve was obtained. Commander Holland of the CIRCE afterwards reported that the class of men enrolled was very good, and much better than had been expected; they all took very keen interest in their work, and were amenable to discipline. The eight days' instruction included sweeping independently in pairs, reeving sweeps, wheeling and slipping the sweep, sweeping up dummy mines, and so on.

At the beginning of April recruiting began at Grimsby, but the results were by no means encouraging. Not more than a dozen men volunteered, and not one of these was a skipper. There was no disguising the fact that Grimsby, which had been the birthplace of this Trawler Reserve scheme, and was also the home of the great fishing industry, showed itself very far from enthusiastic. There was something not quite as it should be. What was it? Anyone acquainted with these rough, hearty fishermen knows that in many ways they are just delightful big children. If one man " throws his hand in," practically the whole crew will do the same. The trouble in this case began with the skippers, some of whom made what the seaman calls " a bit of a moan " over some apparent injustice. Most of their companions took up the same attitude, and the result was failure. It is only fair to state that there were defects in the scheme, which, considering its novelty, was scarcely surprising. For instance, the Admiralty had made the age limit for skippers twenty-five to thirty-five. The Grimsby men objected to this as being too young, seeing that the best skippers in the port were much older than thirty-five. Another grievance was that the pay was not attractive. The Admiralty were quick to see where the trouble lay, and a number of modifications were devised to meet the difficulty. It was afterwards possible to smile at all this, since throughout the long war which was to follow no men did more gallant and persevering service in the minefields and on patrol than the Grimsby skippers and Grimsby crews. These men revealed themselves as no sea-lawyers, but the bravest of the brave. Time after time a Grimsby trawler foundered on a mine, and the first thing that the sole survivor did on getting back to his port was to sign on for a mine-sweeping job. And as to the skippers' ages—well, many of the best men were of the same age as some of the best Admirals!

Down to the autumn of 1911 the recruiting and training went on. In addition to Aberdeen and Grimsby, the fishing ports of Hull, Fleetwood, and Milford were visited. From these there were obtained 52 skippers, 94 second-hands, 198 deck-hands, 88 enginemen, and 94 trimmers; a total of 526.

This was the nucleus of what was to develop into a great Auxiliary Navy. But it was patent that its usefulness would depend very considerably on the rapidity with which it could be mobilised at the time of war's approach. The sphere of utility for these trawlers, as conceived in the mind of the Admiralty, was not to act as fleet sweepers—that is, sweeping ahead of the Grand Fleet. For this purpose the trawlers were too slow of speed, and a number of old gunboats were already earmarked for that duty. But it was for clearing the entrances to harbours and fairways that the trawlers were to be relied on. The moment war was declared the enemy might lay his mines off the entrances to our East Coast ports; perhaps he would not even wait for the declaration of war. Unless ships were to be either blown up or virtually blockaded, sweepers must be ready to work almost at once.

The Admiralty realised in November of this same year that there should be appointed for each of these trawler-ports a mobilising officer, whose duty was laid down. Just before the outbreak of war this officer would, on receipt of a telegram ordering him to take up his mobilisation appointment, proceed to his assigned port. There he would receive in due course another telegram ordering him to take up so many trawlers, call on the Registrar of the Royal Naval Reserve for that port, and warn him to prepare crews for these craft. The Registrar of Shipping and Seamen would furnish the mobilising officer with a list of the trawlers in port, or likely to arrive very shortly. Arrangements would be made to have these craft prepared for sea, coaled, and filled up with water, oil, and provisions to last seven days. The owners were to take out all the fish, the ice, and the fishing-gear, excepting the warps. Having selected from the available trawlers those which were suitable, the mobilising officer was to give the skippers their charts and sailing orders, and away they would sail to their port. Having proceeded thither at full speed, the trawler's skipper would then draw his special sweeping stores, such as his kite, White Ensign, flags, cone, and signal book, and be informed to which group of sweepers he was to belong, as well as the name of the parent ship of the officer in charge of his group. He would also be given a number, which was to be painted n white figures two feet long on each bow, and his ship would in future be known officially by that number. His fishing letters and number were to be painted out. A naval petty officer would also join the trawler in order to assist the skipper with advice, especially in purely naval matters, in signalling and keeping accounts; and this petty officer would be third in command. By this time the ship would also have been painted a navy grey and be flying the White Ensign; she would, in fact, have changed her character from that of a peaceful fisherman to a man-of-war.

Mention must not be omitted of the arrangement which had been made, also prior to the war, between the Admiralty and the trawler-owners. It was realised that in the event of hostilities the fishing industry would, except in certain areas removed from the theatre of operations, automatically stop; that the trawlers would have to remain in port, and therefore the owners would cease to receive dividends. The Admiralty scheme, by taking over these vessels in war-time at a certain rate of hire, was to be considered as offering a sound business proposition. Before the war an arrangement existed between certain owners and the naval authorities whereby such vessels would be chartered in priority of any other trawlers in the event of hostilities. The owners agreed that as soon as possible after receipt of notice they would hire their vessels to the Navy upon terms which had already been arranged. The payment in respect of hire was to be 12 per cent. per annum on the then value of the trawler. The first cost was to be ascertained by valuing the hull and outfit at £18 per ton of the gross tonnage on the Board of Trade certificate, and the machinery and boilers at £40 per nominal horse-power. This estimated first cost was to be depreciated at the rate of 4 per cent. for every year of the trawler's age; the class of vessel aimed at was craft not more than ten years old, and able to carry enough coal to steam at least 1,000 miles at 8 knots.

In the month of March 1912, a number of retired naval officers were selected to take charge of mine-sweeping trawlers at Sheerness, the Firth of Forth, Dover, Portsmouth, Portland, Devonport, and Milford. As soon as these officers should receive a telegram ordering them to mobilise, they were to proceed to their respective ports. They were not, of course, the mobilising officers, but were to go to sea in charge of their respective groups of sweepers. In July of that year a further number were also selected as mobilising officers at Aberdeen, Hull, Grimsby, Milford Haven, North Shields, Granton (near Leith), and Fleetwood; and, in order to leave no loophole for misunderstandings, these officers were required to undergo an annual course of three days at their appointed ports with a view to getting in touch with the Registrars of the Royal Naval Reserve, the local harbour authorities, and trawler-owners, and in order to become acquainted generally with the docks and locality. Prior to these three days, they were to visit the Admiralty for one day each year in order to confer with the Inspecting Captain of Mine-sweeping.

It will be seen with what meticulous care the Navy had prepared against one particular form of warfare which it was suspected the enemy would pursue. For years these preparations had continued, but they were not complete. In September of 1912 another stage was reached, when an allocation of mine-sweeping trawlers was made right away down the coast from Scotland along the North Sea, down the Channel, up the Irish Sea to Milford Haven, and even as far west as Queenstown. In November there were sixty-four trawlers on the Admiralty list, each allocated to one of these ports, each with its skipper and crew trained for sweeping, and with a naval officer ready to take charge of a group whenever ordered to leave his retirement and go to sea. The crew was to consist of the skipper, second-hand, four deck-hands, two enginemen, and one trimmer, in addition to one naval petty officer, whose knowledge of signalling would be found not the least useful of his qualifications.

By August 1914 the Trawler Section had so far advanced that there were already eighty-two trawlers under the above arrangement, to be based on Cromarty, the Firth of Forth, North Shields, the Humber, Harwich, the Nore, Dover, Portsmouth, Portland, and Devonport. In addition to these eighty-two fishing trawlers, there were, of course, the six Admiralty-owned trawlers already mentioned, as well as the surveying trawlers *Esther* and *Daisy* which appeared in the Navy List, for some years before the war, as surveying-vessels. It was intended that on the outbreak of war these two should sweep at the Nore, but as soon as they were relieved by hired trawlers they were to proceed, the one to Harwich and the other to the Humber. Thus the commanding officers of both the *Daisy* and *Esther* were each able to take charge of a unit of detached trawlers.

The Admiralty also owned the trawlers *Javelin, Jasper, Janus*, and had chartered some time prior to the war the trawlers *Alnmouth, Xylopia, Daniel Stroud*, and *Osborne Stroud*. These had been employed in peace-time in towing targets, and were at that period commanded by warrant officers of the Royal Navy. Nor was the Admiralty ignorant of the mining preparations which Germany had been making stealthily and determinedly during the years of peace. It was known that practically every

German man-of-war, from battleship to torpedo-boat, had been fitted to carry mines; and for a long time the personnel of the German torpedo-craft had been trained in mine-laying. It was known, also, that our future enemy possessed over 10,000 mines, chiefly of the horned type, ready to be scattered at our very doors at the earliest moment. The naval authorities were prepared for this. On the other hand, whilst it was realised that the mine would be a serious menace, no one could have foreseen that it would usurp to itself, in conjunction with the submarine, the task of carrying out the main operations of the enemy by sea.

Such, then, was the situation at the outbreak of hostilities. The country possessed a defensive organisation when the first act of warfare by sea occurred in the laying of the minefield off the Suffolk coast by the enemy. This organisation had taken just seven years to create and to perfect. During those years great difficulties had been overcome, for unsuspected obstacles were continually arising. To have created a mine-sweeping fleet ready for service as a reserve force with a minimum of cost to the country was indeed no mean achievement. It is not possible to realise how shipping could have gone up and down the North Sea as it did during the first few months of the war if it had not been for this trawler organisation. Within ten days of the declaration of hostilities there were 100 of these fishing-vessels serving under the White Ensign. They kept a channel up the coast swept clear for tramp steamer and man-of-war alike. They had come straight in from their fishing-grounds, landed their catch and their gear, coaled, turned round, and away they had gone to sea again, with the least possible delay, to begin one of the most dangerous occupations which, in the whole history of marine warfare, has ever been devised by the wit of man. To these men the country owes an immeasurable debt.

CHAPTER VII

THE APPEARANCE OF THE SUBMARINE

THE Germans must have realised at an early stage in the war that they could not hope seriously to interrupt British sea-borne traffic, immense in volume and widely distributed, with the comparatively few men-of-war and armed merchantmen which they had operating on the trade routes. The ultimate fate of those enemy vessels was also certain in view of the large forces which the Allied fleets were able to employ in hunting them down. The Germans may also have been impressed by the confident statements issued by the British Admiralty from time to time as to the flow of traffic, and must have foreseen that month by month the Allies, drawing from the inexhaustible resources of the sea, would continue to grow in strength, while Germany and the Powers associated with her would suffer from increasing exhaustion due to the slow but relentless pressure of superior sea-power. Before hostilities had been in progress three months, there were indications that the German naval authorities were searching for some means by which they could strike an effective blow at the merchant shipping of the Allies, and the United Kingdom in particular, without endangering the existence of the High Sea Fleet.

The whole civilised world was shocked, towards the end of October 1914, by the story of the barbarous attack by a German submarine upon the French s.s. *Amiral Ganteaume*, crowded with Belgian refugees, about forty of whom were killed.[1] A charitable view was at first taken of the incident, it being assumed that this attempt to sink a vessel engaged on an errand of mercy was due to the ill-considered act of an individual naval officer. That opinion

---

[1] Subsequent examination of one of the damaged lifeboats of the *Amiral Ganteaume* led to the discovery of the fragment of a German torpedo.

had, however, to be abandoned subsequently in face of incidents which indicated that the Germans were definitely testing the suitability of the submarine for cutting the sea communications of the Allies.

Six days before this incident, on October 20th, the British steamship *Glitra*, 866 tons, had been attacked in the North Sea. That ship, which was old, slow, and, of course, unarmed, left Grangemouth, at the head of the Firth of Forth, for Stavanger on October 18th with a general cargo; the crew numbered seventeen. She followed the route laid down by the Admiralty, steaming at about 8 knots. When some fourteen miles west-south-west from Skudesnaes on the Norwegian coast, at noon on the 21st, she unsuspectingly hoisted the signal for a pilot, for no suspicious vessel was in view. The response was instant. But as the motor pilot-boat approached a low, long object, about three miles to the seaward, was observed by the *Glitra's* master (Mr. L. A. Johnston) and chief officer, who were on the bridge. It proved to be U17 (Oberleutnant z. S. Feldkirchner). The pilot-boat turned back, evidently fearing trouble, and the master of the *Glitra* altered course more to the north, in order to increase the distance between himself and the submarine. He had no reason to anticipate molestation by the submarine, a thing unheard of hitherto. The submarine, which had 5 knots superior speed, followed the *Glitra*, subsequently describing a complete circle round the defenceless merchant ship, and carrying out a leisurely inspection. A gun mounted abaft the conning-tower of the submarine was then fired, and on the *Glitra* stopping, the Germans approached within a ship's length and launched a collapsible boat. An officer and two men forthwith boarded the merchantman. They were fully armed and evidently in ruthless mood. The master of the *Glitra* was immediately ordered off the bridge, the German officer placing the muzzle of a revolver against his neck and excitedly warning him in passable English that he would be allowed ten minutes in which to get his crew away in the boats, and that then his ship would be sunk.

While preparations were being made to leave the ship, the Germans covered the crew with revolvers, and two guns mounted in the submarine were trained threateningly on the vessel. Captain Johnston and his men were refused permission to [collect their clothes and other belongings, and the Germans, having seized the ship's papers, lowered the British flag, which was torn to pieces and trampled underfoot with maniacal rage. These actions were indicative of the spirit of the enemy's seamen on entering upon the new campaign. As soon as the crew had taken to the boats, the Germans transferred to the submarine the charts and compasses of the *Glitra*, without a word of apology for such acts of theft. In the meantime, the commanding officer of the U17 had sent an engineer into the engine-room, evidently to open the valves, for shortly afterwards the ship began to settle down, her late crew being helpless spectators. The submarine towed the crowded boats for about a quarter of an hour, and, having then cast them loose with directions to the men to row towards the land, returned to complete the destruction of the *Glitra*. The pilot-boat subsequently came to the rescue of the abandoned seamen and towed the boats until the Norwegian torpedo-boat *Hai* appeared. This craft eventually landed Captain Johnston and his men at Skudesnaes, from which place they were taken on by a passenger steamer to Stavanger.

At the time this action of the Germans was regarded as merely an isolated outrage of a despicable character, but later events contradicted that impression. That the officer commanding U17 had acted on instructions received from superior authority, and that a definite policy of attack was being tested before its adoption on a larger scale, was afterwards suggested by the fate of the s.s. *Malachite* (718 tons). This vessel left Liverpool on November 19th for Havre with a general cargo. She was about four miles north by west from Cape la Hève on the afternoon of the 23rd when she sighted U21, commanded by Kapitän-Leutnant Otto Hersing, about two miles away on the starboard beam. Warned by a shot fired across his bow, the British master (Mr. Stephen Masson) stopped his engines. The submarine then closed in, and particulars of the voyage and the cargo were demanded in English. Question and answer were shouted from deck to deck. The Germans, realising that they had the British seamen at their mercy, then hoisted their ensign, and directed the master to carry all his papers to the enemy ship. When the crew were taking to the boats, the officer remarked, as though

SURVIVORS FROM A TORPEDOED SHIP.

ashamed of his conduct, that he was sorry he could not accommodate the men on board the submarine, but "war is war." Meantime the master had asked permission to retain the logbook and the ship's articles. The request was refused. When the men were clear of the ship, the submarine began firing at the *Malachite* at a range of about 200 yards with a gun mounted abaft the conning-tower. As the boats were being rowed towards Havre, which was reached the same evening, the Germans were still firing on the *Malachite*, and incidentally on the German flag, which the doomed vessel continued to fly. It was afterwards ascertained that the ship remained afloat and on fire for twenty-four hours.

Three days later the same submarine encountered the *Primo* (1,366 tons), which was on passage from Jarrow-on-Tyne to Rouen with coal. She was six miles north-west by north from Cape d'Antifer when the submarine, flying no flag, appeared. As in the case of the *Glitra* and *Malachite*, the attack was made by daylight, the *Primo* falling in with the submarine at about 8 a.m. The captain of the submarine adopted the same procedure as before, apologising shamefacedly to the master (Mr. C. A. Whincop) for the trouble caused, remarking that "This is war." The master and crew, cast adrift in their boats, endeavoured to reach a steamer which they saw at some distance, but on hearing the firing of the submarine directed on the *Primo*, that vessel sheered off in order to avoid sharing the *Primo's* fate. The seamen then rowed towards Fécamp, and about two hours later were picked up by the s.s. *Clermiston* and put ashore. The captain of the U21 experienced considerable difficulty in sinking the *Primo*. Gunfire failed to achieve the purpose. When Captain Whincop and his men last saw the vessel, she was still afloat with the submarine standing by. Two days later various vessels reported her as on fire and adrift. The French naval authorities at Boulogne, learning that an abandoned ship was afloat, a danger to traffic, dispatched a division of torpedo-boats on the last day of the month to carry out a search. According to a report from the Vice-Consul at Tréport, the battered *Primo* was ultimately sunk by a French torpedo-boat.

The sinking of these two merchant ships was the result of the first cruise for commerce-destruction carried out in the Channel by Kapitän-Leutnant Hersing. He was dispatched, there is every reason to believe, to test the adaptability of the submarine to a campaign on merchant shipping, being chosen for this mission by reason of the success which he had already achieved in the North Sea. About the same time rumours were current of a German plan to establish submarine bases in Flanders, which had recently passed into the enemy's possession; this intention, however, did not materialise until the following spring, and no other merchant ship was destroyed before the close of the year, though one vessel had a narrow escape. On December 11th, the *Colchester* (1,209 tons), a passenger vessel of the Great Eastern Railway Company, with a speed of about 18 knots, was crossing from Rotterdam to Parkeston Quay, Harwich. When some twenty-two miles from the Hook of Holland, at 8.20 a.m., she saw a submarine on the starboard bow steering approximately south-west by west. The master (Mr. F. Lawrence), being at first doubtful of the nationality of the stranger which was closing on his ship, ported his helm, bringing the submarine on the starboard bow. The submarine then turned to starboard and steamed direct for the *Colchester*, at the same time rising well out of the water. The Germans began to signal, but Captain Lawrence was too busy watching his pursuer to pay attention to signals, and in any case he was determined to spare no effort to escape. As the submarine turned towards his ship, he ported his helm again so as to bring the enemy astern of him. His seaman's instinct prompted him to turn out all the stokers, and the fires were double-banked to obtain the utmost speed. In these exciting conditions the chase continued for about twenty minutes. Finding the British vessel was drawing away from her, the submarine at last steered away south-west. The Admiralty came to the conclusion that the submarine was a German vessel, and commended the master of the *Colchester* for his spirited action.

These incidents indicated the policy which the enemy had determined to adopt. The High Sea Fleet dared not face a general action against superior forces; the whole Austrian Navy was held firmly in the Adriatic; the enemy cruisers—armed merchantmen as well as men-of-war—had been nearly all rounded up, and enemy commerce had been swept off the seas. Driven to desperation by the complete failure to interfere with the transport of the British Army or to interrupt seriously British ocean commerce, the German authorities had searched round for some method of striking a vital blow at the one Power which, encompassed by the sea, they could not reach with their army or navy. When the war opened Germany possessed only twenty-eight submarines; the oldest of these craft, eighteen in number, were built between 1905 and 1912, but ten of them, U19 to U28, of later and improved construction, were thoroughly reliable vessels.

During the early phase of hostilities, the German General Staff was encouraged by events, judging by the comments in the German newspapers, to believe that, with the aid of the submarine, a war of attrition could be pursued until at last the two fighting fleets—the Grand Fleet and the High Sea Fleet—stood at something approaching parity in strength. As early as September 5th, the light cruiser PATHFINDER had been sunk at the entrance to the Firth of Forth by U21. Later in the same month a single submarine, U9, under the command of Otto von Weddigen, had destroyed in rapid succession the armoured cruisers HOGUE, CRESSY, and ABOUKIR, with heavy loss of life. These successes produced a great effect on German opinion, and it was intensified when, on October 15th, the cruiser HAWKE was sunk in the North Sea. Orders must almost immediately have been given to a certain number of submarine commanders to prove whether U-boats might be employed against merchant shipping. The incidents already recorded brought conviction to the German Naval Staff that submarines could, at one and the same time, wage war against the British Navy and the British Mercantile Marine, thus week by week wearing down the essential sea power of the British people.

The attack upon commerce involved the infraction of international law and a denial of the common dictates of humanity, since submarines, owing to their limited accommodation, could not become "places of safety" for the crews of the ships destroyed. But those were not matters to trouble the Germans, ready to believe that the end—a German victory—would justify the means. The subsequent action of the German Government and the character of its pronouncements support the impression that the belief existed that the mere threat of a submarine campaign, supported by a comparatively few ruthless acts, would intimidate British seamen, with the result that the seas would be cleared of British shipping, thus preparing the foundations for the conclusion of a German peace. By that time it had become apparent to the German authorities that their military machine had failed to realise the hopes which rested in it within the limit of time laid down by the General Staff. Germany had become involved, *not* in a short campaign resembling those waged in 1864, in 1866, and in 1870–1, but, owing to the intervention of British sea power, in a long and exhausting war, the issue of which was uncertain. They had under-estimated the influence of sea power, and they hailed the submarine as offering them an escape from an exceedingly embarrassing situation.

In these circumstances, the submarine, with all it implied of inhuman terrorism, was adopted as giving the promise of an early peace on Germany's own terms. The enemy's growing intention was revealed before the end of the year in an interview with Grand-Admiral von Tirpitz, then Naval Secretary, which was published in the *New York Sun* on December 22nd. Referring to the possibilities of a submarine campaign, he declared, " It is difficult to draw conclusions just yet, but it is unquestionable that submarines are a new and powerful weapon of naval warfare." At the same time he confessed—and the confession indicates the restrictions which it was then believed limited the activity of these craft—" One must not forget that submarines do their best work along the coast and in shallow waters, and that for this reason the Channel is particularly suitable for this craft. The successes which have been achieved hitherto do not warrant the conclusion that the day of large ships is past. It is still questionable whether submarines would have made such a fine show in other waters. We have learnt a good deal about submarines in this war. We thought that they would not be able to remain much longer than three days away from their base, as the crews would then necessarily be exhausted. But we soon learnt that the larger type of these boats can navigate round the whole of England, and can remain absent as long as a fortnight. All that is necessary is that the crew gets an opportunity of resting and recuperating, and this opportunity can be afforded the men by taking the boat to the shallow and still waters, where it can rest on the bottom and, remaining still in the water, the crew can have a good sleep. This is only possible where the water is comparatively shallow." He put the further query, "What would America say if Germany should declare a submarine war against all enemy trading vessels?"

That this was something more than a mere academic expression of professional views became clear in the light of later events. After the appearance of this interview, which was no doubt intended to test public opinion in the United States and other neutral countries, a period of nearly a month occurred, during which no British vessel was attacked by a submarine. It was soon apparent that the enemy had devoted attention to the study of the problem which the new policy, directly foreshadowed by Grand-Admiral von Tirpitz, presented. German submarines were provided with bombs to be used in circumstances in which such comparatively cheap and light weapons could be employed, thus economising the expenditure of torpedoes, of which each vessel could carry only a few. At this stage of the war, therefore, the German submarines, particularly susceptible to surface attack owing to the vulnerability of their hulls, depended for offensive purposes on the bomb, and in the last resort on the torpedo, though some of them were provided with light guns.

On January 21st, 1915, in rainy but clear weather, the s.s. *Durward* (1,801 tons) was two days out from Leith, on passage to Rotterdam, when the chief officer, who was on the bridge, reported to the master (Mr. John Wood) that a suspicious submarine was about 1½ points before the steamer's starboard beam. On going on deck and looking through his glasses, Captain Wood saw that the strange ship was flying the signal to stop instantly. The submarine was only about a mile and a half distant and was showing no colours; she was steaming towards the *Durward* on an opposite course. The British ship was travelling at about 12 knots. Captain Wood at once determined to ignore the signal, and, going into the engine-room, gave directions to put on all possible speed. When he returned to the deck, he saw that the submarine had altered course and was heading for the *Durward's* starboard side, at the same time flying the signal "Stop, or I fire." Within half an hour of the first sighting of the enemy craft, the submarine, in spite of the best endeavours of the *Durward's* engine-room staff, had managed to get under the ship's starboard quarter, and shortly afterwards a warning rocket was fired. Captain Wood realised that further effort to escape was impossible, and stopped his engines. The submarine proved to be U19 (which had recently been rammed by H.M.S. BADGER), and the conduct of the commanding officer, Oberleutnant Kolbe, towards the British seamen merits being recalled in view of later events. In reply to a signal, the chief officer of the *Durward* and three men of the crew carried the ship's papers on board the submarine. As soon as the boat got alongside the enemy vessel, a group of German seamen put off, themselves using the *Durward's* boat, and an officer, speaking in good English, ordered Captain Wood to get everyone into the boats as quickly as possible. After the crew had left and while the British master was on board U19, to which he had been taken, the boarding-party placed two bombs against the ship's side. About twenty minutes afterwards explosions occurred, the vessel beginning at once to settle down in the water, to the grief and consternation of the British seamen. The German commander towed the two British boats for about half an hour in a northerly direction. Casting them adrift, he went back to the *Durward*, subsequently returning to give a further tow until he was within one mile north of the Maas lightship, as though anxious to do what he could for members of the same great brotherhood of the sea while conforming to the orders he had received from his superiors. From first to last the British seamen had been well treated, and, having been placed in a position of comparative safety, they were left to their own resources. Eventually a Dutch pilot steamer took them on board and towed the two boats as far as the Hook of Holland. The craft were returned later on to their owners, and, apart from the loss of the ship and the crews' effects, the incident was marked by no exhibition of Prussianism.

On the last day of January no fewer than seven ships were attacked, and only one, the *Graphic* (1,871 tons), escaped. Of the six vessels which were destroyed, three were intercepted by the enemy outside Liverpool, pointing to a carefully prepared plan of attack by the submarine under Kapitän-Leutnant Hersing to test the possibilities of virtually blockading a great commercial port. At 10.30 a.m. the *Ben Cruachan* (3,092 tons; master, Mr. D. W. Heggie) was sunk by bombs, the crew, who had taken to the two lifeboats, being directed to steer towards the sailing trawler *Margaret*, by which they were landed at Fleetwood. About an hour later the same submarine, U21, fell in with the *Linda Blanche*, a small steamer of 369 tons. The procedure was the same as in the case of the *Ben Cruachan*, the crew being advised to steer towards the trawler *Niblet*, by which they were taken to Fleetwood. When the boarding-party reached the *Linda Blanche*, some of the Germans gave cigars and cigarettes to the British crew, as though to indicate that they did not care for their work. At 1.30 p.m. the s.s. *Kilcoan* was sunk. The mate, who was on deck in charge of this little ship of 456 tons, shouted down to the master (Mr. James Maneely) to come on deck, as a submarine wished to speak to him. On going up, Captain Maneely found the submarine close to the starboard side, with a machine-gun trained on the *Kilcoan*. Her hull was painted a dull white, the conning-tower being of a darker colour. Ten men stood on the deck of the enemy craft, most of them armed with revolvers, but two carrying rifles. In face of this menacing exhibition, what could the British seaman do but comply with any demands? Kapitän-Leutnant Hersing shouted in English, "Get into your boats." The men promptly launched the starboard and port boats, and all hands took their places. The boats were then ordered alongside the submarine, and the crew were directed to get on board. The master was asked peremptorily for his papers and, as he had not brought them with him, he was sent for them. Four fully armed German seamen, carrying an explosive bomb fitted with about two yards of fuse, accompanied him. The Germans remained on deck while the master went below to obtain the ship's certificate of register and other papers, which he handed over to a petty officer. The logbook was saved, Captain Maneely suggesting in his answers to questions that he did not know where it was. The enemy, however, secured the ship's ensign and the Union Jack.

In the meantime, one of the German seamen had fixed the bomb amidship and set the fuse alight. The skipper and the boarding-party then left the *Kilcoan* to return to the submarine. While they were on their way back, the bomb exploded, tearing a hole in the port side of the steamer. The members of the crew of the British ship, still on board the submarine and wondering what their fate would be, were ordered back into their boats. Then occurred an unexpected diversion. In the distance the German officer discerned the steamer *Gladys* from Liverpool to Douglas. He made off towards her and directed her captain to pick up the *Kilcoan's* men. He then returned to the *Kilcoan* and fired at that vessel in order to hasten her destruction. The submarine at length disappeared, and late that night the British seamen's adventure ended when they were landed at Fleetwood without further mishap. On the same day the *Graphic*, twenty-two miles from Liverpool Bar light-vessel, was chased, but, thanks to her speed, succeeded in making her escape.

In the meantime, another submarine—U20—was busy farther south, pursuing a policy of torpedoing ships at sight, no warning of any kind being given. The Shaw Savill liner *Tokomaru* (6,084 tons) was sunk seven miles north-west from Havre light-vessel, and the *Ikaria* (4,335 tons) nearly twenty miles farther away, both on January 30th. The former vessel was on her way from Wellington, New Zealand, and Tenerife. At nine o'clock on the morning of that day, in fine, clear weather, the sea being smooth, she was slowly steaming towards Havre looking for a pilot. The master (Mr. Francis Greene) had no suspicion of the menace which threatened him. He was on the bridge, with the second and third mates, an A.B. being on the lookout forward. Suddenly an explosion occurred on the port side, sending the water up over the bridge and filling the stokehold. The ship at once listed heavily and commenced to sink. It was evident that the submarine was watching the effect of its torpedo, for a periscope was seen by Captain Greene three cables away. The commander of the submarine, his act of savagery consummated, then disappeared, caring nothing as to the fate of the British sailors. The experience of the *Tokomaru's* crew was one which no seaman had hitherto suffered, but nevertheless discipline was maintained and all the hands succeeded in getting into the boats—the captain going over the side last in accordance with tradition. Within an hour the men were

CH. VII]   TORPEDOED WITHOUT WARNING   279

safely on board the French mine-sweeper *Saint Pierre*. Before being landed at Havre, Captain Greene and his companions saw their ship disappear beneath the water.

Shortly after noon on the same day the Leyland liner *Ikaria*, which left Santos and other South American ports for Havre, stopped off Cape la Hève to pick up a pilot. The ship still had slight headway on her when the master (Mr. Matthew Robertson), who was on the bridge, saw the wake of a torpedo, fired, there is no reason to doubt, by U20. There was no time to use the helm, for almost immediately afterwards the vessel was struck on the port side abreast of No. 1 hatch and began to sink gradually by the head. The boats were ordered out and the officers and men proceeded on board a tug which happened, fortunately, to be close by. About an hour later, the *Ikaria* being still afloat, Captain Robertson, with some of his men, boarded her. He came to the conclusion that the ship could be saved. She was only about twenty-five miles from Havre, the sea was smooth and there was no wind. With the assistance of a tug, the *Ikaria* was got into Havre and berthed alongside Quai d'Escale, where she remained until midday on January 31st. The port authorities, becoming nervous lest she should sink and thus impede traffic, removed her to the west of the Avant Port, towards the breakwater, where she sank on February 2nd, leaving her afterpart showing.

There is no reason to doubt that the General Steam Navigation Company's steamer *Oriole* (1,489 tons) met her fate also at the hands of U20, but her end was mysterious. The *Oriole* left London for Havre on January 29th, and passed the s.s. *London Trader* off Dungeness on the afternoon of the following day. The distance from Dungeness to Havre being from ninety to ninety-five miles, the *Oriole* should have reached the latter port about ten o'clock that evening. She was never heard of again. Later in the year, Mr. Justice Bailhache had to decide in the High Court the fate of the vessel. In the course of his judgment, he told of two pathetic incidents. On February 6th, two lifebuoys were found on the coast between Hastings and Dymchurch, a little seaside place to the north of Dungeness. The name *Oriole* was painted upon them. In the following month—on March 20th—a Guernsey fisherman picked out of the sea an ordinary beer-bottle containing a piece of paper. On the bottle being broken, the paper was found to be an envelope embossed with the name of the General Steam Navigation Company, and written in pencil was the message, "*Oriole* torpedoed—sinking." The widow of the ship's carpenter identified the handwriting as that of her husband. After considering all the evidence, Mr. Justice Bailhache came to the conclusion that the only reasonable explanation of the disappearance of the *Oriole* was that she was torpedoed by the enemy, the master (Mr. William G. Dale) and his crew of twenty men perishing. The story has an historical interest since, whereas the *Glitra* was the first vessel to be sunk by a submarine—on October 20th, 1914—the *Tokomaru* and the *Ikaria* were the first to be torpedoed without warning, while the *Oriole*, destroyed in the same barbarous way, was the first British loss which involved the death of the crew. Later events were to overshadow this tragedy of the war, presenting a picture of such large, dramatic, and terrible proportions that in a few months the story of the fate of these defenceless British seamen shrank into comparative oblivion.

These first outbursts of terrorism by sea, though succeeded by an interval of a fortnight during which no British vessel was sunk and only two were attacked, proved merely the preliminary acts to the declaration of a definite policy on the part of the enemy. Since the sinking of the *Glitra* the practicability of employing submarines in attacking commerce had been tested under varying conditions. The reports received had encouraged hopes that at last a means had been discovered for bringing the war to a speedy end. A good deal had been written of the submarine and its psychological influence, and the enemy embarked upon the new policy in full confidence that the war would be ended by the severance of the maritime communications of the British people, even if the mere announcement of the intention to employ submarines on a large scale in an attack upon British shipping did not break the courage of the officers and men. Accordingly, on February 4th, 1915, the following memorandum was issued by the German Government:

"Since the commencement of the present war Great

THE GERMAN DECLARATION

Britain's conduct of commercial warfare against Germany has been a mockery of all the principles of the law of nations. While the British Government have by several orders declared that their naval forces should be guided by the stipulations of the Declaration of London, they have in reality repudiated this declaration in the most essential points, notwithstanding the fact that their own delegates at the Maritime Conference of London acknowledged its acts as forming part of existing international law. The British Government have placed a number of articles on the contraband list which are not at all, or only very indirectly, capable of use in warfare, and consequently cannot be treated as contraband either under the Declaration of London or under the generally acknowledged rules of international law.

" In addition, they have in fact obliterated the distinction between absolute and conditional contraband by confiscating all articles of conditional contraband destined for Germany, whatever may be the port where these articles are to be unloaded, and without regard to whether they are destined for uses of war or peace. They have not even hesitated to violate the Declaration of Paris, since their naval forces have captured on neutral ships German property which was not contraband of war. Furthermore, they have gone further than their own orders respecting the Declaration of London, and caused numerous German subjects capable of bearing arms to be taken from neutral ships and made prisoners of war.

" Finally, they have declared the North Sea in its whole extent to be the seat of war, thereby rendering difficult and extremely dangerous, if not impossible, all navigation on the high seas between Scotland and Norway, so that they have in a way established a blockade of neutral coasts and ports, which is contrary to the elementary principles of generally accepted international law. Clearly all these measures are part of a plan to strike not only at the German military operations, but also at the economic system of Germany, and in the end to deliver the whole German people to reduction by famine, by intercepting legitimate neutral commerce by methods contrary to international law.

" The neutral Powers have in the main acquiesced in the measures of the British Government; in particular they have not been successful in securing the release by the British Government of the German subjects and German merchandise illegally taken from their vessels. To a certain extent they have even contributed towards the execution of the measures adopted by England in defiance of the principle of the freedom of the seas by prohibiting the export and transit of goods destined for peaceable purposes in Germany, thus evidently yielding to pressure by England.

"The German Government have in vain called the attention of the neutral Powers to the fact that Germany must seriously question whether it can any longer adhere to the stipulations of the Declaration of London, hitherto strictly observed by it, in case England continues to adhere to its practice, and the neutral Powers persist in looking with indulgence upon all these violations of neutrality to the detriment of Germany. Great Britain invokes the vital interest of the British Empire which are at stake in justification of its violations of the law of nations, and the neutral Powers appear to be satisfied with theoretical protests, thus actually admitting the vital interests of a belligerent as a sufficient excuse for methods of waging war of whatever description.

"The time has now come for Germany also to invoke such vital interests. It therefore finds itself under the necessity, to its regret, of taking military measures against England in retaliation of the practice followed by England. Just as England declared the whole North Sea between Scotland and Norway to be comprised within the seat of war, so does Germany now declare the waters surrounding Great Britain and Ireland, including the whole English Channel, to be comprised within the seat of war, and will prevent by all the military means at its disposal all navigation by the enemy in those waters.

"To this end it will endeavour to destroy, after February 18th next, any merchant vessels of the enemy which present themselves at the seat of war above indicated, although it may not always be possible to avert the dangers which may menace persons and merchandise.

"Neutral Powers are accordingly forewarned not to continue to entrust their crews, passengers, or merchandise to such vessels. Their attention is furthermore called to the fact that it is of urgency to recommend to their own vessels to steer clear of these waters. It is true that the German Navy has received instructions to abstain from all violence against neutral vessels recognisable as such; but in view of the hazards of war, and of the misuse of the neutral flag ordered by the British Government, it will not always be possible to prevent a neutral vessel from becoming the victim of an attack intended to be directed against a vessel of the enemy. It is expressly declared that navigation in waters north of the Shetland Islands is outside the danger zone, as well as navigation in the eastern part of the North Sea and in a zone thirty miles wide along the Dutch coast.

"The German Government announces this measure at a time permitting enemy and neutral ships to make the necessary arrangements to reach the ports situated at the seat of war. They hope that the neutral Powers will accord consideration to the vital interests of Germany equally with those of England, and will on their part assist in keeping their subjects and their goods far from the seat of war : the more so since they likewise have a great interest in seeing the termination at an early day of the war now raging.—Berlin, February 4th, 1915."

This declaration was epitomised in a proclamation of the same date, signed by Admiral von Pohl, Chief of the Admiralty Staff of the German Navy, in the following terms :

" 1. The waters surrounding Great Britain and Ireland, including the whole English Channel, are hereby declared to be a War Zone. On and after February 18th, 1915, every enemy merchant ship found in the said war zone will be destroyed without it being always possible to avert the dangers threatening the crews and passengers on that account.

" 2. Even neutral ships are exposed to danger in the war zone, as in view of the misuse of neutral flags ordered on January 31st by the British Government, and of the accidents of naval war, it cannot always be avoided to strike even neutral ships in attacks that are directed on enemy ships.

" 3. Northward navigation around the Shetland Islands, in the eastern waters of the North Sea, and in a strip of not less than thirty miles width from the northward coast, is in no danger.

"VON POHL,
"*Chief of the Admiralty Staff of the Navy.*

"BERLIN,
"*February 4th*, 1915." [1]

To this announcement the British Government issued the following reply on March 1st, 1915:

"Germany has declared that the English Channel, the north and west coasts of France, and the waters round the British Isles are a 'war area,' and has officially notified that 'all enemy ships found in that area will be destroyed.' This is, in effect, a claim to torpedo at sight, without regard to the safety of the crew or passengers, any merchant vessel under any flag. As it is not in the power of the German Admiralty to maintain any surface craft in these waters, this attack can only be delivered by submarine agency. The law and custom of nations in regard to attacks on commerce have always presumed that the first duty of the captor of a merchant vessel is to bring it before a Prize Court, where it may be tried, where the regularity of the capture may be challenged, and where neutrals may recover their cargoes.

"The sinking of prizes is, in itself, a questionable act, to be resorted to only in extraordinary circumstances, and after provision has been made for the safety of all the crew or passengers (if there are passengers on board). The responsibility for discriminating between neutral and enemy vessels, and between neutral and enemy cargo, obviously rests with the attacking ship, whose duty it is to verify the status and character of the vessel and cargo and to preserve all papers before sinking or even capturing it. So also is the humane duty of providing for the safety of the crews of merchant vessels, whether neutral or enemy, an obligation upon every belligerent. It is upon this basis that all previous discussions of the law for regulating warfare at sea have proceeded.

"A German submarine, however, fulfils none of these

---

[1] A translation accompanying the dispatch of Ambassador Gerard to the Secretary of State, February 6th, 1915. This proclamation was published in the *Reichsanzeiger* of February 4th, 1915. (No. 29.)

obligations. She enjoys no local command of the waters in which she operates. She does not take her captures within the jurisdiction of a Prize Court. She carries no prize crew which she can put on board a prize. She uses no effective means of discriminating between a neutral and an enemy vessel. She does not receive on board for safety the crew of the vessel she sinks. Her methods of warfare are, therefore, entirely outside the scope of any of the international instruments regulating operations against commerce in time of war. The German declaration substitutes indiscriminate destruction for regulated capture.

" Germany is adopting these methods against peaceful traders and non-combatant crews with the avowed object of preventing commodities of all kinds (including food for the civil population) from reaching or leaving the British Isles or Northern France. Her opponents are, therefore, driven to frame retaliatory measures in order in their turn to prevent commodities of any kind from reaching or leaving Germany. These measures will, however, be enforced by the British and French Governments without risk to neutral ships or to neutral or non-combatant life, and in strict observance of the dictates of humanity. . . ."

As already stated, it was evidently anticipated by the Germans that the announcement of their intention to employ submarines in an attack upon British shipping would break the courage of officers and men. That this expectation was ill-founded was proved by the continued flow of traffic to and from the British Isles, and the hardihood and seamanship which were exhibited during the next few weeks, not by one ship merely, but by many. Between the beginning of February and the end of May, 128 vessels were molested by submarines, and more than half of them—sixty-four to be exact—managed to escape. Thirty-one of these ships, slow tramps though they were for the most part, owed their good fortune to their speed, of which the captains took the fullest advantage. At this period of the war the Germans were able to employ only a comparatively small number of submarines, and the surface speed of these was slow. After Grand-Admiral von Tirpitz had relinquished office some months later, he was severely criticised for having failed to provide a sufficient number of submarines of suitable types to insure the success of Germany's policy. Down to the end of April the loss of British tonnage, in comparison with the great volume operating in the waters surrounding the British Isles, proved a great disappointment to the enemy, who was compelled to readjust his estimate of the character of the British seamen and their seamanlike qualities.

The story of the *Laertes* (4,541 tons) provided a conspicuous illustration of the spirit which animated the service. This ship (master, Mr. William H. Propert) left Liverpool on Sunday, February 7th, with a general cargo for Java, being under orders to call at Amsterdam. Captain Propert had been in charge of the ship for two voyages to the Far East, and had come to the conclusion that the vessel's best speed was 11¾ knots. The vessel had a crew of fifty-one officers and men, including twenty-four Chinese. By four o'clock on the 10th, the *Laertes* reached a point about twelve miles from the Schouwen Bank lightship. The master and the second officer were on the bridge, a good lookout was being kept by men stationed on the poop and in the crow's-nest on the foremast, and the ship was making her best speed, when a submarine was seen about three miles away bearing two points on the starboard bow. Captain Propert promptly ordered the helm to be starboarded one point, and almost at the same moment the submarine hoisted a signal directing the vessel to heave to, and threatening to fire if the order was not obeyed. Captain Propert ignored the signal and determined to make an effort to escape; the enemy submarine made straight for the *Laertes* at top speed. What happened can, perhaps, best be told in Captain Propert's own words:

"My engines were well opened out, and I kept starboarding my helm to avoid him, but he gained steadily; and at 4.15 p.m., when he was about one point and a half on the starboard quarter, distant about three-quarters of a mile, he opened fire with a machine-gun, directing his fire on the bridge. I then starboarded further and brought him right astern, keeping the ship going at the highest speed she could make. Just at this time four or five single shots were heard, indicating that we were also being subjected to rifle fire. (Three bullets of different kinds were found later in various parts of the ship.)

"This was about 4.20 p.m., and the firing was kept up continuously until about 5.15 p.m., the submarine being kept all the time as much astern as possible by the use of our helm. In order to deceive him, I also hoisted the answering pennant indicating that I had read his signals. This I did twice, but he did not appear to reduce his speed, and when he had come within less than a quarter of a mile from the *Laertes*, at about 5.15, he gave one continued discharge from the machine-gun and then fell astern. About six minutes later, when he was well astern slightly on our starboard quarter, I ported the helm one point and immediately noticed a torpedo coming straight for the ship about two cables off on the starboard quarter. My helm was at once put hard aport, and the torpedo passed astern very close to the ship.

"The submarine at this time was enveloped in a cloud of steam and appeared to be in difficulties. It was dusk by this time, and a steamer, which came up on my port side steering directly towards the submarine, was given the signal, 'You are steering into danger.' The other ship altered her course, but appeared to resume the former course a little later. I had no means of ascertaining the name of the other vessel, and she made no attempt to speak further with us.

"I now hauled the *Laertes* round and steered in a northerly direction, gradually swinging her in towards the land and taking continual soundings as we approached. When we had reached a point about seventeen miles off Ymuiden, a green light appeared on my port bow three miles distant. I put the helm hard astarboard, and the light suddenly disappeared and was not seen again. As this was suspicious, I put the helm hard aport, but no further lights were observed. I then took in the regulation lights, and, while they were kept ready at hand, they were not again exhibited until we had come close to Ymuiden, which port we reached at about 10.30 p.m. on February 10th. No lives were lost and no injury received by any person on board the *Laertes*. The upper bridge, the casing of the standard compass, two boats, several ventilators, the main funnel, donkey funnel, and exhaust pipe, were pierced by bullets, and there may be some further damage. I cannot estimate the amount of this damage. The Dutch flag had been hoisted at about 4 p.m. on February 9th, and was kept continually flying during daylight. The name of the port of registry had also been obscured. Two boats had been swung out ready for loading and two lifted from the chocks on February 9th."

That is the modest record of an escape from the enemy which suggested, in association with a hundred other incidents, that British seamen were not prepared to surrender to the enemy without a struggle. The Admiralty marked their appreciation of Captain Propert's " gallant and spirited conduct " by granting him a temporary commission as lieutenant in the Royal Naval Reserve, and awarding him the Distinguished Service Cross; a gold watch, with a letter of commendation, was presented to each of the officers, and a complimentary grant of £3 was made to every member of the crew.

By this time it was evident that the enemy, with limited resources—how limited was not known to the British Government at the time—was determined to make a desperate attack on the British Mercantile Marine, paying no regard to the ordinary humanities which in previous wars had restricted the action of belligerents. The number of cases in which torpedoes were fired against ships unarmed, and therefore incapable of resisting visit and search, steadily increased. The *Membland* (3,027 tons) was destroyed in the North Sea either by mine or by submarine; she disappeared about February 15th, together with her officers and men, numbering twenty, and the cause of the loss of this valuable cargo-carrier and the destruction of so many lives will probably never be known. Nothing, perhaps, is more remarkable than the comparatively small loss of life which, in fact, occurred during this early period of the submarine campaign. That immunity must be attributed to the high standard of seamanship maintained in the British Mercantile Marine, and the skill exhibited by officers and men in the management of the small boats to which they were compelled to confide their fortunes after their ships had sunk. Typical illustrations of the hazardous experiences which fell to the crews of ships destroyed at sight are supplied by the stories of the *Dulwich* (3,289 tons) and *Cambank* (3,112 tons), the former attacked off Cape la Hève on February 15th, and the latter ten miles east of Lynns Point, on the north-eastern coast of Anglesey. The *Dulwich* was on her way to Rouen, when an explosion occurred on the starboard side. Night had descended, and it is not difficult to imagine the momentary consternation which was caused as the ship listed slightly to starboard, and then began to settle by the stern. Fortunately, the boats had been swung out and were uninjured. The master (Mr. J. A. Hunter) soon had his men transhipped, twenty-two being allotted to one boat and nine to the other. Within about twenty minutes the *Dulwich* had disappeared in a swirl of foaming water, and then a submarine was dimly seen travelling on the surface of the water, a menacing spectacle for the British seamen who had been left to the mercy of the sea on this winter's night. The enemy, callous as to the fate of these men, was evidently watching the effects of the explosion —making sure that the ship sank. The boats soon afterwards became separated. A French torpedo-destroyer picked up the master and his twenty-one companions shortly after eight o'clock that night and took them into Havre. The other boat, with only seven men on board, reached Fécamp, and thus two lives were added to the death roll of the campaign. How these two men came to their end is uncertain, as they were seen leaving the forecastle to enter the boats by Captain Hunter when he and the chief officer made their final round of inspection.

The loss of life in the case of the s.s. *Cambank* was heavier. This ship was on passage from Huelva to Liverpool with a cargo of copper and sulphur ore. The voyage proceeded uneventfully until February 12th. At midnight on that date a gale from the south-west sprang up and continued to blow throughout the following day. Early on the 14th the wind shifted to the north-west. A heavy sea struck the ship at 9 a.m. on the port side, staving in No. 1 hatch. The master (Mr. T. R. Prescott) kept his vessel away before the wind and sea and was able to reach Falmouth. Temporary repairs were effected at that port, and on the 17th the vessel left to resume her voyage. Three days later, after taking up a pilot at Lynns Point, the *Cambank* saw the periscope of a submarine[1] about 250 yards on the port beam, and immediately

[1] U30, according to German accounts.

afterwards the track of a torpedo was noticed making for the merchantman. The *Cambank's* helm was put hard aport, but, before the ship could answer, the torpedo struck her near the engine-room. It was at once evident to Captain Prescott that the vessel would speedily sink, and he ordered the crew to take to the boats. Midnight, the enemy near at hand, and their ship so fatally damaged that officers and men had no choice but to confide their lives to frail boats! The starboard lifeboat was successfully lowered, and into her scrambled twenty-one of the twenty-five men on board, including the pilot. What happened to the other four men is a matter of speculation. For a quarter of an hour the survivors lay off the doomed ship, which at last broke in two amidships and was swallowed up in the waters. Eventually these men, having been buffeted in a hurricane and then attacked by the enemy, succeeded in reaching port.

On the evening of the same day the steam collier *Downshire* (337 tons) was steaming at about 10 knots off the Calf of Man, when she saw a submarine standing to the northward on the starboard bow, being about one and a half to two miles distant. The enemy gained rapidly on the British ship and, when about a quarter of a mile away, fired a shot from a gun on the fore-deck. The master of the *Downshire* (Mr. W. H. Connor) ignored the warning, and then a second shot was fired. The collier, which was travelling at full speed, still stood on her course. A third shot followed. The submarine was then close up, and as it was apparent that escape was impossible the engines were stopped. The crew were ordered to the boats, a bomb was placed against the side of the vessel by the Germans, and the ship was sunk. Fortunately in this instance there was no loss of life, but that was due to no consideration on the part of the commander of the submarine.

Three days later—on February 23rd—two vessels were sunk without warning, the *Oakby* (1,976 tons; master, Mr. F. J. Bartlett), off the *Royal Sovereign* light-vessel, and the *Branksome Chine* (2,026 tons; master, Mr. F. J. Anstey), six miles E. by S. ¾ S. from Beachy Head—evidently by the same submarine. Within five minutes of the torpedo striking the port side of the *Oakby*, the forecastle was level with the water. It seemed as though the ship must founder rapidly. Nevertheless, the second engineer went below and stopped the engines so as to enable the boats to be lowered.[1] The vessel took so long in settling down that an attempt was made by the patrol-boat ISLE OF MAN, which had come on the scene, to tow her to Dover. The effort was unsuccessful, the *Oakby* sinking near the Varne Lightship. The loss of the *Branksome Chine* was marked by no noticeable incident, the crew managing to make their escape in safety.

On the following day undoubted evidence was furnished that an enemy submarine, commanded by an experienced and daring, if callous, officer, was operating in this part of the English Channel, the *Rio Parana* (4,015 tons) and the *Western Coast* (1,165 tons) being destroyed off Beachy Head. In the first case no submarine was sighted, but the ship was struck on the starboard side, with the result that ports and doors were stove in, jammed, or broken, and a great volume of water entered the saloon. In these conditions, the master (Mr. J. Williams) and the crew prepared to abandon the ship. By the time their preparations were completed, the ship was considerably down at the head, and the water was flush with her deck. It was at first suggested that the casualty was due to a mine, but the Admiralty, in view of all the circumstances, came to a contrary conclusion. This was supported by intelligence as to the fate of the *Western Coast*. This vessel was on her way from London to Plymouth, where warnings of the presence of enemy submarines were given by a destroyer, and shortly afterwards a ship in distress was noticed. The second officer of the *Western Coast* (master, Mr. J. Ratcliffe) was on his way to report the incident when an explosion occurred, a column of water rising forty or fifty feet. The ship immediately began to settle down, but, though she sank in two or three minutes, Captain Ratcliffe and his men managed to make their escape. The month's losses closed with the sinking of another ship—the *Harpalion* (5,867 tons ; master, Mr. A. Widders)—not far from the *Royal Sovereign* light-vessel. A violent explosion occurred which killed three firemen, and then the ship was enveloped in steam and water poured over the port side.

Though enemy submarines secured eight British ships

[1] The second engineer, Mr. Stanley Robinson, was awarded the Bronze Medal for gallantry in saving life at sea.

during the month of February, ten succeeded in escaping. Of these, in addition to the *Laertes*, a notable experience was that of the master and men of the *Thordis* (501 tons). Her case attracted a good deal of attention at the time owing to the fine spirit exhibited by master and men. The *Thordis* (master, Mr. J. W. Bell) left Blyth on the afternoon of February 24th, with a cargo of coal for Plymouth. Everything went well until the 28th, when the ship was about eight or ten miles off Beachy Head, which bore north-east by east. The *Thordis* was steaming at about 5 knots, her maximum being $10\frac{1}{2}$ knots. A heavy head sea was running, and Captain Bell, who was on the bridge, noticed what he thought to be a periscope on the starboard bow, twenty or thirty yards away. Then began a contest between the little steamer and the enemy craft, which ended in the discomfiture of the latter. Captain Bell instantly gave instructions for full speed and all hands were ordered on deck. The submarine crossed the bow of the *Thordis*, taking up a position thirty or forty yards on her port side. Shortly afterwards Captain Bell noticed the wake of a torpedo on the starboard beam. He put the helm hard over to starboard, the engines in the meantime going full speed. The *Thordis* responded well and ran over the submarine's periscope. Everyone on board the merchantman heard a crash, and an oily substance was afterwards noticed on the surface of the water. The submarine was not seen again. The severity of the blow which the *Thordis* had dealt the submarine was suggested by the damage to the keel and propeller, revealed when the vessel was docked immediately afterwards at Devonport. The Germans subsequently asserted that the submarine, though put out of action, had managed to return to port. If that was so, she must have been badly damaged. The Admiralty marked their high appreciation of the master's conduct by conferring on him a commission in the Royal Naval Reserve, and awarding him the Distinguished Service Cross, and £200 was distributed among the officers and men of the ship, Captain Bell—or, rather, Lieutenant Bell, R.N.R., as he had become—receiving half that sum.[1]

The month of February furnished another conspicuous example of British seamanship. On the 17th the *Col-*

---

[1] A reward of £500 offered by *The Syren and Shipping* for the destruction of an enemy submarine was also paid to the officers and men of the *Thordis*.

chester, which had already been under attack, again escaped from the enemy when on passage from Parkeston Quay to Rotterdam, Captain Charles A. Fryatt, who afterwards became the victim of one of the foulest crimes committed by the Germans, having in the meantime succeeded to the command. During a southerly gale, with heavy seas and thick rain, a submarine was sighted about two miles ahead of the ship. The submarine was steering about W.S.W. and the British vessel E. ¼ S. Captain Fryatt had only a moment in which to decide what he should do. In a report to the British Consulate at Rotterdam he explained how, by prompt action, he had saved his ship: "I at once altered my ship's course until her head was north-west by the compass on the bridge, so I brought the submarine right astern of me, and I ordered the chief engineer to get all the steam he could and get all the speed he could with the engines, and after about fifteen minutes steaming north-west, I lost sight of the submarine in the thick rain. I then brought my ship gradually back to her course again E. ¼ S., and proceeded on my passage, and I never saw the submarine again."

During March and April the enemy campaign was evidently conducted with all his available resources, the officers commanding submarines apparently receiving instructions to use their torpedoes freely, discharging them without warning, and without consideration for the lives of British seamen, who had treated all previous threats and acts with contempt. No fewer than sixty-seven ships were attacked by submarines during that period. Aircraft were also called in aid to intensify the sense of terror which it was intended to create, and ten vessels were bombed by aeroplanes near the North Hinder and Galloper light-vessels. But of the ships attacked, all those which were molested by aircraft, as well as thirty-five which attracted the attention of submarines, escaped, in addition to a mined ship, which was towed in, and a merchantman which a Turkish torpedo-boat vainly chased in the Mediterranean.

It is difficult to judge the motives which inspire a nation's policy in time of war, but there are indications which suggest that the Germans anticipated that the aeroplane, or seaplane, would prove a valuable complement to the submarine in closing the North Sea against Allied merchantmen. It was only when the new ruthless submarine policy had failed to intimidate British seamen that attacks by enemy aircraft began. The first ship to be molested was the *Blonde* (613 tons; master, Mr. A. B. Milne), on her way from Cowes to the Tyne in ballast. On the morning of March 15th the ship was about three miles to the eastward of the North Foreland, when the second mate, who was on the bridge, noticed an aeroplane approaching from the east. The master at the time was down below looking for a screwdriver, as was afterwards explained, when he heard the sound of an explosion which caused him to run to the engine-room door, thinking that something was wrong with the engines. The engineer had reached the same conclusion, and immediately stopped the engines. This officer was engaged in searching for the damage when the second mate, running along the deck, called out that an aeroplane of enemy nationality was dropping bombs. It was a novel experience for these seamen, who had certainly never given a thought to such a possibility—representing a fresh menace to navigation. Captain Milne at once gave orders for full speed. The first two bombs fell about twenty feet astern, exploding on reaching the water, and the next about the same distance ahead. During this attack on the vessel, the aeroplane circled about the ship, endeavouring to get immediately above her. The fifth bomb was dropped even closer on the starboard side. The utmost endeavours of the airmen, however, failed. Captain Milne, realising his danger, adopted a zigzag course, and in the meantime kept his whistle blowing. His distress call attracted the attention of a trawler, a single shot from which caused the aeroplane to disappear. The *Elfland* (4,190 tons), a Belgian relief ship, was attacked in very similar circumstances off the North Hinder on the 21st, and the *Lestris* (1,384 tons) fourteen miles east of the Galloper on the same day, when the *Pandion* (1,279 tons) was also bombed without result. On the two following days the *Osceola* (393 tons) and the *Teal* (764 tons) shared the same experience. The *Ousel* (1,284 tons) was attacked on the 29th, and the *Staffa* (1,008 tons) on the 30th.

On April 11th the *Serula* (1,388 tons) was exposed to a determined attack, two machines concentrating on her. The ship was five miles west of the North Hinder light-vessel at 3.50 p.m., when a seaplane of large size and one smaller machine appeared. The large one was first seen coming down towards the ship from high up on the starboard side abaft the beam, and dropped a small bomb showing a white trail of smoke, followed by three bombs which fell just before the bridge on the starboard side. The undismayed master (Mr. J. T. Sharp) ordered the helm to be put hard aport. Shortly afterwards three more bombs came down on the port side, also on the foreside of the bridge, distant about twenty-five feet. The smaller machine, following the example of the larger one, started to come lower down to co-operate in the attack, but, being met with rifle fire from the ship, she straightened up and flew across, dropping bombs on each side of the vessel. The two machines then proceeded aft, on the port side, turned, and came back together, evidently with the intention of dropping bombs all along the steamer. The ship's course was altered backwards and forwards from port to starboard, so as to confuse the airmen. At last Captain Sharp got both machines on the starboard side, and then the helm was put hard aport and the engines full astern. Both airmen dropped their bombs on the port side forward.

So far the enemy airmen had failed, but they were not discouraged. The machines again went aft and attacked a third time. On this occasion they came singly and dropped bombs on each side of the bridge, doing no damage to the ship. On the last occasion the smaller aeroplane, on passing over the vessel, appeared to have been struck by the rifle fire which was then being maintained from the *Serula*, as she tilted up, then recovered herself, and flew directly away to the south with part of the left wing hanging down. The larger seaplane remained around the ship for about ten minutes longer, and then, passing over a Dutch ship which was close by, disappeared to the southward. The attack lasted from 3.50 to 4.30, and twelve shots were fired at the two machines, one rocket distress signal also being sent up. Later events suggested that the Germans regarded these attempts with aircraft as unsatisfactory, and this conclusion reacted on their policy, for such attacks were in future spasmodic—mere casual incidents of the war in the North Sea.

To return to the submarine campaign, the fact that so

large a proportion of the vessels attacked made good their escape from under-water craft was evidently noted by the German Naval Staff. Hitherto crowded passenger liners had not been interfered with, but the failure of the campaign during March and April to realise the expectations formed in Berlin was to lead to a change of policy in this respect. During the first week of March the enemy secured only one vessel—the *Bengrove* (3,840 tons), which was destroyed five miles north-north-east from Ilfracombe on the 7th. During the same period three other vessels succeeded in escaping—the *Wrexham* (1,414 tons) in the North Sea on March 2nd; the *Ningchow* (9,021 tons) in the Bristol Channel on the 4th; and the *Lydia* (1,188 tons) in the English Channel on the 5th.

The experience of the *Wrexham* attracted the attention of the Admiralty owing to the spirited manner in which the enemy was eluded. The *Wrexham* (master, Mr. Charles A. Fryatt)[1] was one of the Great Eastern Railway Company's vessels, running between Harwich and Rotterdam, and this further attack on a ship of this line supports the belief that the enemy was endeavouring to cut communications between England and Holland. The submarine appeared at thirty-five minutes after noon on March 2nd, when the *Wrexham* was approximately in lat. 51° 50′ N., long. 3° 0′ E. The enemy circled to the northward, and then made towards the British ship. Captain Fryatt immediately altered course to south-east by south, and ordered the engineer to increase speed to the utmost. Deck hands were mustered and sent below to assist the firemen, everyone realising that a chase for life had begun. Under ordinary conditions the *Wrexham* was capable of about 14 knots. But, in the face of such a peril, she was soon travelling at nearly 16 knots through the heavy, northerly swell. In these circumstances the chase continued, the submarine in the meantime flying imperative signals. Though the weather was fine and clear, Captain Fryatt kept his ship so far away that the signals could not be read. No doubt they were calling upon him to stop, but this was the last thing he had in his mind, as the *Wrexham* slowly drew away

---

[1] Captain Fryatt (whose spirited action on February 17th has already been mentioned) was taken prisoner by the Germans on June 23rd, 1916, when in command of s.s. *Brussels*, and afterwards shot.

from the submarine. The British skipper had to exhibit a high standard of seamanship owing to the proximity of the Schouwen Bank on his starboard hand. The course was altered time after time so as to keep the enemy on the port beam (abaft), and at a distance of about one and a half miles. For about forty miles the Germans maintained the chase, and only abandoned it when the *Wrexham* had approached within a mile of the Maas light-vessel. The incident provided a fine demonstration of British seamanship and British pluck. In making his report to his owners, Captain Fryatt remarked: "Had it not been for the good work put in by the engineers and the men firing, and the speed they were thus able to get up, I could not have escaped, as the submarine was doing well over 14 knots and chased us for about forty miles, only giving up when we were safe in Dutch waters." The Admiralty commended the conduct of the master, officers, and crew of the *Wrexham*, laying special emphasis on the spirit exhibited by the engine-room complement; the chief engineer, Mr. F. A. Goddison, was " mentioned " in the *London Gazette*.

Throughout the remainder of the month the enemy maintained a vigorous attack upon merchant shipping, alike in the North Sea, in the Irish Sea, and in the English Channel. Two ships were sunk without warning on March 9th—the *Princess Victoria* (1,108 tons; master, Mr. John Cubbin), sixteen miles north-west by north from Liverpool Bar light-vessel; and the *Blackwood* (1,230 tons; master, Mr. John Souter), eighteen miles south-west by south from Dungeness. On the same day the *Tangistan* (3,738 tons) foundered nine miles north from Flamborough Head. The sinking of the last ship was accompanied by the heaviest loss of life which had hitherto occurred, whether due to enemy cruiser, submarine, or mine. The *Tangistan* was on passage from Ben-isâf to Middlesbrough with a cargo of iron ore. The voyage from the Mediterranean had been like scores of other voyages which the crew had previously made; they had seen no enemy ships, and they had run into no mines. As the ship approached Middlesbrough, it was realised that she was early for the tide, so speed was reduced. Night fell, and all on board were anticipating their early arrival in port, when suddenly the ship trembled from end to end and then stopped. The hour of midnight was just striking; the lights went out. All hands rushed up on deck, to find the *Tangistan* was rapidly sinking under their feet. There was little or no confusion as orders were shouted from the bridge for the boats to be lowered. Before this could be done, however, the tragedy was completed; the *Tangistan*, on an even keel, disappeared in the dark waters, with all on board. Several of the men came to the surface, and cries rang out in the night, but only one of them survived the night's horror—a seaman named J. C. Toole. He managed to secure a spar, and he clung to it in desperation as offering him the only hope of life. Benumbed with the cold, he noticed the other voices around him were soon silenced, and he remained the lonely survivor of the whole ship's company! All he could do was to shout in the hope that he might attract the attention of some passing steamer, and this he did with all his remaining strength. One ship had passed in the night soon after he had reached the surface, and then he descried yet another vessel, but failed to attract her attention. Three times hope of rescue was excited, but each time the desperate man was disappointed. He had been in the water for two hours when at last the s.s. *Woodville* passed near him, heard his cries, now faint with increasing exhaustion, and picked him up. He was afterwards landed at West Hartlepool. Of the crew of thirty-nine, consequently, only one man survived to tell the tale of the loss of the *Tangistan*. Whether the *Tangistan* was, as in the case of the *Princess Victoria* and *Blackwood*, the victim of a submarine, or whether she exploded a mine, was a matter of some doubt, but it is significant that "Die Deutschen U-Boote in ihrer Kriegsführung, 1914–18" claims the *Tangistan* as a victim of U12, whose destruction the following day is described in a later chapter (p. 390).

It was indubitably a submarine which was responsible for the destruction two days later of the *Florazan* (4,658 tons; master, Mr. E. J. Cawsey) when fifty-three miles N.E. $\frac{1}{2}$ E. from the Longships, the lighthouse which stands on the rocks off Land's End. In this instance the violence of the explosion of the torpedo not only gave the ship a list to port, but lifted the oil lamps in the cabins from their sockets, with the result that the ship was soon ablaze amidships as she began to settle slowly by the head.

Fortunately the steam drifter *Wenlock*, then about two miles away, noticed that the *Florazan* was in distress, and rescued all the officers and men, who in the meantime had taken to the boats, with the exception of one fireman, who was presumably killed by the explosion. The survivors stood by the burning vessel for two or three hours, but it was impossible to board her on account of the flames, and, no sign of life being observable, the *Wenlock* continued on her course. On the following day the *Florazan* was still afloat and was taken in tow by eight drifters, but she sank on the morning of the 18th.

On the same day the *Adenwen* (3,798 tons) had a curious experience off the Casquets. In the early morning light, submarine U29 appeared, and firing rockets ordered the merchantman to stop. The master (Mr. W. H. Ladd) paid no attention to what was intended to be a peremptory injunction, but, on the contrary, increased speed and steered varying courses in order to keep the submarine right astern. Again the signals were made, and again they were ignored. But the chase was a hopeless one, for the submarine had the advantage of speed and soon overhauled the *Adenwen*. Speaking through a megaphone, the commander of U29 threatened to torpedo the ship unless she was stopped. There was no alternative but compliance with this order. In a few minutes the crew had taken to the boats, and a German party proceeded on board the *Adenwen* and placed bombs in the hold, which subsequently exploded. The crew were towed by the submarine for some time, and were then transferred to the Norwegian s.s. *Bothnia*, which landed them at Brixham the same afternoon. The enemy assumed that the British ship would sink, but, on the contrary, she remained afloat, was noticed by the French destroyer CLAYMORE later in the day, and, having been towed into Cherbourg and temporarily repaired, arrived at Cardiff on April 1st, to be taken later on into the Admiralty service.

The campaign continued on the 12th, when five ships were attacked, four being sunk. One, the *Invergyle* (1,794 tons; master, Mr. D. K. Minto), was torpedoed off the Tyne, and the other three in the neighbourhood of the Scilly Islands. This group consisted of the *Headlands* (2,988 tons), the *Indian City* (4,645 tons; master, Mr.

John Williams), and the *Andalusian* (2,349 tons; master, Mr. L. Malley), and they were all sunk by the U29 under the redoubtable Otto Weddigen. As in the case of the three armoured cruisers ABOUKIR, CRESSY, and HOGUE, this officer profited by the code of humanity which the seamen of the great maritime Powers had always hitherto observed. The s.s. *Headlands* was entering the English Channel from the west when the master (Mr. Herbert Lugg) saw a burning ship about five miles away to the eastward. Without a thought except for the men of the vessel from which the smoke was rising, he altered course in the hope that he might be able to save the lives of brother seamen. He had been steaming towards the mass of smoke for a matter of twenty minutes, when he observed a submarine approaching him at full speed. In the track of the submarine was a patrol-boat, and intermittently flashes of gunfire reminded him that in obeying the humane custom of the sea he had run into danger. When his own ship had disappeared, he learnt that the U29 had attacked the *Indian City*, which had been torpedoed when the patrol-boat came on the scene. As the *Indian City*, which did not sink until the following day, was in no immediate danger, the patrol-vessel had given chase to the submarine. By keeping on the surface, at the risk of being hit by a shell, the German commander was able to outdistance his pursuer. As soon as Captain Lugg realised the danger, he put his helm hard astarboard in the hope of avoiding pursuit. Owing to the *Headlands'* slow speed, it was soon apparent that his case was hopeless. The merchant ship was still holding to her course when the submarine commander drew up close astern and shouted to the *Headlands* to stop. The challenge was unheeded. The submarine then manœuvred for position and fired a torpedo, which struck the *Headlands* abaft the engine-room. The ship began to settle down as the submarine, with a group of patrol vessels in pursuit, made off at high speed. Within a few minutes everyone on board the *Headlands* had taken to the boats, which were afterwards towed into port by a patrol craft.[1]

[1] On March 18th, 1915, Otto Weddigen, who, as a reward for his successes, had been promoted from U9 to U29 since he began his raids on commerce, attempted to attack one of the battle squadrons of the Grand Fleet, and was appropriately rammed and sunk by H.M.S. DREADNOUGHT—" Picked up on her ram like a winkle on a pin," as an

On the following day the *Hartdale* (3,889 tons; master, Mr. Thomas Martin), after being chased off the coast of County Down, was torpedoed, two lives being lost. Four ships were attacked on the 14th; none was sunk, and all managed to escape uninjured except the *Atalanta* (519 tons). This ship was the first defensively armed British merchantman to fall in with a submarine. She was on passage from Galway to Glasgow, and was steaming about eleven miles off Inishturk Island, which lies about half-way between Blacksod Bay and Styne Head, when she sighted a submarine which was coming up astern and gaining rapidly on her. The master (Mr. J. MacLarnon) decided to withhold his fire. But when the submarine had come within a range of three or four thousand yards, the marine gunners could be restrained no longer and action was opened, the submarine replying with guns and rifle. By the time four rounds had been fired by the *Atalanta's* gunners, the ship stopped, rolling heavily in the swell. The submarine, concluding that the short chase was over, came abreast of her on the port beam. As the 12-pounder gun could not be brought to bear owing to the ship having stopped, Private Gilgallon blew away a davit by gunfire; three more rounds were then fired, causing the submarine to submerge. According to a statement subsequently made by the two marine gunners, the boats had in the meantime been lowered; officers and crew got into them and rowed away from the ship, with the exception of Mr. Mackey, first mate, who remained on the bridge and rang orders to the engine-room for steam until it was found that all the men had left; and, as the vessel was now helpless, and the submarine appeared to be preparing to discharge a torpedo at short range from a position in which she could not be fired on, the mate and two marines got into a boat which was lying alongside and shoved off. According to the report of the chief engineer, Mr. James Fraser, the master, after he had got into the port boat, went on board the *Atalanta* again, and while he was there the submarine appeared on the starboard bow. "When the boat got round the starboard side and the master got on deck,

eyewitness expressed it. This incident, one of the most striking in the whole history of submarine warfare, was kept secret from the Germans, who never tired of inquiring the fate of Otto Weddigen, though thousands of people in and out of the Grand Fleet must have known the facts.

he called on those in the boat to go on board, but those who had the oars would not pull back." Captain MacLarnon then left the ship with the rest of the hands. The crew were eventually landed at Inishturk Island. In the meantime the enemy devoted attention to the ship, which was soon well afire. She was subsequently found adrift by the patrol-boat *Greta* and towed into Cleggan Bay, about ten miles to the southward, where, already gutted by the flames, she was beached.

During the remainder of the month of March the campaign was pressed by the enemy with energy and eleven ships were lost, together with 115 lives. Eighteen other vessels were attacked, but managed to escape. None of these ships possessed any armament, but owed their safety in most cases to speed and good seamanship. A typical illustration of resourcefulness under adverse conditions was furnished by the master (Mr. John Horne) of the *Hyndford* (4,286 tons). The *Hyndford* was on her way home from Bahia with a cargo of wheat and oats. On the afternoon of March 15th she was steaming up-Channel at full speed, making for London, and when about twelve miles south of Beachy Head an explosion occurred. The weather was fine and there was a smooth sea. The ship shook from end to end. On rushing out of the charthouse, the master encountered a great volume of falling water and débris. After a moment's delay he was, however, able to reach the bridge in time to see the wake of a submarine, with its periscope showing. The enemy vessel was going away from the ship in a south-westerly direction, and soon disappeared beneath the water. The second officer had also seen the periscope, and there was no doubt, therefore, that the vessel had been attacked by a submarine without warning. The outrage was so unexpected that considerable confusion occurred on board the *Hyndford*. As the ship's head was sinking fast, the engineers left the engine-room, and the crew were hurrying towards the boats, which had already been swung out, when the master took command of the situation. He immediately directed that the boats were not to be lowered, but, owing to an accident, the port lifeboat slipped and two hands were thrown into the water. Captain Horne then endeavoured to calm the men and ordered an engineer to stop the engines. As soon as way was sufficiently off the ship, a boat was put out to rescue the two men who had fallen into the water, and one of them was, in fact, saved. Gradually more or less normal conditions were established on board. In the meantime it had been found that water in the fore hold was at sea-level, but No. 2 hold was dry, so, firing two rockets of distress, Captain Horne put his engines half speed ahead for ten minutes as a test, and, finding the bulkhead stood the strain, he proceeded at full speed towards the Downs, filling the after ballast tanks in order to trim the ship. The *Hyndford* arrived at the Downs half an hour after midnight on March 16th, and eventually was towed to Gray's Flats and beached for temporary repairs.

The attack on the *Delmira* (3,459 tons) on the 25th attracted the special attention of the Admiralty owing to the pluck and resource exhibited by Mr. Jonathan Evans, the master of the s.s. *Lizzie* (802 tons). The *Delmira* had a crew of thirty-two hands, but only eight of these were English, the rest being Chinese. She was proceeding from Boulogne to Port Talbot, and was twenty-three miles north-north-east from Cape d'Antifer, when the U37 appeared aft at a distance of about two miles. The master of the large British merchant ship (Mr. William Lancefield) took no notice of a signal directing him to stop, and the Germans then began firing and gradually gained on the *Delmira*, which was making only about 9 knots. The usual procedure was followed, but in this case the commander of the U-boat showed consideration for the officers and men. He volunteered to tow their boats until some vessel was met with to which they could transfer. For an hour and a half the little procession, consisting of the submarine and the three boats of the *Delmira*, maintained its course towards the English coast, and then the s.s. *Lizzie* appeared to the eastward. The submarine immediately cut the tow and began to dive in the direction of the *Lizzie*. The master of the little British vessel promptly steamed full speed towards the submarine with the intention of ramming her. The *Lizzie* passed over the enemy vessel, but felt no shock, and it is doubtful if even the periscope was struck. In spite of the danger which the presence of the enemy boat must have suggested, Captain Evans of the *Lizzie* stopped his ship and picked up the men out of the three boats, who were eventually landed at Portsmouth. The *Delmira* grounded later on at Cape La Hogue, where temporary repairs were carried out.

By this time evidence was accumulating of the determination of the enemy to break, if he could, the spirit of British merchant seamen, while, on the other hand, the stories that reached the Admiralty bore testimony to the dogged courage with which these men, in face of unparalleled dangers, continued to go about the nation's business. Almost every incident suggested that no amount of frightfulness on the part of the enemy would succeed in terrorising the descendants of the men who had thrown open the navigation of the seas freely to the nations of the world. The record of these days of heroic resistance to a cruel campaign must be studied in the knowledge that these men, untrained for the violence of war, were also, for the most part, unprovided with armament to enable them to defend themselves and their vessels against craft possessing, in addition to the powers of submergence, powerful guns, deadly torpedoes, and easily portable bombs. It was an unequal contest, but British seamen pursued it with high courage and tenacity. The official records reveal the generous feeling of admiration excited in naval officers serving at the Admiralty as tale after tale came in from the sea.

A particularly noteworthy story is that of the *Vosges* (1,295 tons). She was on passage from Bordeaux to Liverpool, carrying a general cargo, with two first-class passengers and five consular passengers, when she was attacked on March 27th, 1915, at 10.15 a.m., by a German submarine in lat. 50° 27′, long. 6° W. The merchantman was unarmed. Immediately the submarine came into view the master (Mr. John R. Green) ordered all the firemen below and asked the consular passengers to volunteer to assist in maintaining steam pressure. This aid was willingly given. A fight was in prospect that made the blood course freely through the veins of every man on board. The submarine opened fire from astern, the first shot being immediately followed by one which hit the British vessel aft. In the meantime the *Vosges* was steaming at her highest speed, Captain Green altering course as necessary to keep the enemy behind him, and with her head to the sea, so that she could not use her gun. On the other hand, the submarine was all the time endeavouring to get on the beam of the merchantman, so as to obtain a good target for his torpedoes. This manœuvring and counter-manœuvring continued for an hour and a half, the enemy, firing as opportunity offered, refusing to abandon her quarry. The British vessel was struck repeatedly by shells, a round hole about two feet in diameter being made in the starboard side, and another about one foot in diameter being pierced on the starboard quarter; there were other small holes about the waterline aft. The funnel was riddled, the bridgehouse smashed, and the engine-room badly holed. The chief engineer, Mr. Harry Davies, was killed instantaneously when standing near the stokehold door exhorting the firemen and volunteers to further efforts, a shell striking him in the chest. The second mate was hit on the arm while on the bridge; a fireman was injured in the wrist; the mess-room boy had a leg hurt; the mate was slightly wounded in the hand; and splinters grazed the captain's hand. Among the passengers, the only injury suffered was in the case of a lady who was struck in the foot.

At about a quarter to twelve, the submarine, having failed to effect her purpose owing to the skill of Captain Green and the manner in which he was supported in the engine-room, sheered off. It was hoped that it would be possible to get the damaged vessel into Milford Haven. Water, however, was gaining rapidly on the pumps, and it became evident that the ship was sinking. At this moment, the armed yacht *Wintonia* (Lieutenant-Commander W. E. Kelway, R.N.R.) was sighted about twenty-two miles north-west of Trevose Head. This vessel immediately bore down on the *Vosges*, and shortly afterwards the boats were manned and lowered, and, by the captain's orders, officers and men took their places. There was no fuss or excitement in spite of the unnerving experience through which everyone on board had so recently passed. After making sure that everyone else had left the ship, Captain Green cast off both painters, and, getting into the starboard lifeboat, rowed over to the patrol yacht. In spite of the strong wind and heavy rain, everyone got on board—a difficult operation in the circumstances. " The only remark I have to make," Captain Green reported, " is that, had I had a gun, I have not the slightest doubt but that I should have sunk the submarine." The *Vosges* disappeared bow first at 2 o'clock after an explosion had occurred. " Gentlemen, I did not give her away," the captain concluded in his report to his owners. The Admiralty, on receiving information, at once expressed their appreciation of the conduct of all concerned, it being remarked that "the chief engineer, both by his energy and his example, was largely instrumental in enabling the vessel to shake off the submarine." Official appreciation was afterwards formally expressed of the gallantry of officers and crew: Captain Green was awarded a commission in the Royal Naval Reserve and received the D.S.O. for "his gallant and resolute conduct"; gold watches were presented to the other officers, the widow of chief engineer Harry Davies receiving the gold watch which would have been handed to her husband if he had lived; and the members of the crew were paid a gratuity of £3 each.

A duel lasting ninety minutes between an old British merchant ship and a German submarine occurred at this period of the war, reflecting the utmost credit on British seamanship. The *City of Cambridge* was a four-masted ship of 3,844 tons, and her compound engines gave her a normal speed when loaded of about 10 knots. She was thirty-three years old, having been built by Messrs. Workmen, Clark & Co. at Belfast in 1882. She left Alexandria for Liverpool on March 16th with a general cargo. The master (Mr. Alfred C. Fry) was determined not to be caught unprepared for an emergency, and on the 27th he mustered all hands at their respective boat stations in order that every officer and man should practise putting on his life-belt in its proper position, "for, believe me," Captain Fry afterwards remarked, "familiarity breeds contempt, and there are numbers of persons on board most ships who do not know how to put on life-belts properly." Strong north-east winds were encountered in crossing the Bay, and at 4.30 on the following afternoon, the *City of Cambridge* passed Bishop Rock at a distance of about thirty-eight miles, and course was then altered to pass about twenty miles west of the Smalls, to the westward of Milford Haven. At noon Captain Fry had doubled the lookout, and he "kept his eye skinned" for any suspicious craft or for the sight of a periscope. At 6.30, nothing being observable on the horizon, he left the bridge to go down to dinner, the third officer with the lookout men and the man at the wheel remaining on the bridge. He had just sat down with the chief and second officers, when a sharp report was heard on the starboard side of the vessel. "I raced from the table to the bridge," he stated in his subsequent narrative of events, "and did it, I think, in record time—say fifteen seconds. I climbed the port ladder and rushed to the wheel. Looking over the side, I saw close to us, say half a ship's length away, the conning tower of a submarine with several men in it. She was heading the same way as ourselves. I at once myself pulled the wheel over to the starboard, shaking them up below at the same time; then, knowing that the bridge would be fired at, I lay flat for a minute. The chief and second officers were with me by this time, and the second officer took the wheel and kept it for the rest of the time of our trial. After a short time I looked for the enemy, and found that he was a couple of points or so on the starboard quarter and our own ship swinging off good to port. This gave us courage and the hope that he would not have it all his own way; if we could only keep her going and the enemy astern, we had a good chance of getting away, unless holed below the water-line. As soon as he understood we were going to make a try for it, he fired a shell, and then for an hour and a half it was very hot work. He would gain on us till one could count the heads in the conning tower. At one time I think he could not have been 200 feet from us, a mass of foam with just the top of the tower showing, and then he was hard aport or starboard (generally port) till he stood at right angles, trying to get far enough out to smash the bridge, at the same time he was shepherding us so that we were before the wind and swell, which, although it was small, probably upset his shooting platform. We managed to baffle him at every move. At one time I was afraid our speed was going down, but with the best of firemen below and the mighty efforts of the engineers, we recovered speed and worked her up to a little over 13 knots (our top speed). At this time we were heading into both wind and sea (he had forced us to turn round the compass twice) and going slowly away from him. The light by now had settled into a bright moonlight night, and as he got farther astern we gradually lost sight of him, but he gave us one parting shot, which did a lot of damage.

"That ninety minutes was such as I do not wish to experience again. Thinking it possible that some of our armed ships might be within range, I fired two distress signals one after another to attract their attention. Then he brought a Morse lamp on deck and started Morsing, but knowing this was only a trick to divert our attention, I took no notice of it."

For the courage and resource exhibited in face of the enemy, Captain Fry was presented with a gold watch from the Admiralty as well as Lloyd's Medal, and was commended in the *London Gazette*, besides receiving a reward from the War Risks Association. Though his ship was entirely without armament, he had opposed his seamanship to all the offensive qualities possessed by the submarine, and, splendidly supported by his officers and the staff in the engine-room, he had won. The devotion of the master, officers, and engineers saved the ship and its cargo, but the *City of Cambridge* did not escape uninjured. One German shell carried away a $6\frac{1}{2}$-inch davit, destroying the boat which it helped to support. Another penetrated the boatswain's room and part of the lamp locker, one of these holes being about 30 inches by 50 inches. The after-works were injured, and one shell which passed over the bridge carried away the signal halyard. "This was a close call," Captain Fry remarked, "as, had it struck any of the short awning spars, it would have exploded, and that would have finished us." Except for a slight splinter wound sustained by a fireman, no one was the worse for the encounter. "With a bit of luck and owing to the hard determination of the officers and men above and below deck," the master related afterwards, "we managed to bring our ship home." [1]

Another incident which occurred in the closing days of March must be noted, because, apart from the loss of life involved, it figured in the Notes which afterwards passed between the Government of the United States and Germany, and was the subject of a special inquiry by the Board of Trade. When approximately sixty miles W. $\frac{1}{2}$ N.

---

[1] The *City of Cambridge*, after a second escape from a submarine in the same year, was sunk in the Mediterranean (July 3rd, 1917) when under the command of another master.

off St. Ann's Head at 12.30 p.m. on March 27th, the master (Mr. George Wright) of the *Eileen Emma*, who was fishing from Milford Haven, sighted the periscope of a submarine. He immediately rang for full speed and tried to cut her off. The enemy, realising what was happening, altered course again and again, trying to avoid collision. The speeds of the two ships were about equal, and for some time these manœuvres continued, until a steamer appeared on the horizon steering south-west. The submarine then increased her buoyancy until she was well above the water, and in this trim outpaced the *Eileen Emma* and proceeded towards a steamship which proved to be the *Falaba* (4,806 tons; master, Mr. F. J. Davies). She was unarmed, and had on board a crew of ninety-five men and 147 passengers, including seven women and an American citizen, when she left Liverpool on the previous evening on her passage to Sierra Leone. Passengers and crew had had insufficient time to adjust themselves to war conditions when they sighted the submarine about two points abaft the starboard beam and three miles distant. In approaching the *Falaba* the submarine at first showed a British ensign, for which the German colours were afterwards substituted. She was noticed by Mr. Pengilly, the *Falaba's* third officer, at 11.40 a.m. The sequence of later events was settled by the considered judgment of Lord Mersey, acting as Wreck Commissioner:

" The captain immediately altered the course of the *Falaba* so as to get the submarine directly astern, and at the same time he rang up the engine-room to increase the speed. The best was done in the engine-room to respond to this call, but it was found impossible to effect any material improvement in the short time available. The captain then sent Baxter to instruct the Marconi operator to signal all stations as follows: 'Submarine overhauling us; flying British flag. 51° 32', 6° 36'.' This message was sent out at 11.50 a.m. Baxter then obtained a telescope and observed that the submarine was flying a German ensign. It is, in my opinion, uncertain whether the ensign had been changed, or whether the ensign already observed was not, in fact, a German flag. The point, however, is not material, because from the first the captain believed the submarine

to be an enemy craft. The submarine was at this time
making about 18 knots and was rapidly overhauling the
Falaba. Shortly before noon she fired a detonating signal
to call attention, and by flags signalled the *Falaba* to ' stop
and abandon ship.' The *Falaba* did not stop, but still
manœuvred to keep the submarine astern. The submarine
then signalled ' Stop or I fire.' The captain and the chief
officer then conferred and decided that it was impossible
to escape. They accordingly rang to the engine-room
to stop the engines. The signal ' Stop or I fire ' was given
a minute or two before noon. The submarine then signalled ' Abandon ship immediately,' and hailed through a
megaphone to the *Falaba* to take to the boats, as they were
going ' to sink the ship in five minutes.' The captain
answered that he was taking to the boats. The Marconi
operator heard the hail, and sent out a second message,
' Position 51° 32′ N., 6° 36′ W.; torpedo ; going boats.'
The warning that the submarine was going to sink the ship
in five minutes was given as nearly as possible at noon.
The *Falaba* stopped at 12.4 or 12.5, and at 12.10 the submarine fired a torpedo into her. At this moment the submarine was within about 100 yards of the *Falaba*. The
torpedo struck the *Falaba* on the starboard side by No. 8
hatch aft of No. 1 lifeboat and just alongside the Marconi house. The blow was fatal. The *Falaba* at once
took a list to starboard, and in eight minutes (namely,
at 12.18) she sank. This was within twenty minutes
of the notice from the submarine of her intention to sink
the ship. An affidavit by Mr. Baxter, the chief officer,
which had been put in has satisfied me that no rockets
or other signals were fired or shown from the *Falaba* on
March 28th."

Lord Mersey held that he was not required to find
whether the submarine was within her rights as an enemy
craft in sinking the *Falaba*, but he was called upon to assume that " in any event she was bound to afford the men
and women on board a reasonable opportunity of getting
to the boats and of saving their lives. This those in charge
of the submarine did not do. And so grossly insufficient
was the opportunity in fact afforded that I am driven
to the conclusion that the captain of the submarine
desired and designed not merely to sink the ship, but, in

doing so, also to sacrifice the lives of the passengers and crew." The Wreck Commissioner added that evidence was given by the witnesses of laughing and jeering from the submarine while the men and women from the *Falaba* were struggling in the water, but Lord Mersey stated that he preferred to hope that the witnesses were mistaken. Corporal Turnbull of the Royal Army Medical Corps, one of the survivors, in a statement to the Press,[1] said that "the barbarity of the crew of the submarine was frightful. They waited to see the last of the *Falaba* before they dived, but, of course, they made no attempt to save any of us. That was not the worst part. The most maddening thing was to see the crew of the submarine after they had torpedoed us. The *Falaba* listed over, and the passengers and crew were clinging like flies trying to get a grip of the deck, and dropping one by one into the water, while the crew of the submarine laughed and jeered at them." The ascertained loss of life was 104.

Continuing his judgment, Lord Mersey added that, " between the first signal of the submarine to stop and the actual stopping of the *Falaba*, the chief officer directed the first and second stewards to assemble the passengers on deck and to tell them to put on their life-belts. The captain also sent the fourth officer below to see that these orders were carried out. After the engines were stopped, the chief engineer and the third engineer ordered all men in the engine-room and stokehold on deck, and the order was obeyed. By the time the *Falaba* was stopped, a large number of the passengers were already on the boat deck. The captain was on the bridge. He sent the third officer and the quartermaster to see to the lowering and filling of the boats, and the order to man the boats was passed round the ship." The Wreck Commissioner then dealt with the " serious complaints which were made by some of the witnesses as to the condition of the boats and as to the launching of them." After referring to these statements and to the technical evidence given before him, he said that he was satisfied " that the witnesses who described the boats as having been ' rotten ' are mistaken, and that, in truth, the boats were sound and in good order up to the time of the attack by the submarine. What, however, the witnesses probably mean, when they

[1] *Times*, March 30th, 1915.

say the boats were rotten, is that when afloat some of them were found to be unseaworthy. And this, no doubt, is true. But this condition of things was, in my opinion, wholly due to the damage sustained by the boats after the operation of launching began, and not to any previous defect. Upon the subject of the launching, it is, therefore, necessary to say a few words. It is to be remembered that the submarine had given the *Falaba* only about five minutes in which to man, to fill, and to launch these boats; in which, in short, to save the lives of 242 persons. This was an operation quite incapable of efficient performance in anything like that short space of time. There was unavoidable hurry and disorder; the falls of one of the boats slipped: the falls of another jammed; some boats were dashed against the side of the ship and damaged; one (No. 8) was seriously injured by the explosion of the torpedo while still hanging from the davits. It is in these circumstances that some of the witnesses apparently desire me to find that the damage done to the boats was due to the neglect of the officers and crew in connection with the launching. I cannot do this. I have no doubt that, had there been more time for the work, it might have been better carried out, but, in my opinion, all on board—captain, officers, crew, and passengers —did their very best. People were fighting for their lives and for the lives of others about them, and in the struggle the captain, half the crew, and a large number of the passengers were drowned. It is impossible for me to fix any man on board the ship with a failure of duty or with incompetence. The responsibility for the consequences of this catastrophe must rest exclusively with the officers and crew of the German submarine."

Two more ships were sunk on the last two days of March, happily without loss of life. The *Flaminian* (3,500 tons; master, Mr. David Cruikshank) was destroyed on the 29th by gunfire, fifty miles south-west by west from the Scilly Isles, and the *Crown of Castile* (4,505 tons; master, Mr. T. S. Fyfe) on the 30th, when thirty-one miles south-west from the Bishop Rock. Submarine U28 was responsible for the sinking of both vessels.

By the end of March the depredations of enemy surface craft had ceased, and no further losses on this account were incurred until the following January; the mine peril had

A TUG'S PLUCKY FIGHT

been for the moment checked; but the destruction due to submarines, which had amounted to 17,126 tons in January, with a loss of twenty-one lives, and had reached only 21,787 tons, with the death of nine persons, in February, had suddenly jumped up to 64,448 tons, and the number of lives lost was 161. After this exhibition of frightfulness, the intensity of the attack became for a time less marked. During April only 22,453 tons were destroyed, thirty-eight lives being lost, and only six other ships were molested. On the first day of the month the *Seven Seas* (1,194 tons; master, Mr. Barnes) was about six miles south of Beachy Head when an explosion occurred forward, the vessel sinking almost immediately. The destroyer FLIRT picked up nine of the crew, but the captain, chief engineer, both mates, steward, three seamen and a boy were drowned. No doubt existed that the ship was torpedoed without warning. The *Lochwood* (2,042 tons; master, Mr. T. H. Scott) fell a victim to the enemy on the following day off the Start. On the 4th four more lives were lost in the *City of Bremen* (1,258 tons; master, Mr. Richard Martin), which was destroyed twenty miles south by west from the Wolf Rock, and the same day the *Olivine* (634 tons; master, Mr. A. Lamont) also went down near St. Catherine's Point. The *Northlands* (2,776 tons; master, Mr. A. S. Taylor) came to a similar end off Beachy Head on the 5th, and then an interval occurred of four clear days, the only noticeable incident being the escape of the tug *Homer*, which furnished further confirmatory evidence of the spirit in which British seamen were determined to meet the enemy's threats and murderous acts.

The *Homer* (150 tons) was proceeding from Queenstown to Sunderland towing the French barque *Général de Santos*. On the afternoon of April 8th, twenty-five miles southwest by south from the Owers Lightship, a German submarine approached within three or four hundred yards of the *Homer's* port side. The enemy vessel was travelling on the surface, and hoisted a signal which the master of the *Homer* (Mr. H. J. Gibson) ignored, although an officer in the submarine shouted and pointed at the flags. The submarine then steamed round the bow of the tug, speed in the British vessel having in the meantime been eased. She soon came up on the starboard side, both vessels steaming in the same direction. A shot was fired over the *Homer* and the German officer resumed shouting in English, ordering Captain Gibson to get into his boat. The enemy craft, considering the issue practically decided, came within a hundred yards, and then the *Homer*, having cast loose the *Général de Santos*, turned towards her. It was a critical moment. As soon as the enemy realised the intention of the master of the *Homer*, he put his helm hard aport and opened fire, continuing a desperate attack until the *Homer* was almost on top of him, missing his stern by about three feet. The *Homer's* head was then reversed, and, the submarine still firing, the vessel proceeded in the direction of the Owers. The submarine followed, firing a torpedo which passed close to the British vessel's starboard quarter. At this time the *Homer* was travelling at about 12 knots. The submarine continued to chase her for half an hour, but had fallen half a mile astern when she abandoned the pursuit and turned back, evidently with the intention of dealing with a French barque which was in sight. The tug, with seven holes as evidence of the enemy's persistency, reached Bembridge some time later. The Admiralty marked their appreciation of the resource and courage of the master by presenting him with a gold watch and a letter on vellum.

Five other ships managed to make their escape during April, *La Rosarina* (8,332 tons) experiencing a narrow escape on the 17th, when she was chased by a submarine, and beat off the attack by gunfire. But during the last twenty days of April the *Harpalyce* (5,940 tons), *The President* (647 tons; master, Mr. Neil Robertson), *Ptarmigan* (784 tons; master, Mr. W. A. W. Hore), *Mobile* (1,950 tons; master, Mr. W. C. Fortune), *Cherbury* (3,220 tons; master, Mr. James Davidson), and *Fulgent* (2,008 tons) were all sunk, with loss of life in the case of the *Harpalyce*, *Ptarmigan*, and *Fulgent*. The end of the *Harpalyce* (master, Mr. Wawn) was marked by some features which appeared particularly revolting to still tender consciences at that early period of the struggle. This ship was working for the Commission of Relief in Belgium. When she left Rotterdam for Norfolk, Virginia, U.S.A., in addition to her Red Ensign she was flying the large flag of the Commission, and painted on her sides in large letters was the name of the Commission. Her status had been recognised by the German

Minister at The Hague, who had issued a safe-conduct, covering risks from attack by German submarines during her voyage. This permit was of the most specific character, but contained a warning " against navigating the waters declared by Germany to be a war zone," especially through the English Channel. In those circumstances there should have been no cause for anxiety. The *Harpalyce* left Rotterdam about 2.30 a.m. on Saturday morning, April 10th, and all went well until the ship was about seven miles south-south-east from the North Hinder light-vessel, when at 10 a.m. a loud report was heard on the starboard quarter. An explosion had blown in the ship's side. In less than two minutes the whole of the poop and afterwell deck were submerged. The ship was doomed. According to the statements of the second officer (Mr. W. J. George) and the second engineer (Mr. J. S. Turnbull), " It was impossible to swing out the boats, as by now the top of the funnel was nearly in the water, the engine-room being filled up and the decks beginning to blow up." Within a short time the ship went down. The crew consisted of forty-four officers and men, including thirty-three Chinese hands. They would all undoubtedly have been drowned but for the fortunate appearance upon the scene of the Netherlands s.s. *Elizabeth* and s.s. *Constance Catherine*, which, in company with the United States schooner *Ruby*, managed to save all but fifteen of the crew. These neutral vessels not only exhibited fine seamanship during this rescue work, but illustrated that chivalry of the sea which, prior to Germany's decision, had united the seamen of the world. Two possibilities called for investigation. In the first place, it had to be settled whether the ship had been sunk by mine or torpedo. As to that, not only was it improbable that a mine would strike the vessel on the starboard quarter, as was the case, but the second mate distinctly saw the periscope of a submarine and its wash as it made off to the northwards; corroborative evidence on this point was also given by the master of the *Elizabeth*. Nor was there any lack of testimony as to the position in which the *Harpalyce* was sunk—well outside the so-called German war zone. No doubt existed that this vessel, engaged on an errand of mercy to " the suffering civil population of Belgium," to quote from the German permit, was torpedoed without warning and in broad daylight outside the area designated by the enemy, although she carried every mark of her distinctive mission.

The last day of April was marked by a tragedy which, conspicuous at the moment, was afterwards to be completely overshadowed by events which focused the attention of the world on the enemy's inhuman campaign. The *Fulgent* sailed from Cardiff on the evening of April 28th under Admiralty orders for Scapa Flow. She was taking a roundabout course for safety, evidently under orders, and had passed the Blaskets Lighthouse, off the coast of Kerry, on the morning of April 30th, when the silence was broken by the report of a gun. It was then noticed that, unobserved by anyone on board, a submarine had crept up within about 200 yards of the *Fulgent*. The master of the merchantman (Mr. C. W. Brown) at once realised the peril in which he stood, and began zigzagging in order to keep the enemy vessel astern of him and thus in an unfavourable position for attack. The contest, however, was an unequal one, as the submarine, stated to be the U7, had the advantage of speed. Captain Brown, with dogged courage, refused to believe that his position was hopeless. Even when the submarine had gained a position about three points on the port quarter, he continued to handle his ship with courage and competency. A flash from the gun mounted on the deck of the submarine told him that a shot had been fired. A few seconds later the vessel's funnel and chart-room had been shattered, an A.B. named Williams, who was at the wheel, being killed, and Captain Brown himself being mortally injured. The struggle was then over, and all that could be done was to get out the boats with all speed, in order that the remaining officers and men might leave the doomed ship. Without a thought for the British seamen, the officer commanding the submarine then sank the *Fulgent* out of hand and disappeared, leaving these unfortunate men to whatever fate might overtake them. During the remainder of the day the two boats managed to keep together and then night fell, and in the darkness they got separated. The most sluggish imagination can fill in the broad details of the sufferings of these men as hour after hour passed and hope of rescue rose and fell as ships appeared on the horizon, to disappear again unconscious of these men's distress. But at last, on Sunday, May 2nd, the s.s. *Tosto* of Newcastle picked up the first mate and eight hands, exhausted physically and mentally by the ordeal through which they had passed, and the trawler *Angle* landed nine other men at Cappa (Kilrush), where the body of Captain Brown was silently borne ashore.

The destruction of the *Fulgent* provided an extreme example of the fate to which at this period the seamen of torpedoed merchant vessels were liable, and in considering the first stage of Germany's submarine campaign as here described it is necessary, in view of the subsequent developments, to preserve a sense of proportion. Grievous as were the experiences of crews set adrift in open boats, their sufferings, generally speaking, were as nothing in comparison with those endured later in the war by survivors from ships torpedoed in mid-Atlantic—a phase of the enemy's savage warfare by sea which is dealt with in the second volume of this work.

CHAPTER VIII

THE AUXILIARY PATROL AT WORK

IN those fateful summer days which immediately preceded the British ultimatum to Germany little information was revealed as to the preparations of the Royal Navy. Of the steps which were taken none was, in fact, more thorough than the precautions against our fleets being blockaded by means of a potential enemy's mine-fields. But the vigilant work of the destroyer flotillas off the coast does not come within the scope of this history.

Allusion has already been made to the flotilla of old gunboats, whose duty was to attend on the Grand Fleet, while the trawlers were relied upon to keep the channels and harbour approaches swept clear. As far back as July 28th, 1914, Commander Lionel Preston, R.N., had received his orders to take charge of these gunboats and to assemble them at Dover. On the first day of August they steamed away from that great national harbour for Queensferry, having been instructed by Admiral Sir George Callaghan, then Commander-in-Chief of the Grand Fleet, to begin sweeping on their way north as soon as they got to the Inner Dowsing, near the Wash. And it was on this same day that the inspecting Captain of Mine-sweepers received his orders in regard to the trawlers. The Admiralty had decided to charter these for mine-sweeping, and preparations were to be made so that they could be sent to their assigned ports as soon as possible. There were then eighty-two such vessels on the Admiralty list, and the ranks and ratings of the trawler section numbered 1,025.

On the next day the Admiralty-chartered trawlers, which had been usually employed in towing targets, were ordered to the Nore from their various ports, where, being completed with mine-sweeping stores, they were

THE FIRST MINE-FIELD

ready for eventualities. On the coast of Scotland, and at the fishing ports of the North Sea and West of England, steam trawlers were being taken in hand as they came in from their fishing, though it had been foreseen that probably 25 per cent. of these would not have succeeded in getting back from Iceland and other fishing waters in time for the commencement of hostilities. Meanwhile Germany was also availing herself of her fishing fleets, and on August 3rd, a telegram from the British Ambassador at Berlin announced that that country had obtained thirty trawlers from Geestemunde, and was equipping them with a couple of searchlights each, and fitting them out as mine-layers.

The first mine-field to be discovered was that which was laid by the KÖNIGIN LUISE, an auxiliary vessel of the German Navy resembling one of the steamers that had been on the service between Harwich and the Hook of Holland. At ten o'clock on the morning of August 5th she was seen laying mines not far from Orfordness, and was herself sunk by the Third Destroyer Flotilla, issuing from Harwich. She had not quite completed her work when her career so suddenly terminated, for survivors stated that many mines were still aboard her. They further asserted that she had laid a long line of mines from a position in lat. 52° 10′ N., long. 2° 25′ E., to the eastward. This position is about thirty miles to the eastward of Orfordness, and it is clear enough that such mines were laid for the express purpose of sinking any British forces proceeding from Harwich towards Germany. In this intention they partially succeeded, for H.M.S. AMPHION foundered on one of them the next day.

Meanwhile the Senior Naval Officer at Harwich was ordered to hasten the preparation of the mine-sweeping trawlers. On August 6th they put to sea and proceeded to sweep from Orfordness to Southwold. The Admiral of the patrols was also directed to send Grimsby trawlers to sweep off Aldeburgh as soon as possible. Nothing could have given a greater impetus to the work of the trawlers than the discovery of a mine-field on the first morning of the war. From the Firth of Forth, Admiral Lowry, the Senior Officer on the coast of Scotland, telegraphed to say that the mine-sweepers which he had taken up had almost completed their equipment at Queensferry and Invergordon, and he had given orders that as many trawlers as possible should be commissioned from the northern Scottish ports for patrolling the Moray Firth. Such was the call on the destroyer flotillas that there was only one torpedo craft patrolling that big bay. To Devonport, Portsmouth, and Portland urgent telegrams were dispatched by the Admiralty for the temporary loan of trawlers for mine-sweeping, and meantime shipping had been warned that mines had been laid off the Suffolk coast as far seaward as the third meridian East, and all vessels were ordered not to enter the North Sea without calling for orders at a South Coast port.

On the third day of the war, Admiral Sir John Jellicoe was informed that a permanent mine-sweeping flotilla of trawlers was being established with a view to ensuring a clear channel from the Outer Dowsing to the South Goodwins. This extensive lane would mean that merchant ships could be guaranteed a safe journey from the eastern entrance of the English Channel almost as far north as the Humber. The flotilla was to consist of eighty trawlers, to be formed as vessels became available. Captain Ellison was summoned to the Admiralty, and instructed to bring this huge flotilla into being. He was at the time commanding officer of the HALCYON, the senior ship of the North Sea Fisheries, based on Lowestoft. He immediately began to get together suitable fishing-craft, and in a short time the North Sea became again a safe highway. The trawlers got to work with such zeal that by August 11th they had swept a channel four cables wide from as far south as the North Foreland to as far north as Southwold. From that night, also, the whole channel from the Outer Dowsing light-vessel to the Downs began to be patrolled by steam drifters, manned by Trawler Reserve officers and men and flying the White Ensign. Night and day, without so much as a gun with which to defend themselves, these little craft kept up their patrol, ever on the alert against enemy mine-laying vessels. No one who passed up the North Sea about this time will ever forget the sight of this continuous patrol of little vessels engaged on a new sphere of work.

And whilst Lowestoft was busily getting craft together, Chatham was also rapidly fitting out mine-sweeping trawlers, so that in about a fortnight seventy-four hired and other trawlers had been equipped on the Medway. Some of

A DRIFTER FLEET AT SEA.

these were engaged in sweeping the Thames Estuary; others were dispatched to Lowestoft; some to Peterhead. These trawlers had been provided with their mine-sweeping gear, given a month's consumable stores, coal and water, as well as rifles, ammunition, charts, tide-tables, Morse lamps, and so on. Free kits had been issued to all deck-hands and trimmers, and a week's pay advanced. Before sailing, both skippers and crews had been taken out in the Admiralty trawlers *Seamew* or *Seaflower* and instructed in sweeping, reeving of gear, and station-keeping.

By the middle of August the special channel from the Outer Dowsing to the Downs was already buoyed, and thirty steam drifters, equally spaced, were patrolling it from end to end. Such duty essentially belonged to our torpedo flotillas, and not to the smallest type of fishing steamers, but what did it matter, seeing that the destroyers and torpedo-boats were wanted elsewhere, and that drifters were the finest little steamships ever built to withstand bad weather? But besides these Lowestoft drifters, other drifters were being taken up on the north-east corner of Scotland. From Banff, Fraserburgh, Port Mahomack, and Wick, they were being speedily sent to sea to look for mine-layers, and thus afford some protection to Moray Firth. The task which was imposed on some of these Scotch crews was anything but safe. They were unarmed, they were to perform no hostile act, and if captured were to give no indication of their being in the Government service. Their duty was simply to pose as fishermen, keeping their fishing gear on board and their eyes open. The moment they sighted any suspicious movement of ships, they were to run into harbour as fast as they could and report the facts.

At Lowestoft great activity continued. The Commander-in-Chief was calling for more mine-sweeping trawlers for the North. Eight he wanted to sweep round Kinnaird Head, in addition to those already sent to Cromᵤ y. These were being fitted out at Lowestoft, besides some more for the Humber and elsewhere. When on August 15th the Grand Fleet made its sweep down the North Sea, the mine-sweeping gunboats went ahead of the battle-cruisers and battleships, leaving the trawlers to keep clear of mines the approaches to the Grand Fleet's base, and to sweep the Pentlands daily.

Notwithstanding the large number of vessels which had now been taken up, and the speed with which they were being sent forth on their duties, the demand was still far in excess of the supply. For towards the end of August the enemy's mine-layers had been very busy. On the 27th the steam drifter *Barley Rig* had been blown up about thirty-five miles E. ½ S. of Blyth, and thus the existence of the Tyne mine-field was discovered. Two mine-sweeping trawlers, the *Thomas W. Irvine* and the *Crathie*, were also blown up whilst endeavouring to sweep this new field. H.M. Torpedo-boat No. 18 found herself surrounded by mines, being unable to discover a way out, and the same day a mine-field was discovered also off the Humber. On the top of this intelligence came a request for four trawlers to be sent to Admiral Christian, who was flying his flag in the EURYALUS, and was engaged in operations off Ostend. He urgently required sweepers, as the weather had recently been particularly suitable for mine-laying. These trawlers were therefore sent to him; they left Lowestoft in charge of the navigating officer of the HALCYON, but the next day Captain Ellison was compelled to request their return, as it was impossible to carry on without them. On the day that this request reached Ostend, Admiral Jellicoe was also asking for twenty more trawlers, and two days later he expressed a desire for a score of drifters to act as lookouts to Scapa Flow, since the enemy was now mining the salient points of the coast.

The mine-sweeping trawlers were doing yeoman service. Their draught of water, which was in many cases as much as fifteen feet, made them dangerous to themselves in a mine-field, but they went about their work with fine disregard of their own peril. Already the Humber trawlers had been able to sweep from Spurn Head to the Outer Dowsing, and thus connect up with the swept channel running down to the North Foreland, ensuring a safe passage for the heavy traffic from the English Channel to Hull. In the north, the trawlers based on Granton, in the Firth of Forth, had swept fifteen miles to the eastward of St. Abb's Head, and the Scapa trawlers had swept a channel for the Third Battle Squadron into Scapa.

It had been suggested that the opening phase of the war

would be marked by a determined torpedo attack by the enemy, pushed right into the base where the British Fleet might be lying, ready to strike. It was urged that enemy destroyers would rush across the North Sea, penetrate the British line of patrols, torpedo one or two capital ships, and then dash out again. Probably a whole division of German destroyers would be lost in the attempt, but the loss to the enemy would be well worth the gain.

It is clear that something of this strategy was actually attempted, but with two differences: First, the attack was timed to take place only after the first mine-laying had been carried out; and, secondly, the torpedoes were to be fired by submarines and not destroyers. Within four days of the outbreak of war enemy submarines were assuredly seeking out the Grand Fleet. Of this there is no doubt, for on August 8th the battleships MONARCH, ORION, AJAX, DREADNOUGHT, and IRON DUKE, the last-named being Admiral Jellicoe's flagship, each reported having sighted a submarine. It was impossible that the lookouts of all these ships should have been mistaken, and their reports were confirmed by the fact that H.M.S. BIRMINGHAM early the next morning, when off the north-east coast of Scotland, rammed and sank U15.

It was obvious enough that the Navy could not afford to take unnecessary risks. Admiral Sir John Jellicoe was forthwith ordered to move all his heavy ships at once to the western side of the Orkneys, and a few days later he expressed the opinion that, when the Grand Fleet went to sea, its object should be definite, and as soon as that object was accomplished, it should withdraw; for the risk of mines and submarines was not to be regarded lightly. The enemy had already discovered that Scapa Flow was the main anchorage of the Grand Fleet, and a base at Loch Ewe had now to be established.

But that was only a temporary measure. A definite, settled defensive policy was necessary, and in this respect the trawlers and their fishing crews were to prove invaluable, not merely for mine-sweeping, but in protecting the Grand Fleet from the stealthy under-sea boat. A fortnight after hostilities began, on August 17th, the Admiralty decided to form the Northern Trawler Flotilla. This was to consist of sixteen trawlers, each one fitted with a modified sweep, and in addition each vessel was to carry a couple of 3-pounders. These trawlers were to be based on Scapa, and to be used for the special service of hunting submarines off the Eastern Orkneys. Orders were promptly sent to Lowestoft, where the craft were fitted out and manned by ratings of the Trawler Section, Royal Naval Reserve. It was a sound scheme, and their presence fulfilled a real need in the north, for only the day previous the battle-cruiser NEW ZEALAND had sighted another submarine in the North Sea, with her deck almost awash. Within ten days the first six ships of this Northern Trawler Flotilla were on their way to Scapa.

This, then, was an entirely new rôle for the trawlers to play, and one that had not been contemplated prior to the war. It meant that actually they were to perform the duties of destroyers. Inferior to the latter as regards speed, they possessed much superior sea-keeping ability; and their hardy crews, accustomed to North Sea weather and possessing an excellent fighting spirit, now found their vessels transformed into lightly-armed men-of-war. The decision to employ fishing-vessels to hunt submarines was justified by subsequent events. Within a week the Admiralty were considering the advisability of employing even steam-yachts as patrol craft, and Admiral Sir John Jellicoe favoured the suggestion. It was most important that as many small craft as possible should be taken up and used as mine-sweepers or as submarine-chasers. Before the end of August the Commander-in-Chief informed the Admiralty that trawlers were much required off the Orkneys, as the danger of mine-laying in that area was increasing. He wanted twenty more at once. All that the Admiralty could inform Sir John Jellicoe was that they were arming trawlers for patrol duties as quickly as possible; and meantime Lowestoft was working at high pressure and doing the best to meet the heavy demands.

Thus for two purposes the Royal Navy was hastily taking up trawlers, first for mine-sweeping, secondly for harrying submarines and mine-layers. But before the first month of hostilities had come to an end, it was clear enough that this was to be, in the main, a war of small craft. The Admiralty therefore determined at the beginning of September to utilise all available steam-yachts, trawlers, and motor-boats, and to form these into units; each unit was to consist of one yacht, four trawlers, and four motor-boats, which were to be sent where they were required. The first places would be Scapa, Loch Ewe, Rosyth, Humber, and Cromarty. As more vessels became available, additional units were to be formed. The yachts' and trawlers' armament would be either 3-pounders or 6-pounders, the yachts having two guns and the trawlers one.

Forthwith the Admiralty began to take up all the steam-yachts fit for service, and to send them to Portsmouth and Devonport, to have their gun-mountings placed forward and aft. Many of these yachts had but recently finished their summer cruising, and as soon as their guns were in position, their hulls painted grey, and their wireless gear installed, they were dispatched to the North Sea. Prior to this decision, two yachts had already been taken up for other services. The s.y. *Venetia* had been commissioned at the commencement of hostilities and sent to Scapa Flow, where, under the command of Lieutenant-Commander A. T. Wilson, R.N., she was looking after the Northern Trawler Flotilla. The s.y. *Zarefah*, commanded by Lieutenant-Commander Stuart Garnett, and officered and manned almost entirely by Cambridge rowing men and Ratcliffe sea scouts, was at work in the North Sea in connection with the swept channel.

These additional yachts which were now to be taken up were to work inshore, thus enabling the destroyer patrol flotillas to go farther out to sea, and they were to capture any vessel, of whatever nationality, suspected of laying mines. At this time the amount of traffic, both merchant ships and fishing craft, using the North Sea was considerable. The destroyers and torpedo-boats were doing their best, but they could not board and examine more than a small percentage of suspicious ships. At first these yachts were lent by their owners free of charge, the Admiralty paying all expenses of equipment and running. At the end of three months, provided the yachts were found suitable for service, they were chartered at an agreed rate per ton per month. Owners who possessed the necessary qualifications were invited to take command and accept commissions as lieutenants of the Royal Naval Volunteer Reserve, though subsequently they were transferred to the Royal Naval Reserve.

As to the motor-boats, there was already an organisation

in existence. Its origin dated back a year or two before the European crisis developed, and a working scheme was just being completed when hostilities began. For a long time past yachtsmen in England and Scotland had been anxious to place their sea experience at the disposal of the Royal Navy in the event of war. The difficulty was to [discover a way in which their enthusiasm and ability could be utilised. Most of these yachtsmen were experts in the art of handling sailing craft, but the age of sail in the Royal Navy had long since passed. A suggestion, however, came from the principal motor-yacht clubs that in the event of war the Navy might find it useful to have a number of motor craft at their disposal, officered by yachtsmen, and that these craft might prove of service in various capacities round our coasts. Already there were in existence roughly three types. First was the cruiser type of motor-yacht, able to keep the sea in moderate weather and capable of being armed so as to act as a scout against submarines. Secondly there was the small type of craft, about the size of a picket-boat, which would be useful for patrolling harbour mouths and estuaries. Finally came the small motor-boat which could be used in a dozen ways for policing harbours, taking despatches to shipping in the roads, and in other miscellaneous duties.

The Admiralty were approached on the matter, and were so far interested that they formed a Motor-Boat Reserve Committee, under the presidency of Admiral Sir Frederick S. Inglefield, which was instructed to report on the motor-boats in the United Kingdom, and for what services in war they could be utilised. This was in November 1912, and in the following March, Admiral Inglefield reported that the boats would be capable of patrolling and performing examination service in estuaries and harbours; assisting in controlling traffic, berthing and detaining merchant shipping in ports; detecting hostile submarines that might endeavour to enter a harbour; acting as dispatch-boats to ships in roadsteads; attending on aircraft; and, finally, augmenting the present torpedo flotillas. This corps, it was suggested, should consist of commanding officers of divisions, with the rank of Commander; owners of boats with the rank of lieutenant; and their assistants with the rank of sub-lieutenant. The whole organisation was to be a volunteer reserve. As a result of the first report the Admiralty were so favourably impressed that in January 1914 they proposed that the Motor-Boat Reserve should be affiliated to the Royal Naval Volunteer Reserve, and they requested the Committee to send a further report.

In the meantime, Admiral de Robeck, who was about to relinquish his appointment as Admiral of Patrols, made a number of suggestions and worked out a scheme of organisation and of training for both officers and men in the Motor-Boat Reserve. This was to include small-arm drill, 3-pounder and machine-gun drill, signalling, torpedoes, detection of submarines, wireless telegraphy, visits to war-stations, lectures on International Law, and so on. It was realised that a highly educated and intelligent personnel would be available, and that a few would go through a longer course equivalent to the short course undertaken by naval officers. Admiral de Robeck further showed his interest by attending a Motor-Boat Reserve Committee in March 1914, when the various suggestions which had been put forward were considered. The result was so encouraging that just before the end of July the Admiralty appointed a small Committee to draw up a detailed scheme for the training and organisation of the Motor-Boat Section of the Royal Naval Volunteer Reserve. It was to be under the chairmanship of Commodore George Ballard, the new Admiral of Patrols, and included officers of the three leading British Motor-Yacht Clubs.

That stage of affairs had been reached when suddenly the country was plunged into the European War. The scheme for training had to be dropped, and there were other duties to occupy the attention of the Admiral of Patrols. Still, it was fortunate that the organisation had been developed so far, for the time had arrived to act; and, unless this preliminary spade-work had been done quietly and thoughtfully in peace, it would have been impossible to produce at once so useful an organisation. Motor-boats were forthwith lent by their owners, and during the first few days of the war the little craft were employed principally in acting as despatch-boats in connection with the transports that were carrying the British Army from Southampton across to France. But towards the end of September 1914, the first eight armed auxiliary patrol units had been established at Loch Ewe, Dover, the

Humber, the Tyne, the Shetlands, and at Cromarty. The biggest and best sea-going motor-yachts were selected and sent to these stations. The officers had been given commissions in the Royal Naval Volunteer Reserve, the ratings being known as motor-boatmen.

Arrived at their bases, these motor craft patrolled the harbours, estuaries, and coasts in conjunction with the steam-yachts and trawlers. There was work enough for every sort and description of vessel, for the enemy was engaged in extensive operations with both submarines and mine-layers. Before the end of August already three known German mine-fields had been laid. There was the Southwold mine-field, of which the first mines had been laid by the KÖNIGIN LUISE; then the Tyne mine-field; and, lastly, the mine-fields off Flamborough and the Humber. It is true that a swept and buoyed channel existed at the beginning of September from the Goodwins as far north as Flamborough, and was being patrolled. But outside this narrow lane, four cables wide, the risks to shipping were considerable. On September 3rd the patrol drifter *Linsdell* had struck a mine near the Outer Dowsing (that is, to the eastward of the Humber) and sunk; fifteen minutes later the gunboat SPEEDY also struck a mine, with fatal results. Reports were received that this Humber mine area was an extensive one, the mines being within three feet of the surface. Similarly, from Newcastle came the significant news that four vessels, apparently drifters, had been seen forty-four miles east-south-east of the Tyne, and three more thirty-five miles off. This was on September 7th; and inasmuch as there are no herrings in that part of the North Sea at that season, the local fishermen drew their own conclusions. British fishing skippers recognised them as vessels which three months before were German, and were fishing in the North Sea. Now, in the track of merchant shipping, they were laying mines.

Four days after the loss of the SPEEDY and *Linsdell*, the fishing-vessel *Revigo* foundered on this Humber mine-field, and the s.s. *Runo* had just been sunk on the Tyne mine-field, a disaster that was followed next day by the loss of the fishing-vessel *Imperialist* in the same manner forty miles east-north-east of the Tyne. Admiral Jellicoe pointed out that the difficulty of keeping the North Sea clear of mines was rendered more difficult because of the impossibility of boarding and examining the East Coast shipping. His opinion was that mine-laying would never be stopped until the East Coast traffic was diminished.

The work of the armed units of the Auxiliary Patrol became now more strenuous than ever. Up to this time the submarine had been a menace—a most serious menace—but nothing more. But on September 5th the first submarine success by the enemy was achieved when H.M.S. PATHFINDER was torpedoed ten miles south-east of May Island, off the entrance to the Firth of Forth. At first it was believed that the loss had been caused by a mine, but the mine-sweeping trawlers sent out by Admiral Lowry from the Forth swept from Inchkeith to May Island, then on to Bell Rock and all round the position where the PATHFINDER had struck, and not a single mine was found. It was evident that a submarine had been lying in wait off the Forth in the hope of catching a warship bound to or from Rosyth, and it was afterwards established that a torpedo from U21 sank the PATHFINDER. Only a few days later, a fishing-vessel called the *Defender* unmistakably sighted a submarine eleven miles east by south of the Isle of May, in practically the same spot where the PATHFINDER had sunk; and, true to her name, this trawler determined to protect the Navy as far as she could. Leaving her fishing, she at once hurried westward, gave the information to Torpedo-Boat 32, and went up to the Forth to report the fact also to H.M.S. RINGDOVE. She thus lost her day's catch, but she had done the right thing, and the Admiralty awarded her the sum of £62 for having so promptly given valuable intelligence.

Three days later another submarine—or perhaps the same one—fired a couple of torpedoes at the destroyer CHEERFUL three miles west of Fidra, in the Firth of Forth; the destroyer STAG had also reported that torpedoes had been aimed at her a few hours before off the Isle of May. But nothing brought home the submarine peril more acutely than the loss of the three big cruisers HOGUE, ABOUKIR, and CRESSY, which were sunk in the southern portion of the North Sea by U9 on September 22nd. This triple disaster showed to what dangers British ships were exposed. More than ever the demand was for small armed craft.

On the Humber a special anti-submarine trawler flotilla

was being got ready. From Grimsby, too, four more trawlers, specially fitted with a modified explosive sweep, were sent to the Forth to act as submarine-hunters. These were additional to the armed patrol. Rear-Admiral George Ballard,[1] the Admiral of Patrols, was ordered to have the entrance to the Humber patrolled by trawlers with their modified sweep in addition to his armed trawlers; and finally, with a view to checking mine-laying and the dissemination of information useful to the enemy, the Admiralty announced on September 27th that all East Coast ports would be closed to neutral fishing craft from October 1st. This was a sharp measure, but it was absolutely necessary if success was to attend the plans for dealing with mine-layers and potential supply-ships acting as tenders to German submarines.

When Sir John Jellicoe informed the Admiralty that his destroyers were all too few for stopping and examining traffic, he advocated the employment of armed trawlers, fitted with wireless, in certain areas. He expressed his belief in the freest possible use of these vessels. Some, he urged, should be armed, but as their stems were a good weapon for ramming, it was not necessary to arm all, and there were not at the time sufficient guns to go round. The Germans, he remarked, were making the greatest use of trawlers, and we should do the same. Much the same opinion came from Admiral Lowry at Rosyth, in whose area the submarine activity in the Firth of Forth still continued. On September 29th one submarine had been seen as far up the Forth as Burntisland, and, owing to this and other incidents, he had been compelled to suspend in that neighbourhood all mine-sweeping operations. Altogether no fewer than nine torpedoes had within a few days been fired at British torpedo craft in the Forth, and in view of the value of such vessels and their numerous crews, he considered it was advisable to replace them by armed trawlers or drifters as far as possible. Nor was the menace confined to the North Sea; for on September 27th, H.M.S. ATTENTIVE had been attacked by two submarines in the Straits of Dover.

Mines were being reported frequently in the North Sea, and steamers were still foundering on them. But by this date the whole organisation for dealing with mines, mine-

[1] Now Vice-Admiral George Ballard, C.B.

FLAGSHIP OF A DRIFTER FLEET.

CH. VIII] THE MINE-SWEEPING SERVICE 381

layers, and submarines was well in hand. So important had the mine-sweeping service become that it had been decided to appoint a flag officer in charge, and Rear-Admiral E. F. B. Charlton, C.B.,[1] was selected, with the title "A.M.S." (Admiral of the East Coast Mine-sweepers). This was in the middle of September.

Under this scheme the Mine-sweeping Service was to consist of gunboats, drifters, trawlers, and other vessels employed in mine-sweeping; the sphere of operations extending from St. Abb's Head to the South Goodwins, exclusive of the Nore and Harwich areas. Under Admiral Charlton were the Port Mine-sweeping Officers at Lowestoft, Eyemouth, Grimsby, and North Shields, the Inspecting Captain of Mine-sweepers continuing his duties in connection with the chartering of trawlers as before. This concentration of the whole of the mine-sweeping on the East Coast under one senior officer was essential, owing to the very large increase in mine-sweeping trawlers and other vessels. It was a service quite distinct from the armed patrol trawlers, yachts, and motor craft. It did, however, include the drifters and armed trawlers which were engaged in watching the swept channels.

During this first autumn no seamen more thoroughly earned the gratitude of their nation than those of the busy mine-sweepers, whose work was never finished. From each East Coast port, day after day, six of them steamed out in line ahead just before dawn to their stations; and then they would get sweeps out and go rolling down the North Sea until relieved a few days later by another six; all the time they offered an easy target for the enemy's submarines, and were equally liable to be blown up on an unseen mine.

From the North Foreland to Flamborough Head they were now hard at work, keeping a clean highway a couple of hundred miles long and eight hundred yards wide. Every day this long road was swept twice. In the extreme north, three pairs of trawlers were sweeping two channels at each end of the boisterous Pentland Firth twice daily, necessitating an actual steaming distance of eighty-five miles for each trawler during the daylight hours of a short autumn day. The Cromarty and Peterhead trawlers were sweeping round the headlands of their own area, lest the enemy should have laid his snares; and all down the

[1] Now Vice-Admiral Sir Edward F. B. Charlton, K.C.M.G., C.B.

coast—from the Forth, the Tyne, the Humber, Lowestoft, Harwich, the Nore, Dover, Portsmouth, Portland, and Devonport—they issued forth on their monotonous and dangerous routine.

The sea was witnessing some strange sights. Scarcely had the excursion paddle-steamers which used to ply from so many piers been laid up, little expecting to be brought into use until the return of peace, than they were placed under the White Ensign. What earthly good did the Navy expect to find in a Bank Holiday paddler? When the first of these ships came churning up the muddy waters of the Humber and bumped into Grimsby Docks alongside the steel trawlers, every seaman rubbed his eyes and wondered. And yet those craft, drawing only about seven and a half feet, did splendid work as mine-sweepers. They could go into a mine-field with half the risk of the deep-draught trawler, and they could steam at good speed. The result was that two or three pairs soon cleared up any suspected area and set merchant ships free to proceed to their destinations. The first of these paddle sweepers to be taken up were the *Brighton Queen* and *Devonia*. They were sent round from Bristol to Devonport, where they were fitted out, and thence they steamed up the Channel and North Sea, encountering very heavy weather on the way. In this manner still another type of small craft was pressed into the Service. Built for the purpose of giving pleasure, they were now engaged in war. Some of them ended their days on mines, but not before they had been the means of thwarting certain of the enemy's best-laid schemes.

By the end of September good progress had been made in adding to the number of auxiliary craft. Already fifteen armed yachts were in commission, and about another fifteen were being fitted out. There were roughly 300 trawlers and drifters and 100 motor craft at work, but all the while the enemy was increasing his activities. It was impossible to estimate exactly the intensity of the submarine warfare, owing to the fact that the submarines were mostly invisible. The only absolute evidence of their activities was found in the number of ships sunk, the number of times such craft were sighted, or in the number of torpedoes whose wake might momentarily be seen. It was equally impossible to say whether in a given area, at a given time, these attacks were the work of one or more submarines.

But the next month brought ample indication that Germany was embarking whole-heartedly on a submarine campaign of great dimensions, and scarcely a day went by without supplying evidence. On the 2nd, 5th, 6th, 7th, 9th, 11th, 12th, 13th, 15th, 16th, 17th, 21st, and 24th of October, His Majesty's ships either sighted or were attacked by enemy under-water craft. In this one month alone enemy submarines made attempts on such varied types of British warships as cruisers, destroyers, a gun-boat, a monitor, a torpedo-boat, and a submarine, apart from the refugee ship *Amiral Ganteaume* and s.s. *Glitra*, mentioned in a previous chapter. Nor was this danger in one area only, for in the Dover Straits the British submarine B3 was attacked on October 2nd. During the next few days in the same locality the destroyers COQUETTE and MOHAWK chased submarines; several drifters sighted a submarine off the Smith's Knoll Buoy—that is, off Great Yarmouth; and a submarine was seen in Loch Ewe. On the 9th, the cruiser ANTRIM was attacked off Skudesnaes, and the next day the destroyer ATTACK off the Schouwen Bank had a similar experience. A few hours later a British torpedo-boat chased a submarine off the Isle of Wight, the monitor SEVERN was attacked in the Straits of Dover, and the destroyer GOSHAWK was molested off the Dutch coast. On the 15th the cruiser HAWKE was sunk in the North Sea, and the THESEUS, another cruiser, was molested, both vessels belonging to the Tenth Cruiser Squadron; and the destroyer leader SWIFT was actually attacked three times whilst engaged in picking up the HAWKE's survivors. Next day the destroyer ALARM just missed being hit by a torpedo, and the destroyer NYMPHE, off the Orkneys, possibly struck a submarine. On the 17th the mine-sweeping gunboat LEDA, and again the SWIFT, had torpedoes fired at them whilst entering Scapa Flow, and on the 21st the destroyer LYNX saw a submarine off Cromarty Firth. Three days later the destroyer BADGER was fired at. The torpedo missed her, and the destroyer managed to ram the submarine. Although the BADGER's bows were damaged, the enemy claimed that the submarine got home safely, and this seems probable. The same day submarines were seen off the west coast of Scotland in the neighbourhood of Loch Ewe and Loch Shell. Finally, on the 31st the seaplane-carrier HERMES was torpedoed and sunk not far from Dunkirk.

Such, then, was the enemy with whom the British Navy had to contend. He showed respect neither for a refugee ship nor for a merchant ship. What were the steps taken to meet this violence ? All that could be done, besides laying a British mine-field across the Straits of Dover at the beginning of the month and extinguishing all lights on the East Coast at the end of the month, from Orfordness to Wick, was to strengthen the armed auxiliary patrol in every way possible—in numbers, in organisation, and in offensive devices. More and more guns were wanted for these craft, but, unfortunately, they were not available. The Royal Navy had never counted on so many demands being made upon it, and the Army in France called for every gun that could be turned out. But as an anti-submarine device, the Admiralty attached great importance to the explosive sweep. These sweeps were being made in large numbers, and fitted to patrol trawlers. At Portsmouth alone fifty trawlers were thus being fitted, two dozen more were prepared at Lowestoft, and Commander L. A. B. Donaldson, R.N., was specially appointed to the Admiralty to look after this device, his title being " Commander Superintendent of Modified Sweeping."

Similarly, an improvement was made in jurisdiction, the Dover and the East Coast being divided into two separate commands. On October 12th Rear-Admiral the Hon. H. L. A. Hood was appointed in command of the Dover Patrol as Senior Naval Officer at Dover. In addition to a destroyer flotilla and two submarine flotillas, he had some trawlers and drifters placed in his command, and the latter were presently to increase to considerable numbers. Rear-Admiral George Ballard, the Admiral of Patrols, now became responsible for the area extending from the Naze to St. Abb's Head, an area in which were working many trawlers fitted with explosive sweeps.

Admiral Jellicoe continued to ask for more trawlers for Scapa Flow, Pentland Firth, Loch Ewe, and Moray Firth. Submarines were still reported off the Grand Fleet's northern base and in the Minch. Destroyers, he said, were unsuitable for searching out the lochs and creeks, and only got badly knocked about ; he also wanted trawlers for examining neutral ships in the Minch and vicinity of Pentland Firth, as the submarines prevented such work being done by cruisers. Small flotillas of trawlers working under a yacht were required, and so, on October 28rd, a yacht and the trawlers were sent to him.

Three trawlers specially fitted with the explosive sweep were also sent to the Straits of Dover under Lieutenant-Commander George E. Tillard, R.N., to hunt submarines. More motor-boats were being fitted out and sent to the East Coast to examine the estuaries, harbours, and inlets, but the demand still exceeded the supply. Seven were working at Scapa Flow in connection with the local defences, and the Rear-Admiral at Cromarty was asking for eight to perform the duties of the Auxiliary Patrol. Before the end of the month, the Admiralty were able to inform Sir John Jellicoe that they were increasing the number of armed trawlers at Cromarty, Peterhead, Methil (Firth of Forth), Scapa, Rosyth, Loch Ewe, Great Yarmouth, and Dover. The geographical position of these places is a sufficient indication of their strategical value in regard to submarines. As more trawlers became available, they were armed with one or more guns and an explosive sweep, and organised into divisions of six trawlers to the unit. From each unit one trawler was to be selected as divisional leader. She was to be fitted up with a suitable officer's cabin, then placed under the command of a lieutenant or sub-lieutenant of the Royal Naval Reserve, and to be given also wireless telegraphy. In addition, an armed yacht was to be attached to each unit, and at certain important bases captains-in-charge were to be appointed.

Granton, on the Forth, was becoming an important war base for trawlers and yachts, and was destined soon to be one of the largest auxiliary stations on the coast. Sixty additional trawlers were now taken up as armed patrol vessels. There were a hundred of these already in the Service or being fitted out, and the full 160 were being organised into twenty-six divisions of six vessels each, and one of four vessels. These, of course, were quite apart from the mine-sweeping trawlers and the watching drifters. In fact, before October was ended—that is to say, within less than three months of the declaration of war—there were 130 armed trawlers either in commission or nearly ready; and thirty-seven armed yachts either patrolling or fitting out, in addition to 246 mine-sweeping trawlers, two paddle mine-sweepers, and forty-two drifters. With admirable zeal and energy a new navy had been created in a few weeks which already exceeded in numbers the navy that flew the White Ensign at the beginning of August. In spite of the haste with which the ships and men had been assembled and sent out to their strange duties, in spite of the dangers from weather, fogs, submarines, and mines, only half a dozen trawlers and drifters had been lost during the period. The decision to use for warlike purposes, under modern conditions, ships which were never intended for the contest of organised violence, and men without war training, had abundantly justified itself, to the great advantage of the country and the welfare of British shipping.

Warfare by means of the mine, and warfare by means of the submarine, are practically identical. The aim in each case is to sink the ship attacked by a violent explosive without the victim having so much as a chance of escaping. The only difference between the torpedo and the mine is that the former goes to meet the ship, and the latter waits for the ship's coming. The result in the two cases is the same.

There were only two courses open to the Admiralty. The first was to make mine-laying for the enemy as difficult as possible, and the second was to continue increasing the resources of mine-sweeping. These obvious measures were carried out. To begin with, not only had all the East Coast ports been closed to neutral fishing-vessels from October 1st, but any neutral fishing-vessel found fishing west of a certain line in the North Sea was regarded as under suspicion of mine-laying. The British Government were determined to take no half-measures, and gave warning that any trawlers not in the exclusive employment of the German Government found illicitly laying mines would be sunk, while their crews would be liable to be treated as war criminals and shot after trial by court martial.

It will be recollected that when discussing the pre-war arrangements the Admiralty had established the principle that trawlers were suitable for sweeping fairways and the entrances to harbours, but not for sweeping ahead

MINE-LAYING RAIDS

of the Fleet, owing to their comparatively slow speed. Before the end of the autumn, after Commander Preston's gunboats had been doing much service in the North, Admiral Jellicoe asked for some Fleet sweepers. He insisted that they should possess good speed and be seaworthy, and be capable of standing the heavy weather which prevails off the north of Scotland. The Admiralty, therefore, took up four pairs of steamers owned by various railway companies and fitted them out with the requisite gear. These vessels were the *Reindeer*, the *Roebuck*, the *Lynx*, and *Gazelle*, all owned by the Great Western Railway; the *Folkestone* and *Hythe* belonging to the South-Eastern and Chatham Company, and the *Clacton* and *Newmarket*, which were the property of the Great Eastern Company. The first pair was taken in hand at the beginning of October.

The policy adopted by the Admiralty in regard to the mine-fields was as follows: The trawlers were to sweep the North Foreland to Flamborough Head channel clear and safe; the limits of all suspicious areas were to be defined and therefore avoided; the mine-fields, once their extent and position had been discovered, were to be left intact, and not swept up. Thus the three mine-fields off the East Coast acted as a means of protection against the enemy's possible aggression. Inasmuch as the safe channel for shipping ran between the coast and the mine-field, it was obvious that the enemy was doing us a good turn in laying mines, when once the limitations of these areas had been ascertained. For his measures to be effective, he should have gone close inshore and fouled the swept channel. But to lay mines inshore was not so easy as it seemed, for there were only three possible methods. The first was to employ small craft, especially fishing-vessels, but this sort of thing had already been rendered too risky a proceeding, owing to the careful watch maintained by the British patrols. The second method was to lay the mines invisibly, but the submarine mine-layer had still to be commissioned. Lastly, there was always a possibility of a strong raiding force coming across and overpowering the British patrols, leaving German mine-layers free to do what they liked. It was this third alternative which was adopted by the enemy at the time of the Scarborough and Gorleston raids, when, under the feint of bombarding the coast, dangerous mine areas were laid. These developments will be considered separately in so far as they concern this History, but for the moment attention must be devoted to another locality.

Germany now developed on fresh lines her campaign against ocean traffic. From the Dominion of Canada a number of transports would soon be crossing the Atlantic on their way to England, bringing troops to aid British arms. If Germany could lay a mine-field in the path of these vessels, and blow any of them up, that would be sound strategy. It was on October 3rd that the first Canadian convoy left Canadian waters, and on the very day that this convoy began to arrive in Plymouth Sound an exceptionally large mine-layer was leaving Germany. This auxiliary vessel was the Norddeutscher Lloyd liner BERLIN, of over 17,000 registered tonnage, and a speed of about 17 knots. In peace-time she had been well known on the New York service, and the reasons for employing her in mine-laying were twofold. If she were seen in the track of Atlantic shipping she would not excite much suspicion, for she looked what she was—an Atlantic liner. Moreover, she had ample capacity for carrying many hundreds of mines, and a long after-deck from which to lay them. She was, however, a little unfortunate at first, for she acted on faulty information. She arrived too late to interfere with the big convoy of thirty-one transports, and she had erroneously assumed that the transports would come to Liverpool via the North of Ireland.

She had already made one attempt to pass through the North Sea at the end of September, when, having got up towards the Norwegian coast, she sighted a number of British men-of-war, and therefore put back to Germany. On October 14th, however, she steamed away from Wilhelmshaven with 2,000 mines on board, being escorted by a couple of submarines. Passing round the north and west of Scotland, she arrived off the North of Ireland and laid a big mine-field off Tory Island on October 22nd and 23rd. It happened that there steamed out of the Manchester Ship Canal, on October 24th, a 5,000 ton steamship called the *Manchester Commerce*, bound for the River St. Lawrence, whence the Canadian convoy had started, and on the afternoon of the 27th she struck one of the mines off Tory Island and sank; the explosion occurred between Nos. 2 and 3 holds, the ship drawing

CH. VIII] THE TORY ISLAND MINE-FIELD 339

at the time 19 feet 5 inches forward and $22\frac{1}{2}$ feet aft. Next day at 9 a.m., whilst the Second Battle Squadron was steaming in this locality, the third ship in the line, H.M.S. AUDACIOUS, struck a mine and eventually foundered.

This event suggested more work for the trawlers in an unexpected quarter. It happened that at this time part of the Grand Fleet, with Admiral Jellicoe's flagship, had anchored in Lough Swilly, and until this mine-field was cleared the ships were practically blockaded—the very thing, as has been explained already, that was feared would happen when war broke out. Admiral Jellicoe the same day telegraphed to the Admiralty asking for eight mine-sweeping trawlers to be sent to Lough Swilly at once. Nothing was then known about the *Berlin* having been there; the only information was that a mine-field was in existence about eighteen to twenty miles N. $\frac{1}{4}$ E. of Tory Island. To what extent and in what direction it spread, absolutely no information was available. In response to the Commander-in-Chief's request, four mine-sweeping trawlers were at once ordered to leave Milford Haven for Lough Swilly. For an enemy wishing to mine the shipping track to Liverpool and the Atlantic the obvious strategic points are firstly that strip of sea called the North Channel between the north-east coast of Ireland and the Mull of Cantyre; and, secondly, the St. George's Channel. As it was suspected that the enemy might have fouled these approaches, orders were sent the day after the disaster to the AUDACIOUS that two groups of six trawlers, each attended by an armed vessel, were to be dispatched from Lowestoft to the westward. Of these two groups, one was to proceed to Larne in order to sweep the North Channel, the other was to go to Milford to sweep the St. George's Channel. Nor was this all. The Admiralty decided at once that energetic action was essential in order to cope with this mine-laying on the West Coast and on the trade approaches. Two additional squadrons of about twenty trawlers each, with a proportion of mine-sweepers, were to be formed without delay for the purpose of searching and picketing these areas.

As this dramatic revelation of the Tory Island death-trap suggested that other new mine-fields might be laid off the anchorages used by the Grand Fleet, Sir John

Jellicoe, on October 28th, ordered the Vice-Admiral commanding the Orkneys and Shetlands to send trawlers to sweep for mines up to within thirty miles of the bases. The same day, also, special instructions were sent to the Senior Naval Officer at Liverpool to proceed with the utmost dispatch with the organisation of a special auxiliary patrol for the prevention of mine-laying. Thus yet another type of merchant vessel came to be pressed suddenly into the war. Who is there familiar with ships and seafaring matters that has not heard of the wonderful achievements of the famous Liverpool tugs, which can go anywhere and do almost anything? These powerful little craft have made some wonderful voyages across the world towing floating docks, disabled liners, or dismasted sailing-ships. The war was certainly becoming far-reaching when it needed these craft. However, two days after the AUDACIOUS had foundered, a dozen of these Liverpool tugs were commandeered, six of them to patrol the North Channel, board suspicious ships and prevent mine-laying, while the other six were to be sent to Milford to patrol the southern part of the Irish Sea. This was only a temporary measure until more trawlers could be chartered, and before the end of the year the tugs were sent back to Liverpool. Meanwhile, in addition to the tugs, the armed yacht *Oriana* and a number of drifters were ordered to patrol the vicinity of the Mull of Cantyre, and to search such places as Loch Indail, the west coast of Islay, and its northern side.

Within three days of the AUDACIOUS disaster, six mine-sweeping trawlers were hard at work sweeping from Lough Swilly entrance to the west and south of Tory Island, but found no mines; they had yet to learn that the mines were farther to the northward, but their first duty was to insure a safe channel close to the coast. While the Grand Fleet was unable to leave its anchorage, the entrance to Lough Swilly was being patrolled by the armed yacht *Lorna* and six trawlers; more drifters were also taken up at Kingstown and sent to swell the list of small craft. The experience of war had upset many preconceived ideas, but it was a strange fact that, while yachts, tugs, trawlers, and drifters could use the sea, it was not safe for battleships and cruisers to venture forth.

CH. VIII] WEAKNESS OF THE WESTERN PATROL 341

An inquiry into the manner by which the BERLIN managed to pass through the North Sea and down the Atlantic right to the coast of Ireland, without being intercepted by any of the vessels belonging to the Grand Fleet, would yield interesting reading, but it is foreign to the present purpose. It is, however, pertinent to ask what our Auxiliary Patrol vessels in the neighbourhood of Ireland were doing at the time the *Berlin* was acting as she pleased. The answer is simple. This incident happened within the first few weeks of the war, when every available patrol craft had been sent to the North Sea, for the obvious reason that that was the main theatre of war. It had scarcely seemed credible then that the coast of Ireland could have much strategical value, and the western areas were almost bare in respect of patrols. At the time when the *Berlin* paid her visit, the only auxiliary craft in Ireland were: at Queenstown, an armed yacht, four drifters, and two or three motor-boats; and at Belfast, the armed yacht *Ilex* and four armed trawlers. That was all. There were two bigger craft patrolling to the westward and eastward of the North of Ireland. The old-fashioned light cruiser Isis was cruising about remarkably close to where the mine-layer had been; for the noon position of the Isis on October 22nd was seventy miles west of Tory Island, and at noon of the following day she was forty-five miles west by north of Bloody Foreland. The *Tara*, another of the commissioned railway steamers, was also patrolling the North Channel, and she proceeded to Larne on the 21st to coal. To the north was the armed yacht *Hersilia*, on her way from Peterhead to Loch Ewe, her station; on the 24th she sighted a submarine off Loch Shell, and the same day a submarine had also been sighted five miles north-east of Iona Island. It is probable that these were the two submarines which had accompanied the *Berlin*.

There were, too, four armed trawlers and four motor-boats based on Loch Ewe, but there were only the armed yacht *Oriana* and four drifters working out from Liverpool. The auxiliary force, then, was inadequate for keeping the trade approaches in this part of the British Isles well patrolled and shipping watched for suspicious movements. But the foundering of the *Manchester Commerce* and AUDACIOUS had shown that it was impossible to treat this area as almost negligible; it needed plenty of patrol craft and proper organisation. So Commander H. Berkeley, R.N., was selected and sent to Larne to act as Senior Naval Officer, and to organise for the North Channel the patrol force now being dispatched. At first he had only the *Oriana* and her four drifters and six Liverpool tugs, until other vessels could be obtained. While each drifter carried a 3-pounder gun, the tugs had nothing beyond rifles for weapons, but they had been provided with explosive signals and flares, so that, if a mine-layer or other suspicious ship was sighted, they could instantly warn the other patrols.

Meanwhile, the greatest activity was being manifested to increase the patrols at the most important points. Four more yachts and forty-eight additional trawlers were ordered to Scapa from various ports within a week of the *Manchester Commerce's* sinking, and the dockyards were being asked how many trawlers they could fit out for service. It was no easy problem for the Admiralty, as already the resources of our fishing fleets had been called upon to an extraordinary extent. More patrol vessels, the Director of Operations pointed out, were required for the West, but he confessed that it was difficult to see where they could be obtained. Considerable progress was being made with the manufacture of the modified sweep explosive charges for dealing with the submarines. These sweeps were being prepared for another seventy trawlers, and orders had been placed for a still further supply of sixty; but the manufacture took time, and Woolwich could not turn out more than a hundred a week.

The Admiralty needed nearly a couple of hundred more trawlers, despite the large number of the little ships they had already chartered. It was a strange experience for these fishing craft suddenly to find themselves everywhere in so much demand. Off the North Irish coast they were having a strenuous time sweeping for mines in the heavy Atlantic swell; it was certainly no yachting trip, and presently a long series of gales interfered considerably with their operations. Some of Commander Preston's old mine-sweepers had been sent down from Scapa to assist. The CIRCE and LEDA came first, and by October 29th they had been joined at Lough Swilly by the

JASON, the SPEEDWELL, and the SKIPJACK, which swept the channel along the shore to the east and west of the entrance of Lough Swilly. Thus at length a safe passage inshore of Tory Island and Inishtrahull could be guaranteed, and the Grand Fleet was freed to put to sea once more.

On November 2nd six trawlers again endeavoured to find where the BERLIN's mine-field began and ended. They made an exploratory sweep from Fanad Point, the western headland of Lough Swilly, well out into the Atlantic, but found nothing; and then, having swept out as far north as the fifty fathom line, they swept in three directions from Tory Island, north-north-west, north, and north-north-east, but still without result. Six drifters, which had been sent with their nets to search for mines, had no better fortune. In the last week of November another six mine-sweeping trawlers under the command of Lieutenant Sir James Domville, Bart., R.N., arrived. These craft had come from Scapa Flow to locate the mine-field. It was important that no time should be lost, but exceptionally heavy weather set in, and it was not till late in December that the trawlers could get to work again. A special sweep was carried out from Skerryvore to the Mull of Cantyre, a route likely to have been fouled because it was that traversed by Grand Fleet ships bound for Liverpool for docking or repairs. No mines were found. Then, on December 19th, another disaster occurred, when the Donaldson liner *Tritonia* foundered on a mine in almost the same spot where the AUDACIOUS and *Manchester Commerce* had been sunk.

Fortunately during the next three days the trawlers at last succeeded in finding the dangerous area, a task that is far harder than may be realised by those unfamiliar with such work. Search for mines in the Atlantic in the winter, and never finding them until they suddenly appear in the sweep or blow the trawler to destruction, is an operation not to be undertaken either lightly or inadvisedly. It needs determination to stick it out, enduring the monotonous routine and boisterous weather; but it also needs pluck to go blindly where mines may be found, and a special kind of intuition to guess where the enemy may have laid them. Between December 20th and 22nd, Sir James Domville's trawlers managed to sweep up and explode no fewer than a dozen of the *Berlin's* mines. Five of them were discovered sixteen miles north-east by north of Tory Island, and three more eighteen miles north-north-east of the same island. It was many weeks before the whole mine-field was completely cleared up, but a good beginning had been made, and the trawlers kept doggedly at work. The danger was increased by the heavy weather, which had caused many of the mines to drift in roughly a north-easterly direction. On December 2nd one was even found by the battleship NEPTUNE on the direct line between Oronsay and Skerryvore, and was sunk by her, but others drifted up the west coast of Scotland.

And whilst all this increased activity in regard to patrols and mine-sweepers was proceeding in the North of Ireland, a similar impetus had been created also in the south of the Irish Sea. About the time when Commander Berkeley was appointed to Larne, the Admiralty instituted another base for auxiliary craft. This was at Milford, and thither Captain K. C. Gibbons, R.N., was sent to take charge of the patrol vessels working the St. George's Channel and the outer part of the Bristol Channel. Milford began [to [develop into a most important base, and before very long its spacious haven was alive with all sorts of auxiliary craft. As a beginning, twenty armed trawlers, in addition to some mine-sweepers and armed yachts, were ordered there, as well as six Liverpool tugs. The armed yachts *Aster* and *Greta*, both small enough for the work, and typical fine-weather pleasure vessels, were based on Milford temporarily. But the mine-sweeping trawlers had an equally important office to perform as soon as they could get to sea. It was essential that they should ascertain whether the enemy had laid a mine-field in the south of the Irish Sea, as he had in the north. They were accordingly ordered to sweep the Irish coast from the Tuskar and Coningbeg against the tide, and then work across the St. George's Channel in about six tides. This exploratory sweep was duly carried out, but happily no mines had been laid there.

Reference has been made to the increasing difficulty which the enemy was finding in laying mine-fields in the North Sea, consequent on the improvement of the British patrols. The line of demarcation which the Admiralty had ruled down this sea suffered neutral fishing craft to proceed no farther west than the Dogger Bank, unless they wished to be treated as suspicious ships. The Dogger Bank for hundreds of years has been one of the most productive fishing areas in the world, and the British fisherman continued to use it in war-time, even though he went there knowing full well the risks he ran. Farther down the coast, the Lowestoft and Yarmouth men went on fishing pretty much as usual, and the Ramsgate smacks also sailed up the coast, trawling as they went. These men had nothing to gain by the war, and everything to lose, for if the freedom of the seas were denied to them, their means of livelihood disappeared and people ashore would have no fish. As the demand for crews and ships increased, the younger men joined the Trawler Section of the Royal Naval Reserve, but the older men carried on with that fine spirit which had always been the glory of British seamanhood. Their co-operation with the British Navy was admirable. They realised all that the war by sea meant to them. Moreover, their spirit had been roused by the way the enemy had laid his mines in the areas which they, as peaceful fishermen, had always frequented, and though these fishermen had little regard for the niceties of international law and the subtleties of regulations, they were determined to do their utmost to hinder the enemy to the full extent of their ability.

At the beginning of November there existed in the North Sea one British and three German mine-fields. There was the Tyne area, the Flamborough Head to the Spurn area, the Southwold area, and the area which included the British mines laid across the Dover Straits. But it had become evident towards the end of October that the enemy was at work on some undefined fresh attack. Three suspicious vessels had been seen to the north of the area where the upper end of the Southwold mine ended—that is to say, not far from Smith's Knoll, in the vicinity of Yarmouth. A report came in that, when a Ramsgate smack which was fishing in that neighbourhood approached these suspicious ships, she was fired on. Very shortly afterwards this smack, whilst sailing about, got a couple of mines in her trawl, and one of the mines blew up. The incident was a little mysterious at the time, but in the light of after-events it became intelligible.

A few miles off Yarmouth is the Smith's Knoll shoal, which runs parallel with the shore. It was marked by a lighted buoy at its southern end. From this buoy a short channel had been kept swept, so that it formed a safe highway for ships from the North Sea into the other swept channel which ran from the North Foreland to Flamborough. It was evident, from what subsequently occurred, that the enemy had obtained information of this secret channel, and he certainly was about to make use of it in connection with the Gorleston raid. It is significant of both the raid on Gorleston, and that which occurred a few weeks later on the Yorkshire coast, that the actual bombardment was of secondary importance, and the laying of mines was the main object, for the enemy realised that as soon as he opened fire on the shore the British naval forces would be sent to attack the Germans. In other words, it was an obvious invitation to battle, but without any intention on the part of the enemy to fight; since before the two forces could engage, the German squadron would have scattered plenty of mines across the line of pursuit, thus imperilling valuable warships whose loss we could not afford.

The scheme also included the laying of additional mine-fields just before the raid took place, with the same intention of entrapping His Majesty's ships. Thus the enemy hoped to inflict on us losses from three separate traps. He reasoned that, as soon as the news of his bombardment was telegraphed up and down the country, some of the Grand Fleet squadrons and flotillas would come steaming down from the North across the Dogger Bank; local patrol-ships would emerge in haste from Yarmouth; and some of Commodore Tyrwhitt's destroyer force would steam north from Harwich up the Suffolk coast to the scene of the bombardment. For each of these three forces a mine-field was to be laid, and there is circumstantial evidence that this project was carried out.

The suspicious ships seen by the Ramsgate trawler had almost certainly been laying some of the mines. It was the definite opinion of Admiral Charlton, in charge of the East Coast mine-sweepers, that the mines, on which later on the British submarine D5 foundered, had been laid just prior to the raid, " with the intention of trapping any of our vessels leaving Yarmouth in pursuit." Be that as it may, on November 2nd, the Smith's Knoll Light Buoy was found to have mysteriously disappeared, and that same afternoon a so-called "neutral" fishing-vessel was reported in circumstances which were at least suspicious. The spot was sixty-five miles north-east of the Spurn, at the south-west corner of the Dogger Bank. It was just inside the imaginary line drawn by the Admiralty, so neutral fishing-vessels sighted were not necessarily suspected as mine-layers.

About three o'clock the Hull steam trawler *Alonso* was in that neighbourhood. She was not a patrol vessel, but had come out there to fish, and as she was steaming, her skipper, Mr. Charles Read, who was on the bridge, noticed another vessel about four miles away to the southward with her mainsail and mizzen set. She appeared to be a foreign sailing drifter. It was a hazy afternoon and there were no other vessels in sight, but when half an hour later he got nearer he noticed that the strange ship had steam as well as sail and that she had white bows. She had lowered her mainsail and hoisted a flag on her mizzen. Skipper Read, having been all his life familiar with the ways of trawlers and drifters, decided in his own mind that she was acting suspiciously. He therefore steamed up to her and found that she was riding to a floating anchor. She had no nets out, nor were there any buoys or pellets visible such as one would expect to find on a drifter's deck. The *Alonso* passed right under her stern, and her skipper noticed that the drifter had a derrick swung out from her bridge with a tackle from the end of the derrick to the mizzenmast head. This derrick, which reached out from the ship's rail about eight feet, was made either of iron or steel, and caused the vessel to appear still more suspicious.

What was the obvious inference to be drawn from a drifter with no nets, lying practically stationary, and with a heavy derrick already swung out for use? Appearances suggested to Skipper Read that she was there for the purpose of laying mines during the haze. For twenty-five years he had been fishing, but he had never before seen a drifter with a derrick; "Nor," he remarked, "is a derrick used by drifters in their fishing." He expressed his suspicions to his crew, and suggested that the best thing to do would be to run her down. The evidence, however, was insufficient to warrant his taking such a drastic step, so, to quote his own words, "As I could not see any mines I decided not to do this, but to break my voyage by ceasing fishing operations and make for the Humber as quickly as possible, to give the information to one of the Admiralty vessels." He steamed back to the Spurn and came up the Humber, where H.M.S. VICTORIOUS was lying as guardship, and gave her the information. He had done the right thing, had patriotically sacrificed his fishing, and wasted no time. The Admiralty showed their appreciation of his devotion to duty by making a present of £25 to the skipper and crew, in addition to another £25 to the owners.

The next morning the Gorleston raid occurred.[1] Briefly, the facts are as follows: Just after seven o'clock in the morning of November 3rd, H.M.S. HALCYON, which had just left Yarmouth to look for mines, sighted a four-funnelled cruiser steering south-south-west towards the shore, and two minutes later there appeared four German Dreadnought vessels as well. This was an enemy squadron, which is supposed to have left Heligoland Bight the previous evening. Within a quarter of an hour of being sighted the enemy opened fire, and it was seen that there were two cruisers following astern of the Dreadnoughts. About the same time two British destroyers, the LIVELY and LEOPARD, also came under fire, but the former made a smoke-screen to windward of HALCYON and thus shielded her. At twenty minutes to eight, by which time the HALCYON's steering compass had been shot away, but practically no other damage done, the enemy ceased fire, and was seen to be steering to the south-eastward. Shortly afterwards the squadron was lost sight of. The enemy had come down from Smith's Knoll, and having proceeded thence towards the shore, had begun to lay mines from the rearmost ship just before altering course to the south-east. The LEOPARD endeavoured to keep in touch with the enemy, but he was soon lost to sight. Presently the submarine D5 came out from Yarmouth in pursuit, but she had only covered a couple of miles south-east of the South Cross Sand when she struck a mine and was lost.

[1] Fuller and later information supported the conclusion that all the mines discovered after the Gorleston raid were laid by enemy men-of-war.

As to the raiding squadron, they had apparently dropped mines as they approached Smith's Knoll, then all the way down the swept Smith's Knoll passage, for six or seven miles towards the Cross Sand Lightship; and, having altered course, they continued to lay mines as they proceeded seawards. They had thus laid a veritable trap, but again a fisherman, by his intelligence, rendered excellent service and saved valuable lives and ships. About 3.30 in the afternoon a fishing-vessel returned to Lowestoft, and her skipper reported that the enemy had laid these mines. He had seen the Germans engaged in the very act, and had observed that one of the ships had her quarter-deck covered with mines ready to be dropped overboard.

The object of the enemy became clear. He had fouled the Smith's Knoll passage, and had scattered mines in the track of any pursuers. The actual shore bombardment had been little more than a blind. For our part, the first duty was to save British ships, and the *Columbia* was forthwith recalled to Lowestoft, bringing with her all the minesweepers available, and ordered to keep well to the northward of the Smith's Knoll buoy. Unfortunately, three fishing-vessels the same day foundered on this new minefield; but the next day the mine-sweeping trawlers went out on their dangerous job, groping about to find where the mines had been strewn. To add to their dangers a fog settled down, and on the following day, November 5th, the *Mary*, one of the mine-sweeping trawlers, struck a mine whilst at work and sank. This put an end temporarily to the sweeping operations, but before long the passage was cleared and a new channel was in existence. Once again the best-laid scheme of a ruthless enemy had been brought to naught by the good work of the trawlers, though at the expense of valuable lives. Not a single merchant ship or big man-of-war had fallen into the trap, though, unhappily, a submarine, besides several fishing craft, had been lost.

So much for the mine-laying efforts of the enemy. During the first week of November the Admiralty became aware that he was increasing his submarine attacks. Almost simultaneously twenty armed trawlers reached Scapa Flow for local defence, but still the Commander-in-Chief required more. Eighteen he was using to work in the Minch and between Cape Wrath and Pentland Firth, those wild, boisterous waters where seaworthy, well-built craft are thoroughly tried. The Shetlands Patrol had been further strengthened by six trawlers, but another dozen trawlers were required for the Moray Firth, to provide for the safety of the battle cruisers. Nor was this all. The Admiralty began to take up a number of stoutly-built Scotch motor fishing-boats for patrol work. They are wonderful sea-boats, double ended, though rather slow. Sixteen of them were soon put into service by the Motor-Boat Reserve, each manned by a crew of five hardy Scotch fishermen, with two officers of the Royal Naval Volunteer Reserve. These boats were about sixty feet long, and were sent to Lerwick, Scapa, Cromarty, and the Firth of Forth, but presently there were also to be based on Cromarty three armed yachts with wireless, and eighteen trawlers fitted with the explosive sweep, in addition to ten motor-boats for patrolling narrow waters. Granton, too, now became a very important naval base for trawlers, under Captain Cecil Fox; and having regard to the extent to which submarines had frequented the vicinity of the Firth of Forth, its development was undertaken none too soon. Within eight weeks eighteen enemy submarines had been sighted inside the limits of Rosyth Naval Centre, apart from those which had been seen up the Forth itself. At least six submarines had been identified near the Longstone, and it seemed probable that they were using this spot for making the land. Though the Longstone light had been extinguished in the first week of September, submarines continued to be sighted off there during the next two months.

Before attention is devoted to the North, something must be said of what was happening in the English Channel. It was expected that submarines were about to operate off the South Coast, and with the limited available auxiliary patrols efforts were made to cope with this activity. The task was most difficult. Prior to the war there had been a disposition to underrate the capacity of the submarine, and when its offensive ability was demonstrated only too forcibly, it was painfully realised that our countermeasures were by no means adequate. The Grand Fleet had to be preserved intact, at all costs, on the principle

CH. VIII] INCREASED NEED FOR AUXILIARIES 351

that the final contest is decided by the capital ship. Consequently, nearly all the destroyers, and a great part of the armed auxiliary patrols, were attracted to northern latitudes. Small ships on the South Coast were few in numbers, and the problem to be solved was rendered no easier by the fact that the enemy had developed a type of mine-laying submarine which could do its work without breaking the surface.

Portsmouth was asking for eight drifters to patrol outside the Solent; Portland required trawler patrols for the Dorset coast; and we were compelled to invite the French to organise a trawler patrol in order to pursue submarines by day and night in the area between the lines Dungeness–Boulogne and Beachy Head–Dieppe. The submarine came and went like a will-o'-the-wisp. On November 6th three torpedoes were fired at H.M. Torpedo-boat 91 while patrolling off the Girdler in the Thames Estuary; the same day H.M.S. DRAKE sighted a periscope off Hoy Sound at the western entrance to Scapa Flow. Five days later H.M.S. NIGER, an old-fashioned gunboat, was torpedoed close to Deal Pier. On the 18th H.M.S. SKIPJACK chased a submarine north of the Orkneys. Submarines continued to be reported off the Hebrides and Cape Wrath. H.M.S. AJAX also sighted a periscope about midway between the Faröe Islands and Cape Wrath.

These incidents in no wise lessened the demand for auxiliary craft. Yet again the Commander-in-Chief asked for more and more trawlers—twelve to be based on Stornoway for patrolling the east coast of the Hebrides and the west coast of Skye and Mull; six to be based on West Loch Tarbert for the west coast of the Hebrides; and twelve to be at Loch Ewe for the outer coast of Scotland. He also desired one yacht for the west coast of the Hebrides, one at Stornoway, and one at Loch Ewe. But already the Admiralty was working out a bold and comprehensive scheme for dealing with the whole coast-line, and meanwhile everything possible was done by improvisation to strengthen our defensive measures against the mine and submarine. Instructions were issued to accelerate the fitting out of trawlers with modified explosive sweeps. Admiral Sir Percy Scott, who, just prior to the war, had suggested in the face of some criticism the great possibilities of the submarine, was in the middle of November appointed to the

Admiralty to investigate the best methods for counteracting this invisible vessel. As a further step, the Admiralty elaborated a scheme for modifying the lighting and buoyage from Great Yarmouth to the Isle of Wight, and this came into force early in December.

Meanwhile the task of the mine-sweeping trawlers grew no lighter. For, besides keeping clear that long lane from the North Foreland to Flamborough Head, they had to meet many demands made upon them. Towards the end of November Rear-Admiral Stuart Nicholson had been directed to bombard Zeebrugge with the battleships RUSSELL and EXMOUTH. To sweep ahead of his ships he required eight trawlers, and so, at a time when they could ill be spared, four had to be sent from Lowestoft and another four from Great Yarmouth. They proceeded to Dover and thence to Dunkirk, sweeping a clear way for the battleships, but such craft were hardly suited for this kind of work, as they were wanting in speed. Presently trawlers were sent from Dunkirk to sweep the West Deep, off Nieuport, clear of floating mines, work which they could perform admirably. But the strain put upon the East Coast mine-sweepers became intolerably heavy. Many of them had been taken away to Lough Swilly, to Milford, and now to the Belgian coast, with the result that it was possible to sweep the North Foreland–Flamborough lane only once a day instead of twice. This, of course, increased the risks to our coastwise traffic, but in view of the limited number of trawlers and the demands made upon their services, such risks could not be avoided.

On November 17th, 1914, there came out from Heligoland a submarine with the number "U18" painted on the hull. Never did a craft leave port with so much hatred of her enemy, nor with greater assurance of achieving success. She was a vessel of about 200 feet length, with surface speed of 20 knots and radius of 3,000 miles. Her crew consisted of a Kapitän-Leutnant, a Leutnant zur Zee, and a Marine Oberingenieur as officers, and twenty-four ratings. All were animated with the firm intention of seeking out the Grand Fleet and attacking it, no matter at what cost. Proceeding across the North Sea, the submarine arrived off the southern end of the Dogger Bank at night, running on the surface, but when a British destroyer approached at high speed soon after

U18'S DISAPPOINTMENT

4 a.m., she was compelled to submerge to a depth of 9¼ fathoms, and did not dare to rise again to the surface until about half-past eight. While awash she had sighted many fishing craft on the Dogger Bank, and had avoided them successfully, though one had signalled to her. At nine o'clock on the morning of the 19th, U18 was off Whitby, and she continued on her northerly journey, coming up to the surface every hour for her commander to look round and take bearings. Two days later she was off the Moray Firth, and patrolled there all day at slow speed, sighting one of the mine-sweeping gunboats in the distance.

Off the Pentland Firth the submarine observed the armed trawlers towing their explosive sweeps, and saw also some destroyers. Then her commander perceived how difficult it would be for him to penetrate the close screen protecting the Grand Fleet. In Germany among naval officers no place was so much talked about at this time as Scapa Flow, but so far no submarine had succeeded in getting right inside. It was the fixed intention of this U-boat captain to succeed where others had failed, and to torpedo the Iron Duke. Having proceeded farther north, the submarine was off Fair Island about midnight of November 22nd–23rd, and in the early hours of the morning, whilst it was still dark, she passed through the British patrol lines and made towards Scapa Flow. At 7.30 a.m. she entered Pentland Firth, having waited till slack water, and then, in the sure hope of finding the Grand Fleet and of attacking it, passed north of the Pentland Skerries. A steamer was seen to be heading for Scapa Flow, so the submarine followed in her wake, making for the entrance, and hoping to be able to slip into the harbour astern of her unobserved. Looking through his periscope, the German captain noticed that Scapa Flow was protected by means of an anti-submarine boom, and he took his craft close up towards it until he could scan the whole of the harbour.

This was the crest of his success and the beginning of his downfall; for the nest which he had hoped to foul was empty; the Grand Fleet was not there! It was a bitter disappointment after so long and trying a voyage. The men had not been out of their clothes since leaving Heligoland. The captain at once surmised that the Fleet was at Cromarty, and he determined to follow there. His supposition was incorrect; for, had he but known it, the Grand Fleet had coaled during the night of the 21st and put to sea early on the following morning, to make a sweep down the North Sea towards Heligoland. The helm of the U18 was now put hard over, and she came out again, intending to get to the Moray Firth. She had not run more than about a mile and a quarter from Hoxa Head, which is on the eastern side of the entrance to Scapa Flow, when suddenly a violent blow was felt. The captain and first lieutenant realised the situation when the submarine took a list of fifteen degrees. What was worst, the most effective periscope had been carried away. The fact was that above them, on the surface, thanks to a good lookout and skilful handling, the Scapa mine-sweeper *Dorothy Gray* had been able to ram the periscope, bending it over, and to strike the submarine's hull aft, causing considerable damage. Another trawler, the *Tokio*, had been the first to see the periscope. The *Dorothy Gray*, being nearer, acted promptly and effectively. The ramming happened at 12.20 p.m., and the submarine was not seen again for another hour, during which time twenty-seven German officers and men spent some of the most anxious and exciting moments of their lives.

After the blow struck by the *Dorothy Gray*, the lower tube of the damaged periscope at once filled with water, but the submarine went on in a mad endeavour to escape. She submerged to eleven fathoms. Half an hour later she managed to fix her position, and then, getting on to her course, submerged again to the previous depth. Life thereafter to those confined in U18 became an unceasing struggle to escape from the most horrible of deaths. The trawler's attack had put much of her mechanism out of gear. First, the hydroplane motor gave out and suddenly jammed. The result was that the craft could not be controlled to a normal depth. She rose and sank erratically, at alarming angles, so that at one time she was rushing upwards and about to break surface, whilst the next moment the vessel nose-dived towards the bed of the sea. Tanks were emptied and again flooded; the submarine descended to $27\frac{1}{2}$ fathoms—165 feet ! Then twice in quick succession there came a bump, indicating that the hull had touched the hard bottom of the sea. Up the submarine came to the surface, and then followed another crash. This time she had been rammed by the destroyer GARRY.

What happened during the ensuing period is best described in the words of Oberleutnant Neuerburg, second in command: "The boat shot upwards and downwards; the men rushed forward and aft; the flooring became slippery with the oil carried out of the engine-room by the men's feet; the men slipped." Down the craft went again, striking the sea bottom, then rose, and descended once more, this time to over 230 feet. "Then," declared Oberleutnant Neuerburg in his narrative, "we shot upwards so violently that I gave up all hope. . . . From the conning-tower came the report, 'Steering gear jammed—man the hand wheel.' And then from the engine-room: 'The motors have broken down!'" The boat eventually began to rise, and then suddenly the captain pushed open the conning-tower hatch. She had a heavy list, a hole torn in her starboard tanks, rudder gone, propellers badly damaged. "As I came on deck I saw how the periscope was almost broken off short. . . . Suddenly there was a smell of burning. Someone shouted, 'The battery is on fire!' The captain gave orders that the boat was to be sunk. We drifted helplessly in the currents of Pentland Skerries. No. 2 fired star-signals to draw the attention of the signal-station . . . two destroyers were approaching at full speed. The captain fired off the stern torpedoes in order to allow the water to enter through the tubes. . . . Spreuger (the engineer officer) tore open the flooding valves . . . then the boat sank. . . ."

It was at 1.30 p.m. that the submarine had for the last time come to the surface, and the crew were seen on deck with a white flag flying. She had foundered about five miles east by south of Muckle Skerry, the largest of the group of rocks which lie at the eastern entrance to the Pentland Firth. The two destroyers which came up were the ERNE, with Admiral Sir Stanley Colville on board, and the GARRY. The latter picked up all the officers and men with the exception of one man, a stoker, who was drowned. So ended the career of the craft which had proposed to sink Admiral Jellicoe's flagship.[1] Up

[1] "Die Deutschen U-Boote in ihrer Kriegsführung, 1914–18," states (vol. i, p. 16) that U18, as she was returning from Scapa Flow, was sighted and chased, and that she struck the rocks whilst proceeding submerged, and was compelled to come to the surface and surrender owing to the damage sustained.

to this date, though the Auxiliary Patrol had been doing most excellent work, no chance had come their way of sinking a submarine, and to trawler *Dorothy Gray*, No. 96, belonged the honour of being the first auxiliary vessel in naval history to achieve such a feat. This incident was most wholesome in its effect; it convinced the Admiralty that these small ships and fishermen crews could do all that might be asked of them, and to the crews themselves it imparted an increased confidence in their ability. A healthy spirit of rivalry was excited, and amidst the depressing monotony of the patrol there was no man who was not cheered by the belief that some day he might help to send a submarine to the bottom.

"I wish," wrote Admiral Colville to the Admiralty, "to draw their lordships' attention to the excellent work done by Trawler No. 96, the skipper of which worked his craft most successfully in chasing and ramming the submarine." "Hearty congratulations to Trawler 96," telegraphed the First Lord, "for brilliant service, which their lordships will mark by a substantial reward." In due time came the reward: £500 to the skipper (Chief Skipper A. Youngson, R.N.R.) and crew of the *Dorothy Gray*, and £100 to *Tokio*. But, apart from any pecuniary prize, there was the knowledge that a fishing-vessel, manned by a fishing crew, had performed distinguished service in ridding the sea of a dangerous enemy, and had created a most encouraging precedent. That the enemy was determined to penetrate into the area known to be frequented by the Grand Fleet was made evident by the persistence with which submarines cruised off the Orkneys. On the day after U18 was rammed and sunk another of these craft was seen by H.M.S. DRYAD off the east side of the Orkneys, and again on the following day the trawlers won the praise of the Royal Navy. That day, off the same part of the coast, a submarine was netted, though she was not destroyed. As soon as she was sighted trawlers gave chase, whilst an outlying trawler got the intelligence through to H.M.S. SKIPJACK, which followed the submarine till, as she was approaching gun range, the craft dived and was not seen again. "I consider most praiseworthy," reported Commander Preston of the incident, "the way these two trawlers, 79 and 80, carried out the chase and promptly gave information." Such evidence of the trawler's effective value was as welcome to the Commander-in-Chief as to Whitehall. The Lords of the Admiralty wrote to Sir John Jellicoe that they noted with satisfaction the apparent increase in the value of the trawler patrols, and desired that he would cause an expression of commendation to be transmitted to the commanding officers of these two trawlers.

The raid on the Yorkshire coast on December 16th was in strategy, and to a great extent in tactics, practically a repetition of the raid which had occurred off Gorleston a few weeks before. In results, however, this Yorkshire raid was the more serious. Each of these raids revealed the same deliberate, well-planned scheme; in each occurred the arrival off the coast at dawn, the bombardment, and the endeavour to entice British squadrons on to mine-fields in carefully chosen areas, mines being sown close inshore in the hope of destroying British flotillas and light forces, as well as out to sea where the battle fleet might be expected to pass. But the mines laid off Flamborough Head were far more numerous than those which had been scattered off Yarmouth.

On the morning of December 15th a portion of the Grand Fleet left Scapa, Cromarty, and Rosyth, and swept down the North Sea, accompanied by seven destroyers. About 5 a.m. these destroyers suddenly encountered a German force, consisting of cruisers and destroyers, to the eastward of the Dogger Bank, proceeding in an opposite direction—that is to say, on a north-westerly course. An engagement ensued, and three of our destroyers were badly hit, though one of the latter claimed to have torpedoed an enemy cruiser. This proved to be the advanced screen of the German High Sea Fleet, and just before eight o'clock, as it was getting light, enemy cruisers appeared off Scarborough. Whilst three of them bombarded the town, the fourth cruiser steamed east-south-east towards Flamborough Head and laid an extensive mine-field. These four ships represented only part of the main force, for prior to reaching Scarborough the squadron had split up, the VON DER TANN and DERFFLINGER making for this seaside resort; the other division, consisting of the SEYDLITZ, MOLTKE, and BLÜCHER, steering for Hartlepool, which was also bombarded till just before nine o'clock, when these vessels made off to the eastward. A few minutes later, the two Scarborough raiders appeared off Whitby and also bombarded that place, after which the whole of the force made its escape. It had come via the open passage existing between the Tyne and Humber mine-fields, and the ships which had gone north to Whitby and Hartlepool had kept shoreward of the Tyne mine area. But on their return journey, between these two old mine areas, the enemy's light cruisers and destroyers, forming the German screen, were sighted and fired on by the British light cruisers about 11.30 a.m. Owing to the mist they escaped. About midday the Second Battle Squadron also sighted enemy cruisers and destroyers steering east by south at full speed; and again the raiders eluded pursuit. It was a very fortunate adventure for the Germans; but for the bad luck in regard to the mist and rain, they would have been severely handled.

This raid is of immediate interest as illustrating the part which the Auxiliary Patrol had in the affair. There was afterwards reason to assume that the force which had encountered British destroyers in the morning had steamed up to the north-west corner of the Dogger Bank, and there laid some mines to entrap the Grand Fleet. At any rate, a quarter-past nine that morning, the fishing trawler *Blanche*, which had come to the Dogger Bank to fish, sighted a mine, the position being about seventy miles N.E. ½ E. of Flamborough Head. The skipper, Mr. John Wilson, took his ship close up to it, and as he had no weapons for sinking it he dropped a dan-buoy to mark it, lay alongside it for an hour, and definitely ascertained that it was a moored mine and that it had five horns. The trawler then steamed half a dozen miles, when she sighted a destroyer; there is a reason to think that this was a German destroyer which had accompanied the first squadron, encountered at five o'clock farther to the south-east, and had just finished laying mines. " As we altered our course to go to him," stated Skipper Wilson, " he steamed away in the east by north direction. When we first saw him he had his head on the east-south-east course, and the wind was north-north-west, fine breeze and rain. I saw it was no good steaming after him, so proceeded homewards, as I think he was the one that laid the mine. If he had been English he would have waited, as he could see we altered our course towards

A DRIFTER ON PATROL.

him." This destroyer had evidently been in action, for her mast appeared to have been shot away, but the *Blanche* at this time was unaware of the Scarborough raid. Skipper Wilson acted as one might have expected him to do; and as he could not sink the mine, he abandoned all thought of fishing, steamed back to the Humber, and gave information to the guardship H.M.S. VICTORIOUS in the river. Then he steamed out to his fishing-ground again, and when about sixty-five miles N.E. $\frac{1}{2}$ E. from Flamborough, shot his trawl and fished all night. When daylight came he found another mine waiting for him. He was determined to sink it, though many men would have been content to leave it alone. " We hove our gear," he said, " and then made fast a liver barrel half filled with water, attached to a 50-fathom wire buoy-line, and this we towed with the object of bursting the mine." The intention was by this means to strike the horns and so explode the mine. The attempt was made four or five times, and then, as the effort failed and darkness was coming on, he gave it up, buoyed the mine with a dan-buoy, and for the next two or three days continued fishing in its vicinity. It was a risky thing to do, for his ship might at any moment have been blown up by striking a mine, or his trawl might have caught the mooring wire and brought about an explosion. There can be no question that these were mines. Within a few days the fishing-vessel *Ocana*, in almost the very spot where the *Blanche* buoyed her first mine, hit one of the horns of a mine and foundered.

Another fishing steam trawler, the *Cassandra*, had an excellent view of the retreating enemy on the day of the raid. This Hull trawler suddenly found herself in the midst of a modern naval engagement between powerful ships, while she was quietly trawling as if the sea were as safe as in peace-time. Her skipper, Mr. H. Pegg, afterwards related his experience: " On December 16th, 1914 at noon, I had just left the bridge to get a bit of tobacco, when the mate shouted down the cabin that he could hear the firing of big guns. I immediately went on deck, and there rushing towards us was a big German cruiser accompanied by a torpedo flotilla, steaming about southeast. About seven or eight miles to the westward were our Fleet, firing as hard as they could. Immediately we were surrounded by flying shells. You could hear them whistling overhead and see them falling all round us. As the Germans were passing us, the big cruiser fired a shot which passed between our bridge and funnel and hit the water about fifty yards away from us. Simultaneously I saw two shells hit one of their destroyers, and all I saw was a tremendous upheaval of water and then nothing more. This all lasted about fifteen minutes." By this time the trawler's skipper had got in his gear and was steaming towards the land. "About 3 p.m., no warships then being in sight, I saw what looked like a mast sticking up out of the water, about south-west of us, and immediately bore away towards it. Getting a better view, I made it out to be a submarine with two masts, the fore one longer than the after one, and having a cross-tree to it (the fore one). This I surmised must be a German, and we kept after him for about a quarter of an hour, but he outdistanced our ship easily. Last seen, he was going about south by east to south, time being 3.45 p.m."

It was not long before the mine-field laid by the raiders off Scarborough began to bring forth disaster upon disaster. Happily the battleships, battle cruisers, cruisers, and destroyers, in spite of the risks they ran in the chase, had escaped the danger. Thus one portion of the enemy's plan had miscarried; but the losses to merchant shipping were to be alarming, and the toll of human life was great. The enemy had barely finished laying his mines when the Norwegian s.s. *Vaaren* struck a mine about three and a half miles north-east by north of Filey and foundered, her crew being picked up by the trawler *Clon* at 9.15 a.m. Twelve hours later the British s.s. *Elterwater* also ran on a mine and foundered three miles east of Scarborough; and the same evening the *Princess Olga* went down five miles east-north-east of Scarborough. Still further to increase the peril to our shipping, three German torpedo-boats at sunset laid more mines on the Dogger Bank, seventy miles north-east by east of the Spurn. Next day the *City*, which had on board several of the dead seamen from the collier *Elterwater*, reported that the sea off Scarborough was strewn with mines. The extent and direction of this latest mine-field was then, of course, unknown, but the day after the raid all traffic between Flamborough and the Tyne was stopped, except during the hours of daylight.

Down to the day of the Scarborough raid, as has been

stated, a swept channel existed from the North Foreland to Flamborough. Up and down this channel streams of ships passed. Owing to the existence of other mine-fields already mentioned, vessels were practically restricted to this lane. It had been swept daily and patrolled daily and was used with confidence. But now the enemy had laid snares along this sea road, and the results were serious. Until the *Clon* had picked up the *Vaaren's* crew it was not known that a new mine-field had been laid, and only the disappearance of the other merchant ships that day gave even a vague indication of the mine-field's actual position. It was now the duty of the mine-sweepers to ascertain the limits of this danger area, and to get rid of the mines as quickly as possible. Orders were sent by Admiral Charlton instructing the mine-sweepers to work from Flamborough Head to Hartlepool, with a pair of Fleet sweepers, and destroyers from the Ninth Flotilla were sent to sea so as to stop all south-going ships from entering the mine-field.

Although arrangements were made to extend the swept channel northward from Flamborough, and the passage of merchant shipping was stopped, the situation was embarrassing. A hold-up of cargo vessels throttled trade, besides causing an inconvenient congestion of traffic at focal points. On the other hand, if they were allowed to proceed, they ran considerable risk. It was therefore decided to make a compromise, and to allow ships to pass by daylight, warning them to keep within two miles of the shore. The actual mine-sweeping commenced on December 19th. From Grimsby came groups of trawlers which not many weeks ago had been fishing for food. There came, too, the paddle-steamer *Brighton Queen*, which had early that summer been running excursion trips on the South Coast. From Lowestoft were sent eight sturdy drifters to assist in keeping merchant ships off the mine-field; and, as if to complete the representative character of the auxiliary craft, from the northward came a motor-vessel usually engaged in summer cruising which at the beginning of the war had been transferred to the White Ensign. H.M.S. SKIPJACK, under Commander L. G. Preston, R.N., also arrived to assist the trawlers. The personnel engaged on this big scheme had come from most parts of the world. North Sea fishermen who had been trawling off Iceland, sportsmen fresh from fishing in Canadian waters, seamen working in cross-Channel packets or liners when the war broke out, others, again, who were yachting as recently as the preceding July, as well as naval officers, were soon busy, all bearing testimony to the great brotherhood of the sea.

In order to ascertain how the mines lay, it was essential to sweep at all states of the tide. None except those who have served off this inhospitable coast during the few daylight hours of a December day can realise the anxieties and difficulties of the task. Gales spring up at short warning, and as Bridlington and Scarborough, the only adjacent harbours, could not be entered at all states of the tide, Grimsby—involving a long passage for small craft along an unlighted coast—was the nearest port available. Trawlers keep the sea in almost any weather, but they draw a good deal of water, especially aft, and thus at any moment they were in peril of falling victims to the hidden mines.

Thus the operations began, Commander R. H. Walters, R.N., in the *Brighton Queen*, being the officer in charge. The trawlers passed out with their sweeps to clear the seas of hidden death. It was not long before the inevitable happened. The mine-sweeping trawler *Passing*, commanded by Lieutenant G. C. Parsons, R.N., ran into a mine, which blew a hole into her bow so large that a small motor-car could have been driven through it. She was a magnificent type of trawler, stoutly built, and fortunately her bulkheads held. The *Brighton Queen* was able to take her in tow and beached her on the Scarborough sands, whence she returned later on to Grimsby to be repaired. But immediately after the accident to the *Passing*, the mine-sweeping trawler *Orianda* (Lieutenant H. Boothby, R.N.R.) hit a mine a mile and a half south-east of Scarborough Castle and blew up. One of the crew was killed, but Lieutenant Boothby got the rest of his men away safely. The next trawler to suffer misfortune was the *Star of Britain* (Lieutenant C. V. Crossley, R.N.R.), three violent explosions revealing the cause of the injuries she had received. On the first day's sweeping, and within ten minutes, three trawlers had struck German mines. Commander Preston took the SKIPJACK very gallantly to the middle of the mine-field where explosions had taken place, and there anchored his ship between the trawlers and the mines which had been swept up. The mines which had occasioned so much trouble were then sunk.

The first day's sweeping failed to define the extent of the dangerous area, but at least it was established that mines had been sown thickly from a position in lat. 54° 18′, long. 0° 15′ W. to the shore. Next morning the sweeping was continued, and further disasters occurred, the first about 9 a.m. The steam-yacht *Valiant*, under the command of Admiral Barlow (one of a good many retired flag officers who had volunteered for this, or other, perilous work), on passage up the coast on her way to Cromarty, struck a mine near Filey, disabling both her propellers and rudder; she soon began to leak badly. Two trawlers, at no mean risk, crossed the mine-field to her assistance, bringing her to anchor off Scarborough. This action was all the more meritorious since it was low water at the time. Next day the *Valiant* was taken in tow by the steam-yacht *Eileen*, commanded by Admiral Sir Alfred Paget, who had also returned to the Service on the outbreak of war. After temporary repairs in the Humber, she was towed down the North Sea and English Channel and up the Irish Sea for overhaul.

About an hour after the *Valiant's* accident, the armed patrol trawler *Garmo* also struck a mine off Scarborough. She turned right over and sank, one officer and five men being lost. So the dangerous work went on during the cold, depressing December day. Groups of trawlers under Lieutenant G. C. Parsons, R.N., and Lieutenant-Commander Bernays, R.N., worked their hardest under most trying conditions. By December 22nd, Commander Walters was able to report a safe passage from Flamborough Head to Filey Brig buoy within half a mile of the shore; but north of that point the channel was only partially swept. Meanwhile the Humber had become crowded with shipping. Unable to proceed on their voyages, merchant vessels had run up the river and come to anchor in its sandy waters. No fewer than forty-eight commercial vessels of all sizes—tramp steamers, transports, colliers, food ships, timber ships, oilers—were waiting, and the numbers were daily increasing. But, again, there was a difficulty. Serious as was this delay financially to the owners and others, yet it could not have been avoided,

as was suggested by the further report that the Norwegian
s.s. *Boston* had struck a mine three miles east-south-east
of Scarborough. She was beached on the north side of
Filey Brig.

Already a flotilla of fourteen trawlers was sweeping
off Scarborough, in addition to the drifters and the motor-
boat *Euan Mara*. No fewer than thirty-five mines had
so far been destroyed, and it was impossible to tell how
many more might be hidden. Christmas Day, 1914,
will long be remembered by East Coast fishermen as a day
of tribulation, but a day on which these fishermen made
heroic history. At 11 a.m., whilst sweeping south from
Whitby, the trawler *Night Hawk* struck a mine and foundered about five and a half miles east of Scarborough.
Only seven of her crew of thirteen were saved, including
the commanding officer, Sub-Lieutenant W. A. Senior,
R.N.R. The s.s. *Gem* came along, struck a mine and blew
up seven and a half miles south-east of Scarborough Rock,
with the loss of ten lives, including her master. The
s.s. *Eli*, under the Norwegian flag, also struck a mine and
eventually sank three miles south-east of Scarborough.
The day was marked by a fine exhibition of pluck on the
part of these Lowestoft drifters. The " Commodore "
was Skipper E. V. Snowline, of the Trawler Reserve.
Although a gale was blowing, this seaman, instead of
running for shelter, stuck it out and kept his station in
order to prevent other vessels getting into the mined area.
In spite of the heavy seas, his drifter, the *Hilda and Ernest*,
faced the weather and the risk of being mined and stood
by the *Gallier*, a British steamer which had also struck
a mine, Skipper Allerton in the drifter *Eager* showing
the same hardihood. Not to be outdone by the drifters,
Skipper T. W. Trendall, in the mine-sweeping trawler
Solon, on his own responsibility went to the assistance of
this ship. It was low water; it was dark; the *Gallier*
was showing no lights. The *Solon* had to search for her
during the gale in the middle of the mine-field, yet in
the end she was safely brought into Scarborough. Never
did British sailors in peace or war perform a more unselfish
and heroic act on Christmas night. For their gallantry
the King awarded the D.S.C. to both Skipper Snowline
and Skipper Trendall.

The following day a channel had been cleared, and traffic

was permitted to pass, but only in daylight. The s.s. *Linaria* next foundered two and a half miles north-northeast of Filey Brig. Destroyers were sent from the seventh and Ninth Flotillas to patrol the extremity of the Scarborough mine-field until the channel had been completely swept and buoyed, to prevent commercial traffic from passing through at night or by any unauthorised routes, and to check further mine-laying. But on the last day of the year 1914, still another steamer was blown up four miles north-north-east of Filey Brig. By that date, however, a channel had been swept and the principal buoys laid; most of the work had been done, and the paddle-steamers, which drew less water than trawlers, were pressed into the Service. The trawlers were, indeed, wanted everywhere. They were required to sweep up the Tory Island mine-field, and still more were needed for service in the North Sea in order to prevent mining activity being resumed. The sweep off Scarborough continued, and on January 6th the *Banyers* struck a mine off that port and sank. Her commanding officer, Lieutenant H. Boothby, R.N.R., had already been blown up on December 19th in the *Orianda*, but again he escaped death, and afterwards he was awarded the D.S.C. Next day the s.s. *Elfrida* also hit a mine and went down two miles north-north-east of Scarborough. But at last, in spite of the hindrances through heavy weather, this dangerous mine-field was so far swept up that a buoyed channel was established right up to a point abreast of Hartlepool, and the merchant traffic, thanks to the vigilance of our patrols and the daily diligence of the mine-sweepers, was able again to carry on right away down the North Sea to the English Channel.

Such is the narrative of the Scarborough mine-field. Although it brought about the loss of valuable lives, as well as of a few trawlers and merchant ships, it did not diminish the strength of the Grand Fleet by a single unit. Undoubtedly the laying of mines on the Dogger Bank, just before and on the day of the raid, was part of the scheme to entrap the Grand Fleet. On December 11th and the two following days, Skipper W. Pearce, of the fishing steam trawler *Dane*, sighted seven floating mines in various positions approximately between seventy and ninety-eight miles north-east by east of Scarborough, and, as has already been mentioned, the trawler *Blanche* found a mine on the day of the raid and a German destroyer near-by in a position roughly seventy-five miles north-east by east of Flamborough, where on December 23rd the trawler *Ocana* foundered on a mine. On December 18th the *Blanche* observed another mine in much the same position. On January 31st mines were also reported between eighty-five and 100 miles north-east of the Spurn. These may or may not have been laid in connection with the Scarborough raid. At any rate, the Dogger Bank mine-field was in existence, in addition to the other areas, and thus the lot of the fisherman was rendered still more dangerous.

CHAPTER IX

THE GROWTH OF THE SUBMARINE MENACE

As the war progressed, the Royal Navy became increasingly dependent upon the ships of the Auxiliary Patrol. The chances of the Grand Fleet ever meeting the High Sea Fleet in decisive action, so long as German hopes rested on the war of attrition, grew more than ever remote. Warfare by means of mine and submarine was seen to be the enemy's settled policy, and therefore the demand for small craft continued unabated. The trawlers and paddle craft, employed in great numbers, were proving effective in keeping down the mines, but the problem of the submarine presented greater difficulties. In November 1914 it became manifest that the Germans were about to make a determined attack on vessels using the English Channel; in other words, they would try to cut the lines of communication with France, and thus strike a deadly blow at the British armies.

The object of the Germans, apart from any damage which they might inflict upon merchant ships and transports, was to draw away to the south anti-submarine craft which could not be spared from the north, and thus cause a dispersion of British effort. The naval authorities were consequently confronted with an embarrassing situation, for the condition in northern waters had not improved. As an illustration, on December 3rd another effort was made by the enemy to attack the Grand Fleet, when a submarine penetrated the eastern entrance of Scapa Flow. The patrol was on the alert; the destroyer GARRY, which had been in at the death of U18, engaged this other submarine twice. The enemy fired a torpedo and then managed to escape. Simultaneously, therefore, the war of attrition was being conducted with energy in the North Sea as well as in the

English Channel. The immediate needs of the Grand Fleet, so far as enemy mining operations were concerned, was met by dispatching further railway steamers to act as Fleet sweepers, and in the meantime attention was also directed to the protection of the main base of the Fleet against submarines.

An incident on November 23rd concentrated attention on the English Channel. On the afternoon of that day submarine U21 sank by gunfire the s.s. *Malachite*, near Havre. Two days later three trawlers, *Cleopatra*, *Jackdaw*, and *Warter Priory*, were ordered from Yarmouth to Portsmouth, with three R.N.R. officers in command. Twelve armed trawlers fitted with guns and the modified explosive sweep were also sent. This flotilla was intended to operate in the English Channel against submarines, to sink drifting mines, and to board any suspicious small craft which might be supplying submarines. These trawlers were directed to patrol the transport route between Spithead and Havre. Thus began a new system of coastal patrols which was to make for increased efficiency in combating the submarine.

By the first week of December about sixty lieutenants and sub-lieutenants R.N.R., trained in the Merchant Service, had been drafted to bases of the Auxiliary Patrol for the command of armed trawlers and as leaders of units; another fifty officers of the same force were also undergoing instruction in Torpedo School ships preparatory to being sent to trawlers. In vessels where there was no suitable cabin a temporary cabin was being erected, and one in every six trawlers was fitted with wireless telegraphy, although the supply of telegraphists had become temporarily exhausted. Trawlers were still being taken up and fitted out with the utmost dispatch. Four were sent to Queenstown, though some time was yet to pass before submarines penetrated Irish waters.

Prior to the war, there existed at the Admiralty a Committee which dealt with the submarine problem; but for some reason this had been disbanded when hostilities broke out. It was now obvious that the submarine menace had to be carefully studied and guarded against. Early in December a Submarine Attack Committee was set up at the Admiralty, Captain Leonard A. B. Donaldson, R.N., being president. At this date there were only four known methods of dealing with the submarine. A patrol vessel could sink it by ramming; she could blow it up with the explosive sweep; she could sink it by gunfire; or she could entrap it by means of nets, which were then being evolved. Owing to the shortage of guns, many patrol vessels were still unarmed, and thus their only weapon was their stem. But ramming, as every student of past naval history is aware, is a far more difficult operation than appears at first sight. Modified sweeps, for the purpose of exploding over a submarine, were being supplied as fast as possible, but before an enemy can be blown up it must be known where he is. It was on the development of the net that attention was now centred. Preliminary experiments had been going on for some time. As far back as October a scheme had been suggested by Captain H. M. Doughty, the commanding officer of the Devonport Gunnery School, for the employment of nets and floating buoys with or without explosives; and experiments with nets were made at Harwich and Lowestoft under Captain Ellison and Lieutenant Menzies, the original idea being to employ fishing-nets such as are used by drifters. These soon developed into what were technically known as "indicator nets," the purpose of the buoys being to indicate or "watch" as soon as the submarine got into the net. The idea was that when a submarine became entangled, the section of the mesh would be broken off and thus the propeller would be fouled. Simultaneously, the submarine would announce its presence by causing the buoys to "watch." Nets are employed in peace-time by drifters which put to sea for the herring fishery. Drift-net fishing is quite different from trawling along the sea-bed. Just as the trawlermen's experience had so happily fitted them for sweeping up mines, so the driftermen with their ships were the experts at hand to go out and entrap submarines. During the winter of 1914–15 the Admiralty took up a considerable number of drifters from the east coast, forty-four being hired from the little port of Lossiemouth alone. Instructions were sent to Lowestoft that these craft were to be fitted out with the utmost dispatch. This task was to go on day and night, all other work being deferred if necessary. Thus by January the Admiralty had quite a large flotilla of these vessels ready for service.

The increasing efficiency of the yacht and trawler patrols had already impressed the Board of Admiralty, and a scheme was planned for the armed patrol of the entire coasts of Great Britain and Ireland by auxiliary craft. It had been drawn up by the Admiralty in conjunction with the War Staff, and was modified slightly in detail to meet the criticisms of Admiral Jellicoe. In the fewest words, the scheme divided the British Isles into twenty-one areas, plus the Clyde and the Nore areas. These different areas were to be patrolled by 74 yachts and 462 trawlers and drifters. Their duty was to prevent mine-laying, and capture or destroy mine-layers; prevent the operations of submarines and destroy such craft; prevent spying and capture spies. Motor-boats were to assist in these duties in sheltered waters. The needs of each area strategically were carefully considered, regard being paid to the indented nature of the coastline, the proximity of trade routes, and the opportunities for submarine activity and successful mine-laying. Under the scheme every part of the British Isles would be systematically patrolled, thus making the work of the enemy more difficult. With this improved organisation was instituted a general revision of the allocation of auxiliary ships. Some stations had their numbers increased, others had vessels taken away, according to the strategical necessity. The Northern Trawler Flotilla came under the same control as the Scapa Flow Flotilla, thus making it possible for trawlers to be detached in case the Grand Fleet left the Scapa base. The following were the areas now constituted, provision being made to ensure rapid transmission of the intelligence gained by the yachts and trawlers:

I. Loch Ewe and Stornoway.
II. Shetland Islands.
III. Orkney Islands.
IV. Cromarty.
V. Peterhead.
VI. Rosyth.
VII. Granton.
VIII. Tyne.
IX. Humber.
X. Yarmouth and Harwich.
XI. Dover.
XII. Portsmouth.
XIII. Portland.
XIV. Devonport.
XV. Milford (with base at Rosslare).
XVI. Liverpool, Kingstown, and Belfast.

CH. IX]   SUBMARINES IN THE CHANNEL   371

XVII. Lough Larne.   XX. Galway Bay.
XVIII. Lough Swilly.   XXI. Queenstown   and
XIX. Blacksod Bay.   Berehaven.

In addition there were the Clyde and Nore areas, as already mentioned.

Submarine activity rather than mine-laying was at this period causing the Admiralty the greatest amount of anxiety, and especially in the English Channel. At one time it had seemed almost unthinkable that German submarines would dare to penetrate the Straits of Dover and sink merchant and passenger ships at their will. Gradually the awakening came. First on October 14th a submarine torpedoed the *Amiral Ganteaume* carrying refugees from Calais to Havre; on October 31st H.M.S. HERMES was torpedoed in the Dover Straits; then on November 11th H.M.S. NIGER was torpedoed close inshore near Deal; on November 23rd the *Malachite* was sunk, as has been already mentioned, not by torpedo, but by a submarine's gunfire near Havre; and finally, on November 26th, the s.s. *Primo* was destroyed also by submarine gunfire off Cape d'Antifer. These incidents, which have already been described, showed that the enemy was able to disregard the British mine-field across the Dover Straits, and was determined to attack any kind of ship, without restricting himself to the recognised limitations of legitimate warfare. On December 22nd Admiral von Tirpitz forecasted a submarine campaign against our commerce. The crisis was reached when in the dark hours of the morning of January 1st H.M.S. FORMIDABLE was sunk off the Devonshire coast by U24. Thus the submarine operations had developed in a brief space from a dangerous menace into an offensive campaign of a deadly nature. If, for the moment, the English Channel seemed to be the chief area of attack, evidence was not wanting that the North Sea was not being neglected. On Christmas Day two torpedo-boats patrolling well up the Firth of Forth had torpedoes fired at them, and submarines were sighted out at sea by three of the Town class light cruisers which had come from Rosyth. Such places as the Farne Islands in Area VIII, Kinnaird and Rattray Heads were being used as points of arrival by enemy U-boats from the other side of the sea. There was, therefore, wide scope for the work of the Auxiliary Patrol in watching wherever submarines were likely to operate. In the twenty-three areas mentioned patrol vessels maintained constant vigilance, and in addition to these the mine-sweepers carried on their routine duties wherever required. Thus, by the end of the year 1914 there were in all 750 yachts, patrol trawlers, mine-sweeping trawlers, drifters, paddle sweepers, motor-drifters, and motor-boats, in which 190 officers of the Royal Navy and Royal Naval Reserve and 250 officers of the Royal Naval Volunteer Reserve were serving. Officers and men were keen and needed only improved devices for the arduous work entrusted to them, and these gradually were perfected.

On January 2nd, 1915, the First Lord of the Admiralty (Mr. Winston Churchill) made a request for four drifters to be sent to Dover. They were to carry out a number of experiments under Captain E. C. Carver, R.N., in the laying of nets under a system devised by Admiral of the Fleet Sir A. Wilson. Four drifters were accordingly ordered next day from Lowestoft, and formed the nucleus of a huge fleet which was presently to be transferred to the White Ensign for the special service of entrapping submarines.

To those unfamiliar with ships the difference between a trawler and a drifter may not be evident. They are built for entirely different purposes, and have distinctive features in size, construction, design, and personnel. The drifter is smaller than the trawler, and usually is built of wood, though a few are of steel; she has no powerful winches and but one capstan; in lines she is but slightly modified from the old sailing drifters; and, unlike the steam trawlers, she relies very much on her mizzen, not for speed, but for sea-keeping ability in bad weather and for riding to her nets. Her engine speed is rarely more than 9 knots, and she puts to sea for only a few days at a time, returning to port to land her fish and take in coal and water before going out again. The drifter's crew is small, usually numbering not more than eight or nine all told; and she is more often than not manned by members of one family. Frequently the skipper is the father or father-in-law of the mate. The engine-man is as likely as not the latter's cousin, and the rest of the crew, if not having some sort of relationship to the skipper, at least come from the same fishing-village. The result in

CH. IX]   DRIFTERS AND THEIR CREWS   373

working is that the drifter, while nominally in command of the skipper, is actually run by a kind of committee. To split up this co-operation would have impaired the efficiency of the ship. Consequently, when the Admiralty took over hundreds of drifters they usually accepted the crews *en bloc*, and the men served in most cases till the end of the war.

Nothing afloat is more clannish than a drifter crew, especially if the men happen to come from the same village on the north-east coast of Scotland. The very names of the drifters are typical of the crews—a curious mixture of Old Testament piety blended with modern ambitions and family pride. Such names as *Integrity, Breadwinner, Courage, Diligence, Direct Me, Effort, Enterprise, Faithful Friend, Friendly Star, Girl Margaret, Boy Bob, Golden Effort, Good Tidings, Hope, Peacemaker, Present Help, Protect Me, Star of Faith, Sublime*, suggest the simple, straightforward, plucky, homely men usually found in these craft. The four drifters sent to Dover as the forerunners of the great fleet that was to follow were the *Young Fisherman, Sedulous, Nine Sisters*, and *Ocean Comrade*. Dover became the cradle of the indicator-net method of anti-submarine warfare. Large numbers of drifters were taken up at Lowestoft and Yarmouth, thirty of which were sent to Dover alone.

Their arrival, fresh from their fishing occupation, came rather as a surprise to naval men at Dover, accustomed to smartness and well-found gear. These were an ordinary group of fishermen in their warm jumpers, without naval kit, unaccustomed to discipline, and banded together in ships that obviously needed a refit, for they had defects in hull and machinery and were ill-found in respect of lamps, warps, and other gear of the sea. But the main thing was to get the ships to Dover, and then as soon as possible to train the crews, so that with no avoidable delay nets might be strung across the Dover Straits and submarines prevented from entering the Channel to sink our shipping. Captain Humphrey W. Bowring, R.N., was appointed to take charge of this new drifter organisation, and the first trial at shooting indicator nets from these craft was made on January 15th, 1915, under the superintendence of Rear-Admiral the Hon. Horace Hood,[1]

[1] Rear-Admiral the Hon. Horace L. A. Hood, C.B., M.V.O., D.S.O. lost his life in the Battle of Jutland.

commanding the Dover Patrol. Day after day the drifters went out into the Channel to learn their lesson, and as if to show the urgent need for nets, submarines were being reported from all parts of the English Channel—from Christchurch Bay, the Channel Islands, West Bay, Berry Head, and elsewhere.

A hundred miles of nets were sent to Dover. More and more drifters kept arriving, together with sinkers with which to moor the nets, dan-buoys with which to mark them, clips with which to secure them. There were all sorts of difficulties to overcome. The clips, for instance, were a constant source of trouble. They had to be strong to stand the strain when the nets were being hauled in; at the same time it was necessary that they should be weak enough to carry away as soon as the strain of the submarine in the nets came. Then there were the strong tides in the Dover Straits to contend with. Nets disappeared under the water and were carried away; others caught on wreckage. For a time the whole scheme seemed doomed to failure. However, by dint of dogged perseverance, the co-operation of many brains, and the adaptability of the fishing crews, one after another of the problems approached solution. By the middle of January nets had been moored just N.N.E. of the Varne Buoy, and it was found that a drifter could shoot 300 yards of nets in a heavy sea within half an hour, though eventually this time was very considerably shortened. By the end of January Dover Harbour was becoming pretty full of these small craft; for there were already fifty or sixty drifters and more were arriving.

A really satisfactory net-ship had yet to be designed, but with improvements in apparatus and training it had become possible to shoot 800 yards of nets in eight minutes. At that speed a submarine could quickly be surrounded by an awkward mesh. Preparations were soon on foot to send a few of these drifters to lay their nets off the Belgian coast. On February 3rd the *Sedulous* and four other drifters, escorted by destroyers, left Dover in charge of Captain Bowring for a rendezvous two miles south of the North Hinder Lightship, where they arrived early next morning. The drifters shot their nets in the neighbourhood of Thornton Ridge, the destroyers meanwhile patrolling. On the 5th the drifters returned to Dover.

NET MINES BEING THROWN OVERBOARD.

NETS ACROSS THE STRAITS

No submarines had been trapped, but valuable experience had been gained. Next day a conference took place at the Admiralty on the laying of indicator nets, at which Admiral Hood was present, and a week later the Dover Net Drifter Flotilla was in full working order, endeavouring to close the Straits to hostile submarines. Thirty little drifters stretched across the Channel, riding to their nets and forming a curtain between England and France in the strong tideway that goes rushing by. Every evening the drifters took their nets aboard, and at daylight shot them again. Having regard to the force of the tides, the bad weather, and the difficulties of working the nets, the Admiralty considered the progress made to be encouraging. It was determined to employ drifters and indicator nets in other areas as well. Preparations were made for establishing net-bases at Cromarty, Peterhead, Firth of Forth, Yarmouth, Harwich, the Nore, Portsmouth, Portland, Poole, Falmouth, and Devonport. The nets used were of two types, one 30 feet deep and the other 60 feet deep, each net being 100 yards in length. So quickly did the organisations grow that by the third week in January there were sixty-three drifters stationed at Poole, twenty at Falmouth, fifty-four at Dover, a dozen at Scapa, and four each at Portsmouth, Firth of Forth, and Cromarty. Sixteen drifters were also sent to Harwich to lay eight miles of indicator nets two miles on either side of the Cork Lightship in case a submarine were to be sighted inside the Cork, and two miles on either side of the Shipwash in case the U-boats were seen inside the Sunk.

It appeared for a time as if the Navy had in the indicator net the solution of the main submarine problem. The Admiralty wasted not a moment in equipping every suitable base. And then occurred a series of events, sudden and ominous, which gave a still further impetus to this newly-adopted device. Hitherto submarines had penetrated to the north of Scotland and well down the English Channel, but at last a submarine appeared in the Irish Sea and acted pretty much as she liked. On January 28th the armed drifter *R.R.S.*, when about three miles northwest of Bardsey Island, sighted what she believed to be two submarines. Next day, at 1.45 p.m., Walney Island Battery, Barrow, sighted a submarine about 7,000 yards out at sea. The enemy craft opened fire, but all her shots fell short. The battery returned the fire with eleven rounds, and the submarine disappeared.

It proved to have been the U21, commanded by that enterprising officer, Kapitän-Leutnant Hersing, whose destruction of the *Malachite* and *Primo* in the English Channel has already been described. She had travelled much farther to the westward than a submarine had attempted before. U21 was not long in the Irish Sea, but during her stay she caused havoc and consternation. From Walney Island she cruised about for a while, and on the next day, January 30th, hovered off the approaches to Liverpool and sank three merchant ships, the *Ben Cruachan*, the *Linda Blanche*, and *Kilcoan*, in practically the same position. From there she may have taken a tack over towards the Irish coast, for on January 31st the Holyhead-Kingstown packet *Leinster*, which was at last torpedoed and sunk in the autumn of 1918, sighted a submarine twenty miles east of the Kish Lightship. Thence the U21 probably cruised south, for at 8.30 a.m. on February 1st she had an unsuccessful encounter with a vessel of the Auxiliary Patrol. The yacht *Vanduara* was on passage from the Clyde to Portsmouth, and, when well down the Irish Sea, about thirty-three miles north-west of Fishguard, she sighted a submarine on the surface, trying to head her off. The sea at the time was fairly smooth. The *Vanduara* altered course so as to bring the yacht's bow on to the enemy, and the submarine began to submerge. The yacht opened fire at 3,000 yards, and finally closed at 2,000 yards, her last four shots falling extremely close. The submarine, however, was not hit, and got back safely to Germany, to spread a false report that the " auxiliary war vessel " did not hoist the British " war flag." This was denied by the British Admiralty on the strength of a statement by the *Vanduara's* captain : " I was flying no colours, but hoisted the White Ensign before opening fire."

It was reported that all the crew of U21 received from the Kaiser the Iron Cross as a reward for their work for the Fatherland. This cruise undoubtedly gave a great stimulus to the enemy and suggested endless possibilities for the overseas submarine. The immediate affect was twofold. All shipping was forbidden to enter or leave Liverpool, and the Holyhead-Kingstown service was suspended for the next few days. It proved also the necessity of strengthening the patrols in an area in which under-water craft had not been expected. Admiral Jellicoe suggested the use of indicator nets across the North Channel, to which the Admiralty agreed. Meanwhile, British merchantmen were instructed to keep a sharp lookout for submarines, display the ensign of a neutral country, and show neither house-flag nor identification marks.

On January 21st submarine U19 had overhauled and sunk by bombs the s.s. *Durward*, twenty-two miles northwest of the Maas Lightship—that is, well off the Hook of Holland. Admiral Hood stated that there was little doubt that enemy submarines were passing through the Downs at night-time, and one was reported every few days. On February 1st, the day of the *Vanduara's* engagement, the hospital ship *Asturias* was attacked by submarines fifteen miles north-north-east of Havre, but happily the torpedo missed. On the following day trawlers fired on a submarine off Dieppe.

Evidence accumulated on every hand that submarine warfare was increasing in intensity. At the beginning of February three large submarines left Cuxhaven to operate in British waters. It was well known to the British Admiralty that Germany had become possessed of submarines capable of going to and operating in the Mediterranean. This was not a little alarming, and to meet the menace still more small craft were required. Many yachts had voluntarily been offered for charter, others had to be requisitioned; and of these last one fine vessel was taken compulsorily because the owner, a lady with a fine spirit, refused to let the yacht go unless she was allowed herself " to share the perils of the crew." As the number of yachts in the service increased, the shortage of guns became an embarrassment, and some of the bigger yachts had to surrender part of their armament. No yacht could be spared more than a couple of guns, and the net drifters received none. Some drifters were given the modified explosive sweeps, and all were supplied with bombs.

Not only was the number of patrol vessels increased, but simultaneously improvements were made in the organisation of patrol areas. For instance, Area I, which had been originally based on Aultbea, an out-of-the-way place forty miles from the nearest railway-station, was now based on Stornoway, and Admiral Sir Reginald Tupper was appointed in charge there. Alterations were also made in Areas IV, V, and VI, it being realised that enemy submarines desiring to attack British warships in Cromarty or Scapa Flow would probably seek the very convenient landfall in the vicinity of Buchan Ness, Rattray Head, and Kinnaird Head, after the voyage across the North Sea from Heligoland or the Skaw. By placing the various units of Auxiliary Patrol craft in the modified Areas V and VII, an off-shore squadron was available to prevent submarines making a landfall or entering Areas IV and VI. The Admiral of Patrols was relieved of the control of all auxiliary vessels in Area X, these being placed under Commodore George C. Cayley [1] at Harwich, whilst the northern portion was allotted to Captain Alfred A. Ellison, C.B., at Lowestoft.

Simultaneously with a careful reconsideration of anti-submarine patrols, the ever-present mine question had to be studied afresh. In order to safeguard ships, especially mine-sweepers, various mine-catching devices were tried, affixed to the ships' bows, but they were clumsy and in bad weather soon carried away. Mines were being found in unexpected places, some of them having drifted from their original areas. From the Tory Island field mines had been carried up the west coast of Scotland and had become a menace to the Tenth Cruiser Squadron, employed on important patrol duties; several ships had sighted and sunk some of them; and the armed merchant cruiser CLAN MACNAUGHTON of this squadron, which mysteriously disappeared on the night of February 2nd, 1915, almost certainly struck one of these mines off the Hebrides. Mines were reported off Whitby. Some had exploded in fishermen's nets out in the North Sea twenty-four miles east-north-east of Smith's Knoll. The sailing trawler *Fleurette* caught mines in her trawl whilst fishing forty miles east of Lowestoft.

Early in February the Admiralty commissioned at Barrow two paddle steamers, the *Queen Victoria* and *Prince Edward*, and fitted them to lay nets on a very extensive scale. Each could carry no less than 4,680 feet of net

[1] Afterwards Rear-Admiral George C. Cayley, C.B.

ORGANISATION OF PATROLS

of a specially designed heavy mesh, with sinkers and buoys complete. The intention was to lay the net in the quickest possible time without stopping. The secret of quick net-laying is to arrange that the net shall run out freely without any check. For this purpose these two vessels had all superstructures removed, and special troughs were fitted from which the nets could run out over the stern whilst under way. Acetylene lamps, carefully screened, were provided, as the net-laying was to be done at night.

After six months of war Germany's naval position was already determined, and then came the " war zone " declaration of February 1915. The British Admiralty was not unprepared for this development. All round the coasts of the British Isles the various patrols were active, having had the advantage of several months' experience in their duties. Two routes were possible for enemy submarines seeking to get far afield. They would penetrate either via the North of Scotland or through the Dover Straits. The organisation at the time was as follows: Assuming the enemy should proceed north of the Shetlands, the Shetlands Patrol, consisting of three yachts and eighteen trawlers, was on duty. It was considered more likely that a submarine would pass through the Fair Island Channel, the north side of which formed part of the Shetlands Patrol area, the southern part being controlled by the Orkneys Auxiliary Patrol. The duty in this area was divided among three patrols: the Northern, the Western, and the Southern Patrols, based on Kirkwall, Stromness, and Longhope respectively. These three patrols comprised between them no fewer than ten yachts and seventy-two trawlers. Drifters with indicator nets were also employed in the northern portion of the Orkneys and at the entrance to Scapa Flow. As it was known that enemy submarines were accustomed to dive to about eleven fathoms when harassed by small craft, the patrol vessels fitted with the single sweep were ordered to tow it at this depth.

Similarly in the South of England there was a detailed organisation. Besides the British mine-field across the Dover Straits, which actually proved of little practical or moral effect, for the reason that most of the mines drifted away, there were a number of armed drifters guarding the northern approach to the Downs, patrolling north and south in line abreast. These craft, under Captain H. E. Grace, R.N., were based on Ramsgate. They were worked in three divisions, each under its own leader, and two divisions were always on patrol, the third resting in harbour. They patrolled four days and nights, spending the two next in port. A few miles below them was the Dover Net Flotilla, riding to their nets across the Straits.

Having received intelligence of impending activity in the English Channel, the Admiralty issued instructions on February 11th warning the bases that submarines were expected to pass through the Straits on the next and following days, and that they had been lately making the Varne Lightship and Buoy when so passing into the Channel. Captain E. C. Carver, R.N., was given orders to keep as many as possible of his Poole drifters cruising on February 12th and the following days between St. Alban's Head and St. Catherine's and twenty miles to seaward. The Commodore at Portland was similarly advised that his trawlers should cruise between Portland Bill and St. Alban's Head and twenty miles to seaward. The Commander-in-Chief at Devonport was directed to have his trawlers patrolling between the Eddystone and Start and twenty miles to the seaward. But, in spite of this vigilance, submarines passed through the patrols. On the 13th one was sighted off St. Valery-en-Caux, and another twenty-five miles west-south-west of Cape Gris Nez. On the 15th U16, while on her way south from Heligoland, chased the s.s. *Laertes* between the Schouwen Bank and the Maas, after having been compelled to remain submerged for some hours owing to fog off Calais, afterwards torpedoing the British collier *Dulwich* six miles north of Cape d'Antifer. On the same day H.M.S. UNDAUNTED and eight destroyers had a torpedo fired at them when off Dungeness. Next day, at 2 p.m., U16 sank the French steamship *Ville de Lille* close to Cape Barfleur. On February 18th she torpedoed the French s.s. *Dinorah* north of Dieppe, and then returned to Heligoland.

Already twenty-five net drifters were on their way from Falmouth to Larne, where they were to operate in the North Channel, as suggested by Admiral Jellicoe, and to deny that passage to submarines. They started with only their fishing-nets on board, but as soon as they could be supplied wire indicator nets were to be sent. Another twenty-five drifters were under orders for Milford, this number being increased eventually to fifty. Their mission was to foil the enemy at the southern end of St. George's Channel. Indicator nets were also laid in the Firth of Forth, from the east end of Inchgarvie to Longcraig Pier.

On the day that the German submarine blockade began the Admiralty were already making bold alterations in the organisation of the Auxiliary Patrols, in order to meet this intensive warfare. It was obvious from recent events that the patrols in the Irish Sea required strengthening considerably. Rear-Admiral H. H. Stileman,[1] of Liverpool, had enough to do in looking after the local Liverpool area, for which duty his force consisted of a yacht, two armed trawlers, and ten armed drifters. Hitherto he had been in command also of the Kingstown and Belfast patrol craft, but these areas were to be modified as follows: The Auxiliary Patrol force in Area XVII (Larne) was placed under a flag officer, Admiral C. J. Barlow, late in command of the yacht *Valiant*, being appointed. He was stationed at Larne and given general control of Areas XV and XVI—that is to say, the whole Irish Sea. At his disposal was a " flying squadron " of six large armed yachts, in addition to his other auxiliary craft. These were the *Valiant*, *Jeanette*, *Marynthea*, *Medusa*, *Narcissus*, and *Sapphire*, based on Belfast, but available for use anywhere in Areas XV, XVI, and XVII for concerted action or otherwise. The motor-boats at Belfast remained there, but the Belfast Patrol unit was withdrawn to Kingstown, where Rear-Admiral E. R. Le Marchant[2] was appointed in charge of the base and in immediate command of Area XVI. For this purpose he was allotted three yachts and eighteen trawlers, with an additional two dozen drifters shortly to be sent out to him. Besides these two flag appointments, Rear-Admiral Charles H. Dare[3] was appointed to command the auxiliary base at Milford Haven and in immediate charge of Area XV, the force assigned to him being four yachts, twenty-four

[1] Afterwards Rear-Admiral Sir H. H. Stileman, K.B.E.
[2] Afterwards Vice-Admiral E. R. Le Marchant, D.S.O.
[3] Afterwards Admiral Sir Charles H. Dare, K.C.M.G., C.B., M.V.O.

trawlers, and fifty drifters; ten of the latter were armed.

Strategically the North Channel between Antrim and the Mull of Cantyre resembles the Straits of Dover between England and France. The instructions to Admiral Barlow were to deny the North Channel to enemy submarines and mine-layers. For this purpose he was to have a yacht, eighty drifters, and eighteen armed trawlers, and from February 22nd all merchant ships were forbidden to use the channel. These drifters were to be disposed about a parallelogram thirty miles long and twenty-two miles wide, towing their nets across the channel, thus making it a very unhealthy place for a U-boat. A five-mile space at each end of the area was to be occupied by advanced patrol lines. Thus, it was hoped, a submarine would either have to pass through the channel south of Rathlin Island, or else, having dived to a depth of 90 feet, would reach the vicinity of Lough Larne almost at the end of her diving powers. Orders were given that the passage south of Rathlin Island should be thoroughly patrolled and denied absolutely to the enemy. Each drifter carried at least 800 yards of net, which when laid out would be almost invisible to a submarine at a distance of three cables.

The instructions to Admiral Le Marchant were that his principal duty was to watch the mail route from Holyhead to Kingstown against submarines and mine-layers. Admiral Dare was to hold the southern end of the Irish Sea and the Bristol Channel, and always to have nets down in positions where submarines might be expected to make landfalls. When opportunity offered, the St. George's Channel was to be netted, and he was to be ready to send out all his drifters to shoot their nets across this channel. On March 15th it was decided to establish a sub-base for the Auxiliary Patrols at Rosslare. Larne and Dover, because of their strategical similarity, now became the two greatest net-bases. In both areas net-drifters were at work in a strong tideway, at the entrance to a region where submarines had proved exceptionally dangerous. The tactical principle was identical in the two areas. If the submarine should get into the nets, each section of net was so easily detached that the one in which the craft was entoiled would come away from the rest and foul the propellers, causing the enemy craft to rise to the surface. For this purpose two things were necessary: satisfactory clips that would allow the nets to be detached at the right amount of strain, and indicator buoys to announce that the net was about the U-boat. It was only after weeks and months of experience and much experimenting that these two essentials were achieved.

By the last week of February the nets were in operation. Across the Dover Straits they were kept in position by night as well as day, except in bad weather. Each drifter watched its own eight nets, and altogether there were many miles of nets in use. Across the North Channel the nets were working satisfactorily, except that the kapok floats soon became waterlogged. This difficulty was experienced in many other areas, so gradually kapok gave way to small glass globes, which answered the purpose very well.

The working of the indicator nets was a task entirely new to officers of the Royal Navy; the only people who were at all expert were the drifter crews themselves, and to their suggestions and skill the success achieved was largely due. Without the fisherman and his drifter, it would have been impossible to carry out this particular method of harassing the submarine. Before February was out, the merchant steamers on their way up and down the English Channel and North Sea saw these wooden ships with mizzen set looking after their nets near the Shipwash Lightship, the Downs, Dover Straits, St. Alban's Head, Start Bay, and in the vicinity of Falmouth, as well as up the Irish Sea off the Smalls and North Channel.

There were many difficulties to contend with apart from the securing of efficient clips and indicator buoys. Nets were frequently lost in bad weather; at Dover no fewer than ninety nets were lost in a three days' gale. Another sixty-eight nets were lost within two days and nights of fine weather owing to various causes, especially by fouling submerged objects. There was, moreover, a shortage of officers, most of whom were junior Royal Naval Reserve officers, to take charge of drifter divisions. The drifter skippers themselves were found, generally speaking, to be good, competent men, keen and enthusiastic in their work. They stuck to their job in all sorts of weather, risking destruction from mines and submarines, and keeping a vigilant watch for the enemy.

The outlook was promising at this period. On February 20th a submarine was reported by H.M. Destroyer VIKING to be in the nets near the Varne. " It is quite certain," stated Admiral Hood, "that a submarine was in the net when it moved away from the VIKING. I believe the net tore away, and when the buoy stopped, the submarine got away." Nor was this the only incident of the kind at this early stage. Information came to hand that a submarine had been sighted fifteen miles south of St. Alban's Head, and on February 19th a Royal Naval Reserve sub-lieutenant was sent from Poole with three drifters to lie to their nets near this spot for twenty-four hours. They shot the nets about 2.30 p.m. Nothing occurred until about twelve hours later, when the skipper of the drifter *White Oak* saw a bright white light to the northward crossing his bows to the west-north-west. It was visible for a quarter of an hour, and then disappeared. Twenty minutes later he saw a dark object moving towards him, and called the ship's boy to confirm his opinion. The indicating buoy of the net next to the drifter then flashed, thus showing there was something foul of the nets. The skipper called the sub-lieutenant. For five minutes the light burned, and then disappeared, and the nets seemed to move towards the *White Oak*, the engines of which were moved slowly astern for a couple of minutes to keep clear. Shortly after this the warp began to tauten, and in order to prevent its parting, three bladders were bent on to the warp and the end let go. While this was being done, several more lights were seen flashing in the direction of the nets, but these and the buoyed end of the warp disappeared almost at once. The drifter was then turned to the eastward, and when daylight came she steamed round about, but nothing more was seen of the buoys or nets. Next day the same officer was again sent to the spot, and repeated the procedure at 7.30 a.m. on the following morning. He shot his nets, and they again fouled some obstruction. This incident, though not conclusive, made it highly probable that a submarine had got entangled in the nets. At the least, it afforded some encouragement to the drifters. This was by no means unwelcome, for the submarines were unusually active. Steamships were being attacked in the English Channel and the Irish Sea. The neighbourhood of Beachy Head was becoming a favourite resort for the enemy, five ships having been sunk in that locality within two days. The hospital ship *St. Andrew* was attacked ten miles north-west by west from Boulogne, probably by one of the same submarines, and three days later the s.s. *Thordis* had an experience which has already been described.

In another area a trawler sealed the fate of a submarine in somewhat exceptional circumstances. At about 3 p.m. on February 23rd the steam trawler *Alex Hastie*, though a Government vessel, was fishing 105 miles east-north-east of the Longstone Lighthouse. She had recently put down her trawl, and all available hands were working at the catch which had just been hauled in, when a periscope was seen approaching at great speed. It was too late to slip the fishing-gear and try to ram. The submarine's captain must have been either very inexperienced or else certain that this was a disguised trawler, and showed anxiety to keep astern of her, so that the trawler's gun would not bear. The *Alex Hastie*, however, was neither disguised nor armed. The submarine, in attempting to pass close under the trawler's stern, apparently did not count upon the trawl wires leading down from the ship many feet below the surface. Suddenly she fouled the wires, and on board the trawler the crew listened expectantly to the twanging and creaking of the gear as it withstood the heavy strain. Then after a brief interval there rose to the surface a strange object, with no periscope or conning-tower showing. The U-boat was on her beam ends. Having been caught in the trawl wires, she had capsized, and twenty minutes later she sank to the bottom, leaving a large quantity of oil on the water.

What had probably happened was that the submarine had caught her periscopes in the wires. As trawler wires are of $2\frac{1}{2}$ inch, they stand a good deal of tension. Thereupon the periscopes were badly strained, causing the glands through which they pass into the hull to leak. Water poured into the vessel, and prevented her attaining her upright position on coming to the surface. Furthermore, whilst on her beam ends the batteries would have capsized their contents, and before long the ship's company must have been asphyxiated. The *Alex Hastie* came into port a proud ship, having by good fortune performed a most valuable service, and the Admiralty divided £100 between the owners and crew.

This experience was followed by another curious incident. On the last day of February 1915, a number of drifters, based on Portland, shot their nets at daylight in a position between the Skerries Buoy and Combe Point, Start Bay. This was an area which it was believed was being used by submarines. These drifters were under the command of Sub-Lieutenant E. L. Owen, R.N.R. About 4 o'clock in the afternoon of March 1st, when twenty nets were down, a section of them was seen to sink, form a bight, and then travel in a south-west direction. This was an extraordinary phenomenon, because the wind was blowing from the west, and the west-going tide had not yet begun to make. There was no possibility of mistake, for the nets travelled about a mile and a half, and then were found to be foul and could not be hauled in. Occasionally they had to be veered out in response to violent pulls, as if playing a fish. Vibration also was noticeable. A cast taken with the lead showed only six fathoms, whereas the chart gave nine and a half fathoms at that spot. It was noticed, moreover, that the lead struck something hard. This was followed by a sharp pull on the net, about thirty yards being suddenly dragged out of the hold. A dan-buoy was made fast to the net, which was then let go. The nets continued to travel to the south-west inside the Skerries until about 10.30 p.m., when they were made fast to the stem of the drifter *Sarepta*, and she anchored.

Early on the morning of March 2nd Sub-Lieutenant Owen proceeded into Dartmouth in the drifter *The Boys* to make his report, and then returned to the *Sarepta*, finding her still at anchor with the strain on the nets. He presently ordered her to let the nets go. At one end of the nets the armed trawler SHELOMI had been patrolling. An explosive charge was made fast to her sweep wire, with a $1\frac{3}{4}$-cwt. sinker. This was towed over the position marked by the dan-buoy. About noon the wire fouled twenty yards south-south-west of the buoy, and the charge was exploded. A black patch of oil then came to the surface, and widened to an area of over a hundred yards in diameter. Two more ships also fired their explosive sweeps over the spot. A diver was sent down on the following day, and was unable to find anything; yet it seems extremely likely that a submarine had been in the nets and was blown up, for oil was observed two days after the explosion in thick patches about a mile away from the spot, and large bubbles about a foot in diameter rose and burst, spreading oil on the surface. Sweeping operations continued throughout the day, but no obstruction was found. This was one instance in a long list of highly probable sinkings of submarines, though the fate of the craft could not be ascertained with certainty.

On the day that these operations closed, another enemy submarine farther up the Channel met with certain destruction, the best possible evidence being forthcoming in the shape of German prisoners. The craft was U8, commanded by Kapitän-Leutnant Stoss, the second in command being Leutnant Morgenroth. The captain was a very experienced submarine officer, having been in that branch of the service for seven years. U8 was a vessel of about 800 tons, fitted with four torpedo tubes, and at various times she had been in most of the waters of the British Isles. She had come out of Ostend in company with another submarine, and the sequence of events was interesting. March 4th was a day such as is often experienced in the English Channel during the early spring. Periodically fog settled down. About 1 p.m., during a sudden lift, a submarine was sighted five miles east-north-east of the north-east Varne Buoy, by the officer of the watch in the destroyer VIKING, whose captain at the time was Commander E. R. G. R. Evans, second in command of Scott's last Antarctic Expedition, who was destined to add to his laurels in the famous BROKE and SWIFT destroyer action in 1917. As soon as the VIKING saw the submarine out of the fog, she attempted to ram her, and promptly opened fire with the foremost gun. It was too late, however, as the U-boat dived immediately. The destroyer circled round, passed over the submarine's wash, and began to follow a series of swirling pools which moved north-west slowly for half an hour. The pools then turned to the westward, and were followed for fifteen minutes, when they turned west-south-west until about

4 p.m. The sea was calm, and the track of the underwater craft was quite clear, so the modified explosive sweep was fired by the first lieutenant. The swirl continued for about 150 yards, and then ceased. Although the VIKING waited near the spot for forty minutes, nothing more was seen except some patches of oil. This may have been the companion vessel of the U8, as Admiral Hood suggested on examination of all the available facts. No corroborative evidence, however, exists as to the sinking of any U-boat as a result of this operation.

As to the U8 herself, the first incident in the narrative is that the drifter *Roburn* got separated from the rest of the drifters. When found, she was four miles south-east of Dover, and she reported that about 12.30 p.m. she saw a line of five pellets proceeding in a westerly direction against the tide at about four knots. The skipper informed the destroyer COSSACK, giving the bearing of the object when last sighted. Undoubtedly there must have been a submarine in the nets, for the movements of the pellets indicated the struggle made by a U-boat to get clear by going ahead and astern. At 1.15 p.m. wireless signals from the VIKING concerning her submarine reached Dover, and the stand-by destroyers of the Sixth Flotilla at once proceeded to sea.

The information to the COSSACK was that a drifter had caught something in her nets six miles north-east from the north-east Varne Buoy. When Captain C. D. Johnson, in the destroyer MAORI, with the stand-by destroyers left Dover, he found the VIKING getting out her sweep. At 2.17 the destroyer KANGAROO sighted a buoy moving fast to the eastward. An hour later a periscope was sighted one mile north of the north-east Varne Buoy, and at 3.51 the VIKING exploded her sweep four and a half miles N. 30 E. of the north-east Varne Buoy. Five minutes later a periscope was again sighted one mile N. 20 E. of the centre Varne Buoy. The destroyers were now ordered to close on this position, and at 4.10 a periscope was seen a mile from the centre Varne Buoy. The destroyer GHURKA got out her explosive sweep and ran on a line of bearing north-west from the Varne Lightship at right angles to the submarine's course, which was signalled as S. 65 W., speed about six knots. At 4.40 the MAORI again sighted a periscope proceeding in the same direction. At 5 p.m. the GHURKA fired her explosive sweep. Half a minute later the stern of the submarine—U8—appeared out of the water at an angle of 45 degrees. Then gradually she came to an even keel, with her conning-tower showing. The MAORI and the GHURKA each fired a shot, hitting the conning-tower. Several Germans came on deck, holding up their hands in token of surrender, whereupon the order to cease fire was given. The destroyers closed to the rescue, as the submarine's crew, emerging from the conning-tower, rapidly followed one another on to the deck. A German officer was seen to throw documents overboard. The submarine sank within ten minutes of breaking the surface. Meanwhile, ten men were taken off by the destroyer NUBIAN's boat, and four officers and fifteen men by the MAORI's boat. These twenty-nine, the German captain declared, composed the whole of the crew.

After the submarine went down, a large quantity of air rose to the surface, but no oil. The prisoners admitted that for four hours they had been chased by destroyers. Whilst U8 was travelling submerged at a depth of 65 feet, an external noise was heard, which some of the men likened to a slight explosion and others to a jar, as if a lump of iron had been dropped on the deck. Later a violent explosion occurred, which had the effect of causing the vessel to leak. Water entered two compartments, and there was a bad hole in the ship's hull. Orders were given to blow out the main ballast tank, whereupon the submarine came to the surface, the second engineer remaining below to sink her after the rest of the crew had made sure of their lives. The captain appears to have lost his presence of mind, the explosion having been so violent that the bull's-eyes of the conning-tower were either cracked or blown in; some sea-water connection was also shattered; and, owing to a short circuit, the engine suddenly stopped. Though the drifters had not actually sunk the U8, they had rendered most valuable help in her destruction. It was the opinion of Admiral Hood that she had got foul of the drifters' nets, and so eventually was forced to come to the surface. "The destruction of the submarine," wrote the Admiral, " is a great proof of the value of the modified sweep. It appears that, in conjunction with the indicator nets, it is of the greatest value." The Admiralty rightly considered that the crews of the trawlers and drifters which took part in the hunt had contributed to the destruction of the submarine, and they awarded £500 to be distributed among them.

A day or two later Admiral Hood reported that eleven miles of net had been laid across the Straits. " I am quite confident," he stated, " that they form a real obstacle for the enemy's submarines in the Straits. I was sure of this before the destruction of U8, and I am quite certain now. One of the most certain reports received from prisoners of U8 was that she had been harried for a considerable time ; she can only have been harried by the drifter fleet and their destroyer support. . . . The destruction of U8 has caused a real encouragement to the officers and men of the flotilla."

Six days after the sinking of U8, another enemy submarine, U12, met with a like fate. Again the Auxiliary Patrol co-operated with the destroyers. For the best part of four days the patrol yachts and trawlers hunted this craft, the chase extending over 120 miles, until at last, on March 10th, U12 was rammed by the destroyer ARIEL outside the Firth of Forth and sunk. " Great perseverance and skill," wrote Admiral Lowry to the Admiralty, " were displayed by the officers and men of the yachts and trawlers concerned. . . . The yachts and trawlers, by their skill and steady persistence in anticipating the probable movements of the submarine, and sighting her when she again came to the surface, materially contributed to her destruction." Not only the Auxiliary Patrol vessels, but private fishing trawlers as well, helped in bringing about this satisfactory result of a long chase. It was directly owing to information given by the private trawler *May Island* that the submarine was sunk, and to her owners and crew the Admiralty awarded £500. To each of the three private trawlers *Strathisla*, *Ben Strome*, and *Olive Branch* they sent £62. In addition, five vessels of the Auxiliary Patrol received awards. The armed trawlers *Duster*, *Coote*, *Chester*, and *Martin* were each paid £62, and a similar amount went to the armed yacht *Portia*.

There is reason to believe that on the day when the ARIEL sank the U12, still another submarine was destroyed in the Dover Straits. On the previous day a submarine had shelled and sunk the French steam fishing-vessel *Grisnez*, belonging to Boulogne, at a spot twenty miles west-south-west of Beachy Head. On the same day, also, the s.s. *Blackwood* was torpedoed eighteen miles south-west by south of Dungeness, and five minutes later a second submarine was sighted. There was, therefore, plenty of evidence that the enemy was still able to use the Straits. Commander Evans, of the VIKING, observed a chain of swirling pools one mile north-east of the northeast Varne Buoy, and he proceeded to follow them. This was at 1 p.m. At 4.8 p.m. the destroyer GHURKA came along to assist, and the swirls eventually settled down to a course N. 75 E. Both ships got out modified explosive sweeps, and at 4.25 p.m. the GHURKA fired hers right in line of the track three miles from the Varne Buoy. The track immediately ceased. All the circumstances were thus similar to those of the second submarine encounter of March 4th. Again the drifters gave help. They were with their nets to the east of the Varne, and the peculiar track of the submarine suggested that she was trying to avoid them on the west side of the Buoy.

The fighting spirit of the fishermen could scarcely have been better in any age of our country's history. There is something suggestive of Elizabethan sea-hardihood in some of these fights against heavy odds. Nothing is more typical of their daring than the cool audacity of the unarmed drifter *Rival*. In the month of March submarines were again infesting the Irish Sea, and in order to thwart them, drifters were operating off the Smalls. One of these was the *Rival*. On March 16th reports were received of a submarine which obviously was lying in wait for a large steamer that was making up-Channel. The *Rival*, though she had no gun, determined to attack the enemy with her stem, and the skipper did his best to ram with such determination that twice she narrowly missed hitting the submarine, which, after a pursuit lasting a quarter of an hour, dived and was not seen again. The Admiralty so highly regarded this prompt action that they sent the skipper an expression of their appreciation.

By the end of March the issue was made to Auxiliary Patrol vessels of bomb-lances intended to be thrown at submarines whenever the latter came near enough. Meanwhile an improved type of indicator buoy was required, and experiments were being made at various bases. The difficulty was to devise a buoy that would not strip its piece of tin in a tideway and so expose its calcium phosphide, thus causing a light, and yet would strip and show the light at the slow speed of a submarine dragging on the nets.

There are no fishermen more hardy than those who earn their livelihood in drifters; they are unacquainted with fear, and their ships, with their bold sheer and pleasing lines and easy behaviour in a seaway, are exactly suited for the crews who sail in them. April 3rd supplied an illustration of courage and resource on the part of one of these crews. The drifter *Boy Willie* was proceeding down the English Channel bound for Milford, where a very large flotilla of these craft were collecting to serve under Admiral Dare. It was a wild day, with a westerly gale blowing, showers of heavy rain, and thick weather generally. At 8.30 a.m., the *Boy Willie*, when five miles west-north-west of the Lizard, sighted a submarine. Near the enemy vessel was a neutral steamer, whose conduct seemed suspicious to the skipper of the drifter. The submarine was travelling at such a pace that chase was useless; the drifter, too, had no gun, so the only thing to do was to pass the news on. The *Boy Willie* put her helm hard over, and hastened to inform the Falmouth net-drifters which were operating off the Lizard. They set to work to look for the enemy in spite of the nasty sea that was running. At 1.30 p.m. a submarine was reported off the Runnelstone. Four hours later she was again sighted, the vessels of the Auxiliary Patrol keeping her busy. Orders were sent for ten drifters to lay nets from Lamorna Cove to the south-west before daylight, in case the enemy craft should go into Penzance Bay. Nothing was actually found, but one of the drifters, the *Lily Oak*, on returning from patrol the next day, brought convincing evidence that a submarine had gone through her nets on April 4th, causing damage.

It was known at the Admiralty that in consequence of our use of indicator nets the German submarines were being fitted with a net-cutting device at the bows, by means of which it was hoped to cut a way through these entanglements. On more than one occasion a U-boat

THROWING LANCE-BOMB.

made her escape by this means, after having been well caught in the nets. In other instances the submarine seems to have got away with the nets about her, either to sink or, with good fortune, to manœuvre herself free. Some such escapes were narrowly separated from total destruction. Three days before the submarine had got entangled in the *Lily Oak's* nets, the drifter *Jeannies*, based on Yarmouth, Isle of Wight, was operating off Christchurch Head in company with Torpedo-boat No. 027. At 6.30 p.m. she had shot her nets. Two hours later the *Jeannies'* skipper was standing by, when he noticed a violent tug on the net wire. This could only mean a submarine. The fast-revolving propellers were at the same time distinctly heard, as if a submarine were right underneath the drifter. Everyone familiar with the sea knows that down in the hull of a ship sounds can be heard much more distinctly than on deck. Wooden ships have been known to pick up warning signals in foggy weather by sending a man below, when nothing was audible above. In this case so clearly were the noises heard in the drifter's hull that the engineer came running up on deck, expecting the ship every moment to be rammed by an approaching vessel. The skipper fired a couple of green rockets to inform the torpedo-boat that a submarine was in the nets. The searchlight was switched on, whereupon the submarine's engines stopped immediately and were not heard again. It was found that the strain on the wire warp had gone, and when it was hauled in the nets were gone also. Unfortunately at this early period in the war the depth-charge was not in use, or another would certainly have been added to the long list of destroyed submarines.

Attention must now be turned to another aspect of the enemy's offensive. German seamen were never favourites with British sailors. Among the "square-heads," to use sea language, there were undoubtedly some first-rate sailors, principally to be found in full-rigged ships trading across the Atlantic, round the Horn, and up the west coast of South America. But these men were the exception. The outrages and horrors committed by the German Army in its advance towards Paris, the sinking of peaceful craft, with their passengers and crews, by submarines, and the losses caused by the German raiders on the high seas—all these incidents served to increase the dislike of British seamen of everyone and everything of German origin. In proportion as the submarines sank British trawlers engaged in fishing, so the racial antipathy deepened. The flame of resentment burnt not only among the fishermen crews; it was not less strong with the trawler-owners. One firm wrote to the Admiralty: " We beg respectfully to suggest that an Admiralty representative at the principal fishing-ports might have the trawler skippers before them, and instruct them as to how they should act on sighting a submarine." This was a practical suggestion, and the Admiralty at once acted on it. Arrangements were made to give instruction to skippers of fishing-vessels in anti-submarine tactics. They were advised not to work alone, but to navigate and fish in close company for mutual support. They were warned to keep a sharp lookout and maintain a good head of steam, always being prepared to cut away their gear; if a periscope were sighted, the trawler was to be headed straight for the submarine. Where ramming was impracticable, the skipper of a trawler was advised to blow his whistle, fire a rocket, steer to windward of the enemy, and stoke the furnaces so as to place a dense cloud of smoke between the submarine and trawler, thus increasing the chances of escape.

The sinking of our fishing craft during the spring and summer of 1915 became a most serious menace, not only because of the loss of ships, often accompanied by valuable lives, but for the reason that it might cripple the fishing industry, already reduced by the requisitioning of so many hundreds of fishing-vessels for Admiralty service. Between April 18th and May 4th eighteen fishing-vessels had been lost in the North Sea by the action of submarines. How to protect the industry was not an easy problem to solve. There were two alternatives: either all the fishing-vessels must be concentrated into a very few fleets, with an Auxiliary Patrol operating close to hand, or else, in order to prevent further disasters, they must be kept in port. This second alternative, if adopted, would have deprived the country of a valuable food commodity, caused distress along the coast, and ruined trades dependent on fishing; in short, it would have brought about the very conditions which the enemy was anxious to produce.

CH. IX] PROTECTING THE FISHING FLEETS 395

In these circumstances a conference was held on May 8th, 1915, at the Admiralty. Officials from the British Vessels War Risks Club of Hull, from the Board of Trade and the Board of Agriculture and Fisheries were present, in addition to the Admirals of Patrols and the Fourth Sea Lord. The whole subject of naval protection of fishing-vessels of the North Sea was thoroughly investigated. Roughly, the North Sea fishing craft were divided into four classes, each of which required special consideration. The largest number of craft were those which fished on the Dogger Bank. These fleets comprised 150 to 200 vessels, and so far neither mines nor submarines nor enemy warships had prevented them from going about their business. It was decided that the best means to protect the Dogger Bank craft was to have naval patrols; later Auxiliary Patrol trawlers and steam-yachts were sent out to ensure their safety.

The Aberdeen Fleet of about seventy vessels presented somewhat different conditions. These vessels were accustomed to fishing some distance off the coast, and arrangements were made to protect them by two or three of Admiral Simpson's armed trawlers from Peterhead. The Granton and Dundee fleets, it was suggested, should be concentrated near Bell Rock. These vessels numbered about forty-five. Finally, there were some fifty English vessels working from Scarborough, Shields, Hartlepool, and Sunderland, which fished between Sunderland and Whitby. These also had to be concentrated in a place convenient for patrol vessels. Experience had shown that submarines usually avoided fishing fleets which kept well together. Thus, in addition to its special work of hunting and destroying submarines, the Auxiliary Patrol was now charged with the duty of protecting the fishing fleets.

The need for protection had been brought home by several unhappy experiences. A case in point may be cited. On May 3rd the steam trawler *Coquet* was fishing 160 miles north-east of the Spurn. It was a fine, clear day, with a light north-east breeze and a moderate swell. Two miles away in one direction was the trawler *Progress*, while the *Hector* was two and a half miles distant in another. During the afternoon the *Coquet* was steaming ahead at 3 knots, with her trawl out, when the conning-tower of a submarine came up a mile away. The German vessel headed straight for the trawler, and brought up quickly on the *Coquet's* port beam, with engines going astern and deck awash. On the submarine's deck were seven men, holding on to the wire lifelines which ran from the top and on the conning-tower to each end of the craft. In the conning-tower were five others, who were peering through Zeiss glasses. The submarine captain hailed Skipper Odell, saying in good English, " I will give you five minutes to leave your ship and come on board here." The skipper stopped his engines and the crew of nine got the trawler's boat over the side, amid repeated shouts to them to " hurry up," and rowed alongside the submarine, the men being then hauled up on her deck. Five of the submarine's crew thereupon jumped into the boat with an explosive charge and a coil of time fuse. Meanwhile the submarine headed for the trawler *Progress*, who had taken her for a British submarine. The *Progress* now realised her mistake, and getting in her trawl steamed away as hard as she could go. For a while it was a keen chase, but the submarine soon overhauled her. Skipper Odell and his men were cleared from forward of the conning-tower to aft, as the submarine was about to use her gun. During this chase the water was washing the *Coquet's* men up to their waists, their hold on the lifelines alone preventing them from being washed overboard.

When at effective range of a quarter of a mile, the submarine fired four shots at the *Progress*, whereupon the latter stopped her engines, and the submarine brought up about twenty feet off the trawler's starboard side. Again the submarine gave the trawler's men five minutes in which to leave their ship, and removed them to the U-boat, from which a demolition party set off. After the Germans had returned to the submarine, the *Progress's* crew pulled away in their own boat, and when 300 yards away they saw the port side of their ship blown right out, and she sank like a stone. The submarine returned to the *Coquet*, having been away half an hour. The demolition party had rummaged the ship, and brought off all the charts, including one of the North Sea which had marked upon it all mine-fields, both German and British, as well as the fishing-areas. This chart the submarine captain opened and scanned with great interest.

Then, having taken the trawler's provisions and other articles, the Germans gave the men a few biscuits and some butter and milk, in addition to the binnacle compass, and cast them off in their own boat. The *Coquet* sank, and the submarine, staying only to send the *Hector* to the bottom with twenty rounds of gunfire, made away to chase two more craft to the north-west. This incident furnishes a typical instance of the way the enemy sank fishing craft and cast their crews adrift. Such conduct fired these fishermen's patriotic endeavours to co-operate with the Navy.

Enthusiasm in the work was exhibited as much by the Brixham smacks as by the Humber steam trawlers. Information given by the Brixham smack *Addax*, when fishing in the English Channel, to the armed boarding steamer *Sarnia* brought about a spirited engagement with under-water craft. The submarine was not sunk, but, thanks to the prompt intelligence given, a valuable ship was saved. The smack reported at 7 o'clock on the morning of April 11th that half an hour previously she had seen a submarine following a steamship going southeast. The *Sarnia* made off at full speed to search for the enemy, and soon after 7.30 sighted the French s.s. *Frédéric Franck*, bound for London. The crew had already left her, and were in the boats, and a submarine, U24, was seen alongside the steamer, then about three and a half miles off. As soon as the *Sarnia* approached, the enemy submerged. The *Sarnia* then commenced to circle round the steamer at 20 knots. At 8.15 the periscope was seen about 800 yards away two points abaft the port beam. Fire was opened on the U-boat, and the *Sarnia* made towards her, but the periscope disappeared. At 8.20 the periscope again appeared 700 yards distant six points on the *Sarnia's* port beam, and a torpedo was fired which the vessel avoided by skilful use of the helm. The wake of a second torpedo was recognised, and this torpedo was also avoided by the use of the helm and engines. This torpedo, the *Sarnia's* captain reported, " would have been a certain hit had there been one moment's delay in carrying out my orders either with helm or engines." The *Sarnia* then made a signal by wireless for destroyers to come to her assistance, and proceeded to zigzag at full speed close to the *Frédéric*

Franck so as to prevent the enemy from completing the destruction of the French ship, and to keep him from attacking other steamers which were passing within a short distance, one of them being a Donaldson liner bound down-Channel.

Every time the captain of the *Sarnia* sighted a periscope he did his best to ram, but without success. At 9.15 it became certain that two submarines were operating, as the periscopes of both were seen simultaneously, one four points on the port bow and the other two points on the port quarter. Fire was opened, and the *Sarnia* turned to starboard to avoid exposing her beam to either enemy. A shot from the after-gun struck the periscope of one of the submarines, and a few seconds later the conning-tower was just awash. The second shot fell a little short. Nothing else occurred until 9.55 a.m., when the *Sarnia* missed ramming one periscope by only a few seconds. The *Sarnia's* captain concluded that the submarine with the damaged periscope then headed away, and the second also broke off the action, for after 10.20 a.m. no trace was seen of either of them. The destroyers presently arrived and took the crew of the French ship on board. The destroyer BITTERN towed the *Frédéric Franck* until a couple of tugs came out and brought her safely into Plymouth. The *Sarnia's* captain, Commander H. G. Muir, R.N.R., had fought his ship with great skill and determination, and received an expression of appreciation from the Lords of the Admiralty. The *Addax* having given accurate information which enabled the *Frédéric Franck* to be salved, the Admiralty awarded the Brixham men £120.

These incidents illustrate the manner in which every branch of the nation's sea services contributed to harass and defeat the enemy. Fishermen, with their wonderful eyesight, combined with alertness of movement and quickness of decision, supported with fine loyalty the Royal Naval Reserve officers, themselves possessed of an intimate knowledge of merchant shipping and its ways; destroyer officers and men showed a devotion beyond praise; the masters and men of handy tugs marshalled all their peculiar knowledge and experience in coaxing into port ships which could scarcely float; and finally, officers and crews of merchant ships, threading their way among unforeseen perils, played their part nobly in the

CH. IX] THE WESTERN END OF THE CHANNEL 399

struggle. Never before in the world-seas had the great brotherhood of seamen co-operated with such singleness of purpose.

At the beginning of the campaign nothing was known of the enemy's submarine strategy and tactics, and it was only after many losses had been incurred and much careful consideration given to the facts disclosed that these began to be revealed. It was made clear by actual events that Germany regulated her submarine operations with characteristic thoroughness and system. The persistence with which her under-water craft endeavoured to penetrate into the northern bases of the Grand Fleet, and waited day after day to entrap squadrons and single ships, showed that part of her plan was to reduce our preponderance in sea-power. Collaterally with this attack on the men-of-war she designed to destroy merchant shipping. To this end Germany sent her U-boats to operate off those points where merchant vessels most thickly congregated—off the approaches to Liverpool, at the western mouth of the English Channel, in the neighbourhood of Beachy Head and Dungeness.

The enemy's plan having been revealed, at least partially, the task which fell upon the Admiralty was so to arrange the Auxiliary Patrol as to defeat the submarine strategy. To be strong at every part of the coast was impossible, but to have strong concentrations at likely points of attack was at least feasible. The great drawback was that the naval authorities were compelled to act largely on the defensive. The defence of the English Channel at its eastern end became daily more efficient through the increased activity of the patrols and the use of the indicator nets. In order to improve conditions at the western end, trawlers were ordered to hasten from Devonport to the Scillies, where shipping was being sunk with impunity. By the middle of April a complete reorganisation had been made of Area XIV, which included the Scillies and the Plymouth neighbourhood. Falmouth became the headquarters for the yachts, trawlers, and drifters, Captain V. E. B. Phillimore, R.N., being placed in charge of them. In this reorganisation the principle of decentralisation was carried out. The area was subdivided into four sections: (*a*) Newquay to the Lizard; (*b*) Lizard to Looe; (*c*) Looe to Dartmouth; (*d*) the

Scilly Islands. To each of these sections was allotted a steam-yacht and one and a half trawler units, excepting the Scillies, which had two and a half trawler units. A wireless station was installed at St. Mary's, Scilly.

Similarly, the Beachy Head vicinity in Area XII was reorganised. This section extended from St. Alban's Head to Dungeness. In order to strengthen it, the yacht *Conqueror* and two divisions of trawlers were sent from Great Yarmouth to Newhaven. From St. Alban's Head to St. Catherine's the patrol of the area was maintained by patrol drifters; from St. Catherine's to Beachy Head by a division of six trawlers; from Beachy Head to Dungeness by two divisions of eight trawlers. In addition, the northern section of the transport route from Spithead to France was watched by a division of six trawlers, and an anti-submarine boom across the Channel from Folkestone to Gris Nez was being constructed, to be watched by the yacht *Diane* and her armed trawlers. From Dover nearly 200 trawlers and drifters were working in the Straits by the beginning of April. But though the improvement in the working of the nets there caused enemy submarines to get caught and run away with the nets almost every day, yet, as no satisfactory type of indicator buoy had been evolved, it was almost impossible to tell when the submarine had fouled the nets. However, in the course of time the right kind of buoy was devised.

The Admiralty concluded that, since the sinkings off Beachy Head had become so numerous, submarines were accustomed to go to ground for the night in an elevenfathom hole two miles west of the Horse of Willingdon Shoal. Before April was out they laid a number of submerged mines off Beachy Head, hoping thereby to destroy the enemy. These mines were safe for vessels travelling on the surface, but dangerous for any submerged vessel or for one anchoring or fishing. The area was consequently forbidden for the last-named purposes. At the same time still more fishing-vessels were being taken up for the patrols. A hundred were ordered to increase the Dover Fleet. It was estimated that the total available number of steam-trawlers in the United Kingdom was about 1,400. Of these the Admiralty had already taken up 975. In some ports as much as 90 per cent. of the fishery fleets had thus been requisitioned, in others practically the whole number. Admiral Jellicoe again telegraphed that the apparent increase in the number of enemy submarines passing north about rendered the Orkneys, Shetland, and Stornoway patrol specially important, and he asked for more trawlers. The vicinity of the Butt of Lewis and Cape Wrath required strong forces to protect the colliers and other ships which supplied the Grand Fleet. On April 29th the collier *Mobile* had been sunk by a submarine off the Butt of Lewis, although a special patrol had been established in that vicinity.

With the design of entrapping enemy submarines as they emerged from their own waters, the two paddle-steamers, the *Queen Victoria* and *Prince Edward*, already mentioned, were employed in April in a special operation. On the evening of April 7th they left Harwich under Commander Maurice Evans, R.N., escorted by the destroyers LAERTES and LYSANDER, with orders to lay their nets off the Belgian coast. For this operation they had long been rehearsing. During the night they reached the Belgian coast, but it was not possible to begin work until dawn, as all the sea-marks had been removed. At 4.50 a.m. a mile and a half of nets were laid off Ostend in twelve minutes, the nets being 24 feet deep. Then, just as the paddlers were finishing their task, the enemy's forts opened fire and got off a hundred rounds at the *Queen Victoria* and *Prince Edward* and the destroyers, as it happened without causing damage. The intended surprise failed, but the paddle-steamers and their escort made home safely. On April 12th the *Prince Edward* laid a "trot" a mile long east of the South Goodwins, to which indicator nets were presently moored.

While developing their submarine attacks upon the British merchant ships, the Germans in no way relaxed their activities in mine-laying, and to meet the menace the British Admiralty, by the summer of 1915, had five separate classes of mine-sweepers in the Service. They were (1) the Fleet sweepers, including the old gunboats SKIPJACK and JASON; (2) eight auxiliary sweepers chartered from the railway companies for the Grand Fleet; (3) the paddle-steamers which had been taken up for rapid sweeping near the coast; (4) the mine-sweeping trawlers; and (5) another class lately introduced bearing the old historic name of "sloop."

It being known to Germany that the armed merchant cruisers of the Tenth Cruiser Squadron, engaged upon its assigned mission to the north of Scotland in intercepting ships, were using Liverpool for coaling and refitting, it was deemed likely that mines would be laid on the route to this base. The duty accordingly fell to the Lough Swilly sweepers from Barra Head to Inistrahull periodically to sweep this area. There was also reason to suspect that mines had been laid between the Humber and Southwold mine-fields, and on April 17th the suspected area was swept. No mines were discovered, though on the way out from Grimsby, whilst crossing the centre of the Humber area, the paddle-ships destroyed five moored mines. A curious incident occurred on the day following the exploratory sweep. Near the spot where the five mines were found, two British trawlers, the *Vanilla* and *Fermo*, were fishing. Three miles south-west of the Swarte Bank a submarine torpedoed the *Vanilla*. The *Fermo* was only 300 yards off, and she immediately went to pick up survivors; whereupon the submarine fired a torpedo also at her, forcing her to abandon the rescue and escape. The explanation of this incident was that the *Vanilla* was suspected to have witnessed the laying of the mines, and for this reason the enemy was determined that none of her crew should live to tell the tale. From quarters far and near the enemy's activities in mine-laying were continually being reported. On April 26th the British fishing trawler *Recolo* foundered on a mine south of the Dogger Bank.

In preparation for an intended bombardment of the Belgian coast from the sea, four Grimsby paddle-steamers were sent to sweep from April 26th to 28th, and on their way back across the North Sea they commenced a sweep four cables wide in an area where the *Sutterton* had found a mine in her trawl a few days before. Whilst the *Sagitta* and *Westward Ho!* were turning south, a mine exploded in their sweep. A few minutes later another mine rose to the surface in the same sweep. It was very desirable that a specimen of these mines should be salved for examination by British naval experts. The commanding officer of the *Sagitta* was Lieutenant-Commander W. H. S. Garnett, R.N.R., a Cambridge wrangler and an enthusiastic yachtsman, who had volunteered and received a commission at the beginning of the war. This gallant officer, disregarding the peril, went overboard, swam to the mine, and dexterously cut the electric wires about it, after which it was hoisted inboard without further incident. For this plucky act the Admiralty sent him an expression of appreciation. It is to be regretted that some months later Lieutenant-Commander Garnett, having in the meantime transferred to the Royal Flying Corps, met his death in a flying accident.

From the condition of the paint on these Swarte mines, it was evident that they had been laid quite recently. Meanwhile the Tory Island mine-field was being swept up; seven more mines had been destroyed by the Lough Swilly sweepers, and altogether forty-five mines had been accounted for in the mine-field, seventy-one others having drifted away and been destroyed on the Irish and Scottish coasts. On April 23rd still another ship had blundered into the field, hit a mine, and foundered. This was the Norwegian s.s. *Caprivi*, which was sixteen miles north-north-east of Tory Island at the time, just a mile to westward of where the sweeping was going on. Although the eastern part of the area had been pretty well cleared, yet many mines still remained, and prolonged spells of bad weather did not lessen the difficulties of the task.

In the meantime, enemy submarines were engaged upon many daring enterprises, in spite of the persistency of the patrols. They were seen south of the Goodwins and near the Lizard; a ship was torpedoed off the Start, in a strong south-west wind and rough sea. They were operating successfully off the French coast, and in mid-Channel, and a ship was chased twenty miles south of the Eddystone. Other merchant ships were sunk south of St. Catherine's, off the Wolf Rock, and off Beachy Head. Submarines were reported in the Irish Sea, off the entrance to the Bristol Channel, and off the Owers. A cork life-jacket picked up at Trevose Head, Padstow, marked U21, with an impression of the Iron Cross, and a torpedo picked up off Farn by a steamer and marked U22, showed where the enemy had been. Off Hartlepool two trawlers sighted U16 on the surface about the middle of April; another trawler sighted a submarine east of Aberdeen; an armed yacht attacked still another near May Island; the Newhaven Patrol vessels had chased yet another off Beachy

Head; and a Falmouth drifter pursued one for two hours, a torpedo being fired at her which passed under her forefoot. On the same day a trawler reported having seen and run over a submarine off Land's End. It was even reported, with some show of credibility, that two German officers had come ashore in a collapsible boat and landed at Cairn Ryan, near Stranraer. Ships were being attacked or sunk near the North Hinder and other parts of the North Sea. Auxiliary Patrol vessels were in action with submarines off Fair Island and Anvil Point; and off St. Abb's Head the trawler *Ben Lawers* fired forty rounds at an enemy craft and claimed to have hit her. Dense black smoke was observed, and the submarine, apparently damaged, made off, being chased by the trawler until lost to sight. She was unable to dive, and only her fast surface speed saved her. At the end of April the enemy sank a couple of ships off the west coast of Ireland, near the Blaskets, supplying further evidence of the radius of action of these craft. The Auxiliary Patrol in these embarrassing conditions had to maintain its operations with vigilance and alertness. Surprise followed surprise, but it was never long before each new development was countered by fresh strategy, novel tactics, or improved weapons. Scarcely had the patrols become accustomed to mine and submarine warfare than they had to prepare for offence and defence against aeroplanes and Zeppelins. Harwich and Lowestoft trawlers, in consequence of repeated flights of Zeppelins over Lowestoft and the neighbourhood of Orfordness, were fitted with anti-aircraft guns. By night and by day, below the surface and on the surface, there was little rest for the already overworked patrol craft, and to their routine duties was added, this month of April 1915, and in the first days of May, that of protecting the lines of communication when the 10th Division of the British Army crossed the Irish Sea from Kingstown to Holyhead. The whole of this route was carefully patrolled by auxiliary ships in the following manner :

At intervals a chain of trawlers was placed just outside Kingstown, past the Kish Lightship right across until near Holyhead. In addition, five steam-yachts guarded the route, while a division of drifters, with their indicator nets, were stationed to the west of the South Stack (at the approach to Holyhead) and off the Codling Bank, to the southward of the Kish. Actually no transport was torpedoed, but on the day when the last of the troops crossed, a submarine was seen by the trawler *Garu* three miles west-north-west of the South Stack, that is close to the route of passenger ships. The trawler gave chase, but the enemy dived.

That these troops were moved without the loss of a single life furnished further proof of the increasing efficiency of the patrols and of the respect in which these craft were held by the enemy. The keenness exhibited by the crews was all the more notable in view of the exacting conditions of service which war imposed upon them, in association with many days on end unvaried by any incident to relieve the creeping feeling of boredom. But the imagination of these fishermen had been stirred by events at sea since the opening of hostilities, and they did not fail to realise the possibilities of disaster associated with the passage of this division of the British Army, whose safe crossing from Ireland to England constituted a further conspicuous success to the credit of this improvised force which had already shown its value as an extension of the long arm of the British Fleet. From the outbreak of war down to the end of April 1915, twenty-seven trawlers and three drifters of the great fleet of auxiliary craft engaged in fighting the enemy had become total losses. Having regard to the risks of mine-sweeping in dangerous areas, attacks by submarines, and losses incidental to navigation during winter months off unlighted coasts, the Auxiliary Patrol had been fortunate in suffering so lightly. The immunity which the vast majority of these vessels had experienced was due not to any want of daring and resource on the part of the enemy, but to the seamanship, courage, and adaptability which the officers and men of these British auxiliary craft had exhibited in conditions of uninterrupted danger and difficulty.

With the passing of the long nights of the winter of 1914–15 and an improvement in weather conditions at sea, it was expected that the enemy would redouble his attack upon sea-borne commerce. The construction of better types of submarines and the manufacture of thousands of additional mines had kept the German shipyards and engineering shops busy since the outbreak of war.

Simultaneously the strength of the British patrols had increased as fast as ships, guns, and men were available. In the summer of 1915 a new type of British mine—the "Cruiser" mine, which was the direct ancestor of the depth-charge—was being distributed among trawlers and drifters, the idea being that, when circumstances were favourable, it should be dropped upon submarines from shoots specially fitted for the purpose. In the North Channel a dozen sections of net drifters were denying the passage to the enemy, each section consisting of ten or eleven drifters, commanded by a sub-lieutenant Royal Naval Reserve, whose ship was armed with a gun, a bomb, a mine, and, later, with the depth-charge; so that the chances of escape of any submarine which found itself entangled in the nets became fewer.

The whole organisation was improving and increasing. At the end of the first nine months of war there were either at their stations or fitting-out 63 armed yachts and 524 trawlers and drifters; arrangements were in hand to increase the number to 83 and 631 respectively. Apart from these, about 350 trawlers and drifters were employed in mine-sweeping and watching the cleared channels, the auxiliary craft were co-operating in the Dardanelles operations, and there were the motor-boats.

At Dover Rear-Admiral Hood had been succeeded by Rear-Admiral R. H. S. Bacon, D.S.O.,[1] who had disposed his drifters in a four-sided area in the Straits where submarines were very likely to be caught. The limits of this area were:

(a) Lat. 51° 3′ 10″, long. 1° 19′ 0″ E.
(b) Lat. 51° 8′ 50″, long. 1° 29′ 10″ E.
(c) Lat. 51° 5′ 20″, long. 1° 51′ 30″ E.
(d) Lat. 50° 54′ 30″, long. 1° 31′ 20″ E.

The Scarborough area, after being most carefully swept, was by the end of April declared free of mines. The clearing-up had been a long and arduous task, but it was a satisfaction to know that the passage of this Yorkshire coast was at length freed from the mine peril. Almost simultaneously with the elimination of this mine-field it became known that another had been laid in the Swarte area, the beginning of which has already been noticed. It was

[1] Afterwards Admiral Sir Reginald H. Bacon, K.C.B., D.S.O.

discovered, as has been stated, by the trawler *Sutterton*. Apparently the enemy had assumed that this channel was being used by vessels of the Grand Fleet, or at least of Commodore Tyrwhitt's Harwich force, as a short-cut when bound north. Possibly the new mine-field was laid with the intention of another raid, or the design was to entice out the capital ships and thus cause losses. It was significant that the mines were found at a greater depth than was usual, allowing merchant ships—mostly neutral —which were accustomed to pass along this route in considerable numbers, to steam over them in safety. Obviously it was desirable, from the enemy's point of view, that nothing should happen which would cause the new mine-field to be prematurely revealed. The chance discovery by the *Sutterton* of a mine in her trawl disclosed the enemy's plan, and was the means of saving lives and ships, although not before two British fishing craft had foundered in the field. On May 3rd the trawler *Uxbridge* caught a mine in her trawl and the explosion destroyed the ship. Three days later, very near to the same position, the trawler *Don* shared a like fate.

On the Swarte mine-field being reported, large numbers of the auxiliary craft were sent out to ascertain its boundaries, and meantime merchant traffic between Britain and Holland was suspended. The northern limit was found to be somewhere south of lat. 53° 32′, and the eastern limit to be long. 2° 40′ E. Mines were destroyed in plenty. The effect of the enemy's activity was to disarrange the routine work in the swept channel on which the coastwise traffic was dependent. The menace of the Swarte area was met with imagination and insight, and it soon became known that the lines of mines had been laid in an easterly direction from a position in lat. 53° 26′, long. 2° 25′ E. By the end of the first week in May most of the mines for the first seventeen miles had been destroyed, the only other casualty being the loss of the fishing-trawler *Hellenic*, which had blown up with a mine in her trawl. The mines were observed to be newly painted, and of a type hitherto unknown. The line extended for about thirty miles.

Other areas at the same time required constant attention. The Northern Dogger Bank area was examined and found to be clear; but there was a very large area under suspicion right in the middle of the North Sea, bounded by lat. 54° 40′ and 56°, and long. 2° 30′ E. and 5° E., and covering a space of 6,000 square miles. From this it may be seen with what thoroughness and sound strategy the enemy had laid his mines. Lines joining the points given bring out a four-sided area embracing that through which the Grand Fleet must have passed in making a sweep towards Heligoland down the North Sea. Had the High Sea Fleet come out as far as the southern boundary of this area, refused action, and then run back home, the mine-field, it was calculated, would have caused heavy losses to the Grand Fleet engaged in the pursuit.

Large numbers of mines were found. In addition to forty-one mines which quite early had been swept up and exploded, the trawler *Reverto* on May 18th fished up a newly-painted mine in her trawl. The gear was cut away and the mine sank without exploding. Two days later the s.s. *Maricopa* struck a mine in the field, but did not sink. The *Sagitta* and her group of trawlers proceeded to sweep from close to where the *Maricopa* had struck, and promptly destroyed forty-three mines. This was on May 23rd. Next day ten more mines were accounted for. Two were actually brought into port by the *Sagitta*, having been found floating, only just awash and nearly full of water. They had been set to a depth of 5·4 metres. Mine-sweeping gunboats, which also were engaged in the search, destroyed a number of mines. Once more the new Navy was in the happy position of having saved the old from possible disaster. For some days the *Sagitta* and her paddlers continued to search the field, escorted by destroyers and supported by light cruisers, the destroyers being of great service in examining and warning passing vessels. By the end of May eighty-six mines had been swept up between lat. 54° 40′, lat. 55° 20′, and long. 3° E. to 3° 20′ E. The lines of mines had been laid just inside the 20-fathom line, with a very pronounced tongue running diagonally across the great area throughout its whole breadth.

The Lough Swilly sweepers proceeded to clear the area west of Tory Island before continuing to sweep the northern part, in order to ensure a passage across the field on an east and west course passing within thirteen miles of the island. This work was desirable, it being seven months since this field had been laid ; several ships had foundered upon it, and the mine-field was placed in a most important position. Bad weather during the winter months had interrupted operations.

Simultaneously with more intensified mine-laying, the enemy's submarine activities became more pronounced. During May submarines sank fishing-vessels in the North Sea, and merchant ships in areas as widely scattered as the North Sea, off the Scillies, the south of Ireland, the Irish Sea, Bristol Channel, and the western end of the English Channel. Six fishing-vessels were sunk on May 2nd off Aberdeen and May Island ; eight more the next day off the Dogger Bank and east Scottish coast, all by submarines. Between May 13th and May 18th four more trawlers met the same fate near the north-west corner of the Dogger Bank, the crews being taken prisoners. Altogether there were no fewer than twenty-two fishing-vessels destroyed in the North Sea in the month of May.

CHAPTER X

THE SINKING OF THE "LUSITANIA"

THE month of April 1915 had proved an unsatisfactory month for the enemy; only seventeen merchant ships had been attacked, and of these six had escaped. It must have been apparent to the German authorities that neither the threats nor the acts in which they had indulged had produced the desired effect on British merchant seamen. Hitherto the farthest the declared policy of Germany had gone was the announcement that, " on and after February 18th, 1915, every enemy merchant ship found in the said War Zone will be destroyed without it being always possible to avoid the dangers threatening the crews and passengers on that account." The suggestion was that loss of life would be due to accidental causes, and would not be deliberately pursued as a feature of German submarine policy. But towards the end of April a demonstration of " frightfulness," exceeding anything hitherto recorded, was determined upon, and on May 7th the great Cunard liner *Lusitania* was sunk without warning by U20, commanded by Kapitän-Leutnant Schwieger, resulting in the loss of 1,198 lives. During the six preceding days the enemy had destroyed six ships, of which three went down on the 6th. In only one case did loss of life result, two of the crew of the *Minterne* (3,018 tons) being drowned on the 3rd of the month. There was evidence, however, that enemy submarines were working off the Irish coast, for the s.v. *Earl of Lathom* (132 tons) was sunk eight miles south by west from Old Head of Kinsale, where, two days later, was enacted the greatest maritime crime in history, revealing the full significance of Germany's new policy. It would scarcely be an exaggeration to say that no single event of the whole war, whether by sea, by land, or in the air, produced

DETAILS OF THE GREAT LINER

such an instant universal and ineffaceable impression, or was more pregnant in its moral and ultimate political significance, since it was probably the determining factor in America's decision to intervene on the side of the Entente Powers, although this event did not actually take effect for another two years.

Several factors combined to make the sinking of the *Lusitania* the touchstone, as it were, of civilisation's judgment, and to confer upon the event a tragic representative value in respect of Germany's whole assault upon merchant shipping. One of the largest, swiftest, and most lavishly equipped vessels afloat, the *Lusitania* at the time of her sinking was only eight years old. Built by Messrs. John Brown & Co., Ltd., of Clydebank, in 1907, she was a vessel of 30,393 gross tonnage. She was 785 feet in length, 88 feet in breadth, 60 feet $4\frac{1}{2}$ inches in depth, and with a load draught of 36 feet, her displacement being 41,440 tons. She had nine decks, including the hold, and accommodation for 550 first-class, 500 second-class, and 1,300 third-class passengers. The crew numbered 750 in normal conditions, and with all berths filled the *Lusitania* could therefore carry a population of no fewer than 3,100 persons. Built to attain a speed of 25 knots, she was driven by six Parsons turbines, four ahead and two astern, the former being capable of developing 68,000 indicated horse-power. The twenty-five boilers, twenty-three of them double-ended, were fitted with eight furnaces apiece, the boilers being divided into four groups, and each stokehold having its uptake with a funnel. The four funnels rose to a height of 184 feet above the keel, their diameter being 24 feet. The navigating bridge stood 110 feet above the keel, while the masts were 210 feet high. The initial cost of this great vessel was estimated at £1,250,000, and insurance, maintenance, depreciation and other charges amounted to £30,000 per month. As a moderate estimate, the cost of running the *Lusitania* on a voyage to New York and back, including wages, victualling, and coal supplies, was about £20,000, and an agreement with the British Government stipulated that at least three-quarters of the crew must be British subjects. With her sister-ship, the *Mauretania*, she had been built at the suggestion of the British Government at a time when the North-German and Hamburg-

American liners were making a strong bid for the commercial mastery of the Atlantic; and though she was not, in the acutal event, employed on war service, she had been definitely subsidised as a reserve merchant cruiser, the Government having placed at the disposal of the Cunard Company, at a moderate rate of interest, the sum of £2,600,000 for her construction and that of the *Mauretania*. The *Lusitania* stood, therefore, for somewhat more than a merely up-to-date Atlantic liner, in that by her means the British Mercantile Marine had regained what was known at the time as the " blue ribbon " of the Atlantic.

Though little heed was paid to the matter either by the general public or even by responsible persons, rumours had been very widely spread in New York that the *Lusitania* was to be attacked, and indeed an advertisement had appeared in several American newspapers on May 1st in the following terms :

" NOTICE.—Travellers intending to embark on Atlantic voyages are reminded that the state of war exists between Germany and her Allies and Great Britain and her Allies ; that the zone of war includes the waters adjacent to the British Isles; that in accordance with formal notice given by the Imperial German Government vessels flying the flag of Great Britain or of any of her Allies are liable to destruction in those waters; and that travellers sailing in the war zone in ships of Great Britain or her Allies do so at their own risk.—Imperial German Embassy, Washington, D.C., April, 22nd, 1915."

No direct warning was given either to the Cunard Company or to the captain of the *Lusitania*. Judge Mayer, of the Federal District Court of New York, was subsequently called upon to investigate the circumstances of the sailing of the *Lusitania*, a petition having been lodged by the Cunard Steamship Company, Ltd., for limitation of liability. In the course of his judgment on August 24th, 1918, Judge Mayer stated that " the captain was fully justified in sailing on the appointed day from a neutral port with many neutral and non-combatant passengers, unless he and his company were willing to yield to the attempt of the German Government to terrify British shipping. No one familiar with the British character would expect that such a threat would accomplish more than to emphasise the necessity of taking every precaution to protect life and property which the exercise of judgment would invite. And so the *Lusitania* sailed undisguised, with her four funnels, and a figure so familiar as to be readily discernible not only by naval officers and mariners, but by the ocean-going public generally." Few intending passengers of any nationality believed that such a threat as had been made by the Germans could be meant seriously or would ever be carried out. When the *Lusitania* sailed, it was with a total of 1,959 people on board, including 440 women and children. The crew on this voyage numbered 702 instead of 750. With regard to the cargo, this was a general one of the usual kind, but, as was entered on the ship's manifest, a certain number of cartridges were carried. These were stowed well forward in the ship on the orlop and lower decks and about fifty yards away from where the torpedo struck the vessel. There was no other explosive on board.

It was afterwards alleged by the German Government that the *Lusitania* was equipped with guns, trained gunners, and special ammunition, that she was transporting Canadian troops, and that she was violating the laws of the United States. The investigation subsequently held by Lord Mersey proved that all these statements were untrue. The *Lusitania*, in fact, carried neither guns nor gunners, and no troops, and in no wise violated the laws of the United States. In response to the suggestion of the German Government, the United States in a subsequent note stated:

" Fortunately these are matters concerning which the Government of the United States is in a position to give the Imperial German Government official information. Of the facts alleged in Your Excellency's Note, if true, the Government of the United States would have been bound to take official cognizance. Performing its recognised duty as a neutral Power and enforcing its national laws, it was its duty to see to it that the *Lusitania* was not armed for offensive action, that she was not serving as a transport, that she did not carry cargo prohibited by the statutes of the United States, and that if, in fact, she was a naval vessel of Great Britain, she should not receive a clearance as a merchantman. It performed that duty. It enforced its statutes with scrupulous vigilance through its regularly constituted officials, and it is able therefore to assure the Imperial German Government that it has been misinformed. If the Imperial German Government should deem itself to be in possession of convincing evidence that the officials of the Government of the United States did not perform these duties with thoroughness, the Government of the United States sincerely hopes that it will submit that evidence for consideration. Whatever may be the contentions of the Imperial German Government regarding the carriage of contraband of war on board the *Lusitania* or regarding the explosion of that material by a torpedo, it need only be said that in the view of this Government these contentions are irrelevant to the question of the legality of the methods used by the German naval authorities in sinking the vessel."

Judge Mayer, of the Federal District Court of New York, referring to this allegation by the Germans, declared that the *Lusitania* did carry some eighteen fuse cases and 125 shrapnel cases consisting merely of empty shells without any powder charges, 4,200 cases of safety cartridges, and 189 cases of infantry equipment, such as leather fittings, pouches, and the like. All these were for delivery abroad, but none of these munitions could be exploded by setting them on fire in mass or in bulk, nor by subjecting them to impact. He learnt in evidence that the ship " had been duly inspected on March 17th, April 15th, 16th, and 17th, all in 1915, and before she left New York the boat gear and boats were examined, overhauled, checked up, and defective articles properly replaced."

The great liner set out from New York on May 1st, under the command of Captain W. T. Turner, an old and trusted servant of the Cunard Company. The voyage across the Atlantic was uneventful, and was accompanied by smooth seas and fine weather. The name of the ship and port of registry were painted out in accordance with Admiralty advice to merchant shipping generally; no flag, not even the house flag, was flown. An average speed of about 21 knots was maintained throughout the Atlantic crossing. This was lower than the usual pre-war speed of the *Lusitania*, for reasons that were made clear by Mr. (afterwards Sir) Alfred Allen Booth, Chairman of the Cunard Company, in his evidence before Lord Mersey's Commission, on June 16th, 1915. From this it appeared that, after the rush of homeward-bound American traffic was over, towards the end of October 1914, it had become a serious question as to whether or not the Cunard Company could continue to run their two large steamers, the *Lusitania* and the *Mauretania*. Having gone into the matter very carefully, the directors came to the conclusion that it would be possible to continue running one of these vessels at a reduced speed, once a month, paying expenses, but without the hope of making a profit. They decided, therefore, to run the *Lusitania* with eighteen boilers out of the total of twenty-four, reducing the speed from 24 to 21 knots, this reduction, however, still leaving the *Lusitania* considerably the fastest steamer in the Atlantic trade.

In common with other masters, Captain Turner was, of course, familiar with the various Admiralty Notices to responsible officers of the Mercantile Marine that were periodically issued for purposes of advice. Dealing generally with such matters as that of the number of lights to be shown, precautions as to lifeboats, and various other matters, these Admiralty Notices embodied the growing experience of those who were responsible for studying and combating the German methods of submarine warfare. In view, however, of what happened, and of certain criticisms to which the master of the *Lusitania* was afterwards subjected, one such notice is particularly important.

On March 22nd a warning had been issued from the Admiralty in the following terms: " Warn homeward-bound British merchant ships that when making principal landfalls at night they should not approach nearer than is absolutely necessary for safe navigation. Most important that vessels passing up the Irish or English Channel should keep mid-channel course. War experience has shown that fast steamers can considerably reduce the chance of a successful surprise submarine attack by zigzagging—that is to say, altering course at short and irregular intervals, say ten minutes to half an hour. This course is almost invariably adopted by warships when cruising in an area known to be infested by submarines. The under-water speed of a submarine is very low, and it is exceedingly difficult for her to get into position to deliver an attack unless she can observe and predict the course of the ship attacked. It is believed that the regulations of many steamship lines prescribe that the master shall be on deck whenever course is altered. It is for the consideration of owners whether, in the present circumstances, some relaxation of rules of this character is not advisable in the case of fast ships, in order to admit zigzagging being carried out without throwing an undue strain upon the master." At the same time it has to be borne in mind that these notifications were in the nature of general advice rather than imperative orders, and were not intended to cramp the initiative of responsible masters.

By May 6th the *Lusitania* was approaching dangerous waters, and at 5.30 a.m. on that day all the lifeboats under davits were swung out. All bulk-head doors were subsequently closed, except such as were required to be kept open in order to work the ship. Scuttles were closed. The lookout on the ship was doubled, two men being sent to the crow's-nest and two men to the " eyes " of the ship. Two officers were always on the bridge, and a quartermaster on either side, with instructions to watch for submarines. That these were indeed to be feared became clear just before 8 o'clock on the evening of that day, the Admiral commanding at Queenstown having signalled to the *Lusitania* that submarines were active off the south coast of Ireland, and had been reported four miles to the south-west of Copper Point, near Castlehaven. A little later on the same night a second wireless message was received by the *Lusitania* in the following terms : " Take Liverpool pilot at Bar and avoid headlands. Pass harbours at full speed, steer mid-channel course; submarines at Fastnet."

From lat. 40° 10′ N. and long. 49° W., the *Lusitania* was navigated on a great circle in the direction of Fastnet, and upon a course that, when approaching Ireland, would take her some twenty miles distant from this point. At 8 a.m. on May 7th, for reasons that will be referred to later, her speed was reduced to 18 knots ; and shortly after this, owing to the presence of fog, her speed was further reduced for awhile to 15 knots. About 11 o'clock the fog began to clear, and speed was again increased to 18

THE CUNARD LINER "LUSITANIA" OFF BROW HEAD.

knots. At 11.30 an Admiralty wireless message was received from Valentia: "Submarines active in the south part of Irish Channel and last heard of twenty miles south of Coningbeg." The *Lusitania* was then on a course S. 87 E. magnetic, and land was sighted at about 12.10 p.m., two points abaft the beam, and about twenty-six miles distant. Although the weather was clear, Fastnet, owing to the distance, had not been sighted, and the land seen was believed, and probably rightly so, to be Brow Head, the next headland after Mizen Head. The sea was smooth, there was a light breeze, and this course of S. 87 E. was maintained until 12.40 p.m., when Galley Head was sighted, a long distance away, on the port bow. Owing to the fact that submarines had been reported twenty miles south of Coningbeg, and thus about midway between the Tuskar and the Smalls, the channel up which the *Lusitania* must pass on her way to Liverpool, Captain Turner had now decided, when he had assured himself of the exact position of his vessel, to steer a course that would bring him past Coningbeg, some half a mile south of the lightship, thus giving as wide a berth as possible to the enemy submarines of whose presence he had been notified. At 12.40 p.m., therefore, and in order to fix his position as exactly as possible, he gradually altered course thirty degrees more to the northward to N. 63 E. magnetic. Shortly before 1 p.m. he received another wireless Admiralty message to the effect that submarines had been sighted off Cape Clear, near Fastnet, at 10 a.m., when they were heading for the westward. This point was, of course, now behind him; he was proceeding himself in an opposite direction; and he therefore concluded that at any rate he had escaped these particular submarines. At 1.40 p.m. the Old Head of Kinsale was in sight on the port bow, about ten miles distant, and Captain Turner then altered his course back to S. 87 E., intending to take a four-point bearing off the Old Head of Kinsale before altering his course to the Coningbeg lightvessel, which he had resolved, as has been indicated, to leave about half a mile on his port hand. The twelve to four watch was that of the *Lusitania's* first officer, Mr. Arthur Rowland Jones, who was relieved at 1.40 p.m., the second officer, Mr. Hefford, who was unfortunately drowned, and the junior third officer, Mr. Albert Arthur

Bestic, being on the bridge. The latter, who was engaged in taking the four-point bearing, was relieved at 2 p.m. by another officer, Mr. Stephens, also afterwards drowned, and it was while the four-point bearing was still being taken, approximately at a quarter-past two, that the ship was torpedoed.

The first torpedo struck the ship on the starboard side, somewhere between the third and fourth funnels, breaking, as it did so, one of the lifeboats to pieces. The second torpedo struck the ship almost immediately afterwards, apparently about 100 feet aft of the first.[1] Both torpedoes exploded with terrible effect, the engine-rooms being almost immediately flooded, thus making it impossible to take way off the ship, and thereby considerably adding to the great difficulties of launching the lifeboats. This was further increased by the listing of the ship to the starboard side, thus causing all the port side lifeboats to swing inboard, and those on the starboard side to swing outwards to distances that made it very difficult for passengers to be placed in them. Wireless messages for help were at once dispatched, received, and answered, but no vessel of any sort, as it happened, was near the scene of the disaster, and within twenty minutes the great liner had disappeared beneath the waves.

One of the most graphic narratives of the course of events was that of Mr. James Brooks, of Bridgeport, Connecticut, an American business man, who was a saloon passenger, and who described his experiences as follows:

"None of my fellow-passengers," said Mr. Brooks, "regarded a submarine attack as a serious possibility, and we had a very comfortable voyage, favoured by pleasant

[1] We have a German denial of the fact that a second torpedo was fired. In a publication entitled "Die deutschen U-Boote in ihrer Kriegsführung, 1914–18," by Kapitän-Leutnant A. Gayer, it is stated: "On May 7th, between 2 and 3 p.m., Schwieger sighted in fine clear weather on the south coast of Ireland, near the Old Head of Kinsale, so many masts and funnels that he thought at first he had before him a first-rate destroyer flotilla proceeding in line ahead." But it soon appeared that "all belonged to *one* steamer only." But the commander was not able to make sure that it was the *Lusitania* before the shot had already hit. Although the sinking of the ship was doubtful at first, Schwieger did not allow the second torpedo, which was all ready, to be fired, as he saw that there were an immense crowd of passengers to be saved. As though he had a foreboding of the tragedy which lay in his success, he went with his boat to a depth of twenty metres, "moved by mixed feelings."

weather. A good many passengers were still at lunch when, on Friday afternoon, the attack came in reality. I had just finished a run on deck, and had reached the Marconi deck, when I glanced out over the water. It was perfectly smooth. My eyes alighted on a white streak making its way with lightning-like rapidity towards the ship. I was so high, in that position, above the surface of the water that I could make out the outline of the torpedo. It appeared to be about twelve feet long, and came along possibly three feet below the surface, its sides white with bubbles of foam. I watched its passage, fascinated, until it passed out of sight behind the bridge, and in another moment came the explosion. The ship, recoiling under the force of the blow, was jarred and lifted, as if it had struck an immovable object. A column of water shot up to the bridge deck, carrying with it a lot of débris, and, despite the fact that I must have been twenty yards from the spot at which the torpedo struck, I was knocked off my feet. Before I could recover myself, the iron forepart of the ship was enveloped in a blinding cloud of steam, due, not, I think, to the explosion of a second torpedo, as some thought, but to the fact that the two forehold boilers had been jammed close together and 'jack-knifed' upwards. This I was told by a stoker afterwards. We had been in sight of land for some time, and the head of the ship, which had already begun to settle, was turned towards the Old Head of Kinsale. All the boats on the ship had been swung out the day previous, and the work of launching them was at once commenced. The attempt in the case of the first boat was a tragic failure. The women and children were taken first, and the boat was practically filled with them, there being only a few men. The boat was lowered until within its own length of the water, when the forward tackle jammed, and the whole of its occupants, with the exception of three, were thrown into the water. The *Lusitania* was then on an even keel. On the decks of the doomed vessel absolute coolness prevailed. There was no rushing about, and nothing remotely resembling a panic. In just a few isolated cases there were signs of hysteria on the part of the women, but that was all."

Captain Anderson, the second-in-command, who was lost,

and whose body was afterwards recovered, appeared on the bridge deck as soon as he could reach it, and informed the saloon passengers that there was no immediate danger, for everyone was confident that the ship would remain afloat, in spite of the damage received. Everybody had, of course, rushed on deck, and this statement was reassuring.

"Meanwhile," said Mr. Brooks, "the ship had taken a decided list, and was sinking rapidly by the head. The efforts made to lower the boats had apparently not met with much success. Those on the port side had swung inboard and could not be used, while the collapsible boats, which were lashed beneath them, could not be got at. The ladies were standing quite coolly, waiting on board to enter the boats, when they could be released by the men from the davits. The davits, by this time, were themselves touching the water, the ship having sunk so low that the bridge deck was only four feet or so from the surface of the sea. Losing no time, the men passed the women rapidly into the boats, and places had been found by now for all the people about the midship section. I stepped into one of the lifeboats and attempted to assist in getting it clear. I saw the list was so great that the davits pinched the gear, rendering it improbable that they could be got away when the ship went down, so I stepped on to the gunwale and dived into the water. I had no lifebelt and am not a good swimmer, but I decided to take the risk. I had been wetted right through when the explosion occurred, and I believe that, had I gone in dry, I should have swallowed so much water that I should not have lasted long. I swam as hard as I could away from the vessel, and noticed with feelings of apprehension the menacing bulk of the huge funnels as they loomed up over my head. I expected them momentarily to fall on me and crush me as I swam, but at last I judged myself to be clear, and I turned around and trod the water in order to watch the great hull heel over. The monster took a sudden plunge, and, noting the crowd still on her decks, and the heavily-laden boats filling with helpless women and children yet glued to her side, I sickened with horror at the sight. The liner's stern rose high out of the water; there was a thunderous roar as of the collapse of a great building during a fire; and then she disappeared, dragging hundreds of fellow-creatures into the water. Many never rose again to the surface, but the sea rapidly grew black with the figures of struggling men, women, and children. The wireless installation came over with a crash into the sea. It struck my uplifted arm as it fell, and I felt it pass over my body as it sank, almost dragging me under.

"The rush of water over the steamer's decks swept away a collapsible boat, and I swam towards it. Another man reached it shortly after, and, after we were rescued, I found him to be Mr. Charles E. Lauriat junior, of Boston. Two seamen also managed to swim to the boat and to climb on it. One had a knife, and the other asked me for mine, and together they set about cutting away the canvas cover of the boat. When they had finished, I climbed inside, and the two of them followed me. We started to rescue the unfortunate people in the water, or at least those of them who were still living. We quickly had about thirty of them in the little craft. Around us in the water were scores of boats. There were no oars in our boat. We managed to raise the sides of the boat as they should be raised when the boat is in use, and we collected five oars from the mass of floating timber in the water. Then we started to row towards the lighthouse, which we could see in the distance. At the time the liner was torpedoed there was absolutely no ship of any kind in sight, with the exception of a trawler, the *Peel* 12, of Glasgow. She was close inshore under the lighthouse, and, owing to the lightness of the wind, she was of no use so far as the rescue of persons actually in the sea was concerned. She came along as fast as she could, however, and was able to pick up about 110 persons from lifeboats and life-rafts. Her limited capacity was pushed to the utmost, and I even had to sit with one leg hanging over the side because there was no room to put it on the inside. We took in tow a lifeboat and a raft, which were also filled to the gunwale, and, when the occupants were able to be taken out, they were cast off. The auxiliary boat *Indian Prince* had arrived by that time from Queenstown. The *Peel* 12 was the first boat on the scene, and she was followed by a tramp Greek steamer, which came up from the west, and was able to pick up several lifeboats which had got away."

From this account given by an American, and then neutral, eyewitness, it is clear that there was neither any warning from the submarine nor any opportunity afforded either to the passengers or crew of the *Lusitania* to secure their personal safety before the ship was sunk; and these facts were further confirmed at the official investigation by Lord Mersey in the following June. Material witnesses to this, apart from Captain Turner, who was on the bridge at the time, were, of course, the seamen on the lookout, all of whom acted with admirable courage and promptitude, and of whom one especially, Leslie N. Morton, an able seaman, only eighteen years of age, was singled out in the Commissioner's Report for the highest commendation.

Morton, whose first voyage it was on the *Lusitania*—he had previously been an apprentice for four years on the sailing-ship *J. B. Walmsley*—was an extra lookout on the forecastle head, starboard side, during the two to four watch, and seems to have been the first person actually to observe the approach of the two torpedoes. This began, as he described it, with a " big burst of foam about 500 yards away." This was followed by a " thin streak of foam," as he said, " making for the ship at a rapid speed," followed by another, " going parallel with the first one and a little behind it." Having reported this to the bridge with a megaphone, Morton then made for the forecastle to go down below to call his brother, who was asleep at the time; and on the way there he saw what appeared to him to be the conning-tower of the submarine just submerging.

Having called his brother, Morton returned to the deck to give assistance in lowering the boats and rescuing the passengers. Having helped to fill No. 11 boat, he then went to another boat, into which he scrambled, after passengers had taken their places, and which he endeavoured to launch. Unfortunately, owing to the well-intentioned but ill-directed efforts of some of the passengers, this boat was capsized, and, just before she turned over, Morton, in his own words, " swam for it." After swimming for some little time, he saw an empty collapsible boat, and, with a sailor named Parry, he climbed into it. Having done so, he ripped part of the cover off, and picked up about fifty persons. With these on board, he then made for a fishing-ketch, about five miles away, which he successfully reached, and in which he placed his passengers. He then dropped astern from this smack, and took another twenty or thirty people from a lifeboat that was sinking, Parry and himself and his second boat-load of passengers being then picked up by a mine-sweeper which had arrived on the scene as the result of the wireless messages. In all, these two boys saved nearly 100 lives.

Equally noteworthy for courage, judgment, and a fine display of seamanship, was the conduct of Mr. Arthur Rowland Jones, the *Lusitania's* first officer. This officer, who had been in the Cunard Company's service for seven years, was in the first-class dining-saloon at the time of the explosion. Going immediately on deck, he found that the ship was already severely listing, and he was only able to make his way to his boat-station hanging on to the rail and with great difficulty. He loaded two boats, one with eighty, and one with about sixty-five passengers, and successfully lowered both of them, entering the latter himself, just as the boat deck of the *Lusitania* was level with the water, and only about fifteen seconds before she actually went down. With very great skill, he enabled his boat to keep afloat in spite of the tremendous suction and turmoil caused by the sinking liner, and the fact that the Marconi aerial wire came down across the top of his boat and very nearly sank it. After that, having observed near him an almost empty boat, he secured this, and, manning her with the boatswain's mate, a seaman, the assistant purser, and about ten stewards, he counted out about thirty passengers from his own overcrowded boat and put them in it. He then ordered them to go back to the wreck in order to pick up as many people as possible, and this they did, saving a good many lives. Taking his own boat back again, he once more filled her up, and then pushed off to the *Bluebell*, a little fishing-smack about five miles away, in which he placed his passengers.

Having thus emptied his boat of passengers, he again pulled back towards the wreck, and, after having made about two and a half miles, he fell in with a broken collapsible boat in a bad condition, with about thirty-five injured and exhausted people lying in its bottom. All these he took on board his own boat, the collapsible boat then drifting away in a sinking state. Shortly after this he was overhauled by a trawler, in which he placed all these people. This trawler took him in tow, Mr. Jones himself remaining in the lifeboat until the spot was reached where the *Lusitania* had sunk. He then pulled off and saved another ten people, two of whom, however, died before he could get them ashore. These he placed on board the *Flying Fox*, a Queenstown tender. By this time, nearly eight o'clock in the evening, his crew was at the last point of exhaustion, and, since a large number of cruisers, destroyers, and patrol-boats had in the meantime arrived on the scene, Mr. Jones took his men on board the *Flying Fox*, ultimately reaching Queenstown about eleven o'clock at night.

From the foregoing narratives, which are typical of the behaviour of the whole crew, it will be seen that the high standard of courage of the British Mercantile Marine was never more signally illustrated than in the case of the *Lusitania*; and this was all the more admirable when it is remembered that, at the commencement of the war, the Cunard Company had lost all its Royal Naval Reserve and Fleet Reserve men, and the managers had had to engage the best men they could get, and to train them as well as possible in the time at their disposal.

With regard to Captain Turner, certain criticisms, as already stated, were afterwards made as to his judgment in handling his vessel before the disaster occurred. These were mainly based upon four considerations—that he had approached somewhat near to the neighbouring headlands, that he had reduced speed to 18 knots, that he was not pursuing a mid-channel course, and that he had not, as the Admiralty had advised, zigzagged his vessel. In reply to these criticisms Captain Turner asserted that he had reduced speed in order that he should not have to delay outside the Bar at Liverpool, in a position where he had reason to believe he might be especially vulnerable to enemy submarines; that he had remained at what he believed to be a safe distance from headlands consistent with obtaining an accurate knowledge of his vessel's position, and that, in view of the Admiralty message as to the submarines that had been sighted twenty miles off Coningbeg, he was fully justified in resolving upon a course that would bring him close to the

LORD MERSEY'S CONCLUSION

lightship and as far as possible from the enemy submarines. In respect to the advice as to zigzagging, Captain Turner admitted that he had misunderstood the Admiralty notice, believing that these tactics were to be adopted only in the actual presence of hostile submarines, and not also in waters where they were merely suspected to be operating. After the disaster occurred Captain Turner, as was unanimously admitted, bore himself according to the best traditions of the British Mercantile Marine. He was on the bridge when the vessel was struck, and he remained there to the last, going down with his vessel. His first order was to lower all the boats to the rail—a command obeyed as far as possible—and he then ordered " Women and children first." He also had the ship's head turned towards the land, but the vessel had become unmanageable owing to the damage to the engine-room. It was not until he had been in the water for three hours that Captain Turner was rescued.

On the question of his conduct in view of the various Admiralty Notices, Lord Mersey, after expert advice, expressed himself in the following terms:

" The conclusion at which I have arrived is that blame ought not to be imputed to the captain. The advice given to him, although meant for his most serious and careful consideration, was not intended to deprive him of the right to exercise his skilled judgment in the difficult questions that might arise from time to time in the navigation of his ship. His omission to follow the advice in all respects cannot fairly be attributed either to negligence or to incompetence. He exercised his judgment for the best. It was the judgment of a skilled and experienced man, and although others might have acted differently and perhaps more successfully, he ought not, in my opinion, to be blamed. The whole blame for the cruel destruction of life in this catastrophe must rest solely with those who plotted and with those who committed the crime."

Such was the sinking of the *Lusitania*, and its effect upon the whole civilised world was immediate and unforgettable. As the late Mr. Theodore Roosevelt said, it represented " not merely piracy, but piracy on a vaster

scale of murder than any old-time pirate ever practised."
This was the verdict of practically every neutral nation,
vividly reflected in the almost universal condemnation
of their representative Press organs. Thus the well-known
Dutch newspaper the *Handels Blad* stated, " This act is
opposed to every law and every sentiment of humanity,
and we raise our voice, however powerless it may be,
in protest. A seafaring people which has any self-respect
does not make war of annihilation against defenceless
people." The Swedish paper, the *Nya Dagligt Allehanda*,
condemned it as an " unpardonable crime against humanity," and a Norwegian paper, the *Aften Posten*, spoke
for them all in saying, " The mad and reckless action of
the German submarine has now reached its culminating
point. The whole world looks with horror and detestation
on the event."

In Germany, on the other hand, the sinking of the
Lusitania was received with practically unanimous approval. In the words of Mr. J. W. Gerard, then American
Ambassador in Berlin, "A great wave of exultation swept
over Germany. It was felt that this was a master-stroke,
that victory was appreciably nearer, and that no power
on earth could withstand the brute power of the Empire."
The *Kölnische Volkszeitung* of May 10th, 1915, said:
" The sinking of the *Lusitania* is a success for our submarines which must be placed beside the greatest
achievements of the naval war. . . . The sinking of the
great British steamer is a success the moral significance of
which is still greater than the material success. With
joyful pride we contemplate this latest deed of our Navy,
and it will not be the last." Five days later, the *Kölnische
Zeitung* endorsed this statement by proclaiming that
" the news will be received by the German people with
unanimous satisfaction, since it proves to England and
the whole world that Germany is quite in earnest with
regard to her submarine warfare."

Not only did the city of Magdeburg propose to honour
the officers and men who had committed this murder,
but a committee was actually formed there for the purpose
of collecting money as a national gift for those who had
thus slaughtered so many hundreds of helpless men,
women, and children, and inflicted the anguish of bereave-
ment on so many hundreds more. Nor was that all,

GRAVE OF VICTIMS OF THE "LUSITANIA" AT QUEENSTOWN.

for a medal was struck in Munich, and widely distributed throughout the whole of Germany, in commemoration of an act which, outside its borders, had brought down upon the German peoples the execration of the world.

Upon whom ultimately the responsibility for issuing the order that led to this tragedy must rest may never with certainty be known. But, according to Mr. J. W. Gerard, there was no question of a mistake, or of orders exceeded or disobeyed.[1] Count von Bernstorff had, in Mr. Gerard's words, "Frankly, boldly, definitely, and impudently advised to the world, with the authority of the German Government, that the attempt to sink the *Lusitania* would be made." Admiral von Tirpitz " openly showed his approval of the act, and threw all his influence in favour of a continuation of the ruthless tactics. But a question that involved a breach of International Law, a possible break with a friendly Power, could not be decided by even the Foreign Office and Navy together. . . . All the evidence points to the Emperor himself as the responsible head who, at this time, ordered or permitted this form of murder. The orders were given at a time when the Emperor dominated the General Staff, not in one of those periods when the General Staff, as at present, dominated the Emperor. When I saw the Kaiser in October 1915, he said that he would not have sunk the *Lusitania*, that no gentleman would ever kill so many women and children. Yet he never disapproved the order. . . . A man is responsible for the logical results of his own acts. It may be, too, that Charles IX, when he ordered, perhaps reluctantly, the massacre of Saint Bartholomew, did not know that so many would be killed, but there can be no Pilate-washing-of-the-hands; the Emperor William was responsible, he must bear the blame before the world."

This record of one of the foulest crimes in the history of the war would be incomplete were nothing said of the fate of the German Kapitän-Leutnant Schwieger, who was responsible for the loss of so many lives. In September 1917 he was in command of U88 and the hero of the German people, having stepped into the place occupied at an earlier stage by Otto Weddigen. U88 was proceeding in company with another submarine from a German port when she entered a mine-field. The escort having

[1] *Four Years in Germany*, by J. W. Gerard.

left them, both the submersible vessels were travelling submerged. What happened to the U88 is uncertain, but the commander of the other submarine afterwards reported that he found his vessel embarrassed by a heavy chain, suggesting to him that he had invaded a recently-laid British mine-field. He was about to rise to the surface, his only chance of safety, when he felt a heavy explosion. On reaching the surface, he tried to communicate by wireless and other signals with U88, but got no replies. Nothing was ever heard of the vessel. Presumably Kapitän-Leutnant Schwieger, in company with his crew, paid the full penalty for the ocean crimes which, with unexampled ferocity and callousness, he had committed.

CHAPTER XI

THE ADVENT OF THE OCEAN-GOING SUBMARINE

DURING the winter of 1914–15 Germany had built a number of ocean-going submarines, able to keep at sea for longer periods and more formidably armed than those with which she commenced the war. By the end of April these improved craft had begun to pass down the west coast of Ireland; with results on British shipping which have already been indicated. Submarines were also seen off the approaches to Queenstown and the River Shannon. But all the embarrassing incidents of these days with which the Auxiliary Patrol grappled manfully were to be overshadowed by the work which the sinking of the Cunard liner *Lusitania* threw on these craft.

There was ample evidence that submarines were hovering about the south coast of Ireland. As early as 3.30 a.m. on the day of the disaster, a U-boat was seen near Dunmore, Waterford; a second at the entrance to Gascanane Sound, just to the east of Cape Clear, where such low-lying craft could easily hide behind rocks; and at 5.40 a.m. a submarine was sighted—probably the one that was near Gascanane Sound—eight miles north-west of Brow Head going north-west, possibly to meet the *Lusitania* as she approached the latitude of Mizen Head. Still another was seen at 4.30 a.m. near Castlehaven, proceeding slowly, this probably being the one which was reported five hours later by the Auxiliary Patrol Motor-boat No. 47 off Cape Clear. At 1.45 p.m. a submarine was seen off the entrance to Glandore Harbour. Meanwhile the great Cunarder was approaching land, and before another hour had passed the *Lusitania* had been torpedoed and sunk, probably by the U-boat which was cruising off Glandore, which lies between Galley Head, and Castlehaven.

The disposition of the Auxiliary Patrol vessels in this

area was as follows: the Queenstown trawlers *Sarba*, *Bluebell*, and *Heron*, under the orders of Admiral Coke, Vice-Admiral commanding the coast of Ireland, patrolling between Kinsale and Ballycottin, and the trawlers *Indian Empire*, *Clifton*, *Maximus*, and *Reliance* between Ballycottin and Carnsore Point. The area through which the *Lusitania* passed, Mizen Head to Kinsale, was patrolled by the trawlers *Freesia*, *Verbena*, and *Restango*. Motor-boat No. 47, *Seagull*, had at 9.50 a.m. chased a submarine for ten minutes five miles south of Cape Clear, and then gone into Baltimore to report this fact. This information was sent by wireless to the *Lusitania* at 1 p.m., but was not acknowledged by her. In addition to the above craft, the trawler *Luneda*, based on Berehaven, was patrolling off the Mizen. With the exception of the above vessels and the motor-boat *Aptera*, which was somewhere near Kinsale, there were no other patrols in the neighbourhood, as, at the time, the yachts *Greta* and *Aster* were undergoing repairs; the trawlers *Brock*, *Margate*, and *Bradford* were coaling; and the trawlers *Congo*, *Ebro*, *Reindeer II*, and *Lucida* were also in port owing to defects.

At eleven minutes past two o'clock the Valentia wireless station picked up the *Lusitania's* " S.O.S." signal, and a few minutes later Queenstown received the message. All tugs and small craft and the Queenstown trawlers on patrol were ordered to proceed immediately to the rescue. The Admiralty tugs *Stormcock* and *Warrior* were the first to get out of Queenstown, but the trawler *Brock* (Lieutenant-Commander T. B. H. Whytehead, R.N.R.), which was coaling at the time, got away very smartly, and the Queenstown drifter *Golden Effort* (Commander Birchan, R.N.V.R.) was also soon under way. In addition the trawler *Bradford*, the tug *Flying Fox*, the examination ship *Julia*, and three torpedo-boats proceeded to the spot. Some time was taken in informing the trawlers at sea, the *Indian Empire* being the only vessel of this class near Queenstown which was fitted with wireless.

No time was lost in getting to the scene of the disaster and picking up survivors. At 8.30 p.m. the *Stormcock* arrived back with her complement, followed by the *Indian Empire* (Lieutenant W. H. Wood, R.N.R.), which had on board 170 souls, the largest number of survivors brought in by any one vessel. In this party were only three of her crew, the remainder having been left behind in boats. These trawlers had seen many dead bodies; and men and women with little clothing left to them, whom they picked up, they readily furnished with their own blankets and most of their clothing. The trawler *Bluebell* arrived in port bringing Captain Turner, the master of the *Lusitania*, together with another officer and some passengers. Later another trawler rescued the third intermediate officer.

The patrol-vessels had done all that was possible having regard to the paucity of their numbers. In the original disposition of the vessels throughout the British Isles none could have foreseen that within a year of the war this area about Ireland would become such an important zone. Elsewhere the demands for destroyers and auxiliary patrol craft was so incessant that few could be spared. Now that the enemy had shown that he had ocean-going submarines, and was determined to use them ruthlessly so far away from his base, the Admiralty had to reconsider the whole subject, and make important modifications.

In the afternoon and evening following the sinking of the *Lusitania* submarines were sighted several times between Baltimore and Kinsale off the coast. Four days later the trawler *Brock* saw the conning-tower and wash of a submarine four miles south-west of Daunt Rock Lightship, at the entrance to Queenstown, and fired on her. On May 25th another steamship—an American—was torpedoed off the Atlantic coast. This happened at 8.24 p.m., fifty miles west of the Fastnet. The *Nebraskan* had left Liverpool the day before in ballast. Suddenly a violent explosion occurred, bursting the hatch and deck at No. 1 hold, and throwing the cargo derrick thirty feet into the air. No submarine was seen, but the chief engineer had sighted the wake of a torpedo. An S.O.S. signal was sent out, and at 9.30 p.m. the patrol-vessel *Scadaun*, a drifter converted into a yacht and commanded by Lieutenant W. Olphert, R.N.R., picked up the message from the *Nebraskan* asking for help. The *Scadaun* at the time was patrolling off Castlehaven not far from where the *Lusitania* had been torpedoed, and instantly proceeded at full speed, meeting the *Nebraskan* twenty-six miles west of the Fastnet. Instructing the American ship to obscure all lights, the *Scadaun's* commander informed her that he would stand by her, and then, steaming at $9\frac{1}{2}$ knots, he escorted her to Liverpool, where she arrived well down by the head. Probably it was the same submarine which fourteen hours later torpedoed the s.s. *Morwenna* when 160 miles west by south of St. Ann's Head, at the entrance to Milford Haven.

The incident has significance, as once again an unarmed fishing-vessel was able to render magnificent service. The *Morwenna* was bound from Cardiff to Sydney, Cape Breton, Canada, when she sighted the conning-tower of a submarine. Course was immediately altered to get the submarine right astern, extra firemen were sent below, and the engineer was ordered to get a full pressure of steam. In spite of these efforts, the submarine gained upon the merchantman, and fired shots at a range of about three-quarters of a mile, signalling the steamer to stop. Already one man had been killed and two others wounded when a vessel was sighted on the starboard bow, making straight for the *Morwenna*. Thereupon the enemy fired a couple of shells at the approaching ship, which turned out to be the Belgian fishing trawler *Jacqueline*, of Ostend, which had been fishing out of Milford. Both the submarine and the *Morwenna* took her to be a patrol trawler. Whilst the submarine continued to fire, the *Morwenna* was able to get out her boats, and thus save her crew. After having torpedoed the *Morwenna* the submarine made off, still firing at the Belgian, and then submerged. The skipper of the trawler, Eugène Blonde, had performed a most plucky act in coming to the rescue, having no other weapon than the stem of his ship. Although provided with neutral flags by his agent at Milford to display in the presence of an enemy submarine, he proudly hoisted his national colours, and advanced to attack with the greatest determination and courage, as Admiral Dare bore testimony. "I consider the action of Captain Blonde of the *Jacqueline* was most creditable," wrote the *Morwenna's* captain, "his intention being to ram the submarine if possible; and the courageous manner in which he kept running evidently gave the German commander the impression that the trawler was armed, as when they were about 200 yards from each other, the submarine made off with all speed, and shortly after dived out of sight. Then the trawler picked up the boats, and after getting all on board, including the body of one sailor killed, proceeded to Milford Haven.". For this gallant act in life-saving, skipper Blonde was awarded the silver medal of the Royal Humane Society, and the sum of £2 was sent to each of his crew. " I regret," wrote this Belgian skipper, " that I had no gun on board of my ship; otherwise the submarine had been sunk without doubt, our speed being insufficient to ram her. I beg to submit to the competent authority the proposal to put a gun on board of my vessel," one more proof that fishermen are much the same all the world over. It was just such a petition that our own fishermen were always presenting, and they showed themselves ready enough to attack the enemy, even though no gun could be afforded them. The school of the sea is the finest of all for the development of character and courage.

And now we may pause to take a survey of the activities of the Auxiliary Patrol at this period of the war. Two routes only were available to the enemy by which to get out to the Atlantic approach—either by way of the Dover Straits, or by a course round the north of Scotland. In the latter case there was a choice of coming down the west coast of Ireland and continuing to the latitude of the Fastnet, and so to the Scillies; or alternatively, after leaving Scottish waters, of negotiating the North Channel, thence passing down the Irish Sea and St. George's Channel and on to the Scillies.

Many difficulties beset the submarine on these routes. Local destroyer and torpedo-boat patrols might at any time be met issuing from various bases, and apart from all attacks on the way by these craft, the penetration of the Dover Straits, when reached, was a most perilous undertaking. Off the East Goodwins were armed drifters; another division patrolled near the Ruytingen shoal; a third division guarded a boom in the Downs; whilst yet a fourth division was on patrol at the northern end of the Downs. A British mine-field lay across the Straits, and the Dover drifters with their nets stretched towards the French coast, the nets at this time being made more dangerous by the attachment of explosive mines. The German Intelligence Service was good; the general position of the net area no doubt was known to the enemy, and those submarines which operated well up the English Channel most likely felt their way through the obstacle by night, travelling semi-submerged, taking account of the period of the moon and the state of the tide when choosing the most suitable opportunity. It was an exceedingly difficult task to detect a submarine at night in this trim. As a means of assisting the patrols, instruments known as hydrophones were early in May installed in the Gull, South Goodwin, and Varne Lightships. These hydrophones were a scientific contrivance by means of which the movements of a submarine could be heard. A long series of experiments had been carried out in the Firth of Forth; the instruments were not yet thoroughly efficient, and it was not until a later date that they became of importance for trapping the U-boat.

As the submarine came down the English Channel westward bound, there were armed yachts and trawlers based on Dover, Newhaven, and Portsmouth to be evaded. If a course were taken past the Wight, drifter nets lay out in Christchurch Bay, where the craft might be tempted to rest at night. Inshore, towards Anvil Point, off Poole, two motor-boats made a nightly patrol in case a submarine should be on the surface charging batteries or communicating with the land. To seaward towards Portland the Poole drifters worked their nets; over a hundred of these vessels operated in relays, one section relieving the other for return to harbour to replenish and refit. Beyond this area were the Portland drifters and trawlers. The former cast their nets across the Channel from Portland to the Casquets; and at the centre of the Channel—that is to say, about twenty miles south of the line joining Start Point to St. Catherine's Point—which was known to be frequented by submarines, the Portland trawlers patrolled. Similarly, while protecting their part of the trade route, Portsmouth craft were watching the route between twenty miles south of St. Catherine's and twenty miles south of Beachy Head.

Off Plymouth were the local auxiliary craft, and farther west the Falmouth trawlers slowly beat up and down the Channel. These Falmouth vessels worked in pairs, and as far as possible steered the same course (or its contrary) as the merchant steamers, so as to be in any neighbourhood where an attack by submarines was likely to occur. Between the Lizard and Gribbin Head, the coast was patrolled by the Falmouth drifters to a distance of five miles from the shore, trawlers operating outside that line. All patrols were ordered to be not more than a mile apart from each other. Submarines when in the neighbourhood of the Scillies were hunted by armed yachts, trawlers, and drifters; whilst in Admiral Dare's area between the Welsh and Irish coasts were the Milford patrol-vessels. These were on duty from the Coningbeg Lightship to Newquay; from the Smalls to the Barrells off Carnson Point; from Coningbeg northward along the Irish Coast to Wicklow Head; from the Smalls northward through Cardigan Bay to Bardsey Island and across to Wicklow Head; and from St. Govan's Lightship to Lundy Island and Hartland Point. For this purpose the Admiral had under his command a couple of armed yachts, two dozen armed trawlers, and forty-nine net-drifters—a complete striking force with which he could always keep in communication by means of signal-stations and wireless telegraphy. In addition, the Belfast yacht squadron, consisting of the armed yachts *Marynthea*, *Jeanette*, *Sapphire*, *Medusa*, *Narcissus*, and *Valiant*, was before the end of May placed under Admiral Dare's orders. These six yachts worked wherever submarines might be reported in the area east of long. 10° 30′ W. and north of lat. 50° N. Their duty was to prevent submarines from frequenting any particular locality or destroying successive merchant ships; and the yachts, armed with 12-pounders, and remaining six days at sea, followed by two days in harbour, were so stationed as to harass the enemy and keep him continually on the move.

Farther up the Irish Sea, drifters worked their nets between twenty and thirty miles north-east of Great Orme's Head, attended by armed craft, and some more drifters operated their nets five miles off the Liverpool Bar. Thus any renewed attacks on Liverpool shipping would be greatly hindered. Nets were also used off Holyhead, off the Calf of Man, and off the Mull of Galloway. Between Dublin and the Kish Lightship one unit patrolled each night from six o'clock till 10.30 p.m., acting as scouts prior to the departure of the cross-Channel steamers from Dublin to Holyhead. During the daytime this unit patrolled the Irish coast from St. John's Point to Wicklow Head.

It is extremely doubtful if submarines were able to penetrate the netted area of the North Channel. Nine sections of twelve drifters guarded this area, some of them having been fitted with "cruiser" mines, ready to be dropped on any submarine which might get foul of the nets. The drifters, now using the glass balls instead of the kapok, steamed continuously towing their nets across, so as to form a perpetual double line by day and by night. By these means the whole of the English Channel and the Irish Sea was rendered as dangerous for submarines as was possible, although it proved difficult in practice to shut out a foe that could render himself invisible by submersion. Along the south and west coasts of Ireland, from Carnsore Point away to Sybil Point, there were only four units; the leader of each unit disposed his ships, according to the number available, by sections of three, each section cruising in line abreast two miles apart in fine weather. The general principle observed was to keep out during the daytime on a line of traffic averaging from ten to fifteen miles off the coast, and to close the land and patrol the coast and bays during the night.

In the North Sea, whilst the trawler mine-sweepers continued to keep clear the channels along the shore, and the paddlers and other craft swept up mine-fields laid farther out, patrol-vessels navigating the waters from the Downs to the Orkneys maintained incessant watch for the appearance of U-boats. In order to avoid such patrols, the enemy, bound via the North of Scotland for his cruising-ground off Ireland, was forced to keep well away from the Scottish shore until he made the land about Rattray Head. From there northward to Lerwick the submarines operated, and they were able, not without difficulty, to push through the Fair Isle Channel and so round the north of Scotland and past the Hebrides to Ireland. To counteract this movement, trawlers were sent to cruise well eastward of Rattray Head, in the expectation that they might pick up the enemy before he altered course for the northward; and in order to increase the efficiency of the patrols in the Fair Isle Channel and strengthen the Shetlands Patrol, drifters were sent with indicator nets into these waters.

In short, wherever the enemy went, whether proceeding north or south, he was beset by vessels of an enormous new navy, manned by officers and men possessing the British fighting spirit, though not yet supplied with the apperfected paratus which three years later proved the most effectual means of combating the submarine. The Royal Navy had been prepared by long years of study and experience for fleet actions and for destroyer engagements, but for a long submarine war it possessed neither the data from which to deduce principles nor the means to put such principles into practice. Much shipping was lost, many valuable lives were sacrificed, before a really satisfactory method of attacking the submarine was evolved. Circumstances necessitated that the Navy should carry on a new form of sea warfare with its old weapons until new and more effective ones could be devised.

In spite of all these drawbacks, the Auxiliary Patrol did remarkably well and maintained the best traditions of the older Navy whenever opportunity presented itself. Such occasions were frequent. The spirit animating the Service, of determination to make the best use of its available resources and to miss no opportunity for battle, whatever the odds, was well displayed in an engagement in which the armed trawler *Limewold* figured. On May 8th she was patrolling twenty miles east of Peterhead. Her own commanding officer being on shore sick, the trawler was in charge of Acting Skipper C. C. Bond.

At 4.30 in the morning, Mr. Bond, when on duty in the wheel-house, was startled by the bursting of a shell close to his bows, causing water to splash aboard. He then saw a submarine about a mile and a half away right astern, overhauling him fast. The skipper at once manned his 6-pounder, brought his ship three points to port so that the gun would bear, and proceeded to engage the enemy. Before the trawler was able to get into action, the submarine fired her second shot, which again passed very near. A third shot from the German was well directed, passing between the *Limewold's* bridge and mast. The trawler's first two or three shots fell just over her opponent. By this time the alteration of the patrol-vessel's position and the sheering about of the submarine to starboard, in order to keep herself astern of the trawler, exposed the German's port side. The trawler's fifth shot hit the submarine square on the water-line, abreast of the conning-tower, the shell bursting with a cloud of flame and black smoke. The distance was 600 yards, an effective range for a 6-pounder. A few seconds later, as the trawler fired her sixth shot, the submarine submerged, her stern having risen fifteen feet into the air, and was not seen again. The *Limewold* sounded her steam whistle to attract other vessels, and proceeded to the spot where the enemy had been last seen, then making for Peterhead. The circumstances were investigated, and were not deemed to afford conclusive evidence that the submarine had been sunk. The Admiralty sent an expression of their appreciation to Acting Skipper Bond and the crew, together with a sum of £100 to be divided among them.

A fortnight later the trawler *Ontario* (Skipper G. Garland), patrolling in the neighbourhood of Fair Isle Channel, sighted a submarine steering to the south-west, about four miles off. The trawler put on full speed, and at a range of 3,000 yards opened fire with her starboard gun. It could be seen that the submarine was a vessel of a large type, painted a slate grey, with a gun abaft the conning-tower. The *Ontario's* shots fell all round the enemy ship, and the eighth and eleventh appeared to strike the hull and explode there, though there was doubt about the matter. No fewer than twenty-one rounds in all were fired by the trawler. Finally the submarine made away on the surface at high speed.

On the evening of May 25th, net-drifter *Unity* left Yarmouth, Isle of Wight, for her station, and at 8.30 p.m. shot her mine nets three miles south-south-west of the Needles, and drifted with them through the night. Next morning she commenced to haul the nets aboard, but when most of them were got in, a violent pull was felt, the force being so great that the *Unity* was towed stern first through the water until the 2½-inch strop, to which the nets were secured, parted. Three nets then ran out rapidly back into the sea, but they were cut adrift. Before the strop had parted, the warp and foot-rope, which had been secured together, were seen to be taut on the top of the water, and a swirling eddy such as would be caused by a revolving propeller was also observed. Furthermore, a dan-buoy which had been made fast to the end of the net was towed under water for a short distance and then reappeared and remained stationary. In order to mark the spot, the skipper dropped another dan-buoy with its sinker, and being quite certain that a

LAYING NETS FROM DRIFTERS TO CATCH SUBMARINES.

AN ESCAPE FROM THE NETS

submarine was foul of the nets, fired seven rockets and two sound rockets. Unfortunately these were not observed. The drifter *New Dawn* being sighted two miles off, the skipper steamed up to her and requested her to report the incident to the signal-station. The *Unity* then returned to her nets and remained steaming round them, assisted later by the *New Dawn*. Subsequently the senior naval officer from Yarmouth arrived, and seven torpedo-boats and three destroyers made search for some miles around, but nothing was discovered.

Examination of the nets revealed the fact that fifty yards of the lower half of the end net had been completely torn away, the foot-rope had been broken away from the warp, and nearly all the broken parts of the net showed distinct signs of having been cut by a sharp instrument, the towing-rope being marked in several places. There was no question whatever that a submarine had passed through the nets, that the nets had held him for a few minutes, and that the cutting of the wires of the net had been done by a sharp net-cutter fitted for this purpose to the submarine. It had saved the U-boat on this occasion; and when nearly four years later the great surrender of the German Navy took place, a swan-like erection was noticed on some of the U-boats, securely fastened at the bows on deck, with a series of knife-like cutters. This was the German's antidote to one of our most exasperating traps. Had depth charges been in use at this time, certainly one more German submarine would have failed to return to its base.

Experience had proved the value of light-draught paddle excursion steamers for mine-sweeping, their speed enabling them to make a sweep of 495 miles on the Dogger Bank area in four days, and four more of these craft were taken up and fitted out at the Royal Albert Docks, London, and manned by ratings of the Trawler Reserve. The ships were sent subsequently to Dover. Later one of the paddle-steamers was sweeping when a mine exploded under her stern with such force that her hull was damaged and the remains of her kite were sent up into the air, to come crashing down over the engine-room just above the head of the assistant engineer, Royal Naval Reserve, making a hole six feet by four. The assistant engineer fortunately escaped.

Throughout this period, when the enemy was waging war with mine and submarine with ruthless persistency, fishermen in the North Sea still continued to bring back the fish which the nation so badly needed. Every voyage was accompanied by risk, for many trawlers had foundered on mines, or were taken unawares by submarines, as we have already recorded. The danger was reduced as far as possible by the plans which the Admiralty, realising the need, had made. Armed yachts and armed trawlers, the latter disguised to resemble fishing craft, operated on the Dogger Bank with such alertness that the enemy considered discretion the better part of valour and rarely attacked. Farther north in Scottish waters, where fishing continued, a Peterhead trawler was detailed to steam off the coast between Aberdeen and Buchaness, and to use her trawl occasionally in order to entice a submarine. Two other trawlers were stationed among the Aberdeen fishing fleet, making themselves units of the fleet for the same purpose. For during May submarines had been sinking vessels from fourteen to seventy miles east of Aberdeen, and forty miles to the south-east of Peterhead.

May Day, 1915, was marked by "a certain liveliness"—the phrase of the First Lord—in the southern portion of the North Sea. During the forenoon the British destroyer RECRUIT was torpedoed and sunk by a submarine two miles east-south-east of the Galloper Lightship, but rescuing trawlers saved many of the crew. The same afternoon another loss occurred, this time a trawler and her gallant crew, farther across the North Sea. Four trawlers were on patrol: the *Miura* (Sub-Lieutenant L. W. Kersley, R.N.R.) was on a course a little to the north-east of the North Hinder Lightship; the *Chirsit* (Sub-Lieutenant A. Stablefold, R.N.R.) a little farther to the south-east of the lightship; and the *Columbia* (Lieutenant-Commander W. H. Hawthorne, R.N.R.) about four miles to the west-north-west of the position. Beyond the *Columbia* still farther to the west-north-west was the trawler *Barbados*, commanded by Lieutenant Sir James Domville, Bart., R.N., the senior ship of the four. The division was searching for a German submarine which had fired a torpedo at the *Columbia* that morning off Thornton Ridge. About 3 p.m. a couple of torpedo-boats were sighted approaching from the west-south-west, in quarter-line formation, flying no ensign. When little more than 500 yards distant they hoisted the German flag, and the leader fired a torpedo at the *Columbia*, which missed. Thereupon Sir James Domville, from the *Barbados*, opened fire. Very shortly afterwards a second torpedo was fired at the *Columbia*, striking on the port side abreast of the wheel-house, and she sank. Two torpedoes were also aimed at the *Barbados*, but just missed, and a heavy fire was kept up by the enemy from machine guns and 6-pounders. By this time the trawlers *Chirsit* and the *Miura* also joined in the action at long range, whereupon one of the torpedo-boats sheered off towards the *Chirsit*.

It was an unequal fight from the beginning, but the little trawlers, their Royal Naval Reserve officers, and their senior officer, Lieutenant Sir James Domville, fought with characteristic spirit. At the outset the skipper of the *Barbados* was wounded, so that Sir James Domville had to carry on in the wheel-house by himself. This part of the ship was the enemy's target, and inside this structure Lieutenant Domville was being hit by splinters. On several occasions he was knocked down. But the trawlers put up such a stiff fight that after twenty minutes the nearer of the torpedo-boats was compelled to increase the range to 1,200 yards. Shortly afterwards volumes of steam were seen issuing from her and she stopped. The *Barbados* then closed her, but the German craft got her machinery going, and together with the other torpedo-boat escaped to the south-south-east. Had the affair finished there, it would have been a victory for the trawlers, who with inferior speed and armament kept the enemy engaged until he declined to fight any longer. But this was not the end.

Half an hour later, the *Barbados*, by firing her gun and blowing her siren, was able to attract the attention of the destroyer LEONIDAS, which came up from the south-west and was informed of what had occurred. Thereupon the LEONIDAS and two other destroyers gave chase, whilst the *Barbados* returned to where the *Columbia* had been sunk, and discovered that only one survivor had been saved, the man, a deck-hand, having been picked up by the *Miura*. The destroyers pursuing the enemy torpedo-boats succeeded in sinking both of them; so retribution came quickly. In accordance with British ideas of the chivalry of the sea, efforts were at once made to save human life. Lieutenant Hartnoll himself went into the water to rescue a German.

Two officers and forty-four men of the German torpedo-boats, out of a total of fifty-nine, were picked up, and from these prisoners was learnt something of the callousness of the Germans to the sense of honour respected by seamen. They admitted that from the *Columbia* they had picked up a " two-striped officer " and two men. This officer must have been Lieutenant-Commander Hawthorne, but when asked what had become of him they casually remarked that their prisoners were below and time was short; so whilst they took the first opportunity to save themselves, they left three British sailors to their fate.

Another member of the German crews saved had had an extraordinary experience. As the German torpedo-boats were altering course, this man was swept overboard by the wash. A lifebuoy marked " A6 " was thrown to him, and picked up. He was then rescued by the Norwegian s.s. *Varild*, which happened to be passing, and from her he was handed over to the *Miura*. This prisoner stated that the torpedo-craft had come out from Zeebrugge at noon that day. It was learnt from the solitary British survivor that when struck the *Columbia* immediately broke in half, and sank in less than a minute, whilst the enemy all the time kept up fire from his machine guns and six guns, and did not neglect to fire even on a few men in the water who were endeavouring to save themselves.

The death of Lieutenant-Commander Hawthorne was a great loss to the Auxiliary Patrol Service. At the beginning of the war he had come to England from Canada at his own expense as a volunteer, and he had been constantly employed in most dangerous work ever since. The trawlers had fought most gallantly. In the *Barbados* the little 3-pounder was fired with excellent direction and rapidity by Petty Officer A. H. Hallett; the deck-hands and engine-room staff showed conspicuous courage. The *Miura* and *Chirsit*, by their effective long-range gunnery, had undoubtedly helped to save the *Barbados* and to cause the enemy to retire. The Admiralty expressed their appreciation of the way in which the trawlers had fought a superior force, and sent a letter on vellum to Lieutenant Sir James Domville, at the same time awarding Petty Officer Hallett the D.S.M. It remains only to observe that this incident was intended as another of those " tip-and-run " expeditions favoured by the enemy. During the forenoon considerable activity by hostile aircraft had been noticed, and undoubtedly the latter had informed Zeebrugge, from whence had been dispatched the two torpedo-boats with the intention of destroying all four trawlers.

In order to confuse the enemy when endeavouring to decide what craft was a fishing trawler, and what an armed trawler, various methods were adopted for concealing the gun. In some cases this was done by the addition of a foresail. Some of the Portsmouth trawlers thus added to their disguise, and they also painted the gun with an ingenious patchwork, according to primitive ideas of camouflage, which later were so much developed. There was always a hope that by hiding the gun a trawler might lure the submarine on till the latter was within range of gun-fire.

The enemy proved often enough the truth of the axiom that the bully is generally a coward. What, for instance, could be more cowardly than the following incident ? The steam-trawler *Victoria* had left Milford Haven on May 25th bound for the Labadie Bank, where she was going to trawl. About five in the evening of June 1st the sound of firing was heard astern, and a submarine was observed a long distance away. The *Victoria* was at the time about 130 miles west by south of St. Ann's Head. The submarine was painted grey, and as she had a mizzen set she had the appearance of a drifter. Without giving the trawler's crew time to leave the ship, the Germans shelled her. Even after the *Victoria* had stopped, the submarine, from a range of a mile and a half, maintained a rapid fire. By this time the scene on board the fishing-vessel was heartrending. A boy named Jones, who had come with the skipper for the pleasure of the trip, and had been sent on to the bridge, was killed. The skipper and chief engineer were also killed, both by one shell. In addition another shell struck the mate and the trimmer, who were also killed, a deck-hand being wounded.

Those who survived found themselves caught in a trap, as they could not get away from the ship, their boat having been smashed by the enemy's shells. They therefore jumped overboard with planks to save themselves.

The submarine went alongside the trawler, placed explosive charges aboard, removed the wounded deck-hand, and picked up the other survivors after they had been an hour and a half in the water. Having been cross-examined as to whether they were in the Navy, whether there were any arms on board, and whether they had seen any patrol-boats, these unhappy men were sent below. During the night they were given coffee and a biscuit each, and the deck-hand had his wounds dressed. All night they remained aft near the submarine's engines, and next morning to their surprise were joined by some more British fishermen from another West Country trawler, which had steamed out of Cardiff the previous day. This was the *Hirose*, a vessel built only that year. At 5.30 a.m., when about 130 miles west by south of Lundy Island bound for her fishing-grounds, her career was brought to a quick end. She was proceeding at a steady 9 knots, the third hand and the boatswain being on watch. Her skipper, Mr. Francis Ward, was below and was called by the boatswain, who shouted: "Come up, skipper. There are shells flying all round." He immediately came on deck, ordered all hands to be called, and rang down for the engines to be stopped. The shelling then ceased. The skipper rang down again for full speed ahead, but again the enemy put him under a heavy fire. Once more the trawler's engines were stopped, and the boat was ordered out. The submarine came up astern, and a man in the conning-tower called out to the men to leave the ship within five minutes. The crew got into their boat and were ordered to the submarine, where they found the four men from the trawler *Victoria*. Three of the submarine's crew were sent with bombs to destroy the trawler, and brought back with them the chart-room clock and binoculars. Then, about 6 a.m., the ten men from the *Hirose*, with four from the *Victoria*, were put into the boat of the *Hirose* and cast adrift to manage as best they could. They rigged up a sail with the boat's cover and hoisted an oar for a mast. Under this rig they ran all day, before a strong west-south-west wind and a heavy sea. Twenty-four hours later they were sighted by

CH. XI] THE SINKING OF FISHING CRAFT 445

the s.s. *Ballater*, of Liverpool, who picked them up with difficulty, owing to the heavy sea running, and landed them at Milford at four the same afternoon. The men were found by the *Ballater* just in time, for they were in an exhausted state, consequent on exposure in an open boat at the mercy of rough seas, with food that was sodden by the salt water. The submarine was U34, whose commanding officer had added one more to the long list of crimes committed by Germany on the high seas.

On the day that the *Hirose* was sunk, a submarine destroyed the Belgian fishing trawler *Delta B*, about ten miles south-west of the Bishop Rock. In the North Sea the attacks upon fishermen were even more frequent than in western waters. Altogether no fewer than forty-eight fishing-vessels were sunk during June by submarines, the principal localities being off the north-east coast of Scotland, fifty miles east of Lowestoft, and off the Dogger Bank; though sinkings of these craft also took place forty miles south-west of the Lizard, at the approaches to the Bristol Channel, and at the mouth of the English Channel.

A few examples of these attacks on fishing craft may be taken as typical of the rest. On June 4th the Aberdeen fishing-trawler *Explorer*, when about seventy-three miles north-east by north of Buchaness, saw a big submarine come under her stern. It was 7.30 p.m. A shot having been fired, the submarine commander called out to the skipper in good English : " Get your boat out at once. I have no time to lose." Left without choice, the trawler's crew had no course but to obey. Launching their boat, they pulled clear, when the U-boat promptly sank the fishing-vessel with eight shots and then disappeared to the north-east. The castaways were afterwards picked up by the sloop ACACIA.

On June 5th the fishing-trawler *Japonica*, forty-five miles north-east of Kinnaird Head, was also attacked and sunk by a submarine. The story is best told in the words of her skipper, Mr. William Henry Butler :

" It was about eleven o'clock at night, and we were just shifting watches. The mate had just got on to the bridge, and we heard a gun fire. Looking to starboard, we saw a shell explode ahead, which shook the ship. All hands got aft to get the boat out, the submarine coming along at full speed.

The captain of the submarine sang out, 'Hurry up! Clear out! I'm going to sink you.' We all got into the boat and pulled towards him, and he said, 'I don't want you here. Clear out!' 'Can I go back and get some sails or some food?' I asked. 'No,' he answered; 'clear to —— out of it!' He was about 200 yards from the ship, and fired two shots, which both missed. The third one went through the cabin, and the next one went through the boiler. She sank at twenty-five minutes past eleven."

On the following day H.M.S. ACACIA picked up the *Japonica's* crew and took them into port. That same day U14 was sunk off Peterhead. Later the five Peterhead patrol trawlers *Limewold, Hawk, Oceanic II, Vigilant*, and *Gull* received the sum of £932 to be divided between them for their success in bringing about her destruction.

Also on June 5th, another patrol trawler, which was destined to perform magnificent work during the war until she foundered on a mine many months later, did conspicuous service. There is reason to believe that the enemy assumed at first that this vessel was a fishing-boat, whereas she had a 12-pounder mounted forward. The incident occurred at 7 p.m. about eleven miles west of Mizen Head. The trawler *Ina Williams* was steaming towards the Cahirmore Signal-Station, which is perched on a high hill a few miles to the west of Berehaven. A large submarine came to the surface about a couple of miles away on the port beam. The trawler's commanding officer, Sub-Lieutenant Nettleingham, R.N.R., at once mustered his crew and headed for the enemy with all possible speed, whereupon the U-boat quickly fired four or five shots. All these fell short on the starboard side. She next fired a torpedo, which was seen to pass within ten feet of the *Ina Williams'* starboard quarter. The trawler fired six shots in rapid succession. Of these the first three fell astern of the submarine, but each shot got nearer. The enemy, becoming nervous, called his guns' crews in, but the trawler's fourth shot struck the submarine squarely at the water-line about half-way between the conning-tower and the stern. The fifth shot also appeared to strike, just abaft the conning-tower. The submarine was going down when the sixth shot hit her again at the water-line by the conning-tower, the decks being awash. This last shot was fired at 3,400 yards, the engagement having lasted about fifteen minutes. The trawler then steamed over the position, and bubbles of air and a large quantity of oil were seen to rise. For an hour the *Ina Williams* continued to cruise round the spot; and at the end of that time there were still bubbles coming up, and the oil had spread over about 500 yards. The fight, short and sharp, was much appreciated by the Admiralty, who considered the shooting remarkable, although there was afterwards reason to believe that the submarine was not sunk. Mr. Nettleingham received the D.S.C. and was promoted Lieutenant, and the seaman gunner was also decorated with a D.S.M. and promoted.

On June 10th, at 1.30 afternoon, the armed trawler *Yokohama*, commanded by Sub-Lieutenant C. C. Humphreys, R.N.R., and based on Stornoway, was on patrol west of the Butt of Lewis. Submarines had been frequenting these waters, lying in wait for supply ships bound for the Grand Fleet, or passing to or from the West of Ireland. The *Yokohama* sighted a submarine on the starboard bow three miles towards the land. Both vessels opened fire at the same time, the trawler having nothing better than a 3-pounder. The enemy had partially submerged so as to decrease the target. The firing was the extreme range for the 3-pounder, and the first few shots seemed to fall close. This annoyed the enemy, who rose fully out of the water, discharging a torpedo which passed some ten feet ahead of the trawler. A second torpedo was also fired, and went under the hull aft. It was the narrowest possible escape, for the track was seen by two of the crew aft making straight for the ship, and the engineer, who was on watch, heard the torpedo scrape the bottom of the trawler. Thereafter the enemy made away to the westward at high speed, firing as he went. Altogether the Germans had fired about thirty rounds, not one of which had hit; her gun was of a size corresponding to our 12-pounder. Some of the shells, however, had passed near the trawler; one went between the trawler's bridge and the funnel, and another passed just under the mizzen, which happened to be set at the time. As soon as the U-boat made off, the *Yokohama* gave chase, but owing to her inferior speed was soon left behind.

30

The *Yokohama's* conduct was considered by the Admiralty to merit a monetary reward.

Like the trawlers, the gallant little drifters never showed hesitation in doing their utmost to defeat the enemy. An example may be cited of the way they saved a valuable ship and still more valuable cargo.

On June 12th the U35 was operating about seventy miles west-south-west of St. Ann's Head, in which neighbourhood were two fine barques, the *Crown of India* and the *Bellglade*. The former was British. She had left Barry Dock on the previous day bound for Pernambuco with 3,000 tons of coal. Unfortunately light southerly winds had prevailed, with misty weather. Owing to these circumstances and the strong set to the northward, her master, Captain C. Branch, had endeavoured to keep well off the island; otherwise he would have hugged the shore and evaded attack. A submarine opened fire upon the *Crown of India* from half a mile distant. The sailing-ship was defenceless, and the crew hoisted out their two boats, in which all twenty-three men took refuge, and, abandoning their vessel, rowed away towards a Norwegian barque, the *Bellglade*, which was lying practically becalmed about three miles away. The submarine fired again at the *Crown of India*, which she sank within half an hour. Not content with this destruction, U35 then approached the Norwegian, a vessel which was bound from Halifax, Novia Scotia, for Sharpness with a cargo of timber, and her master was ordered to come aboard and bring his papers. This was done, and the Norwegian master was examined. He was then ordered to abandon his ship, and the submarine proceeded to fire three shots amidships and then one at the stern. As the German was so engaged a steam fishing drifter, the *Queen Alexandra*, was seen approaching. The submarine, mistaking her for a patrol-vessel, abandoned the *Bellglade* and disappeared.

The drifter picked up the crews of both sailing-ships and brought them into Milford, leaving the *Bellglade* still afloat. About 11.30 the same morning she was sighted by Milford patrol-vessels, who boarded her and found her stern submerged to a depth of four feet. Three Milford drifters, the *Cromorna* (Sub-Lieutenant Prestridge, R.N.R.), *Ivy Green*, and *Marys*, all vessels which had been taken up from Scottish fishing ports, determined to try and save her if possible. With a hundred-fathom tow rope of three-inch wire, the *Cromorna* and *Marys* towed ahead, the *Ivy Green* keeping a lookout astern for submarines, and in this way the *Bellglade* succeeded in making about 4 knots. The wind was now easterly, and there was a moderate sea. At five o'clock next morning the hawser parted. Efforts were made under very trying conditions to resume the towage, but the barque listed heavily in the trough of the sea and capsized, turning keel up. The party which had been placed on board her managed to scramble off and were all picked up. More could not be done by the drifters; but seven days later the derelict was towed into St. Bride's Bay, where she was anchored.

[END OF VOLUME I]

INDEX

Aberdeen, course of training, 262, 265; vessels at, 395
ABOUKIR, H.M.S., sunk, 241, 254, 273, 329
ACACIA, H.M.S., 445, 446
ACTÆON, H.M.S., 260
Addax, the Brixham smack, 397, 398
Aden, Gulf of, 137
Adenwen, the s.s., experience of, 299
Admiralty, relations with the Merchant Navy, 227; directions to shipping, 239, 415; policy, 241, 245; dispersal of ships, 243; charters trawlers for mine-sweeping, 260, 265, 318; conferences, 375, 395
Aeroplanes, German, bomb British ships, 293-5, 404
AJAX, H.M.S., 323, 351
Alabama, the s.s., 82, 180, 213
ALARM, the destroyer, 333
Aldeburgh, 319
Alex Hastie, the trawler, sinks a submarine, 385
Algoma, the trawler, experiments with mine-sweeping, 258; size and speed, 258; crew, 259
Allerton, —, skipper of the drifter *Edgar*, 364
Alleyne, G. T., master of the s.s. *Farn*, 162 *note*
Alnmouth, the trawler, 266
Alonso, the, 347
Alva, Duke of, massacres, 24
Amazon River, 140, 153
America, discovery of, 19
Amerika, the German s.s., 125
Amiens, Peace of, 46
Amiral Ganteaume, the s.s, sunk, 268, 333, 371
AMPHION, H.M.S., founders, 319
Andalusian, the s.s., sunk, 300
Anderson, —, assistant master of the s.s. *Lusitania*, drowned, 419

Andes, the trawler, experiments with mine-sweeping, 258; size and speed, 258; crew, 259
Angle, the trawler, 317
Anstey, F. J., master of the s.s. *Branksome Chine*, 290
Antelope, the Falmouth packet, action, 60
Antifer, Cape d', 271, 303
ANTRIM, H.M.S., attacked by a submarine, 333
Antwerp, 16; fall of, 198
Anvil Point, 404
Apprentices, register of, 105
Aptera, the motor-boat, 430
Aragon, the s.s., armed, 120
Araz, Mr., Governor of Chatham Island, 183
Archangel, 22
Archdeacon, L. N., master of the s.s. *Chilkana*, 198 *note*
ARIEL, the destroyer, sinks U12, 390
Arlanza, the s.s., released, 151
Armada, Spanish, defeat of the, 38
Arthur, George, master of the s.s. *Glanton*, 166
Arucas, the German tender, 152 *note*
Aster, the armed yacht, 344, 430
Asturias, the hospital ship, attacked by a submarine, 377
Asuncion, the German s.s., 154, 159, 160, 167
Atalanta, the s.s., attacked by a submarine, 301; beached, 302
Athelstan, King, naval policy, 8, 10
Atlante, the French privateer, 60
ATTACK, the destroyer, attacked by a submarine, 333
ATTENTIVE, H.M.S., attacked by submarines, 330
Atternave Island, 182
AUDACIOUS, H.M.S., founders, 339, 341

Aultbea, 378
Austria-Hungary, man-of-war in foreign waters, 127 *note*
Auxiliary Patrol, vii; organisation, 6, 255-7, 406; work, 329, 404; changes, 381; issue of bomb-lances, 391; protection of fishing fleets, 395; efficiency, 405; disposition of vessels, 430, 433-6; measures against the submarine, 433-6; spirit of the, 437
Ayesha, the s.v., capture of, 208, 209 *note*
Azores, the, 28

B3, British submarine, attacked, 333
Bacon, Admiral Sir Reginald, 406
Baden, the German s.s., 142, 143; sunk, 185
BADGER, the destroyer, rams a submarine, 276, 333
Bailhache, Mr. Justice, on the fate of the s.s. *Oriole*, 279
Ballard, Rear-Admiral George, Admiral of Patrols, 327, 330
Ballater, the s.s., 445
Ballycottin, 430
Baltic Fleet, 110
Baltic, the, 10; trade with, 23
Banff, 321
Bankfields, the s.s., sunk, 184
Banyers, the trawler, sunk, 365
Barbados, the trawler, 440
Barbarossa, the German s.s., 125
Bardsey Island, 375
Barfleur, Cape, 380
Barley Rig, the drifter, blown up, 322
Barlow, Admiral C. J., in command of the steam yacht *Valiant*, 363; in command of Larne Area, 381; instructions to, 382
Barnes, —, master of the *Seven Seas*, 313
Barr, H., master of the s.s. *St. Egbert*, 200, 201
Barra Head, 402
Barry Dock, 448
Bartlett, F. J., master of the s.s. *Oakby*, 290
Battenberg, Prince Louis of, 211; *see* Milford Haven
Battleships and submarines, 256
Beachy Head, 47, 64, 290, 302, 385, 403; patrol area, 400
Beck, Sir Raymond, member of the Committee on insurance of ships in war, 228
Belfast, patrol, 341, 435
Bell, J. W., master of the *Thordis*, damages a submarine, 292; awarded the D.S.C. and made Lieutenant R.N.R., 292
Bell Rock, 329, 395
Bellevue, the s.s., capture of, 173; sunk, 174
Bellglade, the Norwegian barque, attacked by a submarine, 448; fate of, 449
Bembridge, 314
Ben Cruachan, the s.s., sunk, 277, 376
Ben Lawers, the trawler, attacks a submarine, 404
Ben Strome, the trawler, 390
Bengal, Bay of, 187
Bengrove, the s.s., sunk, 296
Ben-isâf, 297
Benmohr, the s.s., sunk, 198
Bennett, Henry J., master of the s.s. *Potaro*, 174
Berehaven, 430, 446
Beresford, Admiral Lord, 123; Commander-in-Chief of the Channel Fleet, 257
Berkeley, Commander H., R.N., 342
Berlin and Milan Decrees, 58, 67
Berlin, the German s.s., lays mines, 338; escapes, 341
Bernays, Lieutenant-Commander, R.N., 363
Bernsdorff, Count von, on the sinking of the s.s. *Lusitania*, 427
Berry Head, 374
BERWICK, H.M.S., 126, 171
Bestic, Albert Arthur, third officer of the s.s. *Lusitania*, 418
Bethania, the German s.s., 126
Bethke, J., master of the s.s. *Cornish City*, diary on board the s.s. *Rio Negro*, 155-66; transferred to the German s.s. *Crefeld*, 165
Bieberstein, Baron Marschall von, at The Hague Conference, 118
Birchan, Commander, R.N.V.R., 430
BIRMINGHAM, H.M.S., rams U15 submarine, 322
Biscay, Bay of, 10
Bishop Rock, 312
BITTERN, the destroyer, 398
BLACK PRINCE, H.M.S., 126
Black Sea Fleet, 110

INDEX

Blacksod Bay, 301 ; armed patrol at, 371
Blackwood, the s.s., torpedoed, 297, 391
Blanche, the trawler, 358, 366
Blaskets Lighthouse, 316, 404
Blonde, Eugène, skipper of the Belgian trawler *Jacqueline*, 432 ; awarded a medal, 433
Blonde, the s.s., bombed by an aeroplane, 294
Bloody Foreland, 341
Blücher, the German s.s., 127, 357
Bluebell, the fishing smack, 423, 430
Blyth, 322
Bolton, Sir Frederick, 228
Bomb-lances, issue of, 391
Bond, Acting-Skipper C. C., of the trawler *Limewold*, 437
Booth, Sir Alfred Allen, Chairman of the Cunard Company, evidence, 415
Boothby, Lieutenant H., R.N.R., of the trawler *Orianda*, 362 ; awarded the D.S.C., 365
Booty, Commander E. L., R.N., of H.M.S. KING EDWARD VII, 258
Bordeaux, equips corsairs, 46
Bordelais, the privateer, 46
Bosanquet, Admiral Sir Day Hort, 210
Boston, the s.s., strikes a mine, 364
Bothnia, the s.s., 299
Boulogne, 47, 64
Bowes Castle, the s.s., sunk, 153
Bowring, Captain Humphrey W., R.N., in charge of drifters, 373, 374
Boy Willie, the drifter, 392
Boyck, George R., master of the s.s. *City of Winchester*, 137
Boys, The, the drifter, 386
Bradford, the trawler, 430
Branch, C., master of the barque *Crown of India*, 448
Branksome Chine, the s.s., sunk, 290
Brazil, Island of, expedition in search of, 19
Bremen, the German s.s., 124
Brenton, Captain, *Naval History*, 48 *note*, 58 *note*
BRESLAU, the German cruiser, 128
Brest, blockade of, 47
Bridge, Admiral Sir Cyprian A. G., 211 ; on the protection of shipping, 213
Brighton Queen, the s.s., as minesweeper, 332, 361

Bristol, 13, 19
Bristol Channel, submarine in, 409
BRISTOL, H.M.S., 170, 185
British Army, 71 ; the 10th Division of the, cross the Irish Sea, 404
British commerce, campaign against, in the Revolutionary and Napoleonic Wars, 44-6, 50, 57
British Corporation for the Survey and Registry of Shipping, 95 *note*
British Government, reply to Germany, 284
British Isles, system of patrol, 370
British Merchant Navy ; *see* Merchant Navy
British Museum, gold noble of Edward III, 15
Brock, the trawler, 430
Brooks, James, on the sinking of the s.s. *Lusitania*, 418-21
Brow Head, 417, 429
Brown, Captain, R.N., Registrar-General of Seamen, scheme of a voluntary Naval Reserve, 106, 111 ; report on the register ticket, 107
Brown, C. W., master of the s.s. *Fulgent*, 316 ; killed, 316
Bruges, 16
Buchan Ness, 378, 445
Bülow, the German s.s., 126
Burchart, Friedrich, Lieutenant-Captain, of the German cruiser DRESDEN, 141
Buresk, the s.s., 199 ; capture of, 195 ; sunk, 195 *note*
Burgh, Herbert de, 9
Burntisland, 330
Butler, William Henry, skipper, on the sinking of the trawler *Japonica*, 445
Butt of Lewis, 401, 447
Byron, the s.s., 168

Caborne, Commander W. F., R.N.R., 113 ; lecture on the Royal Naval Reserve, 113 *note*
Cabot, John, voyages, 19
Cabot, Sebastian, voyage, 21
Cadogan, Anthony, master of the s.s. *Vandyck*, 166
Cairn Ryan, 404
Calais, 47, 64 ; loss of, 23
Calcutta, 193
Calf of Man, 290, 435
Callaghan, Admiral Sir George A.,

President of the Mining Committee, 259; Commander-in-Chief of the Grand Fleet, 318
Callao, 146
Cambank, the s.s., 288; attacked by a submarine, 289; sunk, 290
Campbell, Rear-Admiral Henry, appointed to the Trade Division, 224; memorandum, 120, 225
Canada, transports from, 338
Canary Islands, 27, 244, 246
Candish, Thomas, voyages, 39
Canynges, William, fleet, 18
Cap Finisterre, the German s.s., 124
Cap Poloni, the German s.s., 124
Cap Trafalgar, the German s.s., 127
Cape of Good Hope, 37, 40
Cape Verde Islands, 28
Caprivi, the s.s., founders, 403
Cardiff, 13
Cardigan Bay, 435
Cargoes, insurance of, 236; total value of, 236
Carmania, the s.s., 127
Carnsore Point, 430, 435, 436
Caroline Islands, 204
Carthagena, 30, 35
Carver, Captain E. C., R.N., 372, 380
Caspian Sea, 23
Cassandra, the trawler, 359
Castle of Comfort (Hawkins's ship), 28
Castlehaven, 429
Castro, the s.s., case of, 131
Cawdor, Lord, First Lord of the Admiralty, "Statement of Admiralty Policy," 113
Cawsey, E. J., master of the s.s. *Florazan*, 298
Cayley, Rear-Admiral George C., 378
Ceramic, the s.s., 121
Cervantes, the s.s., sunk, 164
Ceylon, 194
Chagos Islands, 197
Chair, Rear-Admiral Sir Dudley de, in command of the Tenth Cruiser Squadron, 125
Chalcheford or Calshot Castle, 15 *note*
Challis, Captain H. J., R.N., 112
Chamberlain, Rt. Hon. Austen, Committee on War Insurance of Shipping, 228
Chamberlain, Rt. Hon. Joseph, Shipping Bill, 78
Chancellor, Richard, Pilot-Major, 21; Arctic voyage, 21; at Archangel, 22; Moscow, 22; wrecked, 22
Channel Fleet, 47
Channel Islands, submarines in, 374
Chapra, the s.s., 194
Charcas, the s.s., capture of, 178
Charles I, naval policy, 44
Charlton, Vice-Admiral Sir E. F. B., appointed Admiral of the East Coast Mine-Sweepers, 331, 346
Chasehill, the s.s., capture of, 176
Chatham equips mine-sweeping trawlers, 320
CHATHAM, H.M.S., 198
Chatham Island, 182, 183
CHEERFUL, the destroyer, 329
Cherbourg, 47
Cherbury, the s.s., sunk, 314
Chester, the trawler, 390
Chili, 37
Chilkana, the s.s., captured, 198; sunk, 201
China, 39
Chirsit, the trawler, 440; fight with a submarine, 441
Christchurch Bay, submarines in, 374
Christian, Admiral A. H., request for trawlers, 322
Christiania, the Norske Veritas, 95 *note*
Churchill, Rt. Hon. Winston, First Lord of the Admiralty, Navy Estimates, 121–4; request for drifters, 372
Cincinnati, the German s.s., 125
Cinque Ports Fleet, 9; defeat of the French Armada, 9; continual feuds, 10
CIRCE, H.M.S., 262, 342
City of Bremen, the s.s., sunk, 313
City of Cambridge, the s.s., attacked by a submarine, 306–8; sunk, 308 *note*
City of Rangoon, the s.s., 192 *note*
City of Winchester, the s.s., captured, 137; sunk, 139
Clacton, the s.s., 337
Clan Grant, the s.s., sunk, 198
CLAN MACNAUGHTON, the armed merchant cruiser, founders, 378
Clan Matheson, the s.s., captured, 192; sunk, 193
Clark-Hall, John, Registrar-General of Seamen, 111
CLAYMORE, the French destroyer, 299

INDEX

Clear, Cape, 417, 429
Clegg, Robert, master of the s.s. *Lovat*, 189
Cleggan Bay, 302
Cleopatra, the trawler, 368
Clermiston, the s.s., 271
Cleveland, the German s.s., 124
Clifton, the trawler, 430
Clon, the trawler, 360
Clopet, A., master of the s.s. *Southport*, 204
Clyde, the, 75; armed patrol at, 370, 371
Coastal patrols, new system of, 368
Coastal shipping, losses in French wars, 62
Coasters, size of, 55
Coasting trade, 80
Coasts, ancient system of protection by contract, 17
Cochin, 201
Cocos Islands, 195 *note*, 203
Codling Bank, 405
"Coffin-ships," 78
Coke, Admiral Sir Charles H., 430
Colchester, the s.s., escapes from a submarine, 272, 293
Coleby, the s.s., captured, 176; sunk, 177, 252
Collingwood, Admiral Lord, 59
Colomb, Sir John C. R., 210
Colomb, Vice-Admiral P. H., *Essays on Naval Defence*, 68 *note*
Colonial Defence Committee, policy, 217-19
Columbia, the trawler, 349, 440; attacked by a submarine, 441; sunk, 441, 442
Colusa, the s.s., 177
Colva, the German s.s., 124
Colville, Admiral Hon. Sir Stanley, 355
Commerce, international, expansion of, 89, 100
Comorin, Cape, 195, 201
Comoro Islands, 40
Condor, the s.s., captured, 165
Congo, the trawler, 430
Coningbeg, 417, 435
Connor, W. H., master of the s.s. *Downshire*, 290
Conqueror, the armed yacht, 400
Conscription, result of, 4
Constance Catherine, the s.s., 315
Constantinople, report of the British Consul on the merchant seamen, 102
Consuls, British, reports on the condition of the Merchant Navy, 100-103
Convoy Acts, 52
Convoys, British, system of, 52, 215, 226, 241, 242
Conway Castle, the s.s., 145; captured by the German cruiser DRESDEN, 146; sunk, 147
Coote, the trawler, 390
Copper Point, 416
Coquet, the trawler, 395; sunk, 397
COQUETTE, the destroyer, chases submarines, 333
Corbett, Sir Julian S., vi; *Drake and the Tudor Navy*, 29 *note*, 31; *Naval Operations*, 210 *note*; *Official Memorandum*, 66 *note*
Corcovado, the German s.s., 126
Cordilleras, the, 35
CORMORAN, the German gunboat, 128, 177, 188
Cornish City, the s.s., captured, 154; sunk, 156
CORNWALL, H.M.S., 152
Cornwallis, Admiral, 48
Correntina, La, the s.s., sunk, 172
COSSACK, the destroyer, 388
Courage, the drifter, 373
Cradock, Admiral Sir Christopher, 153, 170
Craigforth, the s.s., 135
Crathie, the trawler, blown up, 322
Crefeld, the German s.s., 154-65
CRESSY, H.M.S., sunk, 241, 254, 273, 329
Crighton, William, master of the s.s. *Coleby*, 177
Cromarty, armed patrol at, 266, 328, 335, 370; net-bases at, 375
Cromorna, the drifter, 448
Cromwell, Oliver, naval policy, 43, 44
Crossley, Lieutenant C. V., R.N.R., 362
Crown of Castile, the s.s., sunk, 312
Crown of India, the barque, sunk, 448
Cruikshank, David, master of the s.s. *Flaminian*, 312
"Cruiser" mine, 406
Cruiser Squadron, the Tenth, 125
Cruisers and submarines, 256
Cruisers on service, 1804-14, 59
Cubbin, John, master of the s.s. *Princess Victoria*, 297
CUMBERLAND, H.M.S., 127, 152
Currey, Captain Bernard, R.N., Director of Naval Ordnance, 259

456 INDEX

Customs and Excise, Board of, 242
Cutters in the Revolutionary and Napoleonic Wars, 64
Cuxhaven, minefield, 135

D5, British submarine, founders, 346, 348
Daisy, the surveying trawler, 266
Dale, William G., master of the s.s. *Oriole*, 279; torpedoed, 280
Dane, the trawler, 365
Daniel Stroud, the trawler, 266
Danube, the s.s., 184 *note*
Danzig, report of the British Consul on the merchant seamen, 101
Dare, Admiral Sir Charles H., in command of Milford Haven Area, 381, 435; instructions to, 382
Darien, Gulf of, 32, 35
Dartmouth, 13, 399
Daunt Rock Lightship, submarine at, 431
Davidson, James, master of the s.s. *Cherbury*, 314
Davies, F. J., master of the s.s. *Falaba*, 309
Davies, Harry, chief engineer of the s.s. *Vosges*, killed, 305
Davis, John, voyages, 39, 41
Day, E. M., master of the s.s. *Galician*, report on the capture by the German armed merchant cruiser KAISER WILHELM DER GROSSE, 148-51
Declaration of London, 119, 281, 282
Defence, Imperial, Committee of, 217, 219-23, 228; report, 230-37; " War-Book," 221
DEFIANCE, H.M.S., 260
Delmira, the s.s., attacked by a submarine, 303; grounded, 304
Delta B, the trawler, sunk, 445
DENVER, the cruiser (U.S.A.), 182
Deptford, 42; Naval Arsenal at, 21
Depth-charge, 406
Derfflinger, the German s.s., 127, 357
Destroyers, shortage, 256
Devonia, the s.s., 332
Devonport, armed patrol at, 265, 266, 370; net-bases at, 375
Dewar, Captain K. G. B., R.N., 66, 68
Diane, the armed yacht, 400
Diego, a runaway slave, 35
Diego Garcia, 197
Dieppe, 64
Diligence, the drifter, 373

Dinorah, the s.s., torpedoed, 380
Diplomat, the s.s., captured, 187, 190; sunk, 191
Direction Island, 203
Dobbing, A. E., master of the s.s. *Mary Ada Short*, 178
Dodd, J. C., chief engineer of the s.s. *Southport*, 206
Dogger Bank, 345, 352, 357, 395; clear from mines, 407
Domville, Lieutenant Sir James, R.N., in command of minesweeping trawlers, 343; of the trawler *Barbados*, 440
Don, the trawler, sunk, 407
Donaldson, Captain L. A. B., R.N., appointed " Commander Superintendent of Modified Sweeping," 334; President of the Submarine Attack Committee, 368
Donovan, W. C., master of the s.s. *Exford*, 200
Dorothy Gray, the mine-sweeper, rams U18 submarine, 354, 356; rewarded, 356
Doughty, Captain H. M., R.N., in command of the Devonport Gunnery School, 369
Doughty, Thomas, executed, 36
Dover Cinque Port, 9, 13; armed patrol at, 265, 266, 327, 335, 370; drifters at, 373; net-bases at, 382
Dover Net Drifter Flotilla, 375
Dover Straits, British minefield, 379, 433; netting the, 373, 383
Dovre, the Norwegian s.s., 193
Down, Commander C. E., R.N.R., master of the s.s. *Arlanza*, 151
Downs, the, 47, 383
Downshire, the s.s., sunk, 290
DRAKE, H.M.S., 260
Drake, Sir Francis, 11; in command of the *Judith*, 29; voyages, 32-6; wounded, 34; knighted, 37; reprisals on the Spanish Indies, 38
DREADNOUGHT, H.M.S., 323; sinks U29 submarine, 300 *note*
DRESDEN, the German cruiser, 128, 249; captures and sinks British ships, 139-47, 208, 244; sunk, 147
Drifters, 255, 369; patrol, 320, 321; construction, 372; speed and crew, 372; names, 373; number, 380; skippers, 383; work, 435
Drift-net fishing, 369

INDEX

Driver, the trawler, 262
Drumcliffe, the s.s., captured, 139; released, 140
Drummuir, the s.v., captured, 184; sunk, 185
Drunkenness in the Merchant Service, 74, 77
DRYAD, H.M.S., 356
DUKE OF EDINBURGH, H.M.S., 198
Dulwich, the s.s., attacked by a submarine, 288; sunk, 289, 380
Dungeness, 64, 279, 400
Dunkirk, 26, 47, 64
Dunmore (Waterford), 429
Durward, the s.s., captured, 275; sunk, 276, 377
Duster, the trawler, 390
Dymchurch, 279

Eager, the drifter, 364
Eagles, J. C., master of the s.v. *Drummuir,* 185
Earl of Lathom, the s.v., sunk, 410
East Coast ports, closed to neutral fishing-vessels, 336
East India Company, 39, 41; ships, 42, 48; size of, 54; tonnage, 55
East Indies, 39; trade with the, 40
Easter Island, 178
EBER, the German gunboat, 127, 128
Ebro, the trawler, 430
Ecuador, the s.s., 184 *note*
Edward I, 14
Edward III, victory of Sluys, 13; sovereignty of the sea, 15; commercial policy, 16
Edward IV, commercial treaties, 19
Eileen, the steam yacht, 363
Eileen Emma, the trawler, 309
Elbe River, 135
Elfland, the Belgian relief ship, bombed by an aeroplane, 294
Elfrida, the s.s., strikes a mine, 365
Eli, the s.s., sunk, 364
Elizabeth, Queen, 18; accession, 23; foreign policy, 24, 28; navy, 25; plot to assassinate, 32
Elizabeth, the (Wynter's ship), 37
Elizabeth, the s.s., 315
Ellis, Somers, on the capture of the s.s. *Troilus,* 198-201
Ellison, Captain Alfred A., R.N., 320, 322, 378; experiments with nets, 369
Elsinore, the s.s., captured, 180
Elterwater, the s.s., founders, 360

EMDEN, the German cruiser, 128, 170, 186, 246; sinks British ships, 187-204, 208, 247, 248; destruction, 204
England, expansion of sea power, 43; naval supremacy, 45, 57; privations of the lower classes, 70
English Channel, 350, 368; infested by French buccaneers, 20; mine-laying in the, 371; submarines, 374; defence of, 399
ENTERPRIZE, H.M.S., 57
ERNE, the destroyer, 355
ESSEX, H.M.S., 126
Esther, the trawler, 266
Estill, W. H., master of the s.s. *Royal Sceptre,* saves the ship, 169
Eten, 184
Euan Mara, the motor-boat, 364
EURYALUS, H.M.S., 322
Eustace the Monk, in command of the French Armada, 9
Evans, —, master of the s.s. *Drumcliffe,* 139
Evans, Commander E. R. G. R., R.N., in command of the destroyer VIKING, 387
Evans, J., master of s.s. *Pruth,* 164 *note*
Evans, Jonathan, master of the s.s. *Lizzie,* 303
Evans, Commander Maurice, R.N., 401
Exford, the s.s., captured, 198, 200, 208
EXMOUTH, H.M.S., 352
Exmouth, Lord, 51
Explorer, the trawler, sunk, 445

Fair Island, 353, 404; Channel, 379, 436
Falaba, the s.s., attacked by a submarine, 309; sunk, 310-12
Falkland Islands, battle of the, 185
Falmouth, net-bases at, 375; patrol, 399
Fanad Point, 343
Far Cathay, 19, 22
Farn, the s.s., 165; captured, 162
Farne Islands, 371
Faröe Islands, 351
Farrer, Lord, memorandum on the state of British shipping, 79
Fasnet, 416
Fécamp, 271, 289
Federal Houlders Argentine Line, ships fitted with guns, 124

Federal Steam S. Co., ships fitted with guns, 124
Feldkirchner, Oberleutnant z. S., 269
Fenner, Thomas, trading expedition, 28
Feria, Spanish Ambassador, 24
Fermo, the trawler, escapes from a submarine, 402
Fidra, 329
Filey, 360
Filey Brig, 363, 365
Fisher, Admiral Sir John (Lord Fisher), First Sea Lord, 259
Fishermen, characteristics, 398
Fishing fleet at work, 440
Fishing-vessels, patrol duty, 256; sunk, 349, 394, 409, 445
Flamborough Head, 297, 331, 337; minefield, 328, 357
Flaminian, the s.s., sunk, 312
Flanders, wool trade, 10; submarine bases in, 272
Fleetwood, 263, 265
Fleurette, the trawler, catches mines, 378
FLIRT, the destroyer, 313
Florazan, the s.s., sunk, 298
Flying Fox, the Queenstown tender, 424, 430
Folkestone, the s.s., 337
FORMIDABLE, H.M.S., sunk, 371
Forth, Firth of, mine-sweeping trawlers at, 265, 266; net-bases at, 375
Fortune, W. C., master of the s.s. *Mobile*, 314
Fowey, importance, 13
Fox, Captain Cecil, R.N., 350
Foyle, the s.s., sunk, 196
France, invasion of, in 1415, 14; revolution, 44; capture of British merchant ships, 44; *guerre de course*, 45, 58; tonnage of ships, 82, 85, 87
Franco-Prussian War, 4
Fraser, James, chief engineer of the s.s. *Atalanta*, 301
Fraserburgh, 321
Fraternity of the Holy Trinity, 21
Frau Minna Petersen, German s.v., captured, 209 *note*
Frédéric Franck, the s.s., 397, 398
Freesia, the trawler, 430
French Armada, defeat, 9; buccaneers infest the Channèl, 20; rivalry on the seas, 43; corsairs, 46; fleet, 58; marauding expeditions, 17; depredations of privateers, 63–6
Friedrich der Grosse, the German s.s., 125
Frio, Cape, 173
Frobisher, Sir Martin, 37, 38; voyages, 39
Froissart, Jean, on the battle of Sluys, 13
Fry, Alfred C., master of the s.s. *City of Cambridge*, on the attack of a submarine, 306–8; presented with a watch, 308
Fryatt, Charles A., master of the s.s. *Colchester*, 293; of the s.s. *Wrexham*, 296; taken prisoner and shot, 296 *note*
Fulgent, the s.s., sunk, 314, 316
Fyfe, T. S., master of the s.s. *Crown of Castile*, 312

Galapagos Islands, 181
Galician, the s.s., captured, 148; released, 149
Galley, the oared, 24
Galley Head, 417, 429
Gallier, the s.s., strikes a mine, 364
Galway Bay, armed patrol at, 371
Gama, Vasco da, rounds the Cape, 19
Gare, E. G., master of the dredger *Ponrabbel*, 198 *note*
Garland, G., skipper of the trawler *Ontario*, 438
Garmo, the trawler, sunk, 363
Garnett, Lieutenant-Commander Stuart W. H., R.N.R., in command of s.y. *Zarefah*, 325, 402; plucky act, 403
GARRY, the destroyer, attacks a submarine, 354, 367
Garu, the trawler, 405
Gascanane Sound, 429
Gayer, Kapitän-Leutnant A., 418 *note*
Gazelle, the s.s., 337
GEIER, the German gunboat, 128; captures British ships, 204, 208
Gem, the s.s., blown up, 364
Général de Santos, the French barque, 313
George V, King, tribute to the Merchant Navy, 2
George, W. J., second officer of the s.s. *Harpalyce*, 315
George Washington, the German s.s., 125
Gerard, J. W., American Ambassa-

INDEX 459

dor in Berlin, on the sinking of the s.s. *Lusitania*, 426; *Four Years in Germany*, 427
Germania, the German s.s., 205
Germanischer Lloyd of Berlin, 95 *note*
Germany, submarine policy, v–vii, 399, 410; warfare, 54, 268–80, 285–93, 296–317, 329, 332, 371, 376, 380, 385, 395–7, 402–5, 409, 431–3, 440, 443–9; tonnage of ships, 85, 87, 89; preparations for war, 121; armed merchant ships, 125–8; instructions to, 129; treatment of British ships, 130; naval order, 134; declares war, 135; naval policy, 222, 256, 323, 367; submarines, 254, 273; net-cutting device, 392; measures against, 433–7; construction of minelayers, 261, 266; High Sea Fleet, 272, 357; memorandum on the "War Zone," 280–83, 379, 410; equips trawlers for mine-laying, 319; minefields, 328, 337, 346–9; reception of the news of the sinking of the s.s. *Lusitania*, 426
GHURKA, the destroyer, 388, 391
Giacopolo, —, master of the s.s. *Loredano*, 191; warnings to British shipping, 192 *note*
Gibbons, Captain K. C., R.N., in charge of patrol vessels, 344
Gibson, H. J., master of the tug *Homer*, 313; presented with a watch, 314
Gibson, W. H., master of the s.s. *Foyle*, 196 *note*
Gilbert, Sir Humphrey, expedition to Newfoundland, 39
Gilbert Islands, 204
Gilgallon, Private, 301
Gladys, the s.s., 278
Glandore Harbour, 429
Glanton, the s.s., sunk, 166
GLASGOW, H.M.S., 142, 153
Glenturret, the s.s., 202; captured, 209
Glitra, the s.s., 241; captured, 269; sunk, 270, 333
Glossop, Captain J. C. T., R.N., of H.M.A.S. SYDNEY, 204
GNEISENAU, the German cruiser, 128, 177
Gneisenau, the German s.s., 127
Goddison, F. A., chief engineer of the s.s. *Wrexham*, 297

GOEBEN, the German battle-cruiser, 128
Goeben, the German s.s., 126
Golden Effort, the drifter, 373, 430
Golden Hind, the, 37
Goldenfels, the German s.s., 139
Goodwins, submarines in the, 403
Gorleston, raid on, 337, 346, 348
Goschen, Sir E., 130
GOSHAWK, the destroyer, attacked by a submarine, 333
Gothenburg, report of the British Consul on the merchant seamen, 101
Grace, Captain H. E., R.N., in command of armed drifters, 380
Graham, Sir James, First Lord of the Admiralty, Merchant Service Bill, 98, 105
Grand Fleet, the, 222, 256; mobilised, 6; sweep down the North Sea, 321, 357; anchored in Lough Swilly, 339; at sea, 354
Grangemouth, 269
Granton, 265; base for trawlers, 335, 350; armed patrol at, 370
Graphic, the s.s., escapes from a submarine, 276, 278
Gravelines, 38
Gravesend, 20
Gray, J. R., master of the s.s. *Indian Prince*, 171
Gray, Thomas (Board of Trade), on the condition of the Mercantile Marine, 75 *note*
Great Britain, tonnage of steam-vessels, 85, 87, 88–94; declares war against Germany, 135
Great Orme's Head, 435
Green, John R., master of the s.s. *Vosges*, attacked by a submarine, 304–6; awarded the D.S.O., 306
Green Book, the, 94
Greene, Francis, master of the s.s. *Tokomaru*, 278
Gresham, Sir Thomas, Ambassador at Antwerp, 25
Greta, the armed yacht, 344, 430
Grey, Sir Edward, dispatches from, 130, 131
Grimsby, 265; recruiting for the Trawler Reserve, 262
Gris Nez, Cape, 380
Grisnez, the fishing-vessel, sunk, 391
Grosser Kurfurst, the German s.s., 125

Gryfevale, the s.s., captured, 195; released, 197, 247
Guadaloupe, the French s.s., captured, 176
Guayaquil, Gulf of, 184
Gueran, Spanish Ambassador, 25
Gull Lightship, hydrophone installed, 434
Gull, the trawler, 446

Haddock, Captain H. J., R.N.R., 2
Hague, The, Conferences, 118, 120, 122
Hakluyt, Richard, 21, 27 *note*, 40
HALCYON, H.M.S., 320, 348
Hallaniya, Bay of, 138
Hallett, Petty Officer A. H., 442; awarded the D.S.M., 443
Hamburg, British merchant ships detained, 130
HAMPSHIRE, H.M.S., 198, 201
Hankey, Lieut.-Col. Sir M. P. A., Secretary of the Committee on insurance of ships in war, 228
Hannan, F. S., master of the s.s. *Tamar*, 176
Hanseatic League, 16; decline, 19
Harbours, 74, 76
Harpalion, the s.s., sunk, 291
Harpalyce, the s.s., sunk, 314, 315
Harris, David, master of the s.s. *King Lud*, 194
Harris, William, master of the s.s. *Clan Matheson*, on his capture, 192
Hartdale, the s.s., sunk, 301
Hartland Point, 435
Hartlepool, bombardment of, 357
Hartnoll, Lieutenant H. J., R.N., 442
Harwich, mine-sweeping trawler at, 266; net-bases at, 375
Havana, sacked, 26
Havre, 47, 270, 279, 289
Hawk, the trawler, 446
HAWKE, H.M.S., sunk, 273, 333
Hawkins, John, voyages, 26–32; fight at San Juan de Ulua, 30–32
Hawthorne, Lieutenant-Commander W. H., R.N., 440; drowned, 442
Headlands, the s.s., sunk, 299, 300
Hebrides, the, 351
Hector, the trawler, 395; sunk, 397
Hefford, —, second officer of the s.s. *Lusitania*, drowned, 417
Heggie, D. W., master of the s.s. *Ben Cruachan*, 277
Heligoland, 352
Hellenic, the trawler, blown up, 407
Helsor, the German s.s., 124

Hemisphere, the s.s., captured, 174
Henry IV, 18
Henry V, 17; invasion of France, 14
Henry VI, 17
Henry VIII, establishment of the Royal Navy, 20; the *Great Harry*, 20; fleet, 20, 25; measures of defence, 20
HERMES, H.M.S., torpedoed, 334, 371
Heron, the trawler, 430
Hersilia, the armed yacht, 341
Hersing, Kapitän-Leutnant Otto, in command of U21, 270, 277, 376
Hève, Cape la, 270, 289
Highland Brae, the s.s., captured, 175
Highland Hope, the s.s., sunk, 154
Hilda and Ernest, the drifter, 364
Hill, Sir Maurice, 238
Hill, Sir Norman, member of the Committee on insurance of ships in war, 228, 231, 238
Hill, R. H., master of the s.s. *Holmwood*, 143
Hirose, the trawler, attacked by a submarine, 444; sunk, 445
Hoffnung, the s.s. (*Indrani*), 154, 160
HOGUE, H.M.S., sunk, 241, 254, 273, 329
Holger, the s.s., 174, 176
Holland, Hook of, 272, 276
Holland, rivalry on the seas, 43; tonnage of ships, 82; merchant traffic with, suspended, 407
Holmwood, the s.s., sunk, 143
Holton, E. J., master of the s.s. *Cervantes*, 164 *note*
Holyhead, 404; to Kingstown service, suspended, 376
Homer, the tug, attacked by a submarine, 313
Hood Island, 182
Hood, Rear-Admiral the Hon. Horace L. A., appointed in command of the Dover Patrol, 334; experiments on indicator nets, 373; on the sinking of U8 submarine, 389
Hopkins, Admiral Sir John O., 211
Hore, W. A. W., master of the s.s. *Ptarmigan*, 314
Horne, John, master of the s.s. *Hyndford*, 302
Hospital carriers, 6
Hostilius, the s.s., 139, 140

INDEX

Hotham, Captain Alan, R.N., 226
Howe, E., master of the s.s. *Bowes Castle*, 153
Hoxa Head, 354
Hoy Sound, 351
Huelva, 289
Hull, 263, 265
Humber, the, armed patrol at, 266, 320, 328, 370; minefield, 322, 328; shipping in, 363
Hume, Joseph, on the Merchant Navy, 76, 84
Humphreys, Sub-Lieutenant C. C., R.N.R., in command of the trawler *Yokohama*, 447
Hundred Years' War, 4, 13
Hunter, J. A., master of the s.s. *Dulwich*, 289
Hurstdale, the s.s., captured, 166
Hyades, the s.s., sunk, 142
Hydrophones, use of, 434
Hyndford, the s.s., attacked by a submarine, 302
Hythe, number of ships, 13
Hythe, the s.s., 337

Ikaria, the s.s., sunk, 278, 279
Ilex, the armed yacht, 341
ILTIS, the German gunboat, 128
Imperator, the German s.s., 124
Imperialist, the fishing-vessel, sunk, 328
Impressment, system of, 55–7, 97, 99; unpopularity, 98
Ina Williams, the trawler, attacked by a submarine, 446
Inchcape, Lord, member of the Committee on insurance of ships in war, 228
Inchgarvie, 381
Inchkeith, 329
Indian City, the s.s., sunk, 299, 300
Indian Empire, the trawler, 430
Indian Prince, the s.s., 421; captured, 171; sunk, 172
Indicator nets, use of, 369; experiments with, 374; working the, 383; number lost, 383
Indrani, the s.s., captured, 155, 160; sunk, 208
Indus, the s.s., sunk, 188, 189
Ingham, John, master of the s.s. *Bankfields*, 184
Inglefield, Admiral Sir Edward E. F., 224
Inglefield, Admiral Sir Frederick S., President of the Motor-Boat Reserve Committee, 326
Inishtrahull, 343, 402

Inishturk Island, 301
Insurance Clubs or Associations, 228–39; forms of policy, 238
Invercoe, the s.v., sunk, 178
Invergyle, the s.s., sunk, 299
Iona Island, 341
Ireland, mine-sweeping, 341–4; submarines, 429
Irish Sea, 266, 344, 383; submarines in the, 375, 403, 409; patrol, 435
IRON DUKE, H.M.S., 323, 353
Iron ships, 73, 95
Isdale, John, master of the s.s. *Ribera*, 196 *note*
Isis, the armed yacht, 341
Isle of Man, the patrol-boat, 291
Isle of Wight, 14, 47
Italy, tonnage of ships, 85, 87
Itolo, the German s.s., 127
Itonus, the s.s., 192 *note*
Iversen, Iver, master of the s.s. *Bellevue*, 173
Ivy Green, the drifter, 448

Jackdaw, the trawler, 368
Jackson, Rt. Hon. F. Huth, member of the Committee on insurance of ships in war, 228
Jacqueline, the Belgian trawler, 432
JAGUAR, the German gunboat, 128
Janus, the trawler, 266.
Japan, tonnage of ships, 85, 87
Japonica, the trawler, sunk, 445
JASON, H.M.S., 262, 343, 401
Jasper, the trawler, 266
Java, 41
Javelin, the trawler, 266
Jeanette, the armed yacht, 381, 435
Jeannies, the drifter, 393
Jellicoe, Admiral Sir John (Lord Jellicoe), 320; on the employment of armed trawlers, 324, 330; demand for trawlers, 334, 401; for Fleet sweepers, 337
Jenkinson, Anthony, mission to Persia, 23
John Company, 41
Johnson, Captain C. D., R.N., 388
Johnston, L. A., master of the s.s. *Glitra*, 269
Johnstone, George, master of the s.s. *Rio Ignassu*, 156
Jones, Arthur, master of the s.s. *Lynrowan*, 163 *note*
Jones, A. R., first officer of the s.s. *Lusitania*, 417; rescues passengers, 423

Jones, C. H., master of the s.s. *Nyanga*, 152
Jones, C. H., Registrar-General of Seamen, 111
Jones, H., master of the s.s. *Glenturret*, 202
Jones, Captain Harry, R.N., 224
Jones, James, master of the s.s. *Hostilius*, 141
Jones, Richard, master of the s.s. *Hemisphere*, 174
Journal of Royal United Service Institution, 58 note, 66 note, 68
Juan Fernandez Island, 145
Julia, the, 430

Kabinga, the s.s., captured, 188, 190; released, 192
Kaipara, the s.s., sunk, 151
KAISER WILHELM DER GROSSE, the German armed merchant cruiser, 126; captures and sinks British ships, 147, 151, 152, 208, 244; releases the s.s. *Galician*, 149–51
Kaiser Wilhelm II, the German s.s., 125; gun mountings, 121
Kaiserin Auguste Victoria, the German s.s., 124
KAISERIN ELIZABETH, the Austro-Hungarian cruiser, 127 note
KANGAROO, the destroyer, 388
KARLSRUHE, the German cruiser, 126, 128, 152; captures and sinks British ships, 153–69, 170, 208, 244, 246, 248
Katharine Park, the s.s., 143
Kelway, Lieutenant-Commander W. E., R.N.R., 305
Kersley, Sub-Lieutenant L. W., R.N.R., 440
Kidd, R. H., master of the s.s. *Chasehill*, 176
Kiehne, H. H., master of the s.s. *William P. Frye*, 179
Kigoma, the German s.s., 124
Kilcoan, the s.s., captured, 277; sunk, 278, 376
Kildalton, the s.v., sunk, 178
Killin, the s.s., sunk, 188, 190
KING EDWARD VII, H.M.S., 257
King Lud, the s.s., sunk, 196
King, W. J., master of the s.v. *Invercoe*, 178
Kingstown, 404
Kinnaird Head, 321, 371, 378
Kinneir, Douglas R., master of the s.s. *Ortega*, 144; skill, 145
Kinsale, 430

Kirkwall, 379
Kleist, the German s.s., 126
Kolbe, Oberleutnant, 276
König Albert, the German s.s., 126
König Friedrich August, the German s.s., 124
KÖNIGIN LUISE, the German minelayer, 124; lays mines, 136, 319, 328; sunk, 319
KÖNIGSBERG, the German cruiser, 126, 128; captures and sinks British ships, 137–9, 208, 244
KRONPRINZ WILHELM, the German armed merchant cruiser, 126, 170, 249; sinks British ships, 171–7, 208, 252; interned, 177
Kronprinzessin, the German s.s., 125
Kusaie Island, 204

Labadie Bank, 443
Labrador, 19
Ladd, W. H., master of the s.s. *Adenwen*, 299
Laertes, the s.s., 401; chased by a submarine, 286–8, 292, 380
La Hogue, Cape, 304
Lamont, A., master of the s.s. *Olivine*, 313
Lamorna Cove, 392
Lancaster, James, voyages, 40, 41
Lancefield, William, master of the s.s. *Delmira*, 303
Land's End, 298, 404
Larne, 339
Lauriat, Charles E., 421
Lawrence, F., master of the s.s. *Colchester*, 272
LEDA, the gunboat, attacked by a submarine, 333
Leinster, the s.s., sunk, 376
LEIPZIG, the German cruiser, 128; captures British ships, 180–85, 208
Le Marchant, Vice-Admiral E. R., in command of Kingstown area, 381; instructions to, 382
Lemvin, Cape, 197
LEONIDAS, the destroyer, 441
LEOPARD, the destroyer, 348
Lepanto, Bay of, 24
Lerwick, 436
Leslie, N., master of the s.s. *Clan Grant*, 198
Lestris, the s.s., bombed by an aeroplane, 294
Letters of marque, 14–16
Levant, the, 10
Leveson, Vice-Admiral Sir A. C.,

INDEX

head of the Operations Division of the War Staff, 250
Lighthouses and Trinity House, 76
Lily Oak, the drifter, 392
Limewold, the trawler, fight with a submarine, 437, 446
Linaria, the s.s., founders, 365
Linda Blanche, the s.s., sunk, 277, 376
Lindley, Arthur, member of the Committee on insurance of ships in war, 228
Liners and tramps, in the British Mercantile Marine, 87
Linsdell, the drifter, sunk, 328
Lisbon, the commercial depot for Western Europe, 19
LIVELY, the destroyer, 348
Liverpool, 13, 289; number of privateers, 45; Underwriters' Registry for Iron Vessels, 95 *note*; work of the tugs, 340; armed patrol at, 370
Lizard, the, 392, 399
Lizzie, the s.s., 303
Lloyd's Register of British and Foreign Shipping, 94–7; "ships' lists," 94
Loch Ewe, 322, 333; armed patrol at, 327, 335, 341, 351, 370
Loch Indail, 340
Loch Shell, 341
Lockwood, the s.s., sunk, 313
London, measures of defence, 20; the trading centre of the world, 63; Naval Conference in, 118, 122
London Trader, the s.s., 279
Long, —, master of the s.s. *Troilus*, 199
Longcraig Pier, 381
Longhope, 379
Looe, 13, 399
Loredano, the Italian s.s., 191
Lorna, the armed yacht, 340
Lorton, the Peruvian barque, 147
Lossiemouth, 369
Lotusmere, the s.s., 192 *note*
Lough Larne, armed patrol at, 370; net-bases at, 382
Lough Swilly, minefield, 339; armed patrol at, 370
Lovat, the s.s., sunk, 188, 189
Lowestoft, 320
Lowry, Admiral Sir Robert, 319, 330, 390
LUCHS, the German gunboat, 128, 177
Lucida, the trawler, 430

Lüdecke, Captain (DRESDEN), 140
Lugg, Herbert, master of s.s. *Headlands*, 300
Lundy Island, 435, 444
Luneda, the trawler, 430
Lusitania, the s.s., 123; sunk, 410–27; construction and cost, 411; rumours of attack, 412; cargo, 413, 414; voyage, 414–18; torpedoed, 418–21; "S.O.S." signal, 430; rescue of passengers, 430
Lydia, the s.s., captured, 163; sunk, 164
Lynns Point, 289
Lynton Grange, the s.s., 139, 140
LYNX, the destroyer, 333, 337
LYSANDER, the destroyer, 401

Maas lightship, 276
McKenna, Rt. Hon. Reginald, First Lord of the Admiralty, 115, 260
Mackey, —, first mate of the s.s. *Atalanta*, 301
MacLarnon, J., master of the s.s. *Atalanta*, 301
Madras Harbour, attack on oil-tanks, 193
Magellan Straits, 36, 39, 144
Mahan, Admiral, *Naval Strategy*, extracts from, 3, 4, 5; *Influence of Sea Power on the French Revolution*, 51, 65 *note*, 66 *note*, 67 *note*
Makalla, port of, 138
Makepeace, H., master of the s.s. *Kaipara*, 151
Malacca Straits, 40
Malachite, the s.s., captured, 270; sunk, 271, 368, 371, 376
Maldive Islands, 197
Malekula, 177
Malley, L., master of the s.s. *Andalusian*, 300
Manchester Commerce, the s.s., sunk, 338, 341
Maneely, James, master of the s.s. *Kilcoan*, 277
Manisty, Paymaster-Captain H. Elden, R.N., Organising Manager of Convoys 226
MAORI, the destroyer, 388
Maple Branch, the s.s., sunk, 154
Maraca Island, 153
Margaret, the trawler, 277
Margate, the trawler, 430
Maria, the Dutch s.s., captured, 155
Mariana Islands, 177

Maricopa, the s.s., strikes a mine, 408
Marie, the German s.s., 180 ; sunk, 181
Marine insurance, system of, criticised (1884), 79
Markomannia, the German s.s., 188
Marlvo, the s.s., stranded, 208
Marshall Islands, 177
Martin, Richard, master of the s.s. *City of Bremen*, 313
Martin, Thomas, master of the s.s. *Hartdale*, 301
Martin, the trawler, 390
Mary Ada Short, the s.s., sunk, 178
Mary, the trawler, strikes a mine, 349
Marynthea, the armed yacht, 381, 435
Marys, the drifter, 448
Mason, J., master of the s.s. *Strathroy*, 153
Masson, Stephen, master of the s.s. *Malachite*, 270
Master (Laws of Oleron), qualifications, 10 ; duties, 11 ; relations with the crew, 11
Matthews, J. R., master of the s.s. *Newburn*, 203
Mauretania, the s.s., 123, 411
Max Brock, the German s.s., 127
Maximus, the trawler, 430
May Island, 329
May Island, the trawler, 390
Mayer, Judge, judgment on the s.s. *Lusitania*, 412, 414
Medusa, the armed yacht, 381, 435
Medway, the, 320
Membland, the s.s., fate of, 288
Mercantile Marine Act of 1540, 21 ; of 1850, 111
Merchant Adventurers, Association of, 18, 21, 22
Merchant Navy, British, forerunner of the Royal Navy, vii ; history, 1, 8 ; tributes to, 2 ; responsibilities on the outbreak of war, 6 ; growth, 71 ; report on the condition, 73–8, 100–103 ; reforms, 79 ; progress, 80 ; personnel, 100, 116 ; measures for protecting, 210–16 ; defence policy, 216–23 ; relations with the Admiralty, 227 ; War Insurance Schemes, 228–39
Merchant seamen,campaign against, v ; patriotism, vi, 1, 2 ; characteristics, vii, 1, 2, 304 ; record of services in wars, 7 ; actions with privateers, 48 ; peril of capture, 54 ; seized by the pressgang, 55 ; General Register Office of, 105, 107 ; register ticket, 107 ; abolished, 108 ; taken prisoners, 131 ; antipathy to Germans, 393
Merchant Seamen's Act of 1835, 98, 105 ; Fund, 104, 106 ; wound up, 104 *note*, 108
Merchant Shipping Act of 1854, 111 ; of 1873, 78
Mersey, Lord, Wreck Commissioner, judgment on the s.s. *Falaba*, 309–12 ; on the s.s. *Lusitania*, 422 ; on the conduct of the master, 425
Methil, armed trawlers at, 335
Middlesbrough, 297
Middleton, John, Vice-Admiral, 41
Milford Haven, 263, 266 ; armed patrol at, 265, 344, 370
Milford Haven, Admiral the Marquis of, Director of Naval Intelligence, 211
Milne, A. B., master of the s.s. *Blonde*, 294
Minch, the, 334, 350
Mine, the " Cruiser," 406
Minefields, 267, 319, 322, 328, 337, 338, 339, 344, 345, 357, 360, 402, 406–9 ; method of destroying, 259
Mines, laying of, 118, 135 ; destruction of, 364, 403, 407, 408
Mine-sweepers, British, 320 ; work of the, 331, 343, 361 ; five classes of, 401
Mine-sweeping, experiments with, 258 ; instruction, 260
Minikoi Island, 194, 196, 201
Mining Committee, 259
Minterne, the s.s., sunk, 410
Minto, D. K., master of the s.s. *Invergyle*, 299
Mississippi, the, 81
Miura, the trawler, 440 ; fight with a submarine, 441
Mizen Head, 417, 429, 446
Mobile, the s.s., sunk, 314, 401
MOHAWK, the destroyer, chase of submarines, 333
Moltke, Count von, on wars, 4
MOLTKE, the German battle-cruiser, 357
Moltke, the German s.s., 126
MONARCH, H.M.S., 323
Moray Firth, patrol of the, 320, 350

INDEX

465

Morgenroth, Leutnant (U8), 387
Morrison, John, master of s.s. *Hyades*, 142
Morton, Leslie N., rescues passengers from the s.s. *Lusitania*, 422
Morwenna, the s.s., torpedoed, 432
Motor-Boat Reserve, 326; Committee, 326; organisation, 327
Motor-boats, 255, 325; launches, 255
Mounts Bay, 20
MOUSQUET, the French destroyer, sunk, 203
Mozambique, 139
Muckle Skerry, 355
Muir, Commander H. G., R.N.R., of the boarding-steamer *Sarnia*, 398
Mull of Cantyre, 339, 340, 343
Mull of Galloway, 435
Müller, Captain von, of the German cruiser EMDEN, 186, 202
Murray, Sir James (Foreign Office), report on the decline of the shipping industry, 77, 103
Murrison, A., master of the s.s. *La Correntina*, 172

Nagle, R. F., master of the s.s. *Niceto de Larrinaga*, 163 note
Napoleon, Emperor, method of raising an army, 3; exile, 44; declares a blockade of Great Britain, 58; defeated at Waterloo, 71
Narcissus, the armed yacht, 381, 435
Nauru, 204
Naval and Mercantile Services, difference between, 20, 43
Naval Chronicle, 47 note, 49 note, 50 note, 64 note, 66 note
Naval Intelligence Department, 224
Navigation Acts, 16, 43; Laws, 72; repeal of the, 73, 78; repeal of the Manning clauses, 108
Navy, British Merchant; *see* Merchant Navy
Navy Estimates, 110, 121, 260
Navy, Royal, creation, vii, 1, 20; system of continuous service, 3, 97, 99; inadequate resources, 6; impress service, 56
Naze, the, 334
Nebraskan, the American s.s., torpedoed, 431
Neckar, the German s.s., 126
Nelson, Lord, policy, 5; demand for frigates, 58; on the system of registration, 98
Nelson's Strait, 144; navigation of, 145
NEPTUNE, H.M.S., 344
Netherlands, the, 16; tonnage of ships, 85, 87
Nets, indicator, use of, 369; experiments with, 374; working the, 383; number lost, 383
Nettleingham, Sub-Lieutenant, R.N.R., 446; awarded the D.S.C., 447
Neuerburg, Oberleutnant, on the sinking of the U18, 355
Newburn, the s.s., 203
New Dawn, the drifter, 439
Newfoundland, 39
Newhaven, 47
Newmarket, the s.s., 337
Newquay, 399
NEW ZEALAND, H.M.S., 258, 324
New Zealand Shipping Co., ships fitted with guns, 124
Niblet, the trawler, 277
Niceto de Larrinaga, the s.s., sunk, 163
Nicholson, Rear-Admiral Stuart, bombardment of Zeebrugge, 352
Nicobar Islands, 40
NIGER, H.M.S., torpedoed, 351, 371
Night Hawk, the trawler, founders, 364
Nine Sisters, the drifter, 373
Ningchow, the s.s., escapes from a submarine, 296
Noel, Admiral Sir Gerard H. W., 210
Nombre de Dios, expedition against, 32
Nore, the, armed patrol at, 266, 318, 370, 371; net-bases at, 375
Norfolk, Virginia, report of the British Consul on the merchant seamen, 103
Norman corsairs, activity of, 14 note
Normandy, 47
Norris, A. C., master of the s.s. *Charcas*, 178
North Channel, 339; nets in the, 383; patrol, 435
North Foreland, 294, 320, 331, 337
North Keeling Island, 195 note
North Sea, 47, 266, 320, 344, 357; minefields, 345, 408; submarines in, 404, 409; patrol, 436
North Shields, 265; mine-sweeping trawler at, 266

466   INDEX

North Wales, the s.s., 145; sunk, 146
Northern Patrol, 125
Northlands, the s.s., sunk, 313
Norway, tonnage of ships, 82, 85, 87
NUBIAN, the destroyer, 389
NÜRNBERG, the German cruiser, 128
Nyanga, the s.s., sunk, 152
NYMPHE, the destroyer, strikes a submarine, 333

Oakby, the s.s., 136; sunk, 291
Ocana, the fishing-vessel, founders, 359, 366
Ocean Island, 204
Oceanic II, the trawler, 446
Odell, —, skipper of the trawler *Coquet*, 396
Old Head of Kinsale, 410, 417
Oleron, Laws of, 10
Olive Branch, the trawler, 390
Olivine, the s.s., sunk, 313
Ontario, the trawler, fight with a submarine, 438
Orfordness, 63, 319
Oriana, the armed yacht, 340, 341, 342
Orianda, the trawler, blown up, 362, 365
Oriole, the s.s., fate of, 279
ORION, H.M.S., 323
Orkney Islands, 323; armed patrol at, 370, 379
Oronsay, 344
Ortega, the s.s., escapes capture, 144
Osborne Stroud, the trawler, 266
Osceola, the s.s., bombed by an aeroplane, 294
Ostend, 322; nets laid off, 401
Ostmark, the German s.s., 138
OTTER, the German river-gunboat, 128
Ottley, Rear-Admiral Sir Charles O., Director of Naval Intelligence, 224
Ousel, the s.s., bombed by an aeroplane, 294
Outer Dowsing lightvessel, 320, 321, 322
Owen, Sir Douglas, 239
Owen, Sub-Lieutenant E. L., R.N.R., in command of drifters, 386
Owen, G., master of the s.s. *North Wales*, 145

Paddle-steamers as mine-sweepers, 255, 332, 401, 439

Paget, Admiral Sir Alfred, in command of the steam-yacht *Eileen*, 363
Pandion, the s.s., bombed by an aeroplane, 294
Para, 158, 168
Parker, Admiral Sir William, description of a convoy, 52
Parks, C. W., master of the s.v. *Wilfrid M.*, 175
Parsons, Lieutenant G. C., R.N., in command of the trawler *Passing*, 362
Pascoe, John, 61
Passing, the trawler, strikes a mine, 362
Patagonia, the s.s., 153
Paterson, H., master of the s.s. *Katharine Park*, 143
PATHFINDER, H.M.S., sunk, 273, 329
Pearce, W., skipper of the trawler *Dane*, 365
Peel 12, the, 421
Pegg, H., skipper of the trawler *Cassandra*, in a naval engagement, 359
Pellew, Rear-Admiral Sir Edward, 51; *see* H.M.S. EXMOUTH
Penang, 202
Pengilly, third officer of the s.s. *Falaba*, 309
Pennsylvania, the German s.s., 125
Pentland Firth, 331, 350, 353
Penzance Bay, 392
Pernambuco, 142, 448; report of the British Consul on the treatment of the merchant seamen, 103
Peru, 37
Peterhead, armed patrols at, 321, 335, 370; rewarded, 446; net-bases at, 375
Philip of Spain, marriage, 24; seizes English vessels, 27
Philipps, Sir Owen, Chairman of the Royal Mail Steam Packet Co., 120
Phillimore, Admiral Sir Augustus, 112 *note*
Phillimore, A., *Life of Admiral Sir William Parker*, 53 *note*, 55 *note*
Phillimore, Captain R. F., 258
Phillimore, Captain V. E. B., in charge of patrol at Falmouth, 399
Picton Island, 184
Pilcher, N. B., master of the s.s. *Indrani*, 155

INDEX

Pilot, a defaulting, punishment of, 12
Pine Islands, 33
Piracy, practice of, in home waters, 10, 14, 26
Pisa, first English Consul at, 19
Plimsoll, Samuel, on " coffin-ships," 78
Plymouth, 13, 29 ; patrol at, 434
Pohl, Admiral von, Chief of the Admiralty Staff of the German Navy, proclamation, 283
Pond, R. R., master of the s.s. *Highland Brae*, 175
Ponrabbel, the dredger, sunk, 198
Pontoporos, the Greek s.s., captured, 189, 194
Poole, net-bases at, 375 ; patrol at, 434
Pope, the, partition of the New World, 23
Port Mahomack, 321
Portia, the armed yacht, 390
Portland, 64 ; experiments with mine-sweepers at, 258 ; armed patrol, 265, 266, 370, 434 ; demand for trawlers, 351 ; net-bases at, 375
Porto Rico, 41
Portsmouth, 47 ; armed patrol at, 265, 266, 370 ; demand for drifters, 351 ; net-bases at, 375
Portugal, the first maritime Power, 19
Potaro, the s.s., captured, 174 ; looted, 175, 176 ; sunk, 208
Pratonia, the German s.s., 124
Prescott, T. R., master of the s.s. *Cambank*, 289
President, The, the s.s., sunk, 314
President Grant, the s.s., 125
President Lincoln, the s.s., 125
Press-gang, methods of, 55 ; abolition, 98
Preston, Commander Lionel G., R.N., in charge of gunboats, 318, 361
Prestridge, Sub-Lieutenant, R.N.R., 448
Primo, the s.s., sunk, 271, 371, 376
Prince Edward, the paddle-steamer, 378 ; lays nets off Ostend, 401
Princess Alice, the German s.s., 127
Princess Olga, the s.s., founders, 360
Princess Victoria, the s.s., sunk, 297
Prinz Adalbert, the German s.s., 127

PRINZ EITEL FRIEDRICH, the German armed merchant cruiser, 126, 249 ; sinks British ships, 177-9, 208 ; interned, 179
Prinz Heinrick, the German s.s., 127
Prinz Ludwig, the German s.s., 124
Prinz Oskar, the German s.s., 126
Privateering, system of, legalised, 14
Privateers, French, actions against British ships, 48-50
Prize Code, 132-4 ; procedure, 133
Progress, the trawler, 395 ; chased by a submarine, 396 ; sunk, 396
Propert, William H., master of the s.s. *Laertes*, 286 ; account of the escape from a submarine, 286-8 ; awarded the D.S.C. and made Lieutenant R.N.R., 288
Prussia, tonnage of ships, 82
Prussia, the German s.s., 142
Pruth, the s.s., captured, 164 ; sunk, 165
Ptarmigan, the s.s., sunk, 314
Purdy, S., master of the s.s. *Conder*, 165 note

Queen Alexandra, the drifter, 448
Queen Victoria, the paddle-steamer, 378 ; lays nets off Ostend, 401
Queenstown, armed patrol at, 266, 341, 371

RACOON, H.M.S., 66
Rajput, the s.s., 192 note
Raleigh, Sir Walter, 39
Ramsgate, 63
Rangoon, 193
Ratcliffe, J., master of the s.s. *Western Coast*, 291
Rathlin Island, 382
Rattray Head, 371, 378, 436
Read, Charles, skipper of the trawler *Alonso*, 347 ; gift to, 348
Recolo, the trawler, founders, 402
Record of American and Foreign Shipping, 95 note
RECRUIT, the destroyer, torpedoed, 440
Red Book, 94
Reform Bill of 1832, 98
Reindeer, the s.s., 337, 430
Reliance, the trawler, 430
Restango, the trawler, 430
Reverto, the trawler, 408
Revigo, the fishing-vessel, founders, 328

Rhakotis, the s.s., 146
RIASAN, the Russian volunteer s.s., captured and renamed CORMORAN, 188
Ribera, the s.s., sunk, 196
Richard I, expedition to the Holy Land, 9; last crusade, 10
RINGDOVE, H.M.S., 329
Rio de la Hacha, 29, 30
Rio Iguassu, the s.s., captured, 154, 156; sunk, 157
Rio Negro, the s.s., 154, 155, 156
Rio Parana, the s.s., sunk, 291
Rival, the drifter, attacks a submarine, 391
Robeck, Admiral Sir John M. de, scheme of organisation for the Motor-Boat Reserve, 327
Roberts, J., of the s.s. *Elsinore*, taken prisoner by the German cruiser LEIPZIG, 180; transferred to the German s.s. *Marie*, 181-3; at Chatham Island, 183; Guayaquil, 184
Robertson, Matthew, master of the s.s. *Ikaria*, 279
Robertson, Neil, master of the s.s. *The President*, 314
Robinson, Stanley, of the s.s. *Oakby*, awarded the Bronze Medal, 291
Robinson, Thomas, master of the s.s. *Kabinga*, 190, 192 note
Roburn, the drifter, 388
Rodjestvensky, Admiral, coaling difficulties, 5
Roebuck, the s.s., 337
Romney Cinque Port, 9
Roosevelt, Theodore, on the sinking of the s.s. *Lusitania*, 425
Rosarina, La, the s.s., chased by a submarine, 173 note, 314
Rose, the trawler, 262
Roses, Wars of the, 13, 82 note
Ross, Sir John, *Memoirs and Correspondence of Admiral Lord de Saumarez*, 53 note
Ross, W. H., master of the s.s. *Trabboch*, 191
Rosslare, submarine base at, 382
Rosyth, 329; armed patrol at, 335, 370
Row, Sir Thomas, Ambassador to the Grand Mogul, 43
Rowe, James, *History of Flushing*, 61 note
Royal Fleet Reserve, 113, 115
Royal Mail Steam Packet Co., 120; ships fitted with guns, 124
Royal Naval Coast Volunteers, 112
Royal Naval Reserve, issue of tickets, 109; formation of a voluntary, 110, 111; history, 112; system of training, 114
Royal Navy; *see* Navy
Royal Sceptre, the s.s., 169
Royal Sovereign, the lightvessel, 290, 291
Ruby, the schooner (U.S.A.), 315
Runnelstone, 392
Runo, the s.s., sunk, 328
RUSSELL, H.M.S., 352
Russia, isolation, 7; tonnage of ships, 87
Russo-Japanese War, value of mines, 261
Rye, 41; Cinque Port, 9, 13; ravaged by a French fleet, 17

" S90," the German destroyer, 128
Sabang, 139
Sagitta, the armed yacht, 402, 408
Sailing-vessels, crews, 53; tonnage, 88; number of trading, 92; speed, 117
Sailors, impressment of, 12
St. Abb's Head, 322, 331, 334
St. Alban's Head, 380, 383, 400
St. Andrew, the hospital ship, attacked by a submarine, 385
St. Ann's Head, 309, 443, 448
St. Bride's Bay, 449
St. Catherine's Point, 313, 380, 400
St. Egbert, the s.s., captured, 198, 200; released, 198, 202
St. George's Channel, 339; netted, 382
St. Govan's Lightship, 435
St. Jean de Luz, 46
St. John's Point, 435
St. Julian, port, 36
St. Malo, 47; siege of, 17, 18
St. Nicholas, Bay of, 22
Saint Pierre, French mine-sweeper, 279
St. Valery-en-Caux, 380
Salisbury, Earl of, appointed Commissioner, 17
San Antonio, 185
San Christoval, 207
San Juan de Ulua, 30
San Paulo, the Brazilian s.s., 168
San Wilfrido, the s.s., 135
Sandwich Cinque Port, 9, 13; battle, 9
Sandy Cape, 207
Santa Isabel, the German s.s., 185; sunk, 185
Sapphire, the armed yacht, 381, 435

Sappho, the s.s., detained at Hamburg, 130
Sarba, the trawler, 430
Sarchet, J. B., of the s.s. Benmohr, 198 note
Sarepta, the drifter, 386
Sarnia, the armed boarding-steamer, attacked by a submarine, 397
Satow, Sir Ernest, at The Hague Conference, 118
Saumarez, Admiral Lord de, 53
Savannah, report of the British Consul on the merchant seamen, 103
Scadaun, the drifter, 431
Scapa Flow, 322, 353; armed trawlers at, 335, 349
Scarborough, raid on, 337, 357; minefield, 360–66; free of mines, 406
Sceptre, the s.s., 168
SCHARNHORST, the German battle-cruiser, 124, 128, 177
Schouwen Bank, 286, 333
Schwieger, Kapitän-Leutnant, in command of U20, 410; sinks the s.s. Lusitania, 418 note; in command of U88, 427; drowned, 428
Scilly Islands, 299, 400; wireless station at St. Mary's, 400
Scotch motor fishing-boats, 350
Scott, Admiral Sir Percy, 351
Scott, Captain R. F., 224
Scott, T. H., master of the s.s. Lochwood, 313
Sea power, influence of, 3
Seaflower, the trawler, 260, 321
Seagull, the motor-boat, 430
Seamen of the Cinque Ports, 9; privileges, 9; period of service, 9
Seamew, the trawler, 260, 321
Sedulous, the drifter, 373, 374
Selsey Bill, 47, 63
Semantha, the Norwegian barque, sunk, 175
Semmes, Captain, 186
Senior, Sub-Lieutenant W. A., R.N.R., 364
Serula, the s.s., bombed by an aeroplane, 294
Seven Seas, the s.s., sunk, 313
Severn, the s.s., attacked by a submarine, 333
SEYDLITZ, the German battle-cruiser, 357
Seydlitz, the German s.s., 127, 185
Shannon River, 429

Sharp, J. T., master of the s.s. Serula, 295
Sharp, W., master of the s.s. Kildalton, 178
Sharpness, 448
Shaw, Savill and Albion, Ltd., ships fitted with guns, 124
Sheerman, C. (gunner), 148
Sheerness, mine-sweeping trawler at, 265
Shelomi, the trawler, 386
Shetlands, the, armed patrol at, 328, 350, 370, 379
Ship money, institution of, 43
Shipbuilding, 17, 42, 58, 85
Shipowners, charges against, 84; policy in a naval war, 214; Red Book, 94
Shipping Acts, 78, 84, 111
Shipping, Admiralty directions to, 239
Shipping and Shipbuilding, Report of the Committee on, 85 note, 88, 89
Shipping industry, 72; cause of the decline, 73–8; progress, 80, 84; records, 94; measures of protection, 210, 212, 220; war insurance schemes, 228; instructions against detention, 246; issue of daily voyage notices, 250
Shipping Intelligence Officers, appointed, 242; instructions, 243–5
Shipping, memorandum on the safety, 247
Shipping, Registers of, 110 note
Ships, merchant, regulations, 10–13; captured in the Revolutionary and Napoleonic Wars, 44, 46, 48; tonnage, 54, 68 note, 80, 82, 85–94; losses, 57, 62, 66–9; registered during the Revolutionary and Napoleonic Wars, 69; wrecked, report of the Committee, 73, 76; armament of, 120; fitted with guns, 124; detained at Hamburg, 130; "Traffic Instructions," 242; policy of dispersal, 242, 243; attacked by submarines, 133–209, 268–80, 285–93, 296–317, 330, 333, 416–18, 443–6; by aeroplanes, 293–5; strike mines, 328, 339, 343, 349, 359–65, 402–4, 407, 409, 410, 440
Ships of the Line, number of, 1804–1814, 59

Shipwash Lightship, 383
Shrewsbury, Earl of, appointed Commissioner, 17
Shrovder, Lieutenant, of the German cruiser KARLSRUHE, 154
Siamese Prince, the s.s., 143
Sidonia, Medina, defeat of, 38
Siegal, Admiral (German), 118
Sierra Cordoba, the German s.s., 172 *note*
Sierra Leone, 27
Simpson, H. L., master of the s.s. *Lynton Grange*, 140
Skerryvore, 343, 344
SKIPJACK, H.M.S., 343, 351, 356, 361, 362, 401
Skudesnaes, 269, 333
Slade, Admiral Sir Edmond J. W., Director of Naval Intelligence, 224, 259
Slavery, custom of, 26
Sloops, 64 ; mine-sweepers, 401
Sluys, Battle of, 13
Smaridge, H. S., master of the s.s. *Indus*, 189
Smith, Charles, skipper of the trawler *Tubal Cain*, 147
Smith, Sir H. Llewelyn, Secretary of the Board of Trade, 238
Smith's Knoll, 345, 346, 348, 349
Smyth's Channel, 145
Snowline, E. V., skipper of the drifter *Hilda and Ernest*, gallantry, 364 ; awarded the D.S.C., 364
Soda Island, 139
Solent, the, 255, 351
Solomon Islands, 207
Solon, the trawler, 364
Souter, John, master of the s.s. *Blackwood*, 297
Southampton, ships at, 17
South Cross Sand, 348
South Goodwin Lightship, hydrophone installed, 434
South Goodwins, 320, 331
Southport, the s.s., escape of the, 204–9
South Sea, 36
South Stack, 404
Southwold, 319, 320 ; minefield, 328
Spanish Armada, defeat of the, 38
Spanish Indies, reprisals on, 38
Sparrow, the trawler, 260
Spee, Admiral von, in command of the German Pacific Squadron, 140 ; at the Marshall Islands, 177
SPEEDWELL, H.M.S., 343

SPEEDY, the gunboat, sunk, 328
Spider, the trawler, 260
Spithead, 47, 400 ; fleet at, 20
Spreewald, the German s.s., 126
Spurn Head, 322, 347, 360, 395
Staalbierghuk, 147
Stablefold, Sub-Lieutenant A., R.N.R., 440
Stadt Schleswig, the German s.s., 153
Staffa, the s.s., bombed by an aeroplane, 294
STAG, the destroyer, 329
Star of Britain, the trawler, strikes a mine, 362
Start Bay, 383
Staten Island, 184
Stavanger, 269
Steam-engine, 2, 4, 95 ; invention, 72
Steam-vessels, tonnage, 81, 85–7, 90–94, 236 ; average size, 87 ; number of trading, 92–4
Steam-yachts, 255
Steel, —, master of the s.s. *Gryfevale*, account of his capture, 195
Steel's Navy List, 56 *note*
Stephens, —, of the s.s. *Lusitania*, drowned, 418
Stileman, Rear-Admiral Sir H. H., in command of Liverpool Area, 381
Store ships, 6
Stormcock, the Admiralty tug, 430
Stornoway, base at, 351, 378
Stoss, Kapitän-Leutnant, of the U8, 387
Strathisla, the trawler, 390
Strathroy, the s.s., captured, 153 ; sunk, 154, 159
Stromness, 379
Sturdee, Admiral Sir Doveton, President of the Channel Fleet Committee, 258
Sturton, Lord, appointed Commissioner, 17
Styne Head, 301
Submarine Attack, Committee on, 368
Submarines, German, 212, 216, 254 ; number of, 273 ; warfare, v, 54, 268–80, 285, 293, 296–317, 329, 332, 371, 376, 380, 385, 395–7, 402–5, 409, 431–3, 440, 443–9 ; sunk, 385–91, 441, 446 ; net-cutting device, 392 ; measures against, 433–7
Sudmark, the German s.s., 126

INDEX

Suffolk coast, minefield, 267, 320
SUFFOLK, H.M.S., 170
Supply of Food and Raw Material in Time of War, Report on, 210-16, 224, 227, 228
Surcouf, Robert, 48
Sutterton, the trawler, 402, 407
Swansea, 13
Swarte area, minefield, 403, 406
Sweden, tonnage of ships, 82, 85, 87
SWIFT, H.M.S., attacked by a submarine, 333
Sybil Point, 436
SYDNEY, H.M.A.S., 204; sinks the EMDEN, 195 *note*

Table Bay, 40
Tabora, the German s.s., 126
Tagus Cove, 182
Tainui, the s.s., armed, 121
TAKU, the German destroyer, 128
Tamar, the s.s., sunk, 176, 252
Tangistan, the s.s., sunk, 297
Tara, the s.s., 341
Tarawa, 204
Tasman, the Dutch s.s., 208
Taylor, A. S., master of the s.s. *Northlands*, 313
Taylor, F. G., master of the s.s. *Buresk*, account of the EMDEN, 196-8
Tees, the, 75
Territorial Army, 2
Thames, the, 63, 321
THESEUS, H.M.S., attacked by a submarine, 333
Thierfelder, Lieutenant-Commander, of the German armed merchant cruiser KRONPRINZ WILHELM, 171
Thomas W. Irvine, the s.s., blown up, 322
Thompson, G., and Co., ships fitted with guns, 124
Thompson, J. B., master of the s.s. *Highland Hope*, 154
Thompson, R. J., master of the s.s. *Diplomat*, 190
Thordis, the s.s., 385; damages a submarine, 292
Thornton Ridge, 374, 440
TIGER, the German gunboat, 128, 177
Tillard, Lieutenant-Commander George E., R.N., 335
Tirpitz, Admiral von, on the submarine policy, 274; approval of the sinking of the s.s. *Lusitania*, 427

Tokio, the trawler, 354; rewarded, 356
Tokomaru, the s.s., sunk, 278
Toole, J. C., sole survivor of the s.s. *Tangistan*, 298
Torbay, 47, 52
Torpedo-boat No. 13, surrounded by mines, 322; No. 027, 399; No. 91, attacked by torpedoes, 351
Tory Island, 46; minefield, 338, 378, 403, 408
Tosto, the s.s., 317
Trabboch, the s.s., sunk, 191
Trade, Board of, administration of the Merchant Navy, 1, 227; Marine Department, 78, 84, 238; report on shipping, 82
Trade Division of the War Staff, creation of the, 224; abolished, 225; reformed, 225, 226; instructions to shipowners, 243, 246, 248; memorandum on the safety of British shipping, 247; issue of daily voyage notices, 250
Trafalgar, victory at, 44, 57
Tramps, 87; value of, 88; rate of steaming, 117
Trawler Flotilla, the Northern, 323, 370
Trawler Reserve, recruiting, 262
Trawler Section, regulations, 261
Trawlers, 255, 257; experiments with, 258; chartered for minesweeping, 260, 265, 318, 320; scheme of mobilisation, 264; number of, 260, 335, 372, 400; work of the, 320, 322, 352, 361, 362, 401; demand for, 322, 324, 334, 342, 351; armed, 330, 335, 368; fitted with explosive sweeps, 334, 351; strike mines, 362; methods of disguise, 443
Trendall, T. W., skipper of the trawler *Solon*, awarded the D.S.C., 364
Trevose Head, 305
Tritonia, the s.s., founders, 343
Troilus, the s.s., captured, 198-200; sunk, 201
TSINGTAU, the German gunboat, 128, 205, 206
Tubal Cain, the trawler, captured, 147; sunk, 148
Tulloch, T. T., master of the s.s. *Tymeric*, 194
Tupper, Admiral Sir Reginald, in charge of Area I, 378
Turnbull, Corporal, R.A.M.C., on German atrocity, 311

INDEX

Turnbull, J. S., second engineer of the s.s. *Harpalyce*, 315
Turnbull Martin & Co., ship fitted with guns, 124
Turner, W. T., master of the s.s. *Lusitania*, 414; criticisms on, 424; rescued, 425
Tymeric, the s.s., 194; sunk, 195, 196
Tyne, the, 75, 299; minefield, 322, 328; armed patrol at, 328, 370
Tyrwhitt, Rear-Admiral Sir Reginald, Bt., 346

U7, submarine, sinks British ship, 316
U8, sunk, 387, 389
U9, sinks British ships, 254, 273, 329
U12, sinks British ship, 298; sunk, 390
U14, sunk, 446
U15, sunk, 322
U16, sinks British ships, 380
U17, captures the s.s. *Glitra*, 269
U18, career, 352–4; rammed, 354; sunk, 355
U19, sinks British ships, 276, 377
U20, sinks British ships, 278, 410
U21, sinks British ships, 270, 271, 273, 277, 329, 368, 376
U24, sinks British ship, 371
U28, sinks British ships, 312
U29, sinks British ships, 299, 300; sunk, 300 *note*
U30, sinks British ship, 289
U34, sinks British ships, 445
U35, sinks British ships, 448
U37, sinks British ships, 303
U88, 427; sunk, 428
UNDAUNTED, H.M.S., attacked by a submarine, 380
Underwriters, *Green Book*, 94
United States, Merchant Navy, 81; Civil War, 81; tonnage, 82, 85
Unity, the drifter, 438
Uxbridge, the trawler, sunk, 407

Vaaren, the s.s., founders, 360
Valiant, the armed yacht, 381, 435; strikes a mine, 363
Vanduara, the s.s., fires on a submarine, 376
Vandyck, the s.s., captured, 166–8
Vanilla, the trawler, torpedoed, 402
Varild, the s.s., 442
Varne Buoy, 388; Lightship, hydrophone installed, 434

VATERLAND, the German gunboat, 128
Vaterland, the German s.s., 125
Venetia, the armed yacht, 325
Vera Cruz, 30
Verbena, the trawler, 430
VERNON, H.M.S., 258, 260
Victoria, the trawler, attacked by a submarine, 443; sunk, 444
Victoria Luise, the German s.s., 124
VICTORIOUS, H.M.S., 348, 359
Vigilant, the trawler, 446
VIKING, the destroyer, 384, 387, 391
Ville de Lille, the French s.s., sunk, 380
VON DER TANN, the German battle-cruiser, 357
Vosges, the s.s., attacked by a submarine, 304–6; sunk, 306

Walhalla, the German s.s., 171
Walmesley, J. B., the s.v., 422
Walney Island, 375
Walters, Commander R. H., R.N., of the s.s. *Brighton Queen*, 362
War-Book, the, 221
War Risks Insurance Clubs or Associations, 228–39; forms of policy, 238
War Risks Insurance Office, 239
War Staff, Trade Branch of the Operations Division of the, 225, 250; Trade Division, 226
Ward, Francis, skipper of the trawler *Hirose*, 444
Warrior, the Admiralty tug, 430
Warter Priory, the trawler, 368
Wash, the, 318
Waterloo, Battle of, 71
Watling Island, 170
Wawn, —, master of the s.s. *Harpalyce*, 314
Webb, Rear-Admiral Sir Richard, Director of the Trade Division of the War Staff, 149 *note*, 225, 226
Weddigen, Otto von, 273, 300
Wedgwood, J., master of the s.s. *Willerby*, 178
Wenlock, the drifter, 299
Weselly, A., wireless operator of the s.s. *Kabinga*, 192 *note*
Western Coast, the s.s., sunk, 291
Westerwald, the German s.s., 126
West India Islands, French, 50
West Loch Tarbert, 351
Westminster, the s.s., 207
WEYMOUTH, H.M.S., 198

INDEX

Whincop, C. A., master of the s.s. *Primo*, 271
Whitby, bombardment of, 358
White Oak, the drifter, 384
White Star Line, ships fitted with guns, 124
Whitehead, Captain Frederic A., R.N., Director of Mercantile Movements, 226
Whytehead, Lieutenant-Commander T. B. H., R.N., 430
Wick, 321
Wicklow Head, 435
Widders, A., master of the s.s. *Harpalion*, 291
Wilfrid M., the s.v., captured, 175; fate of, 175
Willerby, the s.s., captured, 178
William I, incorporation of the Cinque Ports, 9
William II, Emperor of Germany, responsibility for the sinking of the s.s. *Lusitania*, 427
William F. Frye, the s.s., sunk, 177, 179
Williams, J., master of the s.s. *Conway Castle*, 145, 147
Williams, J., master of the s.s. *Hurstdale*, 166
Williams, J., master of the s.s. *Rio Parana*, 291
Williams, J., master of the s.s. *Indian City*, 300
Willingdon Shoal, 400
Willoughby, Sir Hugh, Arctic voyage, 21; in Lapland, 22
Wilson, Admiral of the Fleet Sir Arthur, 372; on the policy of the Admiralty, 222
Wilson, Lieutenant-Commander A. T., R.N., in command of the armed yacht *Venetia*, 325

Wilson, John, skipper of the trawler *Blanche*, 358
Wilson Line, ships fitted with guns, 124
Winchelsea Cinque Port, 9, 13
Wintonia, the armed yacht, 305
Wolf Rock, 313
Wood, John, master of the s.s. *Durward*, 275; efforts to escape a submarine, 276
Wood, Lieutenant W. H., R.N.R., 430
Woodville, the s.s., 298
Woolwich, 41
Wrath, Cape, 350, 351
Wrexham, the s.s., escapes from a submarine, 296
Wright, George, master of the trawler *Eileen Emma*, 309

Xylopia, the trawler, 266

Yachts, requisitioned, 325, 377; number of armed, 332, 372
Yarmouth, armed patrol at, 335, 370; net-bases at, 375
Ymuiden, 287
Yokohama, the trawler, fight with a submarine, 447
Yorck, the German s.s., 126
Yorkshire coast, raid on, 357
Younger, A., the skipper of the mine-sweeper *Dorothy Gray*, 356

Zanzibar, 40
Zarefah, the armed yacht, 325
Zeebrugge, bombardment of, 352
Zeiten, the German s.s., 126, 138
Zeppelins, raids, 404
ZHEMCHUG, the Russian cruiser, torpedoed, 202

www.ingramcontent.com/pod-product-compliance
Lightning Source LLC
Chambersburg PA
CBHW031700230426
43668CB00006B/60